*Fifth Edition*

# COMMUNITY PSYCHOLOGY

**John Moritsugu**
*Pacific Lutheran University*

**Elizabeth Vera**
*Loyola University Chicago*

**Frank Y. Wong**
*Emory University*

**Karen Grover Duffy**
*State University of New York, Geneseo*

 Routledge
Taylor & Francis Group

LONDON AND NEW YORK

First published 2014, 2010, 2003 by Pearson Education, Inc.

Published 2016 by Routledge
2 Park Square, Milton Park, Abingdon, Oxon OX14 4RN
711 Third Avenue, New York, NY, 10017, USA

*Routledge is an imprint of the Taylor & Francis Group, an informa business*

ISBN: 9780205255627 (pbk)

Cover Designer: Karen Noferi

**Library of Congress Cataloging-in-Publication Data**

Duffy, Karen Grover.
    Community psychology.—Fifth edition / John Moritsugu, Pacific Lutheran University, Elizabeth Vera,
Loyola University Chicago, Frank Y. Wong, Emory University, Karen Grover Duffy, State University of New York, Geneseo.
        pages cm
    Revision of: Community psychology / John Moritsugu, Frank Y. Wong, Karen Grover Duffy.—4th ed.—Boston : Allyn &
Bacon, ©2010.
    ISBN-13: 978-0-205-25562-7
    ISBN-10: 0-205-25562-0
    1. Community psychology.   I. Moritsugu, John.   II. Vera, Elizabeth, 1967–   III. Wong, Frank Y., 1958–   IV. Title.
RA790.55.D84 2013
362.2—dc23

2013008404

# CONTENTS

## Part III  Community Psychology Applied to Various Settings

### Chapter 6  THE MENTAL HEALTH SYSTEM    120

### Chapter 7  SOCIAL AND HUMAN SERVICES IN THE COMMUNITY    145

# PREFACE

## NEW TO THIS EDITION

- **Heightened readability:** Many chapters have been re-written with the student reader in mind.
- **Updated literature reviews:** You will find references to new terminology, innovative ways of studying the community, new studies of the community as well as new areas of study.
- **Consideration of healthcare disparities:** What are these discrepancies in our care? What is being done to understand and to address them?
- **New materials on obesity prevention:** Is obesity on the rise? What are community-based solutions to preventing obesity in children?
- **Added section on interpersonal violence:** Theories that attempt to explain violence in intimate relationships are presented along with community interventions, aimed to prevent this problem.
- **Addition of healthy aging considerations:** What helps adults enter later stages of life in healthy ways? In what ways are the elderly vulnerable to abuse and exploitation?
- **New considerations of bilingual education and the community:** In what ways are schools attempting to integrate immigrants into the community? Methods that view immigrant communities as assets are discussed.

Community psychology grows from an optimism regarding human nature and a search for truth and meaning in the world. It believes in our basic need for each other and our biologically grounded ability to feel compassion and to desire to help. As community psychologists, we are motivated to improve the conditions for the whole, ameliorating the negative and promoting the positive (Cowen, 2000; Shinn & Toohey, 2003).

There is an appreciation for our individual differences and the diversity of our backgrounds, and at the same time for the commonalities that bind us together. We are able to indulge our curiosity about the world and its complexities.

Driven by questions about ourselves, and the collective entities in which we find ourselves, we derive an understanding that is both complex and nuanced. Simple answers may be easiest, but at the basis to the nature of things, we sense complexity, interactions, and a richness of factors that influence the natural social ecologies we study and in which we work. We believe the answers are to be found both in the empirical data that describe our human and social conditions and in the expression of our values and our spirit (Kelly, 2006).

The direction of our answers is toward the transactional nature of our world. We influence each other for better or worse. And so community theory is driven not just by the individual and his or her personality, but also by the influences of context (Trickett, 2009). It is a humble position to take with regard to our world and our influence in that world.

We have tried to succinctly capture the basic principles, themes, and practices in community psychology. The rest is exposition on the various systems in which these principles, themes and practices can be applied. In the interdisciplinary spirit of community psychology (Rappaport, 1977), the programs and research in these content areas are gathered from a variety of sources within community psychology, outside community psychology but within the discipline (counseling, clinical, educational and school psychology), and finally outside of psychology itself. Among the works cited, you, the reader, might find social work, public health, education, public policy, criminology/police sciences, sociology, and urban planning. This is reflective of where community psychologists are at work.

The text is divided into four parts. The first provides the historical, theoretical, and research framework for the field. Called to action, we are guided by principles of empowerment, ecology, appreciation of diversity, stress, and resilience. The second section looks at social change and how community psychologists might help in that change. The third section examines the variety of systems in which community psychology principles could be applied. The fourth and final section explores community psychology at present and into the future. What has been accomplished and what are potential areas to grow in? And what bits of wisdom might those who have worked in the field provide?

At the beginning of each chapter are quotes from others who pose a challenge or reflection, which may play out a theme within that chapter. Also at the beginning is an opening story or stories, providing an example of what is going on in the chapter. Each chapter is outlined so that students can expect what they are about to read and formulate questions related to the topics listed. Within the chapters are Case in Point examples of how the theory and research are being applied in the community.

Key concepts have been highlighted by boldface in all chapters. And finally, each chapter concludes with a summary. Students are advised to read this summary after they first peruse the outline and chapter so as to direct their attention to important issues in each chapter and to better organize their studying.

We hope that you find both information and a way of thinking about your psychological world emerging from this text. Community psychology is a body of knowledge, a theoretical framework, and a practice of psychology that relates to building a better world. Topics include fellowship and caring, compassion, support, coping, and succeeding against the odds.

Community psychology is also a way of conceptualizing the world and ourselves in it. You will see how thinking contextually, transactionally, systemically, and ecologically might shift your construction of problems and solutions.

Our thanks to Kristin Landon, who helped on the final editing, and all at Allyn & Bacon who facilitated in the completion of this project. Thanks also to the Pearson reviewers Edison Trickett, Peter Wollheim, and Rebecca Francis.

*JM & EV*

As one of the coauthors on this text, I thank the original authors, Karen Duffy and Frank Wong, for their original invitation to join them in this work. I also welcome Elizabeth Vera, the newest coauthor. She brings a wealth of expertise in prevention, social justice, and counseling, as well as work with diverse populations. Besides her research and practice acumen, she is a clear and effective writer. I could not have done the book without her.

I continue to thank my wife and fellow psychologist, Jane Harmon Jacobs, whose positive attitude and support helped in the good times and the hard times, and my son, Michael Moritsugu, who provided informed and very real help in the completion of the text.

We are the product of our own intellectual and emotional communities. Among my early advisors and teachers were Ralph Barocas and Emory Cowen from my graduate school days at the University of Rochester. I thank them for their support and challenges during my time in the snow country of upstate New York and throughout my career.

Among the many colleagues I found in graduate school, three in particular have remained helpful in continuing to engage me in discussions about the field of community psychology. I thank Leonard Jason, David Glenwick, and Robert Felner for their fellowship and connection over the years. Their rich and enlightening research and writing in the field speak for themselves.

*JM*

I thank my family and colleagues for their support in my professional endeavors, which laid the groundwork for my contributions to the text. I am also indebted to the communities with whom I have collaborated over the years in efforts to promote the positive and ameliorate the negative.

*EV*

# 1

# Introduction: Historical Background

*Until justice rolls down like waters, and righteousness like a mighty stream.*
—Martin Luther King, quoting Amos 5:24

*Be the change that you wish to see in the world.*
—M. Gandhi

My dog Zeke is a big, friendly Lab–golden retriever–Malamute mix. Weighing in at a little over 100 pounds, he can be intimidating when you first see him. Those who come to know him find a puppy-like enthusiasm and an eagerness to please those he knows.

One day, Zeke got out of the backyard. He scared off the mail delivery person and roamed the streets around our home for an afternoon. On returning home and checking our phone messages, we found that we had received a call from one of our neighbors. They had found Zeke about a block away and got him back to their house. There he stayed until we came to retrieve him. We thanked the neighbor, who had seen Zeke walking with us every day for years. The neighbor, my wife, and I had stopped and talked many times. During those talks, Zeke had loved receiving some extra attention. Little did we know all this would lead to Zeke's rescue on the day he left home.

As an example of community psychology, we wanted to start with something to which we all could relate. Community psychology is about everyday events that happen in all of our lives. It is about the relationships we have with those around us, and how those relationships can help in times of trouble and can enhance our lives in so many other ways. It is also about understanding that our lives include what is around us, both literally and figuratively.

But community psychology is more than a way to comprehend this world. Community psychology is also about action to change it in positive ways. The next story addresses this action component.

We start with two young women named Rebecca and Trisha, both freshmen at a large university. The two women went to the same high school, made similar grades in their classes, and stayed out of trouble. On entering college, Rebecca attended a pre–freshman semester educational program on alcohol and drug abuse, which introduced her to a small group of students who were also entering school. They met an upperclassman mentor, who helped them with the mysteries of a new school and continued to meet with them over the semester to answer any other questions. Trisha did not receive an invitation and so did not go to this program. Because it was a large school, the two did not have many opportunities to meet during the academic year. At the end of their first year, Rebecca and Trisha ran into each other and compared stories about their classes and their life. As it turns out, Rebecca had a good time and for the most part stayed out of trouble and made good grades. Trisha, on the other hand, had problems with her drinking buddies and found that classes were unexpectedly demanding. Her grades were lower than Rebecca's even though she had taken a similar set of freshman classes. Was the pre-freshman program that Rebecca took helpful? What did it suggest for future work on drug and alcohol use on campuses? A community psychologist would argue that the difference in experiences was not about the "character" of the two women, but about how well they were prepared for the demands of freshman life and what supports they had during their year. And what were those preparations and supports that seemed to bring better navigation of the first year in college?

By the end of this chapter, you will be aware of many of the principles by which the two stories might be better understood. By the end of the text, you will be familiar with the concepts and the research related to these and other community psychology topics and how they may be applied to a variety of systems within the community. These topics range from neighborliness to the concerns and crises that we face in each of our life transitions. The skills, knowledge, and support that we are provided by our social networks and the systems and contexts in which these all happen are important to our navigating our life. A community psychology provides direction in how to build a better sense of community, how to contend with stresses in our life, and how to partner with those in search of a better community. The interventions are usually alternatives to the traditional, individual-person, problem-focused methods that are typically thought of when people talk about psychology. And the target of these interventions may be at the systems or policy level as well as at the personal. But first let us start with what Kelly (2006) would term an "ecological" understanding of our topic—that is, one that takes into account both the history and the multiple interacting events that help to determine the direction of a community.

We first look at the historical developments leading up to the conception of community psychology. We then see a definition of community psychology, the fundamental principles identified with the field, and other central concepts. We learn of a variety of programs in community psychology. And finally, a cognitive map for the rest of the text is provided. But first, back to the past.

## HISTORICAL BACKGROUND

Shakespeare wrote, "What is past is prologue." Why gain a historical perspective? Because the past provides the beginning to the present and defines meanings in the present. Think of when someone says "Hi" to you. If there is a history of friendship, you react to this act of friendship positively. If you have no history of friendship, then you wonder what this gesture means and might react with more suspicion. In a similar way, knowing something of people's developmental and familial backgrounds tells us something about what they are like and what moves them in the present. The history of social and mental health movements provides insight into the state of psychology. These details provide us with information on the spirit of the times (**zeitgeist**) and the spirit of the place (**ortgeist**) that brought forth a community psychology "perspective" (Rappaport, 1977) and "orientation" (Heller & Monahan, 1977).

These historical considerations have been a part of community psychology definitions ever since such definitions began to be offered (Cowen, 1973; Heller & Monahan, 1977; Rappaport, 1977). They also can be found in the most recent text descriptions (Kloos et al., 2011; Nelson & Prilleltensky, 2010). A community psychology that values the importance of understanding "context" would appreciate the need for historical background in all things (Trickett, 2009). This understanding will help explain why things are the way they are, and what forces are at work to keep them that way or to change them. We also gain clues on how change has occurred and how change can be facilitated.

So what is the story? We will divide it into a story of mental health treatment in the United States and a story of the social movements leading up to the founding of the U.S. community psychology field.

In colonial times, the United States was not without social problems. However, given the close-knit, agrarian communities that existed in those times, needy individuals were usually cared for without special places to house them (Rappaport, 1977). As cities grew and became industrialized, people who were mentally ill, indigent, and otherwise powerless were more and more likely to be institutionalized. These early institutions were often dank, crowded places where treatment ranged from restraint to cruel punishment.

In the 1700s France, Philip Pinel initiated reforms in mental institutions, removing the restraints placed on asylum inmates. Reforms in America have been attributed to Dorothea Dix in the late 1800s. Her career in nursing and education eventually led her to accept an invitation to teach women in jails. She noted that the conditions were abysmal and many of the women were, in fact, mentally ill. Despite her efforts at reform, mental institutions, especially public ones, continued in a warehouse mentality with respect to their charges. These institutions grew as the lower class, the powerless, and less privileged members of society were conveniently swept into them (Rappaport, 1977). Waves of early immigrants entering the United States were often mistakenly diagnosed as mentally incompetent and placed in the overpopulated mental "hospitals."

In the late 1800s, Sigmund Freud developed an interest in mental illness and its treatment. You may already be familiar with the method of therapy he devised, called **psychoanalysis.** Freud's basic premise was that emotional disturbance was due to intrapsychic forces within the individual caused by past experiences. These disturbances could be treated by individual therapy and by attention to the unconscious. Freud gave us a legacy of intervention aimed at the individual (rather than the societal) level. Likewise, he conferred on the profession the strong tendency to divest individuals of the power to heal themselves; the physician, or expert, knew more about psychic healing than did the patient. Freud also oriented professional healers to examine an individual's past rather than current circumstances as the cause of disturbance, and to view anxiety and underlying disturbance as endemic to everyday life. Freud certainly concentrated on an individual's weaknesses rather than strengths. This perspective dominated American psychiatry well into the 20th century. Variations of this approach persist to the present day.

In 1946, Congress passed the National Mental Health Act. This gave the U.S. Public Health Service broad authority to combat mental illness and promote mental health. Psychology had proved useful in dealing with mental illness in World War II. After the war, recognition of the potential contributions of a clinical psychology gave impetus to further support for its development. In 1949, the National Institute of Mental Health (NIMH) was established. This organization made available significant federal funding for research and training in mental health issues (Pickren, 2005; Schneider, 2005).

At the time, clinical psychologists were battling with psychiatrists to expand their domain from testing, which had been their primary thrust, to psychotherapy (Walsh, 1987). Today, **clinical psychology** is the field within psychology that deals with the diagnosis, measurement, and treatment of mental illness. It differs from **psychiatry** in that psychiatrists have a medical degree. Clinical psychologists hold doctorates in psychology. These are either a PhD, which is considered a research degree, or a PsyD, which is a "practitioner–scholar" degree focused on assessment and psychological interventions. (Today, the practicing "psychologist," who does therapy, includes a range of specialties. For example, counseling psychologists, who also hold PhD or PsyD degrees, have traditionally focused on issues of personal adjustment related to normal life development. They too are found among the professional practitioners of psychology.) The struggle between the fields of psychiatry and psychology continues today, as some psychologists seek the right to prescribe medications and obtain practice privileges at the hospitals that do not already recognize them (Sammons, Gorny, Zinner, & Allen, 2000). New models of "integrated care" have been growing, where physicians and psychologists work together at the same "primary care" site (McGrath & Sammons, 2011).

Another aspect of the history of mental health is related to the aftermath of the two world wars. Formerly healthy veterans returned home as psychiatric casualties (Clipp & Elder, 1996; Rappaport, 1977; Strother, 1987). The experience of war itself had changed the soldiers and brought on a mental illness.

In 1945, the Veterans Administration sought assistance from the American Psychological Association (APA) to expand training in clinical psychology. These efforts culminated in a 1949 conference in Boulder, Colorado. Attendees at this conference approved a model for the training of clinical psychologists (Donn, Routh, & Lunt, 2000; Shakow, 2002). The model emphasized education in science *and* the practice of testing and therapy, a "**scientist–practitioner**" model.

The 1950s brought significant change to the treatment of mental illness. One of the most influential developments was the discovery of pharmacologic agents that could be used to treat psychosis and other forms of mental illness. Various antipsychotics, tranquilizers, antidepressants, and other medications were able to change a patient's display of symptoms. Many of the more active symptoms were suppressed, and the patient became more tractable and docile. The use of these medications proliferated despite major side effects. It was suggested that with appropriate medication, patients would not require the very expensive institutional care they had been receiving, and they could move on to learning how to cope with and adjust to their home communities, to which they might return. Assuming adequate resources, the decision to release patients back into their communities seemed more humane. There was also a financial argument for deinstitutionalization, because the costs of hospitalization were high. There was potential for savings in the care and management of psychiatric patients. The focus for dealing with the mentally ill shifted from the hospital to the community. Unfortunately, what was forgotten was the need for adequate resources to achieve this transition.

In 1952, Hans Eysenck, Sr., a renowned British scientist, published a study critical of psychotherapy (Eysenck, 1952, 1961). Reviewing the literature on psychotherapy, Eysenck found that receiving no treatment worked as well as receiving treatment. The mere passage of time was as effective in helping people deal with their problems. Other mental health professionals leveled criticisms at psychological practices, such as psychological testing (Meehl, 1954, 1960) and the whole concept of mental illness (Elvin, 2000; Szasz, 1961). (A further review of these issues and controversies can be found.)

If intervention was not useful, as Eysenck claimed, what would happen to mentally ill individuals? Would they be left to suffer because the helping professions could give them little hope? This was the dilemma facing psychology.

In the 1950s and 1960s, Erich Lindemann's efforts in social psychiatry had brought about a focus on the value of crisis intervention. His work with survivors of the Cocoanut Grove fire in Boston demonstrated the importance of providing psychological and social support to people coping with life tragedies. With adequate help provided in a timely manner, most individuals could learn to deal with their crises. At the same time, the expression of grief was seen as a natural reaction and not pathological. This emphasis on early intervention and social support proved important to people's ability to adapt.

Parallel to these developments, Kurt Lewin and the National Training Laboratories were studying group processes, leadership skills for facilitating change, and other ways in which social psychology could be applied to everyday life (www.ntl.org/inner.asp?id=178&category=2). There was a growing understanding of the social environment and social interactions and how they contributed to group and individual abilities to deal with problems and come to healthy solutions.

As a result, the 1960s brought a move to deinstitutionalize the mentally ill, releasing them back into their communities. Many questioned the effectiveness of traditional psychotherapy. Studies found that early intervention in crises was helpful. And psychology grew increasingly aware of the importance of social environments. Parallel to these developments, social movements were developing in the larger community.

## Social Movements

At about the same time as Freud's death (1930s), President Franklin D. Roosevelt proclaimed his New Deal. Heeding the lessons of the Great Depression of the 1920s and 1930s, he experimented with a wide variety of government regulatory reforms, infrastructure improvements, and employment programs. These efforts eventually included the development of the Social Security system, unemployment and disability benefits, and a variety of government-sponsored work relief programs, including ones linked to the building of highways, dams, and other aspects of the nation's economic infrastructure. One great example of this was the Tennessee Valley Authority, which provided a system of electricity generation, industry development, and flood control to parts of Tennessee, Alabama, Mississippi, Kentucky, Virginia, Georgia, and North Carolina. This approach greatly strengthened the concept of government as an active participant in fostering and maintaining individuals' economic opportunities and well-being (Hiltzik, 2011). Although the role of government in fostering well-being is debated to this day, newer conceptions of the role of government still include an active concern for equal opportunity, strategic thinking, and the need for cooperation and trust (Liu & Hanauer, 2011).

There were other social trends as well. Although women had earlier worked in many capacities, the need for labor during World War II allowed them to move into less traditional work settings. "Rosie the Riveter" was the iconic woman of the time, working in a skilled blue-collar position, doing dangerous, heavy work that had previously been reserved for men in industrial America. After the war, it was difficult to argue that women could not work outside the home, because they had contributed so much to American war production. This was approximately 20 years after women had gained voting rights at the national level, with the passage of the 19th Amendment to the Constitution (passing Congress in 1919 and taking until 1920 for the required number of states to ratify it). Throughout the 1950s, 1960s, and 1970s, women—once disenfranchised as a group and with limited legal privileges—continued to seek their full rights as members of their communities.

In another area of social change, the U.S. Supreme Court in 1954 handed down their decision in ***Brown v. Board of Education of Topeka, Kansas.*** This decision overturned an earlier ruling that racial groups could be segregated into "separate but equal" facilities. In reality, the segregated facilities were not equivalent. School systems that had placed Blacks into schools away from Whites were found to be in violation of the U.S. Constitution. This change in the law was a part of a larger movement by Blacks to seek justice and their civil rights. Notably, psychologists Kenneth and Mamie Phipps Clark provided psychological research demonstrating the negative outcomes of segregated schools (Clark, 1989; Clark & Clark, 1947; Keppel, 2002). This was the first time that psychological research was used in a Supreme Court decision (Benjamin & Crouse, 2002). The *Brown v. Board of Education* decision required sweeping changes nationally and encouraged civil rights activists.

Among these activists were a tired and defiant Rosa Parks refusing to give up her bus seat to a White passenger as the existing rules of racial privilege required; nine Black students seeking entry into a school in Little Rock, Arkansas; other Blacks seeking the right to eat at a segregated lunch counter; and students and religious leaders around the South risking physical abuse and death to register Blacks to vote. The civil rights movement of the 1950s carried over to the 1960s. People of color, women, and other underprivileged members of society continued to seek justice. The Voting Rights Act of 1965 helped to enforce the 15th Amendment to the Constitution, guaranteeing citizens the right to vote (www. ourdocuments.gov/doc.php?flash=true&doc=100&page=transcript).

In the 1960s, the "baby boomers" also came of age. Born in the mid-1940s and into the 1960s, these children of the World War II veterans entered the adult voting population in the United States in large numbers, shifting the opinions and politics of that time. Presaging these changing attitudes, in 1960, John F. Kennedy was elected president of the United States (www.whitehouse.gov/about/presidents/johnfkennedy). Considered by some too young and too inexperienced to be president, Kennedy embodied the optimism and empowerment of an America that had won a world war and had opened educational and occupational opportunities to the generation of World War II veterans and their families (Brokaw, 1998). His first inaugural address challenged the nation to service, saying, "Ask not what your country can do for you—ask what you can do for your country." During his tenure, the Peace Corps was created, sending Americans overseas to help developing nations to modernize. Psychologists were also encouraged to "do something to participate in society" (Walsh, 1987, p. 524). These social trends, along with the increasing moral outrage over the Vietnam War, fueled excitement over citizen involvement in social reform and generated an understanding of the interdependence of social movements (Kelly, 1990).

One of President Kennedy's sisters had special needs. This may have fueled his personal interest in mental health issues. Elected with the promise of social change, he endorsed public policies based on reasoning that social conditions, in particular poverty, were responsible for negative psychological states (Heller, Price, Reinharz, Riger, & Wandersman, 1984). Findings of those times supported the notion that psychotherapy was reserved for a privileged few, and institutionalization was the treatment of choice for those outside the upper class (Hollingshead & Redlich, 1958). In answer to these findings, Kennedy proposed mental health services for communities and secured the passage of the Community Mental Health Centers Act of 1963. The centers were to provide outpatient, emergency, and educational services, recognizing the need for immediate, local interventions in the form of prevention, crisis services, and community support.

Kennedy was assassinated at the end of 1963, but the funding of community mental health continued into the next administration. In his 1964 State of the Union address, President Lyndon B. Johnson prescribed a program to move the country toward a "Great Society" with a plan for a "War on Poverty."

President Johnson wanted to find ways to empower people who were less fortunate and to help them become productive citizens. Programs such as **Head Start** (addressed in Chapter 8) and other federally funded early childhood enhancement programs for the disadvantaged were a part of these efforts. Although much has changed in our delivery of social and human services since the 1960s, many of the prototypes for today's programs were developed during this time.

Multiple forces in mental health and in the social movements of the time converged in the mid-1960s. Dissatisfaction with the effectiveness of traditional individual psychotherapy (Eysenck, 1952), the limitation on the number of people who could be treated (Hollingshead & Redlich, 1958), and the growing number of mentally ill individuals returning into the communities combined to raise serious questions regarding the status quo in mental health. In turn, a recognition of diversity within our population, the appreciation of the strengths within our communities, and a willingness to seek systemic solutions to problems directed psychologists to focus on new possibilities in interventions. Thus we have the basis for what happened at the Swampscott Conference.

### Swampscott

In May 1965, a conference in **Swampscott,** Massachusetts (on the outskirts of Boston), was convened to examine how psychology might best plan for the delivery of psychological services to American communities. Under the leadership of Don Klein, this training conference was organized and supported by the National Institute of Mental Health (NIMH; Kelly, 2005). Conference participants, including clinical psychologists concerned with the inadequacies of traditional psychotherapy and oriented to social and political change, agreed to move beyond therapy to prevention and the inclusion of an ecological perspective in their work (Bennett et al., 1966). The birth of community psychology in the United States is attributed to these attendees and their work (Heller et al., 1984; Hersch, 1969; Rappaport, 1977). Appreciating the influence of social settings on the individual, the framers of the conference proceedings proposed a "revolution" in the theories of and the interventions for a community's mental health (Bennett et al., 1966).

## WHAT IS COMMUNITY PSYCHOLOGY?

Community psychology focuses on the social settings, systems, and institutions that influence groups and organizations and the individuals within them. The goal of community psychology is to optimize the well-being of communities and individuals with innovative and alternate interventions designed in collaboration with affected community members and with other related disciplines inside and outside of psychology. Klein (1987) recalled the adoption of the term *community psychology* for the 1963 Swampscott grant proposal to NIMH. Klein credited William Rhodes, a consultant in child mental health, for writing of a "community psychology." Just as there were communities that placed people at risk of pathology, community psychology was interested in how communities and the systems within them helped to bring health to community members.

Iscoe (1987) later tried to capture the dual nature of community psychology by drawing a distinction between a "community psychology" and a "community psychologist." He stated that the field of community psychology studied communities and the factors that made them healthy or at risk. In turn, a community psychologist used these factors to intervene for the betterment of the community and the individuals within it. In the 1980s, the then Division of Community Psychology (Division 27 of the APA): was renamed the Society for Community Research and Action so as to better emphasize the dual nature of the field.

The earliest textbook (Rappaport, 1977) defined community psychology as

> an attempt to find other **alternatives** for dealing with deviance from societal-based norms . . . [avoiding] labeling differences as necessarily negative or as requiring social control . . . [and attempting] to support every person's right to be different without risk of suffering material and psychological sanctions . . . The defining aspects of this [community] perspective are: **cultural relativity, diversity, and ecology,** [or rather] the fit between person and environment . . . [The] concerns [of a

| **TABLE 1.1**  Four Broad Principles Guiding Community Research and Action |
|---|

1. Community research and action requires explicit attention to and **respect for diversity** among peoples and settings.

2. Human competencies and problems are best understood by viewing people within their social, cultural, economic, geographic, and historical **contexts.**

3. Community research and action is an **active collaboration** among researchers, practitioners, and community members that uses multiple methodologies. Such research and action must be undertaken to serve those community members directly concerned, and should be guided by their needs and preferences, as well as by their active **participation.**

4. Change strategies are needed at **multiple levels** to foster settings that promote competence and well-being.

*Source:* From www.scra27.org/about.html.

community psychology reside in] **human resource development, politics, and science . . .** to the advantage of the larger community and its many sub-communities. (pp. 1, 2, 4–5; boldface ours)

This emphasis on an alternative to an old, culture-blind, individual-focused perspective was restated more recently in Kloos and colleagues (2011), who provide two ways in which community psychology is distinctive. It "offers a **different way of thinking** about human behavior . . . [with a] focus on the **community contexts of behavior;** and it [**expands**] the topics for psychological study and intervention" (p. 3).

Both Kofkin Rudkin (2003) and Kagan, Burton, Ducket, Lawthom, and Siddiquee (2011) have noted that continual reconsiderations of the definition of community psychology accommodate a **flexible and dynamic conceptualization** of a field that is sensitive to the continual input of science and theory as well as considerations of the **details of time and place.**

Community psychology is born out of dissatisfaction with the limitations of the traditional psychotherapy approaches. The "radical" theory- and research-based position it took was that individuals were best understood within the contexts in which they were embedded, that these contexts demanded an appreciation of the cultural and ethnic diversity of backgrounds, and that the individual and the context provided both opportunities and problems for health and well-being. Studying communities would yield a better understanding of this position and would provide new approaches to programming toward the health of those communities and the individuals within them.

At the beginning of the 21st century, the Society for Community Research and Action (Division 27 of the APA) surveyed its membership. From those results, a divisional task force compiled four basic principles for community psychology (see Table 1.1). These principles may be summarized as a respect for diversity, a recognition of the power of context, an appreciation of a community's right to empowerment, and an understanding of the complexity of ecologically relevant interventions. The following exploration of these four fundamental principles provides us with a good example of community psychology in application.

## FUNDAMENTAL PRINCIPLES

"Principles" are (1) the theoretical assumptions on which a concept (i.e., community psychology) is built, or (2) the values that influence and motivate action in the field. The framers of these principles hoped to portray what were commonly agreed-on fundamentals of a community psychology, but they also noted that these were aspirations.

---

**TABLE 1.2   The ADDRESSING Framework for Diversity**

**A**ge,

**D**evelopmental and acquired **D**isabilities,

**R**eligion,

**E**thnicity,

**S**ocioeconomic status,

**S**exual orientation,

**I**ndigenous heritage,

**N**ational origin,

**G**ender.

---

*Source:* Adapted from material in Hays, P. A. (2008). *Addressing cultural complexities in practice: Assessment, diagnosis, and therapy* (2nd ed.). Washington, DC: American Psychological Association.

## A Respect for Diversity

At one time, psychology was in search of universal principles that would transcend culture or ethnicity. However, the group sampled to establish these universals tended to be White, middle-class college students. The irony in this did not escape psychologists in the 1960s or today (Gutherie, 2003; Pedersen, 2008; Rappaport, 1977; Trimble, 2001). Recognizing and respecting differences in people and their cultural and ancestral heritage is important to a community psychology. Trickett, Watts, and Birman (1994) and Hays (2008) have noted that diversity extends beyond culture, ethnicity, and race and includes considerations of gender, disability, sexual orientation, and those who have been marginalized and oppressed. Hays (2008) included 10 categories in her system for noting diversity (Table 1.2), the ADDRESSING system. Okazaki and Saw (2011) would add to this list an 11th category, that of Immigrant Status.

Rappaport (1977) called for the acceptance of "the value of diversity and the right of people to choose their own goals and life styles" (p. 3). If diversity is respected, how might that affect our thinking? Certainly, *different* would not mean *inferior* (lower) or *deficient* (lacking). Early models of abnormality that assumed such positions would have to be discarded, and new models that appreciated the contribution of social and cultural factors would have to be incorporated into our conceptions of health and pathology (Sue, Sue, Sue, & Sue, 2013). The assumptions of merit and achievement would also need to be reconsidered, along with resource distribution and the criteria for allocations. From a belief in the diversity of people also comes a recognition of the distinctive styles of living, worldviews, and social arrangements that are not part of the perceived mainstream or established traditional society but that more accurately characterize our society's diversity. Moreover, a recognition of these distinctions keeps diverse populations from being compared with perceived mainstream cultural standards and then being labeled as "deficient" or "deviant" (Snowden, 1987). Such a recognition of diversity increases our ability to design interventions that are culturally appropriate and thus more effective (e.g., Dumas, Rollock, Prinz, Hops, & Blechman, 1999; Marin, 1993).

Sue (1977), early in the community mental health movement, pointed out the differential treatment and outcomes for ethnic minority group clients in the system. He called for provision of responsive services to these populations. These demands for more cultural competency in treatments, emphasizing the importance of understanding relationships and context in our interventions, have continued over several decades (Sue, 2003). Sue believes these variables of cultural capacity to be just as important, if

| **TABLE 1.3**  Framework for Culturally Centered Interventions | |
| --- | --- |
| **Language (Native language skills)** | A carrier of culture and meaning |
| **Personal relationships** | Especially as might be influenced by similarities or differences in ethnicity and race |
| **Metaphors** | The ways in which meaning and concepts are conveyed |
| **Cultural knowledge** | Traditions, customs, and values |
| **Theoretical model for intervention** | The psychological bases for action |
| **Intervention goals** | Need for agreement as to what is to be accomplished |
| **Intervention methods** | Culturally sensitive and respectful of the community |
| **Consideration of context** | The historic, social, political, and economic setting are seen as important to the person, the setting, and the intervention |

*Source:* Adapted from material in Bernal, G., & Sáez-Santiago, E. (2006). Culturally centered psychosocial interventions. *Journal of Community Psychology, 34,* 121–132.

not *more* important, than specific treatment techniques. Padilla, Ruiz, and Alvarez (1975) also called attention to the barriers of geography, class, language, and culture that led to a lack of Spanish-speaking and -surnamed populations in mental health systems. The recommendations of barrio- (neighborhood) and family-focused services have been models for what community-based services should be. In particular, the emphasis continues to be on respect for cultural context in devising treatments. When interventions fail, it is not necessarily the fault of the client or patient. The system and its assumptions can also be at fault and must be examined. Bernal and Sáez-Santiago (2006) described a framework (Table 1.3) for deriving what Pederson (1997) called a "culturally centered" community intervention. The APA has adopted *Guidelines on Multicultural Education, Training, Research, Practice and Organizational Change for Psychologists* (APA, 2003) in recognition of the importance of diversity in psychology.

In terms of research, the recognition of diversity within populations has slowly but steadily been rising. In early issues of community psychology journals, about 11% of the articles addressed ethnic minority populations (Loo, Fong, & Iwamasa, 1988). Martin, Lounsbury, and Davidson (2004) found this rate to more than double in the time period from 1993 to 1998, with approximately 25% of the articles in the *American Journal of Community Psychology* addressing diversity issues.

The study of ethnic minority groups is really the practice of **good science** (Sue & Sue, 2003). Given our understanding of population (the people in whom we are interested) and sample (a subset of those people), accurate sampling requires recognition of who is the population. The cultural variations in ethnic groups make them different "populations" for study. Considerations of culture and community are integral to one another (Kral et al., 2011; O'Donnell, 2006). O'Donnell proposed the term *cultural–community psychology* because all communities were best understood within their specific cultural contexts. Building on the work of Trickett (1996), who described the importance of both culture and context in understanding and working in diverse communities, O'Donnell commented that all community phenomena and interventions should be preceded by the phrase "it depends."

Given the emphasis on diversity and the appreciation of cultural and ethnic factors, it is not surprising that 23% of the membership of the Society for Community Action and Research self-identifies as ethnic minority (Toro, 2005). In comparison, approximately 6% of the APA membership self-identifies as ethnic minority.

Notably, certain marginalized groups continue to be ignored or underserved—for example, homosexuals, individuals with disabilities, and women (Bond, Hill, Mulvey, & Terenzio, 2000). Bond and Harrell (2006) caution that there is little work on the subtleties, contradictions, and dilemmas that arise from working with the many diversities that exist within our communities. Along with the obvious issues of competing ethnic groups, there are the intersections of gender and ethnicity, the combinations of sexual orientation and class, or all of these considerations together creating practical challenges to the practice of community psychology. Although diversity has a history of recognition within the field, its implications are still being worked out and understood.

The appreciation of diversity has been important to community psychologists' work in various groups and communities. However, research has found that community is created most easily within homogeneous populations. This tension between diversity and homogeneity is an area that community psychology must better address (Townley, Kloos, Green, & Franco, 2011).

Of note is Toro's (2005) comment on how the field has become so diverse. This diversity extends to the many theories, approaches to problems, issues addressed, and populations served. Although some may call this a lack of focus, Toro believes it to be an indication of health and vitality as the field expands its boundaries and takes on new challenges.

You will see numerous studies on specific ethnic groups in this text. There are also growing numbers of studies focusing on other aspects of diversity. We will not reference one particular chapter that deals with this topic. That is because diversity is integral to any of the considerations within the field. This is very different from what was found in the 1960s. Community psychology was one of the areas in psychology that championed the need for inclusion of diversity in the mainstream of the discipline.

## The Importance of Context and Environment

Our behaviors are governed by the expectations and demands of given situations. For example, students' behavior in lecture classes is different from their behavior at a dance. Even the levels of our voices are governed by where we happen to be. At a ball game or sports event, we are louder. At a funeral, or in a church or temple, we are quieter. Raising our children, we may tell them to use their "inside" voices, or allow them to use their "outside" voices when the occasion permits it.

Kurt Lewin (1936) formulated that behavior is a function of the interaction between the person and the environment $[B = f(P \times E)]$. A social–gestalt psychologist, Lewin intended to capture the importance of both the individual and his or her context. To consider the individual alone would provide an incomplete and weak description of the factors influencing behavior. It would be like a figure without a ground. Therefore, any study of behavior must include an understanding of the personal dispositions *and* of the situation in which the person finds him- or herself.

Roger Barker (1965), one of Lewin's students, studied the power of "**behavior settings**" in guiding the activities of a setting's inhabitants. People in a given setting acted in prescribed ways. Violation of these environmentally signaled patterns was punished. As a result, these patterns persisted over time. Barker observed and analyzed the social and psychological nature of these settings. For example, in a dining room, we dined. We did not play football there, or so we were told. If we were to go up to a person and rub his shoulder instead of shaking his hand, we would get curious looks. If we were to get into an elevator and face inward instead of outward, people would become nervous. These behavior settings held a powerful influence on what we did.

One aspect of the setting that Barker studied was the number of people it took to maintain that setting. To run a grocery store requires a certain number of people—for example, the checkout clerk, the stocker, and the people to make and accept deliveries. We have all been at a checkout area when there were not enough checkout clerks. There is a demand on people to work harder, and everyone feels that there are not enough people to do what needs to be done. If there are more customers, there might be a call for more checkers to come to their stands. The number of people required is flexible, and the store has made provision to have more or less as the needs change.

Each setting has an optimal level of staffing. When there are too many staff members, it is likely that the setting will be more selective about who is allowed to perform the tasks. There will be competition to fill those positions. Barker (1965) called this a case of **overmanning,** or rather, too many people for the situation. Newcomers are less likely to be welcome, because they would add to the competitive pool. On the other hand, if there are not enough people to complete a task, there is more environmental demand to use every available individual and to recruit more. With a lot of work to be done and not enough personnel to do, there will be less competition for positions. As we might guess, new members will be welcome. This is a case of **undermanning,** or insufficient personnel to accomplish the required tasks. In this case, the social environment is more open and positively inclined to newcomers.

It might be noted that in economically difficult times, where there is competition for scarce jobs, the attitude toward newcomers and immigrants is usually negative. When there is a need for more workers, there is more willingness to take in new people. Often these positive or negative attitudes toward newcomers can be manipulated by perceptions of overmanning or undermanning. For example, attitudes toward new workers can be made more negative by instilling a belief that there are too many people, even though newcomers might be performing tasks that others would not do.

Barker's and Lewin's works have underscored the importance of environmental factors in behavioral tendencies. Regularities of behavior are not determined solely by personality and genetics. Behaviors are also the result of environmental signals and pressures on the individual. Different environments bring different behaviors. Change the environment, change the behavior.

Behavioral community psychology reinforces the importance of context from a learning theory perspective. **Discriminative stimulus** and **setting control** are contextual terms. In behavioral terminology, the "context" can be construed as the discriminative stimuli within a setting that, as individuals or groups have learned, signal the display of certain behaviors leading to consequences that are desirable or undesirable. The expectation of reinforcement or punishment for the behaviors is the basis of the community learning. Certain behaviors are reinforced in a given setting, increasing the probability of those behaviors in those settings; if other behaviors are punished in that setting, the probability of those behaviors decreases (Figure 1.1). A "No Smoking" sign usually suppresses smoking behavior. People drinking usually increases the likelihood of others drinking in that setting. When picking up dog waste on a walk through certain urban neighborhoods was reinforced, people picked up their dog waste in those neighborhoods (Jason & Zolik, 1980). This is a Skinnerian explanation of setting control (Skinner, 1974).

Beyond this strict behavioral interpretation of context, Mischel (1968) argued for the importance of setting as well as personality in determining behaviors. That is, certain behavioral tendencies might appear stronger in particular settings and weaker in others. For example, we might not see friendly behaviors in one setting (final exams), but in another setting, friendliness overflows (parties). Behavioral community

**FIGURE 1.1**  Setting Control and Behavior

| Expectation of Reinforcement | ⟹ | Increase Behavior |
| **Setting** | ⟹ | **Behavior** |
| Expectation of Punishment | ⟹ | Decrease Behavior |

programs have been a part of the community psychology tradition for many years, contributing to the understanding of context and the power of learning theory in devising interventions (Bogat & Jason, 1997, 2000; Fawcett, 1990; Glenwick & Jason, 1980). The emphasis on clear goals, the importance of settings, and the impact of consequences can be seen in community psychology today.

The conceptualization of context is more typically in terms of process and systems (Seidman & Tseng, 2011; Tseng & Seidman, 2007). Here, consideration is given to "resources," "the organization of resources," and "the social processes" within a given environment. Resources are defined as material, personal, or social "assets" that can be of help to an individual or group (http://oxforddictionaries.com/definition/resource). Examples of resources include personnel, expertise, supplies, and money. The organization of resources addresses who has the resources, how they are distributed, and how within the system they are accumulated and managed. Finally, the social processes are the interactions (back and forth) and the transactions (exchanges) between and among the members of a system. For example, in a particular organization we might consider the amount of money in the system (its resources), the rules governing how and when it is distributed (organization of resources), and the discussions around these issues (processes). Although psychologists typically focus on the processes within a system (who talks to whom, how people communicate with each other, the clarity of communications), the context can be changed just as dramatically by alternations in resources (more or less money) or the organization of resources (who has it, how it is decided who gets it).

As we have described, context can be as simple as the stimulus controls in a setting, or as complex as the consideration of means, rules, and participatory patterns of a given setting; context can also dictate behavior patterns and influence motivation for accepting new or rejecting old members. An example of using contextual frameworks for understanding events is our portrayal of the historical events within mental health and social movements leading up to the Swampscott Conference. The social, political, and historical events leading up to Swampscott helped to define the "spirit" of the times (zeitgeist) and of the place (ortgeist) that led the founders of community psychology to bring change (Kelly, 2006).

No matter what the theoretical framework, the importance of context or setting is an essential part of a community psychology (Trickett, 2009). A person does not act except in ways that are determined by his or her setting. In turn, those actions are best understood when viewed in the framework of context.

## Empowerment

**Empowerment is another basic concept of community psychology.** It is a value, a process, and an outcome (Zimmerman, 2000). As a value, empowerment is seen to be good. It assumes that individuals and communities have strengths, competencies, and resources and are by nature nonpathological. As a process, empowerment is a way in which individuals and communities feel that they have some say in and control over the events in their lives, the structures that shape their lives, and the policies that regulate those structures. Community psychology emphasizes the value of the democratic process. As an outcome of democracy, people can feel empowered. In psychological terms, a feeling of efficacy is the belief that one has power over one's destiny. It is the opposite of helplessness. It is what Bandura (2000, 2006) has called agency (being an actor within one's world, and not merely a passive observer), self-efficacy (a belief that one can make a difference), and collective efficacy (a belief of a group or community that together they can bring about change). Beyond these cognitive components, empowerment includes action on one's own behalf.

> Empowerment is viewed as a process: the mechanism by which people, organizations, and communities gain mastery over their lives. (Rappaport, 1984, p. 3)
>
> At the community level, of analysis, empowerment may refer to collective action to improve the quality of life in a community and to the connections among community organizations and agencies. (Zimmerman, 2000, p. 44)

Empowerment is a construct that links individual strength and competencies, natural helping systems, and proactive behaviors to social policy and social changes. Empowerment theory, research, and intervention link individual well-being with the larger social and political environment. (Perkins & Zimmerman, 1995, p. 569)

Perkins and associates (2007) note that empowering individuals through learning and participation opportunities eventually leads to higher level organizational and community transformations.

There are many ways to feel empowered within a work setting (Foster-Fishman, Salem, Chibnall, Legler, & Yapchai, 1998). Job autonomy (control over and influence on the details of the work setting), gaining job-relevant knowledge, feeling trusted and respected in the organization, freedom to be creative on the job, and participation in decision making were examples found through interviews and observations at a given work site. Studies of empowering organizations found that inspiring **leadership,** power role **opportunities,** a socially **supportive environment,** and **group belief** in the power of its members all contributed to feelings of empowerment in community organizations (Maton, 2008; Wilke & Speer, 2011).

And yet, empowerment processes are not simply giving initiative and control over to people. We are reminded that attempts at youth empowerment have come in a variety of forms with differential success. Reviewing relevant youth programs, Wong, Zimmerman, and Parker (2010) noted that empowerment attempts took forms ranging from total control by youth to total control by adults, and included a shared-control model involving both youth and adults in decision making and action as the middle ground. Empowerment was found to be a transactional process, with both adult and youth contributing to the outcomes (Cargo, Grams, Ottoson, Ward, & Green, 2004). Adults contribute by creating a welcoming and enabling setting. Youth contribute through engaging with others in positive and constructive change. Actions by both adults and youth are required. Together, their contributions build on each other's behaviors and produce an empowering and productive environment.

As an example of empowerment outcomes, Zeldin (2004) found that youth increase in their sense of agency and in their knowledge and skills when they participate in community decision-making activities. This reminds us that agency, or the feeling that a person can influence a situation, is linked to self-efficacy, a cognitive attitude that has been shown to result in better persistence, effort, and final success in dealing with problem situations (Bandura, 1989, 2006). Empowerment situations may lead to feelings of self- or collective group efficacy.

Maton and Brodsky (2011) make the distinction among **psychological empowerment,** where individuals gain a sense of mastery; **social empowerment,** where individuals rise in status; and **civic empowerment,** where there is a gain in rights and privileges. Although related to each other, these forms of empowerment are different. Such distinctions need to be considered in examining both processes and outcomes.

The concept of empowerment has not gone without criticism. Empowerment often leads to individualism and therefore competition and conflict (Riger, 1993). Empowerment is traditionally masculine, involving power and control, rather than the more traditionally feminine values and goals of communion and cooperation. Riger (1993) challenged community psychologists to develop an empowerment concept that incorporates both empowerment and community. We will see a variety of attempts at empowerment in our exploration of community applications throughout the text. It is interesting to note to what end? With what results?

## The Ecological Perspective/Multiple Levels of Intervention

In the developmental literature, Urie Bronfenbrenner (1977) described four layers of ecological systems that influence the life of a child. At the center of the schema is the individual, and in ever-growing circles lie the various systems that interact with and influence him or her. The "immediate system" contains the person and is composed of the particular physical features, activities, and roles of that person. This is called the **microsystem.** Examples of microsystems include a playroom, a home, a backyard, the street in front of the house, or a classroom. Microsystems could include the school or one's family. These microsystems directly influence the individual, and the individual can directly influence the system.

At the next level out is the **mesosystem,** which holds the microsystems and where the microsystems interact with each other. Examples of this would be places where one microsystem (school) and another microsystem (family) come together. A mesosystem is a "system of microsystems" (Bronfenbrenner, 1977, p. 515). Note that the child/individual is an active member within the mesosystem. Research has shown the advantages of clear and demonstrated linkages between the school and the family for the child's school adaptation and academic performance, and this has led to direct calls for better collaboration between schools and communities (Adelman & Taylor, 2003, 2007; Warren, 2005). In turn, there are also findings that schools seen as a part of their community are more likely to be supported and less likely to be the target of vandalism. Children who feel connected to family, school, and neighborhood may feel the responsibilities of membership and the supportiveness of their holistically integrated social and psychological environment. The "system" then can lead to feelings of connection or disconnection among the microsystems; to the collection of social, material, and political resources; or to the alienation of the various components from each other.

The next circle out is the **exosystem,** an extension of the mesosystem that does not immediately contain the child or individual. The exosystem influences the mesosystem. Examples would be government agencies that influence the meso- and microsystems (school boards, city councils, or state legislatures, which influence the schools and families but do not have them as members) or work situations for family members (who in turn populate the micro- and mesosystems).

At the furthest level outward is the **macrosystem,** which does not contain specific settings. The macrosystem contains the laws, culture, values, or religious beliefs that govern or direct the lower systems. Being in the southwestern United States brings certain cultural and legal assumptions that may differ markedly from those in Vancouver, Canada; Barcelona, Spain; Auckland, New Zealand; or Hong Kong, China. Bronfenbrenner (1977) proposed that any conceptualization of a child's development needed a comprehensive examination of all these systems to provide an adequate understanding of the processes that influenced the child. Interventions to address this progress should have a comprehensive and conceptual basis addressing multiple levels. Anything less provides an artificial perspective on what really happens in the life of an individual or a group of individuals. Graphic descriptions of Bronfenbrenner's ecological model showed circles embedded in larger circles. This described the nature of the systems embedded in larger systems.

Kelly (2006) saw the ecological model as an alternative to the reductionistic attempts to describing phenomena. If the world was complex and dynamic, it required concepts and processes that captured those qualities. Among the ecological principles were **interdependence, cycling of resources, adaptive capacity,** and **succession.**

With **interdependence,** the elements of an ecosystem are seen to be related to each other. Changing one element affects all elements in some way. Kelly (1980) described a baseball game as a good example of interdependence. Billy Martin, the onetime manager of the New York Yankees, said that every pitch in every game was different (Angell, 1980). Each pitch required calculations of factors such as weather, wind, time of day, ballpark, personnel, positioning, order at bat, pitcher, and number of pitches. You can see the shifts in the infield and outfield, types of signals given, types of swings attempted, and other changes in strategy and tactics. Everything is interdependent. To the uninformed or uninvolved, baseball can seem a quiet, leisurely sport with which one can be intermittently engaged. To those who know, its complexity is never-ending and a source of continuing fascination. Action in the community requires a similar calculation of various interacting parts. Resources, players, activities, traditions, values, history, and culture are some of the interdependent elements of community psychology.

The second principle of Kelly's ecological model is the **cycling of resources.** This follows the first law of thermodynamics, which states that the amount of energy in a system remains constant: If there is an expenditure of energy in one area, it is the result of transfer of energy from another area. In the ecological model, for resources to be dedicated to one area, they must come from another area. Therefore, the community must choose where to attend and where to expend its energy or resources. To provide more funds for education, some roads may not be repaired; to provide more funds for roads, schools may have to get by with less money. This becomes especially apparent in economically lean times.

The third ecological principle deals with **adaptive capacity** to a given environment. Those who are better able to deal with their environment are more likely to survive, and those who can deal with a broader range of environments should find more settings in which it is possible to live. What matters is not just adaptation to one environment, but also the adaptive range that enables the organism to survive across more situations. One might figure that the argument for flexibility and openness to social and cultural variation would allow a person to do well in more social and physical situations. Community cultures allowing us to learn and to live and to change our living situations across a wide array of settings allow for more successful adjustment to change. If our weather changes, how open are we to changing what we do? One of the authors went from Hawaii to upstate New York. When winter came, it got cold. One day, the winter skies cleared. In Hawaii, clear skies meant warm weather. Blue skies in upstate New York in the middle of winter meant the exact opposite. It was colder. Much colder. Make that mistake once, and the person who lives to talk of it again learns very quickly, or risks death. A community that notes warming or cooling, changes in economic opportunities, or shifts in demographics needs to adapt to deal with these changes, or it will fail. Those who do this better survive and thrive.

Kelly's final ecological point is that of **succession.** One thing follows another in a fairly predictable manner. Consider the queen of England and who will succeed her when she is gone. Which of the princes or princesses comes next? And after him or her, who else? They have it all worked out. This person follows, and when they are gone, the next in line follows, and so on and so on. A similar type of consideration is made with the president of the United States. If he or she is incapacitated while in office, the vice president takes charge, and if the person who is vice president is unable to do the job, the Speaker of the House is next in line. Of course, the president can also be succeeded after an election: The process of moving from one president to the next is laid out in predictable fashion, from the elections in November to the inauguration in January. All of this is to say that with time, changes occur. These changes follow a predictable sequence, just as the queen of England will not always be queen, or the president remain the president. With the passage of time, there will be someone new. Settings and organizations change as well. Just as a college student moves from freshman to senior, and spring follows winter, a decline in one industry leads to opportunity for new industries, and particular groups of people decrease and other groups increase in an area. Succession requires the community psychologist to pay attention to these changes. We can see these ecological principles summarized in Table 1.4.

---

**TABLE 1.4    Ecological Principles**

1. Interdependence—Elements of the environment influence each other.
2. Adaptation—An organism must be able to change as the environment changes.
3. Cycling of resources—Resources are exchanged in a system, such as money for goods.
4. Succession—Change occurs; nothing is static.

---

*Source:* Adapted from material in Kelly, J. (2006). *Becoming ecological.* New York, NY: Oxford University Press.

The ecological model also calls attention to person–environment fit. Does the person have the characteristics to succeed, given the environmental expectations and demands? Will someone who is short do well in a place where all the important objects are placed seven feet off the floor? Or (and one author has observed this) can a tall person live comfortably in a basement apartment with six-foot ceilings? This person–environment fit works in psychological terms as well, being quiet when appropriate and loud when appropriate. The person–environment fit concept is well embedded in community psychology (Pargament, 1986; Trickett, 2009). Early on, Rappaport (1977) explained that the ecological perspective required an examination of the relationship between persons and their environments (both social and physical). The establishment of the optimal match between the person and the setting should result in successful adaptation of the individual to his or her setting.

Moos measured **person–environment fit** by assessing a person's perception of the environment and that person's desired environment according to Social Climate Scales (Moos, 1973, 2003). The discrepancies between the real and the ideal could be compared. Where there were few differences (good fit), we would expect the person to be happier. In contrast to this, most psychological evaluations focus on the person alone. The assumption is that people are the most important contributors to their own well-being. This purely trait-type focus has been critiqued by social–behavioral personality theorists Mischel (1968, 2004) and Bandura (2001), where the person and what he or she carries within them is the sole determinant of success or failure. The more recent social–behaviorist personality theories are interactionist or transactionalist.

Labeling the person who does not fit the setting as a "misfit" and blaming the problems on the individual alone is not helpful or realistic. Rather, the ecological perspective recognizes that with people and environments, the influence is mutual. Individuals change the settings in which they find themselves, and in turn, settings influence the individuals in them (Bandura,1978, 2001; Kelly, 1968, 2006; Kuo, Sullivan, Coley, & Brunson, 1998; Peterson, 1998; Seidman, 1990). If something is awry with the individual or the environment, *both* can be examined and perhaps *both* changed. A study of the person–environment fit of urban Mexican American families in the southwestern United States yielded several findings supporting the importance of setting and families. Economically distressed families did better in low-income neighborhoods, and successful, acculturated families did less well in a nonmatching neighborhood. Although single-parent families were generally at risk and dual-parent families generally more adaptive to settings, the match of neighborhoods influenced adjustment capabilities (Roosa et al., 2009).

Given the ecological framework, community psychology research and action must consider more than the individual. It must include the environment that contains the individual. That environment, or context, needs to be expanded to include the variety of situations that influence behaviors. The more completely the ecology can be understood, the more effectively the interventions can be devised and implemented. Communities are complex and reciprocal systems by nature and must be dealt with as such. A more recent description of ecological thinking included (1) thinking **interdependently** (as before); (2) understanding the **cultural contexts** (macrosystemically); (3) ensuring the development of **trust** between the researcher and the community; and (4) realizing that the researcher is **transformed** in the discovery process, just like the communities he or she studies or intervenes in (Kelly, 2010).

We think systemically, ecologically, and with appreciation for the differences we bring to our social milieu. Beyond the principles outlined here, several concepts have high currency within the field. We examine them next. Note that the differences between clinical and community psychology are elaborated in Case in Point 1.1.

## CASE IN POINT 1.1

# Clinical Psychology, Community Psychology: What's the Difference?

Clinical psychology and community psychology both grow out of the same motivation to help other individuals using the science of psychology. Clinical psychology's orientation has traditionally been on the individual and the internal variables that influence their lives. Among those internal variables are emotions, cognitions, neural structures, and behavioral tendencies. Clinicians tend to speak of personality and what has influenced personal qualities. Given the assumption that a clinician is called into service when there is an identified personal problem, clinical skills include testing and assessment, diagnosis, and psychotherapy (Plante, 2011). Essentially, a clinician is trained to deal with psychopathology.

Among the clinical psychologist's work settings may be a hospital, a health clinic, a group or private practice office, a university, or a research setting. You may note the medical nature of most of these sites. American clinical psychology traces its origins back to the late 1800s. Lightner Witmer is credited by many as the father of American clinical psychology. His work in the first part of the 20th century focused on schoolchildren and their treatment, learning, and behavioral problems in the psychological clinic.

In contrast to clinical psychology, community psychology is oriented to groups of people and the external social and physical environments' effects on those groups—that is, communities.

External variables include consideration of social support, peer and familial environments, neighborhoods, and formal and informal social systems that may influence individuals or groups. There is interest in social ecology and public policy. The orientation is toward prevention of problems and promotion of wellness. Skill sets include community research skills; the ability to understand community problems from a holistic perspective; skills in relating to community members in a meaningful and respectful manner; attention to the existing norms, system maintenance, and change; appreciation for the many ways in which context/environment influences behaviors; being able to assemble and focus resources toward the solution of a community problem; and training that enables thinking outside the established normative world. A review of three community psychology texts support these descriptions. Among the earliest of texts on community psychology, Rappaport (1977) dedicated many of his chapters to social interventions and systems interventions. A few years ago, Kofkin Rudkin's (2003) book included chapters titled "Beyond the Individual," "Embracing Social Change," "Prevention," "Empowerment," and "Stress." Kloos et al. (2011) had chapters entitled "Community Practice," "Community Research," "Understanding Individuals within Environments," "Understanding Diversity," "Stress and Coping," "Prevention and

Promotion," and "Social Change." None of these community texts had sections on psychopathology, assessment, or psychotherapy.

Community psychologists might be working for urban planners, government offices, departments of public health, community centers, schools, or private program evaluation agencies, as well as universities and research centers. They are not usually found in medical settings doing therapy but might work there examining delivery systems and community accessibility programs.

There are clear differences between clinical and community psychology topics. Common interests include providing effective interventions for the human good and understanding phenomena from a psychological perspective. Many community psychologists were trained as clinical psychologists. The Swampscott Conference attendees were clinicians. Clinical psychology has taken on the themes of pathology prevention and health promotion in a significant way. The discussion of the limitations of traditional one-on-one clinical psychology has continued among clinicians (Kazden, 2010). The questions remain the same. How can we more efficiently and more effectively bring psychological and physical health to larger segments of the population? Community psychology argues that its approach brings new perspectives to help answer this question.

## OTHER CENTRAL CONCEPTS

Besides the principles that have been identified as foundational to a community psychology, several concepts are central to the field. Among them are the ideas of prevention, a strength focus, social change and action research, a sense of community, and an interdisciplinary perspective.

## Prevention Rather than Therapy

The Swampscott Conference's focus on **prevention** rather than treatment was inspired by public health (Heller et al., 1984; Kelly, 2005) and work in child and social psychiatry (Caplan, 1964). In very basic terms, prevention is understood to be "doing something now to prevent (or forestall) something unpleasant or undesirable from happening in the future" (Albee & Ryan, 1998, p. 441). What one specifically does may be determined by what one is specifically trying to prevent, of course, but the underlying premise remains.

The main argument for prevention is that traditional psychological interventions often came too late in the illness development process; they were usually provided long after the individual already had developed a problem. Emory Cowen (1980) stated,

> We became increasingly, indeed alarmingly, aware of (a) the frustration and pessimism of trying to undo psychological damage once it had passed a certain critical point; [and] (b) the costly, time-consuming, culture-bound nature of mental health's basic approaches, and their unavailability to, and effectiveness with, large segments of society in great need. (p. 259)

Such concerns continue to this day (Vera & Polanin, 2012).

On the other hand, prevention might counter any trauma before it begins, thus saving the individual and perhaps the whole community from developing a problem. In this regard, as stated earlier, community psychology takes a proactive rather than reactive role. For example, community psychologists believe it is possible that sex education *before* adolescence, teamed with new social policy, can reduce the teenage pregnancy rate. Kirby (2007) provides clear research-based guidelines on pregnancy prevention programs. In the following chapters, you will read about a variety of techniques in prevention: education, altering the environment, development of alternate interventions, and public policy changes.

Community psychologists recognize that there are distinctions among levels of preventive intervention. **Primary prevention** attempts to prevent a problem from ever occurring (Heller, Wyman, & Allen, 2000). Levine (1998) likened primary prevention to an inoculation. Just as a vaccination protects against a targeted disease, primary preventive strategies can help an individual fend off problems altogether. *Primary prevention* refers most generally to activities that can be undertaken with a healthy population to maintain or enhance its physical and emotional health (Bloom & Hodges, 1988)—in other words, "keeping healthy people healthy" (Scileppi, Teed, & Torres, 2000, p. 58). Which preventive strategies are best (or whether they are equally efficacious) is part of the current debate in community psychology (Albee, 1998).

Cowen (1996) argued that the following criteria must be met for a program to be considered truly *primary* preventive:

- The program must be mass- or group-oriented.
- It must occur *before* the maladjustment.
- It must be intentional in the sense of having a primary focus on strengthening adjustment of the as yet unaffected.

Levine (1998, 1999) added further characteristics. Primary prevention interventions should do the following:

- Evaluate and promote synergistic effects and consider how to modify countervailing forces.
- Be structured to affect complex social structures, including redundant messages. They should be continued over time.
- Examine institutional and societal issues, not just individual factors.
- Recognize that whatever the program, it is just one part of a much larger cultural effort.
- Acknowledge that because high-risk behaviors tend to co-occur, several behaviors should be targeted.

Later, once there are some signs of problems beginning to arise (e.g., risk factors emerge or are identified), **secondary prevention** attempts to prevent a problem at the earliest possible moment before it becomes a severe or persistent problem. In other words, at-risk individuals are identified and an intervention is offered because of their increased likelihood of developing the problem. This is different from primary prevention, which would be targeted at all individuals, regardless of whether they were at risk. For example, students at a particular high school whose parents are substance abusers or addicts might be helped by secondary preventive efforts directed at keeping the students from becoming habitual users.

**Tertiary prevention** attempts to reduce the severity of an established problem and prevent it from having lasting negative effects on the individual. It is seen as similar to therapy, in that it attempts to help the affected person to avoid relapses (Heller et al., 2000). An example of tertiary prevention would be designing a program to help hospitalized persons with mental disorders return to the community as soon as possible and keep their symptoms under control (Scileppi, Teed, & Torres, 2000) or a program that helps teen mothers reduce the likelihood of having more children during their adolescence. Many argue that this is not really a form of prevention, in that it is conceptually different from primary prevention and the methods used may vary dramatically from those for primary prevention. Whereas psychoeducation, or teaching skills or information about a particular problem, might be effective for individuals who are not involved in risky activities, it is likely to be ineffective for those already exhibiting a particular problem.

A second method for defining prevention is provided by Mrazek and Haggerty's (1994) Institute of Medicine (IOM) report. They describe three types of prevention based on the target populations involved. The first is a **universal** prevention program, which addresses the general public. Here the effort is to help the total population, as is the case with most primary prevention efforts. The second is a **selective** program, aimed at those considered at risk for future development of problems, as is the case with most secondary prevention efforts. These risk factors may be biological, social, or psychological. Last, there are **indicated** prevention programs for those who are starting to show symptoms of a disorder. This category is not analogous to tertiary prevention, however. The IOM definitions of prevention are clear that once a problem has already manifested, the intervention is no longer considered prevention; thus, relapse prevention would be considered *treatment* in this model. The definitions also make a distinction between illness prevention programs and health promotion programs. The authors point to the difference between programs that focus on the avoidance of symptoms and programs that focus on the development of personal potential and sense of well-being. The first type of program is successful when a phenomenon does not appear (e.g., a symptom), and the second type of program is successful when a phenomenon (e.g., a new skill set) does appear. Cowen (2000), Romano and Hage (2000), and Weissberg, Kumpfer, and Seligman (2003) argue for a synthesis of the prevention and promotion components. They point out that promotion of well-being does have a positive effect on the prevention of disorder. Romano and Hage (2000), for example, broadened the definition of prevention to include the following: (1) stopping a problem behavior from ever occurring; (2) delaying the onset of a problem behavior; (3) reducing the impact of a problem behavior; (4) strengthening knowledge, attitudes, and behaviors that promote emotional and physical well-being; and (5) promoting institutional, community, and government policies that further physical, social, and emotional well-being. This more inclusive definition of prevention emulates the evolution that has occurred within the field in conceptualizing the different facets of prevention.

A review of the literature (see Case in Point 1.2) examining the efficacy of primary prevention programs has come to the conclusion that primary prevention works. These reviews also highlight an important differentiation in the prevention literature, namely the difference between person-centered

# Does Primary Prevention Work?

Community psychologists respect prevention efforts, especially those aimed at primary prevention. Can one demonstrate, however, that primary prevention works? As mentioned previously, it is complicated to show that a problem that does not (yet) exist has been successfully affected by a prevention program. Primary prevention programs, however, have been around a long time. Some have been individually evaluated, but not until the 1990s did researchers set out to determine whether, overall, primary prevention works. Fortunately, several major statistical reviews of the literature, called **meta-analyses,** have been performed in the past 20 years. Each set of researchers came to the same conclusion: Primary prevention *does* work! It is helpful to understand why the converging conclusions of these studies are rather astonishing.

In the early 1990s, at the request of the U.S. Congress, the Institute of Medicine (Mrazek & Haggerty, 1994) performed a statistical review of the mental health literature. Using "reduction of new cases of mental disorder" (p. 9) as its definition of *primary prevention,* the Institute of Medicine gathered 1,900 journal citations on primary prevention of mental health problems. Overall, the institute found that primary prevention, as previously defined, does work. A quote from the final report divulges their conclusions: "With regard to preventive intervention research . . . the past decade has brought encouraging progress. At present there are many intervention programs that rest on sound conceptual and empirical foundations, and a substantial number are rigorously designed and evaluated" (p. 215).

Durlak and Wells (1997) completed a statistical review of the litera- ture on primary prevention of mental health disorders. In this instance, the researchers examined programs only for children and adolescents. Using 177 programs designed to prevent behavioral and social problems, such as depressive reaction to parental divorce, they, too, found empirical support for primary prevention. For example, the average participant in primary prevention programs surpassed the performance of between 59% and 82% of children in control groups, depending on the study. In their journal article, Durlak and Wells summarize their findings supporting the notion that primary prevention, at least of mental disorders, is effective: "Outcome data indicate that most categories of primary prevention programs for most categories of primary prevention programs for children and adolescents produce significant effects. These findings provide empirical support for further research and practice in primary prevention" (p. 142).

Psychologist Emory Cowen (1997a) compared both of these statistical literature reviews and concluded that although there was amazingly little overlap in the citations each set of researchers used, the concept of primary prevention is sound. One other point he made is that each meta-analysis used a different definition of *primary prevention.* Recall that the Institute of Medicine's study definition was "reduction of new cases of mental disorder." Durlak and Wells defined *primary prevention* as reducing potential for mental health problems (like the Institute of Medicine) *as well as* increasing the competencies (or well-being) of the prevention program participants. After his comparison, Cowen con- cluded that research on primary prevention programs is both positive and encouraging for the future.

In 2010 and 2011, Durlak and his colleagues updated the literature on whether programs that increase specific competencies for children and adolescents work. One study (Durlak, Weissberg, & Pachan, 2010) looked at the success of after-school programs that seek to promote personal and social skills in children and adolescents. Results from 75 reports evaluating 69 different programs (the majority conducted after 2000) were included in the meta-analysis. In general, after-school programs yielded positive effects on participants compared to control groups. Furthermore, the researchers found that programs that contained all the following characteristics were more effective than those that did not: *Sequenced:* Does the program use a connected and coordinated set of activities to achieve their objectives relative to skill development? *Active:* Does the program use active forms of learning to help youth learn new skills? *Focused:* Does the program have at least one component devoted to developing personal or social skills? *Explicit:* Does the program target specific personal or social skills? After- school programs that had these charac- teristics were associated with significant increases in participants' positive feelings and attitudes about themselves and their school (child self- perceptions [effect size = .37] and school bonding [effect size = .25]) and their positive social behaviors (.29). In addition, problem behaviors were significantly reduced (effect size = .30). Finally, there was significant improve- ment in students' performance on achievement tests (.20) and in their

*(Continued)*

## (Continued)

school grades (.22). In 2011, Durlak, Weissberg, Dymnicki, Taylor, and Schellinger conducted a meta-analysis of 213 school-based, universal social and emotional learning (SEL) programs involving 270,034 kindergarten through high school students. Compared to controls, SEL participants demonstrated significantly improved social and emotional skills, attitudes, behavior, and academic performance that reflected an 11-percentile-point gain in achievement. Thus, these more recent studies suggest that policy makers, educators, and the public can contribute to healthy development of children by supporting the incorporation of evidence-based SEL programming into standard educational practice and the availability of after-school programs as a mechanism for prevention.

and environmental-centered prevention efforts. Person-centered interventions are those that work directly with individuals who may be at risk for developing disorders and typify many prevention strategies (e.g., skill building, psychoeducation) (Conyne, 2004). Environment-centered interventions work indirectly to benefit individuals by affecting the systems in which those individuals reside. Metaphorically, this process involves enriching the soil so that plants will thrive. The systems targeted in environment-centered interventions may be familial, community, or organizational. Based on Bronfenbrenner's Ecological Systems Theory (Bronfenbrenner, 1979), which you just read about, environment-centered interventions might be aimed at the participants' microsystem, which includes peers, school, family, child care, and neighborhood; the mesosystem, which contains the relationships among entities in the microsystem; the exosystem, which includes places of business and industry, federal and state governments, social media, health and social services agencies, school organizations, and extended family members; or last, the macrosystem, which includes cultural values, attitudes and ideologies, and dominant belief systems. Although community psychologists have a preference for environment-centered prevention over person-centered, you will read about both types of prevention in forthcoming chapters.

Throughout this text, you will also read about the uses of preventive programs in various settings in which psychologists work, whether they are industrial settings, law enforcement agencies, mental health agencies, or sports programs in communities. It is incumbent on psychologists, no matter where they work, to be knowledgeable about appropriate interventions and prevention techniques (Price, Cowen, Lorion, & Ramos-McKay, 1988). As Felner (2000b) cautions, the true preventive program is one that is intentional with regard to its theoretical basis, its understanding of causal pathways, and the purposeful planning and execution of programs to intercept those pathways to gainful ends.

## Social Justice

Another core value of community psychology is the goal of social justice. Social justice is a value or aspiration that is best understood in contrast to social *injustice*. Examples of social injustice abound within our society and around the world. Inequality in educational opportunities, racial disparities in many categories of health and well-being, discrimination experienced by members of particular ethnic, gender, or religious groups, and the homophobia to which gay, lesbian, and bisexual individuals as exposed are examples of social injustices that you will read more about in this text. Although society has developed many laws intended to protect people from being harmed by injustices, it is unfortunately true that we do not yet live in a world of legitimate "equal opportunities" for all to reach their potential. In other words, the playing field in our society is not yet level.

So how then is social *justice* to be defined? On the one hand, it could be argued that when resources are all equally distributed and all citizens experience a level playing field of opportunity, social justice has been achieved. This was the philosophy behind communism. However, others have argued that true social justice is not merely examining how resources are ultimately distributed, but rather creating equitable processes to determine the allocation of resources (Vera & Speight, 2003). In a definition of social justice that focuses on process versus outcome, some groups may temporarily have more resources than others, but it will be because the group as a whole has decided that this should happen, perhaps for a particular reason.

Various definitions of social justice are found in theology, political science, and education, but for our purposes, the overall goal of social justice is "full and equal participation of all groups in a society that is mutually shaped to meet their needs. Social justice includes a vision of society in which the **distribution of resources is equitable** and all members are physically and psychologically safe and secure" (Bell, 1997, p. 3). Note that in this definition, the word *equitable* is used instead of *equal* when talking about resources. Resources should be **fairly distributed,** but perhaps not equally. This allows for the possibility that in some situations, we may want some groups to have **greater access** to a set of resources, in the case of affirmative action, for example. A community may decide that it wants to encourage more women to have careers within science or technology fields, so it may decide that creating college scholarships for women who have such interests is an equitable distribution of resources. The point is that if the society as a whole decides that this is a good policy (i.e., until there are more women in the fields of science and technology), it would be considered a socially just decision.

So how do community psychologists contribute to this goal? Vera and Speight (2003) argued that psychologists can make the most meaningful contributions to social justice by attending to the **societal processes** through which injustices result. For example, in Young's (1990) conceptualization of social justice, social structures and processes are evaluated to elucidate practices of domination, privilege, and oppression. Thus, inequities are not solved by merely redistributing wealth or resources. Rather, the processes that facilitated unequal outcomes to begin with must be scrutinized and **transformed.** Typically, **marginalization** (i.e., **exclusion**) is the main process by which social injustice is maintained. Young argued that in the United States, a large proportion of the population is expelled from full participation in social and political life, including people of color, the elderly, the disabled, women, gay men, lesbians, bisexuals, transgendered people, and people who are involuntarily out of work. Thus, issues of social justice are important for the statistical majority of the population, not just minority groups. Such a conceptualization of justice, then, is logically related to issues of multiculturalism and diversity.

Many community psychologists have contributed to the discussion of social justice within the field of psychology. Prilleltensky (1997) argued that human diversity cannot flourish without notions of justice and equality. Several other prominent community psychologists have articulated the connections among social justice, underserved populations, and the overall profession of psychology in recent years (Albee, 2000; Martin-Baró, 1994; Nelson & Prilleltensky, 2010; Ramirez, 1999). Martin-Baró (1994) discussed a form of psychology called liberation psychology that is specifically concerned with fighting injustice. He noted that liberation psychology focuses "not on what has been done [to people] but what needs to be done" (p. 6). This is relevant for action-oriented community psychologists, who may seek to transform the world, not just understand the world. Efforts to engage in such transformations are described throughout this text.

## Emphasis on Strengths and Competencies

Closely related to the idea of empowerment (see Principles) and prevention is the notion of competence and strength. The field of clinical psychology has historically focused on individuals' weaknesses and problems. Freud planted the seed of pathology focus that was cultivated by later clinicians.

| **TABLE 1.5**   Jahoda's Positive Mental Health Attributes |
| --- |
| Positive and realistic sense of self |
| Orientation to growth and development |
| Integrated and coherent self |
| Grounded in reality |
| Autonomous and independent |
| Successful adaption to the environment (in love, relationships, and problem solving in general) |

*Source:* Adapted from material in Jahoda, M. (1958). *Current concepts of positive mental health.* New York, NY: Basic Books.

Marie Jahoda (1958) directed a turn in focus toward mental health following a review of clinical research. She highlighted the advantages of examining our strengths. In particular, she pointed out that **the absence of mental illness did not make one mentally healthy.** Health was defined by the presence of positive attributes—such as a healthy sense of self—and an orientation to growth and development (Table 1.5). Soon after, Robert White (1959) wrote on the importance of **competence,** by which he meant a sense of mastery when interacting with the environment. Jahoda's and White's ideas offered a conceptual change for psychologists concerned with how clinical psychology was mired in its focus on negative behavior.

Ryan (1971) claimed that our usual response to problems was to "blame the victim." It might be blatant, such as claims of laziness, lack of intelligence, incorrect priorities, or "asking for it." It could also be more subtle, such as claims of inferior cultural opportunities, lack of adequate mentoring, or the need for more services. These all place the individual victim in a place of inferiority. What if the individual's problem was not seen as the result of "deprivation, deficits, or weakness"? What if these populations had strengths and had the resources to make the break from their confines? Ryan argued that the cause of many problems is the *lack* of power.

These historic challenges to the pathology-focused fields of psychiatry and psychology have more recently been joined by the Positive Psychology movement (Seligman, 2007; Seligman & Csikszentmihalyi, 2000). Positive psychology primarily focuses on the strengths of the individual (Seligman & Csikszentmihalyi, 2000). The parallels with community psychology's shift to a wellness focus (Cowen, 1994) are apparent but not clearly described (Schueller, 2009). Positive Psychology's research has been on the individual and thus has lacked consideration of positive environments. Those in community psychology have studied the necessary components of a high-functioning environment (Moos, 2003). Three environmental factors working together led to well-being and productivity: **strong social ties, emphases on personal growth,** and **a clear structure.** And as Keyes (2007) pointed out, "mental flourishing" has been a better indicator of well-being than has the absence of mental illness.

A strength and competence focus was embraced from the very first days of the Swampscott Conference (Bennett et al., 1966). This orientation had linkages to empowerment and to ecological principles. The focus on positives in communities and in their members shifted research and interventions toward the ways in which people were successful. These strengths can be commonly found, can be readily mobilized, and are both effective and appealing to the community (Masten, 2009). We will see examples of the research that contributed to these conclusions in Chapter 3 when we look at Stress and Resilience.

### Social Change and Action Research

Community psychology has called for **social change** from its beginnings (Bennett et al., 1966; Hill, Bond, Mulvey, & Terenzio, 2000; Rappaport, 1977; Seidman, 1988) and continues to incorporate it within its operational frameworks (Revenson et al., 2002; Tseng & Seidman, 2007). Social change may be defined as efforts to shift community values and attitudes and expectations as well as "opportunity structures" to help in the realization of the inherent strengths of all within a population. The promise of community psychology is that of social change (Prilleltensky, 2008, 2009).

Research grounded in theory and directed toward resolving social problems is called **action research.** In community psychology, much action research is *participatory,* where affected individuals are not merely "subjects" in a study but participate in shaping the research agenda (Nelson, Ochocka, Griffin, & Lord, 1998; Rappaport, 2000). An active partnership between researcher and participants is the norm (Hill et al., 2000; Nelson, Prilleltensky, & McGillivary, 2001). Ryerson Espino and Trickett (2008) presented a framework for ecological inquiry, which incorporated input from those under study into the process.

Chapter 2 describes and discusses how action research is conducted. At this point, it is important to remember that social problems are difficult to resolve, and research in community settings is complex. For instance, if one wanted to change a human services agency so that it better addresses community needs, one would probably have to research the whole agency and the people involved, including clients and staff, as well as all of their interrelationships and processes within the agency. A special issue of the *American Community Psychologist* presented articles reviewing the state of the science-practice synthesis reached in community action research. Although community psychology has successfully influenced a variety of fields within the larger psychology discipline, there continue to be creative tensions between the search for empirical validation and the need to be relevant to the context. Linney (2005) pointed to four themes arising from the science-practice issue:

1. Effective strategies to bridge science and practice, so as to strengthen the capacity to do both within the community
2. Changing who determines what is important, that is, giving the community power in determining what is important and useful, the direction of the decision making changing from a science directing practice, to a model where the community is a full partner in decision making
3. A broadening of the definition of good science beyond the "narrow" laboratory-based experimental designs
4. Dealing with the difficulty of implementing the values and ideals given the contingencies under which many psychologists work—for example, publish or perish, the valuing of true experimental designs, and the devaluing of quasi- or nonexperimental designs

As you will see in this text, community psychology sees social change and action research as an integral part of its conceptual and intervention framework.

### Interdisciplinary Perspectives

Community psychologists believe social change can be better understood and facilitated through collaboration with other disciplines (Kelly, 2010). Multidisciplinary perspectives are a means of gaining more sweeping, more thorough, and better reasoned thinking on change processes (Maton, 2000; Strother, 1987). Community psychologists have long enjoyed intellectual and research exchanges with colleagues in other academic disciplines, such as political science, anthropology, and sociology, as well as other areas of psychology, such as social psychology (Altman, 1987; Jason, Hess, Felner, & Moritsugu, 1987a). There are renewed calls for interdisciplinary efforts (Kelly, 2010; Linney, 1990; Wardlaw, 2000) with other community professionals, such as substance-abuse counselors, law enforcement personnel, school psychologists, and human services professionals.

Kelly (1990) believed that **collaboration** with others gives new awareness of how other disciplines experience a phenomenon. A benefit of consultation with others such as historians, economists, environmentalists, biologists, sociologists, anthropologists, and policy scientists is that perspectives can be expanded and new perspectives adopted. Kelly believed that such an interdisciplinary perspective helped to keep alive the excitement about discovery in the field (Kelly, 2010). In that same article he acknowledged the influence of philosophy, anthropology, social psychiatry, and poetry on his work.

Stokols (2006) described three factors necessary to have strong transdisciplinary research among researchers: (1) a sense of common goals and good leadership to help deal with conflicts that can arise; (2) proactive arrangement of contextual supports for the collaboration (institutional support, prior collaborative experience, proximity of collaborators, electronic linkage capabilities); and (3) "preparation, practice and refinement" of the collaborative effort. Stokols cautioned that work between researchers and the community increases the potential for misunderstanding. Participation of both researchers and community members in all phases of project development is helpful in these circumstances, deemphasizing status differences and establishing clear goals and outcome expectations.

Case in Point 1.3 demonstrates integration of social and community psychology theories, and Case in Point 1.4 provides us with an example of anthropological concepts and methodology contributing to a community psychology intervention.

## CASE IN POINT 1.3

# Social Psychology, Community Psychology, and Homelessness

You have learned in this chapter that community psychologists have issued a call for collaboration with other disciplines both within and outside of psychology. In response to that, we agree that community psychologists and social psychologists have much to learn from each other (Serrano-Garcia, Lopez, & Rivera-Medena, 1987). In some countries, community psychology evolved from social psychological roots. This was the case in New Zealand and Australia (Fisher, Gridley, Thomas, & Bishop, 2008).

**Social psychologists** study social phenomena as they affect an individual. They may have the answer as to why the media, the public, and other psychologists blame a person's homelessness on the person. Social psychologists have developed an explanation using **attribution theory,** which explains how people infer causes of or make attributions about others' behaviors (Kelly, 1973). Research on attribution has demonstrated that people are likely to place explanatory emphasis on the characteristics of the individual or use trait explanations for another's shortcomings (Jones & Nisbett, 1971). That is, when explaining the behavior of others—especially others' problems— people are less likely to attend to the situation and more likely to blame the person for what is happening.

Does this theory apply to homelessness? Can this theory explain why the media and the public often blame the victim, the homeless person, for his or her problem? *Victim blaming* (Ryan, 1971) is a phrase that describes the tendency to attribute the cause of an individual's problems to that individual rather than to the situation the person is in. In other words, the victim is blamed for what happened to him or her. Social psychologists believe that blaming the victim is a means of self-defense (e.g., if a bad thing can happen to her by chance, then it can happen to me; on the other hand, if the person was to blame for what happened, then it won't happen to me because I am not that way). In the case of the homeless, did their personalities create their homeless situations? Did something in their environment contribute to it? The average person who blames the victim would blame homeless people for contributing to their homelessness.

Shinn, a prominent community psychologist, reviewed research on homelessness and conducted a monumental and well-designed study on the issue (Shinn & Gillespie, 1993). She concluded that person-centered explanations of homelessness, although popular, are not as valid as situational and structural explanations of homelessness. Specifically, Shinn suggested that the researched explanations for homelessness are twofold—that is, person-centered and environmental. She reviewed the literature on each and concluded that person-centered or deficit explanations for homelessness were less appropriate than environmental or situational explanations.

Shinn found studies suggesting that structural problems offer some of the most plausible explanations of homelessness. For example, Rossi (1989) found that between 1969 and 1987, the number of single adults (some with children) with incomes under $4,000 a year increased from 3.1 to 7.2 million. Similarly, Leonard, Dolbeare, and Lazere (1989) found that for the 5.4 million low-income renters, there were only 2.1 million units of affordable housing, according to the U.S. Department of Housing and Urban Development standards. Poverty and lack of affordable housing seem to be far better explanations for today's phenomenon of homelessness than person-centered explanations. Solarz and Bogat (1990) would add to these environmental explanations of homelessness the lack of social support by friends and family of the homeless.

What is important about Shinn's review is not so much that it illustrates that the public and the media may indeed suffer from **fundamental attribution error**—the tendency to blame the person and not the situation—but rather that Shinn offers these data so community psychologists can act on them. Public policy makers need to understand that situations and structural problems produce homelessness. Psychologists and community leaders need to be convinced that temporary solutions, such as soup kitchens, are merely bandages on the gaping wound of the homeless. Furthermore, shelter managers and others have to understand that moving the homeless from one shelter to another does little for them. Families and children, not just the stereotypical old alcoholic men, are part of today's homeless (Rossi, 1990). Being in different shelters and therefore different school systems has negative effects on children's academic performance and self-esteem (Rafferty & Shinn, 1991); homeless children lose their childhoods to homelessness (Landers, 1989).

Something must be done about the permanent housing situation in this country. On this point, both community and social psychologists would agree.

## CASE IN POINT 1.4

# The Importance of Place

Anthropological methodologies were used in a study of communities recovering from a forest fire in British Columbia, Canada (Cox & Perry, 2011). Case studies presented ethnographic data, using intensive and longitudinal interviews, observations, and documents in natural settings aimed at understanding the "meanings" of a group's or culture's behaviors. A participant–observer approach was used, where the data collector became an active engaged member of the group being studied (Genzuk, 2003). The role of social capital (a sociological concept), which related to a sense of place in the land, seemed to mediate the communities' ability to adjust to the changes brought about by the fire. Social capital is defined as those supports, assets, or resources that come to a group or an individual as the result of social position within a system. The studies' findings illustrated a process of disorientation and a search for reorientation in individuals and in their communities. The assumptions as to home and its meanings were reexamined and either reinforced or discarded. The assumptions of social capital also had to be reexamined and adjusted. Identity and sense of place as defined socially and physically were challenged and required rebuilding. The research noted that rebuilding efforts were focused on material and individual-oriented goals—the survival of the person and restoration of their property. Ignored in the restoration efforts were the community's own social capital, that is, natural residential resource networks. As well, there was little attention to recovery of members' "sense of place" in their world. Recommendations were made for attention to these details at the policy level and in direct interventions.

## A Psychological Sense of Community

Early discussions of community psychology noted the seeming contradiction in the terms *community* and *psychology*. Community was associated with groups and psychology with individual experience. Proposing a possible answer to those unfamiliar with the field, Sarason (1974) suggested the study of a "psychological sense of community" (PSC). PSC has become one of the most popular concepts to emerge from community psychology: it is an individual's perception of group membership.

If environments and individuals are well matched, a community with a sense of spirit and a sense of "we-ness" can be created. Research has demonstrated that a sense of community, or what is sometimes called *community spirit* or sense of belonging in the community, is positively related to a subjective sense of well-being (Davidson & Cotter, 1991).

In an optimal community, members probably will be more open to changes that will further improve their community. On the other hand, social disintegration of a community or neighborhood often results in high fear of crime and vandalism (Ross & Jang, 2000), as well as declines in children's mental health (Caspi, Taylor, Moffitt, & Plomin, 2000) and increases in school problems (Hadley-Ives, Stiffman, Elze, Johnson, & Dore, 2000), loneliness (Prezza, Amici, Tiziana, & Tedeschi, 2001), and myriad other problems. Community disorder may intensify both the benefits of personal resources (such as connections to neighbors) and the detrimental effects of personal risk factors (Cutrona, Russell, Hessling, Brown, & Murry, 2000).

Interestingly, research has demonstrated that happiness and the sense of satisfaction with one's community are not found exclusively in the suburbs. People living in the suburbs are no more likely to express satisfaction with their neighborhoods than people living in the city (Adams, 1992) or small towns (Prezza et al., 2001). Many laypeople and psychologists believe that residents of the inner city are at risk for myriad problems. However, research has found that some very resilient individuals are located in the most stressful parts of our cities (Work, Cowen, Parker, & Wyman, 1990).

**Community** has traditionally meant a locality or place such as a neighborhood. It has also come to mean a relational interaction or social ties that draw people together (Heller, 1989b). To these definitions could be added the one of community as a collective political power. Brodsky (2009) also notes that we have multiple communities to which we may have allegiance.

If those are the definitions for *community,* what is the sense of community? **Sense of community** is the feeling of the relationship an individual holds for his or her community (Heller et al., 1984) or the personal knowledge that one has about belonging to a collective of others (Newbrough & Chavis, 1986). More specifically, it is

> the perception of similarity to others, an acknowledged interdependence with others, a willingness to maintain this interdependence by giving to or doing for others what one expects from them, the feeling that one is part of a larger dependable and stable structure. (Sarason, 1974, p. 157)

If people sense community in their neighborhood, they feel that they belong to or fit into the neighborhood. Community members sense that they can influence what happens in the community, share the values of the neighborhood, and feel emotionally connected to it (Heller et al., 1984).

A sense of community is specifically thought to include four elements: membership, influence, integration, and a sense of emotional connection (McMillan & Chavis, 1986):

1. *Membership* means that people experience feelings of belonging in their community.
2. *Influence* signifies that people feel they can make a difference in their community.
3. *Integration,* or fulfillment of needs, suggests that members of the community believe that their needs will be met by resources available in the community.
4. *Emotional connection* implies that community members have and will share history, time, places, and experiences.

Although there have been a variety of criticisms and alternatives to this conceptualization of psychological sense of community (Long & Perkins, 2003; Tartaglia, 2006), the operational definition of this sense by McMillan and Chavis (1986) remains the definitive model for this concept. Long and Perkins (2003) found a three-factor structure for their data: social connections, mutual concerns, and community values. Tartaglia (2006), using an Italian sample, produced a three-factor measure that included attachment to place, needs fulfillment and influence, and social bonds. In its newest evolution, Peterson, Speer, and McMillan (2008) have produced an eight-item Brief Sense of Community Scale, which produces all four of the McMillan and Chavis (1986) elements with significant statistical validity.

A scale developed by Buckner (1988) measured neighborhood cohesion or fellowship. Wilkinson (2007) found validation of Buckner's conceptualization of neighborhood cohesion, and a three-factor structure to his data, taken from a Canadian sample. In Wilkinson's study, "cohesion" was based on a psychological sense of community, neighboring (visiting others and being visited), and attraction for the community ("I like being here.").

Among the many groups whose psychological sense of community has been studied are Australian Aboriginals (Bishop, Colquhoun, & Johnson, 2006), Native American youth (Kenyon & Carter, 2011), Afghan women (Brodsky, 2009), German naval cadets (Wombacher, Tagg, Bürgi, & MacBryde, 2010), gay men (Proescholdbell, Roosa, & Nemeroff, 2006), churches (Miers & Fisher, 2002), university classrooms (Yasuda, 2009), and the seriously mentally ill (Townley & Kloos, 2011). As Peterson and colleagues (2008) said, sense of community is a "key theoretical construct" of community psychology.

A related but separate concept to sense of community is that of **neighborhoods.** These are defined as local communities that are bounded together spatially, where residents feel a sense of social cohesion and interaction, a sense of homogeneity (or sameness), as well as place identity (Coulton, Korbin, & Su, 1996). Research has demonstrated the utility of conceptualizing "sense of community" separately from "neighborhoods" (Prezza et al., 2001), but they can be related. Although neighborhoods are primarily based on geographic boundaries, they are best defined by their inhabitants and do not necessarily conform to political or formal maps. They are psychologically defined. One can see from the description found in Table 1.6 that the questions relate to individual's perceptions.

## Training in Community Psychology

There are established training programs for those interested in studying community psychology. Students are trained to conduct research and to intervene from a set of community psychology theories and values. Just as the practice of community psychology is varied, so are the perspectives provided. See the accompanying four tables of graduate training programs (Tables 1.7 through 1.10).

---

**TABLE 1.6**

**The Brief Sense of Community Scale** by Peterson, Speer, and Hughey (2006) seeks information on:

   **Relationships/Social Connection**—I talk to others; I know others here

   **Mutual Concerns**—We want the same things

   **Bonding/Community Values**—It feels like a community to me; I like it here

---

*Source:* From Peterson, N. A., Speer, P., & Hughey, J. (2006). Measuring sense of community: A methodological interpretation of a factor structure debate. *Journal of Community Psychology, 34,* 453–469.

**TABLE 1.7    Doctoral Programs in Community Psychology**

- DePaul University, Department of Psychology—Chicago, IL
- Edith Cowan University, School of Psychology and Social Science—Joondalup, Australia
- Georgia State University, Department of Psychology—Atlanta, GA
- Instituto Superior de PsicologiaAplicada, (ISPA), Department of Psychology—Lisbon, Portugal
- Michigan State University, Department of Psychology—East Lansing, MI
- National-Louis University, Department of Psychology—Chicago, IL
- Pacifica Graduate Institute, Department of Psychology—Carpinteria, CA
- Portland State University, Department of Psychology—Portland, OR
- University of Hawaii, Department of Psychology—Honolulu, HI
- University of Illinois at Chicago, Department of Psychology—Chicago, IL
- Université Laval, Department of Psychology—Québec City, Canada
- University of Maryland, Baltimore County, Department of Psychology—Baltimore, MD
- University of Quebec, Department of Psychology—Montreal, Canada
- University of Virginia, Department of Psychology—Charlottesville, VA
- University of Waikato, School of Arts and Social Sciences—Hamilton, New Zealand
- Wichita State University, Department of Psychology—Wichita, KS
- Wilfrid Laurier University, Department of Psychology—Waterloo, Canada

*Source:* From www.scra27.org/resources/educationc/academicpr.

**TABLE 1.8    Doctoral Programs in Clinical–Community Psychology**

- Arizona State University, Department of Psychology—Tempe, AZ
- Bowling Green State University, Department of Psychology—Bowling Green, OH
- California School of Professional Psychology, School of Professional Psychology—Los Angeles, CA
- DePaul University, Department of Psychology—Chicago, IL
- George Washington University, Department of Psychology—Washington, DC
- Georgia State University, Department of Psychology—Atlanta, GA
- Michigan State University, Department of Psychology—East Lansing, MI
- Rutgers University, Graduate School of Applied & Professional Psychology—Piscataway, NJ
- University of Alaska, Department of Psychology—Anchorage or Fairbanks, AK
- University of Illinois, Champaign-Urbana, Department of Psychology—Urbana-Champaign, IL
- University of La Verne, Department of Psychology—La Verne, CA
- University of Maryland, Baltimore County, Department of Psychology—Baltimore, MD
- University of South Carolina, Department of Psychology—Columbia, SC
- Wayne State University, Department of Psychology—Detroit, MI
- Wichita State University, Department of Psychology—Wichita, KS

*Source:* From www.scra27.org/resources/educationc/academicpr.

| **TABLE 1.9    Doctoral Programs in Interdisciplinary Community and Prevention Programs** |
| --- |

- Clemson University, "International Family and Community Studies," Institute on Family and Neighborhood Life—Clemson, SC

- Georgetown University, "Psychology and Public Policy," Department of Psychology—Washington, DC

- North Carolina State University, "Psychology in the Public Interest," Department of Psychology—Raleigh, NC

- Penn State University, "Human Developmental and Family Studies," Dept. of Human Development and Family Studies—University Park, PA

- University of California—Santa Cruz, "Social Psychology with a Social Justice Focus," Department of Psychology—Santa Cruz, CA

- University of Guelph, Ontario, "Applied Social Psychology," Department of Psychology—Ontario, Canada

- University of Kansas, "Applied Behavioral Science," KU Workgroup for Community and Health Development—Lawrence, KS

- University of Michigan, "Health Behavior and Health Education," Department of Health Behavior and Health Education—Ann Arbor, MI

- University of North Carolina, Charlotte, "Community Health Psychology," Department of Psychology—Charlotte, NC

- University of North Carolina, Greensboro, "Community Health," Department of Psychology—Greensboro, NC

- University of Wisconsin–Madison, "Human Development and Family Studies," School of Human Ecology—Madison, WI

- Vanderbilt University, "Community Research and Action," Department of Human and Organizational Development—Nashville, TN

*Source:* From www.scra27.org/resources/educationc/academicpr.

One might note that programs can be selected from around the world. The doctoral programs include both community psychology and clinical–community specialties. There is also a category of interdisciplinary doctoral programs, which include areas such as public health, family studies, and applied social psychology.

Clinical–community programs train in both the traditional clinical skills of testing and therapy, and the community-oriented skills of preventive community interventions. Freestanding community psychology programs emphasize ecological and systems orientations to assessment and interventions. Courses at the graduate level might include program evaluation, social action research, applied social psychology, consultation, grant writing, and community field work.

O'Donnell and Ferrari (2000) collected essays on community psychologist employment from around the world. They found that the training of community psychologists had prepared them for a diverse set of opportunities. Although university positions were among the jobs mentioned, individuals found many other types of work: for example, as consultants, evaluators, grant writers, directors of people's centers, researchers, and policy makers.

**TABLE 1.10    Master's Programs in Community Psychology**

- The Adler School of Professional Psychology—Vancouver, Canada
- The American University in Cairo, Psychology Unit—Cairo, Egypt
- Antioch University, Department of Psychology—Los Angeles, CA
- University of Brighton, School of Applied Social Science—Brighton, UK
- Central Connecticut State University, Department of Psychology—New Britain, CA
- Edith Cowan University, School of Psychology and Social Science—Joondalup, Australia
- Manchester Metropolitan University, Faculty of Health, Psychology, and Social Care—Manchester, England
- University of Massachusetts Lowell, Psychology Department—Lowell, MA
- Metropolitan State University, College of Professional Studies—St. Paul, MN
- University of New Haven, Department of Psychology and Sociology—West Haven, CT
- Pacifica Graduate Institute, Department of Psychology—Carpinteria, CA
- Penn State Harrisburg, School of Behavioral Sciences and Education—Harrisburg, PA
- Portland State University, Psychology Department—Portland, OR
- The Sage Colleges, Department of Psychology—Albany, NY
- Instituto Superior de Psicologia Aplicada, Department of Psychology—Lisbon, Portugal
- The University of the Incarnate Word, Psychology Department—San Antonio, TX
- Victoria University of Technology, School of Psychology—Melbourne, Australia
- University of Waikato, School of Arts and Social Sciences—Hamilton, New Zealand
- Wilfrid Laurier University, Department of Psychology—Waterloo, Ontario, Canada

*Source:* From www.scra27.org/resources/educationc/academicpr.

## PLAN OF THE TEXT

Now that you are on your way to understanding community psychology, you probably would like to know what the rest of your journey through this text will be like. The remainder of Part I, which is the introductory portion of the text, introduces you to research processes (Chapter 2) and the stress and resilience models (Chapter 3) from which work in community settings takes direction. Researchers in community psychology employ some of the venerated methods used by other psychologists as well as techniques that are fairly unique and innovative. You then explore the stress and resilience models for understanding adaptation and adjustment to the social environment.

Part II consists of two chapters on social change (Chapter 4) and interventions (Chapter 5). The first chapter outlines some of the reasons for social change. The second chapter describes some strategies for community interventions.

Part III (Chapters 6–12) examines systems to which community psychology can be applied. From mental health settings and issues, community psychologists have easily moved into social and human services, school systems, criminal justice, health care, and organizational settings.

Part IV, the final chapter of the text, looks ahead at what the future holds for the field of community psychology.

## Summary

Community psychology evolved from social science attempts to understand the human condition and effectively improve it. Lewin's and Lindeman's legacies have been apparent in the themes of social change and community research. With a belief in the power of diversity, an understanding of the influence of context on individual actions, a realization of the advantages of a multilayered ecological perspective on behavior patterns and how they can be effectively changed, and a conviction that empowered individuals can be healthier individuals, community psychology addresses the prevention of pathology and the promotion of health. Embedded in these principles is the assumption that we all seek and need community. Without it, we are alone and alienated. With it, we are grounded and secure. The area has grown from a set of ideas to an organized and developing approach to psychological research and interventions. For those interested in pursuing graduate studies in this area, there are a variety of options available. Finally, the text organization is outlined to provide a cognitive map of what is to come.

# 2

# Scientific Research Methods

*The essential point in science is not a complicated mathematical formalism or a ritualized experimentation. Rather the heart of science is a kind of shrewd honesty that springs from really wanting to know what is going on!*

—Saul-Paul Sirag

*The connection between cause and effect has no beginning and can have no end.*

—Leo Tolstoy, *War and Peace*

*It's tough to make predictions, especially about the future.*

—Yogi Berra

Larry liked to take a walk around his neighborhood every evening. The sidewalk was busy with foot traffic, even late at night. The one great annoyance was having to navigate through dog waste that littered the block. Larry sometimes wondered how much of this was deposited every day around his block, and whether there was anything he could do to decrease the amount left on the street. When he brought up the topic in a conversation at work, he found that some research on the problem had been done many years earlier. The research found that wherever dog litter was allowed, the dogs' owners would leave a good deal of it behind. Looking further, Larry also found that a fairly simple program of modeling and prompting could greatly reduce this problem.

Arun and his family had planned on buying a house for several years. When the time came to decide on neighborhoods to explore, he asked questions not only about transportation options, but about the schools as well. What were they like? What were their strengths and weaknesses? What programs were available to his children? How successful were the schools in educating beyond the basics of mathematics, reading, and writing? Did graduates go on to higher education? Where? For Arun, who saw his home as more than a building to house a family, these seemed reasonable questions to ask. The neighborhood and the community could be measured by the success of its institutions. How was the community doing in terms of educating its children? Arun wanted to know so he could make an informed choice as to what his neighborhood would be like. He was asking for data he believed answered some basic questions about the social environment into which he was bringing his family.

## THE ESSENCE OF SCIENTIFIC RESEARCH

### Why Do Scientific Research?

Science is for the curious. We seek information about our world and make decisions on how to act based on that information. We have come to assume that our experiences in life help us determine what is true and real. This assumption, that experience is our window on reality, is called *empiricism*. The tradition of examining the world around us for evidence of what to believe goes back to the Greek philosophers, to the astronomers of the Middle East, and later to the observational studies of the Renaissance. We have come to accept this tradition as the science on which our modern world is built. How do we understand what is around us? We observe it, note its regularities and patterns, test its possibilities, and determine the likelihood that particular events predict or cause other events. Among our questions might be: What makes a community? What about a community makes it a healthy and happy one?

A major intervention strategy in the field of community psychology is to create or engage in some form of social change so that individuals and communities can benefit. To distinguish effective from less effective changes, psychologists need a way to understand and assess these changes. Scientific research provides that mechanism; thus, it has been an essential part of community psychology from its conception and throughout its development (Anderson et al., 1966; Lorion, 1983; Price, 1983; Tolan, Keys, Chertak, & Jason, 1990).

For example, how can researchers be sure that decreases in a risky behavior such as unprotected sex are solely due to people's participation in some form of prevention program? Although we might find that the men and women who enroll in such programs are less likely to engage in unprotected sex than are those who do not, further analysis might indicate that those with spouses who are willing to use condoms are the ones who benefit from the programs. That is, for many, enrollment in a prevention program is not sufficient to reduce unprotected sex *unless* they can go back to a home environment or community with some support (the ecological perspective). The validity of the program's effectiveness needs to be closely examined to determine what makes it work.

Price (1983) pointed to areas in which the community psychologist would need to do research. First, problems or areas of concern must be identified and described. Second, the factors related to these problems and concerns must be articulated. Based on this articulation, possible interventions or solutions can be constructed and tested. Once a program has been found to be effective, it must still be determined whether the intervention can be successfully implemented in particular community contexts. If the implementation succeeds, then the issue of successfully launching the program on a broader scale needs to be studied. If the program is successful, the researcher is left to reexamine the community status and see what other needs may exist. The research cycle provides guidance from identification of community problems to community-wide dissemination of answers. This process is an integral part of community psychology.

The notion that a research process should inform our actions seems both reasonable and practical. If we can know and predict our world, we are at a clear advantage in what we do. The most recent concerns within community psychology are over the best ways to capture data; no voices speak against the advantages of empirical research as a valuable guide to the field (Aber, Maton, & Seidman, 2011; Jason & Glenwick, 2012; Jason, Keys, Suarez-Balcazar, Taylor, & Davis, 2004). If anything, the focus is on how to gather better—that is, more ecologically meaningful—data.

## What Is Scientific Research?

On a daily basis, people observe and make attributions about many things. For example, you might have some hunches as to why men do or do not use condoms or why people abuse alcohol and drugs. Scientists see research as the way to go beyond hunches. In other words, when scientists conduct research, by using a set of related assumptions and activities, they effectively come to understand the world around them. Figure 2.1 depicts the process of scientific research.

Theory and theory-based research are an integral part of all scientific disciplines (Kuhn, 1962/1996), and the field of community psychology is no exception. The early applied social psychologist Kurt Lewin once said, "There is nothing more practical than a good theory." We agree. Why is theory so powerful? That is because theory directs our research and helps us to avoid some common pitfalls in the conducting of scientific inquiries.

**THEORY.** At one time or another, you probably have heard people use the terms *theory, model,* and *paradigm.* The words are often used interchangeably, but they are not quite synonymous. A **theory** is a systematic attempt to explain observable or measurable events relating to an issue such as homelessness or alcoholism. More exactly, a theory is a "set of interrelated constructs (concepts), definitions, and propositions that present a systematic view of phenomena by specifying relations among variables, with the purpose of explaining or predicting the phenomena" (Kerlinger, 1973, p. 9). The goal of a theory is to allow researchers to **describe, predict,** and **control for** *why* and *how* a variable or variables relate to observable or measurable events pertaining to an issue.

**FIGURE 2.1** The Process of Scientific Research

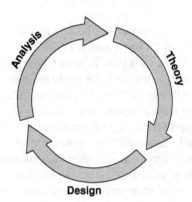

Analysis

Theory

Design

Bear in mind that social science theories serve best as guideposts for studying observable or measurable events. In other words, description and prediction of as well as controls for these events are based on suggested *rules* rather than *absolute laws* like those found in the physical sciences (Kuhn, 1962/1996).

**MODELS AND PARADIGMS.**   Models and paradigms influence research in that they provide a framework for our studies. In a formal science, preconceptions and assumptions resulting from earlier work help to guide current work. Thus, science does not start from the beginning, with no idea of how to proceed and no "understanding" of the world. Rather, previous work helps to formulate the questions and the manner in which they are answered. We might liken it to a child exploring the world. The experiences of the child's ancestors, social group, and others influential in the child's world serve as guides in this process of discovery.

A **model** is a working blueprint of how a theory works. A **paradigm** is a smaller component from within the model that guides researchers to conceptualize specific event sequences. Figure 2.2 depicts these relationships. (In his classic but controversial essay on science and scientific revolutions, Kuhn, 1962/1996, uses the term *paradigm* with two meanings. The first is to describe a set or collection of ideas, values, and theories that are commonly agreed on in a sociological way to guide the direction and conduct of scientific inquiry. The second sense is as the "concrete puzzle solution" to a given problem. We use the term *paradigm* in our description of the progression from theory to model to paradigm. In this case, we intend the paradigm to be the "concrete puzzle solution." However, when we speak of "paradigm shifts" in psychology, *paradigm* is used in the first sense of the word—that is, the sociologically based collective and group-oriented definition of the term. Initial reactions to Kuhn criticized his mixing of definitions, which was confusing. He tried to clarify and correct this in an apologetic postscript in the later edition of his book.)

A theory may develop more than one model. These models guide researchers' understanding of the various observable events. In the case of undeveloped theories, observable events can be explained by more than one theory. Of course, this can be confusing.

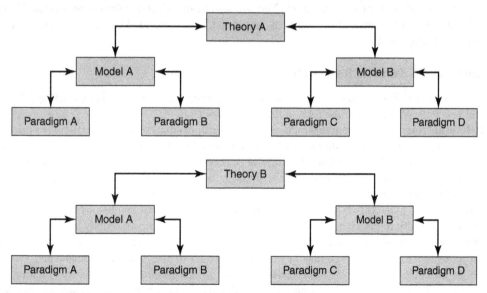

**FIGURE 2.2**   The Relationships among Theories, Models, and Paradigms

**FALSIFIABILITY.** According to Popper (1957/1990), the hallmark of a science is continuous testing of the proposition or theory at hand. The testing assumes that it is always possible that the proposition or theory being tested is false. This *falsifiability* calls for a reliance on observable events to help support or reject any given concept.

**EXAMPLE.** For decades, researchers investigating alcoholism or alcohol abuse conceptualized excessive drinking as a consequence of a genetic predisposition, using the medical explanation of alcoholism as a disease (the theoretical perspective). This theory helped shape the development of various models about alcohol abuse, all of which described individual tendencies totally out of the control of the individual.

In recent years, some researchers have begun to challenge the genetic disease theory of alcoholism. Instead, they argue that some aspects of excessive alcohol use (the observable or measurable event) may be a consequence of something in the environment, such as stress from losing one's home, a difficult life on the streets, prolonged unemployment, or some traumatic life event. Thus, a new theory emerges—the distress or disorder theory of alcoholism. This sociological *paradigm shift* or refocusing of thinking or conceptualizing from genetics to environment leads to the development of new models. One model specifies that socioeconomic status might influence alcoholism. Another suggests that social stress plays a role. In other words, this theory allows for the prediction and description of differential alcohol use for individuals with different environments. On the other hand, the first theory—the disease theory—offers prediction and description of individual differences based on genetics.

**SCIENTIFIC REVOLUTIONS.** This example illustrates the dynamic nature of scientific theories. Kuhn (1962/1996) argued that major scientific development is not linear, or a step-by-step accumulation of facts. Such is the case with the development of community psychology as an alternative theory concerning the development of mental health and mental illness. Within a scientific discipline, a crisis may cause a shift in thinking; such a sociological paradigm shift may shape the development of a new theory. Recall that just such a crisis (discouragement with traditional methods of conceptualizing and treating mental illness) gave birth to the field of community psychology. We should expect the development of new theories and models, as well as new methods for studying human phenomena in the psychological realm.

You will read about many of the current theories, models, and paradigms in the field of community psychology in other chapters of this book. You will also be introduced to the research related to each theory; through research, one makes judgments about theories. Case in Point 2.1 introduces an integrated theory of drug abuse.

## The Fidelity of Scientific Research

Reliability, internal validity, and external validity are the three sets of related issues that speak to the fidelity of research. We now examine each of these in more detail.

**Reliability** refers to the extent to which measurable features of a theory are trustworthy or dependable. When two observers rate or describe what they saw or heard, will they agree? If so, we tend to believe their description. This is called *inter-rater* or *observer reliability*. When a question is asked two times, does it get the same or a similar answer? If it does, then we trust that the answer will remain consistent. If the question is asked twice within the same set of questions, we call that *internal reliability*. If the question is asked twice at two separate occasions across time, we call that *test–retest reliability*.

**Internal validity** refers to the degree to which we believe the results of a study truly describe what happens in a given set of research circumstances—that in an experiment, the independent variable is indeed responsible for any observed changes in a dependent variable (Campbell & Stanley, 1963). In other words, research is said to have high internal validity when confounding effects are at a minimum. **Confounding effects** are extraneous variables that influence the dependent variable and invalidate the conclusions drawn from the research. For example, using Wong and Bouey's (2001) theory of drug

# A Theory of Substance Abuse and HIV/STDs that Incorporates the Principles of Community Psychology

There are more than 40 theories for studying drug abuse (see Lettieri, Sayers, & Pearson, 1984). Some of these theories are person centered, such as the medical or genetic theory of alcoholism; other theories are environmental, such as the stress or disorder theory.

On the basis of 24 studies, Flay and Petraitis (1991) identified a number of determinants of drug abuse. They concluded that the determinants are some combination of the following: the social environment; social bonding of the individual to the family, peers, and community organizations such as schools; social learning and learning from others; intrapsychic factors such as self-esteem; and the individual's own knowledge of, attitudes toward, and behaviors related to alcohol and drugs. Flay and Petraitis argued that most theories about substance abuse address only one of these domains. For the field to advance, an effort needs to be made to integrate more of these domains into one coherent theory. Community psychologists would heartily agree.

Responding to this challenge, Wong and Bouey (2001) proposed an integrated theory for studying substance abuse as well as human immunodeficiency virus (HIV) and sexually transmitted diseases (STDs) among American Indian/Alaska Natives (AI/ANs). This population was singled out because, compared to other racial/ethnic groups in the United States, many AI/ANs have a more serious substance abuse problem (National Household Survey on Drug Abuse, 1999, in Substance Abuse and Mental Health Services Administration, 2000; Improving HIV Surveillance, 2013), which places them at risk for STDs, including HIV.

Most substance abuse and HIV prevention and intervention programs have enlisted psychosocial models of individual behavior. These models, however, tend to isolate individuals and assume that they all follow regular and rational decision-making processes (e.g., DiClemente & Peterson, 1994; Leviton, 1989; Valdiserri, West, Moore, Darrow, & Hinman, 1992), a position consistent with the reasoning of the dominant medical model in health-related programs (Singer et al., 1990). Although individuals are undeniably the key component of such programs, individual behavior occurs in a complex social and cultural context, and analysis that removes that behavior from its broader setting ignores essential determinants (Auerbach, Wypijewska, & Brodie, 1994). Individuals may, in fact, behave rationally, but they do so within the confines of their own sociocultural milieus. Attempting to address this breadth of factors leads to the recognition that responses to typical knowledge, attitude, and behavior measures are constructions by individual actors situated within the interplay of political, economic, social, and cultural realms (Bouey et al., 1997; Nemoto et al., 1998; see Figure 2.3). These forces create opportunities and obstacles for individuals and define the parameters within which they function (Connors & McGrath, 1997). Bouey and others (1997) and Nemoto and others (1998) asserted that it is also necessary to recognize that although these domains are frequently isolated as conceptually distinct entities, they have multiple dimensions and they overlap each other. If we are to understand and address solutions to drug–HIV risks, we must perceive clients as participants in these systemic contexts. Also, these contexts are dynamic. They and their constituent ele-

ments evolve rapidly within themselves and within their encompassing milieus. Thus, historical processes are of great significance in helping us to understand the choices made by individuals. In brief, it is useful to understand substance use/abuse, sexual risk practices, and HIV/STDs among AI/ANs as outputs of a *process* that involves or moves through at least *five domains*. This research can help in deriving preventive models for dealing with particular problems (Figure 2.3).

Within this theoretical setting, all populations are subject to factors associated with the distribution of power and resources (Connors & McGrath, 1997). This applies to all individuals in the larger scale of political-economic systems, as well as to those same persons in smaller-scale personal relationships (Connors & McGrath, 1997). Marginalized inner-city populations provide the extreme examples of these relationships. Unemployment, homelessness, substandard nutrition, violence, substance abuse, lack of health care access, stress, class, race, gender relations, family, community organizations, support networks, sex-partner networks, and culture among other features of inner-city life contribute to this imbalance (Connors & McGrath, 1997; Singer, 1994a; Singer et al., 1990; Weeks, Schensul, Williams, Singer, & Grier, 1995).

As a consequence of these extremes, inner-city conditions represent one example of international manifestation of acquired immunodeficiency syndrome (AIDS) as a disease of poverty, wherein AIDS is just one of a host of community problems (Singer & Weeks, 1996). These circumstances also exhibit tremendous structural variability, supporting the notion that the AIDS pandemic is more adequately described as thousands of

(*continued*)

## CASE IN POINT 2.1

### (Continued)

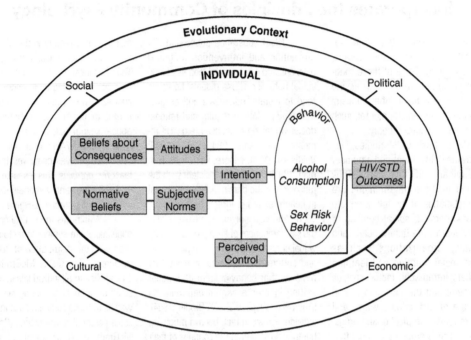

**FIGURE 2.3**  A Conceptual Model of HIV/STD Prevention

separate epidemics (Mann, Tarantola, & Netter, 1992). Exploratory models need to address individuals and communities through these unique circumstances, and these models have to possess the capacity to adjust to each "micro-epidemic and its particular route(s) of transmission, subpopulation at risk, and socio-behavioral context" (Singer & Weeks, 1996, p. 490; also see Singer, 1994b).

Inner-city populations also constitute one class of "hidden populations" (Lambert, 1990; Watters & Biernacki, 1989), groups that are out of the mainstream and little known to those outside their boundaries. These communities are a particular challenge for research and program development, because they can be hard to define, difficult to understand, and especially complex. The first step toward project goals is to engage the communities in the process, opening a dialogue to

define their needs and priorities (Wallerstein & Bernstein, 1998; Weeks, Singer, Grier, Hunte-Marrow, & Haughton, 1991). Through this form of participation, for example, we can learn how people assign meaning to their encompassing networks and communities, how they perceive risk and vulnerability, how they behave in particular ways, and how they are most likely to respond to prevention and intervention efforts. These models also must reflect the "micro-epidemics" and must use cultural information in a culturally competent manner (Singer & Borrero, 1984; Trotter, 1995; Weeks, 1990).

Although it is clear that context has a tremendous influence on each individual, context alone does not account for all relevant aspects of the model. *Individuals* themselves play an important role, not only in the perpetuation of risky behaviors but also in constructing the

parameters of those behaviors as well as their resolutions. Various psychosocial learning and behavior theories apply to these circumstances, and although their specific labels and categories might differ, they share the same basic components. For example, the health belief model (e.g., Becker, 1974; Becker & Maiman, 1980; Janz & Becker, 1984) and the theory of planned behavior (e.g., Ajzen, 1985, 1991; Ajzen & Fishbein, 1980) both incorporate aspects of an individual perspective, of a societal or normative perspective, of an individual's desire to behave in a particular manner, and of an individual's actual behavior. Versions of both models also integrate self-efficacy (Bandura, 1986, 1994) or "perceived control" (Ajzen, 1985; also see Jemmott & Jemmott, 1994) as key elements, and both identify nonspecific external factors as having some influence on any segment of the central, "individual" section of the model.

These learning/behavior models have been successfully used for decades and continue to be instrumental in contemporary efforts to describe, explain, and alter health-related behaviors. Wong and Bouey (2001) incorporated the theory of planned behavior into a more inclusive political–economic model with the intent of obtaining an improved understanding of substance use/abuse, sexual risk practices, and HIV/STDs (see Figure 2.3). The theory of planned behavior holds that HIV/STD infections are determined by behavior, which in turn is predicted by

intentions. The latter are a product of individual attitudes and subjective norms, both results of more inclusive individual perceptions of social group expectations and of behavioral consequences. This particular model has been selected because it has a long history of development and because it has been used successfully in prevention and intervention efforts related to general health, sexual risk behaviors, and substance abuse. For interventions focusing on individuals, this model directs attention to specific attitudinal and normative components that are salient to certain behaviors. Simultaneously, with the expanded

scope of our political–economic model, one can isolate contextual and structural factors that predict beliefs/attitudes and norms related to behaviors. Individuals integrate these inputs, in addition to those they carry with their personal histories, and construct their perceptions of behavior and norms. Attitudes and subjective norms are derived from these exchanges, ultimately defining intentions with commensurate behavioral correlates. This framework is directly applicable to substance use/abuse, sexual risk practices, and HIV/STDs, facilitating the identification of linkages surrounding and coupling those behaviors.

---

abuse, pregnancy status (an individual characteristic) is said to have high internal validity if it is related to the number of days of sobriety (the results) of women participating in primary and secondary substance-abuse prevention or treatment programs. On the other hand, pregnancy status might not be related to sobriety because some other factor (e.g., brain size or the presence of friends who use drugs) is related instead. Researchers would then acknowledge that pregnancy status is not internally valid.

**External validity** refers to the generalizability of results from one study to other settings and outside the laboratory. Can we generalize the findings to people living in the real world? Do the results apply to larger community settings? Sue (1999) argues that the consideration of external validity is not given a high enough priority in research where diverse populations are not represented by diverse study samples. Where diversity matters in the variables under investigation, the study's methodology should account for it. Many psychology studies are done with first-year college students. They are not representative of the population of the United States, much less the population of the world. Using Wong and Bouey's (2001) work on drug abuse as an example, one may find that women in New York City (urban dwelling) who enroll in substance-abuse prevention or treatment programs are less likely to abuse drugs during pregnancy compared to those in Long Island (suburban or rural dwelling), who may not follow the same pattern. Until these results are replicated with similar samples in other cities and settings, the study results must be interpreted as applicable only to New York City women.

A number of factors may also influence the fidelity of research. Most studies hoping to generalize their results to a given population assume a representative sample from that population. The classic manner to achieve representativeness is through **random sampling,** where all potential participants have an equal chance of being selected for a study. A biased sample occurs when those selected for a study are somehow disproportionally weighted so that the sample is not representative of the population. If we were interested in the opinions of both males and females at a school and got mostly males in our sample, we could not honestly say the study was fair.

A consequence of biased sampling is **diffusion of treatment,** meaning that it is difficult to draw definitive conclusions about the respective efficiency and effectiveness of a program because the program is not pure. The effects of one treatment have spilled over into the other. Participants in such programs are also likely to have other problems (e.g., homelessness) in addition to substance abuse, which make them likely to drop out of the study. This is known as **experimental mortality.** Enrollment in such programs is no guarantee that participants' subsequent abstinence or recovery is solely due to components of the programs. Possibly certain client characteristics (e.g., less physical tolerance of the drug) can naturally lead to abstinence or recovery over time. In other words, the desirable outcome is due to some form of **maturation.** Certain historical events might also influence results (e.g., a terrorist attack influencing people's attitudes toward the right to privacy).

## TRADITIONAL SCIENTIFIC RESEARCH METHODS

There are traditional group research strategies that are used by all psychologists, including community psychologists. The usual first step in devising a study is to conduct a review of the scientific literature. The researcher then draws what appears to be the logical conclusion from reading the past work. A statement of what might be expected from a study is called a **hypothesis.** (More formally, it is a tentative assumption made to draw out and test its logical or empirical consequences—a definition adapted from the *Merriam–Webster Online Dictionary*.) The researcher chooses which of two research designs to use in the study to examine the hypothesis, the correlational or the experimental design. The **design** is the systematic plan to test this hypothesis.

Researchers use these designs to guide what kinds of data are gathered from groups of people, and how data gathering is carried out. Assumptions are made regarding what these group data represent. This takes us into definitions of population and sampling.

We now look at these definitions, explore the two traditional research designs, and then look at a third category called the quasi-experimental design, which attempts to gain the explanatory advantages of the experimental design while dealing with the situational limitations that such a design sometimes presents to the researcher (see Table 2.1). We follow the descriptions of

**TABLE 2.1   Characteristics of Three Scientific Research Designs**

|  | Correlation | Quasi-experimental | Experimental |
|---|---|---|---|
| Type of question | Are the variables of interest related to each other? | Does an independent variable that the researcher does not completely control affect the dependent variable or the research result? | Is there a relationship between independent and dependent variables that addresses the cause? |
| When used | Researcher is unable to manipulate an independent variable. Sometimes used in explanatory research. | Researcher wants to assess the impact of real-life intervention in the community or elsewhere. | Researcher has control over the independent variable and can minimize the number of confounding variables in the research. |
| Advantages | Convenience of data collection. May avoid certain ethical and/or practical problems. | Provides some information about cause–effect relationships. Permits assessment of more real-world interventions. | Ability to demonstrate cause–effect relationship. Permits control over confounding variables and the ruling out of alternative explanations. |
| Disadvantages | Cannot establish a cause–effect relationship. | Lack of control over confounding variable. Strong causal inference cannot be made. | Some questions cannot be studied experimentally for either practical or ethical reasons. May lead to artificial procedures. |

*Source:* Adapted from Wong, Blakely, & Worsham (1991). Copyright 1991 by Guilford Press. Used with permission.

these designs with an exploration of other research methods likely to be used by community psychologists.

## Population and Sampling

Social research attempts to understand human behavior. A **population** is defined as the group of people that the research is attempting to understand. If we want to know how people in New Zealand think and behave, the population is "all the people in New Zealand." If we are interested in males in Seattle, the population is "all the males in Seattle." Psychology's ambition is to understand all human beings, in which case the population is all human beings. That is the ambition—but getting data on an entire population is difficult. We therefore use a sample of those in whom we are interested.

A **sample** is a subset of the population that is supposed to represent that population. A **random sample** is a sample in which every member of a population has an equal chance of being selected. In contrast, a **convenience sample** is chosen for no other reason than it is available. College students represent a convenience sample, because the students are readily available to participate in research conducted in psychology departments at colleges and universities. A **stratified sample** tries to match the known characteristics of the population; for example, if we know that 40% of the population is male, we would try to get a sample that is 40% male. A **purposive sample** is one chosen for a specific reason. In a test of drug use among pregnant women, only pregnant women would be chosen to be assessed; they represent a purposive sample. Random samples are the revered form of sampling in psychology.

## Correlational Research

**Correlational methods** include a class of designs (e.g., surveys) and measurement procedures, as well as techniques (e.g., self-report), that allow one to examine the *associations or relationships* between two or more variables in their natural environments. In other words, correlational methods do not contain active manipulations of the variables under study; rather, they are usually descriptive. For example, using Wong and Bouey's (2001) theory of drug abuse, one might want to investigate the relationship between the number of months a woman has been pregnant and the severity of her substance abuse; these variables are not manipulated. The fact that one has no control over them means that the distinction of independent from dependent variables may be arbitrary, albeit dictated by a theory.

Causation cannot be determined from correlational studies, because intervening or other unstudied variables could have produced the effects noted. Associations can be **spurious** (false while giving the appearance of being correct) when intervening or confounding variables are responsible for the relationships. In experimental research, intervening variables are controlled for by randomly assigning participants to groups, holding conditions constant, and manipulating the independent variable. In correlational research, the methodology seldom if ever achieves these conditions.

In its simple form, the associations between two or more variables are quantified using a statistic known as the **Pearson correlation coefficient,** which ranges from +1.00 to –1.00. The sign (+ or –) indicates the direction of the association. For example, if the sign is positive (+), both variables move in the same direction, or as one gets smaller, so does the other. A positive correlation can also mean that as one variable increases, so does the other. A negative or inverse correlation means that the variables move in opposite directions. For example, as one variable increases, the other decreases. The number (e.g., .35) indicates the magnitude or intensity of the relationship, with 1.00 being the largest correlation and .00 indicating little or no relationship.

Using Wong and Bouey's (2001) research of drug abuse in pregnant women, a Pearson correlation coefficient of –.80 between the number of months pregnant and substance abuse means that women who are at more advanced stages of pregnancy are less likely to abuse drugs (a strong negative association).

## BOX 2.1
## Research across Time

Lorion (1990) emphasized the importance of the time dimension in analyzing human behavior. Developmentally we know that with the passage of time, things change, children grow and mature, and interventions may take hold with seemingly small changes leading to significant differences. While correlations do NOT show cause and effect, they do demonstrate predictability. A correlation across time suggests that an event at time 1 is related to an event at time 2—i.e., if a positive correlation—then event 1 occurs, event 2 is likely to occur. While not demonstrating cause and effect, it does help predict.

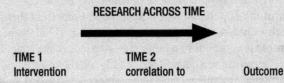

RESEARCH ACROSS TIME

| TIME 1 | TIME 2 | |
| Intervention | correlation to | Outcome |

However, one *cannot* conclude that advanced stages of pregnancy *cause* decreases in substance abuse. Also, this association may be artificial when there is reason to suspect that pregnant women's perceived support from their spouses later in pregnancy is largely responsible for decreases in substance abuse, rather than the pregnancy itself. You can find a further description of the issues related to research comparing data collected at two points in time in Box 2.1.

## Experimental Research

**The experimental design is considered by many to be the "gold standard" for research.** Experiments include a class of designs (e.g., between-groups designs where no two groups receive the same treatment) and measurement procedures that allow one to manipulate independent variables and observe the resulting effects on dependent variables. An **independent variable** is the condition that is varied between groups (e.g., people in one group receive a treatment; people in the other do not). The **dependent variable** is what the scientist measures to see the effects of the independent variable (e.g., doing better in terms of number of positive social contacts). A common design is the **pretest–posttest control group design** (Campbell & Stanley, 1963; Cook, Shadish, & Campbell, 2002), which involves assessing a dependent variable before and after an experimental manipulation (treatment) in one group (the experimental group) and before and after a no-manipulation condition in the control group. That is, one group of participants is exposed to an independent variable, and another group is not.

In addition to this manipulation of the independent variable, in a true experimental design, assignment to the experimental or control group is **random**—participants have an equal chance of being assigned to either the experimental or the control group. If assignment is random, the two groups, experimental and control, can be assumed to be similar to each other, or rather, equivalent. If there are any differences between the groups at the end of the process, it can be assumed that the independent variable is what brought about the change, because the only difference between the groups is the independent variable's presence or absence.

If the experimental manipulation is functioning as predicted by a theory, the dependent variable should be observable as a change from premanipulation to postmanipulation scores within the experimental but not the control group. In other words, the pretest–posttest observations of participants in the control group should remain relatively constant over time, unless some natural maturation occurs or the initial pretest sensitizes all participants to the nature of the assessment being conducted.

### Quasi-experimental Research

For practical and ethical reasons, many variables studied in the field of community psychology (e.g., school climate or minors being exposed to alcohol or cigarettes) cannot be experimentally manipulated. Similarly, subjects cannot always be randomly assigned to groups. For example, if a participant is pregnant, it is not possible to randomly assign her to the nonpregnant group. In studies of pregnancy, one would probably end up using intact groups. Thus, a compromise is the use of the **quasi-experimental design,** which approximates experimental conditions and random assignment but is not quite able to get all of the necessary conditions for a true experimental design (Campbell & Stanley, 1963; Cook et al., 2002). A common quasi-experimental design is the **nonequivalent pretest–posttest control design,** which involves comparing a group before and after some experimental manipulation or treatment with another group that has not been exposed to the manipulation. As mentioned earlier, this design differs from the pretest–posttest design previously discussed in that participants are not randomly assigned to experimental or control conditions.

The quasi-experimental design allows for more natural or realistic research, where initial differences between experimental and comparison groups may not be balanced. For example, using Wong and Bouey's (2001) research, pregnant women who voluntarily participate in primary and secondary prevention or treatment programs may be more educated than those in the comparison group, which may include more women who are high school dropouts. Thus, differences already exist between the two groups before the study begins. Care must be taken in drawing conclusions about differences found between the two groups—because they may differ at the outset, other explanations for the differences found in the study cannot be ruled out. Although there may be statistical methods to bring treated and untreated groups to greater equivalency, quasi-experimental design results are always viewed with caution.

## ALTERNATIVE RESEARCH METHODS USED IN COMMUNITY PSYCHOLOGY

The reason to do research is to better understand the world in which we live. Although traditional designs and methods continue to hold sway over the field of psychology, there are alternatives that have gained increasing currency. Users of these alternatives hope to gain a better sense of reality and to recognize and overcome the limitations of traditional methods. Although we recognize the power of traditional research designs in our discovery process, there are other ways to gain knowledge about our world. In some cases, these methods come from other disciplines such as anthropology or public health, and in others, there have been evolutions in our understanding of what that reality might be (philosophical or statistical models). We now examine several research methodologies used by community psychologists but not by laboratory-based psychologists.

### Ethnography

Have you ever tried to tell a story and found that you could not because of the constraints placed on you in its telling? Because of the urgency of the issues in the field of community psychology, diverse methods or approaches are often employed. One such research method is **ethnography,** which refers to a broad class of designs and measurement procedures where one speaks directly with participants of the study. The primary purpose of ethnography is to allow one to gain an understanding of how people view their own experiences. The effort is to see the world from their perspective.

Ethnography allows an individual study participant to describe his or her own experiences without having to translate them into the words of the researchers. In other words, the informants or participants use their own language to describe their own experiences. An ethnographic interviewer probably also explains why he or she is asking particular questions so the informants understand more fully. Similarly, in contrast to the more traditional scientific methodological efforts to remain objective or neutral, in ethnography the value systems of the researcher may influence social interactions between the researcher and the informants, and this is acknowledged. As much as possible, the researcher should take a stance of ignorance about the experiences of the informants and should be open to learning about the personal reality of those being studied.

As our models of social reality and research become more sophisticated and are affected by the postmodernist philosophies of the world (which challenge the assumption of objectivity and emphasize the importance of interpretation), a greater appreciation of this type of research has come to the field of community psychology (Bond & Mulvey, 2000; Campbell & Wasco, 2000; Campbell, Gregory, Patterson, & Bybee, 2012; Riger, 1990; Speer et al., 1992; Tebbs, 2012; Trickett, 2009). Ethnography is perhaps most informative when research questions asked do not have a strong theoretical framework and so leave the researcher open to the discovery process. Thus, **qualitative information** that is likely to be gathered from ethnographic studies can inform the researcher about future directions of study (Campbell, 1974). Qualitative information is acknowledged to be more subjective and anecdotal. Its strength is that the ideas and themes emerge from the participant. An examination of articles in the *American Journal of Community Psychology* found an increase in qualitative data–based articles from 4% between the years 1981 and 1983 to 17% between 2001 and 2003 (Luke, 2005). Qualitative data are typically seen in contrast to **quantitative data,** which are by definition numeric, are considered objective, and typically are the kind of data found in traditional research methodologies and designs.

The use of a combination of qualitative and quantitative techniques (**mixed method**) for studying community phenomena has the potential to strengthen community research, according to Cauce (1990). Others have since reinforced the value of such a hybrid methodology (Campbell et al., 2012; Tebbs, 2012). The qualitative information may inform the direction in which the quantitative study might go and then later inform the meaning of those quantitative data (Banyard & Miller, 1998). The mixed-method approach is a way to both empower and transform those being studied and, in a manner of speaking, is an intervention in itself (Stein & Mankowski, 2004). The qualitative methods require more awareness of the relationship between researcher and participant and the potential impact of one on the other (Brodsky et al., 2004). The qualitative data assume a more interactive role between the researcher and participants. Qualitative studies are increasingly accepted as a model of research, especially as a part of mixed-method research (Marchel & Owens, 2007). Case in Point 2.2 is an example of a mixed-method study.

From a feminist psychology perspective, qualitative data allow for capturing richer and more meaningful descriptions of social phenomena (Brodsky et al., 2004; Campbell & Wasco, 2000; Campbell et al., 2012; Hill et al., 2000). Again, we note that the quest is for a better apprehension of social reality and therefore a better understanding of that reality.

**Participant observation** is a special type of ethnographic technique. Although the researcher often assumes the role of an observer, the usual assumption is that the observations are made with detached neutrality. In participant observation, the researcher is actively engaged in the dynamics within the setting. There are assumed to be ongoing dialogues between the researcher and the participants. For example, a researcher who is interested in the study of teenage gangs often needs to "hang out" with the gangs for a period of time. Also, the researcher needs to acquire the language used by the gangs to facilitate his or her investigation of the gangs' social network characteristics as well as to establish trust. Meanwhile, the constant social interactions between the researcher and gang members may affect their perceptions of and relationships with each other. They may become friends. A consequence can be role ambiguity, where it becomes unclear to gang members what role the researcher is adopting. Is the researcher a member of the gang, a researcher, or both? In the meantime, the researcher may live the details and nuances of gang life, yielding a richer and more informed set of data. The ethical dilemmas

## Case Study of a Consumer-Run Agency

Felton (2005) studied a consumer-run agency working on mental health services. She wanted to find the characteristics of that work community. Using a variety of methods, including participant observations, ad hoc interviews, behavioral observations, and the standardized Work Environment Scale (Moos, 1994), she spent two years on site, interacting for periods of time and then retreating to analyze the data.

A content analysis of her qualitative interview data yielded a variety of staff-generated themes: pride in the agency, an understanding and compassionate place, and the feeling that it was family. The quantitative scale measures verified these general themes, yielding comparatively high scores (two standard deviations higher) on worker involvement, task orientation, and cohesion. The scale suggested high "relationship" orientation. There was also a very high score on clarity of work mission. These scores **triangulated** well with the qualitative data. The agency under study seems to be doing well in providing a service setting with which workers feel engaged and to which they are committed.

The idea behind triangulation is a referent to anthropological terminology, which likens social sciences efforts to obtain an understanding of phenomena to geological mapping. To locate a site, one takes two readings from different perspectives/sites, focusing on the site to be defined. The two sites *triangulate* with the one point under examination, yielding a better understanding of the one point. It is a kind of social geometry. In a similar way, the qualitative data, the interviews, yield one "siting" on the social phenomena being examined. The quantitative data, the scale scores, yield the second "siting" on what the agency is really like. The ensuing picture is more comprehensive, sensitive to personal nuance, and yet also more verifiable, given the two sets of data.

of informed participation and blurring of boundaries have been raised in regard to this methodology in particular (Gone, 2006; Trimble & Fisher, 2006). Is the researcher really a part of the group (gang)? What of informed consent? What are the responsibilities for crediting those under study for what is discovered? What are the gains to be made from the research, and how can that be acknowledged? These are questions that could be raised about much of our community research, a point that will be addressed again in our consideration of participatory action research later in this chapter.

### Geographic Information Systems

"The three most important things in real estate are: location, location, and location."

"Everything is related to everything else, but near things are more related than distant things." This is the first law of geography (Tobler, 1970, p. 236). Computers provide us with myriad ways to collect and illustrate data on neighborhoods. Following the logic of the importance of place within our lives, researchers are able to combine and map community data so as to capture social phenomena and their location. Starting with a map of a specified area, structural features such as roads, property lines, and government boundaries as well as social (income, marital status, size of family) and psychological data (happiness, well-being, mental health, mental illness) can be loaded onto the analyses. The data may be from archival sources (school, police, county records, U.S. Census), may come from other research data sources, or may be generated by the researchers themselves through surveys (Morton, Peterson, Speer, Reid, & Hughey, 2012).

### Epidemiology

Dr. John Snow's Ghost Map (Johnson, 2007) of 1854 London showed a pattern of cholera deaths within a district. Using that pattern, Dr. Snow convinced officials that the patrons of particular water sources were at high risk of dying. The wells were closed, and the epidemic stopped. This was before germ theory, or any knowledge of the cause of cholera.

This is an example of **epidemiology**, a research methodology used by those in public health. The research entails "the study of the occurrence and distribution of diseases and other health-related conditions in populations" (Kelsey, Thompson, & Evans, 1986, p. 3). This includes a broad class of designs (e.g., prospective or "futuristic" studies and retrospective or "historical" studies) and measurement procedures and techniques (e.g., records, random telephone samples, or neighborhood surveys).

There are two measures of the rate of illness in the community: prevalence and incidence. The **prevalence** of a disease or health-related condition is the total number of people within a given population who have the disorder. **Incidence** refers to the number of people within a given population who have acquired the condition within a specific time period such as a week, a month, or a year.

Incidence rates can be established using a **prospective design** or investigation of new cases. Here, all new cases for the given time frame are counted, yielding a rate of onset for the disease. Rising incidence rates tell us that the problem is increasing. Declining incidence rates suggest that the problem is lessening. We might think about flu season, when the cases of flu rise. Epidemiologists continue to measure the rate of onset to see when the flu season is over.

Prevalence rates can be established using a **retrospective design** or looking back at all known cases. In this design, we would count all old cases and all new cases. In the case of depression, we would count all old cases, take away all cases that have been cured, and then add all the new cases. This tells us the total number of cases in the population at a particular time.

Prevalence rate is a more inclusive measure than incidence rate and is easier to calculate. However, prevalence rates have the disadvantage that they are difficult to interpret, because they must take into account both the incidence and the duration of a disorder.

Depending on the objectives of the epidemiological investigation, measurement procedures as well as techniques used in the design can range from household interviews to random telephone dialing. Others include the use of archived data such as birth certificates, death certificates, census records, or other previously collected data.

## Needs Assessment and Program Evaluation

**Needs assessment** refers to a set of methods to determine whether a program or intervention can be of use to a given population. Needs assessment could also examine where prevention programs or other interventions might decrease the risk of a problem.

Needs assessments can be conducted via examination of existing sources of data on problems and resources within a community. To these data could be added interviews, surveys, and other observational or descriptive information. Each of these methodologies brings advantages and disadvantages. People may be reluctant to provide information in a face-to-face interview, but willing to disclose what they know on an anonymous survey. On the other hand, during an interview, the interviewer (or the informant, for that matter) can change the direction of the interview and thus reveal information not discovered on written surveys. Case in Point 2.3 provides an example of needs assessment leading to a community program.

When the needs or problems have been identified, and a program has then been developed or refined to address needs related to a particular issue, the program's effectiveness or efficiency should be evaluated. This process is called program evaluation. **Program evaluation** refers to a broad class of designs, methodologies, and measurement procedures and techniques that allow one to examine "social programs ... and the policies that spawn and justify them, [and] aim to improve the welfare of individuals, organizations, and society" (Shadish, Cook, & Leviton, 1991, p. 19).

## Needs Assessment of a Hmong Community

The Hmong are an ethnic hill tribe group in Laos. During the Vietnam War, they sided with the United States against the communist Pathet Lao. When America retreated from Southeast Asia, the Hmong suffered for their earlier alliance, and in time refugees were rescued and resettled in America. Wisconsin has one of the largest Hmong refugee communities in the United States.

The Hmong have low levels of education and high levels of teen suicide and drug abuse (Secrist, 2006). They also have unusually high rates of disability (Pfeifer, 2005). In an earlier Wisconsin-based report, the Hmong who were interviewed stated that their greatest barriers to service were language and literacy (Wisconsin Department of Health, 2001).

Concerned providers in the Eau Claire, Wisconsin, area met and discussed how to better address this population. Among their first actions was to engage the Hmong community in assessing their needs. To this end, individual interviews of "key informants"—that is, those within the community who should know its needs—were conducted. Also, several group interviews were conducted with specific groups from the Hmong community: professionals, men, women, and youth. The groups were identified and invited to discuss their community's needs. Interview content was coded for topics. Following this, group meetings were held to present the findings for identified themes. Attendees were asked to provide feedback on what was found. Results yielded needs related to the following (Collier, Munger, & Moua, 2012):

Intergenerational communication difficulties

Marital discord

Domestic violence

Child abuse

Lack of mental health knowledge

The stigma of mental illness

Problems of elders

It is beyond the scope of this chapter to extensively discuss the processes involved in evaluating a typical social program. We do note that besides needs assessment, there are generally two kinds of evaluations: process and outcome. *Process evaluation* examines what a program is doing. Are things going as planned, with interventions occurring in a timely fashion? What are the day-to-day operations like? Where are the problems of implementation and execution? A good process evaluation should report on what a program is doing well and what it is not doing well. The adjustments to the process can then be made based on the process evaluation findings.

An *outcome evaluation*, on the other hand, looks at the effects of a program. At the end of the intervention, what has been accomplished? Does the program do what it intended to do? Most program evaluations look at immediate outcomes, but community programs may require extended outcome evaluations. Many treatment evaluations now look at outcomes one to two years after the conclusion of the intervention. This tries to answer the question of whether the outcomes endure beyond the period of intensive attention or if the natural contingencies within the environment are sufficient to sustain the benefits that accumulated.

A good evaluation usually consists of four related components: (1) the goals, (2) the objectives, (3) the activities, and (4) the milestones. The **goal** refers to the aim of the evaluation. A good evaluation is likely to be driven by theory. That is, the concept of a goal addresses the question, What does the evaluation hope to achieve? (or *why* should an evaluation be conducted?). The construct of an **objective** refers to the plan. That is, objectives address the question, *How* does one go about achieving the goal? The concept of **activity** refers to the specific task; that is, activity addresses the question, *What* does the plan consists of? **Milestone** refers to the outcome; that is, does the evaluation *achieve* its intended goal?

Using Wong and Bouey's (2001) study of drug abuse, one might want to investigate the differential effectiveness of mainstream versus native-focused prevention and treatment programs for American

Indian/Alaska Native adults (the *goal*). Therefore, one reviews records and interviews clients and staff of the two types of programs (the *objective* or design). Given the voluminous records and possible number of informants or interviewees, only a randomized stratified sample will be used (the *activity,* including analysis). It might be reasonable to hypothesize that a higher enrollment rate will be observed in the native-focused programs than in programs in the mainstream because of culturally competent services. However, the two types of programs may not differ in dropout rates, because, as you know by now, intervention outcomes are often contingent on a host of factors other than program type (the *milestones*).

This example certainly is a very simplistic picture of program evaluation. Although program evaluation may seem more objective, role ambiguity is still possible. Role ambiguity is most likely to occur with internal evaluation. That is, an evaluator who is also on the staff of the agency not only assumes the role of evaluator but also is someone interested in using data derived from the evaluation for future program development or refinement. To guard against this problem, agencies usually establish an advisory panel so that program development or refinement is executed by the group rather than a single, internal evaluator. Another solution is to employ an external evaluator, such as a community consultant. Social dynamics are crucial in evaluating any social program. People do not like to be judged, especially when there may be negative consequences. Many not-for-profit social programs are sensitive to funding issues and public scrutiny. If these programs are shown to be less than effective, they are likely to be eliminated. If they are effective but less efficient (i.e., more expensive to maintain), they may still be eliminated. The potential for bias in favor of maintaining the program is obvious.

The tensions between program evaluators and the programs they evaluate often exist when only "objective" assessment or feedback is used with no active or direct engagement of program staff. Wandersman and colleagues (1998) argued that

> there has been a growing discussion of new and evolving roles for evaluators. . . . Unlike traditional evaluation approaches, **empowerment evaluators** collaborate with community members . . . to determine program goals and implementation strategies, serve as facilitators . . . not outside experts . . . in ongoing program improvement. (p. 4)

Ultimately, it is about program accountability. To that end, eight questions (along with the corresponding strategies for addressing them) serve as guides for program accountability:

1. Are there needs for the program? (needs assessment)
2. What is the scientific knowledge or best practices basis for the program? (consult scientific literature and promising practice programs)
3. How do new program(s) integrate with existing programs? (feedback on comprehensiveness and fit of program)
4. How can the program best be implemented? (planning)
5. How effective is that implementation? (process evaluation)
6. How effective is the program? (outcome and impact evaluation)
7. How can the program be improved? (lessons learned)
8. How can effective programs be institutionalized? (replication or spin-off)

Fetterman (2005) emphasized that empowerment evaluation went beyond regular evaluations in that one of the goals of empowerment evaluation was to center the control with those being evaluated. This was more than working together, where feeling empowered is a possible side effect. If the empowerment evaluation worked as it should, one of the main effects was that control of the work was with the organization and people under study. The evaluator served as a facilitator who helped influence the process but did not control it. Among the principles of this form of evaluation are community ownership, inclusion, democratic participation, community knowledge, organizational learning, and social justice.

Program evaluation can be seen as a form of intervention (Kaufman, Ross, Quan, O'Reilly, & Crusto, 2004; Patton, 1997). Evaluation is not a passive process, because the evaluator helps the organization define and objectify the goals and direction of the program under scrutiny. Beyond the definition of tasks, the evaluator defines which data are important, which are attended to, who is given a voice (administrators, staff, clients, community), and how that voice will be heard (surveys, interviews, focus groups, numeric methods, or personal testimony). The evaluator engages in interpretation, weighting, and summation of the data. This is a great deal of power and can have a significant effect on the direction and functioning of the targeted system.

Kaufman and colleagues (2006) presented an excellent example of the evaluation process and its potential for community change. They worked to increase the likelihood that evaluation findings would be used by developing a clear logic and strategy for the program need; having all relevant parties actively engaged in the process of planning, implementation, and evaluation; using a variety of both qualitative and quantitative data from a variety of sources so all felt they were being respected and heard; working to be as scientifically rigorous as possible in the generation of data; working to increase the community's ability to do its own evaluations; and being sure to share findings with all involved once they had the opportunity to comment on first drafts (which increased the ownership of the data and made for no surprises). Among their efforts to have the evaluation accepted by the community was a conscious decision to become regulars within the community, or as Kelly (2006) called it, "showing up" in the neighborhoods. The evaluators were also open and willing to provide help when needed, even when it was above and beyond what was contracted. One gets the impression the evaluators became a part of the community. Thus, the comments were not from a distant and uninvolved team who examined things without knowing in detail whom and what they were examining. The evaluation in turn helped in bringing about a variety of changes within the community and the service systems it served.

We move now to a type of research that closely resembles the process described here. Whereas the focus of Kaufman and colleagues was evaluation, their goals were community change. The incorporation of community participants in the research and intervention planning process is made even more explicit in participatory research.

## Participatory Action Research

If you want to know something about a community, ask someone who is a part of that community. If you want them to be forthcoming, it helps if they feel that they have a say in the research and if they understand that what they say can ultimately affect them. The participatory action research (PAR) methodology takes these points into account. It is much like the empowerment evaluation described earlier in that PAR seeks a partnership with those it is studying, but its basic intention is to do research. The action research tradition (Lewin, 1946) has always incorporated including the targets of any study in the research process. Participatory action research is a continuation of this tradition. In this model, the studied community helps to define the areas to study, the methods for studying, and the use of the study results. Kidd and Kral (2005) define participatory research as a **sharing of power with the participants** themselves, and emphasize that it is an attitudinal change more than it is a specific methodology. It can include both qualitative–anecdotal and quantitative–numeric data. Participant research

> involves the development of human relationships and friendships with participants as opposed to the supposedly objective disinterest of traditional paradigms. It can be a genuine connection, an 'authentic participation' that is motivational, contributes to personal growth and reduces the barriers between peoples. (p. 192)

Jason, Keys, and associates (2004) elaborate at length on the participatory research tradition and its place within community psychology. The partnership between researcher and participants creates a structure of respect, and the research process can be considered the intervention. Rather than doing research with strangers, it is like working with people you come to know, as they come to know you. As opposed to an imposed set of theories and hypotheses, there is partnership in discerning the important aspects of community to research and how to research it.

We are reminded that the PAR is a process that has to deal with the community's own power structures (Dworski-Riggs & Langhout, 2010; Greenwood, Whyte, & Harkavy, 1993). Power is differentially distributed and determined by structural forces. In working within a given community, it is wise to first come to understand that setting's power structure. As well, we are cautioned that participation may not be the way in which participants in the setting believe they will become empowered (Dworski-Riggs & Langhout, 2010; Foster-Fishman, Salem, Chibnall, Legler, & Yapchai, 1998).

Kelly and colleagues (2004) provided an example of a 10-year relationship with an African American community on Chicago's South Side in which community leadership was both studied and developed. The Developing Communities Project (DCP) wanted to take a community organization approach to preventing substance abuse. In close collaboration with the DCP, researchers and community developed relationships and group mechanisms to define and describe African American church-based organizing and leadership. Admitting to the lack of relevant literature on the topic, the researchers built on information from the citizen–leader panelists. The reliance on community knowledge and feedback in devising appropriate data-gathering procedures was an integral part of the process. Clearly, the development of personal relationships (common interests in jazz) and community-based metaphors (such as "Leadership as making a soup; there being many ingredients needed in its making") was essential to the project. Data were collected and reported to the community and then refined so as to be more useful (the use of oral history videotapes to communicate the findings).

There is a further cautionary tale to go with PAR. In reviewing the experiences of researchers and community self-help groups in the PAR process, Isenberg, Loomis, Humphreys, and Maton (2004) offer several reservations concerning the assumptions involved in this methodology. Among them, they propose that PAR does not necessarily make for better science, but rather is a decision that should be based on social justice considerations. They do note that this can lead to better response rates and more meaningful questions as the result of collaboration (Klaw & Humphreys, 2006), but that is not the reason to adopt the process. They further suggest that "collaboration necessarily includes conflicts, not all of which can be easily resolved" (Isenberg et al., 2004, p. 126).

Although participatory research is acknowledged to be complex and time-consuming, as well as less respected in certain mainstream academic settings, nonetheless its potential for contributing to our understanding of meanings within the communities we study seems great (Kidd & Kral, 2005). As well, a second powerful recommendation for its use is the potential for participatory research to empower the communities it studies (Kelly et al., 2004; Jason et al., 2003). Research on the effects of PAR has begun to demonstrate the effects of this methodology on its community participants, ranging from increased sense of control to developing a change agent identity (Foster-Fishman, Nowell, Deacon, Nievar, & McCann, 2005).

## CAUTIONS AND CONSIDERATIONS REGARDING COMMUNITY RESEARCH

Research in the field of community psychology is often conducted with a sense of urgency not often seen in other areas of psychology. The community concerns are immediate and ongoing. Delay has real-life consequences for the populations involved. (See Case in Point 2.4 for an example of this.) And yet, there are cautions related to doing the research and considerations with regard to the manner in which it is conducted. The following are some of the issues.

## The Politics of Science and the Science of Politics

Most of us assume that social policies and programs are based on a reasoned scientific knowledge of social phenomena and human behaviors. That is, a systematic and vigorous examination of an issue using scientific principles will result in programs producing the most desirable outcome(s) or impact(s). However, as found in real-world community projects, there are systems that must be negotiated and power issues with which to contend. This has been discussed at length for work in neighborhoods (Kelly, 2006), in school systems (Foster-Fishman et al., 2005), and at the highest federal policy levels (Jason, 2012). A review of these articles reminds us that systems can be difficult to access and influence and that there are lessons to be learned in the politics of science. In particular, we should be aware of the existing power structure and those affected by change (stakeholders); look to potential allies and coalitions; remember that "experts" within a community can be very helpful; and understand and be willing to use the natural shifts of power and structures (Foster-Fishman, Nowell, & Yang, 2007; Jason, 2012; Kelly, 2006).

## Ethics: Cultural Relativism or Universal Human Rights?

A major principle of scientific research is that the well-being of research participants must be ensured (American Psychological Association, 1985). Taking part in research should not endanger people in any physical, psychological, or social way. All participants must be **informed** about the purpose of the research as much as possible (without jeopardizing the integrity of the research), and use of deception must be minimized. It is ethically undesirable to do otherwise (see Christensen, 1988). In most research institutions and universities, approval from an **institutional review** board must first be secured, demonstrating that all ethical guidelines (e.g., participants must be fully debriefed about the purpose of the study) have been met before research can be initiated.

These general principles seem straightforward and objective (i.e., research is neutral). However, these principles were created over several decades. Historically, the lack of such guidelines has permitted research atrocities. Among the worst examples was the research conducted in the mid-20th century on 399 African American men for the Tuskegee Syphilis Study (conducted by the U.S. government from 1932 to 1972). The men were deliberately denied effective treatment for syphilis to document its natural progression. Decades later, President Bill Clinton expressed his regret: "The legacy of the study at Tuskegee has reached far and deep, in ways that hurt our progress and divide our nation. We cannot be one America when a whole segment of our nation has no trust in America" (May 16, 1997). However, to many African Americans, as well as other racial and ethnic minorities and oppressed groups, such injustices (as an example, forced sterilization of the so-called mentally feeble) continue to prevail—they have just become more covert (in the name of science). These outrages and debates have also assumed new dimensions, guises, and significance in the AIDS pandemic (see the *American Journal of Public Health, 88,* 1998)—extending the boundaries to international scientific research. These are extremely complex issues, so two related sets of ideas are examined: informed consent and experimental-control (placebo) design.

**Informed consent,** a major principle of scientific research, is ensuring that a clear and articulated procedure and process is in place so that participants understand the nature of the research, including the right to refuse participation without any repercussions. In other words, the process of informed consent has two key components: **comprehension** of materials and voluntary participation. In an HIV testing study conducted in a South African hospital, Karim, Karim, Coovadia, and Susser (1998) found that although participants understood the process of informed consent (i.e., comprehension of materials), many felt that they had little choice about enrolling in the study (i.e., voluntary participation) because participation was their only chance of receiving needed medical care and services. Karim and colleagues concluded that "subtle and unexpected elements of coercion can reside in the perceptions (real or imagined) held by patients being recruited into a research project in a medical care setting... . Ethicists and institutional review boards should certainly explore the issue further" (p. 640).

Beyond these concerns, at a more basic level, community researchers are growing more aware of the implicit or assumed meanings regarding research participation. Among the questions raised are: What does consent mean to the participants in regard to their participation, the data they provide, and its analysis? What are the costs and benefits to the individual and to the group? Is this research on or a social service to those who are recruited? These considerations have been raised in global and community research dealing with medical and psychological studies (Barata, Gucciardi, Ahmad, & Stewart, 2006; Bhutta, 2004; Dixon-Woods et al., 2007; Gone, 2008; Jenkins, 2011; Kral, Garcia, Aber, Masood, Dutta, & Todd, 2011; Levy et al., 2010; Yick, 2006).

Once participants consent to enroll in a study, they may be assigned to an experimental or control (or comparison) group. As noted in our description of experimental design, a true control group is one that does not receive any intervention or treatment (but may receive a placebo). However, what should researchers do when they know that without any intervention or treatment, the participants in the control group will likely be in jeopardy?

A series of group interviews among diverse ethnic groups in southern California yielded differences in the groups' understanding of participation in a study of children (Lakes et al., 2012). These variations could be found across a wide array of assumptions and decision-making processes (see Table 2.2). Although there were many common themes, there were enough differences to provide cautions to any assumptions about the beliefs and expectations related to research in the wider, culturally diverse community. The White, Latina, and Asian American samples differed in their understanding of what participation meant. Table 2.2 summarizes these differences.

## The Continuum of Research: The Value of Multiple Measures

Speer and associates (1992) found that there has been a shift in the field of community psychology toward the use of correlational designs and away from experimentation. This is because we have tried to address broadly based social issues. Even in cases where quasi-experimental or experimental designs can be used, one may have to face a multitude of methodological issues or dilemmas. One class of these concerns the logistics of implementing a research program. For example, how do researchers locate drug-using pregnant women to investigate drug use? Not only are such women hard to access, especially if they do not seek medical attention, but they may also be homeless or change addresses often.

**TABLE 2.2     Understanding Participation in Research**

| Themes | Groups | | |
| --- | --- | --- | --- |
| | White | Latina | Asian American |
| Their anticipation of risks | Emotional impact | Being judged | Possible conflicts |
| Sense of research burden about | Getting ready | Length of visit | Obligations |
| Clarifications needed on | Requirements | Research not a service | How info helps |
| Decisions to participate made by | Parents | Family | Family w/elders |

*Source:* Adapted from material found in Lakes, D., Vaughan, E., Jones, M. Burke, W., Baker, D., & Swansen, J. (2012). Diverse perceptions of the informed consent process: Implications for the recruitment and participation of diverse communities in the National Children's Study. *American Journal of Community Psychology, 49,* 215–232.

## HIV Intervention Testing and the Use of Placebos

Based on findings of a trial in Thailand, the Centers for Disease Control and Prevention, together with the National Institutes of Health (NIH) and the Joint United Nations Program on Acquired Immunodeficiency Syndrome (UNAIDS), announced that placebos should not be used in HIV transmission clinical trials. After discovering the effectiveness of a prevention program, some researchers advocated the use of *equivalency trials* (i.e., a new treatment versus a standard treatment) in place of the use of a non-treatment placebo group. This request was turned down.

For some researchers, such as George Annas and Michael Grodin (cofounders of the Global Lawyers and Physicians), as well as the late Jonathan Mann (former director of WHO Global Programme on AIDS and a well-known advocate for human rights in the context of public health practice), the issue is about universal human rights. Annas and Grodin (1998) argued that "unless the interventions being tested will actually be made available to the improvised populations that are being used as subjects, developed countries are simply exploiting them in order to quickly use the knowledge gained from the clinical trials for the developed trials" (p. 561). In addition, they raised concerns about informed consent similar to those brought up by Karim and associates (1998). It is virtually certain that for many of the participants in these developing countries, enrollment in such trials guarantees access to medical or health care rather than no care at all. Does this mean we should not conduct any global studies? There are no easy answers.

These debates demonstrate the interdependence between the integrity of scientific research and societal forces (cultural norms, economy, racism, sexism, classism, etc.). Bayer (1998) stated:

> The tragedy of the recent (HIV) trials is that they bear a profound moral taint, not of a malevolent research design but, rather, of a world economic order that makes effective prophylaxis for the interruption of maternal–fetal HIV transmission available but unaffordable for many—this is true, as well, for a host of treatment for AIDS and other diseases. In a just world, this would not be the case and the research under attack would be unnecessary. It is the social context of maldistribution of wealth and resources that both mandates these studies, and at the same time, renders them so troubling. (p. 570)

How do researchers increase the probability that pregnant teens will tell the truth when using self-report measures? Another way to further validate self-reported alcohol use would be to count the number of empty alcohol beverage containers that pregnant women discard. A nonreactive measure like this, where people are not contacted face to face, is called an **unobtrusive measure.** Although unobtrusive measures are an effective and creative way to obtain cross-validating information, some consider them ethically questionable because participant consent is often not obtained.

When working with complex social issues such as teen pregnancy, one should always make an attempt to use **multiple methods.** For example, self-reports and nonreactive or unobtrusive measures, as well as umbilical cord blood samples, could be obtained to determine whether pregnant women are using drugs or alcohol. When these diverse types of data agree with each other, the findings are more credible. However, multiple methods take more time than single methods and may generate different conclusions for the same issue.

### The Importance of Cultural Sensitivity

Although this seems obvious, it should be noted that different cultures may think and act differently. If we believe the definition of *culture*, those with different cultures in given situations can also have different assumptive worlds and value orientations (O'Donnell, 2006; Pederson, Carter, & Ponterotto, 1996; Reich & Reich, 2006). Growing from this realization is another class of methodological issues or dilemmas that concerns **cultural sensitivity,** or awareness and appreciation of intragroup and intergroup differences. The authors have chosen to define cultural sensitivity in a very *liberal* sense. People belong to many categories and have multiple expectations or identities. For example, a person can be an African American (racial or ethnic identity) and also a college graduate (educational background) and a white-collar worker (socioeconomic status). This individual may have more in common with White college graduates (of similar educational background) who are also white-collar workers (similar socioeconomic status) than other African Americans who are high school dropouts (different educational background) or living on government assistance (different socioeconomic status).

In other words, cultural sensitivity underscores the diverse ways in which our background and experiences can influence our view of the world and our practices. In turn, this diversity can lead to misunderstandings if it is not recognized and appreciated. An example of how this can lead to confusion is provided by a European friend who was offered a free television. He refused out of politeness, telling us that it should have been offered three times. When the American did not make the offer more than once, our European friend lost the TV. He learned a lesson. When in America (or at least that part of America he was in at that time), don't wait to be asked multiple times. Of course the earlier section on diversity, found in Chapter 1, describes the community psychology principle of recognizing the importance of diversity in any of its studies or interventions. It is notable that cultural variations can lead to misunderstandings (in some cultures, "yes" does not mean "yes" but "I respect you"). In research, these variations must be recognized if we are ever to understand our world. Ecologically valid research hinges on cultural awareness (Gone, 2011; Kelly, 2010; Kral et al., 2011; Trimble, Trickett, Fisher, & Goodyear, 2012).

## Community Researchers as Consultants

When community psychologists conduct research, they often do so in the role of consultant. A **consultant** is someone who engages in collaborative problem solving with one or more persons (the **consultees**) who are often responsible for providing some form of assistance to a third individual (the **client**; Mowbray, 1979). Because consultants *collaborate with* the consultees, those who participate in the research, including the consultees and their clients, are not called *subjects,* as they are in other psychological research, but *participants.*

Consultants work in a variety of community settings: educational, industrial, human services (especially related to mental health), governmental, and others. Some consultants conduct research for the government. A number of universities have developed or are developing public policy research laboratories to assist in public- and private-sector research. Other consultants evaluate programs or conduct needs assessments, and still others lend their expertise to solving social problems by designing preventive education programs or by helping change aspects of agencies and communities. In other words, consultants appear in many different settings and work on a variety of problems, most of them related to research.

A variety of complex issues face most community consultants. Consultants often enter a situation not knowing what the real problem is that they are being asked to help solve. In a business setting, for instance, a consultant might be hired by management because productivity is low. However, the real underlying problem might be that the management style is so much disliked that employee productivity has declined. Would you want to be the consultant who delivers the news to the management team who hired you that management is the problem? Given the nature of the problems for which they are asked to intervene, community psychologists acting as consultants need to weigh the ethical considerations of to whom they are responsible and for what (O'Neill, 1989). The consultation process is described in Chapter 5 as a method of intervention.

Consultants also need to ask, Are the methods and research affordable, workable, and understandable for this set of clients? Furthermore, ethical consultants work *with*, not *for*, those who hire them

(Benviente, 1989; Christensen & Robinson, 1989). In fact, all consultants need to ensure **constituent validity,** which means that those participating in the research or change are considered, not subjects to be acted on, but participants whose perspectives *must* be taken into account in planning and other related activities for the activities to be valid (Keys & Frank, 1987). Consultants need to *empower* the population with whom they are working to create and sustain the change initiated by the presence of the consultant. This means that the consultant needs to find a good way to "wean" the clients or participants, lest they become too dependent on the expert.

Professional change agents or consultants also need to assess the prevailing culture as well as the trust and respect held for them in a particular setting. Such assessment will help consultants determine how visible they should be. Consultants also need to evaluate their own personal values and communicate them openly *before* the consultation or research begins to avoid ethical dilemmas after the collaboration process has commenced (Heller, 1989a). Finally, consultants must evaluate their work with their clients; they need to ask the question, Did I improve the community by my presence? This question can best be answered through research. Without evaluation, how would a change agent know if the change worked and whether it ought to be repeated?

The work of Kaufman and colleagues (2006), cited in the previous section, and the discussion by Kelly and coworkers (2004) of an ongoing consultative–research relationship, as described earlier, seem especially pertinent here. The consultative process is one in which the personal aspects of systems engagement are important. What is becoming clearer in the consultative process is the need to be aware of the larger system with its own agendas and concerns for survival and change. Both Kaufman's and Kelly's work speaks to the establishment of a working relationship in which the client/agency/community comes to understand itself as a partner in the research/consultative process. Whether this requires just being there at significant events, on a regular and longer term basis, or contributing resources and time above and beyond normal expectations, the perception of a consultant as an engaged community member or ally rather than a detached and disinterested party places the research, data, and conclusions or recommendations in an entirely different light. Brodsky and colleagues (2004) highlighted the role of such relationships in the community research context. The skill set that the community psychologist brings to the research consultative process is a knowledge of what makes for good science but also an understanding of what makes for usable science.

## Summary

Community psychology is interested in identifying and understanding the social contexts that contribute to the creation of healthy populations and then helping to create these healthy contexts. In both instances, research plays a crucial role in providing an empirical basis for the building of theory and interventions.

The community psychologist uses both traditional correlational, experimental, and quasi-experimental designs and more adventurous alternative research designs and methodologies. Among the more adventurous techniques are qualitative and ethnographic studies. In a pragmatic turn, needs assessment and program evaluations are valued for identifying problems and providing a feedback on the effectiveness of interventions. There is also growing use of technological innovations such as global information systems to help in examining how location relates to community phenomena. And there is a growing awareness of the value of community partnerships in research, as is found in the participatory action research model.

Other community-driven considerations in the scientific endeavor are the ethics of conducting studies in diverse communities, and especially the need to ensure participants' understanding of study implications and gaining their well-informed consent. Cultural issues are especially important in both research and interventions as we venture into areas whose worldviews and value assumptions may differ from collegiate–academic models.

If you are curious about how communities work from a psychological perspective or in how and if attempts to improve communities can work, then community psychology brings various research approaches and research considerations to you.

And so, longitudinal studies like those of Werner and Smith (2001), which we describe in Chapter 3, can tell us that children who have caring adults around them are likely to grow up and be successful. A very long time frame, lasting more than 30 to 40 years, shows us correlations between caring adults and children who succeed

when they are grown. Cause and effect cannot be inferred, but the linkage is made.

In a second set of studies, on the long-term effects of Head Start, which are presented in Chapter 8, we see the research (Garces, Thomas, & Currie, 2002) as a type of intervention (independent variable) on group child success as measured by graduation from high school and lack of contact with the jail/legal system (dependent variables). Although earlier studies have shown the results to be mixed and to be academically sustainable with continued educational support, the long-term effects described by Garces et al. (2002) demonstrate positive effects much later in life for Head Start participants.

In both the studies by Werner and Smith and those by Garces and colleagues, the longer term data comparisons allowed the realization of the life patterns to emerge.

$3$

# Stress and Resilience

*There is an art to facing difficulties in ways that lead to effective solutions.*

—John Kabat Zinn

Linda was the first in her family to go to college. She had done well in high school, getting mostly A's and an occasional B. At the encouragement of her school counselor, she applied to a number of universities, getting scholarships to several of them.

Once at college, she felt lost. The students were different. The classes were different. The dorms seemed very strange. She slept next to a complete stranger in a double room. The other woman came complete with Nordstrom college accessories, whatever that was. They all dressed a particular way. It was like they had called each other up and talked about what to bring and what to wear. Everyone knew, except her. The rest of the hall seemed comfortable with the setting. Their parents had talked to them about college life. They seemed to know the acceptable language and speech cadence, which signaled that they were on the inside. Everyone seemed to know what to do and when to do it. But for Linda, even the food was strange. The dilemma was what to do.

A community psychologist would analyze this example, look to the systems at work for Linda and others like her in the college setting, and make particular recommendations, which could be based on a stress model and a resilience model. We now pursue what goes into these related models and see what might help Linda and those in her situation.

## THE STRESS MODEL AND THE DEFINITION OF COMMUNITY PSYCHOLOGY

The causes and effects of stress have been intricately tied to community psychology since its inception. Barbara Dohrenwend's presidential address to the Division of Community Psychology in 1977 (Dohrenwend, 1978) described a model that she believed would coalesce the many and varied activities of a new community psychology. Her stress model described a psychosocial process leading to the development of psychopathology. In this model, a particular event or set of events could produce stress reactions. However, the stress event itself was just one of several factors that would determine whether an individual's reaction would be negative. An individual's **personal psychological characteristics** needed to be factored into the process. Examples of relevant psychological characteristics might be a person's temperament or their level of intelligence. There were also **situational characteristics** such as when the stress event occurred, the physical setting, and whether other people were present. In addition, there were intervening factors (i.e., between the event and the reaction) that mediated the impact of the event on the individual. There were **situational mediators,** such as social or financial support, and **psychological mediators,** such as coping skills or pain tolerance. The outcome of the stressful event on the individual was determined, then, by the combination of stress events, characteristics, and mediators. Dohrenwend noted that a stress event could lead to either negative or positive consequences, depending on the combination of factors. With this model in mind, Dohrenwend saw community psychologists intervening at both the characteristics level (education for improving psychological characteristics, political action to change the situation characteristics) and at the level of mediators (community organization to strengthen situational mediators or skills training to positively influence psychological mediators). This stress model could be used to direct community intervention efforts as well as to differentiate how community psychology was distinct from clinical psychology, which focused almost exclusively on the individual and typically occurred after pathological reactions had developed. The community psychologist dealt with both the individual and the situation and intervened early in the process before severe and chronic problems might occur.

In a later article on community psychology, George Albee (1982) reiterated the importance of the stress model and its elements. He believed the incidence of mental disorder took into account organic factors, stress, coping skills, support, and self-esteem. Decreasing stress or increasing coping skills and support reduced the incidence of disorders and increased health. Increasing stress or decreasing coping skills and support heightened disorders and decreased health. Stressors could come from a variety of sources—economic, social, or psychological—but the process remained the same. Hence, Albee outlined ways in which human potential could be promoted in addition to how psychopathology could be prevented.

As we can see from these two examples, the stress model has historically been an integral part of community psychology, used by some of its most respected scholars. However, it has not been without controversy. Rappaport (1977, 1981) believed that stress considerations were too person-focused and clinical in nature. Calling it "old wine in new bottles," he advocated a broader—more group, system, or policy—focus for interventions. Yet Cowen (1985) argued that an understanding of the stress process provided valuable information for those working person-centered interventions in the community. "A significant portion of what we call psychological wellness derives from people's abilities to adapt . . . effectively with stressful events and circumstances" (pp. 32–33). **Situation-focused approaches** look at specific stressful events and intervene in those situations. **Competency enhancement approaches** look to the individual's skills in coping with stress in general and work to increase these skills. In both of these approaches, an understanding of the stress model was central and included those factors that served to protect an individual in risky circumstances and promote general well-being.

This chapter presents the development of stress concepts, explores coping styles in dealing with stress, and reviews some of the work on social support as a mediating factor. We then examine the work on resilience, where at-risk individuals thrive. Although resilience takes stress and its components into account, it goes beyond the stress model. Both the stress model and the resilience model have informed community psychology research and community psychologists' interventions. In Chapters 4 and 5 we look at social change and community interventions. Here, we examine the stress and resilience models.

## STRESS

The term *stress* has been used to indicate the occurrence of three things: a stimulus event, a process, and a reaction. This ambiguity is confusing, so for our purposes, we talk of the stimulus event as a **stressor,** the process as a **stress process,** and the reaction as the **stress reaction.**

### Stressors Events

Stimulus events that evoke distress are known as stressors. In the 1960s, a list of life-changing stressors was devised called the Schedule of Recent Experience (Rahe, Meyer, Smith, Kjaer, & Holmes, 1964), along with a weighted scoring system by which to measure the corresponding levels of stress (Holmes & Rahe, 1967). Forty-two specific life events on this measure ranged from "death of a spouse" to "getting fired at work" to a "minor legal violation." The list of events with their weighting scores is called the Social Readjustment Rating Scale (SRRS). The SRRS is one of the most widely used measures of stressors today. The scale scores have been shown to be related to a variety of measures of stress reactions (Scully, Tosi, & Banning, 2000).

Although the events from the SRRS are typically considered major life changes, a second way of looking at stressful events was proposed by Kanner, Coyne, Shaefer, and Lazarus (1981) and Delongis, Coyne, Dakof, Folkman, and Lazarus (1982). In their research, the smaller, everyday hassles were found to be a better indicator of stress than the major life changes. Hassles could include things like worrying about one's weight, having too much work with too little time, forgetting things, and concerns about home repair needs.

Although it is fair to say that we all experience daily hassles, it is important to remember that community context may influence the specific types of hassles most commonly encountered. For example, Vera and colleagues (2012) conducted a study of frequently experienced hassles experienced by urban ethnic minority adolescents. They found that not feeling safe in one's neighborhood was the most commonly reported hassle. Such a finding would be less likely to occur if the study was conducted on a middle-class suburban sample of adolescents.

**ACUTE VERSUS CHRONIC STRESS.**    There is a distinction made in the stressful event literature between acute, time-limited problems that can arise and chronic, persistent demands on an individual (Gottlieb, 1997; Wheaton, 1997). However, it is not always clear which problems are chronic and which are acute. Wheaton (1997) defines the **acute stressor** as a "discrete, observable event . . . possessing a clear onset and offset" (pp. 52–53). He defines **chronic stressors** as "less self-limiting in nature, . . . typically open ended, using up our resources in coping but not promising resolution" (p. 53). These persistent problems are seen to be "located in the structure of the social environment" (p. 57). These classes of stressors lead to different processes and coping strategies (Gottlieb, 1997), as well as differing physiological results. An acute stressor (e.g., having your cellphone stolen) brings activation of the neuroendocrine system and resultant heightened levels of adrenaline and cortisol. Hence, the individual's physical system is ready for "fight or flight." However, with prolonged stress, such as living in poverty, studies find eventual neurological breakdowns (Compas, 2006; Romeo & McEwan, 2006). Chronic stress has been demonstrated to have destructive effects on DNA and to contribute to aging (Epel et al., 2004). Chronic stressors may directly contribute to the physical and mental deterioration of the individuals or groups affected. Notably, the work on African American psychosocial stress models supports the contention that the presence of a chronic socially based stressor such as racism could be a significant contributor to heightened levels of physical disorders (Clark, Anderson, Clark, & Williams, 1999). Similar claims may be made for those affected by other forms of chronic stress.

**RACISM AND MINORITY STATUS: AN EXAMPLE OF STRESSFUL SOCIAL CONTEXTS.**   Moritsugu and Sue (1983) are among the many authors who have described the negative impacts of minority status for people of color over the past several decades. Two recent meta-analyses documented the link between experiences with perceived racism and decreased mental health among Asian and Asian Americans (Lee & Ahn, 2011), Latinas/os (Lee & Ahn, 2011), and Black Americans (Pieterse, Todd, Neville, & Carter, 2012). From academic achievement to physical health problems, those with minority status may be at greater risk for poorer outcomes due to chronic exposure to the stressor of racism. Mays, Cochran, and Barnes (2007) reported data from physiological measures of stress that supported the contention that perception of racism serves as a chronic social stressor for ethnic minorities. This stress, resulting from a culture of racism (Jones, 1997), may serve as a credible explanation for some of the quality-of-life issues of many ethnic minority groups in America.

Dovidio and his colleagues (e.g., Gomez, Dovidio, Huici, Gaertner, & Cuadrado, 2008) find that subtler, more covert forms of racism may be as harmful as more obvious forms of racism. Instead of outright racist statements, which may be less common today than in decades past, unconscious, nonverbal behaviors may be displayed that reflect racist sentiments. In other words, people's nonverbal behavior is often inconsistent with their verbal behavior. Although this inconsistency can be changed, many people don't know they are behaving so incongruently. This research is explored in more detail in Case in Point 1.2.

Sue, Bucceri, Lin, Nadal, and Torino (2007) are among recent scholars who have uncovered additional types of interpersonal racism to capture the changing nature of the race relations referred to as **microaggressions.** Microaggressions are "brief, commonplace, daily . . . indignities . . . that communicate negative or derogatory slights" (p. 271). Examples of microaggressions include telling Asian Americans that they speak English well or crossing the street when a Black man is walking in a person's direction. These microaggressions may be both unconscious and unintentional and are not limited to expressions of racism. Recent research has documented the existence of gender and sexual orientation microaggressions (Sue, 2010), examples of which are presented in Table 3.1.

**TABLE 3.1   Examples of Racial, Gender, and Sexual Orientation Microaggressions**

|                   | Race                      | Gender                               | Sexual Orientation                                                      |
| ----------------- | ------------------------- | ------------------------------------ | ---------------------------------------------------------------------- |
| Microinsult       | "You speak English well"  | Assume that female doctor is a nurse | Ask a male if has a girlfriend (assumes heterosexuality)               |
| Microassault      | Racial slur/joke          | Catcalls (ogling)                    | Teasing a peer: "You're so gay"                                         |
| Microinvalidation | I don't see color         | Using male pronoun as generic        | Saying marriage is only for a man and a woman (Defense of Marriage Acts) |

*Source:* Adapted from material in Sue (2010).

Three kinds of microaggressions are identified: **microassault** (explicit racial belittling remark or action, e.g., displaying a swastika or telling a racial joke), **microinsult** (racial insult or belittling, e.g., saying the best qualified should get the job when a person of color does not get the job), and **microinvalidation** (excluding or denying one's experiences, e.g., "I do not believe racism exists today"—saying that someone's report of racism is *not* true). Thus, studying stressors such as racism is an example of how chronic and acute stressors continue to affect mental health in our current society.

## Stress as a Process

Lazarus and Folkman (1984) defined psychological stress as "a particular relationship between the person and the environment that is appraised by the person as taxing or exceeding his or her resources and endangering his or her well-being" (p. 19). They saw stress as a process that was influenced by multiple variables and emphasized that the appraisal of a given situation was the first step in this process. **Primary appraisal** determined whether the event represented a threatening situation. The **secondary appraisal** factors in the person's expectations of handling the situation. In the secondary appraisal stage, the individual's coping skills and other resources are evaluated as either helpful or not helpful in contending with the situation. Thus, the stress process was determined by the person's ability to deal with the environmental demands. The resulting level of distress experienced would be influenced by how successful the person was in using the available resources. Thus, in this model, it is possible for one person to experience extreme levels of stress in response to an event and another person to be relatively unaffected by the same event, depending on their appraisal of the situation and their resourcefulness in responding to the event.

## Stress Reaction

Research has examined the variety of ways that people respond in the face of stressful events for many decades. Hans Selye (1936) was the first to note a particular set of physiological reactions to a variety of harmful or noxious stimuli. He came to describe this reaction process as the General Adaptation Syndrome (GAS). This involved an initial alarm reaction, followed by resistance, and if this fails, exhaustion. His approach was physiological, documenting the shifts in the organism when the balanced, "homeostatic state" was disrupted. Selye believed this syndrome was activated by any generalized disruption to the physical system. Since then, the stress reaction has been measured in physiological terms, such as illness, or in psychological terms, such as depression, anxiety, or other measures of multiple symptoms, such as the Symptom Check List (Derogatis & Coons, 1993). For example, Gaylord-Harden, Elmore, Campbell, and Wethington (2011) studied the relationship between stress and anxiety and depression symptoms in African American youths. The authors found that stress related to peer relationships was positively associated with depression in African American girls, but associated with anxiety in African American boys. This study suggests that gender may be an important factor that determines how stress affects an individual.

Regardless of gender, however, the stress process has clear physiological consequences that can vary by how one responds to the stressor. Kuehner, Huffziger, and Liebsch (2009) investigated the effects of induced rumination, distraction, and mindful self-focus on mood, dysfunctional attitudes, and college student participants' cortisol responses. Students were subjected to a negative mood–inducing exercise and then told to ruminate on their feelings, engage in a distraction task, or mindfully self-focus on their mood. Findings of their study revealed that rumination had the most negative impact on the cortisol levels of the most depressed students. Interestingly, distraction showed a clear beneficial effect on the course of dysphoric mood, whereas a mindful self-focus did not. This study suggests that our stress reactions can be influenced by what we do in the wake of being exposed to the stressor. It

CASE IN POINT 3.1

## Contemporary Racism

### IMPLICIT AND EXPLICIT PREJUDICE

In today's world, racial prejudice and discrimination are not socially acceptable. In fact, most people speak explicitly of their non-racist attitudes. That being said, we continue to live in a world where "mainstream" culture still reflects the values and traditions of the majority, namely, White, middle-class, Christian, heterosexual people. This bias results in negative connotations being associated with non-majority groups such as ethnic minorities. While we may not be consciously aware of these connotations,

they do appear to lead to differences in how we behave toward members of different groups (Devine, 1989). Research has found that how people *verbally communicated* to one other in an interracial situation could be predicted by their explicit, stated attitudes on prejudice—that is, the less prejudiced, the more they interacted favorably. However, the way people *nonverbally communicated* was predicted by a measure of their implicit (i.e., unconscious) associations regarding the racial group. In the same interracial situation, less favorable associations lead to less friendly nonverbal

behaviors. These unfavorable nonverbal behaviors were noted by both the interracial partner and an independent observer (Dovidio, Gaertner, & Kawakami, 2002).

The problem for many racial minorities, then, is dealing with the double message. At the same time that nonfriendly, nonverbal behaviors being exhibited, there is friendly verbal behavior and a denial of any prejudicial behavior. That is, at an explicit and conscious level, many believe they are not racist, despite the fact that their nonverbal behavior may suggest otherwise.

---

also supports findings of Dandeneau, Baldwin, Baccus, Sakellaropoulo, and Pruessner (2007), who found that diverting attention away from a social stressor led to a reduction in a physiological measure of stress (cortisol) and self-report of stress. Studies such as these illustrate the critical role that coping plays in understanding the stress process.

## Coping

Compas (2006) defines two specific processes involved in the response to stressors. The first is automatic and for the most part not consciously controlled. The second is a voluntary response to the stressors at hand, which includes "regulation of emotion, cognition, behavior, physiology and the environment in response to stressful events or circumstances" (Compas, Connor-Smith, Saltzman, Thomsen, & Wadsworth, 2001, p. 89). As conceptualized by Compas and others (2001), coping is a part of the self-regulatory process in dealing with environmental demands. Studies of coping have found a variety of ways of describing these responses to stress. We now examine some of those responses.

**EMOTION-FOCUSED AND PROBLEM SOLVING–FOCUSED COPING.** Lazarus and Folkman (1984) point to two different types of coping emerging from the research literature: emotion-focused and problem solving–focused. **Emotion-focused** styles work on lessening or strengthening the emotional impact of an event. These include cognitive activities such as distancing, selective attention, reinterpretation, or self-distraction. **Problem solving–focused** coping seeks to change the environment. Individuals try to deal with what is bothering them by examining the given situation, then weigh options as to possible changes to make within one's self (e.g., lowering one's expectations, seeking support from another friend) and within the environment (e.g., changing jobs, finding a new boyfriend or girlfriend).

Lazarus and Folkman (1984) reported that these two styles of coping related to how individuals felt they could control the elements in their environment. They believed the emotion-focused styles typically are used when there is a feeling that nothing could be done to modify the environment. The problem-solving strategies are more to be expected when a person believes things are changeable.

**ACTIVE COPING AND AVOIDANT COPING.**   Carver, Scheier, and Weintraub (1989) presented a second system for distinguishing coping styles. They constructed a broad, theoretically based measure that presented aspects of **active coping,** where the individual does something to try to solve the stressful situation, and **avoidant coping,** "where responses potentially impede or interfered with active coping" (p. 280). Examples of active coping include planning, seeking social support, turning to religion, restraining oneself, and acceptance of reality. Avoidant coping is typified by self-distraction, denial, use of alcohol, and withdrawing from the situation.

Much research has focused on these distinctions and pointed to their varying effectiveness. The majority of findings suggest that active or problem-solving coping leads to better results than avoiding/ passive coping (Compas et al., 2001). However, it is not fair to conclude that active coping is always the best coping strategy. For example, Rasmussen, Aber, and Arvinkumar (2004) investigated how African American and Latino adolescents coped with urban hassles and whether any particular coping styles were associated with positive mental health outcomes. Results showed that active coping styles were associated with increased perceptions of safety, but in some circumstances also increased exposure to further violence in neighborhoods. Clarke (2006) argues that it is important to take into account whether a stressor is controllable before determining which coping style might be more advantageous. When the situation is controllable, active coping may make sense. However, in cases where stressors are uncontrollable, avoidance strategies may be appropriate. In a sample of urban adolescents of color, Vera and others (2011) found that self-distraction was a significant mediator of the relationship between exposure to urban hassles and negative affect. In other words, the more adolescents used self-distraction as a coping style, the less likely it was that their exposure to urban stressors would lead to negative emotional consequences. The lesson to be learned from these studies is that different problems require different solutions.

**EMOTIONAL APPROACH COPING.**   A study of **emotional approach** coping suggests that there are healthy and productive roles for emotion in the stress process (Stanton, Kirk, Cameron, & Danoff-Burg, 2000; Stanton & Low, 2012). Acknowledging one's feelings and expressing them, for example, is thought to be related to better adjustment. In addition to the cathartic effect of expressing one's feelings, emotions can yield useful information for the resolution of problems. The researchers note that the appropriateness of emotional approach behaviors depends on the actor, the situation, and the receptivity of the listener to such behaviors. When a person is in tune with his or her emotions, in a calm situation that facilitates sharing of those emotions, and is communicating with someone capable of validating the person's feelings, such communication may be an effective way of coping with stress. On the other hand, if a person is in an inappropriate setting or dealing with a volatile person, such communication may exacerbate the situation.

**THREE DIMENSIONS OF COPING.**   Other variations on coping of particular note come from Hobfoil and Vaux's (1993) proposal of a coping scheme that takes into account the **active-passive, prosocial-antisocial,** and **direct** and **indirect** ways that coping could be divided. He argues that such a multidimensional consideration could account for cultural variations in coping. He emphasizes the need to take the context of the problem and the response into account. His system gives prominence to the cultural and community/social contributions to coping and the research literature on active versus avoidant and problem-solving versus emotional styles researched by others. Gaylord-Hardin and Cunningham (2009)'s research on culturally relevant coping has found that African American adolescents benefit from utilizing culturally sanctioned coping mechanisms such as religiosity in the face of race-related stress.

**COLLECTIVIST COPING.** Based on research conducted in Taiwan, Heppner et al. (2006) report a five-factor instrument representing **collectivist coping** activities not usually found in coping inventories. Examples of these collectivist styles are: I tried to accept the trauma for what it offered me; I believed that I would grow from surviving; Shared my feelings with my family; Saved face by not telling anyone. An adolescent coping style that taps Chinese values has been derived by Hamid, Yue, and Leung (2003). This instrument reflects concepts such as "as shui-chi tzu-an (let nature take its course), I pu-pien ying wan-pien (coping with shifting events by sticking to one unchangeable way), and k'an-k'ai (to see a thing through)," which were derivatives of a Taoist philosophy where, for example, nonaction is not seen as avoidance but rather the understanding and acknowledgment of the nature of things.

**A SCHEMA FOR COPING.** It is difficult to represent the plethora of coping styles that have been studied in a succinct way. Skinner, Edge, Altman, and Sherwood (2003) reviewed the literature on coping measures and reported problems with the typical ways of organizing coping behaviors. From this review they identified 13 ways of coping (Table 3.2). Taking these basic categories and organizing them into types of coping proved more difficult. They believed a functional definition, that is, problem-solving versus emotional-focused coping style, was not workable because behaviors could perform more than one function. A behavior may be both emotional and problem focused, as we can see in the "positive emotional focus approaches" described earlier. A topological definition based on what is done, for example, the approach versus avoidance distinction, is then confusing because behaviors have multiple dimensions. A coping response may require both avoidance for a time, to gain perspective, and then approach to directly contend with the problem.

Skinner and colleagues (2003) argue that the method for organizing the specific coping response families might be better conceptualized from an adaptive process viewpoint. They believe the three adaptive processes to be (1) coordination of **action and contingencies** within an environment, (2) coordination of **social and personal resources,** and (3) coordination of **preferences and options.** Note that the emphasis is on coordination, or rather, the efforts of the individual to understand the environment and themselves so as to better fit into the presenting context. Skinner and coworkers propose that these three processes might best describe coping processes in general. Future studies of coping might be

---

**TABLE 3.2    Coping Families**

1. Problem solving
2. Support seeking
3. Avoidance
4. Distraction
5. Positive cognitive restructuring
6. Rumination
7. Helplessness
8. Social withdrawal
9. Emotional regulation
10. Information seeking
11. Negotiation
12. Opposition
13. Delegation

---

*Source:* From Skinner et al. (2003, pp. 240–241).

guided by these distinctions. What we can conclude from this body of research is that coping is an idio-syncratic process, and there is no "one size fits all" approach that can be recommended. Although many of the coping styles discussed in this section are individual, some coping styles are more interpersonal, such as the use of social support.

## Social Support

The concept of social support would seem to be a natural area of investigation for community psychology. Those around us are often a resource. Seeking social support is listed among Lazarus and Folkman's coping styles. It assumes there is a social support system from which to receive assistance.

> Social support might be usefully re-conceptualized as coping assistance, or the active participation of significant others in an individual's stress management efforts. Thus social support might work like coping by assisting the person to change the situation, to change the meaning of the situation, to change the emotional reaction to the situation, or to change all three. (Thoits, 1986, p. 417)

Research has demonstrated the advantages of a good social support system to one's health (Barrera, 2000; Davidson & Demaray, 2007; Stadler, Feifel, Rohrmann, Vermeiren, & Poustka, 2010). Some early research found that social support was even more powerful than stressor measures in explaining the variations in psychopathology in a community sample (Lin, Simonre, Ensel, & Kuo, 1979). This relationship continues to be found in a variety of populations dealing with different kinds of problems. The relationships are not always direct or self-evident (Barrera, 2000) and there are distinctions found between perceived and received support (Haber, Cohen, Lucas, & Baltes, 2007). Keinan (1997) points to several intervening variables that figure into the translation of supportive behavior to the appraisal of support. She finds that for low-anxiety mothers who have had experience in birthing (not a first birth), the presence of a supportive husband during the birth process led to higher levels of mother tension. For mothers in their first birth experience, the presence of a husband was helpful. Keinan believes the situational and personality variables influenced the effects of social support.

Nonetheless, the generally positive impact on adaptation continues to be demonstrated using more and more sophisticated physiological measures of stress reactions (Gallagher, Phillips, Ferraro, Drayson, & Carroll, 2008).

**TYPES OF SOCIAL SUPPORT.** Supportive behaviors are typically divided into three areas: emotional, informational, and instrumental (Helgeson & Cohen, 1996; Thoits, 1985). Emotional support comes in the form of expressing compassion for the person. The support is directed at making the person feel understood and cared for. In the informational dimension, the person being supported is provided with helpful facts or instruction. The knowledge imparted may help the person gain some mastery of required tasks. The third form of support is instrumental, where the person is provided with materials, transportation, or physical assistance.

Support from parents may be particularly important during childhood and, in particular, may be an important coping mechanism when children have problems with their peers. Poteat, Mereish, DiGiovanni, and Koenig (2011) examined the role of parental support for kids who were being bullied by peers. They found that while parental support was linked to lower feelings of suicidality in kids who were being bullied, it did not protect kids from experiencing lower feelings of school belongingness. Finally, they found that parental support was less likely to buffer the effect of teasing in gay, lesbian, bisexual, and transgendered youths. Studies like these demonstrate that social support may be a helpful coping mechanism for people in general, but it is not a panacea for all the harmful effects of stressors and it may be a less powerful coping strategy for some individuals.

**BUFFERING AND ADDITIVE EFFECT.**    So how does social support affect our well-being? Some believed that support raised one's well-being regardless of the stressors in the environment (Thoits, 1984, 1985). We are happier because we have friends. The other explanation is the "buffering" theory (Dean & Lin, 1977; Wilcox, 1981). Social support helps us deal with stressors that arise. When facing a problem, it is good to have people to help so the burden of the problem can be shared—often, "two heads are better than one" when it comes to problem solving. It appears that both explanations have been supported by research. However, individual differences must be taken into account when determining what type of social support is most valuable in a given situation.

Brissette, Scheier, and Carver (2002) studied the reasons social support and optimism were associated with good psychological adjustment. They examined the experiences of first-year college students, measuring optimism, social support systems, number of friends, stress, and depression. They found that the correlation between optimism and well-being (low depression and low stress) was in fact mediated by coping and social support. Optimism was associated with more problem solving and positive-reinterpretation coping. Optimism was also associated with perception of a good-quality social support system and the number of friends within one's network. These coping styles and perceptions of social support are what relate to better overall adjustment. Optimism works through these two mediating mechanisms, coping and social support, to bring about positive results for the individual. The present example illustrates the importance of coping and social support in helping mediate the effects of personality on depression.

Social support continues to prove a powerful factor in predicting health outcomes (Richmond, Ross, & Egeland, 2007). In a national Canadian sample of indigenous people, women reporting high levels of positive interaction, emotional support, and tangible support were more likely to report thriving health. For men, emotional support was the only social support variable related to thriving health. Though gender differences appeared with regard to which specific social support components mattered, the overall trends were clear.

Examining our chapter's example of Linda, the first-year college student, we see high stressor scores for life changes in coming to college. We would expect more hassles as a result of these changes.

---

## CASE IN POINT 3.2

# Mexican American College Student Acculturation Stress, Social Support, and Coping

There has been a 75 percent increase in the number of Latino students entering college. Unfortunately, their rate of graduation has not kept pace with this increase of entrants. A meta-analysis attributed these problems in retention rate to the higher levels of financial and academic preparedness and acculturative stress (Quintana, Vogel, & Ybarra, 1991). However, longitudinal research has revealed a wide range of risk factors that fall within the individual, family, school, and community domains (Prevatt

& Kelly, 2003). Crockett and colleagues (2007) studied the acculturative stress in one group of Latino college students, Mexican Americans. Using data from a university in Texas and two universities in California, Crockett's group studied the relationships among acculturative stress, parent and peer social support, coping (active or avoidant styles), and psychological distress. Among those with low levels of social support, higher levels of acculturative stress were related to higher levels of anxiety and depression.

For those with high levels of social support, acculturative stress was not important to the development of psychological symptoms. There were also significant interactive effects with avoidant and approach coping styles. The authors believe this to be the first time acculturative stress and the buffering effect of social support and of coping styles were demonstrated with Latino college students. The stress model and its components provide a clear framework for the study of this at-risk population.

Her social support would depend on her relationship with her parents, family, and friends and her ability to find new friends and mentors in the college setting. If these support systems are good, she could receive good advice and material support when needed or a "shoulder to cry on" when things get frustrating. As for her coping with the stressors, current research would recommend active and engaged styles of dealing with her environment when the problems are workable. Other styles of coping may be called for if the problems are not so workable. If she finds effective ways to deal with her life changes—for example, meeting new people, finding constructive advice, and building a socially supportive support group—then Linda may find her changes less stressful and more like manageable challenges.

Research on resilience examines how people at risk survive and thrive. The stress model is central to much of the work on resilience. Resilience is what we study next. We reference a number of stress concepts in the following section.

## RESILIENCE

Why is it that in difficult times, some succeed while others do not? There are children born into high-risk situations such as poverty who seem to thrive and succeed, despite the odds. Not everyone is doomed to failure in risky situations, fortunately. Resiliency researchers have delved into who does well in risky situations and why.

### At-Risk to Resilient

One of the interesting facts about resilience is that researchers "discovered" it while they were looking at factors placing people at risk for failure and pathology (Garmezy, 1974; Garmezy & Streitman, 1974; Rutter, 1981). Garmezy was studying families that had at least one schizophrenic parent. Rutter was looking at children from poor urban neighborhoods in comparison to children from a rural setting. From this initial focus came the insight that there were many who did well despite their circumstances (Garmezy, Masten, & Tellegen, 1984; Rutter, 1985, 1987). Rutter (1987) emphasized that resilience is not a characteristic of people, but rather, it is a process affected by many variables. He pointed to the impact of gender (expectations and ways in which upsets are expressed), temperament (likable versus unlikable), marital support in childrearing, the ability to plan, and school successes and their effects on a child's resilience or vulnerability. Rutter also noted the importance of "turning points," or important junctures, in the lives of at-risk children. The direction taken at these critical points had long-lasting influence on the life of the individual. Garmezy and the Project Competence group explored what it meant to positively adapt to the environment, what was effective across multiple tasks, and developmental phases (Masten & Obradovic, 2006).

Among the early studies of at-risk populations was one by Sandler (1980). He found strong social support to be related to lower levels of maladjustment in at-risk inner-city children. It was a good example of the use of the earlier described stress model for examining the resilience process.

### The Kauai Longitudinal Studies

In the 1950s, researchers began a series of longitudinal studies to look at the characteristics of children who eventually did well despite their placement in "risky circumstances." An excellent example of these longitudinal studies was conducted by Werner and Smith over several decades on the island of Kauai in the state of Hawaii. Werner and Smith (2001) reported on this longitudinal study of individuals who appeared to be at risk based on a history of family psychopathology, poverty, lack of education, and/or family alcoholism. Following these at-risk subjects into their middle age (50s), Werner and Smith found resilience to be linked to the individual's capability in dealing with age-appropriate developmental challenges. Because the study was situated on an island, the population was relatively stable and the influence of off-island factors somewhat controlled. Starting in 1955, the researchers looked at the developmental progression of the identified group of at-risk infants as they matured into full adulthood. They found that about two thirds of this at-risk population developed problems. The third that did not were characterized by their ability to engage the environment in an age/developmental stage–appropriate way. They were nurtured by a parent or parent substitute who served as a positive role model for them. The "vulnerable but invincible" children also found support outside their families in a variety of community settings: school, neighborhood, informal friend networks, churches, or youth organizations. By late adolescence, these children had developed internalized resources that aided in mastering their environment (high self-esteem, internal locus of control, a feeling that life made sense, and an effective support system). The more risk factors there were, the more protective factors were needed to deal with the risks raised. Family protective factors related to the parents' ability to be nurturing at critical times. The most important community factor was the presence of caring adults who served as teachers and mentors or later as friends, coworkers, or bosses. Among the protective factors in the environment were emotional support throughout the life cycle and a lower number of stressful life events. By age 30, the resilient men and women were more accomplished in both education and careers and were more likely to be married than their nonresilient counterparts or the national norm. By age 40, they were more likely to be settled and contributing members in their communities. Such studies as these serve as a blueprint for community interventions, because they pointed out those aspects of the children's experience that were predictive of later life success.

## A Useful Model

Masten (2001) pointed to the usefulness of these naturalistic studies on resilience and competence in at-risk populations. From the Kauai studies and the work of Garmezy and Rutter, important protective factors in the developmental life process were identified. These were later used in devising interventions. In particular, prevention program emphases on parent competence, early child preparation for school success, the acquisition of specific child skills, and expanded opportunities for community mentoring were directly in line with resilience findings. Masten stated, "Resilience does not come from rare and special qualities, but from the everyday magic of ordinary, normative human resources in . . . children, in their families and relationships, and in their communities." The natural capacity to build competencies and strengths and their importance in the coping process have shifted community prevention interventions from prevention to promotion efforts. Examples of resiliency factors are presented in Table 3.3.

---

**TABLE 3.3    Short List of Resilience Factors (with Implicated Human Adaptive Systems)**

- Positive attachment bonds with caregivers (attachment; family)
- Positive relationships with other nurturing and competent adults (attachment)
- Intellectual skills (integrated cognitive systems of a human brain in good working order)
- Self-regulation skills (self-control systems and related executive functions of the human brain)
- Positive self-perceptions; self-efficacy (mastery motivation system)
- Faith, hope, and a sense of meaning in life (meaning-making systems of belief)
- Friends or romantic partners who are supportive and prosocial (attachment)
- Bonds to effective schools and other prosocial organizations (sociocultural systems)
- Communities with positive services and supports for families and children (sociocultural)
- Cultures that provide positive standards, rituals, relationships, and supports (sociocultural)

*Source:* Adapted from Masten, A. (2009). Ordinary magic: Lessons from research on resilience in human development. *Education Canada, 49*(3), 28–32. Retrieved from www.cea-ace.ca.

Rutter (2006) reminded us that resilience was more than the development of social competence or positive mental health. Resilience occurred when individuals thrived *despite* their risky circumstances. He cautioned that there were differences in how well people fare. Some thrived, but a significant number did poorly and succumbed to the negative environment. Nonetheless, for some the experience of successfully contending with stressful situations made them stronger.

## The Fourth Wave

Masten and Obradovic (2006) described four waves of resilience research. The first started with the study of the causes of psychopathology and the discovery of children who were healthy and successful emerging from risky circumstances. The research focused on what was associated with such failure and illness or success and health. The second wave examined the processes in developing resiliently. The third wave attempted to apply what had been learned from the descriptive studies through developing and testing the efficacy of interventions. Emerging from these first three waves has come the "discovery" of important adaptive systems—family, school, community relationships, spiritual practices—and important skills—self-control, goal-directed behavior, dealing with affect, motivation to succeed, and dealing with stress.

The fourth wave of resiliency work has started to look at the integration of multiple levels (neurological, personality, social, community) and disciplines (psychology, sociology, biology, neurology). For example, Davis and Cummings (2006) found that parental conflict was associated with heightened risk of childhood adjustment problems. Hypothesizing the wear-down of the neurobiological system in children faced with such conflict, Davis, Sturge-Apple, Cicchetti, and Cummings (2007) examined the level of stress reaction in children of conflicted families. They discovered that children with high-conflict parents had fewer adrenocortical reactions when exposed to a parental conflict incident. Adrenocortical reaction had earlier been linked to typical physiological reactions to stressors as a part of the hypothalamic-pituitary-adrenocortical system linked to stress. This dampened reaction was also found to be related to heightened tendencies for acting out and aggressive behaviors. The neurophysiological reactivity findings and their link to this class of problem behaviors were first steps in understanding a child's risk for acting out. Have these children learned not to get excited when witnessing conflict? Did this in turn make them less sensitive to the effects of aggression? Or did it mean that they required more aggression in their world to be stimulated? Further studies are needed on these links between lowered adrenocortical reaction and aggressive behavior. Future findings would help direct the creation of possible early interventions to decrease the likelihood of aggression in children.

A second example of the multilevel analysis of stress and resiliency was provided by Greenberg, Riggs, and Blair (2007) in a multilayer analysis of the plasticity (openness to being shaped, the ability to be altered) of the brain, and the impact of childhood and adolescent experiences on neural development. Greenberg and colleagues elaborated on the neurological context for the Promoting Alternative Thinking Strategies (PATHS) program, which focused on social and emotional learning. There was clear evidence that neural development was the product of the interactions of genetics and environment. Neuron generation, synaptic formation, pruning, and density were all neurological developments that over time formed the basis of frontal cortex maturation and the increasing power of thoughtful control of behaviors. In addition, the growing complexity of right and left hemisphere communications and the use of language in determining action were well-documented neurological trends.

Greenberg and coworkers (2007) found Moffitt's (1993) distinction between life course–persistent and adolescent-limited (AL) antisocial behaviors provocative to their program development. Life course–persistent patterns started at a young age, were frequently found throughout the life of the individual, and were severe deviations from acceptable behaviors. The AL behaviors did not appear until the onset of puberty, were infrequent, and were not as grave a violation of social rules. The AL behaviors tended to stop after adolescence and might, in fact, be normative to the developmental period. Think of "teenage rebellion" versus criminal tendencies. Given this distinction, the importance of early intervention in problem behavior seemed clear.

The research by Greenberg and associates with their PATHS program suggested that the intervention could have a significant impact on young children's (first- and second-graders') ability to inhibit incorrect responses and to sequence relevant information. In turn, these capabilities have been shown to relate to teacher- and parent-reported problems. The ability to control one's behavior and hold back from acting inappropriately was very important. We might think of how impulsive behaviors have been viewed as immature. The children who received the PATHS intervention were better able to control themselves. In turn, being able to talk things through and work out a problem verbally was important. This skill was positively affected by the PATHS program and, in turn, related to fewer problem behaviors.

An awareness of the multiple levels at which the processes exist and of the interactions among these various processes informs the derivation of new theory and interventions. From this holistic perspective, the resilience literature provides direction for community-based programs. The incorporation of the biological to the sociological is in keeping with community psychology's multidisciplinary traditions as well as to the biopsychosocial models that are gaining currency in psychology.

## Summary

The stress, coping, social support, and resilience literature has contributed to a theory and research base for community programs. The models propose that people face a changing and demanding world full of challenges with which the individual must cope. The existence of social supports and the ability to access these supports are important resources for the individual's coping process. Examination of those who have succeeded in threatening and risky contexts—that is, resilient people—highlights the importance of personal and social resources to those successes.

We have come to understand that humans can successfully deal with a variety of adversities. Our example of Linda dealing with the stress of the first year of college helps point out that in high-risk populations (e.g., those in transition), some fail and some succeed. The resilience research suggests that the qualities needed for success are specific to the developmental tasks. It is not a smooth, continuous process from one point in life to another, but a series of challenges. The difference between those who succeed and those who fail is the ability to self-regulate and meet the challenges placed before us. Toward this end, it is helpful to have the support of mentors. This support comes from the interaction of personal qualities and contextual qualities helping the individual "construct" the opportunities needed. Ask most college students and they will tell you their world is daunting. One college graduate likened it to "entering a dark tunnel" (Candice Hughes, commencement speech, Pacific Lutheran University, Tacoma, WA, May, 2008). What you find there and how you cope with your discoveries in the tunnel is dependent on your resources, including your ability to bring aid when needed. This is a normative process, or rather the result of "ordinary magic," within the community (Masten, 2001).

# The Importance of Social Change

*We are the ones we have been waiting for.*

—June Jordan

—Alice Walker

—Barack Obama

A noted African American psychologist once told a story of traveling with her family as a child (Wyatt, G., personal communication, August 1987). When going on a long car trip, they would pack all their necessities and carefully map out their route. There needed to be sufficient food and water. They needed to plot where they could stop for bathroom breaks and gas. Every detail of the trip needed to be planned. The reason for this detailed planning was that they could not stop just anywhere. If they did not have enough to drink, they could not just go and buy what they needed. They could not use just any lavatory facilities, nor could they go just anywhere to eat. During those times, there were clearly marked places designated "For Whites" and "For Blacks," and they were not free to cross those lines. This story was told by a friend, who is still living and is working at one of the nation's premier research universities.

"Separate but equal" had been set as U.S. law by the Supreme Court decision in the late 1800s. The case of *Plessy v. Ferguson* established that a Louisiana law mandating different facilities for Blacks and for Whites was fair, because these facilities would be equal to each other. The Supreme Court at that time believed that this law did not make one group inferior to the other. This interpretation allowed for separate schools, separate bathrooms, separate entrances, and the basis for a clearly segregated society. In 1954, the Supreme Court decided in the case of *Brown v. the Board of Education of Topeka, Kansas* that segregated schools led to inherently inferior facilities for a targeted group. This decision paved the way for the desegregated society in which we live today. The idea of separate entrances, toilets, or schools is so foreign to us that this story is sometimes met with disbelief. This landmark Supreme Court case of 1954 brought about changes in our society that are still being resolved today. We now consider the idea of separate entrances, or separate restaurants, or separate facilities to be absurd. Social change does occur. In the case of *Brown v. Board of Education,* psychology had a hand in influencing the verdict. The testimony and work of psychologists Kenneth Clark and Mamie Phipps Clark played significant roles in this decision, changing American society and American psychology as we know it (Benjamin & Crouse, 2002; Keppel, 2002; Lal, 2002; Pickren & Tomes, 2002). Social change in its best sense moves us to reconsider our present circumstances, imagine improvements, and aspire toward our overall betterment.

Trickett (2009) noted that since its inception, community psychology has had two objectives, "understanding people in context and attempting to change those aspects of the community that pollute the possibilities for local citizens to control their own lives and improve their community" (p. 396). Change, some planned and some unplanned, seems to be a pervasive condition of modern times, especially when economic divides grow deeper within societies. Actively participating in and fashioning social change is a hallmark activity of many community psychologists (Maton, 2000). Social change is the focus of this chapter.

How is change defined from the perspective of psychologists? Watzlawick, Weakland, and Fisch (1974) believed there to be two types of change: "One that occurs within a given system which itself remains unchanged and one whose occurrence changes the system itself" (p. 10). These two types of change have been called **first order change** and **second order change,** respectively. First order change may describe an individual's alteration of typical behavior within a system such as a family. For example, a mother may choose to ignore her two-year-old son who is throwing a temper tantrum because he wants candy at the grocery store (and she has refused to buy it). If the typical interaction of this mother and child is that the child's tantrum results in him *getting* the candy, probably because his mother is embarrassed by the crying and wants him to stop, one can see how ignoring his crying is a type of behavior change. However, if this is a strongly established behavior pattern, Mom's new ignoring behavior, *the first order change*, is likely the only change we would see in this interaction (probably because the son will fuss even louder when he is ignored). In other words, the entire system at this point has yet to change, even though Mom's behavior has. If the mother in our example were to ignore and/or negatively reinforce her son's future attempts to get his way by throwing a tantrum, eventually he will learn that his behavior is ineffective and he will move onto some new way, ideally more pleasant, of getting what he wants. When the system is no longer characterized by the son acting out and the mother giving in, one could conclude that *second order change* has occurred. As Watzlawick and colleagues (1974) noted, second order change requires the innovator to step outside his or her basic

**FIGURE 4.1    The Nine Dot Problem.** Instructions: Connect the nine dots in the grid, using four straight lines, without lifting your pencil. The solution to this problem may be found at the end of the chapter, in Figure 4.3.

assumptive world and think and act in creative new ways. Second order change requires the change agent to have sufficient perspective-taking ability to perceive the existing problem in its entirety and to come to a solution.

An example of second order thinking is the solution to the nine-dot grid problem found in Figure 4.1. Try the problem to determine whether you can devise a second order solution.

We find reference to the "revolutionary" nature of community psychology in Rappaport's 1977 text and many subsequent definitional articles on community psychology (Trickett, 2009). The revolution typically refers to the shift that occurred within community psychology to preventive mental health and away from remediation, from person-centered to system-centered interventions, and from pathology-focused to wellness-focused work. Social change is an integral part of this shift.

Questions regarding social change for community psychologists are complex and interrelated. Social scientists want to know what causes change; how to predict change; how best to cope with change; and, most of all, how to fashion or direct change that improves the living conditions of community members.

This chapter looks at what creates social change—planned or not—especially in today's complex world. The discussion draws from all areas within psychology, as well as anthropology, medicine, public health, political science, sociology, and other disciplines (Maton et al., 2006; Wandersman, Hallman, & Berman, 1989). In fact, a multidisciplinary approach for examining and intervening in social change is often desirable (Maton, 2000; Seidman, 1983), especially if the diversity (U.S. Department of Labor, 2006) and challenges of our vast population are to be appreciated (Maton, 2000; Trickett et al., 2011).

What are some of the phenomena that induce change in society? Factors such as diverse populations, social injustice, declining resources, demands for accountability, expanding knowledge or changing technologies (Kettner, Daley, & Nichols, 1985), economic changes, community conflict (Christensen & Robinson, 1989), dissatisfaction with traditional approaches to social problems, the desire for choices and the need for diversity of solutions to social problems (Heller, Price, Reinharz, Riger, Wandersman, 1984), and other issues lead the list of reasons for social change. Although the list is not exhaustive, some of these forces need to be considered in more detail to help you comprehend their roles in shaping social change.

## REASONS FOR SOCIAL CHANGE

### Diverse Populations

During the Middle Ages, no one expected a long life. Today, life expectancies in the United States and elsewhere are increasing. The growing population of the elderly, as well as the disabled, the unemployed, and the influx of new immigrants into our country, is an example of how diverse populations create the need for dramatic social changes and new community interventions.

For example, consider that within a democracy, public policy and government are supposed to reflect the needs and wishes of all citizens. However, as we know, some Americans do not vote. The homeless are often denied the right to vote because they do not have fixed street addresses. Many elderly people or individuals with disabilities also do not vote because of transportation costs and other factors (Schur & Kruse, 2000). This situation creates the added problem that individuals who ought to voice their political opinions on nutrition, health care, housing, and other programs do not go to the polls. Finding transportation to the polls for the elderly or disabled on election day, or giving them alternative means of voting, may provide them with a greater voice in issues directly concerning them. Taking the service to the people who most need it empowers them to participate in social change.

Thus, special populations (Fairweather & Davidson, 1986) cause changes in society and, in turn, create more social change by virtue of either their swelling ranks or special situations. Consider the fact that baby boomers, who number in the millions, are now approaching older adulthood. This trend may mean that communities will need to provide more resources for the elderly than they have had to in the past. One should never underestimate the importance of population trends in social change (Duffy & Atwater, 2008; Light & Keller, 1985). If formal, established institutions are insensitive to the special issues of diverse populations, these groups themselves can and will create change (Kettner et al., 1985; Maton, 2000). Grassroots efforts to create or deal with social change are discussed in the next chapter.

The social change described at the opening of this chapter was the result of work across several decades. The lawsuit resulting in the *Brown v. Board of Education* decision had been brought by the National Association for the Advancement of Colored People (NAACP). As pointed out before, the court finding for *Brown* was pivotal in opening opportunities for many groups who had previously been excluded from mainstream society.

## Social Justice: A Moral Imperative for Social Change

One of the reasons that community psychologists are invested in helping society adapt to population changes such as those described above is grounded in the field's commitment to social justice. As described in Chapter 1, social justice is a value that guides the field of community psychology, and a just or fair society is an overall goal of much of what we do.

One of the implications of changes in population trends, such as an influx of immigrants, is not only that societal demographics change, but that the needs and values of such groups must be integrated into the fabric of our democracy. This has happened in the United States throughout history, although not without considerable strife, as was illustrated in the *Brown v. Board of Education* case. Cases such as these are excellent illustrations of how over history, the "status quo" or "how things have always been done" must be revisited if we are to have a socially just society and a bona fide democracy.

Albee (2000) was a prominent psychologist who confronted the field of psychology about its values, or apparent lack thereof, and as a result, its position on social justice. Although community psychology has really always been guided by a value for social justice, the rest of the field was much more ambivalent about the issue. Psychology, like other social sciences, was modeled after sciences such as geology and, subsequently, was grounded in objectivity. However, being objective when investigating rocks may be easier than being objective or neutral when investigating human beings or dimensions of human behavior. Thus, psychologists like Albee thought that to present psychology as a "values-free" discipline was misleading and, perhaps even more troubling, aligned us as a field to validate the status quo.

As Young (1990) described, the status quo in the United States and many other parts of the world is to use marginalization to disempower large segments of the population, which results in nondemocratic decision making. So, if psychology as field was unwilling to take a stand on marginalization, it was undeniably complicit in supporting its existence. This was the heart of Albee's (2000) criticism of the field. Community psychologists such as Prilleltensky have echoed this sentiment (Fox & Prilleltensky, 2007), noting that although some people would like psychology to be apolitical or neutral, that does not mean that it is (or should be).

Therefore, one of the reasons that community psychologists are involved in social change is the value we see in social justice. Valuing social justice requires us to be committed to changing processes and policies in our society that result in injustice or inequities. If some children are receiving a better education than others because of their socioeconomic background, social change is needed. If some racial groups are dying of cancer in larger numbers than other racial groups because they are receiving substandard healthcare, social change is needed. If there is a bias in hiring and promotion decisions that results in women being underrepresented in leadership positions, social change is needed. In other words, it is the inequity *itself* that is the rationale for social change when one values social justice.

This is because the inequity is the signal that social injustice exists and social change is required, just as the dying canary is the signal that there are toxic fumes in a contaminated mine shaft. Promoting and protecting socially just policies and processes are critical to maintaining social justice. If community psychology is led by a value of social justice, then participating in an examination of policies and subsequently, participating in social change is a key element of the work we do. This is illustrated again in our discussion of scarce resources.

## The Perception of Declining or Scarce Resources

When resources are in decline, there is a perception of comparative scarcity. What has been established as a baseline for funding is lessening. Scarcity results in changing social dynamics, with increasing competition for these resources (Foundation Center, 2008; Smart Growth, 2008). This issue not only affects individuals and families, it affects community centers, public education, free health clinics, and many other services that are funded by outside sources such as government funding, grants, private donations, or corporate underwriting. Because so few community service programs are self-supporting, most are highly dependent on external funding sources (Kettner et al., 1985), and most attempts to create social change are limited by lack of funding and other resources (Maton, 2000). External funding for community services, whether it comes in the form of government-sponsored legislation or grants from public or private endowments or foundations, typically is awarded for a limited amount of time through a competitive process in which there are more groups seeking funding than the funding can support. New programs therefore compete with older programs for limited pools of money (Levine, Perkins, & Perkins, 2004; Sarason, 1972/1999). Also, both the federal government and local governments have provided less funding for human services than in the past, thereby creating a sort of "Robin Hood in reverse" effect (Delgado, 1986).

Because government funding for community services is decreasing, there is more pressure on other granting institutions, such as private foundations. Examples of such granting foundations for community services include the Ford Foundation, the Charles Stewart Mott Foundation, the Henry J. Kaiser Foundation, the Robert Wood Johnson Foundation, the MacArthur Foundation, the Carnegie Foundation (Chavis, Florin, & Felix, 1992), and more recently the Bill and Melinda Gates Foundation. More programs and human services agencies are applying for these limited funds; hence, the competition for both government and foundation monies is often fierce.

Although some agencies charge fees to clients for services as one revenue stream for their organization, many are reluctant to become dependent on client fees, because such fees also fluctuate depending on caseload and other factors such as the resources of the clients themselves. Even agencies that charge clients on a **sliding scale** (where fees are tied to income and/or number of dependents) are reluctant to increase charges to their most financially needy clients. The trend toward allocating resources away from the poor (Delgado, 1986) contributes to the perception of declining resources.

When funding issues become severe (and even when they are not so severe), clients and service administrators demand reform or social change in order to increase resources. However, taxpayers often are uncomfortable approving tax increases to fund changes.

Because it is difficult to garner support from taxpayers to increase government support for certain community programs, organizations are often forced to try and raise money from charitable donations. These voluntary contributions from the public also vary as a function of the economy and other uncontrollable factors. Community service directors are therefore reluctant to become too dependent on charitable contributions. Funding issues for community services have been and will continue to be delicate and volatile (Frumkin, 2000).

Case in Point 4.1 discusses in more detail some of the funding dilemmas faced by nonprofit agencies.

## CASE IN POINT 4.1

## Funding Dilemmas for Nonprofit Organizations

The number of nonprofit or charitable organizations and the number of foundations willing to make philanthropic donations to them have grown in the past few decades (Foundation Center, 2008; Smart Growth, 2008). But are they keeping pace with each other? In other words, are funding opportunities shrinking while the number of organizations seeking funding is growing? Or are they growing in tandem?

In the 1950s, foundation startups grew by approximately 195 new funders a year. By the 1980s, the average number of new funders had increased to 348 per year. Between 1980 and 1995, the number of foundations in the United States nearly doubled, from 22,088 to 40,140 (Siska, 1998). Today, there are more than 57,000 such foundations and corporate donors that offer 246,000 different grants (Smart Growth, 2008). These grants are available in the areas of social services, arts and sciences, protection of democracy, support for vulnerable and needy populations, care for victims of natural disasters, health care, and education (Independent Sector, 2006). In recent years, the leading issue in terms of growth is peace and international affairs, which grew by a whopping 72.5% (Foundation Center, 2008).

What about the number of nonprofit organizations that tap into or are dependent on grants from these foundations? Have their ranks grown, too? Yes. There are now more than 1.9 million groups recognized by the Internal Revenue Service as nonprofit organizations (Independent Sector, 2006) and vying for funding. Some are small and have receipts under $5,000; others have receipts of millions of dollars. On the surface, then, it appears there should be fierce competition for charitable funding despite the growth in number of grant makers.

These statistics can be deceptive, however, because of economic and other changes—for example, natural disasters such as the hurricanes that hit the Louisiana coast (Center on Philanthropy, 2001; Foundation Center, 2008). Closer examination shows that money is not evenly distributed among all nonprofit organizations. Some organizations receive very large grants of millions of dollars; in fact, the number of grants over $5 million to nonprofits has grown enormously. Do you think that a small human service organization (such as a church's nonprofit child day-care center) can compete against a large national organization (e.g., the American Cancer Society) for such large

amounts of money? Indeed, DeVita's (1997) study showed that although most nonprofit groups are quite small, the largest organizations obtain the bulk of the finances. More specifically, small organizations with expenses of less than $100,000 accounted for 42% of the organizations, whereas organizations with total expenses of over $10 million accounted for only 4% of charities. The smaller charities received only 3% of the support dollars, whereas the larger organizations received half of all support dollars. This same study demonstrated that a disproportionate share of monies ends up in nonprofit organizations related to educational or health issues. In addition, organizations in the northeastern United States receive the lion's share of support dollars. One fourth of U.S. charities are located in the Northeast, yet they devour one third of the support dollars.

The answer to the opening question, then—Are funding opportunities shrinking?—is likely to be both *yes* and *no:* yes in that the number of foundations pouring dollars into nonprofit agencies is growing (but not fast enough), and no in that the support dollars are probably not distributed equitably.

| **TABLE 4.1   Planning and Evaluation Strategies That Address Accountability** |
|---|

1. *Why* is the intervention needed?
2. *How* does the program include science and "best practices"?
3. *How* will this new program fit with other existing programs?
4. *How* will the program be carried out?
5. *How* well was the program carried out?
6. *How* well does the program work?
7. *How* can the program be improved?
8. *What* can be done to "spin off" or institutionalize the program?

*Source:* Adapted from Wandersman, A., Morrissey, E., Davino, K., Seybolt, D., Crusto, C., Nation, M., et al. (1998). Comprehensive quality programming and accountability: Eight essential strategies for implementing successful prevention programs. *Journal of Primary Prevention, 19,* 3–30. With kind permission of Springer Science and Business Media.

## Accountability

*Accountability* and its sister term, *cost effectiveness,* seem to be the buzzwords of today. **Accountability** is the obligation to account for or be responsible for various transactions, monetary or otherwise. In times of scarce funding, it is especially fair and reasonable to ask for accountability from both new and continuing community programs (Wandersman et al., 1998). Table 4.1 provides a list of questions important to planning and evaluation as they relate to accountability.

**Cost effectiveness** means that money should be spent wisely—that is, there should be some return or profit on money expended. Cost effectiveness often refers to money; accountability can refer to such matters as time expended and quality of decisions made.

Spending has always been an important issue, but it is more likely to be in the forefront of the minds of today's citizens than it was in the past. Who requests accountability? Almost anyone today: clients, staff, administrators, taxpayers, elected officials, licensing boards, and others. Any of these constituencies is likely to want to know the answers to such questions as: Where was my money spent? Did the targeted population benefit? Were goals accomplished, and if not, why not?

When answers to these questions are not forthcoming or are not the ones expected, the parties leveling the query are likely to demand change. Some individuals may want new administrators; others might want new spending guidelines. The list of changes demanded can be so exhaustive that the end result is the demise of any organization not readily accountable to its constituents. Again, the final outcome is likely to be some kind of ongoing change.

## Knowledge-Based and Technological Change

**Technological changes** in the form of web- and network-based communication systems have created new demands on workforces in business as well as in human services. Some organizations and individuals adapt well to technological advances. Others—for a multitude of reasons such as reluctance to use new technologies or lack of funds—do not adapt well or quickly.

People today may think that they are undergoing rapid and extreme technological changes more than ever before. Technological changes, whenever they occur, obligate further changes (Frank, 1983; Kling, 2000). Consider, for example, the technology divide that exists between many youths and their parents today (Kaiser Family Foundation, 2010). Today, you probably complete your term papers, balance your checkbook, keep track of appointments, and perhaps pass your idle time by using the Internet. But, for your parents, there was a time when the Internet didn't exist and computers were only used in business and industry, not in homes. The computer has changed our methods of conducting business, completing homework, and socializing.

If these "galloping technological changes" (Frank, 1983) are not enough, mainstream U.S. society is also experiencing a knowledge explosion. New methods for practicing anything from psychotherapy to landscape architecture, new guidelines for human resources management, additional legislation controlling all parts of people's lives, as well as other innovations and applications—all requiring new understanding and new skills—can overwhelm society's members, create additional change, and perhaps at the same time stimulate anxiety.

Despite the fact that technology is ubiquitous in our occupational, educational, and leisure lives (Brosnan & Thorpe, 2006), many people remain afraid of it, especially older individuals who did not grow up with the Internet. The general fear of technology has been called **technophobia** in the psychological literature (Brosnan & Thorpe, 2006). A specific fear of computers has also been identified and is known as **computerphobia** (Hudiburg, 1990) or, more recently, as **computer anxiety** (Thorpe & Brosnan, 2007). In fact, some claim that this phobia or fear is so strong that it might well be diagnosable (Thorpe & Brosnan, 2007) and in need of treatment (Brosnan & Thorpe, 2006) for success in the modern world.

This so-called digital divide extends to many different people and across international borders (Cooper, 2006). Research has found computer anxiety in older adults (Laguna & Babcock, 1997). Marginalized individuals who are not well educated, are poor or elderly or disabled, and some minority groups remain more technophobic than the general population (Duffy & Atwater, 2008; Karavidas, Lim, & Katsikas, 2005; National Science Foundation, 2003). There remains a dispute in the literature, however, as to whether there are true gender differences in computer anxiety and technophobia (e.g., Cooper, 2006; Popovich, Gullekson, Morris, & Morse, 2008). Perhaps as technological changes advance, these individuals will only fear them more. Few traditional community systems (such as the Department of Health) provide help in coping with technical disasters (Webb, 1989)—a situation that does not help allay fears. One possible way to address these concerns is via community education and information dissemination. These strategies are discussed in the next chapter on creating social change.

On the upside, Wittig and Schmitz (1996) and Kreisler, Snider, and Kiernan (1997) found that community organizing is primarily done electronically. Such technological organizing seems to obscure social boundaries, alter perceptions regarding stigmatized groups, enhance participation of previous nonparticipants in civil life, and empower activism.

## Community Conflict

Some communities experience the strife of conflict—for example, in the demonstrations and riots of the 1960s, some of which were triggered when Whites clashed with Blacks. This is often a function of the perception that in order for one community to "win," the other must "lose." Conflict, however, does not always have to produce negative changes (Worchel & Lundgren, 1991). Sometimes a positive outcome of community conflict is social change. **Community conflict** involves two or more parties with incompatible goals that usually have specific values (positive and negative) attached to them. Because of the strongly held values, power struggles, and varying interest levels of the parties, conflict in the community can be difficult to resolve or manage (Checkoway, 2009). However, such conflict, whether resolved or unresolved, often results in social change, because goodwill alone does not always remove or dissipate the factors that led to the conflict (Fairweather & Davidson, 1986).

Yet, as was discussed in Chapter 1 with regard to social justice, in a process where all parties are represented, the result of conflict may still be just, even if the distribution of eventual outcomes is not necessarily even. When conflict leads to dialogue and collaborative decision making, conflict can lead to positive social change.

## Dissatisfaction with Traditional Services

Probably no other cause has fostered social change more than consumer dissatisfaction with existing community services, especially external expert–dominated approaches (Maton, 2000). In fact, you will recall from Chapter 1 that such dissatisfaction with traditional mental health services spawned the birth and growth of community psychology itself when psychologists at the Swampscott Conference expressed dismay with traditional forms of mental health treatment.

One example of dissatisfaction creating community change relates to this chapter's opening vignette. The African American community was well aware of the prejudices and discrimination present in society. The disadvantages were systemically rooted and pervasive in their social world: a powerful example of institutionalized social injustice.

Closer to the issue of psychological interventions, it is important to look at another example of how dissatisfaction with services leads to change. As you may already know from your training in psychology and related disciplines, one of the earliest forms of psychotherapy (or "the talking cure") was psychoanalysis as developed by Sigmund Freud. Freud's own protégés, such as Carl Jung and Alfred Adler, became disenchanted with Freud's approach to therapy and modified psychoanalysis as they knew it (Phares & Chaplin, 1997). Contemporary therapists, disgruntled with such concepts as pansexuality and the unconscious from Freudian theory, have also developed an array of therapies exemplified by behavior modification, cognitive–behavioral therapy, and existential–humanistic counseling, to name a few. Today, the mental health client has a long menu of therapies from which to choose—yet it was in response to the dissatisfaction with what was then the "status quo" that such changes came about.

Dissatisfaction with traditional pathology-based, individually focused clinical psychology led to the creation of community psychology. As noted in Chapter 1, there were many reasons for the proposal of a strength-based, community-oriented intervention coming out of the Swampscott Conference in the 1960s (Kelly, 2006; Nelson & Prilleltensky, 2010; Rappaport, 1977). Complaints with the lack of services to ethnic minority populations were behind similar moves toward a culturally informed psychotherapy (Pedersen, Draguns, Lonner, & Trimble, 2008; Sue & Sue, 2008). The inadequacies of a male-focused psychological theory gave impetus to the development of feminist theories (Gilligan, 2011). We can find many examples of how dissatisfaction has brought about change in psychology. Case in Point 4.2 is one such example.

## Desire for Diversity of Solutions

Walk into any store in the United States and the display of available goods is overwhelming. Americans are used to choices among brands X, Y, and Z. Americans do not just want diversity in goods, however. They also expect diversity and choice among services. Individuals seeking psychotherapy want to know that they have options in the training of the therapist, the type of therapy, the payment plan, and the length of treatment. Similarly, Americans want to be able to choose between private and public educational institutions for their children and between law firms and lawyers when they want to recover dam-

## Community Conflict: Adversity Turns to Opportunity

In the 1960s, an unfortunate but interesting instance of community conflict occurred in Rochester, New York. Surprisingly, from this adversity grew opportunity. An African American neighborhood decided to hold a neighborhood party. The party occurred on a hot summer night, and many young adults showed up for the festivities. Halfway through the night, a group of White youths came to the party and were seen as intruders. One brusque remark led to another, and the scene eventually erupted in violence. Rochester, like many other cities, quickly exploded in racial conflict.

Several community groups, concerned that such violence not repeat itself, came together in an attempt to find a solution to the city's problems. As a result, the American Arbitration Association was asked to consult on the design of a community program for handling many types of conflict. The **community mediation** program was born. This program manages community disputes between individuals or groups in a peaceful fashion by assigning a neutral third party—a **mediator**—to facilitate discussion and problem solving between the disputants (Duffy, Grosch, & Olczak, 1991). The program also monitors community agency elections as well as urban renewal housing lotteries, "lemon law" (automobile owner-manufacturer) arbitration, and other community projects where a neutral party is needed. The initial community conflict, racial tension, was probably part of the larger national civil rights movement—a movement that created sweeping social changes that are not yet complete.

From the Rochester conflict, however, came more social change in the form of the Community Dispute Resolutions Centers Act (Christian, 1986). This legislation established in every county in New York a mediation center modeled after the one in Rochester. With New York as the pioneer, other states followed. Today, there are hundreds of functioning mediation or neighborhood justice centers in the United States. Some are adjuncts to the courts; others are run by religious and other charities (McGillis, 1997). All hope to inspire the peaceful resolution of conflict. Community conflict, then, creates snowballing social reform and social change, of which the Rochester experience is only one example. You will read more about community mediation in Chapter 9.

ages or close a real estate deal. Americans have come a long way since the 1800s, when one doctor, one school, and one pharmacy served every family in their town. When individuals find that agencies are insensitive or that there are few options from which to choose—and sometimes this is coupled with dissatisfaction with those existing options—they often demand and create change.

Here is an example from the justice system of how the desire for more options creates change. Anyone who has watched one of the several televised courtroom judges hand down a verdict knows that the courts often leave both complainants and defendants disgruntled. Sometimes even the "winner" does not feel as if he or she has won. One answer to handling this dissatisfaction and to providing more diversity for users of the court system is to develop a **multidoor approach,** as is found in Washington, DC (Ostermeyer, 1991). This is a *coordinated* system of assisting citizens involved in the justice system to find the most appropriate option for them: various courts (small claims, city, state, and federal); mediation and arbitration programs; legal aid offices; public, private, and volunteer attorneys; and other agencies, such as those assisting with mental health. The multidoor approach helps citizens and agencies avoid the frustration of multiple and overlapping referrals and lessens the perception that the justice system is a confusing maze of bureaucracies (Ostermeyer, 1991).

The preceding catalog of reasons for social change, which is not exhaustive, is summarized in Table 4.2. It will familiarize you with some of the causes for social changes. The *Brown v. Board of Education* example presented at the beginning of this chapter has multiple causes and multiple solu-

**TABLE 4.2    Reasons for and Examples of Social Change**

| Reason for Change | Example of Social Change |
|---|---|
| Diverse populations | AIDS patients desire emotional support from a group of other AIDS patients, and their families get together and form a support group. |
| Declining resources | The national economy is depressed; less grant money is available from private foundations. |
| Accountability | A taxpayer group attends a public hearing and demands to know how a tax increase will improve community services. |
| Technological advances | A corporation buys new software for midlevel managers who now require training. |
| Community conflict | An agency seeks a halfway house in a residential neighborhood not zoned for multiple-family dwellings; two residents groups, one in support and one against, conflict at a public meeting. |
| Dissatisfaction with traditional services | An area's private practice psychologists charge high fees not covered by insurance, so citizens inquire about funding possibilities for a mental health clinic that will charge on a sliding scale. |
| Desire for diversity of solutions | A multidoor courthouse program offers a variety of options for solutions to neighbors fighting in the neighborhood. |

tions. America's history of social and economic development has provided it with a pluralistic society. We believe in equality and freedom of opportunity as basic rights for all people, yet we struggle with how to honor these rights for both in-group and out-group members of our society (Gaertner & Dovidio, 2005). Though we want to be fair, the common perception is that there are limited resources. Our natural and sometimes unconscious tendencies to categorize or group people can work against this desire for equality and freedom for all (Devine, 1989, 2005). The reasons for our groupings have historic, economic, political, sociological, and psychological roots (Jones, 2003). The solutions to our grouping and prejudgment tendencies and their discriminatory outcomes are also multiple. Political and legal solutions go back to the framing of the U.S. Constitution, the U.S. Civil War, and the 14th Amendment to the Constitution (equal protection under the law) to name but a few. The *Brown v. Board of Education* case was just one of many court decisions to help further equal treatment for all in the United States. In the *Brown* case, it had to do with education, but in fact, it opened the door for many more solutions to the issues of fairness. Through these many legal, social, institutional, and personal solutions have come increased opportunities for contact, interactions, mutual dependencies, and other contexts that we know can psychologically build empathy and change the out-group members into in-group members (Allport, 1954/1979; Dovidio, Glick, & Budman, 2005). We now understand race to be a politically derived category and that differences of skin color or facial configuration have nothing to do with intelligence, social skill, and ambition. Thus, the reasoning for separation of individuals according to this arbitrary categorization does not hold true. The Supreme Court decision helped in the *integration* of groups. This has led to our society as we know it today. There has been significant progress in providing access to opportunities for all, including African Americans, other ethnic minorities, women, those with mental health issues, the economically challenged, the disabled, and many others members of groups categorized as outside.

Next we examine some ways in which change occurs, whether planned or unplanned.

## TYPES OF SOCIAL CHANGE

Forecasting social trends and social changes can be tricky but also very useful in designing prevention programs. For example, the U.S. Census Bureau expected the 2000 census to show demographic changes as well as population increases. The Census Bureau is able to forecast some changes. Projected changes, though, do not always come true and are sometimes more or less dramatic than anticipated. If the 2000 census figures are correct, the population growth of 32.7 million people represents the largest census growth in U.S. history. As another example, educators riding the tide of the baby boom built schools and school annexes in the suburbs until the number of schools had soared. Today, these same schools are witnessing a wave of violence from alienated youth. Community activists have much that they can learn from demographers and other forecasters about where change will occur next, particularly spontaneous or unplanned change.

### Spontaneous or Unplanned Social Change

Naturally occurring change is called **unplanned** or **spontaneous change.** Most disasters are not planned. For instance, no one planned the Great Chicago Fire in 1871, and, more recently, few predicted the epidemic of school violence.

Natural disasters result in much distress as well as social change (Ginexi, Weihs, Simmens, & Hoyt, 2000). Droughts, earthquakes, floods, fires, and other natural events displace community members from their homes and jobs. Although these disasters are not necessarily always distressing (Bravo, Rubio-Stipec, Canino, Woodbury, & Ribera, 1990; Prince-Embury & Rooney, 1995), they typically result in some large-scale change.

Unplanned major shifts in the population also cause social change (Rosenberg, 2006) and, in fact, much social dissatisfaction and divisiveness (Katz, 1983). For example, as the swell of baby boomers moves through time, their needs change. Baby boomers are now middle-aged or older (Rosenberg, 2006), and many are caring for their elderly parents (Carbonell, 2003; Naisbett & Aburdene, 1990). They often find a dearth of community services that provide elder care, and this creates much stress in the boomers' lives (Duffy & Atwater, 2008). Some baby boomers also have young children who require day care, which can be in short supply. The stress of caring for both the younger and older generations in their lives has resulted in such adults being labeled the **sandwich generation** (Spillman & Pezzin, 2000). The baby boomers (born between 1946 and 1965) coming of age for Social Security retirement and Medicare medical insurance adds to further social change in the United States.

Other demographic shifts have created further shifts in lifestyle. For instance, there has been an increase in the number of dual-career families (Cromartie, 2007; see Figure 4.2) that has increased the need for day care (Naisbett & Aburdene, 1990). One social change invariably creates another.

What makes unplanned or unintentional change stressful is that it is often uncontrollable and unpredictable. Uncontrollable events are quite stressful, and unpredictable events even more so. When individuals feel they control their fates, they experience less stress; when they feel they have lost control, they experience distress (Boggiano & Katz, 1991; Duffy & Atwater, 2008; Taylor, Helgeson, Reed, & Skokan, 1991).

African Americans in the civil rights movement may have felt that their lives were not under their own control but under the control of the White majority. Studies performed several years after the *Brown v. Board of Education* decision show African Americans to have a tendency toward an external locus of control (Bruce & Thornton, 2004). However, the study of locus of control suggests that with a more mature, sophisticated, and positive racial identity, an African American sample shifted their locus of control from external to more internal or self-controlled (Martin & Hall, 1992). Ruggiero and Taylor (1997), however, still find the perception of discrimination to be a threat to self-concept and to perception of self-control. Through organization and planned action, elements of the African American community have moved from a feeling of uncontrolled to controlled change.

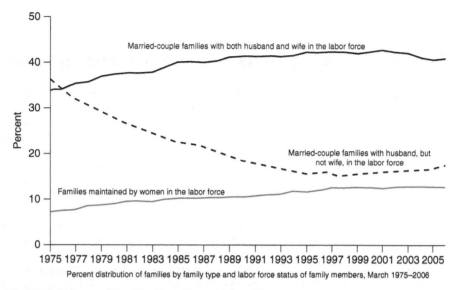

**FIGURE 4.2**  Work Patterns of Families Have Changed Over Time

*Source:* Cromartie, S. P. (July/August 2007). Labor force status of families. A visual essay. *Monthly Labor Review,* 35–41.

Unplanned change is often confined to particular ecological situations in which individuals may unwittingly be placed. For example, crime and natural disasters are generally confined to particular environments (Taylor & Shumaker, 1990), so when individuals find themselves in those environments, they may experience stress. In line with this thinking, individuals walking at night in a neighborhood rife with signs of social disintegration (e.g., graffiti and litter) may well feel distressed.

Besides assisting in the design and development of community services, community psychologists can also assist with coping for unplanned change by playing a role in *forecasting* it. Remember that one of the tenets of community psychology is *prevention*. This does not mean that community psychologists can prevent these changes—obviously psychologists cannot prevent floods—but learning how to predict unplanned changes can enable the community to prepare for the changes as they occur or even before. Such preparation can prevent the change from being as severe and distressing as it otherwise might be.

The science of prediction is complex, and there are scientists who specialize in prediction and forecasting. Census data, for example, can help forecast population changes. By way of example, as the baby boomers age, they will represent the largest group of elderly the United States has ever had. This means that if elder care is in short supply now, it may be in even shorter supply in two decades if no one prepares for it. **Social indicators** are measures of some aspect of society based on combined, corrected, and refined social statistics (Johnston, 1980) and can be used in social forecasting. By using sophisticated statistical techniques, social trends can be forecasted and preventive measures can be prepared (Kellam, Koretz, & Moscicki, 1999a, 1999b). We see an example of studying and dealing with unplanned change in Case in Point 4.3.

### Planned Social Change

Suppose people do not want to wait for change to happen, as in unplanned or unintended change (McGrath, 1983)—suppose that instead they want to intentionally create change, called "planned" or "induced" change (Glidewell, 1976). How could people go about this seemingly monumental task?

## Working with an Indigenous People Experiencing Change

A profound example of unplanned and uncontrolled change is what has happened to the indigenous peoples in many regions of the world. A study with the Inuit in the Arctic Circle of Canada has been provided by Kral, Idlout, Minore, Dyck, and Kirmayer (2011). Tracing an indigenous history and lineage that goes back about 4,000 years (McGee, 2004; Purich, 1992), the authors describe a culture marked by the importance of "kinship, interdependence and cross-generational teaching and support" (Kral et al., p. 427). In the 1950s and 1960s, the Canadian government moved them from family camps to settlements and boarding schools. These changes came quickly and were not planned or controlled by the people themselves.

Presently, infant mortality is 3.5 times the national average for Canada. Unemployment rates run from 15% to 72%. Life expectancy is 12 years lower than the national norm. Youth suicide rates are among the highest in the world (Kral et al., 2011). The numbers speak for themselves.

As a part of a larger suicide prevention project, community psychologists focused on native concepts of well-being, happiness, unhappiness, and healing. They also sought to examine the impact of the changes in communities on residents' experience of well-being.

Following a regional suicide prevention conference, an Inuit steering committee was formed, composed of representatives of the different generations: youth, adults, and elders were on the committee.

An open-ended interview was designed in collaboration with the steering committee and conducted with participants ranging in age from 14 to 94. Before leaving each community, the research team presented summaries of interview data to village leadership. In the end, research team and steering committee members met to consider the results. Only findings about which there was intergroup consensus were reported.

The first and most consistent finding was the centrality of family to life. Being present with, talking to, sharing meals, and just traveling together were all important to interviewees' experiences. Family was mentioned four times more often than anything else in relation to happiness. (Unhappiness was most often related to romantic relationships.) The second most important thing related to happiness was communication. They "believed strongly that merely talking to one or more others was essential to one's well-being" (Kral et al., 2011, p. 430). The third theme related to well-being was connection to traditions, such as how to hunt, go about the land, make tools and clothing, build an igloo, and generally know of one's culture.

The noticed changes were the increase in people, the growing distances between family members with an attendant decrease in talking and visiting, the loss of cultural practices, and finally less parental control. All these changes affected family and the interactions among family. There was less "visiting" and less feeling of being loved.

Chandler and Proulx (2006) noted that disruption in culture and in identity placed people at risk of suicide. The described changes in life certainly place these people at risk.

These findings are being used to inform both new self-determined government policies (Baffin Mandate, Government of Nunavut, 1999), the creation of programs such as Formation of an Elder's Society, the opening of a community wellness center focusing on traditions, and a Health Canada National Aboriginal Youth Suicide Prevention Strategy.

---

There are some venerated strategies suggested in the community psychology literature: self-help, including grassroots activism; networking of services and social support; the use of external change agents or consultants; educational and informational programs; and involvement in public policy processes. All of these issues are detailed in the next chapter. None of these approaches is easy, and each has advantages and disadvantages. With planned change, however, the desired effects are more likely to be obtained than with unplanned or spontaneous change.

Exactly what is planned change? Kettner and associates (1985) wrote a good working definition. **Planned change** is an intentional or deliberate intervention to change a situation—or, for the present discussion, a part of or a whole community. Planned change is distinguished from unplanned change by four characteristics. First, planned change is *limited in scope;* that is, what is to be changed is targeted or earmarked in advance. Second, planned change is directed toward *enhancing the quality of life* of the community members. This is the primary purpose of planned change in communities. Planned change should enhance (not inhibit) community life. Third, planned change usually *provides a role* for those affected by change. Community psychologists should not impose change on community members. Rather, their role is to inform citizens of the viable options, assist them in the selection of appropriate options, and then participate with them in the design and implementation of change. Finally, planned change is often (but not always) *guided by a person who acts as a change agent.* **Change agents** (Lippett, Watson, & Westley, 1958; Oskamp, 1984) are often trained professionals but can also be advocates for or from client groups, political activists, educational experts, or others interested in inducing change (Ford, Ford, & D'Amelio, 2008). Psychologists often act as consultants or change agents. The role of consultants is detailed in the next chapter. The role of the NAACP and the Clarks in the opening story is a very good example of planned change. They targeted the specific school district to bring about intended changes in the law of the land, the quality of life was most certainly improved with increased educational opportunities, and the African American community was clearly leading in determining the goals and intervention.

## Issues Related to Planned Change

A major issue regarding planned change is *who* decides change will occur and *when, how,* and *what* changes will take place. Before the civil rights movement, Whites had pretty much decided what would change in society. Blacks first (and later other less powerful groups) wanted and were eventually provided with equal opportunity to create planned changes in our society. Ask yourself, though—for any planned change, just *who* should decide *what* to do? Any citizen regardless of age? Residents only? All affected voters? Only taxpayers? Elected officials?

Community psychologists advocate for all those involved in the community having a say in their community's development (Fawcett et al., 1996; Fetterman, 1996; Maton, Aber, & Seidman, 2011). Empowerment of the community itself has been a fundamental concept in community psychology (Rappaport, 1977; Zimmerman, 2000).

*Collaboration* is a hallmark of much community work (Bond, 1990; Fawcett, 1990; Maton, 2000; Rappaport, 1990; Rappaport et al., 1985; Serrano-Garcia, 1990; Wolff, 2010). **Collaboration** is where social scientists and clients come together to examine and create solutions for social problems (Rappaport, 1990). Collaboration is also called **participatory decision making, collaborative problem solving** (Chavis et al., 1992; Kelly, 1986a), or **empowerment evaluation** (Fetterman & Wandersman, 2005). As Christensen and Robinson (1989) have suggested, self-determination has practical problem-solving utility in that those who live with the problem can best solve it. Acceptance of change is therefore higher than with imposed changes. Moreover, collaborative decision making helps build a stronger sense of community and avoids client–consultant conflict and duplication of effort because collaboration is a mutual influence process. The key to collaboration is empowerment and networking, which enhance the possibility of self-determination.

Anyone embarking on planned social change needs to prepare carefully for the changes (Maton, 2000). Ongoing, carefully planned change requires a substantial investment of time, talent, money, and other resources that might otherwise be used elsewhere (Kettner et al., 1985). The change agents should also prepare participants for change to take a long time (Fairweather & Davidson, 1986; Seidman, 1990), as it is likely to be resisted by some (Ford et al., 2008). Likewise, the more important the problem, the more difficult it will probably be to solve (Shadish, 1990), and the more numerous the necessary levels of intervention required (Maton, 2000).

Planners also need to consider whether change is really possible (e.g., Will all involved parties cooperate? Are funds available?) and whether, in the end, the desired results can be realistically achieved. For example, although thousands of community programs and organizations exist across the country, many fail (Florin, 1989). Prestby and Wandersman (1985) found that 50% of voluntary neighborhood associations, many of which are designed to create and support social change, become inactive after only one year. Such organizations seem particularly vulnerable to demise or failure (Chavis et al., 1992).

Fairweather and Davidson (1986) have explained that a single attack on a social problem will not create substantial change. A multipronged and continual approach is generally more successful. A once-and-for-all solution probably will not be effective, either (Levine & Perkins, 1987). Fairweather and Davidson have also cautioned that although some old practices might work well, any useless approaches should be discarded. It is worthwhile to remember, too, that *complete* change might not always be necessary.

Besides the preceding dimensions, planners also need to consider the other parameters of beneficial change (Fairweather & Davidson, 1986). Change must be **humane**—that is, it must be socially responsible and represent humanitarian values that emphasize enhancing human potential. Change techniques should also be **problem-oriented**—they should be aimed at solutions of problems rather than theory alone. Similarly, change strategies should focus on **multiple social levels** rather than on specific individuals. The techniques may need to be creative and innovative. **Creativity** is the "friend and companion" of community activists. The change plans also need to be **feasible** in terms of dissemination to other groups or situations. Not all techniques fit all groups, but there are some communities that can adopt tried methods from other communities.

*Context* or *environment* is a concept important to the ecological tradition of community psychology (Trickett, 2009). For example, implementation of planned changes can be influenced by the *social* climate of the settings. In one study, individual school contexts predicted the level of lesson plan presentation of an antiviolence program (Gregory, Henry, & Schoeny, 2007). **Administrative leadership** (e.g., "At this school, information flows smoothly through channels") and a **supportive climate** (e.g., "In this school, even low-achieving students are respected" and "Teachers in this school are proud to be teachers") were found to result in better program implementation over a three-year period.

Change agents also need to value social experimentation and action research. In this regard, planners cannot be timid about innovation—neither can they be afraid to evaluate their innovations. Social experimentation and evaluation go hand in hand (Fairweather & Davidson, 1986). Any interventions and programs developed to create community change need to be honestly evaluated, modified based on the evaluation, evaluated again, and so on. Then and only then do change agents and communities know that they have the best possible ideas in place.

Finally, planners or change agents need to be realists, particularly with regard to the prevailing political climate and the deep system structures that are in place (Light & Keller, 1985; Foster-Fishman & Long, 2009). Change always makes something different that otherwise would not be changed (Benviente, 1989). Some individuals will like the change; others will not. Hence, the power struggles related to change are likely to commence as soon as change is suggested (Alinsky, 1971/1989).

## DIFFICULTIES BRINGING ABOUT CHANGE

Why do programs that are designed to create social change or provide alternative services fail? Why do the most well-intentioned efforts sometimes go awry? What if citizens are divided as to what they should do? A multitude of reasons exist, but only a few are mentioned here.

One of the most important reasons for failure of planned change is *resistance* (Ford et al., 2008; Glidewell, 1976; Levine & Perkins, 1987), which can come from a variety of sources, including administrators, practitioners, clients, or any other community member. Why does resistance occur? Societies tend to have built-in resistance to change (Ford et al., 2008); members of groups seem trained to follow their own ways—the old ways—which they regard as **safe** or superior (Glidewell, 1976). Groups feel their existence is **threatened** by new groups or new ideas. Ellam and Shamir (2005) believed that the acceptance of change is related to the change's concordance with the organizational members' **self-concepts**. If the change is felt to be self-determined, to be in agreement with their sense of self-distinctiveness, to be self-enhancing, and to have some **continuity** with existing self-concepts, changes are much easier to accomplish. In the end, change agents themselves may do something to alienate the community or create resistance to change (Ford et al., 2008).

There are still other reasons for the failure of social change efforts. Psychologists have long documented the effects of in-groups and out-groups in which people favor their own groups (the **in-group**) and stereotype or denigrate outsiders (the **out-group**) (Allport, 1954/1979; Brewer, 1999). In the community, for instance, for-profit businesses, especially big private-sector corporations, often resist social change instituted by small nonprofit businesses or by new government policies because the for-profit enterprises think their revenues will be affected. The assumptions of in-group advantages and out-group disadvantages help maintain in-group cohesion but also add to the reluctance to accept any out-group information or characteristics. The inability to empathize and therefore understand the situation of the out-group members can hamper in-group members' ability to accept information and make changes based on that information (Batson et al., 1995). Helping for the sake of "the other" is very difficult, though not impossible, to find (Strumer, Snyder, & Omoto, 2005).

Sometimes change is resisted by those who would benefit from it because they have been socialized to think change is not possible and the status quo is all that is available to them. The South American liberation educator Paulo Freire (1970) argued that the oppressed are often unaware of the constraints they live under. As a function of the social structure conditioning in which they have grown, they do not see any hope of change. **Conscientization** occurs when the oppressed come to awareness of their oppression. Freire (1994) believed that this occurs when individuals come to a realization of their self-determination and the "unveiling of opportunities for hope" (p. 9). He argued for the value of "the unity in diversity" to create a power base, and of shifting the blame for dysfunction from the "oppressed" individual to the "oppressive" structures (pp. 157–158). These ideas are prescient to—that is, they seem to anticipate—the psychological research and theory related to Bandura's "collective self-efficacy" discussed later and Rappaport's "empowerment" efforts identified in Chapter 1. In many circumstances, conscientization is necessary for the second order change (Watzlawick et al., 1974) described in the first part of this chapter.

Change is often seen as unwelcome, not just by groups but by individuals as well (Kettner et al., 1985). Social perception psychologists know that individual characteristics can lead to resistance to change. So-called **cognitive misers** make decisions based on stereotypical groupings and therefore less information (Fiske & Taylor, 2013; Spears & Haslam, 1997). This is motivated by socially based desires for "belonging, understanding, controlling, self-enhancing, and trusting" (Fiske, 2004, p. 117). Individuals resist information or change for the same reasons as groups—because they feel that change threatens their group, reputation, job security, or well-being. Furthermore, Kuhn's (1962/1996) argument regarding the difficulty of paradigm shifts—or ways of seeing the world—suggests social change, as with worldviews, require people to overthrow that which they have learned to be "real" and to think of things in new ways. Although this can and does occur, a critical mass of evidence needs to accumulate first. The shift in viewpoints is dramatic and therefore is not taken lightly. Vygotsky's concept of proximal development suggests that new learning beyond one level above how we presently conceptualize the world is extremely difficult and fraught with resistance (Hedegaard, 1996). Watzlawick and associates (1974) support this notion of difficulty in finding change. As Foster-Fishman and Behrens (2007) suggest, change requires more than shifts in skill sets—it requires shifts in *mindsets* as well. So we understand that any social change can be difficult to conceptualize, much less execute and find acceptable to the establishment.

Often, agents of change and their programs fail (Ford et al., 2008) because their tactics are uncomfortably confrontational and may be seen to violate "politeness norms." Alinsky (1971), Kettner and associates (1985), and Wolff (2010) see risk taking, including the risk that change will be unwelcome, as part and parcel of all change. However, the reality is that if those people planning change receive only negative exposure (by the media, for example) or fail to suggest their own solutions to the problems they are protesting, their protests are perceived as hollow or disruptive rather than productive. Change comes from the perception of common goals, and commonalities (Gaertner & Dovidio, 1992; Gaertner, Rust, Dovidio, & Bachman, 1994) and the building of **empathic links** to those are negatively affected by existing systems (Batson, Ahmad, & Lisher, 2009; Dovidio et al., 2010). Alternative to these motives are more self-serving ones, of benefit to self or one's group, and avoidance of aversive events.

Saul Alinsky's (1971) community work in Chicago, and later nationally, during the 1940s, 1950s, and 1960s is seen as yet another model for change. Alinsky noted that no power change ever occurred without some struggle. Notably, those involved in creative power struggles can use existing rules to bring about pressure on the status quo. Table 4.3 summarizes some of Alinsky's sometimes radical approaches.

Collective planning for change is construed as good, but this is only true within limits. If the organization or individuals planning change are too loosely structured, if solid leadership does not exist, or if the decision makers show no discipline in their plans, then they can fail. Delgado (1986) reviewed several organizations that had good intent but evaporated because of the inadequacy of their own organizational infrastructures. Maton (1988) found that groups with higher role differentiation, greater order and organization, and capable leaders reported more positive well-being and more positive group appraisal. Many in community psychology now focus on "capacity building" as a way to bring organizational strength to the communities they serve. Examples in the contemporary research literature abound (Miao, Umemoto, Gonda, & Hishinuma, 2011; Nowell & Foster-Fishman, 2011; Vivolo, Matjasko, & Massetti, 2011; Wilke & Speer, 2011).

Foster-Fishman and Behrens (2007) caution that too often the conceptualization of social systems change is too simplistic. When one particular change is targeted without consideration of the multiple levels it can affect, the change efforts can fail or fail to be sustained. Change agents should plan globally or holistically so as to see the *whole* picture rather than disjointed pieces of problems. Pluralistic (Freedman, 1989) or multilevel planning (Maton, 2000) is likely to ensure success because the context or environment within which the change will occur will be more likely to have been considered (Kelly, 2006; Trickett, 2009).

One of the best solutions to *prevent* failure (and, after all, prevention *is* a critical part of all of community psychology) is to lay a good foundation for change by gaining community endorsement for such change and establishing an empirical justification for the need to change. Community psychologists regard research and practice as interdependent on one another (Kelly, 1986b). Action research, as you have already read, is scientific work grounded in theory, accounting for community input to the research and intervention process, and directed toward resolving problems (Lewin, 1948; Jason, Keys, Suarez-Balcazar, Taylor, & Davis, 2004; Primavera & Brodsky, 2004). Action research in the community is not without its problems (Price, 1990; Tolan, Keys, Chertak, & Jason, 1990). Problems include the lack of

| **TABLE 4.3   Ten Rules for Radicals\*** |
|---|
| **1.** Use whatever you've got to get attention. |
| **2.** Don't go outside the experience of your people. |
| **3.** Whenever possible, go outside the experience of the enemy. |
| **4.** Make the enemy live up to its own rules. |
| **5.** Ridicule is a potent weapon, and it makes the opposition react to your advantage. |
| **6.** A good tactic is one that your people enjoy—if they don't enjoy it, there is something wrong. |
| **7.** A tactic that drags on too long becomes a drag. |
| **8.** The threat is usually more terrifying than the thing itself. |
| **9.** Power is what you have and what the enemy thinks you have. |
| **10.** Keep the pressure on. |

\*These are general guidelines. According to Saul Alinsky, they should be adapted to the uniquenesses of each situation.

*Source:* Adapted from Alinsky (1971).

trust in the researcher by community members, breakdowns in negotiating with program and community administrators, the inability to randomly assign subjects to conditions for experimental designs, and the selection of appropriate and adequate measures (Fairweather & Davidson, 1986). Despite all these reservations, "through the collaborative enterprises, we have seen many examples of community members who have gained self-awareness, established important network connections, and achieved social change" (Jason, Davis, et al., 2004, p. 241).

## Summary

We have come to expect change in today's world. There are many reasons why change occurs. Diverse populations, such as the growing number of elderly, have issues that must be addressed but for which society may not be prepared. There can be a decline in resources, or funding due to downturns in the economy or changes in government policies. On the other hand, accelerating technological advances can necessitate change on the part of individuals as well as society. One technology that has caused all sorts of modification in our daily lives and in methods of conducting business is the addition of computers and telecommunications. On the other hand, many people fear the advance of technology (technophobia), and traditional community services do little to help individuals cope with the fear.

Demands for accountability also create change. People expect that funds will be expended wisely, and they grow concerned when spending is not accounted for. Related to accountability is cost effectiveness, which refers to how wisely money is spent (i.e., whether there is a profit).

Community conflict is yet another reason for change. Groups in communities experience ethnic or religious strife, conflict over resources such as land use, and so on to create change. There is growing sentiment against traditional methods for dealing with today's problems—for instance, the treatment of the mentally ill—as well as a desire for choices or diversity among solutions to problems.

There are two types of change: planned (or induced) change and unplanned (or spontaneous) change. Planned change occurs when changes are intentional or deliberate. Planned change is limited by its scope, usually enhances the quality of life for community members, provides for a role

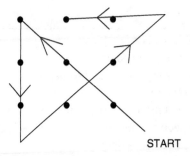

**FIGURE 4.3    The Nine Dot Problem Solution.** The solution requires you to think *beyond* the dots. If you go outside the grid of dots, the solution *is* possible. If you were able to solve this problem, you were engaging in second order thinking.

*Source:* From Watzlawick, P., Weakland, J., Risch, R., & Erickson, M. (1974). Change: Principles of Problem Formation and Problem Resolution. New York, NY: Norton.

for affected groups, and is often guided by a professional change agent or consultant. In unplanned or spontaneous change, change is unexpected, sometimes disastrous (as in a natural disaster such as a flood) and often of a large magnitude (such as when a segment of the population experiences growth, as in the baby boom generation).

Community psychologists are interested in both studying *and* implementing social change for the betterment of the communities served. Some of the tools they bring to this process are discussed in the next chapter. Whether the change is planned or unplanned, the resources of the community can be brought to bear on the problems or issues at hand.

# 5

# Community Intervention Strategies

*I am in Birmingham because injustice is here . . .*
*I am cognizant of the interrelatedness of all communities and states . . .*
*Injustice anywhere is a threat to justice everywhere.*
—Martin Luther King Jr., "Letter from a Birmingham Jail"

The neighborhood had gotten progressively worse over the previous decade. Crime rates had risen, and residential transiency had increased. Neighbors no longer knew neighbors—out of habit, lack of interest, time pressures, or fear. Then the drug dealers moved in. The area became known for crack houses, methamphetamine production, and the violence that comes with their sale and use. It was a neighborhood that commanded sweeping views of the water in places. But no one wanted to move in.

Yet it was an old neighborhood. There were residents who had lived through the decline or had chosen to move in because of affordability, or old loyalties, or the vision of its potential. There were businesses there, there was a hospital there, there was all one would hope for in area conveniences and services. These had been there for a long while. Despite several transitions in economic circumstances, they remained. Yet most talked about the difficulties and risks of business in the area.

Then it happened. A very violent incident in the neighborhood made statewide news. Reporters spoke of the plight of those law-abiding residents, now caught in their homes with little hope of selling and moving. Few wanted to buy and live there. In response to all of these negatives, a group of citizens came together. Some say it started with a block party/barbecue. The neighbors banded together and identified problems and the advantages of working together. They organized block watches and surveillance of the known drug houses. They traded phone numbers and agreed to help each other out. They called on the police, who were encouraged by this and happy to help where possible.

The drugs moved out of the neighborhood, because drug operations require secrecy. The neighbors found common ground and connectedness in the process. They saved their homes and their neighborhood. This was the beginning of Safe Streets and later, the National Night Out, where neighbors come together, talk, have dinner together, and get to know each other.

This chapter reviews some of the ways social change is facilitated by community psychologists. These are planned efforts. They have been studied at the descriptive and predictive levels. From a community psychology perspective, we might better understand the processes. From this understanding, we might better devise interventions to aid in bringing these transformations.

## CREATING PLANNED CHANGE

Sarason (1972/1999) considered at length the importance of "creating settings" for change and the implications of these creations. Some would argue that society has never needed change more than it does today. Multiple reports and commissions have concluded that we are a nation at risk with regard to many social indicators, such as alcohol abuse, drug use, teen pregnancy, and violence (Wandersman et al., 1998). Creating and sustaining social change is not an easy task, but community psychologists are at the forefront of researching the best ways to create and maintain positive societal change. Cook and Shadish (1994) have suggested that there are three ways by which social change can occur. The first (which they believe is the most successful) is by working in increments to bring gradual changes to the system. The second is to test innovative programs and then offer them for acceptance. The third and most dramatic is to start with radical changes to the structure of the system in question.

Participating in social change is a fundamental value in community psychology (Jason, 1991; Maton, 2000) as well as a basic property of social reality (Keys & Frank, 1987). This chapter examines established methods for fashioning both small- and large-scale social change. For each technique, its use, its advantages and disadvantages, and related research are discussed. When change is intentional and considered in advance, it is called **planned change.**

## CITIZEN PARTICIPATION

The Safe Streets Project, described in the opening vignette, engaged neighborhood residents in the solution. They understood the problem in all of its details, because they were daily observers of the environment and its residents. They knew where the drug houses were and the pattern of comings and goings. They could identify the drug makers and drug dealers as well as their customers. In turn, they were the ones who constantly inhabited the environment. It did not take time to respond to things, because they were already there. By reporting what they saw, they could obtain better police intervention. The citizens were the critical variable that changed the course of things in the neighborhood.

Perhaps no other method of creating social change has received as much attention as participant-induced change, and interest in this type of change has been mounting (Linney, 1990). Various authors have given different labels to this type of change, including *citizen participation* (Levi & Litwin, 1986; Wandersman & Florin, 2000), *empowerment* (Rappaport, Swift, & Hess, 1984), *grassroots activism* (Alinsky, 1971), and *self-help* (Christensen & Robinson, 1989). **Citizen participation** can be broadly defined as involvement in any organized activity in which unpaid individuals participate in order to achieve a common goal (Zimmerman & Rappaport, 1988). At the root of this method of change is the belief that people can and should collaborate to solve common problems (Joseph & Ogletree, 1998). In fact, some hold self-help as the most promising mechanism for changing society (Florin & Wandersman, 1990). An example of citizen participation is **grassroots activism,** which occurs when individuals define their own issues and press for social change to address these issues and work in a bottom-up fashion (rather than top-down). For example, when citizens who are tired of lives being senselessly taken on our highways urge policy makers to pass laws with stiffer penalties against drunk driving, the citizens are practicing grassroots activism. Case in Point 5.1 discusses further citizen involvement in community change by introducing the Community Development Society.

Another example of this type of change, but at a more personal level, is **self-help groups** (Levy, 2000), such as Alcoholics Anonymous, where individuals with common issues come together to assist and emotionally support one another. Because self-help groups are often overseen by professionals, some psychologists prefer the term **mutual assistance groups** for groups made up solely of laypeople (Levine, 1988). Shepherd and associates (1999) pointed out, however, that the dichotomy between professionally led and peer-led groups is artificial: the extent of professional involvement in such groups varies on a continuum of minimal to extensive, and the success of such groups comes from the synergy between the members. Often, individuals in these groups learn coping strategies from each other. At a personal level, community members—such as friends, family, and neighbors—can assist in supporting each other through difficult times by providing **social support** (Barrera, 2000). Social support is an exchange of resources (such as emotional comfort or material goods) between two individuals where the provider intends the resources to enhance the well-being of the recipient (Shumaker & Brownell, 1984, 1985). Social support can be another means by which social change occurs.

The usual settings for citizen participation are work settings, health care programs, architectural environments, neighborhood associations, public policy arenas, education programs, and situations applying science (especially social science) and technology. This type of participation can occur by

# The Community Development Society

Community change and citizen participation have become an accepted—in fact, expected—part of daily life in the United States. For this reason and others, the Community Development Society (CDS) was established. CDS recognizes citizens' capacity to build and take democratic action as keys to success in a complex and ever-changing world. Community development is a process designed to create conditions of economic and social progress with the active participation of the whole community and with the fullest possible reliance on the community's initiatives (Bradshaw, 1999; Levine, Perkins, & Perkins, 2004; Rothman, 1974).

CDS members are multidisciplinary and come from the fields of education, health care, social services, government, and citizen groups (to mention just a few). Members believe that community is the basic building block of society (Bradshaw, 1999). In addition, they realize that communities can be complex, growth and development are

part of the human condition, and development of each community can be promoted through improvement of the individual, organizational skills, and problem-solving knowledge. CDS members fervently believe that good practice can lead to sound community development and social change.

In response to these beliefs, CDS has developed several principles of good practice for community development specialists, whether they are citizens or professionals:

- Citizen participation needs to be promoted so that community members can influence the decisions that affect their lives.
- Citizens should be engaged in problem diagnosis so that affected individuals can understand the causes of the situation.
- Community leaders need to understand the economic, social, political, and psychological impact associated with various

solutions related to community problems and issues.

- Community members should design and implement their own plans to solve consensually agreed-on problems (even though some expert assistance might be needed). Furthermore, shared leadership and active participation are necessary to this process.
- Finally, community leaders need the skills, confidence, and motivation to be influential in the community.

According to Maton (2000), these strategies for good practice result in *capacity-building* or *assets-based* change. Do these various principles sound familiar? Many of them are embraced by community psychologists. The significant point here is that there are many community citizens and leaders who adopt community psychology principles and goals without ever having studied community psychology.

electoral participation (voting or working for a particular candidate or issue), grassroots efforts (when citizens start a group and define its goals and methods), or government-mandated citizen participation in which citizens are appointed to watchdog committees or attend public hearings. Table 5.1 provides more examples of mechanisms for citizen participation, which vary in terms of effort expended and commitment.

## Community Participation and Prevention

As was discussed in Chapter 1, prevention is a defining principle of community psychology. In the Safe Streets/National Night Out example, citizens saw a serious community problem and joined together to monitor their neighborhood and make it a safer place for everyone. This type of action could be classified as a tertiary prevention program, in which the problem already exists, and the action is meant to prevent future occurrences. Yet, in some ways, strategies that were used to prevent future occurrences may also be successful in preventing initial occurrences in communities that are not yet experiencing violence or drug problems but may be at risk for such problems (i.e., secondary prevention). When neighborhoods are full of people who demonstrate a concern for and connection to

| **TABLE 5.1   Examples of Citizen Participation** |
|---|
| Voting |
| Signing a petition |
| Donating money or time to a cause |
| Reading media articles on community needs or change |
| Boycotting environmentally unsound products |
| Being interviewed for a community survey |
| Joining a self-help group |
| Participating in a question–answer session or a debate |
| Serving on an ad hoc committee or task force |
| Participating in sit-ins and marches |
| Leading a grassroots activist group in the community |
| Doing volunteer work in the community |
| Conducting fund raising for a community service |
| Offering consultation services |
| Serving in public office or supporting a particular candidate |

the place where they live, it is harder for drug dealers or gang members to find a niche where they can do business and create danger.

So do stories like these lead us to conclude that "good" citizens need to join forces to rid their neighborhoods of "bad" elements? Is it ever possible that community members who were at one point involved in "bad" behavior might be a valuable asset in preventive, grassroots action plans? One approach to prevention that we will see highlighted in several chapters throughout this text is the use of community members as paraprofessional interventionists, which is one of the more committed forms of citizen participation. An example of this would be to have recovering drug addicts reach out to current drug users, or have former gang members attempt to prevent neighborhood violence among current gang members. These types of approaches to prevention are thought to be successful because the community members who are intervening have credibility with those to whom they are trying to reach. A former gang member who reaches out to current gang members may be seen as capable of understanding gang realities in a way that a professional social worker or other professional interventionist may not. In such a situation, the success of a prevention program may be dependent on community members' participation. Fortunately for our purposes, there already exists a program that has demonstrated the merits of such an approach to violence prevention.

An interdisciplinary, now international collaboration, the violence prevention project that we are referring to is known as Cure Violence (http://cureviolence.org). Cure Violence would be considered an indicated approach to violence prevention (i.e., it is offered in specific neighborhoods) that blends elements of person-centered and environment-centered interventions. Developed as CeaseFire by Dr. Gary Slutkin, an epidemiologist at the University of Illinois–Chicago, CeaseFire's original environment-centered strategy was to select ex-convicts who were former gang members and current members of the targeted communities to act as "violence interrupters." These individuals served as neutral parities to mediate conflicts between both individuals and rival gangs and, in doing so, attempt to interrupt the cycle of retaliatory violence that often occurs in the aftermath of a shooting. The person-centered strategies included in CeaseFire involved dispatching outreach workers to counsel targeted youth and connect them to a range of mental health services when necessary. Instead of being a primary or universal approach to prevention, CeaseFire targeted its programs for specific neighborhoods that were known as hubs of violent activity based on police databases. The goals of the project were to decrease future episodes of violent behavior and ultimately, to change community norms surrounding violence. Some people might wonder whether former gang members or ex-convicts could truly change in such a way that they now were true assets to the safety of their communities. The answer to such a questions lies in CeaseFire's successes (http://cureviolence.org/effectiveness/). In 2012, CeaseFire became Cure Violence because the program involved more than guns—it was a broader community approach to violence as a public health problem.

In its evaluation in the United States, the U.S. Department of Justice investigated the effectiveness of CeaseFire/Cure Violence programs in seven cities. Six of the seven CeaseFire/Cure Violence cities assessed showed decreases in the size and intensity of shooting "hot spots." The evaluation (see Skogan, Hartnett, Bump, & Dubois, 2008) also indicated that, in comparison to control-groups, decreases in overall violence occurred in four of the areas where CeaseFire/Cure Violence operated. Reciprocal killings in retaliation for earlier events decreased more in the program areas than in the comparison areas. Additionally, the average gang involvement in homicides decreased in three of the CeaseFire/Cure Violence areas. In some cases, decreases in murder rates were as high as 73%. Thus, the Department of Justice report validated the CeaseFire model as an *evidence-based intervention* that reduces shooting and killings and ultimately creates safer communities.

There are many impressive aspects of the CeaseFire/Cure Violence program. One of those aspects is that it is a prevention program that was modeled after other grassroots, community-staffed, public health programs that had been shown to be effective preventing major public health problems, including tuberculosis and human immunodeficiency virus (HIV), worldwide. The international presence that CeaseFire/Cure Violence has developed now includes programs running in neighborhoods in Iraq, London, South Africa, and Trinidad and Tobago. The program can be successful in such diverse settings because it relies on local community members and accesses local community resources, fostering the message that communities can solve their own problems, a sentiment affirmed by community psychologists. Yet, prevention programs that are so deeply based on community member participation obviously only work when community members feel moved to actually participate. Thus, one must ask the question: Who participates?

## Who Participates?

Not everyone wants to participate in social change or believes that he or she can be effective in fashioning social change, which is known as **helplessness** (Zimmerman, Ramírez-Valles, & Maton, 1999). Research by O'Neill, Duffy, Enman, Blackman, and Goodwin (1988) examined what types of individuals are active in trying to produce social change. The researchers administered a modified I-E Scale and an Injustice Scale to introductory psychology students and single mothers (both of whom were considered nonactivist groups), board members of a day-care center (a moderately activist group), and board members of a transition house for victims of domestic violence (the high activist group). The I-E Scale (Rotter, 1966) measures **internal** versus **external locus of control.** Individuals with an internal locus of control believe that they control their own reinforcers; individuals with an external locus of control believe that other people or perhaps fate (something external to the individual) controls reinforcers. The researchers modified the scale to measure personal power or the sense that a person is in control of his or her fate. The Injustice Scale measures individuals' perceptions about whether the world is just (for example: Do the courts let the guilty go free and convict innocent people?). O'Neill and associates found

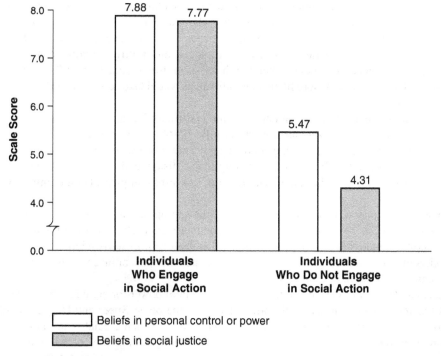

**FIGURE 5.1**   Results of Research on Social Activism

*Note:* Citizens who believe in personal control (or power) and social injustice are likely to be social activists.

*Source:* Data compiled from O'Neill et al. (1988).

that neither personal power nor a sense of injustice alone is sufficient to predict who will be a social activist. Both a sense of personal power *and* a belief in the injustices of society combine to produce social activism. Figure 5.1 reproduces these results in graphic form.

Participation appears to be related to people's sense of rootedness in their neighborhood—that is, the length of time in the area, plans to stay in the area, and having children (Wandersman, Florin, Friedman, & Meier, 1987). Not surprising is a finding by Chavis and Wandersman (1990) that a sense of community seems important to participation in block associations. Perkins, Florin, Rich, Wandersman, and Chavis (1990) proposed an ecological framework for understanding participation. There needs to be a perceived need for coming together and then a set of "enabling conditions," such as neighborly behaviors, that allow the group to do that. Corning and Myers (2002) developed a scale of social action engagement that has been used in subsequent studies of this nature. Research by Sampson and Raudenbush (1999) points to the negative relationship between strong social cohesion and crime. It seems that the residents in the Safe Streets story, which opened this chapter, were correct in assuming that by coming together as neighbors, they would change the climate for crime in their area. Strong neighborhoods equaled less crime.

Kelly and Breinlinger (1996) suggested that community activists identify with the group with which they are associated. They also proposed that individuals need a self-image of themselves as activists to engage in social change projects. Finally, Perkins, Brown, and Taylor (1996) found that community-focused thinking (such as having a sense of civic responsibility or feeling attached to a community) as well as community-focused behaviors (such as volunteering in the community) were consistently and positively predictive of participation in social action efforts within the community. Zimmerman and colleagues (1999) found that African American youths who felt high levels of sociopolitical control were less likely to feel personally helpless (feeling of no or low control) and depressed. **Sociopolitical control** may be defined as beliefs that actions in social and political realms can lead to desired outcomes. Zimmerman and associates believe that sociopolitical control contributes to self-esteem and self-confidence, making it more likely that individuals would take action when challenges appear in other areas of their lives.

Measuring the impact of citizen participation is difficult but necessary if one is to understand the process and to determine whether it works (Kelly, 1986b). The citizens—the stakeholders, so to speak—might want hard evidence that their efforts were worthwhile, but such direct evidence is often difficult to obtain. Involved individuals might also disagree about what is solid evidence: cost savings, increased profits, higher client satisfaction, less stress, improved community relations, and so forth.

Some citizens may want to participate but lack the appropriate skills; few laypeople, for example, know how to lobby for policy change or how to conduct meaningful scientific research. Chavis and associates (1992) noted that citizen groups might also need help in skills relating to group dynamics. Their leaders might need training in strategic planning, negotiations, or incentive management (Prestby, Wandersman, Florin, Rich, & Chavis, 1990).

Speer and Hughey (1995) noted that the development of power for organizations and for individuals went together. Change in one could bring change in the other. Speer and Hughey identified four phases to community organizing. First is *assessment,* through which crucial issues affecting the community are identified. This allows the organization, community, and its members to focus on the other three phases. The second phase is *research.* In this phase, participants examine the causes for the issues identified in the assessment phase. One important piece of information is the ways in which community resources are allocated and how key players exercise their social power.

A third stage, *action,* represents the collective attempt to exercise social power. Actions include public events that demonstrate organizational or citizen power and perhaps attract attention from outside the community. Finally, *reflection* by members is important. Effectiveness of action strategies, discussion of lessons learned, consideration of how power was demonstrated, and development of future plans are explored. The process can then start over again with assessment of other related critical issues for the community. Notably, this process mirrors the action research described by Lewin (1946) and the prevention research cycle espoused by Price (1983). The process of community engagement is a part of the intervention and the research.

Peterson and Reid (2003) found that **personal involvement** (person), a **sense of community** (setting), and **awareness of a community** issue (environment) all contributed to citizen empowerment (a combination of political effectiveness and competence) (Zimmerman & Zahniser, 1991). People seem willing to act when they are involved, feel connected, and are knowledgeable about the problem. These three components of empowerment and action were found again in a study of voluntary counselors to gay–straight youth (Valenti & Campbell, 2009).

## Advantages and Disadvantages of Citizen Participation

Active participation in change efforts usually is highly motivational (Chavis et al., 1992; Yates & Youniss, 1998). People are more likely to accept change that they themselves have generated (Duffy, 1991). Involved individuals are also likely to know the problems that need addressing because they have lived with the problems. For that same reason, this type of community participation often helps build a sense of community (Levi & Litwin, 1986) or social consensus and cohesiveness (Heller, Price, Reinharz,

_advantages:_
_- social_
_cohesion_
_- cheap_

_disadvantage_
_- mistrust_
_+benefits must_
_outweigh_
_cost_

Chapter 5 • Community Intervention Strategies    **101**

Riger, & Wandersman, 1984). Feeling a sense of community also increases participation in grassroots efforts (Chavis & Wandersman, 1990). Exposure to information, fair treatment in discussions, and being a part of an information-gathering process increased citizens' sense of political involvement (Eggins, Reynolds, Oakes, & Mavor, 2007).

Another advantage of citizen participation is that the average citizen often participates in change efforts for little pay but with enthusiasm and a sense of responsibility (Selznick, 2000). For example, it is no secret that many community organizations are dependent on volunteers. The Beacon Hill Institute for Public Policy Research (1997) conducted a survey of executive directors of private charitable organizations and found the following results:

- Ninety percent of the directors say that volunteers are crucial to efficiency because they save the organization money.
- Seventy-three percent said that the time and money spent on training volunteers was well worth the effort.
- Seventy-seven percent said they can depend on their volunteers.

As desirable as this type of participation is, it is not without its pitfalls (Barrera, 2000). Christensen and Robinson (1989) reported that not every citizen wants to participate. Although it is easy to level a charge of apathy against nonparticipants, the rights of those who prefer not to be involved need to be respected. When asked about their willingness to participate for a future unidentified topic, citizens in Italy based their answers on the costs and benefits of returning and the pleasantness of the task, not on a sense of community. Without a clear and defined topic of personal interest, people did not intrinsically want to participate (Eggins et al., 2007).

Finally, because they often are not made up of all members of a community, but rather of a select few, citizen groups can fail. If these individuals are not representative of the affected groups or the population at large, the solutions might not be viable or acceptable for everyone. Recall our discussion of social justice in Chapter 1. The process by which change is pursued can determine whether the outcomes are perceived as just. Thus, if this small group of activists is not **representative** of the larger constituency, then the large group might distrust or reject the smaller group (Worchel, Cooper, & Goethals, 1991), which also causes failure. Participants in community intervention need to recognize the politics of the conflicting goals and interests of the various involved parties (Riger, 1989). Similarly, if the efforts cost more than any benefits that could accrue, individuals are likely to be inactive (Prestby et al., 1990; Wandersman & Florin, 2000). Citizen participation occurs when the **benefits** of action are apparent and the **costs** of such action are outweighed by the perceived advantages of engagement. We see in Table 5.2 the types of things that make for successful participation in block associations.

---

**TABLE 5.2  Summary of Characteristics for Block Associations That Continue**

1. Greater proportion of residents join
2. More activities and participation opportunities
3. More officers and committees
4. More methods of communication, more personalized outreach, more proactive in recruitment and leadership training, used consensus and formal decision making
5. Established ties with external resources
6. More incentives for membership

---

*Source:* From Wandersman, A., & Florin, P. (2000). Citizen participation and community organizations. In J. Rappaport & E. Seidman (Eds.), *Handbook of community psychology.* New York: Plenum, p. 259.

## NETWORKING/COLLABORATION

One means for fostering community development or community change is to develop enabling systems (Chavis et al., 1992). **Enabling systems** are vehicles whereby multiple community initiatives can be simultaneously mobilized, supported, and sustained in an efficient and effective manner by developing specified links among the social actors (Chavis et al., 1992). Chavis (1993) has offered a good example of enabling. He empowered many community groups and organizations to conduct their own program evaluations by teaching them to design, conduct, and analyze research. He has therefore made them independent of the need for reliance on professionals in the future for their research needs.

**Networks** (Chavis et al., 1992; Fischer, Jackson, Stueve, Gerson, & McAllister-Jones, 1977; Sarason, Carroll, Maton, Cohen, & Lorentz, 1977) are confederations or alliances of related community organizations or individuals. Members of networks regularly share funding sources, information, and ideas with one another. Because they network their information and sometimes their clients, their futures are more secure. Another advantage is that clients are less likely to fall through the cracks in the service system. Granovetter (1973, 1983) believed these advantages accrued to those who were even weakly tied to a network. The advantages of strong networks were their durability and usefulness in providing resources to their members (they would share food and babysit for each other). However, the weak ties could serve as bridges to other networks and therefore extend the spread of information and influence beyond the usual strongly held relationships. If one of the functions of networks was the ability to access new information and wield influence beyond the usual circles, then the weak networks have their place in the creation of extended communities.

From the sociological literature comes the concept of **social capital** (resources made available to individuals as the result of their placement within a social structure). "Like other forms of capital, social capital is productive, making possible the accomplishment of certain ends that in its absence would not be possible" (Coleman, 1999, p. 16). Through relationships, the individual is able to do more. This concept is operationalized and used to demonstrate the importance of social ties/networks to the development of building and community organizations (Saegert & Winkel, 2004). Saegert and Winkel's data suggest that there are advantages of frequent face-to-face contact, even if the contacts are brief. Bonding is important, even if it is not at a high level. The concept of networks is a way of linking the individual to larger social systems. Therefore, the creation and understanding of networks seems to be an especially relevant area for community psychologists.

At a higher systems level, **umbrella organizations** are created to achieve this networking among agencies or systems. This overarching organization oversees the health of member organizations. Again, they act as clearinghouses for information that members can share. A concrete example might prove useful. United Way of America is perhaps one of the best-known umbrella organizations in the United States. United Way, through charitable contributions, is known for its financial support of community agencies that might otherwise flounder. In addition, it provides community service agencies with office supplies, furniture, and other desperately needed tangible provisions. However, United Way also offers expert consultation on fund raising, staff training, development of publications, and other issues crucial for community agency survival.

Networking has been used to build collaborative capacity for international participants in the European Union (García-Ramírez, Paloma, Suarez-Balcazar, & Balcazar, 2009). Following a protocol derived by Fetterman (2001), participants from three European nations (Spain, Belgium, Italy) worked together to increase their internal collaborative capacity (i.e., communicate and work with other members of the network) and their external collaborative capacity (communicate and work with those who were not members), using Foster-Fishman, Berkowitz, Lounsbury, Jacobson, and Allen's (2001) framework to guide their work.

**CASE IN POINT 5.2**

# Online Networks for Ethnic Minority Issues

A complaint of many ethnic minority psychologists is that there are not very many of them and they are widely dispersed geographically. Outside of large urban centers such as New York, Chicago, San Francisco, and Los Angeles, there are small numbers of psychologists of color. If there is a question regarding a particular research or clinical issue relating to race or racism, the likelihood of finding someone within a day's drive is small for many parts of the United States. It can feel lonely at times and certainly isolated.

With the development of ethnic minority psychological associations (Asian American Psychological Association, Association of Black Psychologists, National Latina/o Psychological Association, Society of Indian Psychologists) and the Society for the Psychological Study of Ethnic Minority Issues (Division 45 of the American Psychological Association [APA]), psychologists who are interested in these kinds of issues can join online discussion groups and connect with each other. Once on one of these association groups, access to the network of psychologists and graduate students is no more than an e-mail away. These networks are active in sending out information on events, funding opportunities, personal victories, and occasions for sadness. Job announcements that target those interested in ethnic minority issues can be sent out to the entire network with no delay. In turn, questions are asked and answered on the discussions. Who knows a good speaker on microaggressions? What would be a good reading on diversity issues in general? What do people think of a particular psychological test? It is like having access to all who are in the network. Typically, news travels fast. Although the geographic dispersion of psychologists of color continues, the linkage provided by the Internet has provided the kinds of advantages discussed within community psychology.

They first built a good relationship and then worked on building the collaborative capacities. Finally, they evaluated their efforts and discussed future directions for this program. You can read of another instance of good network building in Case in Point 5.2.

## Issues Related to Networks

Networks and umbrella associations offer ongoing support to participants, reciprocally share ideas and resources, provide role modeling for each other, and offer accessible resources to participants (Sarason et al., 1977). For instance, these systems allow small community agencies to share information about grants, staff-training opportunities, and resource libraries; exchange successful publicity ideas; refer clients to each other's services; and build lobbying coalitions. Thus, the health and success of each smaller service is assisted or enabled. Collaborative efforts across agencies and within communities are a well-documented community-level intervention (Foster-Fishman et al., 2001). Wolff (2010) challenges the practitioner to understand, respect, and use the political and the spiritual resources abiding within the communities in which they work.

Enabling systems and networks represent a form of social change because the new systems and networks build on existing resources and develop more productive and creative relationships between already existing services. In other words, such systems reweave the social fabric of what might otherwise be a more tattered and frayed community and its services and thus ensure survival and continued growth of the services.

## Advantages and Disadvantages of Networks

Besides enhancing the viability of many services, networks are advantageous because they ensure that important systems come to know each other better, find effective ways to work together, and learn to plan or advocate for change in a collaborative rather than competitive manner (Wolff, 1987). Likewise, enabling systems better ensure that resources are equitably distributed (Biegel, 1984), help reduce community conflict (Christensen & Robinson, 1989), and focus collective pressure on public policy makers and other decision makers (Delgado, 1986; Seekins & Fawcett, 1987). Networks also enable related services to detect cracks in the service system. **Cracks** are defined as structural gaps in the service systems and are exemplified by missing or inaccessible services and missing information (Tausig, 1987). Granovetter (1973, 1983) described some of the problems of networks that are so strong that they do not structurally encourage linkages to others. If the networks are without connections to other networks, they exclude others and lose the information and access to resources that others might provide.

Few authors have addressed other disadvantages of umbrella organizations, even though several disadvantages exist. For one thing, private-sector businesses might feel threatened by and perhaps launch a successful attack against the collective power of activist community organizations (Delgado, 1986). Similarly, when umbrella organizations grow large, they develop their own set of problems in terms of bureaucracy, conflict, and expense.

Another disadvantage is that when an umbrella organization becomes a controlling, parental organization, member agencies can become dissatisfied. The authors know, for instance, of one rural domestic violence program that broke from a strong countywide coalition of churches over staffing and funding issues, despite the program's already precarious existence. The bad feelings between the smaller domestic violence program and the larger parent organization resulted in the establishment of a second, redundant domestic violence program in the same geographic region.

Another possible disadvantage of community coalitions is that different community services as well as the whole community may be in different stages of development or readiness for change (Edwards, Jumper-Thurman, Plested, Oetting, & Swanson, 2001). The new services need staff training; the older ones may be seeking to expand their client bases. Coordinating the different developmental needs of member organizations can be difficult for the parent organization. Finally, if the reach of the association grows beyond one particular community's boundaries because member organizations have satellites in other geographic areas, existing associations in neighboring communities may feel threatened and subvert each other's purpose. At a personal level, those who network are at a distinct advantage over those who do not. Given the work on social capital, established residents of the "neighborhood" are more likely to be participants and, by definition, may glean the benefits of the network.

## CONSULTATION

In the opening scenario for this chapter, there was a neighborhood in crisis, with high crime rates, high transiency, and a general sense of alienation among its residents. An individual within the neighborhood or some small group of neighbors might have also considered calling a consultant to help them in solving their problems. Some communities write grants, get funding, and hire community organizers or professionals to provide expertise in community functioning and interventions. Sarason (1976b) believed that one of the advantages a community psychologist had over others was access to information.

Professional change agents or expert consultants seek to create social change through assessment, modification, and improvement. Consultation is viewed as one of the basic ways in which community psychologists serve in their communities (Lavoie & Brunson, 2010).

A **consultant** or **professional change agent** is someone who engages in collaborative problem solving with one or more persons (the **consultees**), who are often responsible for providing some form of assistance to another individual (the **client**) (Sears, Rudisill, & Mason-Sears, 2006). Consultants are often professionals well versed in scientific research. They are typically called on to conduct program evaluations and needs assessments for community organizations. The traditional consultant provides leadership to organizations who are interested in demonstrating the successes of their efforts or improving their service delivery.

However, the community model is one that is less hierarchical and expert driven. There is more a sense of collaboration and empowerment to the processes (Maton, Seidman, & Aber, 2011; Serrano-Garcia, 2011; Zimmerman, 2000). The development of relationships (Kelly, 2006) or a type of "joining" with the "consultants" and the community (Lorion, 2011) are more characteristic of most community psychology consultations. This orientation directs the types of consultative actions taken.

Community psychologists seem uniquely qualified to be consultants to community groups because they possess skills in community needs assessment, community organizing, group problem solving, and action research. The community psychologist is also likely to focus on the social systems and institutions within a community rather than on individuals (Nelson & Prilleltensky, 2010). Community psychologists bring a "more consciously and expertly applied" operation of these phenomena, given their familiarity with past research and former attempts to realize the possibilities of a better community (Sarason, 1976b, p. 328). This creates exciting opportunities for community psychology consultants to work with community members to bring about constructive, community-directed change.

## Issues Related to Consultants

An important issue that communities must consider is cost. If the consultant is paid, is that a good use of limited resources? One way the field has tried to answer questions related to the expense of consultants is evaluating whether they really help the client. One early study of the use of consultants was conducted by Medway and Updyke (1985), who reviewed the literature on outcome of consultations. In the better designed studies, the researchers found that compared to control groups (e.g., clients who did not have consultants), both consultees and clients in the intervention groups (where consultants were used) made gains in solving their problems or promoting change as measured by such things as attitude scales, observed behaviors, and standardized scores. In the control groups (in which no consultants were used), there were fewer of these improvements. This literature review therefore offers statistical evidence for the value of consultants. Hylander (2004) provided a more recent study of the impact of consultation in Sweden using a mixed methodology, which included assessing changes such as those mentioned in the Medway and Updyke study, but also conducting focus groups where consultants and consultees were able to talk about the ways in which changes were connected to the work of the consultant. Her study provided additional data on the benefit of consultants. Studies such as these provide evidence that consultation is one viable way that community psychologists can collaborate successfully in community change efforts.

Weed (1990) identified several steps for community psychologists acting as consultants to primary prevention programs that are adaptable for almost all change agents—expert or not. Homan (2010) echoed many of these steps in discussing methods for promoting community change. The first step is *defining the goals* to be accomplished. The second step is to *raise the awareness* of the individuals in the setting under consultation and then to *introduce the new program* or research. At this point, other, related organizations or communities can be networked for collaboration, support, and learning about new techniques and funding sources. Consultants also need to collaborate on effective methods for *evaluating changes*. Favorable evaluation justifies the money, time, and effort expended. Evaluation also leads to modification and fine-tuning, should that be necessary. Unfortunately, evaluation is a step sometimes forgotten in many change situations. Without evaluation, how would people know if the change worked and whether it ought to be repeated?

Sears and colleagues (2006) discussed a critical issue related to consultation: *trust*. It takes time before consultants, who are often not members of the community with whom they are working, to achieve the trust required to act in the role of consultant. It can in fact take years before consultants' ideas are viewed less skeptically by community members. As outsiders, community members often rightly question whether consultants truly understand their community and its goals and whether they will suggest methods that reflect such an understanding. Serrano-Garcia (1994) explained that there are often unequal power relationships between community members and outside professional consultants, with the professional having more power because of specialized knowledge and other resources. She issued a challenge to professionals who act as community consultants to "establish more equitable professional–client relationships" (p. 17) by means of collaboration and empowerment.

This discussion illustrates the fact that consultants, especially when not members of the communities with whom they consult, *must earn* the trust of the community and not assume that it will be implicitly given. This issue is discussed further in the next section.

## Advantages and Disadvantages of Consultants

There are several advantages to expert consultation. The first is obvious—the professional is an expert at what he or she does. The professional change agent has been specially trained and has the knowledge base on which to make wise decisions. One not-so-apparent advantage is that the consultant is a neutral, presumably more "objective" person. Because the consultant is not embroiled in the presenting problems and should have no vested interest in the community, particular members, or the organization itself, he or she can make unencumbered, unbiased judgments and recommendations.

Consultants also generally take a long-term approach to problem solving. Individuals in the community or organization often focus on short-term issues because they are living with them day to day. For the continued health of the community or organization, a long-term approach might be best. As stated earlier, too many community groups fail quickly; fast, ineffective fixes may be one of the reasons. For this reason, most consultants attempt to assess the overall health and well-being of the organization with which they consult, not solely focus on the problem that they were called in to address (Dougherty, 2000).

Finally, if a consultant is experienced, she or he comes with a vast array of ideas, past successes, and relevant ideas because of experiences with past but similar situations. Consultants should neither betray nor create a conflict of interest with past clients, but previous experiences can help them find common ground that might be useful to similar communities or organizations.

Despite these somewhat apparent advantages, professional change agents are not without disadvantages (Maton, 2000); one is cost. Cost can be a major burden and can thwart the best-laid plans of any community or organization needing expert assistance. Ideally, some community psychologists acting as change agents would consider pro bono or voluntary consultations. The American Psychological Association (APA) encourages pro bono work by psychologists. Community psychologists may serve as consultants to the organization and write grants for independent funding of their work, offering awareness of the literature and knowledge of the research process (Suarez-Balcazar et al., 2004), or help in reframing the task or the question based on the expertise that they may bring to the process (Kelly et al., 2004). When the consultant and the community are viewed as equal and reciprocal partners in the process, the community and the consultant are better informed and the problem more effectively addressed.

However, developing cooperation from all involved in the consultation can be challenging and largely dependent on the extent to which community members can trust the consultant. Outside consultants sometimes inspire fear (of job loss or criticism), defensiveness, and resistance to change. Often this is because the organization's leadership has hired the consultant to help solve a particular problem. The employees of the organization may or may not be aware of the problem or may see the consultant as management's "henchman" or "henchwoman." For this reason, consultants are often encouraged to assess the overall well-being of the organization, which allows them to identify problems that may or may not be related to the original issue. Also, consultants might want to consider using less direct or nondirective assessment techniques to avoid these problems (Sears et al., 2006).

In addition, consultants must state up front what type of confidentiality community members can expect in work they do with the consultant. If a community organization's leaders call in a consultant to resolve conflict among staff within the organization, it will be important to be clear about whether the leaders will be privy to the information gathered in fact-finding conversations the consultants have with the staff members. If staff members assume they are speaking in confidence and then learn that the consultant was contracted to share details of the assessment with the leaders, it may damage the working relationship between the consultant and the staff for the remainder of the project. Another issue that affects consultation work is that consultants' contacts with their clients are often time limited. They need to quickly assess the issues, assist in the development of solutions and their implementation, and foster maintenance strategies in a short period of time. Often, the issues on which they are asked to consult are complex compared to the amount of available resources, including time. For example, many communities and their organizations grow haphazardly rather than in a planned fashion. Thus change can be difficult, if not impossible. Some problems defy solutions, or at least would require a total reorganization of the structure of the system (Sarason, 1978). It does also sometimes happen that organizations ask consultants to help them with problems that are outside the competence of the consultant. This can be avoided if consultants carefully match their skills and expertise to client situations (Dougherty, 2000).

Finally, clients sometimes hold high and unrealistic expectations of what a consultant can do. Other clients may use the consultant for their own misleading purposes, especially when there are conflicting views about what ought to be done. In these situations, the ethical consultant will probably leave clients feeling disappointed. Again, careful intake by a consultant to ensure that his or her expertise fits the clients' issues can help. The consultant is wise to be aware of the purpose for which he or she was hired and whether there are multiple and competing interests at work. Bloom's classic principles, found in Table 5.3, provide useful points to community consolidation.

---

**TABLE 5.3  Bloom's Principles to Guide the Development of Community Programs**

**1.** Regardless of where your paycheck comes from, think of yourself as working for the community.

**2.** If you want to know about a community's mental health needs, ask the community.

**3.** As you learn about community mental health needs, you have the responsibility to tell the community what you are learning.

**4.** Help the community establish its own priorities.

**5.** You can help the community decide among various courses of action in its efforts to solve its problems.

**6.** In the event that the community being served is so disorganized that representatives of various facets of the community cannot be found, you have the responsibility to help find such representatives.

---

*Source:* From Bloom, B. L. (1984). *Community mental health: A general introduction.* Monterey, CA: Brooks/Cole, pp. 429–431.

## COMMUNITY EDUCATION AND INFORMATION DISSEMINATION

The terrorized citizens of the neighborhood from the opening example would have benefited from information on police communication procedures and response rules. They soon came to understand the frustration of law enforcement over the lack of willing witnesses, which led to ineffective evidence for prosecution. With the support of the police, the neighborhood learned what they needed to know and how to contact the police in a timely way. Sharing this type of information made for a more effective neighborhood–police partnership.

Information dissemination and community education remain vital parts of social change efforts. In fact, some community psychologists have challenged their colleagues to renew efforts to disseminate useful information and innovative educational programs as a method of addressing social problems (Nelson & Prilleltensky, 2010). Let's address these two related topics one at a time.

### Information Dissemination

Just what is meant by **information dissemination** (Mayer & Davidson, 2000) in community psychology? As you now know, community psychologists seek to prevent, intercede in, and treat (if necessary) community problems with what are generally innovative programs. Typically, information dissemination refers to the sharing of successful programs or beneficial information that has been used to address community problems with new populations. For example, in the creation of the CeaseFire/Cure Violence program discussed earlier in this chapter, researchers who had worked in disease transmission prevention programs used information about "what worked" about those programs and modeled CeaseFire/Cure Violence after those ingredients of success. If innovative prevention programs are researched and found to be successful, but the results are never shared with or adopted by other communities, the results are of limited use (Nelson & Prilleltensky, 2010). In addition, it makes sense to not reinvent the wheel. If researchers can identify "best practices" in preventing violence, risky sexual behavior, or other community problems, then it makes sense to take that information and disseminate it to others who are trying to curb similar problems in other communities. Thus, dissemination of information can save time, money, and effort. However, there has been much debate in the literature about whether successful programs developed in one community can be effectively transferred to other potentially dissimilar communities. Adopters of innovations from community psychology need to be careful in their translation efforts. Although one could argue the importance of being faithful to the initial program, especially to the mechanisms that caused change, there may also need to be some reinventing or modification of the program to fit the unique needs of the community trying to use the program, given that not all settings are the same (Trickett et al., 2011). We discuss this issue at greater length in the section on issues in information dissemination.

### Community Education

*Community education* is a concept related to information dissemination. However, community education is an intervention approach that often integrates psychotherapeutic and educational components (Lukens & McFarlane, 2006; Lucksted, McFarlane, Downing, Dixon, & Adams, 2012) that can be used in both treatment and preventative contexts. Community education may be a focus of some programs that ultimately are found to be successful and disseminated into other community contexts. However, not all community programs involve community education, as will become evident as you read subsequent chapters of this book. For example, some successful programs aimed at reducing car accidents involve policy changes such as making seatbelts mandatory, whereas others may emphasize education about safe driving habits.

Some community education programs that involve psychologists as consultants will be aimed at teaching skills or knowledge that is related to specific disease prevention. Often these programs are referred to as "psychoeducation." Psychoeducation embodies a paradigm of empowerment and collaboration that stresses competence building and coping and that builds on the strengths of the community—all valued components of a community psychology approach. Rather than solely focus on the amelioration or prevention of symptoms, psychoeducation focuses on health promotion, viewing clients as learners and psychologists as teachers (Morgan & Vera, 2012).

Psychoeducation has become a widespread approach to the treatment of a variety of psychological problems. For example, recent reviews of the literature and meta-analyses have been published on the use of psychoeducation in the treatment and/or prevention of eating disorders (Fingeret, Warren, Cepeda-Benito, & Gleaves, 2006), bipolar disorders (Rouget & Aubry, 2006), teenage suicide (Portzky & van Heeringen, 2006), and bullying (Newman-Carlson & Horne, 2004). As a result of the accumulating evidence, psychoeducation is now seen as an important component of treating a variety of medical problems where it is used to enhance treatment compliance and prevent disease progression.

One example of a successful psychoeducational program that was able to demonstrate a reduction in suicidal behavior was Signs of Suicide (SOS) (Aseltine & DeMartino, 2004), whose focus was on peer education and intervention. Peer intervention as a focus of adolescent suicide prevention programs is rooted in studies which have found that adolescents communicate distress more often and more easily with their friends than to family members or other concerned adults (Kalafat & Elias, 1995). The content of SOS includes providing information about incidence rates of suicide attempts and completions, presenting education on risk and protective factors, and describing what is called the "suicide process." The suicide process involves the progression of suicide from ideation (i.e., thinking about suicide) to attempts (i.e., efforts to end one's life) to completion (van Heeringen, 2001). The model is used in psychoeducation because it implies the possibility of intervention and help being valuable at multiple points in the process.

The peer intervention component of the program teaches participants to recognize warning signs of suicidal ideation and behavior and teaches appropriate strategies for intervention (i.e., active listening, encouragement of help seeking). The program also identifies school- and community-based resources such as school counselors or suicide hotlines. The objective of this program is to help adolescents better monitor their friends and peers for signs of suicidal ideation (or intent to attempt suicide) *and* to increase the likelihood that such signs will be reported to adults capable of providing help.

Although psychoeducational suicide prevention programs may not be optimal for use with acutely suicidal teens themselves, such programs appear to be an appropriate intervention to change peers' awareness and ability to identify those among their peer group who may be at risk for suicide (Portzky & van Heeringen, 2006).

Whenever information from community psychology is shared with community members, be it through information dissemination or through community education, its main purpose should be to improve the community, promote prevention, and empower community members to shape their own destinies (Fairweather & Davidson, 1986). These efforts can also be used to direct action in a community, as well as to inform those in a position of power (the **gatekeepers**) about the need for change and share ideas for action plans (Levine, Perkins, & Perkins, 2004). With advances in technology—for example, distance learning—diverse and geographically distant communities can be educated and empowered, and information can be disseminated more easily than in the past (Kreisler, Snider, & Kiernan, 1997).

## Issues Related to Information Dissemination

Several important issues need to be carefully considered by community psychologists hoping to disseminate information about innovative programs (Mayer & Davidson, 2000).

The dominant paradigm of psychology's efforts to prevent and treat community problems such as violence or crime has been to disseminate "best practices," or those programs that have evidence to support their success. However, there is a competing paradigm that is gaining support in the community of scientists working to strengthen community interventions in the United States (Trickett et al., 2011). This "best process" paradigm is in many ways a response to the issues and critiques that have been raised in past dissemination efforts.

One important critique of existing efforts to disseminate program information is that they often treat knowledge of the host community as secondary to the development of the intervention (Trickett et al., 2011). In other words, the process focuses more on what conditions need to be in place to make the program faithful to the original prototype rather than understanding the unique needs of the new community and seeing the program as an event that happens within the community. An alternative perspective, and one espoused in the newer paradigm, is that community interventions are conceptualized as system events (i.e., as complex interactions between the structure, processes, and goals of the intervention and those of the community itself) that emerge from and are defined by knowledge of the community. Hence, community psychologists must begin by gaining knowledge of the community and then shaping programs to reflect the uniqueness of the community. Trickett and his colleagues (2011) call this orientation a "best process" orientation, as opposed to the "best practice" emphasis that has characterized most community interventions in the field of psychology.

The goal of community interventions should then be community capacity building, as opposed to program participant changes per se (Trickett et al., 2011). This is not to say that outcomes such as increases in skill sets or information are irrelevant. However, community interventions should be aimed at developing the community's capacity to address structural and/or policy factors that have served as impediments to healthier functioning. One could argue that a program that is imported (one that has been disseminated) from another community does little to help the community in the long run if its success is solely connected to external resources funding the program (e.g., a grant).

A final issue related to the use of information dissemination as a component of social change is that transferring information from one context to a new community must include cultural sensitivity. The new paradigm of Trickett and associates is one defined by cultural relevance. "Culture is not seen as something to which interventions are tailored; rather, culture is a fundamental set of defining qualities of community life out of which interventions flow" (Trickett et al., 2011, p. 1412). What works for one ethnic group might not work in another. There is a *Handbook of Racial and Ethnic Minority Psychology* (Bernal, Trimble, Burlew, & Leong, 2003) and a sixth edition of *Counseling across Cultures* (Pedersen, Draguns, Lonner, & Trimble, 2008), to name just two of the many texts dealing with this issue. However, it is not sufficient that community interventionists learn about communities by reading books.

> Culture is always changing, and there is considerable variability within any cultural group; moreover, culture is inescapable in the community intervention process, affecting the nature of collaboration, the meaning of constructs, the equivalence of [outcome] measurements, and the salience of intervention goals. (Trickett et al., 2011, p. 1413)

This sentiment echoes Pederson (2008), who warns of the dangers of oversimplifying "multiculturalism." Trickett and colleagues emphasize the importance of investigator immersion in the daily life of the community of interest, to learn about their deep cultural lifeways and thoughtways. Such a perspective reinforces the assertion that interventions are collaborations and are likely to fail if they are not conceptualized as such. How might culture affect the dissemination of information or the importation of a specific community intervention program? As one example, in considering mentoring relationships, Darling, Bogat, Cavell, Murphy, and Sánchez (2006) noted that culture and ethnicity played a significant role in determining the patterns of who was perceived as a mentor and the nature of these relationships. In some cases, parents and extended family members were important; in other cases, the family was on

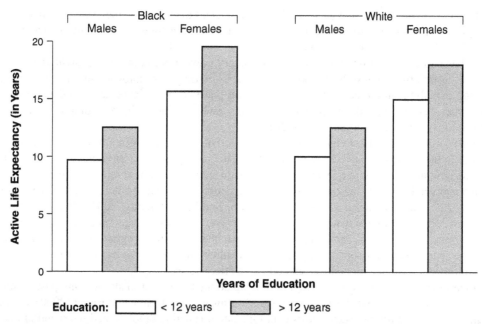

**FIGURE 5.2**   Active Life Expectancy at Age 65 by Education and Race

*Source:* From Kaplan, G. (1994). Reflections on present and future research on bio-behavioral risk factors. In S. Blumenthal, K. Matthews, & S. Weiss (Eds.), *New research frontiers in behavioral medicine: Proceedings of the national conference.* Washington, DC: NIH.

an equal par with nonfamily members; in still other cases, certain family members were the farthest thing from a perceived mentor. A community intervention program aimed at increasing community youths' access to mentors would need to be aware of how the targeted community youths envisioned the potential of various people to act as mentors. Such cultural variations should be carefully considered in the derivation of these programs.

## Issues Related to Community Education

Community education as an intervention strategy brings the advantages of affecting large groups in short periods of time. However, as in the discussion of issues in information dissemination, community education efforts bring the challenge of understanding one's audience and how to most effectively reach them and bring about the desired change. A community psychology may inform these efforts, thus making them more effective.

To be most cost effective and to capitalize on the benefits of group dynamics, most community education and/or psychoeducation occurs with groups of individuals who have certain things in common. For example, parenting groups, stress management workshops for police officers, job search clubs for the unemployed, and biofeedback training for heart patients are examples of groups of individuals who share characteristics, have common needs, and can provide important support to one another. The objectives of many psychoeducational programs are often to promote healthy development or adjustment, rather than to solely stave off psychopathology (Carlson, Watts, & Maniacci, 2006). Although the prevention of pathology may be an added benefit of the interventions, they are often times not evaluated based on such criteria.

For example, a good parenting program might be based on learning theory, offered to parents early in the process (i.e., while their children are very young), and have as goals to increase parents' knowledge of the developmental needs of their children and to encourage the use of positive parenting techniques (i.e., positive reinforcement) (Carlson et al., 2006). A long-term benefit of such a program may be to reduce incidents of child abuse. If the program was offered to parents who might be at risk of such behavior, it would be an example of secondary prevention. However, it might also be able to demonstrate its effectiveness by tracking changes in participants' knowledge base and intentions regarding parenting. In the case of psychoeducation that is used to increase compliance to medical treatment, evaluations may also be based on incidence rates of relapse, disease complication, and other measures of compliance (Morgan & Vera, 2012).

One of the most critical characteristics of effective psychoeducation, however, is its perceived relevance to the participants (Reese & Vera, 2007). This perception is often a function of the extent to which the program has cultural relevance to the targeted audience. Cultural relevance refers to the extent to which interventions are consistent with the values, beliefs, and desired outcomes of a particular group of constituents such as parents (Kumpfer, Alvarado, Smith, & Bellamy, 2002; Nation et al., 2003). Nation and colleagues argued that program relevance is a function of the extent to which a constituency group's norms, cultural beliefs, and practices have been integrated into program content, its delivery, and evaluation. Kumpfer and associates argued that including cultural relevance in psychoeducation programs improves recruitment, retention, and outcome effectiveness.

One of the superficial ways that cultural adaptations have been made in many past community education efforts has been what Resnicow, Solar, Braithwaite, Ahluwalia, and Butler (2000) termed *surface structure modifications*. Such efforts could include translating prepackaged intervention materials into the primary language of the participants, or hiring program staff that have similar ethnic backgrounds to the participants. Such modifications may be one important aspect of cultural adaptation. It may be highly advantageous to have program participants communicate with program staff in their first languages or to interact with staff of the same ethnicity and/or gender. However, when program content does not reflect the reality of the participants' experience, interventions delivered by racially or linguistically similar staff will not make the program relevant or, more importantly, effective.

Rather than surface modifications, it is the "deep structure modifications" (Resnicow & Braithwaite, 2001) that often determine the cultural relevance of community education programs. If education programs can be adapted to their target population, they have achieved measurable successes (Hawkins, Kreuter, Resnicow, Fishbein, & Dijkstraa, 2008). Often, the adaptations required for a program to be culturally relevant result in a program that may be substantively different from its prototype. Reese and Vera (2007), Lerner (1995), and Reiss and Price (1995), among others, have suggested that the most effective, culturally relevant programs include the target program participants in the planning, implementation, and evaluation of the program. If this approach is followed, not only may the content of the program become more relevant, but its very structure may also look significantly different from a program designed for a culturally dissimilar population. Although a preponderance of the literature suggests that a relationship with the target community is a key to acquiring cultural knowledge, there is still a need for large-scale epidemiological research that identifies risk factors and how they affect particular communities. Such studies must be designed carefully and their findings examined responsibly so as to assist community educations researchers and practitioners in more accurately understanding the communities in which they work (Reese & Vera, 2007).

One example of a community education model that was designed to be culturally relevant in its content was the Choices program (Vera et al., 2007). Choices is a psychoeducation program that was developed through a collaboration with a public middle school in a large Midwestern city that serves low-income children of color. The goal of the program was to address the normal challenges of adolescence that are relevant to youth of color and to enhance protective factors that are related to the array of problematic outcomes for which urban youth of color may be at risk. The program was designed from a

## The Choices Program

The Choices Program's goals and curriculum topics were designed with the input of a series of separate focus groups with 12- to14-year-old urban youth of color, their teachers, and their parents. In these focus groups, constituents were asked to discuss their aspirations for the community's youth, the strengths of the community, the potential barriers to success, and their ideas for designing a program that might address these issues. Our confidence in the validity of the participant input was high because of a 10-year relationship between the program leader and the school. The focus groups highlighted issues facing the community (e.g., temptations to drop out of school, lack of hope about the future, a lack of teacher efficacy in addressing the emotional needs of the kids, parental stressors such as intergenerational conflict, or working multiple-shift jobs). Thus, the resulting program had components that addressed the needs of youths, their teachers, and their parents.

The youth program's overall objective was to increase youth's social and academic competencies. We specifically aimed (a) to create opportunities for positive identity development to enhance social and academic self-efficacy by promoting positive self-concepts and cultural identity; (b) to enhance self-awareness and empathy by focusing on productive ways to express difficult emotions (e.g., being disappointed, angry, hurt) and to respond to others' feelings; and (c) to increase students' self-efficacy in responding to peer pressure, which is important in disengaging from and avoiding situations that can compromise well-being. Another aim of the program was to teach communication skills to increase the youth's ability to avoid nonproductive and risky conflict with peers and adults. Finally, we aimed to enhance the youth's academic and career aspirations by examining social barriers, enhancing study and organizational skills, and increasing their knowledge of academic resources in the community.

For the parent program, the goals were (a) to present information on the challenges of adolescent development and the stressors of parenting, (b) to discuss strategies to enhance communication between parents and their children during adolescence, and (c) to present ideas for providing academic and emotional support in the home. For the teachers, we aimed (a) to provide group consultations that would help teachers identify the psychological issues and needs of their students, (b) to brainstorm resources that would help the academic progress of their students, and (c) to better understand the multiple stressors that their students' parents faced, which often affected their ability to participate in the education of their children.

The program was delivered over an 8-week time span, with sessions held during the school day for the youth, before school for the teachers, and after school for the parents. The program was evaluated both qualitatively and quantitatively, and both program leaders and school constituents reviewed the content and outcomes of the program and used that information to make changes for future programming.

---

competency-promotion perspective, guided by Positive Youth Development theory (PYD) (Catalano, Bergland, Ryan, Lonczak, & Hawkins, 1999). PYD theorists contend that children benefit from interventions that enhance their developmental competencies (e.g., social, emotional, academic) independent of the number of risk factors to which they are exposed. This type of program is classified as a primary prevention approach because it is universal in scope, not focused on particular youth who might be more likely to develop mental health problems in the future (Romano & Hage, 2000). Case in Point 5.3 is just such a youth program.

One of the limitations of community education is that many of the underlying causes of problems are not directly affected. For example, the underemployment of parents that resulted in them working multiple shift jobs and being less available to their children was not modified in the aforementioned program. There is a need for community interventions to be directly responsive to systemic barriers to the well-being of community members (Homan, 2010; Trickett et al., 2011) One of the most powerful ways to affect systemic factors is through public policy involvement.

## PUBLIC POLICY

If the besieged neighborhood in our chapter's beginning example had decided to lobby legislators to get particular laws passed that would make it easier to arrest the drug dealers in the neighborhood, or had programs implemented that would address the crime in the area, such social change would be pursued through public policy changes. Public policy advocacy is an example of a community intervention that addresses the contextual barriers to community well-being—in contrast to the approach of community education, which often focuses on changing community members themselves. Though sometimes a lengthy effort, a shift in policies can bring about long-lived changes in the way people live and serve as the most powerful forms of prevention. Public policy interventions are direct interventions at the systems level that require a willingness to participate in the legislative process.

Consider: Did you vote in the last election? It is often surprising how many citizens, college students in particular, do not vote. Voting, drafting legislation, and lobbying for particular interests are actions that change (often dramatically) our national and local social agendas. For citizens and community psychologists alike, participating in public policy endeavors opens a "window of opportunity" (Nelson & Prilleltensky, 2010) for what can often be sweeping social changes.

Just what is **public policy**? The aim of public policy is to improve the quality of life for community members. Although the term is often used for government-mandated legislation, it can refer to policy at a specific agency or at the local community and state governmental levels. Public policy can also influence to what issues various resources are allocated (Levine & Perkins, 1997).

A concept relevant to public policy is **policy science,** which is the practice of making findings from science (and in the case of community psychology, findings from social science) relevant to governmental and organizational policy. A well-known example of this is the use of actual scientific studies on desegregation of schools to shape policies on integration (Frost & Ouellette, 2004). Given the Supreme Court ruling (*Meredith vs. Jefferson County, Kentucky and Parents Involved in Community Schools-PICS vs. Seattle School District*) in June 2007 stating that schools may no longer take a student's race into account in attempting to devise desegregation programs (Greenhouse, 2007), the challenges of integration continue.

Fox and Prilleltensky (2007) note that wishing psychology and politics to be unrelated doesn't make it so. Hence, they argue that psychopolitical literacy is an important prerequisite of public policy involvement. Psychopolitical literacy acknowledges the connections among politics, well-being, and social justice. Psychopolitical literacy promotes a state of affairs whereby individuals, groups, and communities use power, capacity, and opportunity to fulfill personal, relational, and collective needs. *Transformative* psychopolitical validity refers to the extent to which interventions reduce the negative and strengthen the positive political and psychological forces contributing to wellness and justice. Extensive evidence documents the restriction of psychosocial interventions to goals such as skill development, even in fields such as community psychology explicitly concerned with collective phenomena (Fox & Prilleltensky, 2007).

At this point in your reading, you have learned about the variety of techniques that can be used to create social change. Any reliable change agent knows that a multifaceted approach is best. That is, a single change strategy by itself may be weak. Using several change techniques is more likely to result in the desired outcomes. Case in Point 5.4 describes the evolution of rape crisis centers, which generally take this multifaceted strategy of social change. In a later chapter we describe at greater length the efforts to change the educational system in the United States. The research evidence on resiliency shows a clear advantage to early child enrichment and parental education. Long-term outcome studies on Head Start are now coming on line. They support the positive effects of work with young children (Garces, Thomas, & Currie, 2000). You will read more about these issues in Chapter 8.

**CASE IN POINT 5.4**

## Rape Crisis Centers: A National Examination

Campbell, Baker, and Mazurek (1998) hypothesized that many rape crisis centers have undergone significant changes since their beginnings during the feminist movement of the 1970s. The researchers used interviews with center directors to examine the current structure and functions of 168 randomly selected rape crisis centers across the nation.

First, the study demonstrated that there are many avenues to social change. An early goal of rape crisis services was to provide services to survivors of sexual assault. Ancillary to this was the provision of 24-hour crisis intervention hotlines as well as counseling and assistance in negotiating the legal and medical systems. Many (but not all) centers also eventually sought to raise public awareness about sexual assault

in the community. Some centers also became active in public demonstrations, such as Take Back the Night marches. Finally, some centers also sought to conduct large-scale change by lobbying state legislatures for reform. In response, most states did alter their rape statutes in the late 1970s and early 1980s.

Second, although the average center in the study was 16 years old, many were older or younger than this. The older, freestanding, collective centers had larger budgets and staffs as well as a change orientation when interacting with other social services agencies. These centers used participatory decision making for deciding internal issues. Older centers were also more likely to participate in public demonstrations such as Take Back the Night

marches and in prevention programming. The younger centers, especially those that were affiliated with larger service agencies and therefore followed a hierarchical organizational structure, were more likely to engage in political lobbying rather than preventive education and public demonstrations as their forms of social activism.

Both types of centers, then, engaged in social activism or social change, but the types of activities differed by organizational structure and age. In addition, this study also demonstrates that rape crisis organizations and perhaps other service-oriented organizations often need to adapt to the changing political climate to continue to provide quality services to their communities.

## Issues Related to the Use of Public Policy

Politics and community psychology are deeply intertwined (Fox & Prilleltensky, 2007), although changing social policy is a relatively unexplored extension of community psychology (Phillips, 2000). There is general agreement among community psychologists that their science and politics are inseparable. However, community psychologists do not agree on how much science should impinge on policy and how much public policy should pervade science. Some argue that good policies are those based solely on scientific evidence. In other words, one should not attempt to influence any public policy until one has solid scientific evidence. Others argue that pressing social problems such as AIDS and homelessness do not afford the luxury of time for conducting research. Society is not likely to have solutions to this complex situation for some time to come. Choi and associates (2005) urged social scientists who wish to engage in public policy advocacy to understand the differences between the worlds that politicians live in and the worlds that scientists reside in. For example, they argued that policy makers often live in a world that involves putting out fires, managing political crises, and knowing a little bit about a variety of topics. Also, policy makers prefer clear-cut answers and want the essence of an issue laid out for them in bullet points, whereas scientists are apt to equivocate and are often uncomfortable giving a "bottom line." Furthermore, scientists obsess about the quality of evidence available about a particular research question, whereas policy makers are more comfortable using evidence generated more informally. Although these differences may make public policy advocacy more challenging for psychologists, we can learn to speak this language and function within this world to make sure that good policy is developed and guided by sound science.

Most community psychologists do agree that the development of public policy should be a collaborative effort among researchers, affected populations, and the decision or policy makers.

However, the political climate, lobbying groups with cross purposes, and other vicissitudes can often influence the end product in public policy as much or more than science and other logical factors. That being said, when public policy is based on research, it can serve several functions: instrumental, conceptual, and persuasive (Shadish, 1990). When research shapes the direction of change or of public policy, it serves an **instrumental purpose.** Research can also be aimed at changing the way people think or conceptualize social problems and solutions. Research with this function serves a **conceptual purpose.** When research persuades policy makers to support a particular position or solution to a social problem, it then functions in the **persuasive** mode. Finally, when research is designed to forecast what change will occur in the future or predict whether change will be accepted, the function is **predictive.**

Is there any evidence that social science research influences legislators as they develop public policy? Yes, one can see the impact of researchers in part by what type of research is funded by the federal government. Public officials have reported using social science in drafting policies; psychological research was cited as the most influential of all these sciences (Frost & Ouellette, 2004).

While on the staff of the U.S. Senate, Trudy Vincent (1990) reported that the activities in which members of Congress engage are very similar to those of ecologically minded community psychologists. That is, legislators also need to pay careful attention to the people, settings, events, and history of their districts before establishing policy. Directly and indirectly, then, psychology can influence public policy.

Research in the service of public policy is not the only way to address social change. Community psychologists and community members can also **lobby** to change policy. Lobbying means to direct pressure at public officials to promote the passage of a particular piece of legislation or policy. Individuals wishing to influence policy can also disseminate appropriate pieces of information, such as public opinion polls and results of field research, to policy makers in an attempt to educate them (Homan, 2011). Education and information dissemination as a means of social change have already been discussed.

The average citizen hoping to influence legislation may find the process bewildering, whether it is at the local, state, or federal level. Fortunately, there are materials available to the average citizen that will take the mystery out of the legislative process (Homan, 2010). For example, the APA has created a Public Interest Directorate, the mission of which is to advance the scientific and professional aspects of psychology as applied to human welfare. The directorate disseminates reports and other written materials to state and federal governments and legislators. Similarly, the APA also developed a guide to advocacy in the public interest that includes sections on the legislative process and on effective means of communications with congressional staff.

A community psychologist or community member could also seek an elected office, work on the campaign of a particular candidate, or vote for a particular candidate supporting a favored social change program. Holding an important elected office may seem alien to some, but it is often the ideal role for a scientist. Why? The community scientist's training places him or her in the position to be able to demand evidence for proposed programs. Scientists also best know the importance of evaluating change mechanisms, such as new or experimental programs (Fairweather & Davidson, 1986).

Another role for politically active scientists is to act as expert witnesses and *amicus curiae* (friend of the court). A case of the *amicus curiae* role for psychologists in the courts was the use of sex stereotyping research by Susan Fiske in the *Price Waterhouse v. Hopkins* case heard and cited in the local, appellate, and U.S. Supreme Courts. The APA also filed an *amicus curiae* brief in the case. The testimony about the psychology of stereotyping played a crucial role at each court level as well as in the eventual vindication of the wronged female employee (Fiske, Bersoff, Borgida, Deaux, & Heilman, 1991). Community psychologists in these endeavors play a role in shaping case law and setting precedents on which other cases may be based (Jacobs, 1980; Perkins, 1988).

## Advantages and Disadvantages of Public Policy Changes

The advantage of using public policy efforts—including research, lobbying for or sponsoring a particular policy, and elections—is that sweeping social changes can often be induced, especially if the efforts of broad alliances are all aimed in the same direction. Another advantage is that the average U.S. citizen is known to have considerable respect for the law (Kohlberg, 1984; Lempert & Sanders, 1986), and some people may accept the change because it is the law.

Often, the real issues underlying social problems are economic and political rather than psychological, so the policy solution might be the most appropriate anyway (Nikelly, 1990; Wolff & Swift, 2008). Finally, policy makers often (but not always) have a broad perspective on the community that elected or appointed them and are likely to understand the interrelationships between seemingly segregated groups and isolated social problems. Therefore, solutions in the form of policy can take a broad-brush and long-term approach rather than a narrow or short-term focus, which is more likely to fail.

No method of social change is without problems, however, and policy science and public policy are not without theirs. For instance, much social science research is completed by academics operating in a "publish or perish" mode (Phares, 1991) to impress colleagues; the research is often not returned to the community for social change (Vera & Speight, 2003). Similarly, community researchers are often perceived as agents of a traditional system that has historically been oppressive and are consequently not perceived as guests or collaborators in the community (Robinson, 1990; Trimble, Scharrón-del Río, & Bernal, 2010). Therefore, research participation, results, and dissemination efforts are shunned, rendering the research useless.

Another serious problem with using public policy avenues to create social change is the electorate. Bond issues, school budgets, referenda, and other elections are participated in by a select few. Most voters are disproportionately well educated and older than the average citizen. Hence, the voices of the poor, young, and minorities are not heard via voting. This means that those who may most benefit from prosocial change are not participating in the direction of these changes (Hess, Markson, & Stein, 1991), which is a social justice problem, as was discussed in Chapter 1.

Perhaps the greatest disadvantage to using public policy efforts to create social change is that policy shaping can be a slow, cumbersome, politicized process. For instance, the average time span from initial writing to passage of a bill in Congress is about a year. However, less controversial policies pass more quickly. More complex or controversial issues take much longer. In the meantime, the needs of the affected groups may have changed; indeed, the group itself may have evaporated, or its needs may have become more severe so that the original policy solution is insufficient.

## A Skill Set for Practice

Community psychologists can go a long way toward bettering communities. Many community members, however, do not know how to approach them or exactly what they do. To that end, the Society for Community Research and Action (SCRA) of the APA proposed some crucial changes. In a report titled "Finding Work as a New Community Psychologist," the SCRA Practice Task Force (2007) recommended that community psychologists not depend on their title and rather describe what they can do.

By listing competencies, they do not have to deal with a definition, and they broaden their opportunities. These competencies could include:

Political advocacy

Assessment and evaluation

Capacity building for organizations

Collaboration and consultation skills

Communication within organizations and to the public

Report writing

An awareness and appreciation of cultural diversity

Knowledge of group processes

The ability to apply scientific knowledge

The ability to organize and supervise

An understanding of how to build and maintain a positive environment

Research skills

A veteran community psychology practitioner and member of this task force, Alan Ratcliffe (personal communication, January, 2008) stated that he never looked at the job title of what people were looking for. He would describe what he could do for a system, a community, or an organization. He found there to be demand for the skills he brought. Reflecting on a lifetime of working in the "real world," Tom Wolff stated that he knew of no applied community psychologist who worked as a "community psychologist" (Wolff & Swift, 2008).

As for a mind set for community interventions, Kofkin Rudkin (2003) has said it well. It is a matter of realizing the point between contradictions. Her admonitions regarding action in the community include:

- The situation is urgent, so take your time
- The outcome is critical, so don't worry about it
- The problems are huge, so think small
- Social change is complex, so keep it simple
- Social change is serious business, so have fun
- Social change requires staying on course, so relinquish control. (pp. 171–173)

## Summary

Many methods for creating and sustaining social change exist. Each has its own advantages and disadvantages. Activists hoping to fashion social change need to consider what strategies will work best for the issues they address. Some combination of strategies will probably work better than a single strategy, and what worked once might not work again or in a different community or for a different issue.

Planned change, such as grassroots activism and information dissemination, intentionally addresses and prepares the community for changes. The primary purpose of planned change should always be to improve the community. Each method of planned change has disadvantages and advantages. Methods available for induced change include citizen participation, networking with other community resources, the use of professional consultants, education or knowledge dissemination, and participation in public policy efforts by citizens and scientists.

In citizen participation, citizens produce the changes they desire by mechanisms such as grassroots activism, which is a type of bottom-up rather than top-down change. Such change results in empowerment, in which individuals feel they have control over their own lives.

When community agencies come together to aid one another, they are networking. Networking has been shown to directly assist in the longevity of community organizations. Sometimes umbrella organizations, such as the United Way, also provide services to community agencies or enhance their functioning, thus again ensuring their success.

Professional change agents or consultants can also help communities evolve. Community consultants need to be careful not to overtake the community but empower the community to create its own changes.

Education and information dissemination are still more means of producing social change. Although these methods sometimes produce vast changes, care must be taken to use the most appropriate information with sensitivity to the cultural diversity of the community.

Passing new legislation and policies or revamping existing laws and policies are other means of creating social change and are known collectively as public policy. Public policy changes can create sweeping social change, but often such policy is fraught with the politics of competing groups and can take time to fashion and implement.

Community practitioners find it useful to think of what skill sets they bring to social problems. The title of "community psychologist" may be unknown to many. This pragmatism and flexibility are good illustrations of what a community psychology should be.

# 6

# The Mental Health System

*In individuals insanity is rare, but in groups, parties, nations and epochs it is the rule.*

—Friedrich Wilhelm Nietzsche, *Beyond Good and Evil*

Min, age 25, was of Chinese descent and lived in the United States. Not only was she convinced that her psychiatrists did not understand her illness, she was also convinced that they did not understand her Chinese values.

Min had drifted in and out of a large state hospital because of what her doctors called schizophrenia. Each time she entered the hospital, she was given medication that eased her symptoms, particularly her hallucinations and the imaginary voices talking to her. When medicated, Min would develop better contact with those around her, take better care of her daily needs, and then be released from the hospital to her family's care. However, her two parents worked hard to support the family, which included Min's brother and sister. Her siblings were in school. Therefore, Min was alone much of the time. Because her family was not available to supervise her medications, she often forgot to take them. Eventually, she would become out of control, which would prompt the family to call the psychiatrist, who, after some pleading from the family for intervention, would tell them to return Min to the hospital.

Such was Min's state. She would leave the hospital only to return. She would take her medication and be briefly liberated from her symptoms only to forget the medication later. She is one of the country's chronically mentally ill who seem to be in desperate need of long-term, coordinated intervention but who are not necessarily receiving it.

This chapter examines the plight of Min and others like her. It will begin with some historical highlights and move to the issue of deinstitutionalizing the mentally ill. While examining deinstitutionalization, discussions focus on how to measure the success of moving individuals out of institutions as well as the common alternatives to institutionalization. Interestingly, many of the early alternatives have been tantamount to reinstitutionalization. Newer programs are coming into place. The question is whether they do what they have been intended to do. Can there be an effective tertiary prevention program, keeping patients out of institutions and reintegrating them successfully into the community? First we examine the question of how many people are like Min, that is, how many people in our community have to contend with mental health disorders.

## EPIDEMIOLOGICAL ESTIMATES OF MENTAL ILLNESS

In the early 1980s, the National Institute of Mental Health (NIMH) surveyed the psychiatric status of more than 20,000 people in five cities. This study, known as the **Epidemiologic Catchment Area (ECA) Study,** attempted to estimate and describe the incidence and prevalence of psychiatric disorders meeting the criteria of the *Diagnostic and Statistical Manual of Mental Disorders,* 3rd edition (DSM-III). For example, in a comparison of three communities, Robins and colleagues (1984) estimated that lifetime prevalence rate of a given DSM-III disorder was 28.8%, 38.8%, and 31.0%, respectively, in New Haven, Baltimore, and St. Louis. Note that there are variations in numbers, as we would expect different cities to have different characteristics. The researchers' intention is to gather data from enough sites in the United States so as to get a representative sample of rates from across the nation and come to some estimate of problem rates in the United States as a whole. Findings suggest that men and women are equally likely to be afflicted with psychiatric disorders. This study leads us to estimates of 1-year prevalence (having symptoms during the previous year) of anxiety disorders at 13%, of major depression at 6.5%, and schizophrenia at 1.3%. Nineteen percent of the sample is believed to have some psychiatric disorder. A second multiple site study sponsored by NIMH in the 1990s provides estimates based on the DSM-III Revised, a different set of criteria (Kessler et al., 1994). This study is called the National Comorbidity Study (NCS). The 1-year prevalence estimates for this study are anxiety disorder 18.7%, major depression 10%, any psychiatric disorder 23.4%. Lifetime prevalence for having a psychiatric disorder is 50%. However, 17% of the population has multiple diagnoses (comorbid), and the most severe cases have the highest concentration of disturbances. A third estimate of mental health epidemiology was conducted in 2000–2002. This study is called the National Comorbidity Study, Replication (NCS-R), and is based on the *Diagnostic Statistical Manual* IV criteria for psychiatric disorders. Results using these criteria yield an anxiety disorder percentage of 18% for 1-year prevalence, major depression prevalence of 6.7%, and any psychiatric disorder prevalence of 26.2% (Kessler, Chiu, Demler, & Walters, 2005). Again, a small proportion of the population has the worst symptomatology and multiple disorders. In both NCS reports, fewer than half of those with diagnosable disorders are in treatment.

Findings from the ECA, NCS, and NCS-R are consistent with the **Midtown Manhattan Study,** a longitudinal study investigating the prevalence of psychopathology from 1952 to 1960. Across several decades, from multiple sites, using a variety of measurement criteria, the findings seem consistent that mental health issues are a part of our communities. They are not a trivial part, because mental health issues should affect half of us sometime during our lifetime.

Also notably consistent over time, the most recent epidemiological study (Kessler et al., 2005) finds that the general practitioner MD has seen the highest rise in treatment demands. This is reminiscent of the findings by Gurin, Veroff, and Field (1960), who found similar reports of medical doctors being the people most likely to be consulted regarding psychological problems.

## MODELS OF MENTAL HEALTH AND MENTAL DISORDER

In answer to these mental health needs, psychology has traditionally responded by providing individual-focused clinical psychological services. As you may recall, the effectiveness of these services was called into question by Eysenck's (1952) meta-analytic study. We might make note of a more recent review of psychotherapy outcome studies that examined the variety of factors that affected outcome (Lambert & Barley, 2001). The specific therapeutic technique accounted for approximately 14% of the results, a small amount. What did seem to matter was the therapeutic relationship that developed between client and therapist. But we digress. The basic argument against the clinical orientation is that it is an inefficient and reactive model of treatment of well-entrenched psychological symptoms. This was discussed in Chapter 1. We elaborate on some of the treatment models here so as to better understand the traditional systems that are in place and the community applications that have, at times, evolved from them.

### The Medical Model

The standard and traditional model for care is the medical model. Based on the practice of medicine, the assumption is that the patient's illness is based on internally based dysfunctions. The patient is a passive recipient of knowledge from the expert physician, who provides the answer to the patient's problems. The patient obediently follows the advice and partakes of the medicine (a preparation or potion that will bring about a cure of the ailment or relief from the physical symptoms). The tradition has among its roots the Greek and Roman physicians who dealt with physical disorders. Both physical and mental health were the result of maintaining a balance. For the ancient Greek philosopher/physician Hippocrates, this was a balance among the four elements within us: phlegm, blood, black bile, and yellow bile. These traditions are believed to be traced to even older Egyptian and Mesopotamian beliefs.

Of course, modern medicine has come a long way from this elementary model. Yet the procedures are similar in some ways. The patient presents a set of symptoms. These are problems with the patient's physical functioning. Based on the presenting symptoms, there is a diagnosis of what is malfunctioning or out of balance. We might come to understand the etiology or origins and development of the disorder. Once the correct diagnosis is made, the appropriate medicine or therapy is prescribed to cure the problem. The next time you go to the doctor, note how the procedure works. He or she will ask what is troubling you, that is, the set of symptoms; then, based on the fit of symptoms to a set of criteria for the various illnesses, he or she will decide what is wrong. He or she will then make a set of recommendations for therapy (bed rest and fluids, or maybe decrease sugar or salt intake) and may prescribe certain medicines to be taken in a particular pattern so as to alleviate symptoms (e.g., fever, chills, low energy) or strengthen the system (increase level of antibiotics in the body) or cure the illness (correct the imbalance). The patient chooses when to come to the doctor. This is most likely when the patient has experienced enough disorder to make him or her believe that help is needed. Most clinical psychologists use this medical model of investigation of symptoms, diagnosis, and prescription of treatment and therapy.

Given the strength of the biological, or medical, model, two authoritative references about mental illness (*The Diagnostic and Statistical Manual of Mental Disorders* [**DSM**] and the *International Code of Diagnosis* [**ICD**]) have been developed. The medical model leaves at least two important legacies in traditional psychology. One is the reliance on diagnostic labels, as found in the DSM. The other legacy is the assumption of authority and power by the professional over the patient. Both of these legacies, though, are eschewed by community psychologists.

## The Psychoanalytic Model

**FREUD.**  To those of you who are psychology majors or have taken a course in abnormal, child, or personality psychology (or are fans of Woody Allen movies), Sigmund Freud (1856–1939) will be no stranger. Freud is the father of psychoanalysis. Although many people today disagree with his theories, it cannot be denied that Freud's influence is felt in psychology as well as in psychiatry. Although Freud believed that biology played an important role in the development of psyches, he argued that most psychological disorders are treatable or curable with the use of free association or verbal therapy. Psychoanalytic treatment takes the form of individual verbal therapy up to five times a week over several years.

Somewhat later, the psychoanalytic approach began to split into two paths: traditional psychoanalytic individual verbal therapy versus biological psychiatry. A German contemporary of Freud, Adolf Meyer (1866–1950), argued for the importance of the interplay among biology, psychology, and environment, but many others preferred only biology as an explanation for mental disorders, after a strict biological–medical model. The traditional psychoanalytic individual verbal therapy model has consistently failed to show its effectiveness with the severely mentally ill (Wilson, O'Leary, & Nathan, 1992).

**ADLER.**  Among the alternatives to Freud coming out of the early 20th century is Alfred Adler. He emphasized the individual's concern about powerlessness and the person's goal of seeking fulfillment in his or her life. Toward this end, Adler's work was directed at helping people gain this sense of empowerment over their situations. He is credited by some for the psychoeducational movement, which brought knowledge to the people so that they could use it for their lives.

His theory also included *Gemeinschaftsgefühl,* which translates into "community feeling" or what is typically called **social interest.** Social interest is the individual's sense of connection to the people around her. If there is high social interest, the individual feels a part of her family, her neighborhood, her community. If there is low social interest, the individual feels alienated from people and will act in her own self-interest without regard to the consequences for others.

Adler theorizes that these social feelings and our feelings about ourselves are heavily influenced by childhood experiences, so his theory also focused on childhood education. The emphasis in the teacher–child relationship is on encouragement of the child and his curiosity about the world.

As is surely notable from this description, the emphasis is on development of a healthy individual. Pathology is averted through provision of positive social environments that both empower and set appropriate normative limits on the individual. This is reminiscent of community psychology practices.

## The Behavioral Model: The Social-Learning Approach

As you may recall from an introductory psychology course, by using dogs as subjects, Russian physiologist Ivan Pavlov (1849–1936) was able to demonstrate that behavior could be formed as a result of **classical conditioning.** This is the process by which a response comes to be elicited by a stimulus, an object, or a situation other than what is the natural or normal stimulus. Pavlov repeatedly exposed his dogs to a **conditioned stimulus** in the form of a bell whenever the **unconditioned stimulus** in the form of meat powder was present. Although the **unconditioned response** or natural response for meat powder was salivation, eventually these dogs learned to display a **conditioned response** or learned response in the form of salivation *in the absence of* meat powder.

Dissatisfied with the psychoanalytic approach and rejecting the method of **introspection** or self-examination (a method advocated by Wilhelm Wundt, the father of experimental psychology), two U.S. psychologists, John B. Watson (1878–1985) and B. F. Skinner (1904–1990), further developed Pavlov's theory by using humans as subjects. Instead of pairing a conditioned stimulus with an unconditioned stimulus, Skinner developed and preferred the use of **operant conditioning,** in which behavior is more likely to be engaged in when it is **reinforced** or rewarded. Often, the reinforcers and the conditioned and unconditioned stimuli are provided by something external to the organism. Thus, in part, behavioral tradition provides one with a sense that ecology is important.

Extending the principles of learning theory, or the **behavioral model,** Martin Seligman (1975) argued that depression can be explained as a form of **learned helplessness,** or a lack of perceived control due to uncontrollable events in the environment. Other advocates of the social-learning approach, such as British psychiatrist Hans Eysenck, Sr., and U.S. psychologist Joseph Wolpe, have developed techniques such as **desensitization** or step-by-step relaxation training to change phobic or fearful behavior.

Generally speaking, the social-learning model is an effective treatment with many forms of mental distress. However, it is labor intensive because each behavioral treatment must be tailored to match the individual's needs. Moreover, to many critics, the social-learning approach appears to deal with the symptoms rather than the cause of mental distress. Finally, most community psychologists note that this model treats one individual at a time—not a very efficient way to manage change.

However, there have been several successful attempts at translating these learning principles into community analysis and action. Bogat and Jason (2000) review many of these programs, concluding that the behavioral principles provide added "technological tools" to a community psychologist's skill set. In particular, the use of behavioral techniques can provide the small successes on the path toward systems change.

## The Humanistic Model

The 1960s witnessed the growth and emphasis of the movement of human rights, such as the introduction of the Civil Rights Act in 1964. The movement of human rights had a profound impact on how mental health and mental disorders were perceived or defined. That is, to some mental health care experts and professionals, such as U.S. psychologists Abraham Maslow (1908–1970) and British psychiatrist R. D. Laing, maladjustment had more to do with **labeling,** or an individual being told he or she is not healthy or is sick, than with innate determinants. In other words, people sometimes behave in accord with what they are told. Thus, treatments should be designed to help these people understand and reflect on their unique feelings. In conjunction with this notion, U.S. psychologist Carl Rogers (1902–1987) developed **client-centered therapy,** in which the role of the therapist is to facilitate the client's reflection on his or her experiences. Note the word **client** in the previous sentence. To humanistic psychologists, clients are not sick and thus are not labeled **patients.**

Similar to the psychoanalytic model, the **humanistic model** emphasizes the use of verbal therapy. Unlike the psychoanalytic model, both individual and group verbal therapy are common to the humanistic model. However, the humanistic model suffers from some of the same criticisms as does the psychoanalysis theory. Faith, Wong, and Carpenter (1995) found that the effectiveness of a sensitivity training group (a form of humanistic group therapy) is not so much due to the fact that people gain a sense of self-worth but due to improved mental health as a function of social skills learned during therapy.

There are, however, at least two more major ideas derived from humanistic psychology that have been transplanted to the field of community psychology. One is that all people are worthy individuals and have the right to fulfill and discover this worth. The second is that the individual best knows him- or herself and thus needs to provide input on solutions to problematic issues. This directly feeds into community psychology's principle of empowerment and the philosophical justifications for participatory action research.

These models of mental health serve to direct psychotherapy and the field of clinical psychology. Yet there are clear connections that can and have been made between aspects of these models and community psychology principles and practices. The shift in theory and action in community psychology is to the social- and systems-level focus for interventions, as well as an appreciation of the wider ecological contexts that influence human behavior maintenance and change. The interplay of models fits well with community psychology's openness to multiple perspectives and the understanding of multiple levels required for change. It also belies the clinical and counseling psychology roots to some aspects of American community psychology. For example, the Swampscott meeting was a community mental health training conference. As well, there are clinical training backgrounds to many (but not all) of the founders of this area. Nonetheless, we should see the differences between the traditional hospital and office base of clinical psychology and the more broadly ranging community psychology.

## CASE IN POINT 6.1

# Mental Health Care Professionals

Various professional services are available to help people cope with stress. Many of the mental health care services are delivered by individuals from four major professional disciplines. **Psychiatrists** are medical doctors (MDs) who specialize in psychiatry. They can be employed in either the public (governmental) or private sector (such as private practice). In addition to their training, psychiatrists must pass a licensing examination before they can practice the discipline. Within the field, there are subspecialties, such as biological psychiatry and community psychiatry. The role of psychiatry is usually medication maintenance, although mental health patients who are financially capable can often

receive some form of therapy, such as psychoanalytic therapy, up to five times a week.

Many individuals who hold advanced degrees in any subfields of psychology consider themselves psychologists. **Clinical psychologists** are mental health care professionals who have advanced training (a doctoral degree) in clinical psychology. Their training includes exposure to more severe psychopathology and hospital settings. **Counseling psychologists** are required to hold a doctorate and go through practicum training. However, their focus is typically on issues related to normal development and vocational choice. Both are typically licensed at the state level as "psychologists." Similar

to psychiatrists, clinical and counseling psychologists can be employed in either the public or private sector, working privately or for an agency.

Unlike psychiatrists, in most states "psychologists" cannot prescribe medications. A pilot project in the U.S. military trained psychologists in limited use of medications directed at psychological disorders (Sammons & Brown, 1997). There are now a growing number of psychologists trained to provide these services within the U.S. states and territories, although only a few states provide licensure for limited prescription authority to them. This topic is not without controversy (Fox et al., 2009: Gutierrez & Silk, 1998; Lavoie & Barone, 2006; Sammons & Brown, 1997).

*(Continued)*

## CASE IN POINT 6.1

### *(Continued)*

These scenarios are complicated by several other factors. Sometimes, the terms **therapist** or **counselor** are used interchangeably with the terms *clinician* and *psychologist,* although not all clinicians, counselors, and therapists (such as those in social work and psychiatric nursing) have doctoral-level training in psychology. Community psychologists may not necessarily be clinical or counseling psychologists by training or be state licensed.

There are further distinctions within the doctoral-level training in the subfields of clinical or counseling psychology. Traditionally, clinical psychologists were trained using the **scientist–practitioner model.** Under this model, training objectives are to produce a person who is skilled in research/science and in doing therapy . These psychologists hold a doctor of philosophy (PhD), the highest degree in any scientific discipline (Benjamin & Baker, 2004; Farreras, 2005). Professional psychology now has a second model for training people as **practitioner–scholars**. Here the emphasis is on psychotherapy and assessment in practice and less on research. This leads to a different degree, that of doctor of psychology (PsyD) (Murray, 2000).

A third group of mental health care professionals called **social workers** help clients find and access services in the community but also may provide treatment. They usually hold a degree called a master's of social work (MSW). Unlike psychiatrists, they cannot prescribe medication. Similar to psychiatrists and psychologists, social workers can be employed in either the public or private sector. The primary role of a social worker is as a practitioner.

What psychiatrists, psychologists, and social workers have in common is that they treat *individuals* who are experiencing stress. Note that typically these three groups of mental health providers focus on individual functioning. Another common feature is that all of these caregivers operate from a position of authority regarding their clients.

A final and important issue related to these mental health care providers is the one of health insurance or third-party payments. Health insurance companies act as third parties who pay the mental health care provider, whether that professional is a psychiatrist, psychologist, or social worker, for the treatment of the client or person covered by the insurance. In most states within the United States, these three professional groups are licensed and may be covered by insurance.

A growing number of states regulate master's-level counselors (through registration or licensure) and thus allow third-party payments to them as well.

As of 2008, with the passage of the Mental Health Parity Act, levels of insurance coverage for physical and mental health are supposed to be equal. The details are just beginning to being worked out. There appears to be a somewhat disconcerting trend for insurance companies to reduce their payment costs by using providers who charge less (for example, the psychiatric nurses, counselors, and social workers). Community activists need to stay vigilant— for example, by conducting research to ascertain whether there is a relationship between the success of treatment and the cost of the treatment.

Community psychologists, who sit outside most of these insurance issues and professional boundary disputes, believe that an "ounce of prevention is worth a pound of cure" and that prevention is by far the most cost-effective intervention of all. Understanding the causes and progression of psychopathology, encouraging community support systems, and providing mental health education could go a long way toward preventing the need for treatment and health insurance coverage all together.

Acknowledging the need for prevention and other radical shifts in mental health thinking, Kazdin and Blasé (2011a, 2011b) called for a rethinking of the field of clinical psychology.

## THE EVOLUTION OF THE MENTAL HEALTH SYSTEM

### Brief History of Mental Health Care

Although the ancient world has always been portrayed as less than civilized, some older cultures gave more emphasis to the study of mental health than others. For example, to most Chinese (ancient and modern), physical and psychological well-being is thought to depend on a balance of two natural forces:

**yin,** the female force, and **yang,** the male force. Furthermore, these two forces are thought to regulate the five elements—gold, wood, water, fire, and earth—that are responsible for people's daily health. Among other things, the concentration of each element is thought to vary with the type of food group. Thus, a proper diet and regular exercise are important to maintain a balance between these elements.

According to Chinese folklore, a wise king named Sun Lone Tse, whose name meant "to cultivate," in ancient times (circa 600–700 B.C.) was thought to be responsible for the first classification system of herbs used in medicine. Also, Chinese historical texts mention a doctor named Wah Torr as the father of Chinese medicine. On one occasion, he performed minor surgery on a general's arm using **acupuncture** as anesthetic. Needles were used to stick into the **meridians** (pressure points) to facilitate the release of **endorphins** (natural pain relievers) in the brain. Wah Torr wrote many medical texts. These concepts relating mind and body are important to the fields of clinical psychology and behavioral medicine, sister disciplines to the field of community psychology. If Min were in ancient China or even modern-day China, the treatments for her disorder might be different from what they are in the United States.

As one moves through history, one notices that the ancient Greeks are also important. Hippocrates (circa 460–377 B.C.), known as the father of Western medicine, spoke about four natural **humors,** or fluids, that were thought to regulate people's mental health. Specifically, great fluctuations in mood were thought to be caused by an excess of blood. Fatigue was caused by an excess of phlegm or thick mucus. Anxiety was from an excess of yellow bile or liver fluid. Finally, depression was brought on by an excess of black bile.

Whatever medical and psychological advances in theory and practice were achieved by the ancient Chinese, Greeks, and later the Romans, the majority of their contemporaries relied on the supernatural to explain mental illness. After the collapse of the Roman Empire in Europe (in 476 A.D.), supernatural or religious beliefs became model for explaining mental illness in Western society. For example, according to the church and those in power in many Western societies, the mentally ill and other disenfranchised people were thought to be sinners. Religious zealotry reached its peak in the 1480s, when Pope Innocent VIII officially sanctioned the persecution of witches, some of whom were actually suffering from mental illness; many others were just political or social dissenters within the mainstream cultures. This period of almost 900 years in Western societies has come to be associated with the infamous name the Dark Ages.

In many Western societies during the Renaissance (revival) period (circa 1300–1600), the idea of **humanism** developed. Humanism proposed that we should focus on human concerns (possibly as the result of rediscovery and interest in Greek and Roman works). The mentally ill gained indirect benefits from the notion that all people had certain inalienable rights and should be treated with dignity. Furthermore, some doctors began to challenge the concept that mental illness was a defect of moral character. By the middle of the 1600s, institutions known as **asylums,** or madhouses, were established to contain the mentally ill. Perhaps the most famous was London's Bethlehem Hospital, nicknamed "Bedlam," which is now a word meaning chaos and confusion. The first asylum in the United States was established in the late 1700s. Asylums were places where the socially undesirable or misfits were kept. More often than not, residents of the asylums were chained.

The further development of humanism during the American (1776) and French (1789) revolutions provided more incentives to the mental health care reform movement throughout the European continent and in the United States. For example, two pioneers were instrumental in the movement in this country. Benjamin Rush (1745–1813), known as the father of American psychiatry, wrote the first treatise on psychiatry and established its first academic course. The second person was Dorothea Dix (1802–1887), whose experience with mental health care was derived from her teaching of women inmates. During her day, it was not unusual for the mentally ill to be kept in prisons. Dix traveled extensively in the country to raise money to build mental hospitals.

The mental health care reform movement further benefited from the pioneer work of several doctors who devoted their lives to the development of scientific **nomenclatures,** or classifications, of mental illness. These classifications eventually led to the study of the **etiology,** or cause, of mental illness. It was probably a French doctor named Philippe Pinel (1745–1826) who first used the term **dementia** to describe a form of psychosis that was characterized by deterioration of judgment, memory loss, and personality change. A German doctor, Emil Kraepelin (1956–1926), further studied this condition and described it using the term **dementia praecox** (premature dementia). Subsequently, Swiss doctor Eugen Bleuler (1857–1930) gave the same disorder the name **schizophrenia,** which has become a household term in today's psychiatric practice. Also, Bleuler extended previous work by describing several subtypes of this illness.

Meanwhile, the **germ theory,** as advocated by Frenchman Louis Pasteur, had gained unprecedented recognition in the medical and scientific community. That is, many illnesses were thought to be caused by germ infections. Thus, the development of psychiatry as a field was destined to take on a medical or biological tone. In other words, under the influence of germ theory, mental illness was conceptualized as a *disease* rather than a *disorder* or psychological dysfunction.

At about the same time, the American Psychiatric Association and the American Psychological Association were formed in 1844 and 1892, respectively. Although the original mission of the American Psychological Association was not specifically concerned with issues relating to mental health and mental illness, as the subdiscipline of clinical psychology became more dominant, these issues became a priority. This shift in emphasis no doubt does not sit well with the American Psychiatric Association, which has seen itself as the sole guide in the field of mental health and mental illness since its inception. Over the years, these professional conflicts have been further complicated by a number of other factors, including the emergence of social work as a professional field.

After the work of Rush and Dix, mental health care reform in this country can be roughly divided into three more eras: 1875–1940, 1940–1970, and 1970 to the present (Grob, 1991; Shadish, Lurigio, & Lewis, 1989). During the period from 1875 to 1940, the government assumed the major responsibility in caring for the mentally ill. Two-thirds of all the patients were living in state-run psychiatric hospitals. In many ways, this system was an extension of Dix's thesis of moral management. More often than not, these patients received little treatment.

Meanwhile, there were a small number of privately owned psychiatric hospitals, such as the Menninger Foundation and the Institute of Living, providing services or treatments to those who could afford them. Although these services or treatments may be crude by today's standards, they contributed to the development of **community psychiatry,** a subdiscipline of psychiatry that argues that mental patients should be treated using the least restrictive method in the least restrictive environment. Many of these private mental patients lived in small, comfortable units, and they were encouraged to take lessons in cooking, sewing, and other self-improvement skills.

In the 1940–1970s phase, the initial optimism associated with moral management began diminishing in society. In almost all instances, psychiatric hospitals were no more than human warehouses. If treatments were provided, they tended to be **electroconvulsive therapy,** or electric shock to the brain, and **lobotomy,** or brain surgery. Furthermore, the cost associated with these hospitals had become a major strain on society, especially during the Great Depression and World War II. There were concerns that hospitalization itself brought certain self-fulfilling expectations to bear on the patient. This stigmatization was demonstrated in the Rosenhan study of the 1970s (see Case in Point 6.2).

As noted in Chapter 1, beginning in the 1960s, the **zeitgeist,** or atmosphere, of the society began to change. For example, the introduction of **psychotropic drugs** (mood-altering drugs) such as Thorazine (chlorpromazine) rekindled the idea that the mentally ill could be treated with dignity.

## Rosenhan's Classic Study of Hospital Patients' Stigmatization

Researcher D. L. Rosenhan was especially interested in whether mental health professionals (particularly psychiatrists) could tell genuine mental disorders or problems from false ones. He decided to conduct a study. First, Rosenhan (1973) trained his graduate students and others in how to fake symptoms of psychiatric disorders. For example, he instructed the pseudo-patients to tell hospital staff that they heard a thudding sound or a voice saying "thud." Rosenhan then sent his pseudo-patients to a psychiatric emergency facility.

To Rosenhan's amazement, the students were admitted. Soon after their admission to the psychiatric ward, the pseudo-patients were each given diagnoses.

Not long after their admission, the pseudo-patients began to act "normal." Curiously, many of the other patients realized that the pseudo-patients were normal. The staff did not recognize this normalcy partly because they rarely saw it. According to Rosenhan's report, the staff did not spend much time with the patients.

The pseudo-patients began to request release from the psychiatric ward. However, the staff consistently told the students that they were not well enough to be released. Eventually, Rosenhan had to intervene so that some of the pseudo-patients could be released. However, on release, many were labeled *schizophrenia in remission*. The pseudo-patients were kept in the hospital from 7 to 52 days, with an average stay of 19 days.

Without minimizing the agony associated with mental disorders, Rosenhan demonstrated that many perceived disorders are due to the process of labeling. Although some mental health professionals might argue otherwise, Rosenhan demonstrated that once labeled, it is difficult to overcome the label and the expectations and behavioral interpretations that go with it.

In the 1970s, community psychiatry, coupled with the use of medication, once again shifted approaches to the mentally ill. Many of the mentally ill were discharged back into their communities. In this chapter's opening vignette, medications successfully allowed Min to return to her family. When she went off the medication, her problems resurfaced. A consequence was the development of **outpatient treatment,** or nonhospitalized treatment (e.g., community mental health centers), as opposed to **inpatient treatment,** or hospitalized treatment. Also, to accommodate these newly released inpatients, alternative housing such as **community residences,** or group homes, was established—but not without controversy. We now examine the deinstitutionalization of the 1960s and 1970s and the efforts to deal with its implications.

### Deinstitutionalization

**Deinstitutionalization** is defined by efforts to release mental patients back into the community. Recall that Min was institutionalized and sent back to her community—in fact, she was repeatedly released and returned to the hospital (**recidivism**). There is a great deal of controversy about what exactly *deinstitutionalization* is (Grob, 1991; Shadish et al., 1989). A deeper examination of some of these definitions and related issues is in order. John Talbott (1975) argued that the term *deinstitutionalization* is a misnomer. Instead, a better term is **trans-institutionalization** to describe "the chronically mentally ill patient who has his or her locus of living and care transferred from a single lousy institution to multiple wretched ones" (p. 530). Mathew Dumont (1982), another psychiatrist, argued that "deinstitutionalization is nothing more or less than a polite term for the cutting of mental health budgets" (p. 368). Min presents a picture of this phenomenon. She is in and out of institutions, living with her family between institutionalizations.

By the late 1970s and early 1980s, the effects of deinstitutionalization were starting to be realized. The *New York Times* defined *deinstitutionalization* as "moving mental patients from enormous, remote hospitals into small community residences" ("Willowbrook Plan Worked," 1982). Another *New York Times* editorial stated that deinstitutionalization was nothing more than "dumping mental patients out of state hospitals onto local communities, with promises of community treatment that never came true." *Deinstitutionalization* was synonymous with *homelessness* ("Redeinstitutionalization," 1986, p. A24).

Indeed, these definitions illustrate the many different aspects of deinstitutionalization. Reconciling these differences, some mental health care experts (Bachrach, 1989; Rein & Schon, 1977; Shadish et al., 1989) proposed that the term *deinstitutionalization* be understood as a semantic mechanism to frame the complex, often conflicting, and seemingly unrelated sets of issues associated with ongoing mental health care reform. More often than not, the concrete aspects of deinstitutionalization, such as budget constraints, were the impetus behind mental health care reform.

Policy is likely to be the product of practical concern or ideology (Grob, 1991; Kiesler, 1992; Warner, 1989). However, a growing number of mental health care professionals are arguing that society must look beyond the immediate practical concern to develop plans that can anticipate *long-term* consequences. For example, one concern is the growing number of the homeless mentally ill who also have human immunodeficiency virus (HIV) or acquired immunodeficiency syndrome (AIDS). According to a survey conducted in a New York City shelter that housed homeless men, Susser, Valencia, and Conover (1993) found that 12 of 62 (19.4%) of the mentally ill men tested positive for HIV. The severely mentally ill may suffer the triple strikes of mental illness, drug use, and dangerous sexual practices (Dévieux et al., 2007).

What can a society do to anticipate some of these long-term mental health care consequences? To that end, Bachrach (1989) provided meaningful definition of *deinstitutionalization* as

> the shunning or avoidance of traditional institutional settings, particularly state mental hospitals, for chronic mentally ill individuals, and the concurrent development of community-based alternatives for the care of this population. *This definition assumes three primary processes:* depopulation—*the shrinking of state hospital censuses through release, transfer, or death;* diversion—*the deflection of potential institutional admissions to community-based service settings;* and decentralization—*the broadening of responsibility for patient care from a single physically discrete service entity to multiple and diverse entities, with an attendant fragmentation of authority.* (p. 165)

According to Bachrach (1989), this definition of *deinstitutionalization* underscores three related elements: facts, process, and philosophy. That is, sound mental health care policy must be based on credible research or evidence (the facts). To plan for long-term goals, one must know the characteristics of the mentally ill and the resources or systems where they receive their services (process). Historical events and philosophical ideology often determine the direction of mental health care movements (philosophy).

## The Social Context to Deinstitutionalization

What were some of the anticipated and unanticipated issues or deinstitutionalization? In the 1960s, Americans were optimistic about their ability to overcome problems. Indeed, President John F. Kennedy was asking middle-class Americans to give to the less fortunate. Programs were established, such as Project Head Start (including free meals for schoolchildren from low-income families) and the Peace Corps (e.g., teaching people in developing countries about family planning, and building new resources in communities around the world).

Mental health benefited from these efforts, as well as from the advances in medication that brought many symptoms under control. Psychotropic drugs such as Elavil (amitriptyline chloride) and Thorazine controlled the more visible symptoms of schizophrenia. Thus, professionals had more reason to use the least restrictive methods for treating the mentally ill.

This optimism was fueled by negative reports from both professional (Thomas Szasz's [1961] *The Myth of Mental Illness*) and popular writers (Ken Kesey's *One Flew over the Cuckoo's Nest*). People in the legal profession also took up the cause—for example, the American Civil Liberties Union initiated the Mental Health Law Project. A common theme in these writings and legal efforts was opposition to involuntary hospitalization (Torrey, 1997).

However, some mental health care experts (Kiernan, Toro, Rappaport, & Seidman, 1989; Warner, 1989) believed that no matter how admirable and persuasive the philosophical and value-based decisions regarding wide-scale release from hospitals, the more pragmatic explanation to account for deinstitutionalization was **economic**. Investigating deinstitutionalization in various Western countries in the past 30 years, Warner (1989) found that

> the process was stimulated by the opportunity for cost savings created by the introduction of disability pensions and, in some countries, by postwar demand for labor. Where labor was in short supply, genuinely rehabilitative programs were developed. Where cost saving was the principal motivation, community treatment efforts were weak. (p. 17)

Also, Kiernan and colleagues (1989) found that employment was negatively related to both first admissions to state hospitals and case openings in community outpatient facilities. When the economy was good, fewer people had mental problems or were admitted into state psychiatric hospitals.

After World War II, the world economy had been relatively good until the 1970s. The argument that deinstitutionalization is associated with economic stability appears to be consistent with the number of psychiatric hospital beds per 10,000 individuals in the Western industrialized countries. As long as there was a demand for a labor force, more people were deinstitutionalized.

Whether or not one agrees with this interpretation, deinstitutionalization has significant economic impact. The federal budget for care of the mentally ill has continued to rise. States have little financial incentive to provide comparable assistance because significant sources of this care are in the form of Supplemental Security Income, food stamps, Medicaid, Medicare, and so on. This imbalance between federal and state resources directed to the care of the mentally ill has created havoc (Torrey, 1997). Indeed, in a critical analysis of factors associated with deinstitutionalization, Brooks, Zuniga, and Penn (1995) found that financial burden is the principal determinant in this process. These researchers argued that "faced with the increasing costs associated with replacing or upgrading an aging system . . . most changes in services have been the outcome of budget, not medical, decisions, with medical or legal rationalizations applied post hoc or in parallel" (pp. 55–56).

Although these findings appear to explain the reasoning behind deinstitutionalization, they do not adequately account for its falling short of its goal to enhance the quality of life of the mentally disordered. Community psychologists and mental health care experts (Cheung, 1988; Earls & Nelson, 1988; Lovell, 1990; Mowbray, 1990; Mowbray, Herman, & Hazel, 1992; Struening & Padgett, 1990) have argued that sociological factors (such as adequate housing) and psychological factors (such as stigmatization) often hinder the progress of deinstitutionalization. Case in Point 6.2 discussed interesting research on stigmatization—research in which institutionalized patients faked their disorders.

Use of mental health facilities is related to personal poverty. Bruce, Takeuchi, and Leaf (1991) demonstrated a causal link between mental disorder and poverty. They examined the patterns of new disorders that developed over a six-month period in an epidemiological study. Their sample included African Americans, Hispanics, and Whites. The researchers found that a significant proportion of new episodes of mental disorder could be attributed to poverty. In addition, Bruce and associates found that the risk for developing disorders was equal for men and women and for African Americans and Whites— in other words, poverty does not discriminate on the basis of race or gender.

Many people with mental disorders are discharged from hospitals into the community without adequate planning or support systems. For example, Mowbray (1990) argued that many of those discharged did not have adequate living or social skills (e.g., cooking and paying bills) to survive in an unstructured environment. For deinstitutionalization to be effective, adequate and appropriate treatments must be in place (Mowbray & Moxley, 2000). Struening and Padgett (1990) found that homeless adults in New York City had high rates of alcohol and drug abuse as well as mental illness. It is not unlikely that a large portion of these people were mental patients who were discharged from hospitals without adequate planning. Thus, they became homeless and had alcohol and drug-abuse problems (Levine & Huebner, 1991; Susser, Valencia, et al., 1993). Meanwhile, a majority of the mentally disordered are continuously being discharged from hospitals into nursing homes or board-and-care homes that are ill prepared to provide the services these patients need.

A 2006 U.S. Department of Justice report states that 56% of state prisoners, 45% of federal prisoners, and 64% of local jail prisoners have a history of mental disorder (James & Glaze, 2006). Those with mental disorder histories were more likely to be young, female, and White. They are more likely to be violent. In state courts, they are more likely to receive longer sentences. According to Harcourt (2007), within the United States more than 2 million people are imprisoned. This is 5 times Great Britain's rate and 12 times Japan's rate, making for the highest number and rate of prisoners in the world. The point of this is that the idea that deinstitutionalization from hospitals has saved money is very incorrect. The mental patients have not been deinstitutionalized but rather reinstitutionalized in a different setting.

In a study of what happens to the chronically mentally disordered, Diamond and Schnee (1990) tracked 21 men who were perceived to be most at risk for potential violence and were also high users of jails. The men were tracked for two and a half years through various service systems. The men used up to 11 different systems, including the mental health, criminal justice, healthcare, and social services systems. Criminal justice services were the most frequently used, and mental health services were usually only short-term, crisis care services, although some of the men had been hospitalized for long-term psychiatric care. Diamond and Schnee believe that their figure is an *underestimate* and calculated that the cost of care of the 21 men in all service systems totaled $694,291. That figure does not include costs to victims, nor property damaged in the men's violent episodes. The researchers called for a more coordinated effort of the various systems to better assist the men and to reduce costs.

Belcher (1988) suggested that when people with mental disorders are released from hospitals or institutions, they are often unable or unwilling to follow through on their own aftercare. This situation increases the likelihood that these individuals will become involved in the criminal justice system. In addition, because the legal system and the mental health systems view mental disorders differently (Freeman & Roesch, 1989), the mentally disordered are not afforded the same level of therapeutic services for their disorder when they are incarcerated. The legal system narrowly deals with mental illness only as incompetence to testify in one's own behalf or as insanity, which is a defense against guilt.

The U.S. Department of Justice reports that about a third of state prisoners, a quarter of federal prisoners, and 17% of local jail prisoners receive some kind of mental health treatment while they are incarcerated (James & Glaze, 2006). Although hospitalization is very rare, use of medications is most popular.

The solution may be that mental health, criminal justice, and other professionals *need to collaborate in innovative and integrative ways* to prevent the mentally ill from being incarcerated in a correctional facility and to treat their disorders when they are incarcerated (Diamond & Schnee, 1990). Another alternative is to provide treatment and community support for these mentally ill individuals that is strong enough to forestall their ever getting involved in the criminal justice system. Heller, Jenkins, Steffen, and Swindle (2000) argue that the deinstitutionalization of the 1960s has come full circle. They believe the dream of community-based mental health treatment with community-based prevention programs has never been realized. Among the factors they cite for the problems in implementing the vision are a lack of understanding of what would be required for medication maintenance programs, a disregard of natural communities and neighborhoods in setting up program boundaries, and professional resistance to anything other than traditional treatment programs for patients. Heller, Jenkins, et al. (2000) cite the reduction in community support program funding occurred at the same time the economy took a downturn, leaving many of the mentally ill to become homeless.

Seidman and Rappaport (1986) believe that in searching for solutions, we are hampered by a tendency to overgeneralize conclusions regarding a group of people based on extreme examples from that group. Social psychology would add that this tendency to overgeneralize regarding negative aspects of a group is related to our feeling distant from that group, that is, they are considered members of an outgroup (Allport, 1954/1979; McConnell, Rydell, & Strain, 2008). For example, after finding one case of an ethnic minority mother on welfare driving a new Cadillac, people may tend to believe all welfare recipients are members of ethnic minorities who abuse the system. In reality, most of those on welfare are not abusive and are White. Those who have severe mental illness deal with this problem as well. People's preconceptions of mental illness cannot help but influence how they think, feel and act. The **stigma** of mental illness remains and can be found in our communities (Mowbray, 1999; Perry, 2011; Wahl, 2012) and our places of higher education (Collins & Mowbray, 2005).

## Early Alternatives to Institutionalization

The ideal setting for the institutionalized individual would be one that enhances his or her well-being because of the optimal fit between his or her competencies and the support provided in the environment. In reality, many community placements are based as much on what is available and on economics as on the individual's competencies (Mowbray & Moxley, 2000).

If not in institutions, where were the people who with mental disorders placed? They went to nursing homes and home care placements. They were discharged with little community planning and minimal financial support.

Today, they could still be found in a variety of settings, but most often in **unsupervised sites**, that is, on their own (Figure 6.1) Otherwise, the typical community placements have been with **their families**, in **nursing homes** and **halfway houses** (Kooyman & Walsh, 2011). Their care has been typically paid for by Supplemental Security Income (disability checks). As funding for these options dwindled, so did the space for these former clients (Heller, Jenkins, et al., 2000). They have been overrepresented in prisons and among the homeless.

This fragmentation of care and the supposed economization of services implied that society has essentially moved from a mental health system to a welfare system (Kennedy, 1989). The original vision was for a community mental health system that provided "prevention programming, reaching underserved populations, fostering community awareness of social and environmental determinants of psychological dysfunction and consultation to community caregivers to encourage the development of indigenous helping networks" (Heller et al., 2000, p. 446). This vision was never realized.

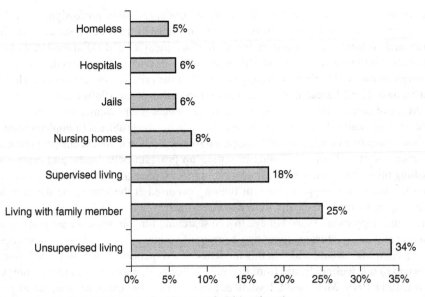

**FIGURE 6.1**   Community Living Situations for Those with Schizophrenia

*Source:* Kooyman, I., & Walsh, E. (2011). Societal outcomes in schizophrenia. In D. Weinberger & P. Harrison (Eds.), *Schizophrenia,* 3rd ed. Hoboken, NJ: John Wiley, pp. 644–665.

## Measuring "Success" of Deinstitutionalized Persons

Many in the mental health field would quickly jump to the conclusion that deinstitutionalization has not been successful. We have reviewed some of the myriad problems that deinstitutionalization has created, including but not limited to trans-institutionalization, homelessness, and jails. How is successful integration into the community measured? The answer depends on whom you ask and what issues you discuss.

Society needs to take a closer look at the measurement of success of deinstitutionalization. Table 6.1 shows the names of famous people who at one time or another experienced mental impairment and were also able to integrate successfully into society.

The typical measures of success are social integration and recidivism. **Social integration** was defined in the last chapter as people's involvement with community institutions as well as their participation in the community's informal social life (Gottlieb, 1981). **Recidivism** means relapse or return to the institution or care—in this case, return to the psychiatric hospital. However, both of these terms

**TABLE 6.1   Famous Individuals with Some Form of Mental Disorder**

| Person | Field | Mental Disorder |
|---|---|---|
| Kim Basinger | Actress | Anxiety disorder |
| Catherine Zeta-Jones | Actress | Bipolar disorder |
| J. K. Rowling | Author—Harry Potter | Depression |
| Abraham Lincoln | 16th American president | Depression |
| John Ford Nash | Mathematician/Nobel prize winner | Schizophrenia |
| Johnny Depp | Actor | Anxiety disorder |

imply limited criteria. Recent efforts in the literature of the field of community psychology indicate that measurement of success is a more complex issue.

For example, Shadish, Thomas, and Bootzin (1982) found that different groups use different criteria for success. Residents, staff, and family members of community care facilities often express that the quality of life (e.g., a clean place to live and something to do) ought to serve as a measure of success. On the other hand, federal officials and academicians cite psychosocial functioning (e.g., social integration and reduction of symptomatology) as good measures of success of community placement.

A Community Competence Scale has been devised to assess deinstitutionalized patients' basic living skills (Searight & Goldberg, 1991; Searight, Oliver, & Grisso, 1986). The questions assess an individual's ability to make judgments related to nutrition and dealing with emergencies, to communicate with others, and to perform simple math and verbal tasks. In their research, Searight and associates found that the scale discriminated effectively between client groups requiring differing levels of guidance in the community.

A very different but also very prominent measure of success for deinstitutionalization is the economic one (Brooks et al., 1995). Arguments for programs are still based on cost efficiencies. Unfortunately, these costs are frequently based on short-term budgeting, without regard to potential long-term savings.

## BEYOND DEINSTITUTIONALIZATION

Certainly, the preceding scenarios do not reflect the optimism when deinstitutionalization began in the late 1960s. It was thought then that the introduction of the **Community Mental Health Act** could "reduce the census of state hospitals and . . . provide treatment to maintain psychiatric patients in the community" (Levine, Toro, & Perkins, 1993, p. 526). Now, with hindsight, it seems obvious that one reason for the existing "patchwork" system is poor coordination and a lack of systematic planning. Heller, Jenkins, and colleagues (2000) would add that problems included "deeply entrenched attitudes and practices" (p. 448), professional resistance, and a general ignoring of local support and/or fears.

### "Model" Programs for Individuals with Mental Disorders

Emerging from the deinstitutionalization movement are several model programs that may be examined for their community psychology properties. These programs range from empowering participatory communities for the severely mentally ill (SMI), to intensive and comprehensive focus on management of each individual case of community-based SMI, to a team effort to provide the multiple levels and multiple areas of services needed for adult SMI or for youth. These are all tertiary prevention efforts, which reflect some of the basic community psychology concepts of respect for the diversity of individuals who need services, the empowerment of individuals or their family systems to deal with problems, and the recognition of multiple levels of intervention required to adequately address the full ecology of mental health needs. Last, for those who continue to require institutional care, we review an effort to shift the social and environmental contexts within the institutions. A program to "reduce the use of restraints" takes an approach to change the physical environments and the social and professional assumptions related to patients and their care, so as to shift the need for restraints in the institutional environment. We begin with an examination of one of the earlier studies of providing an alternative, community-based environment to SMI, the Lodge Society.

**LODGE SOCIETY.**   It is sad to note that community psychologists and mental health care experts know more about what does *not* work rather than what *does* work with people who are mentally disordered. However, coupled with the knowledge gained from pioneer programs such as the **Lodge Society** (Fairweather, 1980; Fairweather, Sanders, Maynard, & Cressler, 1969) and epidemiological investigations, some innovative psychosocial rehabilitation models (Bond, Miller, & Krumweid, 1988; Bond, Witheridge, Dincin, & Wasmer, 1991; Bond et al., 1990; Olfson, 1990) have been developed for treating people with mental disorders. Fairweather's concept of lodge societies encompassed structured *halfway houses* or group homes for the mentally disabled that emphasized *skill building* and *shared responsibility* as well as *decision making*. The concept of empowerment was clearly a central part of his program (Fairweather & Fergus, 1993). Groups of four to eight people would come together around a common business venture, working for **"individual accomplishments"** in a **supportive group setting**. The long-standing effectiveness of the model and its derivatives serves to demonstrate the workable nature of such community interventions. The Coalition for Community Living (http://theccl.org) reported that as of 2012, there were 90 Lodge programs sited across the United States. A study of 25 of these programs in 2007 showed residents' medication compliance rate (staying on their medications) to average 99% and rehospitalization rates to be at 60%.

## Intensive Case Management

Common to the newer models is the use of **intensive case management (ICM),** or intensive case support, including instruction in daily living skills (e.g., cooking and paying bills). Service delivery linking both monitoring and brokering of delivery of a variety of services performed by the case manager is also advocated (Snowden, 1992). In other words, a case manager (usually a social worker) works *closely* with former mental patients, possibly being on call 24 hours a day for any emergency that might arise. Also, case management can easily be integrated into **residential** or outpatient treatments.

It is thought that intensive social support in the form of case management should mitigate recidivism or relapse. Compared to traditional treatments (e.g., outpatient), case management is labor intensive. However, research indicates that case management "repeatedly has been shown to reduce both hospital use and costs across a number of different studies performed in different communities . . . although other desirable effects (e.g., symptom reduction, improved social relationships, . . .) have been less than robust" (Levine et al., 1993, p. 529). These findings are understandable, given the complex nature of mental disorder. As you may recall, even when housing is not a problem, improved social relationships are contingent on many different people—the patient being just one of the many. In examining who most benefits from this form of intervention, a British study of people who were severely mentally ill found that reductions in hospital care were significant for heavy care users. This reduction in use was not found for patients who were did not frequently need hospitalization (Burns et al., 2007).

Nelson, Aubrey, and Lafrance (2007) differentiate ICM from assertive community treatment in that ICM does not employ a team approach. The individual receives close supervision and help in accomplishing the tasks necessary to survive in normal life, but there is not the interdisciplinary perspective that the assertive community treatment approach brings.

**ASSERTIVE COMMUNITY TREATMENT.** One especially powerful variation on the case management model is **assertive community treatment (ACT),** known variously as *mobile treatment teams* and *assertive case management*. It is designed "to improve the community functioning of clients with serious and persistent mental illness, thereby diminishing their dependence on inpatient care while improving the quality of life" (Bond et al., 1990, p. 866). ACT focuses on teaching practical living skills, such as how to shop for groceries and maintain finances. A multidisciplinary team of professionals provides group case management, lending their various expertise and resources to the conceptualization of the case needs and to the interventions called into play. ACT ensures attention to medications, service planning, and coordination, as well as assessment and evaluations. Assertive community treatment uses a low staff–client ratio—approximately 10:1. Moreover, clients do not visit staff offices, but rather, staff visit clients in vivo—that is, in their own environments. Mowbray (1990) viewed assertive community treatment as an embodiment of several community psychology principles:

**Ecological** frameworks for conceptualizing cases

A **systems** level approach to intervention

Working toward integration of **multiple levels** of service

Working for **prevention** of pathology in the client population

**Advocacy** for an underprivileged population

**Promotion of competencies** in the targeted population

In Madison, Wisconsin, Stein and Test (1985) developed one of the first ACT programs in the United States. Wanting more research on ACT, Bond and colleagues (1990) compared ACT clients to clients at a drop-in center. Drop-in centers usually provide an informal meeting place for clients who typically are formerly institutionalized mental patients. These centers offer a range of social and recreational programs in a self-help atmosphere. In sharp contrast to ACT, drop-in centers have a central meeting place, a higher client–staff ratio, and no requirement for frequent staff contact.

Bond and associates (1990) found overall that after one year, 76% of the ACT clients were still involved in ACT, whereas only 7% of the drop-in clients were involved in their programs. The ACT staff team averaged only two home and community visits per week per client, but their clients averaged significantly fewer state hospital admissions and fewer days per hospital stay. The researchers estimated that ACT saved more than $1,500 per client per year. ACT clients themselves reported greater satisfaction with their program, fewer contacts with the police, and more stable community housing than clients from the drop-in center.

One reviewer (Mowbray, 1990) has questioned why community psychologists have not been *more* involved in research on ACT and the seriously mentally ill. For example, Toro's (1990) critique of this type of program led him to suggest that more research was needed on its impact in other domains, such as employment and social relationships. Salem (1990) concluded that a more thorough investigation of consumer- or client-run programs was needed, as well as more diversity among interventions for people with mental disabilities.

Nelson and colleagues (2007) reviewed comparison studies of ACT, ICM, and housing programs for SMI clients. They found that the provision of permanent housing for SMI clients led to reduced rates of institutional recidivism. In addition, the ACT programs resulted in better housing outcomes, with ICM the least successful of the newer models. Otherwise, those in ACT and ICM usually reported better community functioning and better feelings about themselves. One of the studies suggested the provision of ACT to be more expensive than standard treatment. Nelson and associates (2007) remark that ACT and ICM appear to reduce homelessness and hospitalization and improve community functioning. Though the intervention may be initially more costly, the reduction in institutionalization costs compensates for these temporary and superficial up-front expenditures (Rosenhack, Kasprow, Frisman, & Liu-Mares, 2003).

## Wraparound

Wraparound services have been around and developing for a number of years. Burchard, Bruns, and Burchard (2002) believed the evolution to have been at least 15 years in length at the time of their chapter describing the approach. They noted that wraparound services attempted to be "**strength focused, community based**, and **culturally relevant**" (p. 69). The premise was simple: Determine what was needed, and then provide it for a long as it was needed. Developed as an alternative to the medical model, and theoretically based in the ecological principles of Bronfenbrenner (1979), learning principles of Bandura (1977), and systems theory of Munger (1998), it works from the belief that adaptation can be learned just as maladaptation can be learned. Thus, it sets out to create an environment, a mixture of micro and macro settings that provide learning opportunities and support for adaptive behaviors. The systemic understanding is that a change in one part of life influences other parts of life. Therefore, a comprehensive systems approach is taken to each client. The approach is clearly community based, with an emphasis on teamwork and **collaboration across agencies and the family,** the active engagement of families as a part of the intervention, and commitment to the client that is flexible, culturally informed, and long lasting (Burns & Goldman, 1999). A review of studies demonstrates a clear evidence basis to this service approach (Burns, Goldman, Faw, & Burchard, 1999). Ecological, systems oriented, long lived, strength based, outcome focused (Burchard et al., 2002)—the wraparound approach to services is replete with community psychology concepts and practices. Case in Point 6.3 discusses an example.

---

## CASE IN POINT 6.3

### Wraparound Milwaukee

Wraparound Milwaukee is a multiyear program targeting youth with "serious emotional disorders," who are at risk for institutionalization in the mental health or legal system, and their families. The key characteristics of the program are (1) a strengths-based strategy to children and families, (2) family involvement in the treatment process, (3) a needs-based services planning and delivery (see Table 6.2), (4) an individualized service plan, and (5) an outcome-focused approach.

**TABLE 6.2   Services in the Wraparound Milwaukee Benefit Plan**

| | |
|---|---|
| Care coordination | Crisis home care |
| In-home therapy | Treatment foster care |
| Medication management | Residential treatment |
| Outpatient—individual family therapy | Foster care |
| Alcohol/substance abuse counseling | Day treatment/alternative school |
| Psychiatric assessment | Nursing assessment/management |
| Psychological evaluation | Job development/placement |
| Housing assistance | Kinship care |
| Mental health assessment/evaluation | Transportation services |
| Mentoring | Supervision/observation in home |
| Parent aide | After-school programming |
| Group home care | Recreation/child-oriented |
| Respite care | Discretionary funds/flexible funds |
| Child care for parent | Housekeeping/chore services |
| Tutor | Independent living support |
| Specialized camps | Psychiatric inpatient hospital |
| Emergency food pantry | |

*Source:* Adapted from Kamradt (2000).

## CASE IN POINT 6.3

# (*Continued*)

These approaches are structurally integrated into and implemented by four structural components: (1) care coordination, (2) the child and family team, (3) a mobile crisis team, and (4) a provider network. More than "80 mental health, social and support services" are provided within this plan.

The plan differs from others in that it focuses on the strengths of the child and the family systems, building on them so as to maintain the child in the community if possible. It points to the uniqueness of each case and honors it by providing choices and individualized programs for each client/family. It speaks of empowering families to work with their children. Toward that end, there are family social events, satisfaction surveys, and recruitment of families to serve on program committees and in program training. There is a

24-hour Mobile Urgent Treatment Team (MUTT), available to all clients and their families. The outcome focus of the program is to reduce the need for institutionalization.

The program "sustains itself by pooling dollars from its system partners and taking an integrated, multiservice approach . . . based on the Wraparound philosophy and the managed care model, offers care that is tailored to each youth" (Kamradt, 2000, p. 14). An innovative feature is the blending of funding (Medicaid, Supplemental Security Income, and other insurances) to maximize quality of care based on a case management model. It is estimated that "child welfare and juvenile justice systems fund Wraparound at $3,000 per month per child. Prior to Wraparound, these funds were used entirely for residential treatment care

systems [that] paid $5,000 or more per month per child" (Kamradt, 2000, p. 18).

Preliminary results of the program indicate that use of residential treatment has decreased by 60% (from an average daily census of 364 placements to fewer than 140 since the inception of Wraparound Milwaukee). Inpatient psychiatric hospitalization has dropped by 80% (Table 6.3). These positive results have continued. In an annual report for 2005, Wraparound Milwaukee reported seeing more than 1,000 youth (http://www.county.milwaukee.gov/WraparoundMilwaukee7851.htm). The program continues to demonstrate the targeted youth as having decreases in legal offenses, increases in school performance, and more positive parent evaluations. The president's New Freedom Commission on Mental Health named Wraparound Milwaukee as a model program in 2004.

**TABLE 6.3   Recidivism Rates of Delinquent Youth Enrolled in Wraparound Milwaukee (*n* = 134)**

| Offense | 1 Year Prior to Enrollment | 1 Year Postenrollment* |
|---|---|---|
| Sex offense | 11% | 1% |
| Assaults | 14% | 7% |
| Weapons offenses | 15% | 4% |
| Property offenses | 34% | 17% |
| Drug offenses | 6% | 3% |
| Other offenses (primarily disorderly conduct without a weapon) | 31% | 15% |

*Data collected and analyzed as of September 1999.

*Source:* Adapted from B. Kamradt (2000).

## EARLY CHILDHOOD EXPERIENCES AND PREVENTION

Heller, Jenkins, and associates (2000) noted that early community conceptions of mental health issues included a focus on prevention. However, as the saying goes, "We are so up to our eyes in alligators, it is hard to think of draining the swamp." Focus on secondary and tertiary prevention interventions has taken much of the energy and resources of those working in mental health. And yet, there are clear and substantial moves within the field to gather the research and resources necessary to mount preventive efforts.

Cicchetti and Toth's (1998) description of the diverse pathways and multiple factors that bring about psychopathological outcomes underscored the contributions of a developmental psychopathology approach to the understanding of depression and its etiology in children and youth. Considering **developmental pathways** and **trajectories,** the influence of vulnerabilities and events are seen as a **network** of influential factors that affect each other in a complex interplay of variables. Notably, **support systems** that can **coherently** address the life challenges of the individual play a protective role. Conversely, systems that are **chaotic and incoherent** or that are **pathogenic** in nature lead to heightened risk of depression. Preventive interventions have been shown to increase secure mother-infant attachment in an at-risk population (Cicchetti, Rogosch, & Toth, 2006).

These days, our conception of the causes of psychopathology are multifactorial or multipathed (Sue, Sue, Sue, & Sue, 2013). Sameroff and Chandler (1975) described the need for explanatory models that took into account the biological, the psychological, and the social. Sue and associates (2013) argued that a more complete model would include the biological, the psychological, the social, and the social-cultural. The current psychopathology model includes genetics, the environment, and epigenetics—that is, biology/genes affected by critical environmental events, leading to expression or lack of expression of the genetic dispositions (Institute of Medicine, 2009, p. 147).

Among the environmental events that have recently come under scrutiny are adverse childhood experiences (ACEs) (Table 6.4). Based on data first collected in 1995 and 1997, clear relationships were found between ACEs and depression, suicide attempts, drug abuse, alcoholism, and a variety of physical health related disorders (Felitti, Anda, Nordenber, Williamson, Spitz, Edwards, Koss, & Marks, 1998). Even hallucinations have been found related to ACE scores (Whitfield, Dube, Felitti, & Anda, 2005). Sixty-four percent of participants reported at least one adverse event, and 21% had three or more. Early-onset (before age 5) child maltreatment was related to less emotional regulation and more aggressive behaviors, which later led to poorer social relationships (Kim & Cicchetti, 2010). In turn, early-onset physical and sexual maltreatment has also been found to influence cortisol levels (stress) and depressive symptoms (Cicchetti, Rogosch, Gunnar, & Toth, 2010). In a study of adverse life events, social class, area deprivation, and family deprivation, adverse life events independently contributed to child psychopathology (Flouri, Mavroveli, & Tzavidis, 2010). Studies of negative early childhood experiences have shown a pathway to psychological, social and physical problems.

Because behaviors are caused by multiple variables that influence each other, not all who have these negative experiences develop pathology (see Chapter 3, Resilience). Other studies have shown that the combination of risk and protective factors determines the probability of development of pathology (Cicchetti & Toth, 1999; Egeland, 2007). For example, social support provided by fathers, grandparents, and other providers serves as a protective factor against at risk conditions. This was especially so when

| **TABLE 6.4** Adverse Childhood Experiences |
| --- |
| Abuse (Emotional, Physical, Sexual) |
| Neglect (Emotional, Physical) |
| Dysfunctional Household (Violence, Substance Abuse, Mental Illness, Incarceration, Divorce) |

*Source:* Centers for Disease Control and Prevention, Adverse Childhood Experiences Study website, http://www.cdc.gov/ace/prevalence.htm.

there were multiple levels of positive modeling, "higher quantity, higher quality and less disruption of the social support" (Appleyard, Egeland, & Sroufe, 2007, p. 443).

Our understanding of pathological processes has continued to grow. With this understanding has come efforts to prevent the onset of pathology or mitigate the effects of risk factors. One example of these efforts was the Fast Track Program. The Fast Track Program was a 10-year-long intervention for identified at-risk children. The program included parent training in behavior management, child training in social and cognitive skills, tutoring, home visits, mentoring, and peer relation and classroom programming. Early school findings showed significantly **lower likelihood of aggressive** and antisocial behaviors, and fewer diagnoses of conduct disorder and attention-deficit/hyperactivity disorder in middle school (Bierman et al., 2007). A later analysis of adolescent participants showed that those who were a part of the program were **less** likely to use **outpatient mental health** services by nearly 90% (Jones et al., 2010).

A meta-analysis of evidence-based early developmental prevention programs delivered to at-risk populations found stronger support for such programs when they were **multiyear** and **intensive** (more contacts). The review found that such programs showed success at adolescence in terms of **better educational outcomes, lower social deviance, greater social participation, better cognitive development, less involvement in crime, and better social–emotional development** (Manning, Homel, & Smith, 2010). The programs' results encouraged preventive and developmental programs for the mental health system. These findings called for reconceptions of the mental health system as a whole. (Also see Chapter 8 on Schools and Children.) Mental health interventions could and should be proactive, comprehensive, and cognizant of social ecology and epigenetics. The vision of a more broadly defined mental health system (Heller, Jenkins, et al., 2000) makes sense.

*Not just treatment but also prevention*

## THE BATTLE CONTINUES: WHERE DO WE GO FROM HERE?

Although having a mental disorder still incurs a stigma in society, the general public has become more familiar with mental health and mental illness. This awareness is responsible, in part, for the formation of the National Alliance for the Mentally Ill (NAMI). NAMI functions as more than a self-help group; it also operates as a political lobbying body. In 2008, NAMI had about 1,100 affiliates in the country with a membership estimated at 130,000. NAMI is a key player in the ongoing mental health care reform. At the local level, individual chapter members provide support to each other, as well as educational activities for the public on topics such as medication and rehabilitative services.

Some psychosocial models based on the concept of case management and political efforts such as those engaged by NAMI appear to offer hope for the mentally disabled. Mental health care continues to struggle with stigma and stereotype, short- and long-term focus, responsibilities and cost, and the public will to address these issues. Although community psychologists and mental health care professionals can help empower the mentally ill, using appropriate and culturally sensitive intervention models, mental health care reform must *not* be carried out in isolation from other health agendas. Mental health care needs to be framed within a *unified* health care agenda. Research (D'Ercole, Skodol, Struening, Curtis, & Millman, 1991; Levine & Huebner, 1991; Susser, Valencia, et al., 1993; U.S. Surgeon General, 1999) indicates that physical health and mental health are interdependent. D'Ercole and colleagues found that physical illnesses among psychiatric patients tended to be underdiagnosed when using the traditional psychiatric diagnostic tools of the DSM-IV. This was especially true for older and female patients.

Knowledge that community psychologists have gained in the past 30-plus years about health issues (mental health and mental illness in particular) strongly cautions us against the false optimism of the 1960s. No one should be denied mental health care services simply because she or he cannot afford to pay, yet realistic scenarios must take into account the economics and politics of intervention and pre-vention. The community as a whole must address these problems one way or another. In an indirect manner, mental illness is addressed in our policies for the homeless and those in prison—possibly even more so than in programs for the hospitalized or the mentally ill within our communities.

The demands on the system are rising. Torrey (1997) believed that approximately 150,000 people with mental illness were homeless on a given day, and another 150,000 were in jails and pris-ons. The aging baby boomers pose another challenge for caring for the older or elderly mentally ill (Hatfield, 1997). Each of these scenarios demands a somewhat different response or strategy, although the populations are not mutually exclusive. Estimates were that 26% of the U.S. population has a diagnosable mental disorder (Kessler et al., 2005). As of December 2008, the estimated popu-lation for the United States had passed 314 million (http://www.census.gov/population/www/pop-clockus.html). The number 78 million, which is approximately 26% of the population, seems almost incomprehensible.

Proponents such as Breakey (1996) have argued that the pressure of managed care on psychiatry and clinical psychology is likely to limit the role of these clinicians. Although evidence (e.g., ACT, Wraparound, Fast Track) reviewed in this chapter suggests that people at risk of mental illness who receive *integrated services* tend to fare better than those who do not receive such services, integrated care comes with a bigger initial price tag (real dollar and other human capital and resources) (Sharstein, 2000). Can we be farsighted enough to pay the bill? What role does community psychology play in com-municating the advantages of tertiary prevention over traditional services?

On the other end of the continuum, influential psychiatrists such as Torrey (1997) have argued that recent discoveries in biological psychiatry indicated that "severe psychiatric disorders are no more linked to minor mental perturbations than are multiple sclerosis or Parkinson's disease. Their proper treatment demands expertise in brain physiology and pharmacology, rather than human relationships" (p. B5). Torrey argued that resources should be redirected to allow psychiatry to merge with neurology to produce researchers and clinicians who possess expertise on the full spectrum of brain diseases. This would place neuropsychiatry as a single entity exactly where it was 100 years ago, before the Freudian revolution and the mental-hygiene movement led it to focus on general mental health rather than the most severe mental disorders (1997, p. B5).

This is both provocative and ominous! Given the rapid advancement in medical technology, it is all too easy to lose sight of the human side of feelings and behaviors.

And yet, the findings in epigenetics (Fraga et al., 2005; Jaenisch & Bird, 2003) remind us of the importance of the environmental interactions with genetic potentials.

People in community psychiatry and community mental health have the task to argue that inte-grated care (e.g., coordinated, comprehensive, ecologically minded) should be the norm. Meanwhile, the shift to an emphasis on biological psychiatry could hinder work already under way in areas such as social support. We can hope that the work being done on resilience (see Chapter 3), with its emphasis on multilevel interactive processes, will bring better appreciation of the interplay among the biological, the personal, the social, and the institutional variables affecting well-being. The field of mental health ser-vices continues to increase in its use of the ecological model (Bronfenbrenner, 1977; Bronfenbrenner & Morris, 2006; Kelly, 1990, 2002, 2006) for understanding the human experience.

Heller, Jenkins, and associates (2000) mark the neglect of prevention programs in the tradi-tional mental health care programs. Others have noted that one of the problems of prevention pro-grams is the delay in detectable results. A time frame of a decade or two may seem impossible in our minute-to-minute and year-to-year mentality. The economic pressures are to demonstrate pres-ent savings to the system (Felner, Jason, Moritsugu, & Riger, 1983). Nonetheless, prevention has been demonstrated to work, focusing on children and working with systems that are important to the lives of those children—that is, families and schools (Albee & Gullotta, 1997; Durlak & Wells, 1997; Heller, 1990; Ialongo et al., 2006). The aim of these prevention programs is of course to divert the trajectory of the potential mental health client, providing personal and social resources that may aid in dealing with life stressors and in learning life tasks (see Chapter 3 regarding resilience and social support). The present chapter has extensively discussed these programs and their potentials. However, the focus here has been on tertiary prevention for cases within the mental health system, which has a scarcity of prevention programs. The progress in prevention research and action is measurable nonetheless.

The concern raised by Heller, Jenkins, and colleagues (2000) is the lack of natural communities in the first community mental health center formulations (Hunter & Riger, 1986). The concept of a *catchment area* (geographic region that the community mental health center served) used large areas based on street boundaries. There was no sense of **naturally defined neighborhoods** (boundaries used by the members of the community), whose strengths and existing networks could be brought to bear on problems. This shortcoming may now be addressed by the inclusion of communities in devising programs and research for themselves via the participatory action research models that are increasingly used.

## Summary

The presence of mental health concerns in the U.S. population has been studied for several decades, and the results point to a sobering conclusion. The prevalence of mental illness is substantial, and the possibility of some disturbance within an individual's lifetime is nearly one in two. Yet there is a concentration of disorders in a smaller segment of the population, usually with multiple problems co-occurring. For these few, the impact of mental illness is devastating.

Our traditional models of mental health are individual focused and reactive. The shortcomings of these models have led us to the community perspective with its preventive orientation and ecological perspective.

Although a historical overview of treatment for mental illness shows a progression toward more humanitarian and inclusive treatment, the deinstitutionalization of the mentally ill has not come without major problems. A casual review of the field of mental health and illness indicates that there is a great deal of controversy about exactly what deinstitutionalization is. Some have argued that a better term is *trans-institutionalization* to describe the dumping of patients from one setting to another. Also, the characteristics of the mentally disabled have changed in the past 30-plus

years. Now, ethnic minorities constitute a sizable sample of the mentally disordered, and they are likely to be undetected by the existing systems.

The placement for a deinstitutionalized individual is, interestingly, another institution—possibly jail or prison. Many of the deinstitutionalized end up among the homeless. Most are in unsupervised settings, where problems of medical regimen compliance and adverse social influences make successful reintegration into the community very unlikely. We measure successful functioning of the mentally ill in their community in terms of social integration and recidivism, or rate of return to the psychiatric hospital, but the economic indicators of cost have remained important determinants for policy decisions. Most analyses of success focus on problems of the individual, but the environment plays a significant role in successes or failures. Depersonalization of services can also account for problems faced by deinstitutionalized individuals. Lack of adequate or integrated support lead to problems, especially for those who have lost their natural social supports or who have care needs beyond the resources of those supports.

The ideal that led to the enactment of the Community Mental Health Act in the 1960s has not been fully realized. Now it seems obvious that one reason for the existing patchwork system is the lack of systematic planning and poor coordination.

Innovative psychosocial rehabilitation models have been developed for treating the severely mentally ill. Common to these models are the provision of comprehensive, integrated, and personal programs for identified clients, which include forms of daily living skill training and empowerment of the support systems that help these clients. These may be the natural systems, such as families and friends, or might be the formal systems of agencies and programs that offer services. Individualized case management and smaller case loads that allow for that can be very helpful.

Studies of early childhood experiences tell us that experiences in the formative years are important to the development of normal or pathological pathways. Use of what has been learned about these pathways, and of our understanding of what makes for resiliency, has been useful in producing successful programs to reduce pathology in children and adolescents. This challenges us to broaden our conception of the mental health system and the resources it requires.

Although community psychologists and mental health care professionals can empower the mentally ill by using appropriate and culturally sensitive intervention models, mental health care reform must *not* be carried out in isolation from other health agendas. That is, mental health care needs to be framed within a *unified* health care agenda. A holistic approach with an understanding of the interactions of the mind and body and transactions with ecological settings seems the prescription for treatments of the future, based on the extant research in our communities at present. There is a lot of promise yet to be realized.

# Social and Human Services in the Community

*Of all the people in the world, 852 million are chronically hungry; every day, almost 16,000 children die from hunger-related causes.*

—MCC.org/food

*An empty sack cannot stand up.*

—Haitian proverb

Rock was a high school senior. His girlfriend, Monique, was a sophomore in the same school. Both teenagers lived in middle-class suburban homes. Rock was bored with his humdrum life in the suburbs and liked to "live on the edge." He listened to the newest music, had many tattoos, smoked weed, and liked to thrill ride on his motorcycle. His unpredictability and careless living attracted Monique to Rock, although neither set of parents was thrilled with their child's choice of dating partner. Monique's parents were especially displeased because her mother thought several pieces of her gold jewelry were missing and might have found their way into Rock's pockets.

Both Rock and Monique had a history of cutting classes and occasionally not coming home for several days. Rock taught Monique to buy and smoke marijuana early in their relationship, and their use increased as the relationship progressed. They ultimately were caught smoking marijuana behind their school. Because both were minors, the judge ordered them to enroll in a drug-treatment program.

The treatment program was one of a dozen funded by a federal agency in collaboration with two state agencies. The goal of the program was to *prevent* youths from using alcohol and other drugs—not to intervene or treat them. Past research has shown that youths who have various risk factors (e.g., cutting class and stealing) are more likely to use or abuse drugs than those who do not. Thus, youths who have certain risk factors were identified by the child and family welfare divisions of government-sponsored social services and were referred to the drug-treatment programs at another state agency.

In the case of Rock, he was ordered by the court (rather than identified by the child and family welfare agency) to enroll in the drug-treatment program. After intake, he was immediately placed into one of the programs. He was to participate in both individual and group counseling. Family counseling with Rock's parents was provided on a limited basis because the program was mainly designed for drug treatment.

Monique's treatment placement was still pending because during her intake, it was discovered that she was pregnant. The state agency responsible for the drug-treatment programs did not accept pregnant clients. Thus, staff at both state agencies did not know what to do with Monique. Both agencies were also experiencing some difficulty in complying with all of the requirements of the federal agency that funded their drug-treatment programs.

Since the inception of the drug-treatment programs, several major political changes at the state level had led to a leadership vacuum at the state agencies. The two executive directors of the respective agencies resigned after the governor announced that she would not seek reelection. A consequence was the lack of coordination of the patient referral process.

Meanwhile, direct-care staff felt strongly that alcohol and other drug abuse in youths was likely to be symptomatic of other issues, including parent–child and school problems. Moreover, most of these youths were already using or abusing some form of drug; therefore, to talk about prevention was utter folly. However, because the government funding agency focused on prevention, the staff was obligated to comply by educating about prevention of use of drugs.

This true story illustrates that social problems often do not have a single cause and do not develop in isolation. In the case of Rock and Monique, direct-care staff appeared to be correct in that drug treatment for both teens was merely treating their symptom (marijuana use) but not the cause(s) (e.g., school alienation and generational conflicts between parents and children). Moreover, Monique needed a treatment program that specialized in drug rehabilitation for pregnant women. However, staff at the drug-treatment program was limited by resources and expertise. Here is a good example of the inappropriate depletion of limited and sometimes scarce social and human resources. As you can see from this case, effective social services delivery is contingent on good organizational infrastructure and management.

This chapter begins with a review of what poverty is and how social services emerged in Western society to respond to the needs of the poor. Poverty, although not the cause of Rock and Monique's situation, is one of the root causes and complications of many societal problems that ultimately affect all of us, whether or not we are poor (Grogan-Kaylor, 2005; Rank, 2005). The chapter then reviews selected social and human services as well as affected groups.

## HISTORICAL NOTES ABOUT SOCIAL WELFARE IN WESTERN SOCIETY

What is **poverty?** Does poverty merely mean the lack of sufficient money to acquire essential things to survive, such as food? Or does poverty mean being born and living in a ghetto or slum, which might lead to attending a substandard school and might further lead to a vicious circle of unemployment and subsequent homelessness (Hochschild, 2003)? The latter notion is probably what President Lyndon B. Johnson had in mind when he made his 1964 State of the Union address about the War on Poverty. Poverty is not just about lacking money; it is also about a sense of hopelessness and injustice (Yang & Barrett, 2006). For example, without a good education, an individual is unlikely to find a decent-paying job. Poorly educated people are less likely to be well-informed citizens—especially about their basic rights and entitlements—compared to those who are educated. Poverty affects all of us, not just the poor, in myriad ways and is not just about individual shortcomings but about economic structures and failed political policies (Rank, 2005).

Although poverty does affect us all, it clearly harms some of us more than others. The U.S. Census Bureau (2007) reported that the poverty rate for White Americans was 8.62% in 2006, whereas it was 24.3% for Blacks, 20.6% for Latinos, and 10.3% for Asian Americans. For American Indian or Alaskan Natives, the poverty rate was 27% (U.S. Census Bureau, 2007). Scholars such as Smith (2009) have argued that we are living at a time in U.S. history that is what Collins and Yeskel (2005) have termed *economic apartheid*, or a widening equity gap in which increasing numbers of Americans are being left farther and farther behind economically. The Economic Policy Institute conducted an analysis that found since the late 1990s, incomes have declined by 2.5% among the poorest fifth of American families, while they have risen 9.1% among the wealthiest fifth (Bernstein, McNichol, & Nicholas, 2008).

With these thoughts in mind, we are ready to examine the effectiveness of public assistance, one objective of which is to lift people from poverty and from other social problems so that they can move on to a better life. First, Case in Point 7.1 provides some compelling and alarming statistics about poverty in the world and, in particular, the United States.

What has been done to help those who live in poverty? Social welfare is one response that has tried to address the numerous needs of the poor. According to Handel (1982), **social welfare** is "a set of ideas and a set of activities and organizations for carrying out those ideas, all of which have taken shape over

## CASE IN POINT 7.1

# Poverty in America

Community psychologists and other experts consider poverty the number one social problem in the United States as well as the root cause of many other social problems, such as delinquency, substance abuse, school problems, crime, and homelessness. Here are some startling statistics about poverty both in the United States and worldwide. Additional statistics can be found at two websites dedicated to combating poverty (solvingpoverty.com and www.poverty-usa.org). Although being a college student does not necessarily mean that you will live a life of luxury, it may be hard to imagine yourself living in poverty.

- Worldwide, 25,000 people die each day of hunger; every 3.5 seconds, someone in the world dies of hunger.
- In the United States, 1 in 6 or 47.4 million people live in poverty. The 2011 federal poverty guideline is that a family of two that lives on less than $14,710 a year lives in poverty (see http://aspe.hhs.gov/poverty/11poverty.shtml).
- In the United States, 16 million Americans live in *extreme* poverty (that is, they live at less than half of the federal poverty guidelines).

- The United States leads all industrialized nations in child poverty.
- Poverty rates for African Americans, Latinos, and single mothers are the highest—in some cases, twice that of White men.
- Fifty-nine million Americans are without health insurance; that translates into 1 of every 4 Americans between the ages of 18 and 64.
- Food stamp programs provide only $1 per meal per person. Could you live on that?

many centuries, to provide people with income and other social benefits in ways that safeguard their dignity" (p. 31). Without sounding simplistic, this seemingly innocuous statement describes the complex nature of social welfare. Social welfare serves both ideological (e.g., political and religious) and practical (e.g., inability to provide for oneself) concerns.

Until modern times, one major form of social welfare was charity, otherwise known as philanthropy. **Charity/philanthropy** refers to social welfare in which a **donor** (voluntary giver) assists a **recipient** (beneficiary). An example of this is when an individual donates money to Habitat for Humanity so that this nonprofit organization can buy building materials to help a homeless family build a house. The nature of charity/philanthropy is largely a function of the ideology of the time period. For example, research indicates that during religious seasons (e.g., Christmas and Passover), people are more likely to be charitable than during nonreligious seasons. **Public welfare,** on the other hand, is where the government (rather than private donors) assumes responsibility for the poor or for recipients of aid who have not contributed to this particular system of aid.

Charity/philanthropy and public welfare are likely to create social stigmas whereby some individuals hold negative views of those who require such aid (Applebaum, Lennon, & Lawrence, 2006; Cadena, Danziger, & Seefeldt, 2006). Specifically, Handel (1982) succinctly argued that recipients of social welfare

> are widely believed to be lazy and immoral. . . . Although recipients must prove their need, their claims are often thought to be fraudulent. . . . These people receive less social honor than other members of society. Such methods of providing income are therefore regarded as demeaning, as impairing the dignity of the people who depend upon them. (pp. 8–9)

Even recipients of social welfare are likely to have a negative view of themselves (Chan, 2004; Sennett, 2003) or of other recipients (Coley, Kuta, & Chase-Lansdale, 2000). This negative self-concept can translate into self-defeating behaviors. For example, there are millions of students attending public school whose families qualify for free breakfast and lunch programs because they live at or below the poverty level. Yet, imagine that many of these same students would rather skip lunch altogether than to have the stigma of being poor broadcast to their peers in the lunch line. Thus, there are social welfare programs that have been developed with the best of intentions whose effectiveness is questionable.

Moving beyond these so-called traditional forms of social welfare, we now turn to two more modern forms of social welfare: social service and social insurance. **Social services** (*non*material benefits) are an offshoot of charity/philanthropy. In a system derived from the 19th century, the government uses taxes to provide *services rather than direct monetary aid*. A major goal of social services is to ensure and maintain a productive workforce via prevention of or intervention in social problems. Rock and Monique, the two teenagers in the opening vignette, were the recipients of social services (e.g., treatment programs from the substance-abuse agency). It was hoped that these services could prevent both youths from becoming more dependent on marijuana or other drugs in the years to come.

**Social insurance** (or **public assistance,** as it is otherwise known) has its origin in the 19th century, around the time of the Industrial Revolution. The basic premise of social insurance is that the government assumes responsibility for individuals *who may have contributed in some way to the assistance system*. The funds for these systems generally derive from taxes. In other words, the *difference* between public welfare and social insurance (i.e., public assistance) is that "the recipients of social insurance are receiving benefits that have been earned by work, either their own, or work by someone else on their behalf" (Handel, 1982, p. 15), whereas recipients of public welfare do not contribute to this process.

Because Monique had never held a job, if she turned to the government for benefits for her baby, she would be deemed in the strictest sense to be on public welfare, not on public assistance. Some well-known programs of social insurance/public assistance in this country include Medicare (healthcare for the elderly), Social Security (unemployment and disability benefits or old-age pensions for the formerly employed), and veterans' benefits. Eligibility guidelines (e.g., the federal poverty guidelines) are established by the government and can often be cumbersome.

Public welfare programs have changed under the Personal Responsibility and Work Opportunity Reconciliation Act of 1996. Public welfare recipients now have to transition to full- or part-time work and cannot remain indefinitely on government assistance except under certain extreme circumstances. Interestingly, research demonstrates that most welfare recipients would like to work (Allen, 2000; Bell, 2007; Scott, London, & Edin, 2000). Perhaps one reason for their motivation is that such assistance, as mentioned previously, creates a social stigma against the recipients as well as diminishing recipients' own sense of dignity.

This seemingly more enlightened view of public welfare is emerging in the United States among the public and some government officials. First, there is growing concern that people should be less dependent on public welfare. Such assistance is seen as degrading and stigmatizing. Second, recipients should be encouraged to work; that is, incentives to encourage work should be more available than incentives to encourage dependence on public assistance. This appears to be the underlying philosophy of the Personal Responsibility and Work Opportunity Reconciliation Act of 1996, already mentioned (Scott et al., 2000). Third, there is growing recognition that if employment participation is mandatory, employment should make families better off by working rather than by not working. Some recent studies have found that movement into employment and away from public welfare is associated with increases in income and personal well-being but may have little effect on other aspects of family life, such as parenting skills or home environments (e.g., Coley, Lohman, Votruba-Drzal, Pittman, & Chase-Lansdale, 2007). At the time of this writing, results of other studies on welfare-to-work programs are mixed (e.g., Cadena et al., 2006), so more research is needed to sort out the effects of this new effort. In addition, the current economic crisis that has affected the United States as well as the rest of the world has resulted in greater rates of joblessness and underemployment. Thus, transitioning people off of public welfare into work may be more easily said than done. Interestingly, other countries have instituted very different alternatives to welfare as a means of reducing poverty; for example, read Case in Point 7.2 on the award-winning program at the Grameen Bank.

Because welfare-to-work programs appear to have mixed results (Geen, Fender, Leos-Urbel, & Markowitz, 2001), such programs are not without their critics. Piven and Cloward (1996) noted that proponents claim miraculous social and cultural transformations that are unrealistic, such as increased family cohesion and lower crime rates. Piven and Cloward viewed such welfare-to-work programs as nothing more than a class war between the haves and the have-nots. Opulente and Mattaini (1997) suggested that sanction-based programs (such as the Personal Responsibility and Work Opportunity Reconciliation Act) are likely to be ineffective and produce undesirable side effects, such as anger. Wilson, Ellwood, and Brooks-Gunn (1996) and also Cadena and associates (2006) have offered the criticism that the best research methods are not being used to examine the outcomes and processes of such programs. Finally, Aber, Brooks-Gunn, and Maynard (1995) as well as Coley and colleagues (2007) concluded that welfare-to-work programs do little to enhance children of poor parents. In fact, poor children continue to be exposed to more family turmoil, family separation, and instability; come from more polluted environments; live in more dangerous neighborhoods; and experience more cumulative risk factors than wealthier children (Evans, 2004).

## CASE IN POINT 7.2

# The Grameen Bank

Can a small loan (microcredit) of $25 to $50 "cure" poverty? An interesting experiment is under way worldwide. The experiment in microcredit is known as the Grameen Bank. Founder Muhammad Yunus was struck by the extreme poverty, especially of women, in Bangladesh. In 1976, with some difficulty, he took out a loan from a bank and distributed the money to poor women in Bangladesh. In fact, his loans went to the poorest of the poor. The small loans are generally used by the women to begin their own cottage-type industries, such as raising farm animals and producing or creating crafts to sell. Yunus views microcredit as a cost-effective weapon to fight poverty. He could not, however, convince any traditional banks to continue lending money to the poor, so he started his own bank, the Grameen Bank, and continued his microcredit loan program.

The Grameen Bank uses principles that run counter to traditional banking wisdom. It seeks the poorest borrowers. No collateral is necessary for a loan. Instead, the system is based on trust, accountability, participation, and creativity. Borrowers are required to join the bank in groups of five; the group members provide each other with support and advice.

The Grameen Bank is now the largest rural financial institution in Bangladesh, with more than 8.35 million borrowers, 96% of whom are women, in over 80,000 villages. Furthermore, in line with community psychology, the bank brings the loans *to* the people, rather than the other way around. Of course, community problems cannot always be solved by merely throwing money at people, but in this instance, the amount of money is nominal, and the return is enormous.

A cogent question is this: Do the Grameen Bank and microcredit have a positive and long-term effect on these impoverished individuals? The answer is a resounding "yes." First, more than 97% of the loans are repaid, indicating that people are not always looking for a free handout. Second, the bank has a positive effect on both the women and their children. Independent research demonstrates that the women's economic security and status within the family are elevated. The children of the women are better schooled and healthier than other children in the community. Best of all, extreme poverty (as defined by the United Nations) declines by more than 70% within five years of the borrowers joining the bank.

Elsewhere in this chapter, some information on how poverty is measured in the United States (e.g., annual household income for various size families) is provided. The Grameen Bank measures poverty level in completely different and more functional and practical ways. Staff members monitor borrowers to determine whether their quality of life is improving. For example, if a family successfully owns a house with a metal roof, has a sanitary latrine, drinks potable water, finally has adequate clothes for everyday use, eats three square meals a day, gains access to schooling for the children, and has reasonable access to healthcare, then that family is considered to have moved beyond poverty. Would such a program work in the United States? Yunus thinks not. Costs in the United States are such that the operations would be far more expensive. However, individuals from other nations have completed Grameen Bank training so as to create replication programs in dozens of different countries.

The Grameen Bank concept for addressing poverty has been so successful that in 2006 Muhammad Yunus and the Grameen Bank were awarded the Nobel Peace Prize. Muhammad Yunus, by the way, has a degree in economics, not in community psychology. He is living proof that professionals from many disciplines can come together to address serious community issues such as poverty.

Adapted from Yunus (1999, 2007) and www.grameen-info.org.

## SPECIFIC SOCIAL ISSUES AND SOCIAL SERVICES

Many groups access social and human services for a variety of reasons. To evaluate and judge the effectiveness or impact of these services, a consensus of standards is essential. According to Price, Cowen, Lorion, and Ramos-McKay (1988), model programs possess one or more of five characteristics:

1. The programs have a specific target audience.
2. The goal of the programs is to make a long-term and significant impact on the target groups, thus enhancing their well-being.

3. The programs provide the necessary skills for the recipients to achieve their objectives.
4. The programs strengthen the natural support from family, community, or school settings.
5. The programs have evaluative mechanisms to document their success.

Using these criteria as standards, our attention turns to five groups to examine the problems, people, and interventions to the problems within social and human services systems. These groups have been selected for several reasons. First, these groups are large or growing in number. Second, some of these groups are currently receiving much media attention, including maltreated children and pregnant teens. Third, all five groups have received attention to some extent in the field of community psychology. The groups are maltreated and neglected children, survivors of domestic violence, pregnant teens (like Monique), the elderly, and homeless individuals.

## Child Maltreatment

Child maltreatment is a complex and emotionally charged issue. Defining child maltreatment is very difficult, so there is no universally agreed-on definition. One reason for definitional difficulties is that each culture sets its own generally accepted principles of childrearing, child care, and discipline (Elliott & Urquiza, 2006; Runyan, Shankar, Hassan, Hunter, Jain, Dipty, et al., 2010). Child abuse is known to exist universally, however, and there is general agreement across many cultures that child abuse should not be allowed and that harsh discipline and sexual abuse are not allowable at all (Runyan et al., 2010). Also making a clear definition difficult is the fact that some definitions take into account the impact or harm on the child, whereas others focus more on the behavior or actions of the perpetrators.

For now, let's use a broad definition as provided by the World Health Organization (WHO) (2004):

> Child abuse or maltreatment constitutes all forms of physical and/or emotional ill-treatment, sexual abuse, neglect or negligent treatment or commercial or other exploitation, resulting in actual or potential harm to the child's health, survival, development or dignity in the context of a relationship of responsibility, trust or power.

**SCOPE OF THE ISSUE.** The Centers for Disease Control and Prevention (CDC) (2011c) reported that in the United States in 2008, there were nearly 772,000 cases of verified child maltreatment and that 1,740 children died as a result of maltreatment. Worldwide, as many as 40 million children may be abused (WHO, 2004). Though these statistics are alarming, they need to be viewed with some qualifications, because many authorities believe there is underreporting. Why? First, many child injuries and deaths are not routinely investigated, and postmortem examinations are not always carried out, which makes it difficult to establish the precise number of cases (CDC, 2007c; Runyan et al., 2010). Furthermore, many cases of abuse and neglect are concealed from investigators, and there is great variation in how states review and report suspected cases. Also, medical personnel sometimes make inaccurate determinations of the manner and cause of injuries and death of children—for instance, blaming a neglected child's death on sudden infant death syndrome. In addition, investigations are often uncoordinated and not multidisciplinary in their approaches (CDC, 2007c). Although these data are disheartening, recent trends indicate that child maltreatment may be declining. The exact causes for the decline and whether it is permanent or temporary are still unknown (Finkelhor & Jones, 2006).

As shown in Figure 7.1, nearly 80% of victims were abused by a parent acting alone or in conjunction with another person. Approximately 40% of child victims were maltreated by their mothers; another 18% were maltreated by their fathers; and 17% were abused by both parents. Victims abused by nonparental

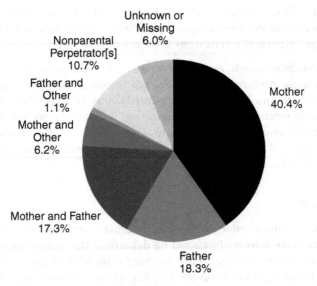

**FIGURE 7.1**  Victims by Perpetrator and Relationship, 2005

*Source:* Administration for Children and Families (2005). Child maltreatment. Washington, DC. U.S. Department of Health and Human Services.

perpetrators accounted for 11%. A nonparental perpetrator is defined as a caregiver who is not a parent and can include foster parents, child day-care staff, nannies, an unmarried partner of a parent, a legal guardian, or a residential facility staff member. Data for victims of specific maltreatment types can also be analyzed in terms of perpetrator relationship to the victim. Of the types of maltreatment children experience, 65.8% were neglected by a parent. Of those who were sexually abused, 30.8% were abused by a relative other than a parent (Administration for Children and Families, 2010).

The toll of child abuse on the victim, family, community, and society are enormous and quite varied. Here are some of the consequences of maltreatment.

- Children who experience maltreatment are at increased risk for adverse health effects as adults, including smoking, alcoholism, drug abuse, eating disorders, severe obesity, depression, suicide, sexual promiscuity, and certain chronic diseases (English et al., 2005; Runyan, Wattam, Ikeda, Hassan, & Ramiro, 2002).
- Child abuse and neglect are associated with an increased risk of major depressive disorder in early adulthood (Widom, DuMont, & Czaja, 2007).
- Individuals with a history of child abuse and neglect are 1.5 times more likely to use illicit drugs, especially marijuana, in middle adulthood (Widom, Marmorstein, & White, 2006).
- Maltreatment during infancy or early childhood can cause important regions of the brain to form improperly, which can cause physical, mental, and emotional problems such as sleep disturbances, panic disorder, posttraumatic stress disorder, and attention deficit hyperactivity disorder (Cicchetti, 2007; Cicchetti & Valentino, 2006; U.S. Department of Health and Human Services, 2001a; Watts-English, Fortson, Gibler, Hooper, & De Bellis, 2006).
- Approximately 1,400 children experience severe or fatal head trauma as a result of abuse each year. Nonfatal consequences of abusive head trauma include varying degrees of visual impairment (e.g., blindness), motor impairment (e.g., cerebral palsy), and cognitive impairments (National Center on Shaken Baby Syndrome, 2011).

- The economy may be contributing to incidents of infant abuse. In a study of children's hospitals, incidents of infant abuse were reported to average 4.8 per month before the recession and 9.3 per month after the recession began (National Center on Shaken Baby Syndrome, 2011).
- Early child maltreatment can have a negative effect on the ability of both men and women to establish and maintain healthy intimate relationships in adulthood (Coulton & Korbin, 2007)
- Emotional and behavior dysregulation, school failure, and antisocial behaviors are consequences to the victims (Olds et al., 2007).

The costs to society are monumental as well. Abused children, in addition to the abusers, are typically the focus of intensive efforts from various social and human services specialists. Suspected cases of maltreatment are often investigated by the Department of Social Services and law enforcement. Abused children and their parents are often referred by judges and other professionals to mental health care providers for treatment. These direct costs are estimated at billions of dollars a year; indirect costs (such as long-term economic consequences) add more billions annually.

Perhaps if we know the causes of maltreatment, we can better design prevention and intervention programs. We'll examine the complex causes next. From what you have learned already, try to determine whether you think Monique and Rock might be at risk to maltreat their expected child.

**CAUSES OF MALTREATMENT.**    There is widespread agreement among family violence experts that multiple factors are responsible for child maltreatment, such as stressors in the parents' lives, poverty, social isolation, and unrealistic expectations by parents of children. Studies have also identified poor prenatal care, dysfunctional caregiving, closely spaced unplanned pregnancies, dependence on welfare, community violence, and parental substance abuse among multiple causes. Researchers, therefore, need to look at several levels including (but not limited to) societal, institutional, and interpersonal factors as providing the explanatory framework for child maltreatment and other forms of family violence, such as partner violence. Societal factors, for example, can contribute to child maltreatment in the following ways. Poverty and economic downturn diminish the capacity for consistent and involved parenting. Parental job loss might produce pessimism and irritability in the parent. The parent might then become less nurturing and more arbitrary in interactions with the children.

Community psychologists would be quick to point out that other ecological factors contribute to child maltreatment. Indeed, child maltreatment may represent one of the greatest failures of the environment to offer opportunities for fostering wellness (Cicchetti, Toth, & Rogosch, 2000; Cicchetti & Valentino, 2006). Garbarino and Kostelny (1992, 1994) investigated community dimensions in child maltreatment. They examined two predominantly African American and two predominantly Hispanic areas of Chicago. Some 60,000 child maltreatment cases were plotted for location for the years 1980, 1983, and 1986. Garbarino and Kostelny found significant location differences in maltreatment. As part of this same research, community leaders from social services agencies were also interviewed. The interviews revealed that high-risk locations were characterized by a lack of community identity, whereas low-risk areas were characterized by a sense of community or greater community cohesiveness. Garbarino concluded that abuse is not necessarily a sign of an individual or a family in trouble but a sign of a community in trouble. Other scientists agree that neighborhood factors, such as impoverishment (Coulton & Korbin, 2007; Euser, van Ijzendoorn, Prinzie, & Bakermans-Kranenburg, 2011) and community violence (Lynch, 2006), affect child maltreatment and child development as much as or more than individual risk factors. You will read more about community disorder and disintegration in the chapter on crimes and communities.

Korbin and Coulton's (1996) research, in which they conducted in-depth interviews with residents in 13 high-, medium-, and low-risk census tracts in Cleveland, Ohio, also demonstrated that intervention efforts can be reoriented to the neighborhood level. They found that neighborhood conditions, such as distrust of neighbors and of social agencies as well as the dangers and incivilities of daily life, limit the abilities of neighbors to help one another act in the best interests of neighborhood children. Neighbors *do* feel that they should be able to help each other; in fact, many participants reported being optimistic that they could help prevent child maltreatment. However, neighborhood conditions often inhibited their willingness to do so. The researchers concluded that because economic and social conditions are inextricably bound together, child maltreatment prevention programs must be embedded within comprehensive efforts to strengthen communities.

Freisthler, Bruce, and Needell (2007) also examined how neighborhood characteristics were associated with rates of child maltreatment. Their study included 940 census tracts in California. Their results demonstrated that for Black children, higher rates of poverty and higher densities of off-premise alcohol outlets were positively associated with maltreatment rates. Percentage of female-headed families, poverty, and unemployment were positively related to maltreatment rates among Hispanic children. For White children, the percentage of elderly people, percentage of poverty, ratio of children to adults, and percentage of Hispanic residents were positively associated with neighborhood maltreatment rates. The researchers concluded that reducing neighborhood poverty may reduce rates of child maltreatment for all children, and efforts to prevent maltreatment at the neighborhood level may need to be tailored to specific neighborhood demographic characteristics to be most effective.

Just what efforts have been made to intercede in child maltreatment and neglect? Traditional efforts at intervention occur at the individual clinical level, where maltreated children and their parents are given counseling to help overcome personal problems and understand the abuse. Although these methods may be laudable, they do little to prevent the abuse in the first place. This method of treatment is also difficult and expensive to implement on a wide scale. Moreover, these methods focus only on the individual or family and not on other ecological systems (e.g., poverty and community violence) that share responsibility.

Some people have argued that the best way to improve the situation for abusers and their victims is through national policies aimed at creating jobs, reducing unemployment and poverty, or providing income maintenance, such as welfare or public assistance. Prevention experts, like community psychologists, believe better and more targeted strategies can be aimed at high-risk groups *before* the maltreatment commences (Olds, 2005, 2006). Prevention of child maltreatment and neglect is certainly the more humane route to take.

**PREVENTION PROGRAMS.** Perhaps one of the oldest, best known, and most highly acclaimed preventive programs is one designed by David Olds and his research team (Olds, Henderson, Chamberlin, & Tatelbaum, 1986; Olds et al., 2007). Their project, known in its earliest form as the Prenatal/Early Infancy Project and more recently as the Nurse–Family Partnership, provides nurse home visitation to prevent a wide range of maternal and child health problems associated with poverty, one of which is child abuse. Despite the usual criticisms of the program (see Chaffin, 2004; Olds, Eckenrode, & Kitzman, 2005), one of the aspects that makes it outstanding is that evaluation research typically is well designed, using randomly assigned experimental and control groups. Likewise, by recruiting a heterogeneous group of participants, these interventionists are better able to compare those who are not at risk for abuse with those who are.

Primiparous mothers (women having their first child) who are young, single parents, or from the lower socioeconomic class are welcomed into the program. The researchers want to avoid the appearance of being a program only for potential child abusers and on the other hand to ensure family engagement and avoid stigmatization. Olds and colleagues, therefore, have actively avoided labeling the program as one aimed at preventing maltreatment. Nevertheless, it was developed explicitly to reduce risk and at the same time promote protective factors associated with child abuse and neglect (Olds et al., 2005).

Nurses typically visit the participants' homes every other week during the prenatal (before birth) and the perinatal (after birth) periods. The mother's primary support person (perhaps her own mother, a friend, or the baby's father) is also invited to attend. Social support from the nurses and significant others is a vital component of this program. The nurses carry out three major activities during their home visits: educating parents about fetal and infant development, promoting the involvement of family members and friends in support of the mother and care of the child, and developing linkages between family members and other formal health and human services in the community. In the education component, mothers and family members are encouraged to complete their own education and make decisions about employment and subsequent pregnancies. Before the baby's birth, the nurses concentrate on educating the prospective mothers to improve their diets and eliminate the use of cigarettes, drugs, and alcohol; recognize pregnancy complications; and prepare for labor, delivery, and care of the newborn. After the baby is born, the nurses concentrate on improving parents' understanding of the infants' temperaments and promoting the infants' socioemotional, cognitive, and physical development. The nurses also provide links to other formal services, such as health providers, mental health counselors, and nutritional supplement programs for mothers and infants (Women, Infants, and Children [WIC] programs) (Olds, 2005, 2006).

One of the most important results of the program is its effect on verified cases of child abuse and neglect. For women with all three risk characteristics of abuse (poor, unmarried, and adolescent), there is usually a remarkable 80% difference in the incidence of verified cases of child abuse and neglect over the comparison (nonintervention) group. Remarkably, these differences persist at the 15-year follow-up. The mothers in the nurse-visited group also report that their infants are easier to care for. The interviewers of the mothers often observed less punishment and restriction of the mothers toward their children and a greater number of growth-promoting playthings in the homes of the nurse-visited mothers. The medical records of the nurse-visited families show fewer visits to emergency rooms for illnesses and fewer childhood accidents. This is true even for the women who reported little sense of control over their lives when they first registered for the program. The results also hint at improved developmental life courses for the nurse-visited mothers, as well. For example, once these mothers become older and more employable, they work at their jobs longer than do their counterparts in the comparison group. Thus, program participants are less dependent on public welfare. The mothers also have fewer subsequent pregnancies, and both the mothers and their children are less likely to become entwined with the criminal justice system. Olds (1997, 2005; Olds, Hill, & Rumsey, 1998) has replicated this program in several communities across the United States with equally impressive results. At present, the program is being disseminated for public investment throughout the United States (Olds, 2007).

Research, however, has unveiled at least one limitation of the nurse home visit program. In homes where other forms of domestic violence are occurring, nurse home visitation is less effective at reducing child maltreatment (Eckenrode et al., 2000; Gomby, 2000). Further research has also shown that other, more long-term programs, such as ones based in schools where children are taught to identify abuse, especially sexual abuse, may be as effective as nurse home visitation programs (Davis & Gidycz, 2000).

The causes of child maltreatment are many. Cases of abuse keep large numbers of social workers and mental health professionals busy with the aftermath. However, Olds' and others' programs demonstrate that child maltreatment can be prevented. Expenditure of human and social service efforts at the outset may be more productive and humane, less destructive, and more cost effective than efforts after the fact.

## Intimate Partner Violence

**SCOPE OF THE ISSUE.** Intimate partner violence, also known as domestic violence, is a societal issue that is often closely related to child maltreatment. According to the CDC (2010b), intimate partner violence (IPV) describes physical, sexual, or psychological harm by a current or former partner or spouse. This type of violence can occur among heterosexual or same-sex couples and does not require sexual intimacy. The overlap between IPV and child maltreatment is often high (Olds, 2010). In other words, in families where children are being abused, there is also a greater tendency for violence among adults in the family to exist. The most common type of interpersonal violence that is experienced globally is violence toward women. Although there are instances of men being abused by women, they are in the minority of total reported cases. For example, the Bureau of Justice reported that in 2005, IPV resulted in 1,510 deaths. Of these deaths, 78% were females and 22% were males (Bureau of Justice Statistics, 2007). Although death may be seen as the ultimate risk of IPV, there are enormous costs and consequences, both physical and psychological, to the survivors and society in general.

In terms of consequences, there are some obvious physical costs of being in a relationship with an abusive partner (e.g., bruises, broken bones, concussions) (Breiding, Black, & Ryan, 2008). However, research has also revealed that there are significant consequences of IPV on the endocrine and immune systems, including fibromyalgia, irritable bowel syndrome, gynecological disorders, central nervous system disorders, gastrointestinal disorders, and heart and/or circulatory conditions (Crofford, 2007; Leserman & Drossman, 2007). Equally disturbing are the emotional and psychological consequences of IPV, including reduced self-esteem, feelings of helplessness, depression, fear, and psychological numbing (Moradi &Yoder, 2012). Although some of the aforementioned physical consequences either heal in time or can be successfully treated medically, the extent to which a survivor of IPV ever completely recovers from the psychological wounds varies from person to person. In addition, for children who are raised in a home where a parent is being abused, the impact of such role modeling can greatly increase the likelihood that they will be in an abusive relationship as an adult (Olds, 2010). Thus, preventing incidents of IPV is of paramount importance to the entire family.

The Duluth Model (Figure 7.2) was conceived in the early 1980s and was one of the first documented IPV models to focus on issues of power and control (Domestic Abuse Intervention Programs, 2008). Their well-known "Power and Control Wheel" was constructed based on the multi-faceted ways in which abusers utilize this power and control through: minimizing, denying, and blaming; using intimidation; coercion and threats; economic abuse; male privilege; using children; isolation; and emotional abuse. The wheel depicts qualities of non-violent relationships such as non-threatening behavior respect.

**CAUSES OF IPV.** Violence toward women is considered both a public health issue and a social justice issue. Because of the gender disparity of prevalence rates, which is exacerbated in certain cultures, and the fact that men hold economic capital that can be used to control their partners, community psychologists view this issue as one that is in need of systemic intervention. There are a variety of theories that have been proposed to explain the abusive behavior of perpetrators of IPV, many of which focus on gender role adherence and conflict (Schwartz, Waldo, & Daniels, 2005) and male privilege (Stanko, 2003). These theories essentially explain IPV as a function of exaggerated, stereotypical male gender role acceptance, which requires women to stay in a subordinate role in the home. There is empirical evidence for all these theories, including international research that has documented higher rates of sexual assaults in countries where there is less occupational and educational equality across genders (Yodanis, 2004).

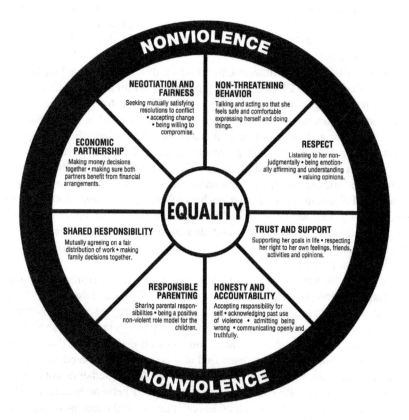

**FIGURE 7.2**   The Duluth Model

Figure reproduced with permission of : Domestic Abuse Intervention Program Duluth, MN 55812

Yet all theories of human behavior are imperfect, and several criticisms of these IPV theories have been leveled. First, there is limited research that has specifically and empirically examined patriarchy (i.e., institutionalized sexism) and its relation to IPV (Woodin & O'Leary, 2009). Second, these theories do not adequately explain incidents of IPV against men, be it by women or other males, nor do these theories apply in the same way to same-sex female couples who exhibit IPV (Burke & Follingstad, 1999). Perhaps the most obvious criticism of these theories, however, is that they do not explain why all, or even most, men are not abusive partners (Healey & Smith, 1998). In other words, similar to our previous discussions of poverty and child maltreatment, just as it cannot be said that poverty "causes" child maltreatment, it also cannot be said that gender inequity "causes" IPV. There are individual and interpersonal factors that must be taken into account when explaining such behavior. Thus, programs that have been designed to eliminate IPV have been focused on both individual/ interpersonal factors that may explain why some individuals are abusive and the community factors that make women vulnerable.

**PREVENTION PROGRAMS.**   According to Davidson, Schwartz, and Waldo (2012), there are two important ways that professionals have attempted to prevent IPV. One way is through early intervention efforts with youths (i.e., person-centered programs) and the other is through public awareness campaigns (i.e., environment-centered programs). An example of the former is a program called the *Youth Relationships Project* (YRP), an adolescent-focused program that aims to prevent abusive behavior as well as promote healthy, nonviolent relationships (Wolfe, Wekerle, Scott, Straatman, Grasley, & Reitzel-Jaffe, 2003). This prevention program is focused on youth who are at risk for IPV because of their history of maltreatment, a research finding that was discussed earlier in this chapter (Olds, 2010). As was discussed in Chapter 1, this type of a program is classified as a *secondary* prevention program in that it targets participants who are higher risk for a specific behavior than the population in general. The content of this program is psychoeducational in that it teaches participants new ways of thinking about and behaving in their romantic relationships. For example, the program teaches participants interpersonal relationship competencies such as conflict resolution and decision making, and nonviolent communication skills within the context of current and future intimate partnerships. To address the influence of gender role adherence, this program also emphasizes awareness of power dynamics and abuse in intimate relationships (Wolfe et al., 1996, 2003). To further model gender role equity, the sessions are cofacilitated by a woman and a man, enabling positive modeling of relationship skills including assertiveness and sharing of power. The program uses a variety of learning approaches including videos, role playing, guest speakers, visits to community agencies, and a community social action project.

Research has shown the YRP program to be effective. Using an experimental, longitudinal design with random assignment to intervention and control conditions, Wolfe and associates (2003) found that program participants demonstrated decreasing severity and frequency of abuse trajectories compared with participants in the control condition. Interestingly, participants in both the intervention and control conditions showed decreases in both abuse perpetration and victimization over time. However, the participants in the YRP intervention condition decreased at a faster rate compared to those in the control condition. This finding suggests that as these adolescents grew older, whether or not they participated in the YRP program, there was a positive trend for relationships to become healthier and less abusive. However, those who were in the program seemed to reach the desired outcome of the program sooner, presumably reducing incidents of IPV along the way.

Another type of intervention that Davidson and associates (2012) describe is environmentally focused, whereby the goal of the program is to change the culture surrounding IPV and attitudes toward violence against women. One example is *Men Against Violence* (MAV) (Hong, 2000), a university-based prevention program that aims to engage men in activism and social change regarding conceptions of masculinity and gender roles, including violence against women. MAV began at Louisiana State University in 1995 as a service organization focused on opposing and preventing a variety of violence-related activities including stalking, IPV, sexual assault, hate crimes, and hazing. Since its inception, other universities have created their own chapters of MAV. According to Hong (2000), the organization uses a community action-based peer education model and is sponsored by the university health center. An elected executive board of undergraduate and graduate students manages the organization with input from an advisory board made up of faculty, staff, and alumni.

The explicit purpose of MAV is to decrease both the frequency and severity of violence among all members of the campus community, with an express emphasis on men's responsibility in this mission. This is accomplished through a variety of activities including media campaigns to the campus and wider community (e.g., a campus-wide newsletter); community action activities including organizing political activism projects; and raising students' awareness of the relationships between sexism, masculinity, and violence by making presentations in university classes, fraternities, and residence halls. In this program, college-aged men are asked to take leadership positions in changing the campus climate (and societal norms) toward IPV. Although this program has not yet undergone the type of evaluation that would determine its long-term impact on the college campus communities it serves, it has promise as a grass-roots approach to prevention of IPV.

While programs such as MAV and YRP attempt to decrease future incidents of IPV by working with individuals whose beliefs about IPV and their experience in actual relationships are still "works in progress," social welfare approaches, often publicly funded, have played an important role in tertiary prevention efforts by offering services to women who escape abusive relationships. Domestic violence shelters are the most common example of these approaches.

**DOMESTIC VIOLENCE SHELTERS.**  Davidson and colleagues (2012) note that there are more than 2,000 community-based programs focused on protecting and supporting victims of IPV in the United States, which provide emergency shelter to approximately 300,000 women and children each year (National Coalition Against Domestic Violence, 2010). According to Walker (1999), the establishment of domestic violence shelters emerged in the 1970s as a community-based crisis intervention. The location of shelters is kept confidential so that IPV perpetrators are unable to locate their victims once they are relocated. Shelters provide physical safety, access to resources (e.g., counseling, medical services), and emotional peace of mind to the women and children they serve and aim to empower women to start new lives with the economic and psychological independence that they often lacked in their lives with their abusers. According to Chronister and colleagues (2009), one of the key factors in permanently escaping violence relationships is economic self-sufficiency. Unfortunately, many women who end up seeking the services of domestic violence shelters have significant disadvantages to overcome on their way to obtaining economic self-sufficiency. Abusers often have directly sabotaged women's attempts to gain employment and access economic resources while they were in the relationship, but they also have denigrated these women, often to the point of destroying their confidence and efficacy for identifying and pursuing economic opportunities in the future (e.g., employment, vocational training), which further exacerbates their emotional and economic dependence (Chronister, 2007).

Recent research (Chronister & McWhirter, 2006) has demonstrated that interventions aimed at career development in domestic violence shelters can positively affect both the women's employment self-efficacy (their confidence in their ability to successfully find and maintain employment) and their progress toward securing work, compared to women who resided in shelters who did not undergo specific career development interventions. Addressing barriers to economic independence is argued to be as important as addressing those that prevent emotional independence. Failure to do so may be part of the reason that some women return to the same abusive relationships or end up in new relationships that are violent. The fact that domestic violence shelters do not provide sufficient services to "guarantee" that women will permanently escape IPV is often leveled as a criticism (Davidson et al., 2012). However, few types of community intervention have 100% success rates, and the reasons that some women stay in violent relationships is a complex interplay of individual, interpersonal, and societal factors.

## Teen Pregnancy

**SCOPE OF THE ISSUE.**  Adolescent pregnancy, such as Monique's, has long been a concern, but the issue has recently become one of the most frequently cited examples of perceived social decay in the United States. Between 750,000 and 1 million teenagers become pregnant each year (McCave, 2007), with over 80% of the pregnancies unintended (National Campaign to Prevent Teen and Unwanted Pregnancy, 2012). Although the rate of teen pregnancy dropped in the mid-1990s, new data indicate that it is again on the rise (National Center for Health Statistics, 2007a). Adolescent birth rates in the United States still remain higher than those in other industrialized countries (CDC, 2011d; Coley & Chase-Lansdale, 1998; National Campaign to Prevent Teen and Unwanted Pregnancy, 2012). Even though U.S.

teenagers do not exhibit different patterns of sexual activity compared with teens from other countries, they use contraception less consistently and less effectively, thereby giving the United States a much higher birth rate (Coley & Chase-Lansdale, 1998).

Teen pregnancy is an important issue because these mothers' babies are often low in birth weight and have a disproportionately high mortality rate (McCave, 2007; National Campaign to Prevent Teen and Unwanted Pregnancy, 2012; Olds, 2005). The young mothers themselves have a high rate of dropout from school and often live in poverty; therefore, they are likely to end up on public assistance (McCave, 2007; National Campaign to Prevent Teen and Unwanted Pregnancy, 2012; U.S. Department of Health and Human Services, 2001b). Monique may be at risk for all of these problems. Teen mothers also have lower levels of marital stability and lower employment security compared to peers who postpone childbearing (Coley & Chase-Lansdale, 1998). Teen mothers and their children are more likely to end up in prison, and their daughters are more likely to become teen mothers themselves compared to other teens (National Campaign to Prevent Teen and Unwanted Pregnancy, 2012). Teen pregnancy can also be hard on teen fathers, such as Rock. The pregnancy can strain fathers' relationships with their girlfriends and their own parents. Teen fathers do not go as far in school and make less money when they go out on the job market than do teens who are not fathers (4parents.gov, 2007). Teen pregnancy costs the United States at least $9 billion annually in public assistance, medical care, and other expenses (National Campaign to Prevent Teen and Unwanted Pregnancy, 2012).

**CAUSES OF TEEN PREGNANCY.**   Some critics argue that the social welfare system in the United States may, in fact, be responsible for the nation's high pregnancy rate among teens. In particular, they believe that such assistance as a source of income actually promotes teen pregnancy and the growth of female-headed households. However, this assumption is not supported by research. Other industrialized countries, such as Sweden and the United Kingdom, that have more comprehensive welfare programs than the United States have *lower* teenage pregnancy rates (Alan Guttmacher Institute, 2004, 2006; CDC, 2007a; Singh & Darrock, 2000). Therefore, public assistance does not appear to cause young women to become or want to become pregnant.

Besides focusing mainly on females, mainstream psychological literature on adolescent pregnancy focuses on the individual and individual deficits as causes, something community psychologists would shun. However, there have been investigations of contextual factors that may influence teenage pregnancy rates in the United States versus other Western countries. For example, Darrock (2001) found that American teens have less access to free or low-cost prescription contraceptives, primary care physicians in the U.S. are far less likely to offer birth control help to teenagers than are physicians in other countries, comprehensive sex education (vs. abstinence only) is favored more in other countries, and other countries have parental leave policies that provide incentives to postpone childbearing. Findings like these highlight the importance of contextual factors in understanding causes of teenage pregnancy.

Community psychologists typically examine different causes—*contextual or ecological ones*—for adolescent pregnancy, such as school alienation that produces low educational aspirations. Another contextual factor is living in poverty (Crosby & Holtgrave, 2005), as experienced by many minorities in America. It is not surprising, given the poverty of many African Americans and Hispanics, that major disparities exist in pregnancy and birth rates by race and ethnicity. Hispanics and Blacks have the highest pregnancy and birth rates of all, nearly 3.5 times higher than White teens (CDC, 2007a). Other ecological reasons for teen pregnancy include perceptions of limited life options as well as exposure to the mass media or to peer pressure to engage in sex (Alan Guttmacher Institute, 2004; Schinke, 1998). These latter reasons help explain teen pregnancies such as that of Monique, a White, suburban teen who was not living in poverty. On the other hand, perhaps Rock, two years older and adored by Monique, put immense pressure on her to engage in sex. Also contributing to teen pregnancy are lack of a support system (parents or peers) and being the victim of sexual assault (Alan Guttmacher Institute, 2004). In addition, social capital, defined in Chapter 4 as resources made available to individuals as the result of their placement within a social structure, is beginning to emerge as another important ecological feature that can prevent teen pregnancy (Crosby & Holtgrave, 2005). In this case, **social capital** includes trust, reciprocity, cooperation, and supportive interaction within families, neighborhoods, and communities. Deficient social capital can contribute to teen pregnancy. Whatever the causes of adolescent pregnancy, the issue is better addressed on a large scale, rather than by individual counseling.

**PREVENTION PROGRAMS.** Although the majority of American teachers and parents agree that sex education is needed in our schools (Alan Guttmacher Institute, 2006), the overly rationalistic perspective that such efforts simply need to expose adolescents to more information or provide them with contraceptives is too narrow (Reppucci, 1987; SIECUS National Guidelines Task Force, 2004). Early in the teen pregnancy intervention movement, Reppucci (1987) reiterated, "The limited effects of these changes are evident in the [still] concomitant high rates of pregnancy, clinic dropouts, and contraceptive nonuse" (p. 7).

What is needed is less focus on individual education (Patterson, 1990) and more focus on an ecological or transactional approach to teen pregnancy (Allen-Meares & Shore, 1986). The ecological approach takes into account the environment surrounding the adolescent. However, the ecological perspective is complicated. It is complex because the adolescent may be confronted by differing viewpoints on sexuality by peers, family members, the community, and the culture. Furthermore, the media to which the adolescent is exposed flagrantly exploit sexuality (Alan Guttmacher Institute, 2004) yet prohibit contraceptives from being advertised (Reppucci, 1987). Early motherhood may be an attractive alternative to low-paying, dead-end jobs available to young, uneducated, and impoverished women (Lawson & Rhode, 1993).

Adding to the conundrum of what to do about sex education, President George W. Bush intensified efforts to direct federal funding to abstinence-only sex education programs as well as to faith-based institutions (rather than schools) (Marx & Hopper, 2005; McCave, 2007). Fortunately, federal funding has now been expanded to include prevention efforts that focus on contraception as well as abstinence (see the Personal Responsibility Education Program, part of the Affordable Care Act). However, in the years where contraception was not included in federally funded prevention efforts, there were undoubtedly some teens who failed to benefit from that information. Monique (but not Rock) was exposed to a little bit of sex education in her health class, but it clearly was not enough to prevent her pregnancy.

Comprehensive sexuality education should cover sexual development, reproductive health (including contraception and sexually transmitted diseases), interpersonal relationships, emotions, intimacy, body image, and gender roles, not just abstinence (SIECUS National Guidelines Task Force, 2004). Moreover, there are important issues related to these more comprehensive types of programs that speak to their significance compared to abstinence-only sex education. First, most teachers believe that topics such as birth control methods, sexual orientation, and other information *should* be taught alongside abstinence. Second, 82% of American adults support comprehensive—not abstinence-only—sex education. Third, research demonstrates that the use of contraceptives explains 75% of the above-mentioned (early 1990s to mid-2000s) decline in teen pregnancies while abstinence explains only 25% (SIECUS National Guidelines Task Force, 2004).

We now focus on one well-known comprehensive program—the Carrera Program. In 1984, Dr. Carrera and The Children's Aid Society developed a comprehensive sex education/teen pregnancy prevention program that centers on the belief that success in school, meaningful employment, access to quality medical and health services, and interactions with high-caliber, adult role models have a potent "contraceptive" effect on teens. The Carrera Program takes a holistic view of adolescents, which is a relatively new direction for the prevention of teen pregnancy (Allen, Seitz, & Apfel, 2007). Specific program components include:

- *Education:* Individual academic plans for each participant, daily one-on-one or small group tutoring, PSAT and SAT preparation, college trips, and a college scholarship fund.
- *Employment:* Job Club is a full introduction to the world of work, including opening bank accounts, exploring career choices, and providing summer and part-time jobs. Participants are paid a stipend and make monthly deposits in their bank accounts.
- *Family Life and Sexuality Education (FLSE):* Weekly comprehensive sexuality education sessions taught in an age-appropriate fashion.
- *Self-Expression:* Weekly music, dance, writing and drama workshops led by theater and arts professionals, where children can discover talents and build self-esteem.
- *Lifetime Individual Sports:* A fitness program emphasizing sports that build self-discipline and can be played throughout life, including golf, squash, swimming, and surfing.
- *Full Medical and Dental Care:* Comprehensive physicals and medical services in partnership with the Adolescent Health Center of the Mt. Sinai Medical Center. Full dental services provided by The Children's Aid Society.
- *Mental Health Services:* Counseling and crisis intervention as needed, and weekly discussion groups led by certified social workers.
- *Parent Family Life and Sexuality Education:* A program that facilitates parents'/adults' ability to communicate more effectively with their [adolescent] children about important family life and sexuality issues (The Children's Aid Society, 2008).

These programs run five days a week during the school year. In the summer, young people receive assistance with employment, and maintenance meetings are held to reinforce sex education and academic skills. There are also occasional social, recreational, and cultural trips (Philliber, Kaye, & Herrling, 2001).

In a multisite program evaluation using random assignment of at-risk youths to either control or treatment groups, researchers (Philliber et al., 2001) determined that the program successfully reduced teen sexuality and teen pregnancy by 50% in the communities served. One way the program produced this latter result was to facilitate effective use of protection (contraception) among young women who became sexually active. The program also resulted in additional benefits, such as linking young people with medical care (private physicians rather than visits to the emergency room), encouraging them to participate in the workforce, enhancing participants' computer skills, promoting higher graduation rates, and increasing certain standardized test scores (Children's Aid Society, 2008).

Community psychologists would remind us that prevention programs need to be culturally sensitive, too—an important topic not yet addressed on the issue of teen pregnancy—because no one program or component holds all the solutions for all groups (Stoiber & McIntyre, 2006). Just as surely as culture and ethnicity influence childrearing, they undoubtedly shape sexual practices and beliefs, such as when, where, and with whom to engage in sex.

To enlarge on the issue of culture, let's focus on Hispanic teen pregnancy, because the rates currently are highest for this group. Several authors have elaborated on values and themes in Hispanic cultures that may account for the higher rates of teen pregnancy in that population. Gilliam (2007) explains that Latina parents rely on fear to dissuade their daughters from pregnancy as opposed to open communication about sexuality and contraception. Wilkinson-Lee, Russell, and Lee (2006) identified other facets of Hispanic culture that may be important to pregnancy prevention. One cultural value is **familismo,** which is a collective loyalty to the extended family that outranks the needs of the individual. **Personalismo,** translated as "formal friendliness," is another important value in which Hispanic individuals expect to have formal but warm personal relationships with any authority figure, such as healthcare professionals or educators. Wilkinson-Lee and her colleagues remind us that Hispanic teens often hear conflicting messages from their traditional culture and religion versus mainstream American culture. Clearly, cultural sensitivity is important to program design and effectiveness. Here we examine a sample program related to these issues.

Méndez-Negrete, Saldaña, and Vega (2006) preliminarily report on a culturally sensitive program in San Antonio, Texas, called Escuelitas for Mexican American girls who are at risk for pregnancy. San Antonio unfortunately leads the nation in pregnancy among girls age 15 and under. Escuelitas provide an after-school organizational and social structure that supplements the formal, social institutions of traditional schools and families. The Escuelitas (translated as "little schools") provide experiences and activities that support and encourage academic, personal, cultural, and social achievements designed to prevent teen pregnancy and delinquency as well as reduce school dropout rates.

Girls come from low-income families and are recruited from schools with high incidences of teen pregnancy, delinquency, and school dropout. In the Escuelitas, students meet after school for three 90-minute sessions each week. Activities consist of guest speakers, tutorials, group discussions, and relational workshops with their mothers or guardians (familismo). University students and adult Hispanic role models act as mentors and presenters (personalismo). Presentations by the Hispanic role models, for example, focus on the cultural assets of the students and on their cultural heritage. Note that students are not randomly assigned to the Escuelitas and are not compared to a no-intervention group. However, the preliminary results point to program successes. As of 2004, *none* of the participants had dropped out of school, and *none* had become pregnant. Though these results are encouraging, we certainly need more data and better designed research on Escuelitas before the program is adopted and disseminated elsewhere.

One of the major problems of teen pregnancy prevention is that although effective and scientifically based programs are available, they are not well known in local communities across the country. Efforts are now under way to build prevention infrastructures in and guide large-scale prevention strategies for various communities, thanks to the efforts of certain community psychologists (Lesesne, Lewis, White, & Green, 2008).

## The Elderly

**SCOPE OF THE ISSUE.** The population of the United States is aging. As the swell of baby boomers moves through time, the ranks of the aged are increasing. Medical advances allow people to live longer, with most women outliving men. At the beginning of the 20th century, only 4.1% of the total U.S. population was elderly (Blakemore, Washington, & McNeely, 1995). Today, the percentage of Americans age 65 and older has tripled, and the total number has increased almost 12-fold (from 3.1 million to 36.3 million). Figure 7.3 illustrates the dramatic increase in our elderly population and provides projections through 2050.

The elderly, unfortunately, have been largely ignored in the community psychology literature. Steffen (1996) reviewed articles in the *American Journal of Community Psychology* from 1988 to 1994 and found a weak emphasis on aging. Over the seven-year period, only 13 articles focused specifically on older adults. Given that in 2005 many elderly lived at (3.6 million) or near (2.3 million) the poverty line, and given the demographics in Figure 7.3, the topic of aging Americans should not be so ignored in the literature. Other professionals agree that as a society, we are way behind in our efforts to study and promote optimal aging (Chapman, 2007).

The stereotype of the elderly in the United States is that of a wrinkled, incoherent person rocking in a chair in a nursing home. Obviously, this negative stereotype, although incorrect, persists (Cuddy, Norton, & Fiske, 2005; Kite, Stockdale, Whitley, & Johnson, 2005). Most elderly, in fact, live and die in their own homes (Steffen, 1996) rather than in hospitals or nursing homes. Separation of the young and the old in American culture is one factor that leads to such stereotyping (Hagestad & Uhlenberg, 2005).

Although these stereotypes often result in adults of any age fearing the prospect of growing old, there is good news to report. The concept of "healthy aging" has emerged in the past several years to provide a new lens through which aging can be viewed. The term *healthy aging* has guided the development of social initiatives to promote quality of life in old age. Peel, Bartlett, and McClure (2004) noted that the concept of healthy aging has received substantial international attention in countries including Canada, Australia, and parts of the European Union. For example, one Canadian initiative embraced a framework supported by three values: (1) the celebration of diversity, (2) a refutation of ageism in all of its forms including economic inequities, and (3) the active creation of opportunities within the community for independence and quality of life (Menec, Button, Blandford, & Morris-Oswald, 2007).

This perspective is very compatible with a community psychology philosophy in that well-being of older adults is significantly influenced by the environments they live in where resources must be accessible and stressors such as ageism must be eliminated.

This is not to say that our aging population, as with any group, is entirely without problems. For example, two frequent and particularly important transitions of aging are loss of health and loss of spouse. Loss of spouse and significant others in an elderly person's life can cause depression and stress (Vacha-Haase & Duffy, 2011). In addition, declining health is exacerbated by perceived lack of control over health matters, personal barriers such as memory deficits, and societal barriers such

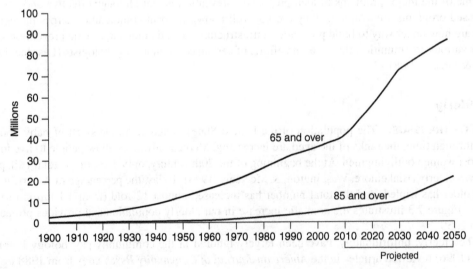

**FIGURE 7.3**  Number of People Age 65 and Over, by Age Group, for Selected Years 1900–2000 and Projected to 2010–2050

*Source:* U.S. Census Bureau (2000), Decennial Census and Projections. Washington, D.C.

as lack of transportation and high-cost healthcare (Dapp, Anders, von Rentein-Kruse, & Meier-Baumgartner, 2005). Families of the elderly who provide caregiving can also find themselves under stress (Hardin & Khan-Hudson, 2005; Singleton, 2000), especially employed family members (Hardin & Khan-Hudson, 2005).

**ELDER ABUSE.**   Unfortunately, because the elderly at some point often do become dependent on others to care for them, they are as vulnerable to maltreatment as are children. Elder abuse is a societal problem in the United States that is defined very similarly to how child maltreatment was defined earlier in this chapter. The one way in which elder maltreatment can manifest differently, however, is in the financial exploitation of the elderly. The National Center on Elder Abuse, an office of the U.S. Administration of Aging (www.ncea.aoa.gov), in a 2005 publication reported that between 1 and 2 million Americans age 65 or older have been injured, exploited, or otherwise mistreated by someone on whom they depended for care or protection. Perhaps more disturbing are the estimates of elder maltreatment that go unreported. For example, current estimates put the overall reporting of financial exploitation at only 1 in 25 cases, suggesting that there may be at least 5 million financial abuse victims each year. Furthermore, it is estimated that for every one case of elder abuse, neglect, or exploitation reported to authorities, about five more go unreported. These statistics suggest that the scope of this problem may be grossly underestimated.

Although most states have laws to protect against elder mistreatment, if elderly people are segregated from others, which may be the case in a homebound or nursing care facility situation, it may be difficult to know mistreatment is happening. Another complication is that those elderly who are frail from physical or mental illnesses are prone to accidental injuries from falling. Thus, it is often not easy to determine whether bruises are the result of a fall or of maltreatment. For this reason and many others, enhancing the well-being of the elderly has been a priority in the prevention arena. Keeping the elderly mentally and physically healthy offers the direct benefit of keeping them socially active and less vulnerable to the maltreatment that confined settings may present.

We concentrate here on two issues that have received attention in the prevention literature that has examined elder health—personal control and social support. Both are postulated to enhance the well-being of the elderly. Note, however, that there are many other factors affecting the welfare of the elderly (Lehr, Seiler, & Thomae, 2000) that we cannot include here because of limited space.

## PREVENTION PROGRAMS

**Social Support.**   Myriad programs exist for the elderly that focus on enhancing the quality of their lives, with only a few mentioned here. One well-examined approach to preserving the emotional well-being and sense of security of the elderly is to provide them with social support (Greenglass, Fiksenbaum, & Eaton, 2006). Social support by means of informal networks of family (Tice, 1991), confidants (Lowenthal & Haven, 1968), or others (Abrahams & Patterson, 1978–1979) has been reputed to increase morale, buffer the effects of loss of loved ones, and slow the deterioration of health (Choi & Wodarski, 1996; Greenglass et al., 2006).

More recently, researchers have made use of the Internet to provide social support to the elderly, especially those who might feel isolated because of age or disability. First, the Internet can be viewed as a preventive tool that might delay or avert age-associated physiological and behavioral changes restricting elderly functioning, for example, isolation. Second, the Internet might help compensate for age-related losses in strength and perceptual-motor functioning, such as slowed eye-hand coordination. Third, it might be a good communication tool for the frail elderly, those too frail or too hard of hearing to leave their homes or use their telephones for social interaction (Fozard & Kearns, 2007).

Shapira, Barak, and Gal (2007) compared older adults in day-care centers and nursing homes trained in Internet use with a comparison group of nontrained individuals. Both groups were administered interviews, health assessments, and life satisfaction, depression, loneliness, and other scales. On all measures (except physical functioning) the Internet group improved while the comparison group declined. The researchers concluded that indeed, Internet use can contribute to older adults' well-being and sense of empowerment by affecting their interpersonal interactions, promoting better cognitive functioning, and contributing to the sense of personal control and independence. This last finding provides an interesting segue to our next topic.

**Sense of Self-Control.**   As mentioned, self- or personal control is one issue relevant to the elderly. Every facet of aging, such as health and cognitive functioning, involves the issue of control (Baltes & Baltes, 1986). **Self-control** is the belief that we can influence events in our environment that affect our lives (Duffy & Atwater, 2008). Increasing the sense of self-control of the elderly is a technique that has proven to produce positive results (Shapira, Barak, & Gal, 2007; Thompson & Spacespan, 1991; Zarit, Pearlin, & Schaie, 2003), such as better mental health (Reich & Zautra, 1991). An enhanced sense of control leads to feelings of empowerment, a coveted principle of community psychology.

In a very early test of this issue, Langer and Rodin (1976) matched two groups of elderly in a nursing home on age, health, and other important dimensions. One group was shown in detail how much control they had over their lives. They decided how to arrange their rooms, when to greet visitors, and how to spend spare time. Each of these residents was given a plant to care for. The second group was told that their lives were mainly under staff control. For example, these elderly were also given a plant but were told the staff would take care of it. Pre- and postintervention questionnaires about feelings of personal control, happiness, and activity level were administered to the elderly and completed by the care staff. Almost all before-and-after comparisons favored the intervention group—the one with a higher sense of self-control. Eighteen months later, Rodin and Langer (1977) conducted a follow-up. Half as many experimental participants had died as had control participants. This study demonstrates that the quality of life for the elderly can indeed be enhanced when they believe they have more control over it (Schulz & Heckhausen, 1996). Subsequent research has replicated the fact that a sense of self-regulation (e.g., Wrosch, Dunne, Scheier, & Schultz, 2006) or self-control (e.g., Zarit et al., 2003) has an enhancing effect on the quality of life and the health of older individuals.

## Homelessness

Some Americans stereotype the homeless as drunk or mentally disabled old men who deserve what they get—a life of misery on the streets. Rock and Monique, for example, would taunt the homeless who lived near subway entrances of the city close to the suburbs where they lived. On the other hand, some people feel sorry for homeless individuals and hand them money. Community psychologists are concerned with homelessness not just for humane reasons but because homelessness carries with it myriad problems for the individual. The issue of homelessness is discussed here for these reasons and because homeless individuals end up interfacing with a variety of social and human services.

**SCOPE OF THE ISSUE.**   The extent of the problem of homelessness is difficult to determine, for one thing because homelessness is difficult to define (National Coalition for the Homeless, 2011; Shinn et al., 2007; Tompsett et al., 2006). According to the U.S. Government's Homeless Management Information System data, nearly 1.6 million people used emergency or transitional shelters between October 1, 2006, and September 30, 2007. However, other agencies estimate the problem to be greater. For example, the National Coalition for the Homeless (2011) estimates that more than 3.5 million men, women, and children are homeless. One reason for the difficulty in making accurate estimates is that the homeless are a heterogeneous group; the group includes people of all races, families with or without children, single individuals, individuals who move from temporary shelters to homelessness and back to some type of shelter, as well as others (National Coalition for the Homeless, 2011).

Who are today's homeless? Rossi (1990) devised an interesting way of classifying the homeless. He suggested that there are old homeless and new homeless. The **old homeless** are the individuals who are generally stereotyped as homeless. These are older, alcoholic men who sleep in cheap flophouses or skid-row hotels. They are "old" because they are the type of homeless who were seen on city streets after World War II. The **new homeless** are indeed truly homeless. They do not sleep in cheap hotels but are literally on the streets or at best may find shelters to escape into during inclement weather.

The new homeless include more women and children than in the past, although the National Coalition for the Homeless (2011) estimates that single men make up over half of all homeless adults (see also Shinn et al., 2007). Likewise, there are age differences between the new and old homeless, with the new homeless being much younger. The National Coalition for the Homeless (2011) estimated that children under the age of 18 account for 1.35 million of the homeless population. Another difference is that the new homeless suffer a much more profound degree of economic destitution than the old homeless. One final difference between the old and the new homeless is that the ethnic and racial composition has changed over the years. Today's homeless are more likely to be from minority groups rather than White, as was true of the old homeless. For example, some databases report racial breakdowns of homeless individuals to be 42% African-American, 39% White, 13% Hispanic, 4% Native American, and 2% Asian (American Psychological Association, 2005; National Coalition for the Homeless, 2011).

As for families experiencing homelessness, homeless children suffer a number of compounding problems, largely due to their homelessness (Burt, Pearson, & Montgomery, 2007). Studies have consistently shown that homeless children have elevated levels of acute and chronic health problems compared to housed children (Gewirtz, 2007; Walsh & Jackson, 2005) as well as poorer nutrition (Molnar, Rath, & Klein, 1990). Homeless children are also more likely to experience developmental delays, such as short attention spans, speech delays, inappropriate social interactions (Rafferty, Shinn, & Weitzman, 2004), and psychological problems such as anxiety, behavior disorders, and depression (Rafferty & Shinn, 1991). In addition, achievement scores on standardized tests for homeless children are well below those of housed children (Rafferty, 1990), primarily because homeless children frequently move from school to school—when they are lucky enough to be enrolled in school.

Zugazaga (2004) and Muñoz, Panadero, Santo, and Quiroga (2005) have also studied homelessness in relationship to stressful life experiences. The latter group of researchers has found that there are distinct groups of homeless based on analyses of stressful life events. Their results revealed the existence of three subgroups of homeless. Group A was characterized by economic problems, such as unemployment; this group functioned well and had few mental health or substance abuse problems. Group B was typified by substance abuse and health problems, resulting in longer durations of homelessness. Psychologists and healthcare professionals have long recognized that poor health and homelessness are intricately intertwined (Flick, 2007; O'Connell, 2007; Smith, Easterlow, Munro, & Turner, 2003). Group C was of lower average age and manifested multiple problems, many stemming from childhood (such as abuse or parental alcoholism). Note that this study was conducted in Spain, but the overarching conclusion is important—the existence of subgroups of homeless people emphasizes the importance of designing different interventions for each group, adapted to their diverse needs. Another stressful life event related to homelessness but not necessarily revealed in the cited research is exposure to trauma or traumatic life events, such as being the victim of violence (Kim & Ford, 2006). Preventing posttraumatic stress disorder and addressing its influence on people in the early stages of homelessness can go a long way toward intervening in homelessness.

Interest in understanding cross-national homelessness is also growing in the field of community psychology because there may be much we can learn from the experiences of other countries. Interest in the United States is mounting, especially in other developed countries and their programs designed to address homelessness. For example, in Great Britain and the countries of the European Union, men and minorities (those discriminated against) are overrepresented among the homeless ranks just as in the United States (Toro, 2007). Case in Point 7.3 provides more information on international perspectives on homelessness.

## CASE IN POINT 7.3

# How Do Cultures Differ on the Issue of Homelessness?

You have been reading the American perspective on homelessness. Because one of the goals of this text is to introduce you to multicultural aspects of community problems, we are well served by examining how other countries are researching and managing homelessness. As we turn our attention to other cultures to learn from them, be mindful that we "cannot transplant policies and programs from one country to another without considering the foreign soil in which the plants must take root" (Okamato, 2007, p. 525).

A 2007 edition of the *Journal of Social Issues* offered articles from authors and researchers from around the world. Understanding what produces homelessness and just who is homeless in other countries might provide lessons and insights for the American public as well as for community psychologists. Two particular authors from seemingly different cultures—the Czech Republic and Japan—offered interesting cultural perspectives on homelessness.

In Japan, there was no word for *homelessness* until after the destruction of World War II (Okamato, 2007). With a changing economy (i.e., movement toward a technological society) and government policy changes, there is now not only a phrase, "rough sleeping," but increased interest in homelessness. The term **rough sleepers** was essentially coined by the media for individuals who sleep in public places, such as parks. Many of the rough sleepers

are minorities, just as they are in the United States. Koreans, for example, are minorities in Japan and are thus more likely to be homeless than are Japanese citizens. As in the United States, the majority of homeless are men—some are even employed—but they are likely to be older than homeless men in the United States. One major cause of homelessness in Japan is that housing was often tied to employment; that is, employers offered housing to employees as a perk, so when jobs were lost, housing was lost. Japanese companies today are less likely to offer the lifetime employment and housing security they offered in the past.

As in the United States and Japan, in the Czech Republic there are personal as well as structural reasons for homelessness. A personal reason might be divorce or loss of employment; a social or structural reason is the problem of runaway or homeless youth for whom there are no shelters. In both Japan and the Czech Republic (and some would argue, the United States) the government provides low budgets for social welfare spending (Shinn, 2007).

There are differences, however, between Japan and the Czech Republic. In the Czech Republic (Hladikova & Hradecky, 2007), rough sleepers are those who are literally roofless; they do not sleep under a roof, as in a shelter. Other nomenclature exists in the Czech Republic for the remainder of the homeless population,

such as those in *insecure* housing (where the housing might be lost at any minute because of job loss) and those who have *inadequate* housing (where an apartment is too crowded or substandard with no heat or running water). To mention a few other differences, homelessness historically became an issue and a larger problem in the Czech Republic with the fall of communism. People today retain a right to work (just as they did under the communists), but continual corruption and bribery make the employment system much more competitive and difficult than in the past. The political breakup of Czechoslovakia also contributed to much social strife; no such massive political upheaval has occurred recently in Japan to contribute to the homeless problem. In the Czech Republic, rather than the government providing social services, nongovernmental organizations (NGOs) or private social services and charities have taken up the banner of helping the homeless. In Japan, the law states that all people shall have the right to maintain minimum standards of wholesome and cultured living. Furthermore, in all spheres of life, the state shall use its endeavors for the promotion and extension of social welfare and security, although this is not a common practice (e.g., low government spending) when it comes to housing. In reality, Japanese families, rather than NGOs and the government, have often taken over the burden of providing housing for those in need.

**CAUSES OF HOMELESSNESS.**    To prevent something from happening, one needs to know what causes it or have the ability to predict in advance when or to whom it will happen; this, of course, applies to homelessness (Burt et al., 2007). Studies show that homelessness is often episodic, or at least is not a chronic condition for all individuals (National Coalition for the Homeless, 1999; Shinn, 1997; Sosin, Piliavin, & Westerfelt, 1990), so focusing only on person-centered factors may not account for all cases of homelessness. Person-centered causes include but are not limited to issues such as mental disorders and life stressors, as previously mentioned. Unemployment is also another major consideration in homelessness (McBride, Calsyn, Morse, Klinkenberg, & Allen, 1998; Shaheen & Rio, 2007; Shinn et al., 2007).

Person-centered explanations such as mental disorders, life stressors, and unemployment are only partially useful for explaining homelessness—regardless of how popular these explanations are in the mass media. We wisely turn our attention to ecological factors. Shinn (1992) conducted some seminal research to expand the understanding of whether structural variables explain homelessness. In her study, a sample of 700 randomly selected homeless families requesting shelter were compared to 524 families selected randomly from the public assistance caseload. The first group represented "the homeless" and the second "the housed poor." Only 4%—a small percentage—of the homeless in the sample had been previously hospitalized for mental illness. Only 8% of the homeless and 2% of the housed poor had been in a detoxification center for substance abuse. Shinn concluded that individual deficits were relatively unimportant in differentiating the homeless from the housed poor.

Shinn also found that only 37% of the homeless, compared to 86% of the poor housed families, had broken into the housing market (i.e., had been primary tenants in a place they stayed for a long time). In addition, 45% of the homeless versus 26% of the housed poor reported having three or more persons per bedroom in the place they had stayed the longest. The researcher regards poor housing opportunities and crowding to be better explanations for homelessness than personal deficits or individual level explanations. (See also Shinn & Tsemberis, 1998.)

In a five-year follow-up on homelessness, Shinn and associates (1998) stated that "subsidized housing is the only predictor of residential stability after shelter" (p. 1655). In other words, the research team found that once a family entered a shelter, five years later many were able to have their own residences, but only with financial assistance. Zlotnick, Robertson, and Lahiff (1999), in a 15-month prospective study, also reported that subsidized housing is one of the most important factors associated with exiting homelessness. Thus, because of the newer welfare laws as well as fewer new units of subsidized housing, future homeless families may not fare so well (Western Regional Advocacy Project, 2006).

Other ecological and structural causes—outside of the person—have been identified. The National Coalition for the Homeless (2007b) identifies lack of affordable healthcare as a cause of homelessness. Individuals who are struggling to pay the rent and also have a serious illness or disability can start a downward spiral into homelessness when payment of medical bills results in lack of funds to pay rent (Burt et al., 2007). Domestic violence also results in homelessness (National Coalition for the Homeless, 2007b). Many women choose to become homeless rather than remain with an abuser. Recently, Shinn and colleagues (2007) also identified a paucity of social capital (defined earlier) as a major contributor to homelessness. Without social support and nearby family members or friends who can provide aid, many individuals find themselves homeless. These factors do not exhaust the list of causes but do help identify the myriad pathways by which individuals and families descend into homelessness. Because no social problem originates from a single cause, clearly, solutions to the problem of homelessness are not simple. Until prevention policies focus on a general strategy against *all* aspects of poverty (Firdion & Marpsat, 2007), focusing on keeping people in their homes or on person-centered factors such as unemployment is less likely to work. Poverty indeed is a primary contributor to nearly every major social problem in this chapter.

**PREVENTION PROGRAMS.**    Several suggestions for addressing homelessness have already been reviewed—planning psychiatric hospital discharges better, addressing unemployment, increasing the amount of affordable housing, and subsidizing housing expenses, to mention a few. Given that these approaches take much time and money or are subject to the caprices of politicians, what else is available to address homelessness?

Many communities in the United States have programs in place to prevent or address homelessness. Some professionals, though, argue that these community programs have yet to provide strong evidence that their homelessness prevention efforts are effective (Burt et al., 2007). Others appear more optimistic and suggest that prevention efforts are promising (Moses, Kresky-Wolff, Bassuk, & Brounstein, 2007). Fortunately for us, Burt and colleagues (2007) have published fairly new, albeit sketchy evidence that community-wide strategies for preventing homelessness, especially among those being released from institutional care, can be successful. The researchers, with great difficulty, identified five possibly effective programs from a multitude of federal grant applications. Not surprisingly, they also found that many of the programs they reviewed but did not include in their analysis did not maintain adequate data on the efficacy or efficiency of their programs. Because the sample is small and because of other design factors, the following results must be balanced with some uncertainty while we await other such studies.

Burt and colleagues found five activities that are useful for preventing homelessness and may be used alone or in combination in community-wide prevention programs:

- Providing housing subsidies (money) for first-time homeless individuals and families
- Coupling supportive social services with permanent housing
- Using housing-court mediation between tenants and landlords to prevent eviction
- Cash assistance for rent or for mortgage arrears
- For secondary prevention, rapid exiting from homeless shelters to housing

Burt and associates—and the American Psychological Association (2005)—also emphasize that merely throwing money and services at high-risk populations will not work *unless* the following key elements are also present in the programs:

- At-risk populations need to be well targeted, using data from multiple agencies.
- The community must accept as important its obligation to assist at-risk populations.
- Relevant community agencies must collaborate with one another on prevention efforts.
- Someone or some agency needs to take the lead collecting data on progress, monitoring gaps in the system, knowing the needs of the population, and contacting agencies so as to establish collaboration.

The best solution to the homeless problem in the United States, though, may be a concerted and organized public policy program at the federal level. Charities and local governments alone cannot meet the growing needs of the homeless (Gore, 1990). One piece of legislation aimed at grappling with the homeless problem on a national level is the McKinney-Vento Homeless Assistance Act. It established an Interagency Council on Homelessness to coordinate, monitor, and improve the federal response to the problems of homelessness. The act established an Emergency Food Shelter Program National Board as well as local boards across the country to determine how program funds could best be used. Grants and demonstration programs—for example, for drug and alcohol-abuse treatment for addicted, homeless individuals—were authorized by the law, and the Temporary Emergency Food

Assistance Program was reauthorized as well (Barak, 1991). A coherent policy of federal legislation needs to pursue increased low-income housing, treatments for mentally disabled and substance-abusing homeless, and education and job training for homeless individuals (American Psychological Association, 2005; Gore, 1990).

What have we learned by examining child maltreatment, intimate partner violence, teen pregnancy, the elderly, and the homeless? Messages for community psychologists and other prevention experts cut across these groups.

- The types of individuals affected by these problems are diverse.
- There are multiple causes for each of these social problems, few of which are created by the individuals affected by the problem.
- Single solutions for these problems will not work; *multifaceted* efforts will yield better results.
- When various social service agencies are involved in interventions—whether the interventions are primary or secondary in nature—their efforts need to be *coordinated* to be effective.
- Government officials, affected individuals, and social service agencies must come together or collaborate in order to address these issues.

## Summary

Social welfare or ideas and activities to promote social good have a long history in Western society. Until modern times, two major forms of social welfare were charity/philanthropy (private assistance) and public welfare (public assistance). During the 19th century (around the time of the Industrial Revolution), two other forms of social welfare were born: social insurance (public assistance derived from taxation) and social service (public nonmaterial human services derived from taxation). To receive social welfare, people must demonstrate their need, usually in the form of a low standard of living or poor economic means.

It is generally believed (i.e., stereotyped) that recipients of social welfare are lazy, despite the fact that they might genuinely need such assistance. On the other hand, donors to community services are perceived to be honorable people, although research indicates that willingness to help is often a function of environmental factors (e.g., people are more generous during religious seasons).

Five groups that interface regularly with human services in U.S. communities are maltreated children and their families, survivors of domestic violence, pregnant teens, the elderly, and the homeless.

Teen parents and others—such as people who themselves were abused children—are predicted to be at risk for maltreating a child. Providing social support, parenting and prenatal education, and links between the parents and services in the community can sometimes prevent child abuse. The Nurse-Family Partnership program has proven to be particularly successful in reducing child maltreatment among first-time, at-risk teen mothers and has been disseminated nationwide.

Women who are being victimized by intimate partner violence are at risk for enormous physical and psychological injuries, including death. Those who are able to escape such situations often face an uphill battle as they attempt to gain emotional and economic independence for themselves and their children. Programs to address this problem include prevention aimed at changing gender role beliefs, improving interpersonal skills, and attempting to provide psychological and career services for women who seek safety in domestic violence shelters.

The problem of pregnant adolescents is major; the United States leads other industrialized countries in this statistic. The prevailing culture does not provide good role models; thus, the problem persists. Programs to reach teenagers before they become sexually active include abstinence-only and comprehensive sex education. Comprehensive sex education (rather than abstinence-only education) provides teens with sex education that better ensures they will not be stuck in the welfare quagmire so frequently found in teen parenthood.

The elderly sometimes interface with services in the community, too, although the elderly are a rather neglected group in the community psychology literature. Declining health, loss of mobility, death of loved ones, and loss of control are problems for the elderly. As is true with other groups, not all community interventions are effective with the elderly. However, providing the elderly with social support and increasing their sense of control or sense of personal efficacy can maintain their self-esteem and health for longer periods.

Homelessness is an increasing problem in the United States. Stereotypically, the homeless are drunk or mentally disabled old men. The new homeless, however, include many children and women as well as previously employed and previously housed individuals. Providing more affordable housing and better and coordinated public policies and social services will go a long way toward solving this problem.

What has been learned from the examination of maltreated children, survivors of domestic violence, pregnant teens, the elderly, and the homeless? For one thing, not all interventions work equally well, and no single intervention works for all groups. Interventions need to be multifaceted; that is, they must address multiple issues and use multiple approaches. Efforts should take into account ecological factors as well, and not just focus on the individual level. Efforts by all affected individuals and groups need to be well coordinated to be effective and efficient.

# Schools, Children, and the Community

*I touch the future. I teach.*

—Christa McAuliffe (teacher, astronaut)

Mi nombre es Roberto. Nací en Mexico y me mude a los Estados Unidos cuando era un niño. En mi casa, solamente se hablaba español. Un día, cuando estaba en el séptimo grado, mi maestra me pidió que leyera en frente de la clase. Yo trate de leer, pero no pude reconocer algunas de las palabras en inglés. La maestra me interrumpió y me dijo que yo no sabía leer muy bien y que debía sentarme. Después, ella llamó a un niño Americano, quien leía mejor que yo. Yo me senti bastante avergonzado.

Could you read this passage? Imagine how frustrating textbooks, television programs, and public announcements are to individuals for whom English is a second or third language. Programs that might help individuals such as Roberto are discussed later in Case in Point 2. For now, we begin again, this time in English.

My name is Roberto. I was born in Mexico, and I moved to the United States when I was a child. In my house, only Spanish was spoken. One day, when I was in the second grade, my teacher asked that I read in front of the class. I tried to read, but I was not able to recognize some of the English words. The teacher interrupted me and told me that I did not know how to read very well and to sit down. After that, she called on an American child who read better than I. I was quite embarrassed.

Roberto's story continues: I had to repeat the second grade, but this time with a different teacher, Miss Martinez. She had experienced much the same embarrassment when she was a child, so she was sympathetic to my situation. Her extra help inspired me to do my best. In no time, I was speaking and reading English well, almost as well as my classmates. By high school, I was a very good student. My good grades and my ability to play soccer well had endeared me to my fellow classmates enough so that they liked me. Unlike some of the other Hispanic students, I was quite popular, which made my life easier than theirs.

Today, I am in college; I am studying to be a lawyer. Actually, I don't want to be a lawyer; I want to be a legislator. I view law as the avenue to a political career. One of my goals as a legislator is to reform American schools so that all children will feel welcome and comfortable in them.

Consider for a moment how it feels to be a child whom others view as different because of a different skin color, a foreign-sounding name, an accent or language other than English, or the use of a wheelchair. This chapter explores the world of schools as it relates to children and families. In a special issue about human capital, the National Behavioral Science research agenda committee of the American Psychological Society (1992) remarked, "There is no better way to invest in human capital than to improve our schools" (p. 17). The schools themselves are small communities as well as integral parts of the communities they serve. Every school issue cannot possibly be covered here, but this chapter touches on some of the more salient ones: child care, diversity in the classroom, and stressful events such as school violence and parental divorce.

## THE EARLY CHILDHOOD ENVIRONMENT

Urie Bronfenbrenner (1979, 1999) presented what he considered at the time to be an unorthodox conceptualization of child development. He formulated the ecological perspective of human development. **Development,** to Bronfenbrenner and other psychologists, involves "a lasting change in the way in which the individual perceives and deals with the environment" (p. 3, 1979). The **ecological setting** refers to a set of interdependent contexts, or settings, embedded within one another. At the innermost level are the immediate settings in which the child exists, such as the home or a classroom. The next layer consists of the interrelationships between these settings, as in the links between the child's home and the school. The third level, interestingly, is the environment in which the child has not direct participation but that has an indirect effect on development, such as the policies of the parents' places of employment (e.g., availability of day care and healthcare). All levels in this conceptualization are interconnected rather than independent. The way the individual interacts with these settings and perceives them is important in influencing the course of the individual's development. As you may already know, the ecological perspective and the transactional nature of the individual's encounters with various elements in the environment are of utmost importance in community psychology.

A concrete example might further your understanding of this model. Suppose Johnnie is having trouble focusing his attention on his studies in the third grade. Using the individual level of analysis, his teacher might believe that Johnnie needs additional assistance with his math and spelling (e.g., tutoring) or medication for his attention-deficit disorder. An ecological perspective would take into account other contexts, such as Johnnie's home situation and neighborhood or even the playground at the school. The reality might be that Johnnie's home life is stressful because his parents are divorcing. Furthermore, his father might be unemployed, which is contributing to his parents' discord and Johnnie's inattention.

Johnnie is also being teased on the playground and thus finds concentrating in the classroom difficult when surrounded by the bullies. Perhaps what would most assist Johnnie is some social support from other children whose parents have divorced or an adult who watches over his safety on the playground—not extra tutoring from the teacher.

As Bronfenbrenner suggested, advances in understanding development require investigation of the actual environments, both immediate and remote, in which human beings live. This chapter examines settings in which children develop—especially educational ones such as day-care centers and schools. Although we review these settings separately, it is important to remember that they are interconnected with each other as well as other contexts not specifically discussed in this chapter. For example, immediately following this paragraph, the topic of child care will be discussed. Research has demonstrated that the triad of family structure (one versus two parents), the day-care structure (in-home care or day-care center), and the day-care process (content of the activities) influence a child's language development in very complex ways (National Institute of Child and Human Development [NICHD], 2006). Research has demonstrated that other ecological factors such as the family environment and teacher perceptions of students predict future academic success (Baker, 2006). Studies generally show that in-school prevention programs have significant positive impacts on children (Durlak, Weissberg, & Pachan, 2010). Because the organization of this chapter is chronological (i.e., human developmental), early childhood care is discussed first.

## Child Care

**Child (day) care** can be defined as ways children are cared for when they are not being cared for by their parents or primary caregivers (NICHD, 2001). In the opening vignette, Roberto did not reveal whether his parents worked during his early childhood. However, if his parents worked and he was left with a neighbor, he would have been in a form of day care. Child-care or day-care providers can include licensed and unlicensed centers, family members or relatives other than the parents, neighbors, informal sitters, and even preschools. Some provide nothing more than babysitting services, whereas others provide healthcare, educational materials, nutritious meals, and field trips (Haskins, 2005). Indeed, we have a mixed system of child care in the United States (Lamb & Ahnert, 2006; Muenchow & Marsland, 2007), making this important issue difficult to research and data difficult to interpret.

**NECESSITY FOR CHILD CARE.**   The need for day care for children in the United States has grown historically over the past half century. Today, more than 90% of all families have at least one parent in the labor force. In two-parent families, 62% have both parents employed. In female-headed households, 72% of the mothers are employed, and in male-headed households, 93.5% of the fathers work. Of mothers with children under a year old, more than 56% work. Because more and more parents are working today than ever before, there are more and more children at younger and younger ages in nonparental child care (Belsky, 2006) as demonstrated in Figure 8.1. Notice that today, not only are higher percentages of children in child care, but child-care centers are used more frequently than any other type of care. This latter point is relevant to later discussions.

Day care in the United States is not without controversy. Some individuals believe that day care can be harmful to young children because it separates them from their parents. Others argue that it is not *whether* care is provided but *the type and quality of care* that makes a difference in the children's lives. Still others comment that the scarcity of *good* care at a reasonable cost is this nation's biggest problem. These and other issues are explored here in more detail.

**EFFECTS OF CHILD CARE.**   In the 1970s, as more middle-class mothers entered the workforce, a popular question asked by parents and researchers was: "How much damage is done to infants and young

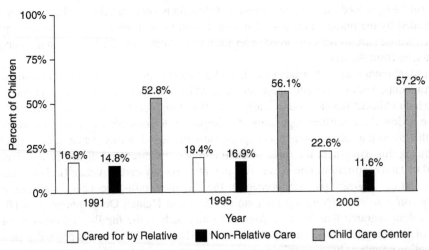

**FIGURE 8.1**  Child-Care Arrangements of Preschool Children by Year and Type of Arrangements

*Note:* Columns do not add up to 100% because children were sometimes in mixed types of care or were cared for by parents.

*Source:* U.S. Census Bureau (2008). *The 2008 statistical abstracts.* Washington, DC: Author.

children by working mothers?" (Scarr & Eisenberg, 1993). What was really being asked, if not assumed, was whether nonmaternal care was a threat to the child. For example, if Roberto was left with a neighbor, would that affect his development differently than if his mother cared for him at home and did not work? A second related issue is what effect nonmaternal care has on the child's development: social, cognitive, language, and other abilities. Scarr (1998) warned that there are no simple answers to these questions. Nonparental child care, for example, includes for-profit (such as the large national chains) and not-for-profit centers (such as church-sponsored centers), as well as family-based care and other permutations. Not only are there different types of care but also differences in the *quality* of care within the same category.

Because high-quality care, whether provided by parents or others, is the cornerstone of child development, we examine the issue of child care in more detail. Only well-designed, large-scale studies allow us to tease out conclusions about the effects of early child care—parental or nonparental—on child development (NICHD, 2001). Fortunately for us, a current, large-scale, well-designed, and ongoing NICHD study (2006) is helping sort out some of the caregiving factors that enhance or hinder optimal child development. The study, known as the NICHD Study of Early Child Care, followed the development of more than 1,000 children from birth through age 3 at 10 different sites in the United States. A second phase of the study followed their development through first grade, and Phase III studies their development in middle childhood (NICHD, 2006).

The primary purpose of the NICHD study is to examine how variations in nonmaternal care are related to children's social adjustment as well as cognitive and physical development. Family characteristics are also a consideration. The life course approach of this study helps focus attention on not only the timing of events but also the transitions in the lives of the young children and their families. The network of researchers has attempted to obtain a sample of children that includes families from diverse geographic, economic, and ethnic backgrounds with parents who have diverse work-related issues. The parents, however, come from higher educational and income levels than census data indicate are typical, and Whites are overrepresented in the sample. However, on many other dimensions the sample is quite representative of the U.S. population (2001).

The study involves researchers making observations in the home and administering various measures of social-emotional as well as linguistic and cognitive development. Several indices of quality of day care, such as training of the staff and child-to-staff ratios, are also assessed. Because of the study's design, the psychologists are able to follow children through a wide range of child-care experiences and to assess combinations and changes in child-care arrangements over time. For example, some infants are cared for at home in the first few months of life, then are turned over to a relative (perhaps a grandmother or an aunt) until the parents decide the child can attend day care or preschool at the age of 2. Some of the early results are in.

A critical first question is, what constitutes high-quality child care? The NICHD (2006) identified the following specific and measurable guidelines as indicating high-quality care:

- Appropriate adult-to-child ratio (e.g., for infants, a maximum of six children to one adult)
- Small group size (e.g., for children one and a half to two years old, a maximum of eight children)
- Appropriate caregiver education (e.g., completed high school and better yet, completed college with a degree in early childhood education or child development)
- Accreditation by state and/or federal agencies

Notably, quality of care has been linked to both good cognitive and social development (Brooks-Gunn, 2004; NICHD, 2006; Ramey, Ramey, & Lanzi, 2006), with high-quality care, of course, enhancing development no matter where it is provided. It is not surprising that NICHD researchers found that when these guidelines are followed (i.e., the standards are high), child care leads to better outcomes for children. For example, the higher the standards, the better the child's cognitive functioning and language development. Similarly, the higher the standards, the more cooperative and sociable the children are. The NICHD study (2006), however, found that most child care in the United States rated only "fair," with a mere 10% of children receiving very high quality care and another 10% receiving very poor quality care. On some quality dimensions (such as child-to-adult ratio), only 20% of the caregiving arrangements met important criteria.

The NICHD study also made clear that beyond these guidelines there are *processes* that also contribute to high-quality care, such as the caregivers':

- Positive attitudes, positive interactions, and warm physical contact (e.g., holding hands) with the children
- Communications to the child, such as asking questions, making comments, or providing answers
- Reading stories, singing songs, and other activities designed to help children learn
- Encouragement of the child's development, such as helping an infant walk
- Social behaviors, such as smiling and laughing

Sadly, the NICHD (2006) study found that only a small percentage of children have access to these positive processes. The study also found that as the child grows older (and thus becomes more sociable), the child receives less positive caregiving. We might conclude, then, that the child-care experience provides both risks and benefits in the United States (Belsky, 2006).

One other finding of the NICHD study is very important. In the end, despite these interesting results, child-care arrangements had less impact on social-emotional and cognitive development than did family characteristics. This finding has been documented by other researchers (de Schipper, Van Ijzendoorn, & Tavecchio, 2004). In fact, the NICHD researchers concluded that family characteristics overall were *better* predictors of child development than any other aspects of the child-care situation. Effective parenting may be the most protective factor a child can experience (Knitzer, 2007). Thus, it is clear that early child care cannot be adequately assessed without taking into account the children's experiences *in their own families*. In addition, one could argue that good child care may not be able to compensate for negative family environments. All of these findings, as ever, hold important implications for public policy and for families making decisions about child care.

**PLANS FOR THE CHILD CARE DILEMMA.**    More than two decades ago, child-care expert Edward Zigler and his colleague Mary Lang (1991) asked how we could make our mixed system of child care effective for all families. The same question persists today: How can we make quality, affordable child care available to the many who need it? The solutions are not simple, but the United States seems to have made some steps in the right direction, even if more needs to be done (Muenchow & Marsland, 2007). Progress can be made on the family, employer, governmental, and societal levels.

At the most immediate ecological level—the parental or family level—parents can and should familiarize themselves with information about quality child care. Recent studies (for example, the NICHD study) have detailed characteristics of high-quality care. Parents, however, might not know where to search for such information, so pediatricians, public schools, health departments, and other agencies need to help them find it. Families also need to understand the value of participating in and asking appropriate questions about their children's care. This may be affected by the sense of empowerment that a parent feels in his/her life in general and in relation to advocating for his/her children. Additionally, many low-income families and single working parents may benefit from higher child tax credits or other subsidies for child care.

At the employer level, there is also much that can be done to improve access to child care and promote healthy child development (Murphy & Halpern, 2006). Generous family leave time, flexible working hours, telecommuting, and in-house child-care centers would help ensure that the organizational climate is family friendly. A menu of these workplace enhancements, rather than just one option, would also demonstrate to employees that they need not be afraid to use them. Working families are here to stay, and what happens to families and children in society should be everyone's concern (Murphy & Halpern, 2006).

Other experts call for sweeping policy changes and rethinking of current policies and funding at the state or federal level (Doherty, Forer, Lero, Goelman, & LaGrange, 2006; Haskins, 2005; Knitzer, 2007; Muenchow & Marsland, 2007) or increased funding for early childhood care and education (Ludwig & Phillips, 2007). Some of these professionals have called our federal policies downright antifamily in comparison to other countries around the world (Murphy & Halpern, 2006). European countries, for example, often provide generous family leave time for the arrival of a new child. Sweden allows more than 400 days of *paid* leave combined for new mothers and fathers. Likewise, based on their research, Burchinal and colleagues (2000) favor more federal intervention because state policies vary from good to nonexistent or unenforced regulations. There is much variety among states in their regulations (Riley, Roach, Adams, & Edie, 2005), and states with more demanding standards house fewer centers providing poor-quality care (Lamb & Ahnert, 2006). Rigorous standards, however, are no guarantee of high-quality care. Doherty and her team (2006) found that because appropriate education of child-care workers translates into better care, requiring people who have no interest in working with children (such as in the work-for-welfare programs mentioned in Chapter 7) to provide care to them is incompatible with providing quality care. Others suggest paying child-care workers higher salaries and requiring that they be trained in early childhood education (Doherty et al., 2006).

Certainly, although it is difficult, child-care research needs to continue. We know relatively less, for example, about after-school care for older children or the effects of day care on children from various cultural backgrounds. Further research into the exact processes that contribute to high-quality care is also needed, although the NICHD study is a good beginning. Among other research issues that are rather neglected are the effect of the child's attachment to the surrogate caregiver, his or her relationship to peers as affected by day care, and how to improve support among the public for high-quality child care

(Lamb & Ahnert, 2006). Furthermore, most research is center based, but much care is provided informally or in family/home settings. More research is needed on this latter type of care, too (Raikes, Raikes, & Wilcox, 2005).

## Enrichment Education and Early Intervention

Many professionals argue that child care alone is not enough for some children to flourish developmentally, because of other factors in their environment such as poverty or elevated levels of family conflict. Research has found that on average, children from low socioeconomic-level families are relatively less well prepared for school (Administration for Children and Families, 2008; Magnuson & Waidfugel, 2005; Stipek & Hakuta, 2007) and are more at risk for later behavior problems (Caputo, 2003; Webster-Stratton & Reid, 2007), such as crime and risky behavior. In addition to these potential risks, there is also serious concern about what is called the achievement gap. The achievement gap refers to the multitude of ways that impoverished children, often children of color, fail to keep up academically with their middle-class or upper-class peers when it comes to test scores or standardized measures of achievement (Ladson-Billings, 2006). Deciding the best way to close the achievement gap is one of the most perplexing problems facing educators today. Many have argued that the key to addressing this problem is in early intervention.

Early intervention programs designed to assist economically disadvantaged children first came to be known as **compensatory education** or **early intervention** programs. Today such programs are more likely to be known as **enrichment education.** Such programs are thought to form an "invisible safety net" (Currie, 2006) to prevent future problems of children at risk (Administration on Children and Families, 2008).

However, in an age of economic crisis, policy makers have to ask, are compensatory education programs really beneficial to these children, especially given their costs, most of which are carried by the taxpayers? For example, if Roberto had attended a preschool designed especially for Hispanic children about to enter mainstream public schools, would his early elementary education have been more beneficial? To address this question, we explore the best-known enrichment education program: **Head Start.**

The Economic Opportunity Act of 1964, as part of the "War on Poverty," established a variety of ways that children might benefit from social programs, one of which was Project Head Start (Ludwig & Phillips, 2007). In many ways a national preschool program, the goal of Head Start is to reach children between the ages of 3 and 5 from low-income families. It is a total or comprehensive program in that it attempts to meet the children's mental, emotional, health, and educational needs (Haskins, 2005). Typically, a child receives a year or two of preschool along with nutritional and health services as part of the program. The federal government picks up much of the cost, although under various administrations the program has fared better or worse (Ludwig & Phillips, 2007; Knitzer, 2007; Zigler, 1994; Zigler & Muenchow, 1992). Head Start is now the largest program providing comprehensive educational, health, and social services to young children and their families living in poverty; thus, it is an important player in the early childhood service delivery system. Here are some program statistics for 2009 (Office of Head Start, 2012), the latest available at the time of this writing:

- More than 904,000 children were enrolled (since its inception, Head Start has served 24 million children).
- Over 39% of the children were White, over 30% were Black, and 36% were Hispanic.
- 77% of Head Start teachers have at least an AA degree in early childhood education.
- 26% of Head Start program staff members were parents of current students or were former Head Start children.

- Nearly 850,000 parents volunteered in their local Head Start program.
- More than 228,000 Head Start fathers participated in organized, regularly scheduled activities designed to involve them in Head Start programs.
- 94% of Head Start children had health insurance.

Head Start historically has been somewhat unusual among early childhood education programs. Because of some of its unique features, the program incorporates some of the principles of community psychology as outlined earlier in the book. First, although it is a nationwide program, Head Start programs can be tailored to each individual community. Second, it was one of the first programs to demonstrate that a single approach or a single intervention is insufficient. For example, Project Head Start is not just a preschool program. One of the revolutionary ideas of this program is to involve parents as decision makers and learners (Zigler & Muenchow, 1992). Parents serve on policy councils, work directly with children in the classroom, attend parenting programs, and receive services for their own social, emotional, or vocational needs. Many Head Start parents have become certified Head Start teachers. Project Head Start was not designed simply to enrich children's environments so as to enhance IQ. Rather, the program was developed so that children would be motivated to make the most of their lives (Zigler & Muenchow, 1992). An important question is, Has it done this?

Head Start has been in existence for more than 50 years, so researchers should easily be able to assess both its short- and long-term effects. Right? Not exactly! Head Start research is extremely difficult to conduct for a number of reasons. First, the programs are rather variable across the country and do not use random assignment for enrolling children (Lamb & Ahnert, 2006). Moreover, Head Start programs have been evolving over time such that today's programs are not identical to the earlier ones; the few long-term evaluations that have been conducted do not take this into account (Ludwig & Phillips, 2007). Third, researchers do not agree on exactly what constitutes "progress" by the children. Is it improvements in school readiness? Social skills? Cognitive skills? Better health? What if gains are so small that the program is not cost effective? In addition, the larger ecological environment surrounding Head Start children is continually in flux—for example, when societal prejudice waxes and wanes, more single mothers enter the workforce, and public opinion about such programs shifts (Ludwig & Phillips, 2007). Given this ever-changing political context, program effects are more difficult to tease out. We examine some of the newest research next, but the Head Start program will probably always fluctuate from site to site, forever have its critics, be subject to research biases, and continue to transform as federal and state policies, the political climate, and funding change.

Many authors claim that Head Start demonstrates that the program provides benefits for children (Administration for Children and Families, 2005; Love, Tarullo, Raikes, & Chazan-Cohen, 2006; Ludwig & Phillips, 2007). Some studies do show short-term gains for the children. For example, a major research study (3,200 children in 40 programs) reviewed by Love and colleagues (2006) concluded that Head Start narrows the gap between disadvantaged children and all other children in vocabulary and writing skills. Another study (Administration for Children and Families, 2006) also resulted in findings that showed Head Start children over time improved social skills and that Head Start led to better word knowledge, letter recognition, and math and writing skills compared to nonprogram children when they reached kindergarten. The same study also showed that Head Start children experienced modest gains in health status as well as improved parenting (e.g., use of more educational materials and less physical discipline).

But what about long-term effects? In a study of some of the earliest graduates of Head Start, the researcher found that as adolescents, Head Start students appeared comparable to other adolescents in regard to the highest grade completed, their sense of personal mastery, health, and mental health (Caputo, 2004). Other studies have echoed these findings (Love et al., 2006; Mashburn, 2008). Another way to look at long-term effects is by means of cost-effectiveness. In these terms, early intervention programs such as Head Start again appear to pay their way. Cost-effectiveness is a measure of great interest to taxpayers and policy makers. Ludwig and Phillips (2007) reviewed the cost-benefit literature on the program. They determined, "There is now an accumulating body of evidence on Head Start's long-term impacts that seems to suggest the program probably passed a benefit-cost test for those children who participated during the program's first few decades" (p. 3).

For example, children from Head Start (as compared to nonparticipating siblings) are more likely to complete high school and more likely to attend college (Mashburn, 2008). Head Start also reduces the chances of being arrested and subsequently being charged with a crime (Garces, Thomas, & Currie, 2002). Many of these results held regardless of the child's race or ethnicity. There are also benefits to parents and society in that high-quality child care is typically provided in Head Start, special education placements are reduced, and grade retention (repeating a year) is lower. In sum, Ludwig and Phillips (2007) and others conclude that Head Start generated benefits in excess of program costs, with the ratio possibly being as high as seven to one. Notably, Ludwig and Phillips also argue that the benefits from each extra dollar of program funding a county spends easily outweigh the extra spending.

Head Start is not the only early intervention program available, but it probably is the best-known one. The High/Scope Perry Preschool program was also designed to intervene in the process that links childhood poverty to school failure to subsequent adult poverty and related social problems, such as involvement with the criminal justice system. The High/Scope program incorporates into its design developmentally appropriate learning materials based on psychological principles of development, small class sizes, staff trained in early childhood development, in-service training for staff, parental involvement, and sensitivity to the noneducational needs of the child and family. What is fairly unique about this program is that it views the child as an active rather than passive, self-initiating learner. Typically, the child selects his or her own activities from among a variety of learning areas the teacher prepares—called **participatory learning** (Schweinhart, 2006; Weikart & Schweinhart, 1997).

Research on the High/Scope Perry Preschool project is impressive. In the short run the High/Scope Perry project improves educational outcomes, such as higher IQ and achievement test scores. The program also reduces the need for academic remedial services (Ramey & Ramey, 2003). In the long run, evidence collected over more than two decades shows that the program results in lowered crime rates, reduced high school dropout, less need for welfare assistance, increased earnings as adults, and higher personal wealth (Schweinhart & Weikart, 1998),including higher likelihood of employment and home ownership and fewer evictions from rental units (Schweinhart, 2007).

Nores, Belfield, Barnett, and Schweinhart (2005) claim that the High/Scope Perry Preschool program returns an amazing $5.67 to $12.90 for every dollar expended, depending on the calculations used. Savings or benefits occur in lowered welfare assistance, lower special education and justice system costs, savings to crime victims, and increased tax revenues from higher earnings by the participants (Nores et al., 2005; Parks, 2000). This research again illustrates that the participants, their parents, the public, and the adult graduates of early interventions programs all benefit from such programs.

### Self-Care Children

Before leaving the topic of child care and its importance, it is appropriate to discuss the fact that for many children of working parents, the need for supervised, structured child care continues even after they enter public schools. Approximately 7 million children between the ages of 5 and 13 lack adult supervision when they come home from school (Durlak & Weissberg, 2007). These children, referred to as *self-care* children, may be on their own because of a lack of after-school child care, which is especially true in low-income neighborhoods (Afterschool Alliance, 2004), or because they are in the home with older siblings who may be charged with the role of babysitter. For low socioeconomic–status families who lack other options, children spend more hours on their own in comparison to families of higher socioeconomic status (Casper & Smith, 2002). Depending on the age of the children who are caring for themselves, the extent to which they are being monitored by adults (e.g., by telephone), and what they are doing with their time (e.g., homework, chores, playing videogames), there is great variability in whether self-care arrangements are problematic for children. For example, younger school-age children who spend more time alone, as opposed to those involved in structured activities, are more likely to have emotional and social problems (Vandell & Posner, 1999). At the same time, there are potential problems for older children who are left on their own in that they may be more vulnerable to peer pressure or the temptation to engage in risky behaviors (Coley, Morris, & Hernandez, 2004).

Not surprisingly, all things being equal, research suggests that being involved in high-quality after-school care is more beneficial than being at home by oneself (Durlak & Weissberg, 2007). In particular for lower socioeconomic–status children, being involved in after-school programs that offer academic assistance (e.g., tutoring) and enrichment activities (e.g., art, physical recreation) seems to result in superior classroom work habits, academic achievement, and prosocial behavior as compared to children who are in self-care environments (Vandell et al., 2006). Thus, community psychologists advocate for increasing the availability of child care and enrichment programs for both preschool and school-aged children.

## THE PUBLIC SCHOOLS

Although education laws vary by state, at the age of 5 or 6, most children in the United States attend public schools: elementary, then middle school, and then high school. Many students breeze through the school system without difficulty. Others experience difficulties on entering school, and some develop problems later in their academic careers. For example, the transition from early childhood—whether the child is reared at home or provided day care or preschool—can be difficult for some children. Transition from middle school to high school can also be troublesome. Such times of transition or milestones help psychologists predict who might be at risk for developing school-related problems (Koizumi, 2000; Warren-Sohlberg, Jason, Orosan-Weine, Lantz, & Reyes, 1998).

In addition, schools are remarkable social institutions shaped by political and social events, such as the civil rights movement, the advent of modern technology, and the changing demographic trends, such as the increase in our Hispanic population. One event of major importance—the desegregation of schools—is reviewed first.

### Desegregation, Ethnicity, and Prejudice in the Schools

Because Roberto, the young man in the opening vignette, is now about 26 years old, he has benefited from the civil rights movement of the 1950s and 1960s. Or has he? It is necessary to examine the complex effects of societal prejudice as well as public policy changes designed to confront prejudice, discrimination, and segregation—in particular, on children and schools. Seymour Sarason (1997), a leading expert on U.S. schools, called the nation's schools our Achilles' heel. He argued that the nearly total failure of the education reform movement has had, and will continue to have, consequences beyond the educational arena, one of these being racism. Has anything improved in the years since Sarason made these comments?

**THE HISTORICAL CONTEXT.**    Despite the fact that amendments to the U.S. Constitution long ago gave equal protection under the laws and the right to vote to all citizens, it was not until the 1950s that events took place that have had a lasting and sweeping effect on our schools. In 1954, the Supreme Court of the United States decided the case of *Brown v. Board of Education of Topeka, Kansas.* In fashioning their decision, the Supreme Court justices heard major testimony from social scientists about the detrimental effects of segregation on African American pupils (see, for example, Clark & Clark, 1947). In the official unanimous rendering, the judges cited social science research as being influential in their deliberations (Levine & Perkins, 1997). The consequence of the decision was that there would no longer be a place for segregation in schools, not even for "separate but equal" educational facilities. Interestingly, the judges were not initially concerned with implementing their decision, or in the precise effects of desegregation on children once it was instituted. Despite school desegregation, the ruling did little to alter a society that remained segregated in housing and other social institutions, such as places of worship (Well, Holme, Atanda, & Revilla, 2005).

Some school authorities scrambled to comply with the ruling. The chosen method for desegregation was often "one-way busing" (Oskamp, 1984), where inner-city children were bused to the suburbs and all-White districts. Some school systems dragged their heels, and some openly defied the ruling; subsequent court-ordered desegregation plans were imposed on them. Public policy changed some discriminatory behaviors, voluntarily or involuntarily, but an important question is, Did it change all related behaviors? An equally important matter was whether the children were really better off with this policy. Social scientists quickly became concerned with these and other issues of desegregation (Maruyama, 2003).

**PREJUDICE AND ITS COMPANIONS.**    In the opening vignette, Roberto revealed that he thought the other children believed he was dumb. Is this a form of prejudice? If yes, how did the children form this impression?

**Prejudice** is an unjustified attitude (usually negative) toward the members of some group, based solely on their group membership. If Roberto's classmates thought he was dumb because he was Hispanic, they were indeed prejudiced. A companion to prejudice is discrimination. **Discrimination** involves prejudiced actions toward particular groups based almost exclusively on group membership. If Roberto's classmates refused to play with him on the playground because of his ethnic background, they would have been discriminating against him. Recall that we discussed in Chapter 3 the changing faces of racism and other forms of discrimination, called microaggressions. Often, discrimination is influenced by stereotypes. **Stereotypes** are beliefs that all members of certain groups share the same or common traits or characteristics. Believing all Asian Americans are good at math is a stereotype. In keeping with the earlier example, if Roberto's classmates classified all Hispanics as dumb, then they would have held a stereotype.

Important historical research on stereotyping in classrooms was conducted by Rosenthal and Jacobson (1968). In their study, teachers were told that perfectly normal children were either "bloomers" or "normal." Teachers were *not* told to treat these two groups differently. By the end of the study, the so-called bloomers showed dramatic improvements in classroom performance and IQ scores, probably because they had been the beneficiaries of positive prejudice. It is important to remember that all children were randomly assigned to the conditions of normal or bloomer. This study demonstrates that teachers' labels and their stereotypes of children somehow fulfill the teachers' prophecies. This phenomenon, where a labeled individual fulfills someone else's forecast, is called the **self-fulfilling prophecy.** Studies have shown that teachers' expectations in a variety of classroom settings *do* influence student achievement and motivation (Weinstein, 2002).

As discussed in Chapter 3, research on contemporary society indicates that people's prejudices and labels may be quite different from those of the generations previous to the civil rights movement

(Hitlan, Camillo, Zárate, & Aikman, 2007). Before 1950, **traditional racism** was more *overt* (Dovidio, Gaertner, Nier, Kawakami, & Hodson, 2004), with open name calling, different laws for certain groups ("Negroes ride in the back of the bus"), and, in fact, mob actions against as well as lynchings of certain groups. In **modern prejudice** (Dovidio & Gaertner, 1998; Duffy, Olczak, & Grosch, 1993), sometimes called **aversive racism** (Dovidio et al., 2004), people's attitudes are more *covert* and subtle. These subtle forms of prejudice and discrimination allow their users to conceal the negative views they really hold.

Prejudice, then, has not disappeared simply because the courts have ruled that desegregation and equal opportunity must prevail. It has simply taken on a different appearance—a more subtle form. Given that prejudice still pervades society and that more diverse groups (e.g., Hispanics and Asians) are being added to the United States (American Psychological Association, 2005), we should devote some attention to immigrant experiences.

Until recently, the United States boasted of its heritage of immigrants (Mahalingam, 2006). Indeed, today, we are still a nation of immigrants (Deaux, 2006). Much of our population is first-, second-, or third-generation immigrants. Census data tell us that since 1970, the number of immigrants living in the United States has tripled, and during the 1990s, the immigrant population grew by more than 50% (Silka, 2007). Census data also reveal that large cities are made up of multiple immigrant populations. New York City's population, for example, was composed of 28% immigrants in 1990; today, immigrants make up 40% of New York's population (Deaux, 2006). What census data do *not* tell us is that arriving immigrants face different cultural traditions and values, different languages, and different religions. They also face different business customs, healthcare practices, art forms, and school systems than in their countries of origin (Silka, 2007). Immigrants also face much prejudice, marginalization, and discrimination that cause myriad adjustment problems for them (Mahalingam, 2006). Immigration undeniably is a "hot button" issue today (Deaux, 2006).

Immigrants of color face the most prejudice (Mahalingam, 2006) compared to immigrants from European countries or Canada. Historically, biases against various immigrant groups have waxed and waned; Japanese citizens, for instance, faced high levels of prejudice before, during, and after World War II. More recently, Arab and Mexican immigrants have faced immense prejudice (Hitlan et al., 2007). White Americans who perceive themselves as truly "American" often manifest the most prejudice (Hitlan et al., 2007), especially those high in social dominance (Danso, Sedlovskaya, & Suanda, 2007). They do so by overincluding strangers in immigrant out-groups (this concept is covered shortly) (Kosic & Phalet, 2006) and by dehumanizing immigrants—not seeing them in personalized ways (Danso et al., 2007)—or isolating them (Silka, 2007). Unfortunately, teachers are not immune to this phenomenon, which is why special efforts have been made to have teachers learn about various immigrant cultures so that they can better understand immigrant students and their families.

The actions that people take toward immigrants occur, for the most part, at the community level (Silka, 2007). For this chapter, then, an important question is, When children from all of these different backgrounds are intermingled in classrooms, do they experience prejudice? Discrimination? Stereotyping? If yes—and you already know the answer is yes—what can we do to lessen the effects of any prejudices children bring from home? Given that children begin to develop ethnic attitudes by age 3 and systematic racial prejudices between 5 and 7 years of age (Houlette et al., 2004), most intervention efforts are directed at young children. Psychologists have some interesting and innovative programs to address this issue.

**FOSTERING ACCEPTANCE OF DIVERSITY IN THE CLASSROOM.** In a famous demonstration with children called "The Eye of the Storm," teacher Jane Elliot told the dark-eyed children that they were inferior to the light-eyed children. In fact, she said they were so inferior that the light-eyed children were not to play or have contact with the dark-eyed children. The light-eyed children soon segregated, taunted, and mistreated the dark-eyed children. Elliot then reversed the roles; the light-eyed children were now the inferior ones. When she debriefed the children and they discussed their feelings, the children talked about how horrible it felt to be the victims of such intense prejudice. This demonstration reveals just one means by which children in schools can be familiarized with what prejudice feels like. What other techniques are in the psychological arsenal for fostering acceptance of diversity in classrooms?

One other approach to reduce prejudice is to *actively* involve children with one another. **Intergroup contact** is when two conflicting groups come together, and the contact enables them to better understand and appreciate one another (Brewer, 1999; Buhin & Vera, 2009; Kawakami, Phills, Steele, & Dovidio, 2007; Molina & Wittig, 2006; Paluk, 2006; Zirkel & Cantor, 2004). Research demonstrates that only certain intergroup contacts enhance people's understanding and acceptance of each other (Kawakami et al., 2007; Marcus-Newhall & Heindl, 1998; Molina & Wittig, 2006).

Stuart Cook has been a leading proponent of the contact hypothesis for reducing prejudice. The **contact hypothesis** states that personal contact between people from disliked groups works to decrease the negative attitudes *but only under certain conditions*. The five conditions are:

1. The groups or individuals must be of equal status.
2. The attributes of the disliked group that become apparent during the contact must be such as to disconfirm the prevailing stereotyped beliefs about the group.
3. The contact situation must encourage, or perhaps require, a mutually independent relationship or cooperation to achieve a joint goal.
4. The contact situation must promote association of the sort that will reveal enough details about members of the disliked group to encourage seeing them as individuals rather than as persons with stereotyped group characteristics.
5. The social norms of contact must favor the concept of group equality and egalitarian intergroup association (Allport, 1954/1979; Cook, 1985).

Of all of these, interdependence appears to be very important (Molina & Wittig, 2006). Molina and Wittig would also add that respected authority figures need to support such intergroup efforts if they are to decrease bias, for example, in the schools. In other words, teachers and school administrators cannot ignore or tolerate any instances of discrimination if these efforts are to be effective. They also acknowledge that knowing which contact conditions are optimal for what outcomes and for which groups will improve success in intergroup contact programs. In other words, one size does not fit all.

Several quasi-experimental and laboratory experimental studies of the intergroup contact hypothesis have been conducted, and they support the hypothesis (Pettigrew, 1998). Only one set of studies are reviewed here. Wright, Aron, McLaughlin-Volpe, and Ropp (1997) examined the hypothesis that if it is known that an in-group member has a close relationship with an out-group member, more positive intergroup attitudes will result. The **in-group** is the group with which one identifies, whereas the **out-group** is the group one perceives as being different from one's own group, as in racial groups to which one does *not* belong (Duffy & Atwater, 2008).

In one study, Wright and colleagues (1997) found that participants who knew an in-group member who had a friendship with an out-group member held less negative attitudes toward the out-group. In another study, competition and conflict were induced to create in- and out-groups. When in-group members discovered that their own group members had cross-group friendships (that in-group members were friends with some members of the out-group), negative attitudes toward the out-group were reduced.

In line with these studies, other authors have found that intergroup contact reduces prejudice or creates a greater appreciation for diverse groups at a variety of grade levels—college, for example

(Gunn, Ratnesh, Nagda, & Lopez, 2004; Hurtado, 2005; Lopez, 2004). Molina and Wittig (2006) recently found that in schools, the opportunity for individualized interactions with members of diverse groups helps reduce prejudice. Kawakami and associates (2007) found that merely approaching members of a certain group can lead to more favorable attitudes toward that group.

Kawakami and colleagues warn, though, that their research addresses only a basic and limited mechanism—approach behavior. In the world at large, their research does not speak to the more general questions related to the impact of contact in everyday settings and over extended periods of time. Research on intergroup contact needs to continue. Undoubtedly, many schools, workplaces, and other organizations promote diversity or provide some form of diversity or cultural sensitivity training (Paluk, 2006). However, because these programs are not always grounded in sound theory—such as intergroup contact theory—and research, nor are they always desired by the participants, they do not always work (Paluk, 2006).

Elliot Aronson (2004) and his colleagues pioneered another technique called the **jigsaw classroom.** In this type of classroom, students initially work on a project in mastery groups. In this first type of group, students all learn the same general material, but each group learns different details about that material. The mastery groups then break into jigsaw groups such that each jigsaw group contains one student from each mastery group. For example, if students were learning about prejudice, one mastery group would learn the definitions and examples for *prejudice, discrimination,* and *stereotypes.* A second mastery group would learn about the detrimental effects of prejudice. A third might learn about ways to reduce prejudice, and so on. In the jigsaw groups, one student from the definition group, one student from the detrimental effects group, and one from the how-to-reduce-prejudice group would come together and teach the others the appropriate module. In this way, isolated students become more central to the group, and competitive students learn to cooperate. Without everyone's interdependence and cooperation in the jigsaw group, the group cannot achieve its learning goals. This process can be particularly useful for English language learners in that students who trip over English words are prompted and assisted by the other children; otherwise, no one can learn (Aronson, Blaney, Stephan, Sikes, & Snapp, 1978; Walker & Crogan, 1998).

In one of the first major experiments on the jigsaw technique, Blaney, Stephan, Rosenfield, Aronson, and Sikes (1977) found that attitudes toward classmates and the school, self-esteem, cooperative learning, and school performance all improved over those of control students in standard classrooms. Of course, competitiveness also declined. Other research has documented that peer teaching, as used in the jigsaw method, improves peer liking, learning, and perceptions of the classroom climate (Slavin, 1985; Wright & Cowen, 1985). Exciting news is that positive results from cooperative strategies such as peer teaching seem to generalize to children not in the immediate school environment (Miller, Brewer, & Edwards, 1985)—for example, to all members of a minority group. Some authors have even suggested that the jigsaw classroom will work with older students, including college students (Williams, 2004).

Since the jigsaw technique was introduced, other similar cooperative learning techniques have been developed (e.g., Houlette et al., 2004; Slavin, 1996). What is important is that the positive results of these forms of cooperative learning have been replicated in thousands of classrooms, thus making cooperative learning "a major force within the field of public education. . . . [Cooperative learning] is generally accepted as one of the most effective ways of improving race relations and instruction in desegregated schools" (Aronson, Wilson, & Akert, 1999, p. 544).

Some states have experimented with **magnet schools** to reduce prejudice, where students from a variety of school districts attend a certain school because it specializes in a particular discipline, such as music or foreign languages. Interested students are thus attracted to the schools like iron to a magnet. These schools create a natural experiment on intergroup contact because students of many backgrounds attend. Rossell (1988) compared the effectiveness of voluntary plans at magnet schools to mandatory-reassignment desegregation plans. She found that magnet schools produce greater long-term interracial exposure than mandatory reassignment, probably because of what she and others have called "White flight" from the reassigned districts. In line with this, Fauth, Leventhal, and Brooks-Gunn (2007) reported that even court-ordered moving of disadvantaged, minority students and their families to higher income neighborhoods (and schools) can have deleterious effects not only on the youths but on their parents and their parenting styles. Forced desegregation does not appear to be working as well as some of the programs described here.

We can conclude that once classrooms are desegregated, by court order or by voluntary design, there are some good, empirically tested means by which children can become more accepting and helpful to one another. But what happens to the academic and social performance of these students? If the courts determined that separate education was not only unequal but inferior for many economically disadvantaged students, does desegregation in any form accelerate the upward path of the targeted children?

**EFFECTS OF DESEGREGATION.**   One noted authority (Pettigrew, 2004) reviewed research on the effects of desegregation and concluded that desegregation does have positive academic effects as supported by research, but *only when the research controls for social class*. As you may have learned in Chapter 7, socioeconomic class is intricately intertwined with race and ethnic inequities (Hochschild, 2003), so it needs to be carefully scrutinized alongside desegregation. Specifically, Pettigrew's review concluded that compared to Black children in segregated schools, Black children from desegregated schools are more likely to:

- Attend and finish college, even White-dominated colleges
- Work with White co-workers and have better jobs
- Live in interracial neighborhoods
- Earn higher incomes
- Have more White friends and more positive attitudes toward Whites

Pettigrew laments, however, that the historic upward trajectory toward equal education for Blacks and Whites was slow and circuitous, whereas the retreat from it has been swift and direct, with much of the backpedaling blamed on court decisions. In fact, some courts have even lifted desegregation orders, for example, in Nashville, Tennessee (Goldring, Cohen-Vogel, Smrekar, & Taylor, 2006). In many of these instances, students returned to neighborhood schools that were closer to their homes. What has been the result of this latest trend? Once again, social scientists have some interesting perspectives and answers.

Goldring and colleagues studied schooling closer to home and found that geographic proximity to school does not necessarily translate into supportive community contexts for children. Black children, they found, were more likely to be reassigned to schools in higher risk (high poverty and crime rates) neighborhoods than were White children. Another noted expert on desegregation, John Diamond (2006), explains that even in integrated (wealthier?) suburbs, the playing field still is not level at school. For one thing, suburban Blacks often teeter on the fence between privilege and peril, as he calls it, because of the difference between "wealth" and "assets." Blacks in suburbs still do not have as many assets (e.g., own their homes) as Whites. Daniel (2004) adds that the new emphasis on "accountability" and "achievement" has undermined the movement toward desegregation by distracting attention away from it. Further-more, Davis (2004) suggests that segregation issues have also become less urgent because Americans are now focused more on school safety issues. Arias (2005) also bemoans that fact that the *Brown v. Board of Education* was designed to assist African Americans, and to date we have little information about whether desegregation and other related strategies are appropriate for Latinos and other ethnic or racial minorities. There is still much to be done to research and overcome these and other educational issues (King, 2004).

## The Schools and Adolescents

Despite nationwide efforts to desegregate U.S. schools, and despite the best-laid plans to provide early intervention programs for targeted children, it remains true that many children isolated in the inner city continue to be economically disadvantaged and receive poor-quality education. These children are usu-ally from a racial or ethnic minority, yet they have never benefited from any of the mentioned programs; thus, inner-city children mature to adolescence still trapped in poverty. Psychologists consider inner-city adolescents most at risk for academic failure, dropping out of school, teen pregnancy, drug use, and myriad other problems that interfere with obtaining an education necessary to break the cycle of poverty (Caputo, 2003; Magnuson & Waidfugel, 2005; Stipek & Hakuta, 2007; Webster-Stratton & Reid, 2007). Eventually, as adults, they are more likely to experience life's stresses and strains (Golding, Potts, & Aneshensel, 1991; Rank, 2005).

In the interest of space, two relevant issues are examined here: dropping out of school and school violence. First, however, we will discuss the role of the school itself in creating some of the problems found within it (Branson, 1998).

**THE SCHOOL CLIMATE.**   It is not just inner-city and minority children who have problems in school. There are multitudes of reasons middle-class students drop out, get pregnant, fail, or underachieve in school. Some of the reasons are the same as for the inner-city students. It would be easy to blame stu-dents for being alienated or for having some personality flaw that makes them restless and unmotivated (Legault, Green-Demers, & Pelletier, 2006), but research shows that even gifted children become bored with, uninterested in, or bullied at school (Feldheusen, 1989; Meade, 1991). One useful way of catego-rizing contextual factors related to school problems (e.g., dropout, failure) is the distinction between "push factors" and "pull factors." *Push factors* are aspects of school environments that cause students to become academically disengaged, whereas *pull factors* are events and circumstances outside of school that compel students to disengage (Lehr, Johnson, Bremer, Cosio, & Thompson, 2004). Because of poor school conditions in high-poverty neighborhoods, such as higher levels of chaos and teacher turnover, students may be pushed out of school during the middle grades. Students may also feel pulled to disengage from school by increased demands in the home and/or temptations to participate in way-ward activities (Shin & Kendall, 2012). Obviously, students at greatest risk for dropout may experience both push and pull factors. Imagine for example, a student whose teacher has underestimated his intel-ligence, who is being bullied by peers, and who feels unsafe in school. This same student might be vulnerable to recruitment by a neighborhood gang that offers a sense of importance, protection, and a source of income. This combination of push and pull factors might be enough to result in the student dropping out of school.

One common factor that is studied by researchers who investigate academic achievement in adolescents is **alienation from school.** According to Bronfenbrenner (1986), *alienation* means lack-ing a sense of belonging, feeling cut off. *School alienation* means lacking a sense of belonging in school. This phenomenon has received much attention in the community psychology literature, but community psychologists focus on the circumstances in which the alienated child finds him- or herself rather than just on the child.

In 1983, Seymour Sarason authored *Schooling in America: Scapegoat and Salvation,* in which he suggested that schools are relatively uninteresting places for both children and teachers. Sarason contended that children often exhibit more intellectual curiosity and learn faster outside of school (Sarason, 1983; Weinstein, 1990). Bronfenbrenner (1986) added that children under stress at home can easily feel distracted and alienated at school. Some 20 years later, Aronson (2004) issued a rather harsh indictment against American schools, particularly our high schools, in his analysis of the Columbine (Colorado) school tragedy in which a teacher and 14 students were killed. He stated that

> the rampage killings are just the pathological tip of an enormous iceberg: The poisonous social atmosphere prevalent at most high schools in this country—an atmosphere characterized by exclusion, rejection, taunting and humiliation. In high school there is an iron-clad hierarchy of cliques. . . . At the bottom are kids who are too fat, too thin, too short, too tall, who wear the wrong clothes or simply don't fit in. . . . My interviews with high school students indicate that almost all of them know the rank ordering of the hierarchy and are well aware of their own place in that hierarchy. (p. 355)

Contemporary authors have identified some of the ecological components of schools or, loosely, of the **school climate**—which encompasses the entire culture of the school and not just educational methods and goals (Van Houtte, 2005)—that contribute to school alienation. Teacher, administrative, and peer support (Gregory, Henry, & Schoeny, 2007), as well as clarity and consistency of school rules and regulations, are some of the features contributing to a school's climate (Way, Reddy, & Rhodes, 2007). Safety in the physical facility, student autonomy, and teacher/administrator abuse of power, among others, are also characteristics that contribute to school climate (Langhout, 2004). Loukes, Suzuki, and Horton (2006) also mention cohesiveness between, friction with, and competition against other students as components of school climate. These and other aspects of school climate are related to student problems such as violence and school dropout. School climate can be experienced in different ways by students with different needs. An example of this is discussed in Case in Point 8.1.

As you can see, the nature of schools is complex, so responses require an array of options that should have their foundations in research (Freiberg & Lapoint, 2006). One sample response to poor school climate and subsequent school alienation is **alternative education**. Alternative education, or alternative schools, have components that differ from traditional schools. For example, in traditional schools, the curriculum and requirements are designed by teachers and administrators. In alternative settings, the students and perhaps their parents in consultation with teachers design the curriculum or select classes in which the student will enroll or help set up rules (Vieno, Perkins, Smith, & Santinello, 2005). Students generally express a desire to have some autonomy, independence, and choice in school (Langhout, 2004). This more democratic type of school environment is reminiscent of the High/Scope Perry Preschool discussed previously and has been identified for being responsible for creating a greater sense of community in the school (Vieno et al., 2005). In addition, in alternative schools, the classes might also be smaller (Boyd-Zaharias, 1999; Muir, 2000–2001), and learning can occur outside a traditional classroom setting (Coffee & Pestridge, 2001).

Solomon, Watson, Battisch, Schaps, and Delucchi (1996) designed an alternative program to provide students with experiences essential to the development of a sense of community in their schools. Students in the alternative program were compared to nonparticipating students to evaluate the program. Specifically, the program included cooperative rather than individual learning, interpersonal

## CASE IN POINT 8.1

# Dual-Language Immersion Programs

After reading the story of Roberto, you will not be surprised to learn that approximately one in every five students in the United States has a native language other than English (National Center for Educational Statistics, 2011). All together, this means that more than 11.2 million children who speak a language other than English at home attend U.S. schools, a statistic that has more than doubled since 1980. Many of these children are not yet fluent in English, creating challenges for school systems, which typically deliver instruction only in English. A common approach to accommodating English language learners such as Roberto has been to teach English as a second language (ESL) as a remedial course that has the goal of English proficiency. Thus, once Roberto's language "deficiency" can be remediated, he can benefit from instruction in traditional subjects such as math, reading, and science. The problem with this approach is that there are both educational and socioemotional consequences to segregating students such as Roberto until they can "catch up" to their English-speaking peers. This approach also sends the message that literacy in languages other than English is not valued in the United States.

The good news is that schools are now considering a new approach to teaching English language learners called dual-language immersion programs. These programs are not remedial programs but rather enrichment programs from which both native English speakers and non–native speakers benefit. The goal of dual-language immersion programs is bilingual proficiency for all students. Typically such programs enroll an equal balance of native English speakers and native

speakers of a second language such as Spanish. Each language group serves as a linguistic resource for the other, an important method of reducing prejudice that will be talked about in the next section of this chapter. Heterogeneous classes address the concern that ESL programs isolate English language learners from other students (Alanis & Rodriguez, 2008). The important difference between dual-language immersion programs and ESL programs for students such as Roberto are that the goal is to retain the native language and promote academic achievement, as opposed to remediating a linguistic problem that interferes with academic achievement. The benefit of such a program for native English speakers is that they have an opportunity for foreign language immersion by being taught traditional courses in a second language.

Typically children begin dual-language immersion programs in kindergarten or first grade, when language acquisition abilities are at their peak, and they remain in them throughout middle school. Traditional subjects are taught in both languages to all students, as is literacy in both languages. Academically, students in these programs, regardless of their native language, outperform their peers in standardized testing. Non–native English speakers make phenomenal academic gains in dual-language programs in comparison to their peers in ESL programs (Thomas & Collier, 2003). For native English speakers, dual-language immersion students even outscore their native English speaking peers in English proficiency. The dual-language immersion program represents a pluralistic view of language and cultural competence that cultivates an understanding

and appreciation of other cultures, instead of an "English only" view that can be very marginalizing for immigrant families.

Studies on dual-language immersion programs by researchers such as Alanis and Rodriguez (2008) have found that such programs are most successful when they exhibit the following characteristics: pedagogical equity, effective teachers, active parent participation, and knowledgeable leadership. Pedagogical equity refers to the rigor of standards used in teaching traditional subjects as well as language acquisition, with attention to not promoting one language over another. Effective teachers must truly understand the philosophy and mechanics of teaching in a dual-language immersion program (e.g., following recommended ratios of linguistic use, ensuring heterogeneous student workgroups, having high expectations of all students). Active parent participation not only refers to the ways in which parents supported their children in the program, but in many programs, the school provides opportunities for parents to learn their nonnative language. Knowledgeable leadership refers to the support and expertise that school administrators have in implementing and supporting such programs.

While dual-language immersion programs are not the norm in U.S. schools, think about the role they could play in reshaping community values about bilingualism and the role of immigrants in society. Imagine, too, how they might help in reducing the injustices and discrimination experienced by children such as Roberto. Keep these issues in mind as you read about strategies to combat prejudice in educational settings.

helping and other prosocial activities, active promotion of discussions about prosocial values (such as fairness), and empathy and interpersonal understanding. Results indicated that the program was successful in heightening the sense of community in the classrooms. Moreover, sense of community related positively to a number of student outcomes, such as ability to manage conflicts with and likelihood of helping others. Further studies indicate that alternative education is successful in creating higher student and teacher satisfaction with the schools and better student achievement (Arnold et al., 1999; Catterall & Stern, 1986; Coffee & Pestridge, 2001; Gray & Chanoff, 1986; Trickett, McConahay, Phillips, & Ginter, 1985).

Just what are the mechanisms by which alternative education creates these effects? Studies have identified the elements of student participation, self-direction, and empowerment (Gray & Chanoff, 1986; Matthews, 1991); innovative and relaxed atmospheres (Fraser, Williamson, & Tobin, 1987; Matthews, 1991); and empathetic teachers (Taylor, 1986–1987). All of these factors are *outside* the student; they are not personality attributes of the students in the alternative settings but factors related to the ecology of the alternative setting, which is in line with principles of community psychology.

One other promising intervention currently receiving attention in the literature is the use of mentors to assist children with their social, interpersonal, and other skills both inside and outside the school (Cassinerio & Lane-Garon, 2006; Durlak, Weissberg, & Pachan, 2010; Novotney, Mertinko, Lange, & Baker, 2000; Phillip & Hendry, 2000). A **mentor** is a caregiver or other adult who develops a close bond with the child. Mentors often make a positive and lasting impression on a child. Cassinerio and Lane-Garon, for example, assigned university-level students to urban middle school children learning to become mediators or neutral conflict managers for their schools. Analysis of results of the mentoring program reveals that at year's end the school climate was rated more positively, and there were fewer reports of violence in the school compared to the previous year. The study is notable because the school enrolled not only White students but many Asians, Hispanics, and African Americans—a situation ripe for student conflicts.

**OTHER FACTORS RELATED TO SCHOOL SUCCESS OR FAILURE.** The school climate is not the only school-related risk factor affecting children. Students who transfer from one school to another and those who are moving from elementary to junior high or junior high to high school (Compas, Wagner, Slavin, & Vannatta, 1986; Koizumi, 2000; Reyes, Gillock, Kobus, & Sanchez, 2000; Reyes & Jason, 1991) are also considered at risk for problems. These and a host of other factors require attention from educators if children are to adjust to schools. Also important is the finding that poor grades in school, absence of positive coping behaviors, and presence of negative coping behavior in the early grades predict mental health problems some 15 years later (Ialongo et al., 1999; Spivack & Marcus, 1987).

One of the most promising approaches to ensure healthy adjustment—not just in school but throughout life—is **cognitive problem solving** (Cowen, 1980) or other programs that teach social skills (Durlak et al., 2010). Cognitive problem solving involves generating alternative strategies to reach one's goal as well as consideration of the consequences of each alternative. Cognitive problem solving also generally includes developing specific ideas for carrying out one's chosen solution (Elias et al., 1986).

Cognitive problem solving can be used for interpersonal problems, such as racial and teacher–student conflicts, school-related problems, and many other areas of concern. When used for interpersonal problems, it is called **interpersonal cognitive problem solving** (Rixon & Erwin, 1999; Shure, 1997, 1999; Shure & Spivack, 1988). Research has uncovered the fact that a significant difference between well-adjusted and less well-adjusted children is that the latter group fails to generate and evaluate a variety of solutions for coping with a personal problem. Training in cognitive problem solving has been used successfully as an intervention to assist children with coping with stressors and reducing student conflict (Edwards, Hunt, Meyers, Grogg, & Jarrett, 2005). Both teachers and parents can be trained to teach children cognitive problem solving.

Well over 50 child and adolescent interventions have been conducted based on the premise that cognitive problem-solving skills mediate adjustment (Denham & Almeida, 1987; Shure, 1999) and improve interpersonal skills (i.e., reduce conflict) (Edwards et al., 2005; Erwin, Purves, & Johannes, 2005). Although many of the studies support this strategy as competency enhancing, cognitive problem solving is not without its critics. Durlak and his colleagues (2010), for example, advocate task-specific rather than generic problem-solving training.

**DROPPING OUT OF SCHOOL.**    In the opening vignette, Roberto wisely chose to stay in school despite his early feelings of frustration and alienation. Some students, however, do not choose to stay in school; they drop out. More than 500,000 public school students drop out of grades 9 through 12 each year (National Center on Education Statistics, 2007). This translates into one in eight students never graduating from high school, and one student dropping out of high school every nine seconds (Christenson & Thurlow, 2004).

Demographic differences exist, just as we might expect. Dropout rates for males are higher than for females, except for Hispanic students (Kaplan, Turner, & Badger, 2007), in particular Mexicans (Olatunji, 2005). The dropout rate varies by race and ethnicity, as Table 8.1 illustrates. Notice that dropout rates have diminished only slightly over time, and Hispanics still have the highest dropout rates of the groups covered in the table. Inner-city youth, especially those living in poverty (Pong & Ju, 2000; Roscigno, Tomaskovic-Devey, & Crowley, 2006), students who are chronically absent (Sheldon & Epstein, 2004), students who repeat a grade (Entwisle, Alexander, & Olson, 2005; Stearns, Moller, Blau, & Potochnick, 2007), those who attend large urban schools (Christenson & Thurlow, 2004), and adolescents who switch schools multiple times (South, Haynie, & Bose, 2007) are at particular risk for dropping out. Family factors, such as English as a second language and the absence of learning materials in the home, have been implicated as well. Students who have friends who drop out are also likely to drop out. Some young people drop out because they would rather work or need to earn money (Entwisle, Alexander, & Olson, 2004; Olatunji, 2005). Recall our discussion of push and pull factors earlier in this chapter. The need to earn money for the family would be a pull factor. In addition to push and pull factors, however, there are individual predictors of school dropout. For example, personality variables such as low self-esteem, loss of sense of control (Reyes & Jason, 1991), and shyness (Ialongo et al., 1999) predict dropping out. Dropout rates are worrisome not only in the United States but around the world, making it a vexing and perplexing issue almost everywhere (Smyth & McInerney, 2007).

**TABLE 8.1**  Percent of High School Dropouts among Persons 16 Years and Older by Race/Ethnicity and Historic Time Frame

| Year | Percent of Total Number of Students | White | Black | Hispanic |
|------|-------------------------------------|-------|-------|----------|
| 1985 | 12.6% | 10.4% | 15.2% | 27.6% |
| 1995 | 12.0% | 8.6% | 12.1% | 30.0% |
| 2005 | 9.4% | 6.0% | 10.4% | 22.4% |

*Source:* National Center for Education Statistics (accessed February 18, 2008).

Perhaps the most daunting task that dropout researchers have grappled with over the years is the question of how to accurately predict which students are most likely to leave school early (Shin & Kendall, 2012). Realizing the fact that there is no one singular risk factor for dropping out of school, researchers have focused on identifying predictive clusters or composites of factors (e.g., Balfanz, Herzog, & Mac Iver, 2007; Gleason & Dynarski, 2002). The findings from the majority of studies demonstrate that the use of groupings of risk factors can increase the probability of accurately identifying students who will drop out of school. However, the relatively low predictive ability reported in most studies (typically around 40%) and the lack of a clear-cut group of factors that can be viewed as the "best cluster" do not warrant the design and implementation of prevention programs focused on specific factor groupings (Hammond, Linton, Smink, & Drew, 2007). In other words, researchers cannot accurately predict which specific students are in most need of interventions to predict dropout—although it stands to reason that the more "risk factors" a student is exposed to, the greater the likelihood that he or she will be one of the millions who end up without a high school diploma. Not only does failure to earn a high school diploma hurt the individual in terms of earning potential, but it also has enormous costs for society in general.

The costs of dropping out of school are immense. High school dropouts experience more unemployment during their work careers, have lower earnings when employed, are more likely to be on public assistance, and are more likely to use illegal substances or commit crimes than those who complete high school or college (Christenson & Thurlow, 2004; Christie, Jolivette, & Nelson, 2007). Young women who drop out of school are more likely to become pregnant at young ages and more likely to become single parents living in poverty (Cantelon & LeBoeuf, 1997). Thus, finding preventions and interventions for those at risk of dropping out are extremely important.

What can be done about the dropout problem in the United States? Early efforts were focused on the individual student and included counseling (Baker, 1991; Downing & Harrison, 1990; Rose-Gold, 1992) or improvement of self-image or self-esteem (Muha & Cole, 1990). Because there are *multiple causes* of dropping out (Christie et al., 2007; Christenson & Thurlow, 2002; Ialongo et al., 1999; Lee & Breen, 2007; McNeal, 1997; Svec, 1987), a more ecological approach is desirable (Oxley, 2000). An ecological approach would take into account situational or contextual factors—for example, characteristics of the schools, including the same push and pull factors mentioned along with school alienation (Christie et al., 2007; Patrikakou & Weissberg, 2000). Community and neighborhood variables (Leventhal & Brooks-Gunn, 2004), such as social isolation (Vartonian & Gleason, 1999), poverty (Christie et al., 2007), and adult involvement with the student (e.g., community mentors) (Sheldon & Epstein, 2004), would also be considered ecological factors that affect students' decisions to stay or leave school.

One of the more successful, better-known prevention programs for students at risk for dropping out is one designed by Felner (Felner, 2000a; Felner, Ginter, & Primavera, 1982). Today the program is known as STEP, or the School Transitional Environment Program. STEP was designed to address multiple issues, and it is discussed here as a model program to address school dropouts. Felner and associates understood that transitions in school are themselves risk factors for children—for example, the transition from junior high to high school, especially when the high school population is made up of students from multiple feeder schools or who have other risk factors, such as low socioeconomic class, minority group membership, simultaneous life transitions, or low levels of family support (American Youth Policy Forum, 2008).

There are two major components to STEP. The first is reducing the degree of flux and complexity in the new high school (e.g., participants or cohorts are in classes together in only one wing or section of the school), so that in essence a smaller school is created within a larger one (Felner, Seitsinger, Brand, Burns, & Bolton, 2007). The second component involves restructuring the roles of the homeroom teachers (e.g., more informal and individualized meetings with the students). Notably, the homerooms are also made up solely of program participants (American Youth Policy Forum, 2008). The teachers, who undergo two-day training, use meetings to discuss students' personal problems, help select classes and schedules, and clarify understanding of school rules and expectations. Teachers also maintain contact with the students' families as well as with other STEP teachers within the school.

The beauty of STEP is that it takes precious little time away from instruction, costs very little, does not change instructional methods or content, and lasts only one year, the transitional year. With these simple ecological changes and short intervention, program participants compared to nonparticipants show better attendance, higher grade-point averages, more stable self-concepts, and lower transition stress (Felner, 2008; National Center on Secondary Education and Transition, 2008). Important to this discussion is the lower dropout rate for STEP participants. Positive effects for the teachers includes higher job satisfaction and higher comfort levels in the school (American Youth Policy Forum, 2008).

**SCHOOL VIOLENCE.**    School violence and aggression is a difficult and complex issue and an important one because of its escalation in the past decade. The National School Safety and Security Services (2008) reports that for the 2006–2007 school year there were 32 school-associated deaths in the United States, with another 171 additional nondeath but high-profile incidents, including shootings, stabbings, and riots. The fact that there have been several high-profile acts of violence on college campuses in the past decade also illustrates the severity of this problem.

The costs to victims of school violence are enormous, not the least of which are emotional, social, behavioral, and academic problems. The costs to society are large, too. In tracking 227 truly troubled youths who were removed from school and placed in special behavioral units, researchers found that the cost of these units to society was over $10 million. This figure did *not* include ancillary costs, such as police work, court appearances, property damage, detention and housing costs, professionals' time spent with the youths (e.g., psychologists and social workers), and treatment programs (Eisenbraun, 2007).

The U.S. Department of Education (1998), out of concern for this epidemic of violence, issued *A Guide to Safe Schools*. Other authors have echoed similar concerns (e.g., Garbarino, 2001). The guide offers warning signs for parents and teachers of potentially violent students: social withdrawal, excessive feelings of isolation and rejection, low school interest and poor performance, a history of discipline problems including aggressive behavior, intolerance for differences and prejudicial attitudes, and access to drugs, alcohol, and/or firearms.

Many of these warning signs appear to blame the individual student and do not address issues of student–school fit or of school climate (Reid, Peterson, Hughey, & Garcia-Reid, 2006), which may inadvertently present challenges to violence-prone children (Baker, 1998). In addition, these warning signs do not directly address prevention—a key concept for community psychologists. Just what can be done in the schools to reduce or prevent violence and aggression among students? Are the schools waiting for violence to occur, or are the schools working with younger children (students not yet in middle or high schools) to prevent violence altogether?

First, research on crime in schools shows that many situational crime-prevention techniques in schools (e.g., installing video cameras or metal detectors) are not working (O'Neill & McGloin, 2007). Second, national data seem to demonstrate that we are waiting too long to introduce nonviolent methods into the schools. Adolescence may be too late, because it is clear that the incidence of aggressive behavior problems in young children is also escalating (Webster-Stratton & Reid, 2007). Until recently, at best, many high schools offered counseling after a particularly violent incident or harsh discipline or increased security as a response to school violence (Klein, 2005). However, such methods do nothing to prevent violence from occurring in the first place.

Clearly, we need to dip earlier into children's academic careers to abate this epidemic of violence (Espelage & Low, 2012). We also need to continue to find ways to improve school climates (Khoury-Kassabri, Benbenishty, Astor, & Zeira, 2004). In particular, violence prevention programs need to take into account family and community characteristics, not just youth or school characteristics (Laracuenta & Denmark, 2005) during program design, because school violence appears to be a multilevel and ecologically nested issue (Eisenbraun, 2007; Farver, Xu, Eppe, Fernandez, & Schwartz, 2005). Poverty, discrimination, lack of opportunities for education and employment, and paltry social capital (as defined elsewhere in the book) are also community risk factors for interpersonal violence (Farver et al., 2005).

Research is demonstrating that school-based programs that are comprehensive (that is, address a variety of problem behaviors with a variety of curricula), holistic (address the whole child), and well integrated with parents and the community are the most successful (Flay & Alfred, 2003). Programs that are also research based, where program participants or schools are compared to nonparticipants over time, are most effective (Scheckner, Rollin, Kaiser-Ulrey, & Wagner, 2004). We examine one sample program here—the Positive Action (PA) program (Flay & Alfred, 2003)—but there are others.

The PA program was developed by Carol Alfred, a schoolteacher, and researched by Brian Flay. The program is comprehensive in that it includes the entire school, staff, teachers, administrators, families, and students. Another component is that students making positive and healthy choices will develop a higher sense of self-worth, which in turn will result in better outcomes for the student and the school (Flay & Alfred, 2003). Starting in the early school years, students are exposed to more than 100 15- to 20-minute lessons designed to focus on multiple behaviors. For example, there is a unit on getting along with others (topics covered include respect, fairness, and empathy among others), a unit on being honest (e.g., not blaming others, finding one's weaknesses as well as strengths), and a unit on the need to seek continual improvement (e.g., better problem solving, the courage to try new things). Working with school personnel, PA attempts to change the school climate to one that focuses on positive actions rather than negative ones (such as violence and alienation). The program also extends itself in that families receive some training in PA and are encouraged to become involved with the school and the program. A program kit is available to the community so that the students, their families, the schools, and the community align seamlessly in their efforts toward promoting student well-being.

One of the positive results of the program, based on well-designed research, is that PA schools, as compared to control schools, experience a dramatic drop in school violence, specifically, 68% fewer violent incidents per 100 students. There are also other behavioral changes—for example, far fewer school suspensions, fewer students absent for multiple days, fewer other problem behaviors (such as substance use), and lower dropout rates. Academically, program participants are far more likely to graduate and continue their education, probably in part because academic scores rise (Flay & Alfred, 2003; Office of Juvenile Justice and Delinquency Programs, 2008a). What is interesting about this program is that many positive effects of PA endured from primary school through to middle school and high school (Flay & Alfred, 2003).

Two other programs designed to reduce school violence that you might want to research further include Safe Harbor (Nadel, Spellmann, Alvarez-Canino, Lausell-Bryant, & Landsberg, 1996; Office of

Juvenile Justice and Delinquency Programs, 2008a) and PeaceBuilders (Embry, Flannery, Vazsonyi, Powell, & Atha, 1996; Office of Juvenile Justice and Delinquency Programs 2008a).

Other ideas for reducing school violence and victimization are appearing in the literature. For example, the violence surrounding children in their own neighborhoods (Raviv et al., 2001) and in the media (Jason, Kennedy, & Brackshaw, 1999) needs to be reduced, perhaps by public policy or otherwise. Likewise, when teachers make salient to their students that there are norms against aggression, aggressive behavior diminishes (Henry et al., 2000; Khoury-Kasssabri et al., 2004). Programs need to be designed for after school as well (Bilchik, 1999; Danish & Gullotta, 2000; Taulé-Lunblad, Galbavy, & Dowrick, 2000), because this is a time when violence escalates. Attempts to control Internet bullying, which is on the rise (Williams & Guerra, 2007), might also prove useful.

There are, of course, many other school problems that we could discuss, such as peer pressure to engage in sex or try illicit drugs. Because of limited space, we include only one other, one that affects a large number of children. Case in Point 8.2 discusses the high divorce rate in the United States and its effects on children even as they cross the threshold of the school's door.

## CASE IN POINT 8.2

# Children of Divorce

One million children each year experience the stress of parental divorce (Pedro-Carroll, 2005a), which suggests that cumulatively, by age 18, 40% of American children will have experienced parental divorce (Greene, Anderson, Doyle, & Riedelbach, 2006). Divorce and subsequent life in a single-parent family have become reality for a large number of children. In fact, children of divorce spend on average 5 years in a single-parent home (Hetherington & Kelly, 2002); most typically they reside with their mothers (Federal Interagency Forum on Children and Family Statistics, 2008). Children's reactions to divorce include (but, of course, are not limited to) anxiety, behavior problems at home and at school, and somatic symptoms (Pedro-Carrolla, 2005a).

Studies of divorce have indicated that in the child's natural environment are several factors that can moderate the effects of stress from divorce, such as the availability of support from other family members (Hetherington, 2003) and peer support (Lussier, Deater-Deckland, Dunn, & Davies,

2002). In fact, there is a consistent and fairly strong correlation between the child's adjustment to divorce and the availability of social support.

Some interventionists prefer not to take a passive role—waiting to see whether there are tools available in the child's natural environment that can help him or her cope. The schools can build and participate in interventions for children of divorce. Cowen (1996) and his colleagues at the Primary Mental Health Project, a comprehensive school-based program that promotes overall mental health in children, did just that. One aspect of the multifaceted project is the Children of Divorce Intervention Program (CODIP). CODIP is based on the premise that timely preventive intervention for children of divorce can offer important short- and long-term benefits. CODIP's goals, simply stated, are to provide social support and to teach coping skills to children of divorce (Pedro-Carroll, 2005a).

The program was initially designed for fourth- to sixth-graders. Newer versions have been tailored to

younger and older children, each with its own unique techniques matched to the developmental needs of the particular age group (Pedro-Carroll, 2005a). Older children, for example, are plagued by loyalty conflicts and anger, whereas younger children experience intense sadness, confusion, and guilt (over having caused the marital breakup). CODIP is conducted in age-matched groups because children who have gone through common stressful experiences are more credible to peers than those who have not had these experiences or, alternatively, authoritative-sounding adults. Developmental factors shape the group size as well as the methods used (e.g., puppets, role-plays, books, discussion, games). For example, younger children have shorter attention spans and are more prone to want concrete activities than are older children.

In a typical group, both a man and woman (selected from school personnel) act as leaders. They are selected because they are interested, skilled, and sensitive to the needs of the children of

## CASE IN POINT 8.2

### *(Continued)*

divorce and are trained in the CODIP program techniques. Modules for a typical fourth- to sixth-grade group might include the following:

- Fostering a supportive group environment (e.g., the importance of confidentiality)
- Understanding changes in the family (e.g., a group discussion that stimulates children to express their feelings about changes)
- Coping with change (e.g., discussing adaptive ways to cope with divorce rather than losing one's temper)
- Introducing a six-step procedure for solving interpersonal problems (similar to interpersonal cognitive problem-solving, discussed earlier)

- Understanding and dealing with anger (e.g., how to use *I* statements)
- Focusing on families (e.g., understanding that there are diverse family forms)

Program evaluations of CODIP demonstrate that the program results in gains for children's school-related competencies and their ability to ask for help when needed. Likewise, the program appears to decrease school-related problem behaviors in children of divorce. Parents also report improvements in their children's home adjustment; for example, they report that the children are less moody and anxious (Cowen et al., 1996; Pedro-Carroll, 1997, 2005a). Follow-up research on early program participants also demonstrates that program effects endure. Program children report less anxiety, more positive feelings, and more confidence about themselves and their families compared with children of divorce who do not participate. Amazingly, teachers "blind" to whether the children have participated in the program or not report fewer school problems and more competencies in program participants than in a comparison group of children of divorce. CODIP and other programs like it (e.g., Children's Support Group) provide evidence that early and systematic intervention—empirically documented—with children of divorce has promising preventive potential (Pedro-Carroll, 2005a). The next steps for these programs may well be concurrent parent programs and/or collaborative partnerships between courts, researchers, and community organizations (Pedro-Carroll, 2005a, 2005b).

## Summary

The world of schools, children, families, and communities is fascinating and complex. Some children enter school at risk for a variety of problems, but innovative programs are available to intercede with the children, their families, and their communities. Traditional interventions have focused mostly on deficits of the child or the family, but the more effective programs usually take into account the setting, such as the school climate or the neighborhood, as well as the actors in it.

Psychologists recognize how important the early childhood environment is. Children who are advantaged economically or otherwise in early childhood often have fewer problems in later life than disadvantaged children. Intervention programs for young children at risk include quality day care and enrichment education programs.

Research has demonstrated that children of working mothers may not be disadvantaged; nonetheless, if they are to stay employed, these mothers need day care for their children. On the other hand, inner-city and some minority children are at risk for a variety of problems day care alone cannot adequately address. Programs designed to give them the early push they need to later succeed in school are often successful. Project Head Start is one such example. Head Start programs are all-encompassing programs; for example, they include parental involvement, healthcare, academic pursuits, and so on. Studies demonstrate that children who have attended Head Start have an easier transition into elementary school, academically achieve at higher levels, and have had their health problems attended to, as compared with children who do not enroll in such programs. Longitudinal studies are now demonstrating some of Head Start's positive long-term effects.

Desegregation has had an interesting effect on U.S. schools. Desegregation touches children of all ages and races. When the courts ordered the schools to desegregate, the Supreme Court justices did not envision the effects of desegregation on children, nor did they formulate methods for fostering acceptance of diversity in schools. Those jobs fell to psychologists and school staff, who have demonstrated that desegregation often has positive effects for minority as well as White children. Various active methods for decreasing prejudice include intergroup contact—for example, the jigsaw classroom. The more passive programs, such as mere exposure to diverse others, are more likely to fail.

Young children are not the only ones facing problems in this country. Adolescents often use drugs, drop out of school, or become pregnant. Most of the programs that are successful in preventing school dropout do not try to change only the at-risk individual but also make adjustments in the school environment or the community to better accommodate the individual student.

School violence is another concern because it is escalating in the United States. Again, appropriate programs and student involvement can enhance school safety and decrease violence. Children of divorce are often considered at risk for a variety of school-related as well as other problems. Once again, intervention programs for children of divorce have proven successful when they provide for appropriate changes and needed social support.

# Law, Crime,
# and the Community

*I am not a therapist . . . but I know one thing. Anger is very expensive.*

—Kyabje Gelek Rinpoche

Mike was only four months old when he was adopted by a middle-class, older couple, Edna and Walt Farnsworth, who had always wanted children but were unable to bear their own. Mike's childhood was uneventful, although his father, Walt, felt that his wife "doted on the boy a bit too much."

During his childhood, Mike was an average student in school. By junior high school, he seemed more interested in sports and cars than in his studies. When Mike reached puberty, he grew quickly, and by the time he was 16, he soared to 6 feet 2 inches, 210 pounds. His imposing size and apparent boredom with school inspired consternation in his teachers, who weren't quite sure how to manage him.

It was at this point that trouble came to the Farnsworth home. Mike realized that his father, who was a slender man of small frame, was intimidated by him. Mike would yell at his mother and disrespect his father. Mike called his father "old man" as often as he could to embarrass Walt. He reasoned that his parents were older than his friends' parents, so why not call them old?

When Mike could finally drive a car, he wanted nothing but to take his parents' car after school and drive around his small town, showing off to his friends or assessing what "action was going down" on Main Street. The town had few organized activities for its youth. He and his father argued often about the car, Mike's coming home late, and his school grades. His mother, Edna, felt torn between the son and the husband she loved.

One night, Mike had been drinking beer despite knowing that he was under the legal age. His father was particularly angry when he smelled his son's breath. When Walt yelled, "You could have killed somebody with *my* car!" Mike struck out at his father. Walt went crashing through the drywall of their small home. Mike fled into the night, leaving Edna intensely worried as to what he would do next and deeply sad that her husband had been injured in the fracas.

This scenario was repeated again and again between Mike and Walt, who raged at both his wife and his son that he "didn't want this kid around anymore." Edna tried to referee these fights, but to no avail. As the conflicts escalated, Mike asserted his size and independence more.

Taking matters into his own hands, and without consulting Edna, Walt went to the local police department to have his son arrested for "anything you can arrest him for—just get him out of my house." The police were used to such domestic squabbles and didn't feel an arrest was in order. Instead, they referred Walt to the probation department so that he could have Mike declared a PINS (Person in Need of Supervision). The Probation Department was not surprised to see Walt; they had interviewed many parents just like him, all making the same request.

Was Mike really headed for a life of crime? Was the family at fault for the turmoil in their home? Were any community systems to blame? For example, was the school environment so alienating that Mike's disenchantment with school was displaced onto his family? How better could the justice system manage this family conflict?

This chapter examines crime and community in the United States. We not only examine the traditional system and how it manages those individuals who interact with it, we also address some alternative and innovative programs designed to humanize this same system that are more in line with community psychology. Of course, as community psychologists, we also examine how the environment or context contributes to crime, fear of victimization, and other justice-system issues.

## THE TRADITIONAL JUSTICE SYSTEM

### Introduction

Pick up any newspaper from a major city in the United States, and you see splashed across its pages reports of crime—crime in the streets, conflict in homes, corruption in business and government, Internet fraud, identity theft—crime just about everywhere.

Yet crime rates appeared to be decreasing as of 2009. The 2010 numbers show a similar drop (Federal Bureau of Investigation, 2010). The total crimes reported in 2010 were a little over 10 million. There were a little over 1 million violent crimes, and 9 million were crimes of property (such as larceny, theft, or burglary). Police made 550,000 arrests for violent crimes and 1.6 million for property crimes. Those arrested were predominantly male (74.5%) and White (69.4%). Total losses from crime were approximately $15.7 million.

These statistics are based on the compilations of reported crimes of local law enforcement agencies, such as city police and county sheriff departments throughout the nation. The data, however, include only crimes *known* to the police. There may be little correspondence between the crimes that are committed in a community and the crimes that are reported. The caution is that the numbers are only as good as their reporting and measurement.

The rate of imprisonment places the United States at the top of the world (Liptak, 2008). The United States accounts for a little under 5% of the world population, yet has 25% of its prisoners. According to Liptak's *New York Times* report, there are more ways one can commit an offense (more laws to be broken), and penalties are usually for longer periods of incarceration. The U.S. had 2.3 million in prison in 2008. The rate of imprisonment is 751 per 100,000. The second highest rate is Russia, with a little over 600 per 100,000. In comparison, Germany jails 88 per 100,000; England, 151; and Japan, 63.

Community psychologists share in citizens' concern about crime and violence from the victims' viewpoint and from the perspective of prevention (Thompson & Norris, 1992). In a special edition of the *American Journal of Community Psychology* many years ago, Roesch (1988) called for increased involvement by community psychologists in criminal justice issues by going beyond the individual level of analysis to the examination of situational and environmental factors that contribute to criminal behavior. He called for community psychologists to help predict problematic behavior and adopt preventive measures for at-risk individuals. Yet today, there is still little involvement by community psychologists in the justice system, or research on it in our journals. In fact, Biglan and Taylor (2000) argued that we have made more progress on reducing tobacco use than we have on reducing violent crime. We lack both a clear, cogent, empirically based analysis and a set of organizations that effectively advocate policies and programs with regard to crime. Melton (2000) added to this emphasis by suggesting that law should be a major focus of study for those who wish to understand community life.

The justice and enforcement systems in our country are multilayered and complex. They involve the various courts (municipal, state and federal, civil and criminal, and higher and lower) as well as the judges, juries, lawyers, plaintiffs, and defendants; the prisons, jails, and corrections officers; the police, sheriffs, and other enforcement agencies; the departments of parole and probation; and the multitude of ancillary services, such as legal aid societies and neighborhood justice centers. We turn our attention to some aspects of this system.

## Crime and Criminals

Did Mike commit a crime because he hit his father? Some would argue he did. Others would suggest that he was simply a confused or frustrated adolescent—a person in need of some counseling, but certainly not a criminal.

Just what is a crime, and who exactly are criminals? It is beyond the scope of this book to argue about definitions of the term *crime*. Just as laws are never perfect, definitions are never perfect. Laws that determine and therefore define crime change from society to society and from one historical era to the next (Hess, Markson, & Stein, 1991), making the definition of the term difficult. Nonetheless, a rudimentary definition of crime might assist you in understanding its complexity. A **crime** is an intentional act that violates the prescriptions or proscriptions of the criminal law under conditions in which no legal excuse applies and where there is a state with power to codify such laws and to enforce penalties in response to their breach.

The uninformed public might well blame Mike for being "a bad kid" or his parents for being "bad parents." Psychologists, sociologists, and criminologists might view the situation in a completely different way. Rather than examining what's "wrong" with Mike or his family, they would turn to ecological or contextual explanations for crime and violence, including Mike's.

One of the first factors to capture the attention of psychologists was the availability of guns in the United States. Gun violence represents a major threat to the health and safety of all Americans. Every day in the United States, more than 90 people die from gunshot wounds, and another 240 sustain gunshot injuries. Incredibly, a teenager in the United States is more likely to die of a gun-shot wound than from the total of all *natural* causes of death. Young African American males have the highest homicide victimization rate of any racial group.

Often, in a particular country, other methods of committing homicide (e.g., with a knife) are more common, yet no one would say that high rates of knife ownership caused the killing (Kleck, 1991). We would need to know more about a nation's cultural and ethnic background, history of racial conflict, rigidity and obedience to authority, subjective sense of unjust deprivation, and so on before we could make claims that gun control within a nation causes fewer handgun deaths (Kleck, 1991; Spitzer, 1999). Guns alone do not cause crime. What else is responsible for the high crime and incarceration rates in the United States?

A well-researched topic is child exposure to violence. This exposure may be in the form of parent physical abuse or media violence. Being physically abused certainly heightens the risk that a child will become aggressive (Connor, Doerfler, Volungis, Steingard, & Melloni, 2003; Dodge, Pettit, & Bates, 1997; Muller & Diamond, 1999). Research over the years has demonstrated that media violence also correlates with violent behavior (Graber, Nichols, Lynne, Brooks-Gunn, & Botvin, 2006). Patchin, Huebner, McCluskey, Varano, and Bynum (2006) reconfirmed this connection among a group that are sociologically at high risk for crime and violence—urban minority youth. Representatives of the American Psychological Association (APA) have also testified before Congress on the impact of media violence on children (McIntyre, 2007). Specifically, the APA warns that repeated exposure to media violence places children at risk for:

- Increased aggression
- Desensitization to acts of violence
- Unrealistic fears of becoming a victim of violence

However, media violence alone does not account for all crime and violence. What else do we know about circumstances related to crime?

Witnessing community violence often leads to delinquency, crime, and more violence (Lambert, Ialongo, Boyd, & Cooley, 2005; Youngstrom, Weist, & Albus, 2003), but this factor is more complicated than it first appears (Bolland, Lian, & Formichella, 2005). In the psychological literature, it is now quite well known that **decaying, disordered, unstable, and disorganized communities** can contribute to delinquency and crime (Patchin et al., 2006). This alone may explain to a significant degree why urban minority youths are more prone to crime and violence than other youths. Beyond these community factors, though, are the pockets of extreme poverty found in some communities. **Poverty** and economic disadvantage are highly related to neighborhood decay and are highly predictive of crime and violence as identified in research by Strom and MacDonald (2007), Krueger, Bond Huie, Rogers, and Hummer (2004), Hannon (2005), and Eitle, D'Alessio, and Stolzenberg (2006). It is not surprising, then, that **unemployment** also corresponds with increased levels of crime and violence, even in relatively crime-free places such as Korea (Yoon & Joo, 2005). The migration of job opportunities to other countries has probably resulted in the increase of low-income Americans and youth participating in the underground economy and the drug trade (Cross, 2006).

What else in communities besides disintegration and economic disadvantage contribute to crime and violence? For one thing, in disorganized and decaying neighborhoods, there may be a paucity of **supportive community institutions** (e.g., religious, social service, and neighborhood organizations) and deprivation of other resources (e.g., recreational programs to provide youths with after-school activities) to help buffer the deleterious effects of economic disadvantage (Hannon, 2005). Thus, an already at-risk individual (e.g., someone maltreated as a child) may be more crime-prone in this type of neighborhood (Schuck & Widom, 2005). Likewise, a poor overall quality of life may lead to more substance abuse and mental health problems (and perhaps criminal activity) (Gabbidon & Peterson, 2006). These environments also contribute to a sense of hopelessness and the fear or perception that one is not in control of one's life (Bolland et al., 2005). Any expectation of reducing such hopelessness would probably require a restructuring of American society—a seemingly difficult task. Research on impoverished African American communities by Bolland and colleagues (2005) found that half of their research participants expressed strong feelings of hopelessness. This in turn increased their tendency to engage in risky behaviors. After all, why care?

**Parental monitoring** has been studied as another possible factor in dealing with high-risk neighborhoods. Studies suggest that when parents know where their adolescents are and with whom they are spending time, risks for actual violence and crime as well as exposure to community violence are reduced. This is not to say that "bad" parenting causes crime and violence, although there is a strong link between **child maltreatment** and later crime activity (Schuck & Widom, 2005). Rather, good parenting (i.e., monitoring of youth) offsets risk trajectories and promotes forms of competence among adolescents (Graber et al., 2006). Essentially, poor parental monitoring increases a youth's opportunity to associate with delinquent peers, to be victimized, or to witness others committing violence (Lambert et al., 2005). Campaigns such as "Do you know where your child is tonight?" and parenting classes where monitoring issues are discussed might go a long way toward preventing youth crime and violence.

Case in Point 9.1 offers an example of what one community did about its high incidence of crime.

## CASE IN POINT 9.1

## Neighborhood Youth Services

Neighborhood Youth Services (NYS) is an award-winning, community-based program for so-called at-risk youth in Duluth, Minnesota. At the outset, a cadre of youth care workers at NYS decided not to use the label "at risk," primarily because they see all of the youngsters as having great potential. The program was established in a neighborhood with the distinction of having one of the highest crime rates in all of northern Minnesota, so it is primarily designed to intervene with and prevent children from becoming involved in the juvenile justice system. The neighborhood is also exceptionally diverse, so program staff is representative of this diversity.

Staff members work daily to:

- Break down stereotypes that each racial or ethnic group holds of each other

- Identify children's strengths
- Teach children new ways to engage in society
- Discover the children's hidden potential
- Encourage the children to express themselves freely and in safe ways
- Explore new ways of relating to others

In the NYS youth center, which was planned to feel homelike, the children involve themselves in art, reading, poetry, and other projects designed to allow free expression. This after-school program also offers tutoring services, computers, and athletic activities. The children and staff exhibit respect for each other. As with some other programs (e.g., Head Start), parents are encouraged to become involved.

NYS is housed in a building with other community services, so referrals to additional resources are easily provided and readily available to families. The program is funded by individual donations, state prevention funds, and grants, so it is free and voluntary for all community children and families. The program lives by the adage that money spent up front (in early intervention) pays important dividends to communities willing to invest. NYS is just one example of the burgeoning programs spawned by mounting attention to prevention and intervention—one of the cardinal principles of community psychology.

*Source:* Adapted from Quigley (2005).

Three other community-level factors are undoubtedly contributing to crime (Caldwell, Kohn-Wood, Schmeelk-Cone, Chavous, & Zimmerman, 2004)—racial/ ethnic prejudice, discrimination, and segregation. Most of these terms were defined earlier. In review, prejudice is an *attitude* toward members of some group; discrimination involves prejudiced *actions* against a particular group; segregation means *isolation* of a group from others in the community. Racial discrimination leads to fewer opportunities (i.e., jobs) and less social support from others and thus may lead to crime or violence (Caldwell et al., 2004). Being African American is not a cause for violence; being subjected to high levels of discrimination and prejudice may be. And of course, along with discrimination and prejudice go high rates of poverty. With the increase in America's Hispanic-Latino population, data are now showing that social isolation (à la discrimination and segregation) may also be contributing to that population's homicide rates (Burton, 2004).

Although this review is not exhaustive, by now you should understand that there exist multiple factors that contribute to violence and crime. Many risk factors are contextual rather than individual, so it does little good to blame Mike or any other person for criminal behavior. Sadly, individuals who experience more than one of these risk factors are exponentially more likely to become involved in crime or violence. Again, however, there is evidence that certain individuals casting about in these environments *do* escape the cycle of crime and violence that such settings can engender (Farmer, Price, O'Neal, & Man-Chi, 2004). We will explore these factors shortly.

## Jails and Prisons

Once an individual commits a crime or act of violence, it may be too late for prevention. It might appear that prevention efforts are few and far between, given the number of Americans locked up in jails and prisons. Let's look first at the traditional U.S. criminal system and its statistics. *Traditional* in this context usually entails a crime, followed by arrest, prosecution, conviction, and imprisonment or **incarceration** of the guilty individual. When Walt Farnsworth approached his local police department in the opening vignette, he had this process in mind. He wanted his son arrested, taken out of the home, and removed from him and the rest of society.

The philosophy behind incarceration is generally retribution, not rehabilitation. **Retribution** in the legal system is supposed to mean repayment for the crime, but it translates in reality to punishment for the crime. If anyone is repaid, it is usually not the victim. Indeed, the victim is the only person who has no official role in the process and so is the "forgotten" participant (Wemmers & Cyr, 2005). Amazingly, the victim need not even appear at the trial. The state is the entity that seeks justice and administers the punishment. For instance, if an individual is found guilty and is fined, the fine does not go to the victim but to the state. If the guilty party is sent to prison, the state decides the sentence and the type of prison. In the past, the victim was rarely allowed to address the offender or have a say in any of these issues.

Does the retribution and punishment approach work? Is the convicted person reformed or corrected in correctional facilities? Or does he or she return to a life of crime? In 2006, 2,258,983 individuals were incarcerated in federal or state prisons or local jails. As stated in the beginning of the chapter, the United States has a higher percentage of its population in jail than any other country in the world. (See Figure 9.1.) In 2006, more than 5 million individuals were being supervised by federal or state authorities (on probation and parole) for crimes committed. This statistic represents a 1.8% increase from the year before (Bureau of Justice Statistics, 2008).

*Recidivism* is the re-arrest of released prisoners. It is a way to measure the effective of the imprisonment. Does time in jail deter future criminal behavior? A report on recidivism issued by the U.S. Department of Justice (Langan & Levin, June, 2002) provided discouraging data. Examining prisoners

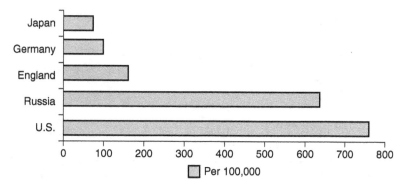

**FIGURE 9.1**  Rates of imprisonment around the world

Source: New York Times, April 3, 2008. http://www.nytimes.com/2008/04/23/world/americas/23iht-23prison.12253738.
html?pagewanted=all.

released in 1994, in a 15-state sample, they found that 67% were rearrested within three years. The highest reoffense rates were robbers (70%), burglars (74%), and automobile thieves (79%). The lowest reoffense rates were held by murderers (40%) and rapists (46%). There were 272,000 released prisoners in this study. Within three years after release, they accumulated 744,000 criminal charges. The length of time in jail did not increase recidivism. There were also mixed results on whether the length of incarceration decreased recidivism. In a European study of prison time versus noncustodial sentencing, the rates of recidivism eight years later were found to be lower for the noncustodial sentencing. This was after other factors related to recidivism had been controlled for (Cid, 2009). So it would appear that spending time in prison increases the likelihood of reoffending. A meta-analysis of studies on predictors of recidivism identified "criminogenic" factors (antisocial attitudes, criminal associates, impulsivity, criminal history, low levels of educational and job achievement, family factors) as the best predictors for return to jail or prison (Gendreau, Little, & Goggin, 1996). Several of these factors can be specifically targeted for psychological intervention. However, this is not done without a shift in focus to deducing recidivism. That would require a shift in our understanding of the criminal justice system, from retribution to rehabilitation.

As for the demographics within prison, many of the inmates were of minority status, with Blacks being by far the most likely to be incarcerated, as illustrated in Figure 9.2. The number of women in prison increased 4.5% and that of men increased 2.7% from the previous year (Bureau of Justice Statistics, 2008). A *USA Today* article (posted July 18, 2007, at http://www.usatoday.com/news/nation/2007-07-18-prison-study_N.htm) stated that Blacks were imprisoned at a rate that was five times that for whites. Hispanics' rate was twice that of whites. The disproportionality is staggering. In 12 states, more than 1 in 10 Black males can be found in jail (Human Rights Watch, February 7, 2002; http://www.hrw.org/news/2002/02/26/us-incarceration-rates-reveal-striking-racial-disparities). Keen and Jacobs (2009) found that perception of racial threat helped to explain some of these prison discrepancies, with political and social factors heightening fear of Blacks in certain localities, which then result in longer prison terms. One might be surprised that community psychology is not more involved in investigating these discrepancies.

A classic study in psychology highlights what occurs in prisons that makes inmate reform unlikely. Philip Zimbardo and colleagues (Haney, Banks, & Zimbardo, 1973) obtained volunteers to act either as prisoners or guards in a mock prison. Subjects were all mentally healthy before the study began and were randomly assigned to their roles. The researchers told the guards to "Do only what was necessary to keep order." The prisoners were all "arrested" unexpectedly at their homes and driven to the mock prison

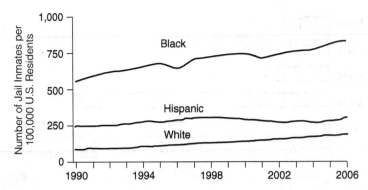

**FIGURE 9.2** Blacks Are More Likely to Be in Jail: Jail Incarceration Rates by Race and Ethnicity, 1990–2006

*Note:* U.S. resident population estimates for race and Hispanic origin were made using a U.S. Census Bureau Internet release with adjustments for census undercount. Estimates for 2000–2006 are based on the 2000 Census and then estimated for July 1 each year.

*Source:* Bureau of Justice Statistics Correctional Surveys (The Annual Survey of Jails and Census of Jail Inmates) as presented in Correctional Populations in the United States, 1997, and Prison and Jail Inmates at Midyear series, 1998–2006.

by real police officers. The prisoners were stripped, searched, dressed in hospital-style gowns, and given identification numbers by the guards. Within a few days of assuming their roles, the guards became abusive of the prisoners. They harassed the prisoners, forced them into crowded cells, awakened them in the night, forced them into frequent countdowns, and subjected them to hard labor and solitary confinement. Conditions in the mock prison became so brutal, the prisoners so depressed, and the guards so involved in their roles that Zimbardo and his colleagues prematurely ended the study. The prison experience, even for these "normal" men, proved overwhelming.

Inmates today often live in overcrowded conditions (Lösel, 2007). This overcrowding has led to early release of prisoners because courts determine the conditions to be cruel and unusual punishment. More and more individuals are living under community supervision, which may be unsettling to community citizens. Additionally, human immunodeficiency virus (HIV) is present in our prisons, and the rates of transmission of this virus and hepatitis are growing rapidly (Myers, Catalano, Sanchez, & Ross, 2006). Inmate-to-inmate violence and a prison culture that is not conducive to successful and productive return to mainstream society are further problems with the prison and jail system (Lahm, 2008). On top of these issues, substance abuse among inmates is increasing (Office of Justice Programs, 2006), and allegations of sexual violence are on the rise in prisons (Bureau of Justice Statistics, 2007). Incarceration is also demonstrated to have negative effects on intergenerational relations (e.g., between children and incarcerated parents) and to create family instability (Bonhomme, Stephens, & Braithwaite, 2006). In fact, one set of justice system experts claimed that local jails serve only to brutalize and embitter individuals, further preventing them from returning to a useful role in society (Allen & Simonsen, 1992). Had Walter Farnsworth known the realities of the corrections system, perhaps he would not have jumped so quickly at the notion of having his son arrested. Not surprisingly, Ortmann (2000), based on his own longitudinal research, contended that prisons are extremely unfavorable places for the positive correction of people.

Courts have ruled that the prison system must be restructured (*Ruiz v. Estelle*), but this restructuring has sometimes escalated inmate–inmate and inmate–guard violence. Inmate lawsuits over the crowded conditions in prisons have led to early release for many, which sometimes results in higher recidivism rates and subsequent return to the crowded prisons (Kelly & Ekland-Olson, 1991). Although legal decrees to change prisons have been issued, there is concern that the decrees do not translate readily into *real* change. In the meantime, the growth in the number of inmates continues to exceed the growth in prison space, which leads to more overcrowding. There must be a better way than to incarcerate all individuals who break the law.

In a cautionary sense, mounting evidence suggests that some alternative forms of punishment outside of the traditional prison system are not good substitutes for incarceration. Several studies have demonstrated that shock incarceration camps or **boot camps** that are run by corrections personnel but resemble intensive army training camps fall short of their goals (MacKenzie, Wilson, Armstrong, & Gover, 2001; Palmer & Wedge, 1989). A report of work by the Office of Juvenile Justice and Delinquency Prevention (U.S. Department of Justice, 1997) revealed that "reoffending youth in the experimental groups (boot camps) committed new offenses more quickly—that is, had shorter survival periods—than reoffending youth in the control group" (p. 23). In programs described in the report, youth in some of the boot camps actually recidivated at rates higher than the control group.

Prison may not be the best solution for dealing with crime and providing the community with productive members for the future. Some promising alternatives include prevention of crime through both social and environmental interventions, and providing conditions that support positive behavioral change. We review some of those efforts later. Let us now turn to the victims of crime and the fears of ordinary citizens about being victimized.

## Victims and Fear of Being Victimized

In 2010, U.S. citizens experienced more than 10 million crimes. The number of violent victimizations alone is about 26 per thousand for men and 23 per thousand for women (Bureau of Justice Statistics, 2006). Given that many crimes are never reported to authorities, the true number is likely to be higher. DeFrances and Smith (1998) surveyed households that had been victimized and found that 44% said the crime problem was so objectionable that they wished they could move out of the neighborhood. One-third of U.S. residents are afraid to walk alone where they live (Rader, May, & Goodrum, 2007).

Community psychologists, sociologists, and criminologists are interested both in fear of crime and in its relationship to actual victimization (Chadee, Austen, & Ditton, 2007; Kruger, Reischl, & Gee, 2007; Thompson & Norris, 1992). Those who are the most fearful are sometimes the least likely to be victimized—a phenomenon called the **fear-victimization paradox.** One reason for this paradox may be that risk perceptions are based on interpretations of the world that are not based on statistical realities (Chadee et al., 2007; Rader et al., 2007). We now discuss data that support the paradox.

Men (compared to women) are more likely to be victimized, yet are less afraid of violent crime (Schafer, Huebner, & Bynum, 2006). **Young urban men** are especially likely to be crime victims but are not very fearful of crime as compared to young women (Bayley & Andersen, 2006; Perkins, 1997; Roll & Habemeier, 1991). The **elderly** are more afraid of crime even though their victimization rate is much lower than they actually perceive (Beaulieu, Dubé, Beron, & Cousineau, 2007; Schuller, 2006). Especially fearful of crime are elderly women. And yet they are least likely to be victimized of any group (Bayley & Andersen, 2006; Mawby, 1986; Perkins & Taylor, 1996; Rountree, 1998). Even though Black-on-Black crime has been frequent, young Black men are less likely to fear crime than are Whites or Hispanics (Bayley & Andersen, 2006).

Thompson and Norris (1992) and Youngstrom and associates (2003) found that victims of violent crimes, especially those of low economic status, suffered alienation, fear, and avoidance. Additional studies have demonstrated that neighborhood deterioration, which can also signal unsafe conditions (i.e., potential victimization), is related to stress and depression (Kruger et al., 2007). Some authors claimed that fear of crime might have helped bring about America's obesity epidemic (Loukaitou-Sideris & Eck,

2007), because fear of victimization could reduce the likelihood of walking around one's neighborhood or enjoying other forms of active and healthy outdoor activities.

Why did some individuals fear crime even if they were not likely to be victimized? For one, people often perceived environments, especially urban ones, as dangerous (Glaberson, 1990; Wandersman & Nation, 1998). City residents with the greatest fear were usually dissatisfied with their neighborhoods or **mistrust** other residents (Ferguson & Mindel, 2007; Schafer et al., 2006). When an area contained **symbols of disintegration** and disorganization such as abandoned buildings, vandalism, graffiti, litter, unkempt lawns, and other signs of "incivilities" (Brown, Perkins, & Brown, 2004; Kruger et al., 2007; Taylor & Shumaker, 1990), its residents were more fearful because these signs suggested neighborhood deterioration (Kruger et al., 2007) and social disorder (Ross & Jang, 2000), both of which they identified with threats to their personal safety. In neighborhoods perceived to be disordered, even indirect victimization, that is, hearing of crime problems, heightened fear. However, if the neighborhood was perceived as **ordered**, neither direct nor indirect victimization affected people's fear (Roccato, Russo, & Vieno, 2011).

Other research demonstrated that adverse neighborhood conditions, such as poverty, also increased the risk of children's emotional and behavioral problems above and beyond genetic predispositions (Caspi et al., 2000). The perception of crime level and risks of victimization could undermine an individual's confidence in the effectiveness of the government, its elected officials, and its enforcement agencies (Williamson, Ashby, & Webber, 2006).

Fortunately, there were factors that reduced fear of crime and actual crimes, such as attachment to one's neighborhood and **social cohesiveness** in a community (Brown et al., 2004). Availability of **social support** networks (e.g., nearby family and friends) and various types of **police presence** (Ferguson & Mindel, 2007) enhanced perceptions of safety. Similarly, high levels of **social capital** contributed to reduced fear of crime (Williamson et al., 2006). Social capital, as defined elsewhere in this book, includes trust, reciprocity, cooperation, and supportive interaction within families, between neighbors, and among those in the community. Prezza and Pacilli (2007), studying Italian adolescents, discovered that the more they **played** independently in public places as children, the less their fear of crime in those areas and the more they felt a sense of community. These in turn related to feeling less lonely. This is an interesting finding in that it suggests we might lessen fear of a neighborhood by having residents become familiar with and frequent sites within that community.

Aside from fear of crime, there are other concerns about victims. Victims often do not know their rights; because of this, many **victims' assistance programs** have flourished in the United States. There are more than 3,000 such organizations today, but only a fraction of crime victims receive much-needed services (Turman, 2001). Victim assistance can include crisis intervention, counseling, emergency transportation to court, and support and advocacy during the justice process. Because of fairly new public policy, victims in most states now have the right of notification of all court proceedings; the right to participate in proceedings; the right to be reasonably protected from the accused; the right to have input at sentencing; and the right to information about the conviction, imprisonment, and release of the offender.

## Enforcement Agencies

Some see the police as peace officers, keeping communities harmonious and free of crime. Perhaps this attitude led Walt Farnsworth to the police when the conflict with his son escalated. Others see enforcement officers or the police as dishonest, unethical, prejudiced, and prone to misconduct (Ackerman et al., 2001; Dowler & Zawilski, 2007; Ross, 2006; Weitzer & Tuch, 2005). This is particularly true of America's racial and ethnic minorities, with Blacks and Hispanics holding far more negative attitudes toward the police than do Whites.

Regardless of one's views of the police, interesting research has demonstrated how difficult the job of policing communities can be. In fact, there is mounting interest in police burnout and stress (Anshel, 2000; Goodman, 1990). Why is the career of an enforcement officer so difficult? One reason is that the police force and community citizens hold different views of the role of the officers. New police recruits often maintain a serve-and-protect orientation toward the community, but after training, their attitudes often shift toward one of remoteness. In fact, police officers increasingly see themselves as hampered by community attitudes and constraints (Ellis, 1991) and as holding differing views from the community as to what police actually do (Salmi, Voeten, & Keskinen, 2005).

The police force and citizens also hold different views as to which community incidents ought to involve the police. Police are often called by citizens for public nuisance offenses (e.g., loud noise or drunkenness), traffic accidents, illegally parked vehicles, and investigation of suspicious persons. Answering such mundane calls is surely not the kind of exciting role portrayed in television dramas about the police. In fact, heavy users of the media are more likely to believe that police use unpopular methods (such as racial profiling) and participate in misconduct than are low-level users (Dowler & Zawilski, 2007; Weitzer & Tuch, 2005). The police are also likely to be called to intervene in family conflicts—a role for which they need more training—which can sometimes lead to assault on the officer if managed ineffectively. Another frequent role of the police is to intervene in mental health crises; that is, the police are asked to intercede in an incident involving someone with a mental disorder, then make a quick evaluation, and promptly decide whether to use placement in a hospital or a jail based on whether the person is a danger to self or others. Police officers do not relish this job and are often required to make such decisions without much training in mental health issues (Borum, 2000; Cordner, 2000).

A primary question about policing is whether *active* enforcement and a police presence in a community affect its actual crime rate and the fear of crime as well as residents' perceptions of their community. In one study of the use of police foot patrols in violent crime hotspots, reductions in violent crime were found in comparison to control sites. The mere presence of police "increased certainty of disruption, apprehension and arrest" (Ratcliffe, Taniguchi, Groff, & Wood, 2011, p. 795) and thus served to deter crime.

In another vein, community policing emerged in the early 1980s as a response to criticism regarding the stiff and professional style of policing used at the time (Roh & Oliver, 2005). **Community policing** involves forming partnerships or collaboration between police and community citizens. A major tenet of community policing is to identify problems based on the needs of the particular community and then deal with those problems with the cooperation and participation of the residents and related agencies (Zhong & Broadhurst, 2007). For example, the police might casually drop in on businesses to see how things are going, stop and talk to citizens on the street even when no crime has been reported, or provide talks to schoolchildren in an effort to gather knowledge about the community in general and crime in specific.

Salmi, Voeten, and Keskinen (2000) found that seeing police on foot patrol around the neighborhood (rather than in patrol cars) increased police visibility and improved the relationship between the police and the public. Later, these same researchers demonstrated that many citizens responded more positively to the police simply because of community policing (Salmi et al., 2005). Community policing also appeared to reduce fear of crime, but it seemed to do so in indirect ways. Specifically, community policing reduced the perception of "incivilities," as mentioned before (Roh & Oliver, 2005). Reducing residents' dissatisfaction with their community and quality of life (Roh & Oliver, 2005) as well as decreasing neighborhood disorder and disintegration (Wells, 2007) accounted for positive views of the police.

Yet, research has demonstrated that in the highest crime neighborhoods, citizens were least likely to become involved in crime prevention strategies such as community policing (Pattavina, Byrne, &

Garcia, 2006). It appears that where crime reduction is needed most, the community policing program is least likely to succeed.

A case study of a department shifting from traditional methods to a community policing model focused on capacity building (Ford, 2007) found that, organizationally, the shift required team involvement and decision making, and an active learning environment. The change was possible given good leadership with regard to the preparations for the change and patience and willingness to work through the problems it brought.

Community psychologists, of course, believe that crime prevention is better than police patrols, citizen arrest, prosecution, and possible incarceration after a crime has been committed. In the next section, we examine programs designed by community psychologists and other prevention experts interested in tackling the diverse needs of the citizens, victims, offenders, and relevant professionals involved in the criminal justice system.

## ADDRESSING JUSTICE SYSTEM ISSUES

Was there anything in Mike Farnsworth's background that would have helped someone predict he would turn into an irascible and difficult adolescent? Perhaps his adoption, being placed with older parents, his large size, school alienation, and other factors contributed to his family difficulties. Maybe there were community-level factors, such as befriending delinquent peers, that would have helped us predict he would eventually turn aggressive toward his father.

Earlier in this chapter, we examined some of the predictors of criminal and violent behavior. Knowing of them, we might be able to intercede better with prevention programs. In review, some of the factors alluded to include access to guns, lack of parental monitoring, family instability, child maltreatment, exposure to violence in the community or in the media, prejudice and its horrific companions (discrimination and segregation), and especially poverty and neighborhood disorder. What can be done about these issues so as to prevent crime or to improve a community to make it safer?

### Primary Prevention

**PREVENTION WITH AT-RISK INDIVIDUALS.** Given the list of risk factors just mentioned, you can probably guess some of the suggested methods for reducing risk for violence and crime. Removing violence from the media might go a long way toward changing the cultural norms for violence. Similarly, the nurse home visitation program developed by David Olds and colleagues (see Chapter 7) is also helpful. These programs align with the principles of community psychology, but first we examine what has traditionally taken place with adjudicated or delinquent youth.

You probably already know there are juvenile "correctional" facilities dotted around every state—each meant to "reform" juvenile "offenders." In large part, these facilities do *not* work. Some states report that recidivism rates for youth emerging back into the community are as high as 55% (Woodward, 2008). Research also demonstrates that many youth in these facilities are uncertain about their ability to change their behavior, and they think their incarceration will not deter future delinquent activity. In addition, most youth, when interviewed, articulate that there is a major disconnect between what they learned on the "inside" and the reality of life on the "outside" (Abrams, 2006). When youth are released from these facilities, their families are considered critical to interrupting the pattern of delinquent and criminal behavior, but other research shows that follow-up, face-to-face family visits by youth service workers are few and far between (Ryan & Yang, 2005). Youth service workers and community psychologists—indeed, anyone working with such youth—can have a difficult time interacting with these individuals, not just because of their backgrounds and their sense of hopelessness, but also because of the subculture that they live in. Case in Point 9.2 offers some insight into how difficult it is to work with at-risk youth.

## CASE IN POINT 9.2

# Working with At-Risk Youth

Working with youths at risk for delinquency, running away from home, and dropping out of school can be extremely challenging. Such youths live in a rather closed subculture where "squealing" is not only looked down on but can be downright dangerous. Community psychologists and other professionals are learning how to work better and smarter with street youth, who can be resistant to the most well-intentioned efforts.

In an interesting project, Hackerman (1996) recognized that just as a country has its own language, so do street youth. Street gangs in particular, such as the Crips and the Bloods, use their own symbols and words to communicate. Psychologists and others (such as ministers, school officials, and youth probation officers) need to be able to speak the unique street language of these young people if they are to work with and design programs for them. In essence, they need to become cultural anthropologists in addition to their other training. Over a two-year period, Hackerman put together a much-needed glossary of terms for individuals working with this target group. She noted that not all terms were used by all youth. Hispanic youth in Los Angeles often speak a language different from African American youth in New York City. Hackerman's work demonstrates the importance of ethnography in community psychology. Some of the terms from her glossary are shown next. Cover the right side and see how many terms on the left side you know. Based on your awareness of terminology, how successful do you think you would be working with street youth?

| Street Terminology | Meaning of Term to Youth |
| --- | --- |
| Blue light | Order someone killed |
| Bo | A marijuana cigarette, a joint |
| Flying colors | Wearing gang colors |
| Jack up | Rob someone |
| Strap | A gun |
| Jankin' | Teasing |

Taylor and Taylor (2007) identified hip hop as an important, evolving youth subculture with its own language. Because hip hop has gone somewhat mainstream, it is essential that community psychologists and other adults (parents, social workers) understand the words. Much of the language used in the hip hop movement expresses what young people encounter in their struggle to find meaning in home communities that too often leave them feeling hopeless (Taylor & Taylor, 2007). Here are some examples of this language. See if you know any just from listening to hip hop music or by walking around your community.

| Street Terminology | Meaning of Term to Youth |
| --- | --- |
| Running a train | Multiple men engaging in sex with one woman |
| Blazing | Violence |
| Hurting someone | Gun violence |
| Ho | Whore |
| Bitch | Woman |
| Punks | Adults |

What do you think the effects are on young people of hearing such terms over and over again?

On the other hand, although a **positive adult role model** cannot single-handedly change families or whole communities (Broussard, Mosley-Howard, & Roychoudhury, 2006), research with at-risk youth who are involved with a **caring, consistent adult** suggests that such youths are more likely to withstand a range of negative influences, such as poverty, family conflict, and impoverished neighborhoods (Rhodes, Spencer, Keller, Liang, & Noam, 2006; Southwick, Morgan, Vythilingam, & Charney, 2006). Positive adult role models are considered preventive in that they contribute to the completion of future important milestones, such as high school graduation or employment (Broussard et al., 2006). In general, positive adult role models are considered to enhance a young person's development by providing successful models for coping and thus influencing the youth's resiliency. **Resiliency** can be defined as the capacity of those who are at risk to overcome those risks and avoid long-term negative outcomes (Masten, 2009). Specifically as related to this chapter, a close bond with a supportive caregiver or other adult—in other words, a **mentor**—might help prevent a young person from entering a life of delinquency and crime. A mentor, as defined in the chapter on schools, is a caring and responsible adult role model who can make a positive and lasting impression on a child.

Mentoring can be informal, such as when a neighbor has frequent, unstructured contacts with a child over a period of time, or it can be formalized, as in a community mentoring program. Informal mentoring occurs spontaneously in the form of attentive and caring athletic coaches, teachers, neighbors, or clergy. Research reveals that informal mentoring can and does occur quite naturally (Hamilton et al., 2006; Helping America's Youth, 2008; Masten, 2009) when an extended family member (e.g., an uncle) or even a shopkeeper or municipal worker (Basso, Graham, Pelech, De Young, & Cardy, 2004) watches over a particular child's safety and well-being when the parents are not around. In fact, some studies indicate that over 50% of youth report having a natural mentor (Helping America's Youth, 2008). For children who do not have a naturally occurring mentoring network, a formal mentor can supply the extra attention, affection, supervision, and prosocial role modeling that is not always available in other environments (Bilchik, 1998). Formal mentors tend to come from youth development, service-learning, or faith-based organizations (Hamilton et al., 2006).

**Mentors,** formal or informal, play various roles, such as providing tutoring for school subjects, attending or participating in recreational activities with the child, and talking to the child about various personal issues. On a more psychological level, mentors appear to help children **escape from daily stresses** (such as parental discord), provide **positive interpersonal relationships** that may generalize to the child's other relationships (peers and parents), assist in **modeling** better emotional regulation (e.g., when and why not to lose one's temper), and bolster the child's self-esteem (Rhodes et al., 2006).

There are now an estimated 3 million young people who have an adult, volunteer mentor (Rhodes, 2008). One of the best-known and oldest formal mentoring programs is Big Brothers/Big Sisters. This program primarily connects middle-class adults with disadvantaged youths, or a fatherless boy with an adult male, or a motherless girl with an adult female. Another federally sponsored program is JUMP (Juvenile Mentoring Program). In both programs, mentors are selected, trained, and matched to children (often by race and/or gender). The mission of such mentoring programs is usually to prevent delinquency and/or improve school performance by providing a caring adult role model. JUMP also involves coordination among community resources (referrals to human service agencies in the community), the schools, and the families, although there is variation from program to program (Bilchik, 1998).

Two meta-analyses of mentoring programs concluded that mentoring has several positive effects (Dubois, Holloway, Valentine, & Cooper, 2002; Eby, Allen, Evans, Ng, & Dubois, 2008).

Tierney, Grossman, and Resch (1995) compared data from mentored youths in the Big Brothers/Big Sisters Program to youths on a waiting list. At the end of the 18-month study period, several positive results were documented for the mentored youths. Mentored youth were less likely to use or initiate use of drugs and alcohol, more likely to attend school (missing half as many days as the wait-list group), and less likely to report hitting someone. Subsequent research has illustrated that the program does have beneficial effects in other areas, such as reduced emotional problems and social anxiety as well as better self-control (De Wit et al., 2007). Research also found that a mentor's **inconsistent** presence might be **detrimental** to the children (e.g., lower the child's self-esteem) (Helping America's Youth, 2008) and in fact do more harm than good (Karcher, 2005). Before assigning "Bigs" and "Littles," careful screening should occur for this and many other reasons.

Some preliminary data are also available for JUMP (Bilchik, 1998). Both youths and mentors responded positively on a survey about the mentoring experience, with youths being more positive than their mentors. When mentors and youths were asked whether mentoring improved or prevented problems, they generally responded "yes" to varying degrees. Adults and children reported that the mentored child was getting better grades; attending classes; staying away from alcohol, drugs, gangs, knives, or guns; avoiding friends who start trouble; and getting along better with his or her family. Mentoring, then, holds great promise for reducing the risk of delinquent behavior. Community psychologists are continuing their efforts to sort out the literature and continue researching the best practices for youth mentoring programs (Rhodes, 2008).

Mentoring is not the only solution to juvenile delinquency problems. A much newer program is Safe Start. In 2000, the Office of Juvenile Justice and Delinquency Prevention of the federal government launched **Safe Start** to address the needs of children exposed to community violence. Recall that witnessing community violence often leads to delinquency, crime, and more violence (Lambert et al., 2005; Youngstrom et al., 2003). Safe Start is designed to reduce the negative consequences of exposure to violence and create conditions that enhance the well-being of all children and adolescents through prevention interventions. Safe Start's definition of exposure to violence includes direct exposure (such as child maltreatment) and indirect exposure (such as witnessing family or community violence). The Safe Start Initiative envisions federal, state, and local governments working together (Office of Juvenile Justice and Delinquency Prevention, 2008b). Some local programs have been established in early child-care centers so as to reach children as early as possible (Hampton, Epstein, Johnson, & Reixach, 2004). Safe Start sometimes engages classroom teachers who have been mentored by a trained professional to model appropriate strategies for children's socioemotional development. Other programs use social workers who arrive on the scene of violence to which young children are witnesses, and other programs establish groups of parents of children who have been exposed to violence that are facilitated by a trained leader. Each program depends greatly on the community and its unique issues with crime and violence, as well as on local agencies available to participate. Programs such as Big Brothers/Big Sisters and Safe Start show great promise as crime prevention programs because they address multiple and complex risk factors and target appropriate subgroups of children and adolescents (Case & Haines, 2007).

**DESIGNING THE ENVIRONMENT TO PREVENT CRIME.**  The issue of how the environment contributes to whether an individual is likely to fear crime or be an actual victim needs to be examined here. **Environmental psychologists**—those who study the effect of the environment on behavior—have much to offer community psychologists in terms of recommendations for arranging the environment so that crime is less likely to occur.

Do characteristics of the environment influence crime? Traditional approaches to crime deterrence in various environments include installing burglar alarms, motion sensors, and other devices designed to prevent or catch someone in the act of breaking the law. Schools have made a particularly concerted effort to reduce crime by widening corridors, limiting the number of entrances to the building, using landscaping to define campus boundaries, and keeping up the facility to deter vandalism and crime (Kennedy, 2006). However, some of the solutions to altering the built environment (e.g., gated communities) are purchased at the cost of loss of movement and even greater fear of crimes (Zhong & Broadhurst, 2007). Many of these techniques simply do not completely prevent crime, whereas others prevent one type of crime but not others (Farrington, Gill, Waples, & Argomaniz, 2007). Short of creating the perception of a community or building as a fortress (Davey, Wootton, Cooper, & Press, 2005), there must be other aspects of environments and communities that can be altered to help reduce crime and fear of crime.

The pioneer and rebel urban planner **Jane Jacobs** (1961/2011) argued that it was not the physical aspects of design itself so much as what the design accomplishes on the human level. As opposed to the planners of her day who emphasized highways and large parks, Jacobs argued persuasively with her human-level stories of urban dwellers that city planning should be about the opportunities for face-to-face interactions and ownership of public spaces. What she noted were those aspects of the settings that helped people feel safe and to use their environment. Among her findings was that **use** and **ownership** were important to places. When there were people using spaces, observing and interacting with the users of the space, people felt more comfortable. Ownership of that space was also most helpful to get people to take responsibility for what happened there. The ownership did not have to be literal—they did not have to own the property. Rather, the owners/participants/observers had to understand that they had a stake in what happened in those spaces. The danger was apathy. Her solution was to have naturally evolving designs of space that facilitated "liveliness." Although Jacob's work is not without its modern critics (Zukin, 2010), her work provided narrative evidence of crime prevention in urban design/sociology/psychology and is still cited among the classics of urban design.

When citizens and residents feel a lack of social solidarity and attachment to the community, traditional approaches to altering the built environment simply create indifference, suspicion, or even outright hostility. Furthermore, such approaches isolate prevention activities from the surrounding social context—such as citizen diversity—and fail to take into account community needs, priorities, and capacities. Merely altering the physical environment by means of better lighting or redesign will not work, because such projects reflect top-down decision making where outsiders bring prevention to the community, without an understanding of the psychological impact on those who people that setting (Kelly, Caputo, & Jamieson, 2005).

Many community psychologists and criminologists echo this feeling—that citizens need to feel an attachment to (Brown, Perkins, & Brown, 2003) and ownership of their communities to prevent crime. Research on the effects of crime on citizen participation or empowerment is ambiguous at present, with some studies indicating that crime has a chilling effect on participation and others demonstrating that it has an energizing effect (Dupéré & Perkins, 2007; Saegert & Winkel, 2004). However, several authors suggest that citizens can become more interested in and empowered to do something about crime in their particular building or their own community (e.g., Dupéré & Perkins, 2007). One approach is to empower citizens to design their *own* programs so that the response comes from an integral knowledge of the social fabric of the community (Kelly et al., 2005). One means for empowering and involving citizens is to take advantage of or build the social capital of community citizens. Social capital helps groups achieve both individual and collective goals. **Social capital** is exemplified by a sense of shared obligation, shared norms, trustworthiness, and information flow (Dupéré & Perkins, 2007). Let's examine two ways to build social capital—one at the building level and one at the community level.

An example of a building-level intervention (which could also be used at the community level) designed to increase social capital is the development of **neighborhood crime watches** (National Crime Prevention Council, 1989). In neighborhood crime watches, neighbors are on active alert for suspicious activity or actual break-ins to each other's homes (Bennett, 1989). Certain environmental factors predict who will and will not join neighborhood watches (Perkins, Florin, Rich, Wandersman, & Chavis, 1990; Sampson, Raudenbush, & Earls, 1997). Crime watches are a collaborative activity among neighbors, which helps to build a sense of community (Levine, 1986). These watches introduce neighbors to each other, provide information on how to communicate with each other, and serve as the basis for common agreements to be "watchful and responsible" around the neighborhood. Researchers found that a sense of community was one of the most important variables related to lower fear of crime (Schweitzer, Kim, & Mackin, 1999).

A second sample program of social capital building is at the community level. We have already reviewed the discrepancies between police attitudes and community citizens' attitudes about how the police should serve their communities. Programs that reduce these differences might give citizens more confidence in their police and allow the police to better service each individual community. Walker and Walker (1990) have described a **Community Police Station Program** in which citizens play a major role in the determination, design, and delivery of crime-prevention programs. Citizens from the community see to the daily operation of the station and to the delivery of specific programs, such as Seniors Calling Seniors, a program designed to give shut-in or isolated seniors a sense of contact with others as well as a sense of safety. The program also includes a citizens' advisory board that helps identify the neighborhood crime-prevention needs of each area of the city and sees that programs are developed to address those needs. In the Community Police Station Program, the police and citizens collaborate to make police services more acceptable and effective. In other communities, citizens and community members have been used to help recruit and select new police officers, again allowing collaboration and building a sense of community among citizens and enforcement personnel.

## Secondary Prevention

This section explores exemplary measures designed to intercede as early as possible after a crime. Primary prevention at this point is too late. The strategy thus becomes secondary prevention. In the case of the Farnsworths from the opening vignette, when Mike first argued with his father, stayed out beyond the agreed-on curfew, or missed school, someone should have or could have intervened before the situation deteriorated. As it was, Mike struck his father and, in so doing, committed a crime. Primary prevention was too late.

**EARLY ASSISTANCE FOR CRIME VICTIMS.**   Victims need their concerns addressed as early as possible after the victimization. They may experience a wide variety of emotions, ranging from fright, rage, a sense of violation, and vengefulness to sorrow, depression, despair, and shock. Victims can also experience an array of health consequences after the crime—for example, HIV infection after a rape (Britt, 2000). As mentioned earlier, the justice system does little for the victim, who does not even have an official role to play in the trial, if there is one (Wemmers & Cyr, 2005). The National Victims Resource Center is a national clearinghouse that provides victims with educational materials, funds victim-related studies, makes referrals to assistance programs, and provides information on compensation programs. Some state governments have also developed victim assistance programs (Woolpert, 1991) in which victims are compensated for their injuries or awarded money from the offender's selling his or her story to the media, or where victims can participate in decisions on their offender's parole (Educational Conference on Psychiatry, Psychology and the Law, 1990). (**Parole** is supervision of the offender in the community after incarceration.) However, victim compensation programs are rare because an offender in prison does not earn much money that could be used for restitution.

Financial compensation alone, though, cannot take away the psychological pain of being victimized or the victim's vengeful or angry thoughts. Even with a trial, victims may have to wait months or years before their side of the story is aired in court. There are at least two types of programs available to victims that afford early and substantially successful interventions. The programs are crisis intervention and neighborhood justice centers.

**CRISIS INTERVENTION FOR VICTIMS.**   One program available to victims is **crisis intervention,** which is a set of procedures used by a trained individual to help others recover from the effects of temporary or time-limited but extreme stress. Early efforts at crisis intervention were focused on potential suicides, victims of violence, unpredictable or dangerous situations, and natural disasters. Since its early days, crisis intervention has expanded to assistance of victims of major school incidents (Eaves, 2001; Weinberg, 1990), sexual assaults (Kitchen, 1991), individuals with chronic mental disorders (Dobmeyer, McKee, Miller, & Westcott, 1990), and even victims of international terrorism (Everly, Phillips, Kane, & Feldman, 2006). Every year, millions of individuals are confronted with crisis-producing events that they are unable to resolve on their own, so they frequently seek help from crisis intervention specialists. Crisis intervention has become the most widely used, time-limited treatment in the world. Although its potential uses seem limitless, not all situations are appropriate for it (Roberts & Everly, 2006).

Crisis intervention is usually a face-to-face or phone (hotline) intervention that uses *immediate* intercession in the form of social support and focused problem solving to assist a person in a state of elevated crisis or trauma. Its immediate purpose is to avert catastrophe and quell distress, so in this way it is a sort of psychological first aid (Everly et al., 2006). Crisis intervention centers can be staffed by professionals or trained volunteers and are often open 24 hours a day. Note, though, that crisis intervention is not designed to be a stand-alone intervention; usually it is the beginning of a continuum of future interventions for the same individual. For example, many people witnessed the September 11, 2001, terrorist bombings or lost loved ones in the collapse of the World Trade Center towers. Others were traumatized when they visited the devastated site or witnessed news reports over and over again. Although crisis intervention teams were available to many affected individuals and helped them in about 90% of the cases (Jackson, Covell, Shear, & Zhu, 2006), some required ongoing therapy or other interventions.

A pertinent question about crisis intervention is whether it is an effective means of providing help at the onset of the crisis and thus of preventing future problems. Mishara (1997) examined the effects of different telephone styles used with suicidal callers. Using calls from 617 callers, nearly 70,000 responses by crisis counselors were categorized and then evaluated for success of the crisis intervention. Mishara found that Rogerian-based, nondirective (rather than directive) interaction with the caller resulted in better outcomes—that is, it resulted in decreased depressive mood and in contractual behavior as to how to manage the crisis. Crisis counseling is even being conducted electronically (Wilson & Lester, 1998), but whether this is as effective as phone contact remains to be determined. Campfield and Hills (2001) found that the sooner the crisis intervention occurs after an actual crime, the lower the number and severity of symptoms for the victim in the long run.

Because of the maturation of the crisis intervention field and proliferating research on it, Roberts and Everly (2006) were able to conduct a literature review (meta-analysis) of well-designed crisis intervention studies to determine whether it is superior to psychiatric hospitalization and other long-term interventions. The 36 studies they examined all had pre-post designs or an experimental and control group matched on multiple variables. The researchers concluded that "adults in acute crisis or with trauma symptoms and abusive families in acute crisis can be helped with intensive intervention [crisis intervention]." (p. 10).

**RESTORATIVE JUSTICE PROGRAMS.**    You have already learned that recidivism rates for inmates of correctional facilities (juvenile detention centers, prisons, and jails) are quite high. Once these individuals are released, they often return to a life of crime. What can be done to reduce recidivism? This question speaks to the issue of secondary prevention. Although community psychologists much prefer primary prevention, secondary prevention becomes an important issue in this chapter because of the likelihood of recidivism, especially when the person is released into the same environment and the same peer group that may have cued crime in the first place.

Recidivism remains just one of the problems when crime-prone individuals emerge from any of the traditional forms of justice (e.g., incarceration). The traditional system is designed to administer

**retribution** or punishment. You read earlier that incarceration generally does not deter a person from committing a subsequent crime. In fact, some studies find that very few persons who experience retribution or punishment from the traditional system are deterred from crime, so the rate of recidivism may be as high as 90% at times (Bradshaw & Roseborough, 2005). What the traditional system offers in the form of secondary prevention is supervision in the community, such as parole. Less frequently, **rehabilitation services** might be offered to the juvenile delinquent or adult offender and are designed to reform or dissuade the individual from crime-prone activities such as using illegal drugs.

Neighborhood justice centers or community mediation centers, on the other hand, comprise a category of secondary intervention for both the offender *and* their victims where a third type of justice is offered—**restorative justice,** a method for making right the wrong that was done (Wemmers & Cyr, 2005). Restorative justice can involve victim compensation, but in this case, restoration also includes repairing the psychological harm done by the crime. The process aims to benefit the victim, the offender, and the community. Victims are able to express their feelings, emotionally heal, get questions answered regarding the crime, and have input into a reparation plan. The offender is held personally accountable for the crime (Rodriguez, 2005) by providing restitution as well as details about the crime and his or her plans to reintegrate into the community. **Neighborhood justice centers** are almost always linked to courts, where judges or intake workers refer cases away from adjudication and to mediation. **Community mediation centers** are often nonprofits that use volunteer mediators to facilitate discussion among individuals involved in conflicts. Both types of centers are established in the local community and are designed to handle cases from criminal, juvenile, family, and civil courts or from other community agencies, such as community mental health centers and religious organizations (Hedeen, 2004). Although the exact number of such programs is elusive, estimates range from between 500 and 1,000 centers in the United States that manage a remarkable 100,000 cases a year (Hedeen, 2004).

At these centers, a special type of mediation is used to provide restorative justice when crimes have been committed. **Victim-offender mediation** is attempted. In this type of mediation, a trained person hears the case as presented by both the victim and the offender. This neutral person, the **mediator,** assists the two parties in understanding their involvement and fashioning a resolution that is satisfactory to each. Mediators use a variety of strategies to facilitate discussion and guide the parties toward restoration (Carnevale & Pruitt, 1992; Heisterkamp, 2006; Ostermeyer, 1991). Mediators are supposed to use reality testing (a process in which one person is asked to "get in the other person's shoes"), a futuristic (rather than retrospective) orientation, turn taking, compromise, reciprocity in concession making, and active listening, among other skills. Analysis of the process of mediation demonstrates that mediators generally do remain neutral and use unbiased paraphrasing as well as invitations to take the other person's perspective. In some respects, mediation and psychotherapy are parallel processes, but mediation focuses more on problems and issues than on emotions or relationships (Forlenza, 1991; Milne, 1985; Weaver, 1986). The resolutions in most programs are legally binding, do not require decisions about guilt or innocence (thus can "clear" an arrest record), and must be mutually agreed (Duffy, 1991).

The centers and the process of mediation embody many of the values of community psychology. The centers are generally available to the parties in or near their own neighborhoods. The centers provide an alternative to the sometimes oppressive, bureaucratic, and almost always adversarial court system (Duffy, 1991). Mediation empowers the parties to play a major and active role in determining their own solutions. Research on compliance with the contracts suggests that they usually prevent conflicts and crimes from recurring in the future (Duffy, 1991). Similarly, the centers are generally available to every community citizen regardless of income, race, or creed (Crosson & Christian, 1990; Duffy, 1991; Harrington, 1985), and the mediators are trained to *respect the unique perspective* and *diversity* of the parties (Duffy, 1991). Empirical research has demonstrated that mediation is a humanistic process because it enhances the functioning of both participants as measured by Maslow's hierarchy of needs (Duffy & Thompson, 1992).

These centers hold several advantages over more traditional forms of seeking justice. For one thing, the centers dispense with cases in a more timely fashion than the court system (Duffy, Grolsch, & Olczak, 1991; Hedeen, 2004). One state reports a 15-day turnaround time from intake to resolution at its mediation centers (Crosson & Christian, 1990; Duffy, 1991), so in essence they offer early intervention. Second, victims no longer have to play a passive role in the justice system; in mediation, the victim plays an active role (Smith, 2006). Third, some studies have shown that victims demonstrate very little knowledge about the justice system and services available for them (Sims, Yost, & Abbott, 2005), so referral to mediation, where subsequent referrals to helping services can be made, educates victims about their rights and about other available supports. Furthermore, other research has found that victims are very dissatisfied with more traditional forms of justice (such as trials). They often are not told the full facts of the case and frequently have difficulty trying to recover personal property or even a loved one's remains because the police view these items as evidence (Goodrum, 2007). Additionally, many crime victims can achieve emotional repair, even forgiveness, in the mediation process (Armour & Umbreit, 2006; Strange, Sherman, Angel, & Woods, 2006). Charkoudian (2005) found that community mediation reduces repeat police calls for the same or continuing problem. Importantly, recent studies have found that offenders who take part in restorative justice programs such as victim-offender mediation are far less likely to recidivate (Bradshaw & Roseborough, 2005; de Beus & Rodriguez, 2007; Rodriguez, 2007). One study followed parties in victim-offender mediation for three years and found that restorative justice programs are related to significantly better outcomes (e.g., less recidivism) than are traditional programs (e.g., parole).

Most victims are highly satisfied with the process of mediation (Bazemore, Elis, & Green, 2007; Carnevale & Pruitt, 1992; Duffy, 1991; Hedeen, 2004; McGillis, 1997; Wemmers & Cyr, 2005) because they get to tell their version of the story soon after their victimization. They are also allowed to vent their emotions (something usually prohibited in court), and they are given the opportunity to address the person they believe caused their distress. Respondents or offenders appreciate the process because they typically do not come out of it with a guilty verdict or an additional criminal record. Likewise, they are afforded the opportunity to provide evidence that the other party may have played a role in the "crime" (as in harassment, where both parties may have actually harassed each other). From the victim's perspective, the mediation process helps by allowing them to share with others their tale of victimization, get more information, and receive a sincere apology from the perpetrator (Choi, Green & Kapp, 2010). This is viewed as a reempowering process and a way to achieve restorative justice.

The end result in about 85% to 90% of the cases is an agreement or contract between the parties (Duffy, 1991; Hedeen, 2004; McGillis, 1997). What is equally important is that 80% to 90% of victims and defendants emerge from the process satisfied (Duffy, 1991; Hedeen, 2004; McGillis, 1997). The agreements can contain anything from restitution and apologies to guidelines as to how the parties will interact in the future. Just about anything that both parties agree to that is legal can be part of the mediated settlement. Mediation has been successfully used in landlord–tenant and consumer–merchant disputes; neighborhood conflicts; crimes such as assault, harassment, and larceny; family dysfunction; racial conflict; environmental disputes; school conflict; and a host of other areas where individuals disagree or infringe on each other's rights.

In fact, the opening vignette of Mike Farnsworth is a true story; Mike and his parents were referred to a mediation center by the probation department. Although the hearing was long, Mike and his parents eventually agreed on rules (e.g., curfews) and a reward system (which had been missing before the mediation). A punishment system had long been in place. The reward system would be used when Mike's grades were good or when his behavior was positive. During the hearing, Mike and his father finally listened to one another (rather than bellowed) and began to better understand each other's perspective. Mike's mother, Edna, learned some valuable skills from the mediator, such as compromise and reciprocity of concessions, for use in refereeing future disagreements between Mike and his father, should they arise. The Farnsworths (whose name we changed to protect their anonymity) have lived much more harmoniously since the mediation.

Neighborhood justice centers have experienced tremendous growth in the past three decades (Duffy, 1991) but are not without their critics (e.g., Greatbatch & Dingwall, 1989; Presser & Hamilton, 2006; Rodriguez, 2005; Vidmar, 1992). Some critics argue that mediators hold too much control over the process and the parties and fail to challenge attitudes conducive to crime (Presser & Hamilton, 2006). Others point out that Hispanic/Latino and Black juveniles are less likely than Whites to be referred to restorative justice programs (Rodriguez, 2005). Finally, Latimer, Dowden, and Muise (2005) argue that some of the research on restorative justice is poorly designed, and because it is often voluntary—even for the offender—there is an important self-selection bias in the research. The foregoing information, then, needs to be considered in light of these criticisms.

**REINTEGRATION PROGRAMS FOR INCARCERATED INDIVIDUALS.**    You know now that Mike Farnsworth's story had a fairly happy ending. Imagine, though, how Mike would feel if he had been imprisoned because of his repeated assaults on his father and then released after five years. He would have learned much in prison, most of it counterproductive. He may have learned how to fashion weapons out of ordinary household implements, such as mirrors and pens. He may have learned how to intimidate others merely by staring at them in a certain way, and he may have learned how to commit more heinous crimes than the assault on his father. Even though prison might have hardened Mike, he might also have felt intimidated about his reentry into society and insecure about his newly acquired freedom. Where would he find a job? How would he feel about going to see his parole officer? Would his parents allow him to come home? What would the neighbors and his friends think?

Each year, thousands of individuals are released from prisons and jails to communities (Byrne & Taxman, 2004; Mellow & Dickinson, 2006). The increase in number of parolees over the past few years is indicated in Figure 9.3. Although crime rates are declining somewhat, inmate numbers continue to rise because many are serving longer sentences or sentences that are now mandatory rather than discretionary on the part of a judge or jury (Bracey, 2006). For most inmates, returning to the community is problematic. First, their lives and decisions are totally controlled by the correctional staff while they are incarcerated. Thus, day-to-day prison life runs counter to the day-to-day life inmates will face outside of prison (Taxman, 2004). Furthermore, inmates probably lack skills to obtain employment. They may emerge from incarceration with some of the same problems (i.e., substance abuse) that got them there in the first place. Some inmates reappear in the community with health problems they did not have on entry to the prison (i.e., HIV/AIDS). Some of them have learned negative institutional behaviors (e.g., gang behavior), have lost contact with family members and friends, and will be stigmatized by community members and potential employers so that they cannot find housing or employment (Byrne & Taxman, 2004). Heap on top of these issues the stigma of having lost personal rights such as voting and parental rights, compounded by not being able to run for elective office and being unable to sit on juries, and the parolee can experience a profound sense of disconnection from the same community in which the crime was committed (Bazemore & Stinchcomb, 2004). Also, predictably, the longer the individual remains incarcerated, the more likely there will be changes in the family, peers, and neighborhood dynamics (Byrne &

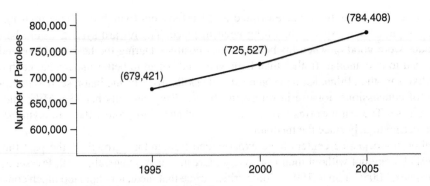

**FIGURE 9.3** Number of Individuals on Parole in the Community

*Source:* Bureau of Justice Statistics (Glaze & Palia, 2004). One in every 32 adults is now on probation, on parole, or incarcerated. Retrieved from http://bjs.gov/index.cfm?ty=pbdetail&iid=1109.

Taxman, 2004). It should not be unexpected, then, that recidivism occurs. Criminologists project that more than two-thirds of all parolees will eventually be rearrested, and 40% of them will likely return to jail (Byrne & Taxman, 2004).

As already mentioned, the typical program for those being released from incarceration is parole. Some previously incarcerated persons are also court-ordered into treatment programs, but data reveal that they are unlikely to attend. Correctional personnel have known for decades that the high rate of recidivism is largely related to ineffective transition programs (e.g., parole) for inmates released back to the community (Bonhomme et al., 2006). Better pre- and postrelease programs are necessary. Research clearly shows that getting "started right" immediately on return to the community is extremely important (Bullis, Yovanoff, & Havel, 2001) if recidivism is to be reduced and the former inmate is to become a successful community member (Baltodano, Platt, & Roberts, 2005).

As for prerelease programs, we know little about them empirically (Byrne, 2004). Many prisons and jails now offer mental health counseling and substance abuse rehabilitation, as well as educational programs, to inmates. It is well known that the prison population is less well educated than the general population. There are, however, limited data on how well schooling programs work or how much education actually takes place. What we do know is that such programs are quite variable (Byrne & Taxman, 2004), depending on the state, the community, and available funding. Some states do not offer educational programs. The existing studies, however, do indicate that **prison-based education programs** have positive effects on reducing recidivism (Vacca, 2004). Unfortunately, the number of prison staff dedicated to providing inmate education has declined over the years (Bracey, 2006).

Another well-known factor that enhances positive reintegration to the community is **family and social support.** Formerly incarcerated individuals who return home or live with relatives have a lower probability of rearrest and reincarceration than those who do not (Bahr, Armstrong, Gibbs, Harris, & Fisher, 2005; Baltodano et al., 2005). Of course, having stable housing and being employed also reduce the likelihood of running into trouble with the law. Practical prerelease programs designed to help former inmates secure housing and jobs *before they are released* would be advantageous because most inmates enter the community with no money, a poor work history (Bahr, et al., 2005; Shivy, Wu, Moon, Mann, & Eacho, 2007), and no housing options because they are expected to make all such arrangements while they are still in prison (Taxman, 2004). An interesting attempt to bring the one's community and culture into the jail release process is described in Case in Point 9.3.

# Huikahi: The Restorative Circle

One promising program designed to address all these needs and to reduce recidivism is the *Huikahi* (*hui* means "group"; *kahi* means "individual") **restorative circle.** These circles empower the inmate to choose how he or she will live on the outside—which may create higher compliance with such programs (Taxman, 2004). Circle programs were originally developed in Hawaii for foster children aging out of the foster care system. In prison, the restorative circle is a group planning process for inmates, their families, significant others, and prison staff. In restorative circles, the professional facilitators do not tell inmates and their families how they should deal with problems but instead ask appropriate questions so that the involved parties can find solutions themselves. In many instances, family members or other emotionally supportive individuals reach out with suggestions for the inmate in developing the plan (Walker, Sakai, & Brady, 2006).

Circles can occur when the individual is first incarcerated and detail who will visit the inmate, how often, and so forth. On the other hand, a community reentry circle might include topics such as where the inmate will live,

how much interaction he or she will have with the family, where a job or job skills training will be sought, and what the inmate will do to remain crime-free and drug-free once in the community. In both cases (on admission or on release), circle plans can also describe how the inmate will restore justice (e.g., write a letter to the victim, return stolen items). Identifying strengths of the inmate is also a key feature of this solution-focused approach. For example, if the inmate is identified as being highly intelligent, family members might encourage him or her to include an education component in the plan while in prison or after release. The program eventually results in a written plan (Walker et al., 2006). A recircle meeting is also planned for a later time where the written plan is reviewed to tweak its various components. Restorative circle programs certainly feature many of community psychology's tenets (such as empowerment and social support), but the programs are so new that we await sufficient literature on their efficacy (Walker et al., 2006). In a two-year follow-up to this prison reentry program, recidivism rates were at 30% (versus typical rates of 50-80%). Admittedly, the number of prisoners in this study was small,

and no final conclusions could be drawn with regard to recidivism. Other data from the program did point to its desirability to the population of prisoners trying to reenter their communities. Of the participants (prisoners, families, prison staff) in this program, all evaluated it as a positive experience. The demand for the program outstripped the capabilities of the prison. Only 37% of those who requested it were able to be seen. This program is seen as a "public health" approach to criminal behavior—that is, one that emphasizes learning and prevention (tertiary and targeted) (Schwartz & Boodell, 2009).

In conclusion, criminal justice is a complex system made up of many different players with a variety of motives and functions. Effectiveness of programs dealing with criminality can be influenced by many different individual, relational, or community factors (O'Donnell & Williams, 2013). Community psychologists are collaborating with individuals involved in the justice system, and together they are making headway on preventing crime and assisting those involved in the crime once it occurs. Better yet, community psychologists and others hope to keep the community and its members "whole" before, during, and after the crime.

## Summary

The traditional justice system includes enforcement agencies such as the police, the courts, the prisons, and related programs. Such programs allow only a small role, if any, for the victim and tend to seek retribution or punishment for the offender.

Psychologists who have tried to parcel out the causes of crime know that guns, gun control,

and related factors are not the only predictors of crime. Certain ecological settings and certain groups of individuals are likely to be involved in crime. Young African American men are most likely to be victimized by crime and most likely to be convicted of and incarcerated for crime. Societal prejudice and the history of African

Americans in the United States may in part be what underlies some of the statistics. Poverty and community disorder are other good predictors of crime rates.

Prisons are bleak, overcrowded institutions often fraught with problems such as violence, AIDS, and illegal substances. Prisons do not tend to rehabilitate or treat offenders. Thus, recidivism rates remain high.

Victims and those who fear crime have been neglected populations in the traditional criminal justice system. An interesting phenomenon, the crime-victimization paradox, which has tempered support in the literature, suggests that those who fear crime the most are often least likely to be victimized. An example would be an elderly woman who fears crime but is very unlikely to be a victim.

Police are asked to play a variety of roles in a community. Some are roles for which they are ill prepared, such as intervention in domestic disputes and mental health issues. Police officers often report that they feel alienated from the communities they serve and feel that their superiors offer little understanding for street life.

Community psychologists believe that criminal behavior can be predicted. Some studies have successfully predicted delinquent behavior in at-risk youths. Environments can also be altered to reduce the probability of crime. An example is removing violent cues from the media, which tend to bias reports of crime.

Community programs, such as neighborhood crime watches, are successfully reducing the fear of crime. Other innovative programs involve citizens in collaborative efforts with officers at enforcement agencies.

In terms of secondary prevention, community-based programs show much promise for intervening in the cycle of delinquency and recidivism. There also exist programs for early assistance to actual crime victims. Two such programs include crisis intervention and neighborhood justice centers or community mediation centers.

Victims, for example, may need follow-up services long after the crime. One new and interesting program is the victim-offender mediation program in which the victim and offender meet face to face and discuss their impact on one another as well as plans for restitution to the victim.

Programs comparing incarceration to alternative community services are difficult to assess with research because of confounding issues, but many community programs offer hope that even chronic offenders can be assisted. An especially important type of program is one, such as a restorative circle program, that is designed to ease adjustment of an incarcerated person returning into the community.

# 10

# The Healthcare System

The speaker was a famous Black American figure. He was being honored by the association for his work and accomplishments. The band played, and the audience came to its feet. The speaker spoke in stentorian tones about the honor and his life. But before he did so, he dedicated the time there and his comments to his recently departed uncle. Dearly remembered, the uncle had been a friend and a grounding force in the famous person's life.

As the story unfolded, it became apparent why this uncle was the point of dedication. It turned out that he had had health problems for a while. However, like many, he put off going in to see a doctor. It was too expensive. It seemed a needless cost when times were difficult economically, or at least it did not seem worth the extra expense. By the time the uncle made it to the doctor's office, the cancer had progressed to the point of irreversibility. Then it was just a matter of time. The family came together. People said their goodbyes. The uncle died. The speaker had nearly canceled his engagement with the award ceremony. He was grieving. Yet he decided to come and to speak about his uncle. He hoped to point out the example this presented for us all. Was the delay in seeking healthcare necessary? Was it a function of poor habits? Was it a pattern of behavior that was culturally established long ago? Were the concerns about money justified? What was the cost in the end? These are the questions he put to the audience that evening. These were the challenges the speaker wanted to present to those who honored him. Where are the answers? Would they come from those to whom he spoke that night? What could we, would we contribute to solving this problem, made personal by his uncle, but otherwise found in data collected every year in the United States?

A second story completes our picture of a healthcare system looking for answers. In this story, we find a successful clinical psychologist, working in a large metropolitan area. When she went for a checkup for symptoms she could not explain, her physician discovered over the course of several days and many tests that she had a rare form of cancer that was quite aggressive. To receive the cutting-edge treatment that could provide her with the best chance of survival, she needed to go to where the treatment was being tested. Unfortunately, the medical center where this treatment occurred was in another state, several hundred miles away. At first she was able to travel between her home and the other site. However, besides the travel expenses, her medical expenses mounted quickly. Soon, she discovered that the regimen of therapies cost in the hundreds of thousands of dollars. While her insurance decided if she qualified, and if her treatment qualified, she had to bear the cost herself. Eventually, the determination was that the insurance did not believe they were responsible for her treatments. Meanwhile, the psychologist had to close down her practice because she was not able to adequately care for her patients. Soon she had run through her savings and was looking at the choices of death or going further into debt. She also had to decide whether to stay in her home city with her circle of friends or move to a strange city where she knew no one.

So what, then, of our healthcare system? What could community psychology contribute to making it better? That is what we explore in this chapter.

## THE AMERICAN HEALTHCARE SYSTEM

### National Health Indicators

The World Health Organization reports on global health indicators. Among them are life expectancy and neonatal mortality rates. The 2011 World Health Statistics state that the average life expectancy for those who live in the United States is 79 years, slightly lower than many European countries, Japan, and Canada. However, these numbers still look much better when compared to global life expectancies (World Health Organization, 2011). Neonatal mortality rates per 1,000 follow a similar pattern (Table 10.1).

In the 2011 annual report on health within the United States, life expectancy was at an all-time high. Life expectancy in 2009 was four years greater for males and two years greater for females than in 1990. Given the 2009 figures, the United States ranks 32nd in the world for life expectancy (Japan is ranked first, and Singapore is second). Infant mortality is also low at 7 infants per 1,000 or 4 neonates per 1,000, making us 30th in world rankings (Singapore and Sweden are first and second). However, these health status indicators were not uniformly found throughout the U.S. population, with ethnic minority groups faring less well. In particular, African Americans had more than double the norm for both infant and neonatal deaths. Blacks or African Americans also had lower life expectancies than their white counterparts by approximately 5 years (White males—75 years, Black males—70 years; White females—80 years, Black females—76 years) (National Center for Health Statistics, 2011). Also cited in the report were concerns over the problems of rural health. Despite increasing sophistication in medications and interventions that could help treat a variety of physical illnesses, access to healthcare is still more easily attained in urban centers. For example, we see in Figure 10.1 that in the specialty area of obstetrics and gynecology, there were large (mostly rural) sectors of the nation without any identified physicians with this specialty. These shortages mean that patients have to travel far to obtain services, and these services, in turn, were placed under extraordinary demands to meet the health needs of the wider geographic area, which may mean greater delays between seeking and receiving services.

**TABLE 10.1** Comparative World Health Status Statistics: Mortality Measures, 2010

| | Life Expectancy (Age in Years) | | Neonatal Mortality (Number Who Die per 1,000, Birth to 28 Days of Age) |
|---|---|---|---|
| | **Male** | **Female** | **Both Sexes** |
| Canada | 79 | 83 | 5 |
| Cuba | 76 | 80 | 5 |
| France | 78 | 85 | 3 |
| Germany | 78 | 83 | 3 |
| Ireland | 77 | 82 | 3 |
| Japan | 80 | 86 | 2 |
| Mexico | 73 | 78 | 14 |
| Spain | 78 | 85 | 4 |
| Switzerland | 80 | 84 | 4 |
| United Kingdom | 78 | 82 | 5 |
| United States | 76 | 81 | 7 |
| Global | 66 | 71 | 24 |

*Source:* World Health Organization. (2011). *Global health indicators.* Geneva, Switzerland: Author.

In addition to concerns about unequal access to healthcare, there is still an overall concern about unhealthy lifestyles, which include diet, exercise, risky behaviors, and alcohol- and drug-related habits. The combination of these lifestyle risk factors contributed to a formidable portion of health-related concerns. For example, it was estimated that in 2006, approximately 39% of the population over 18 years of age were inactive during their leisure time (p. 286). Among those 18 years and older who drank, more than a third reported consuming more than five alcoholic drinks in one day during the past year (p. 9).

Given these health statistics, one can conclude that the United States does well in healthcare, although it is not the best, and there are national behavior patterns that place us at risk. It is also true that the benefits of living in the United States are not evenly distributed, with health advantages going to the upper- and middle-class White ethnic majority, those in urban centers, and those who have insurance.

## Observations on the System

In the not too distant past, access to healthcare more or less depended on one's ability to pay for it. The establishment of federally funded programs, such as Medicaid and Medicare, in the 1960s, as well as the institutionalization of employment-based healthcare, has been a significant step forward for a healthy nation. However, health maintenance organizations (HMOs) have the potential to place restrictions on doctor–patient discourse.

Given the aforementioned issues of inequity in healthcare, however, there continues to be a need for a meaningful discourse on healthcare reform. This conversation would need to include four elements: financing healthcare, implementing appropriate public policy, working with healthcare providers, and partnering with patients. Typically, most conversations about healthcare reform focus on one

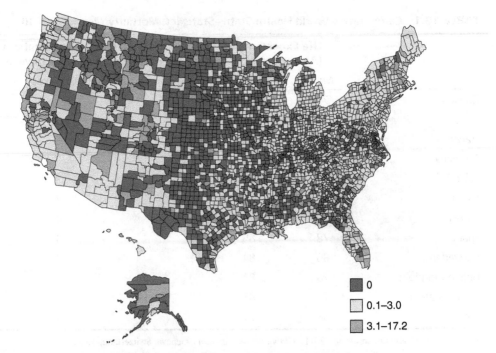

**FIGURE 10.1**    OB/GYNS per 10,000 Female Population Age 15+, by County (2004)

*Sources:* Centers for Disease Control and Prevention; National Center for Health Statistics (2007b), Fig. 23. Data from the Area Resource File.

or two elements. Often, the first, the economics of the situation, dictates ability to access healthcare. Until this barrier is removed, there will always be less than optimal health among some segments of the population.

Although the United States spends more money than any other country in the world to pay for its citizens' healthcare, the country has found itself in a state of flux over the past few decades, struggling to contend with the expenses of healthcare and the manner in which patients can pay for it. For example, in 2009, 32% of costs were paid by private insurance, 35% by the federal government, and 12% as "out of pocket" expenditures. However, there have continued to be problems for people who are not covered by private insurance or federal programs such as Medicare and Medicaid. Uninsured individuals who do not qualify for Medicaid still get sick and, as explained in this chapter, the cost of their care when they go to an emergency room is indirectly passed along to taxpayers and those who are insured. Thus, in an effort to reform healthcare in at least several significant ways, in 2011, the Obama Administration developed and the Congress passed the Affordable Care Act. As is the case with much legislation, many compromises were made in order to pass the law, and political infighting delayed that passage.

Many positive changes are contained in the act, to be phased in from 2011 to 2014. Among the highlights of the act are that insurance companies can no longer deny coverage to individuals with pre-existing conditions and that adult children up to the age of 26 can continue to be covered by their parents' health insurance policies. Perhaps the most controversial aspect of the act is its mandate that all citizens must have health insurance coverage or be willing to pay a fee as a penalty for being out of compliance. Given that the major focal point of the act is to increase the percentage of citizens who are covered by healthcare insurance, the government has already begun collecting data on changes in insured citizens. The National Center for Health Statistics has tracked changes to the rates of uninsured citizens that are encouraging, despite the fact that the mandate has yet to be enforced (this will not occur until 2014). For example:

- The percentage of people with employment-based private health insurance increased from 15.6% in 2007 to 26.9% in the first six months of 2011.
- The percentage of people covered by directly purchased private health insurance increased from 39.2% in 2007 to 53.2% in the first six months of 2011.
- The percentage of adults aged 19–25 who were uninsured decreased from 33.9% (10 million) in 2010 to 28.8% (8.7 million) in the first six months of 2011.
- The percentage of adults aged 19–25 covered by a private plan in the first six months of 2011 increased to 55.0% from 51.0% in 2010.

**COST AND ACCESS.**   While the Affordable Care Act attempts to rectify inequities in cost and access to healthcare, there is still a demand to minimize the overall costs associated with healthcare, especially the healthcare that is subsidized by taxpayers or paid out of pocket by those lacking coverage. Ross, Bradley and Busch (2006) noted that lack of health insurance places none-too-subtle pressure on the potential patient to be frugal with healthcare usage. The threshold for seeking help may be higher because of the drain on resources that occurs when a person seeks medical help. In other words, when individuals lack coverage, they may practice far less preventative care, waiting to see a doctor only if they are already symptomatic. Because people without insurance also typically do not have a regular physician, many patients seek treatment in emergency rooms, which are typically the most costly places to receive care. What results, then, is a more passive form of healthcare from the patient's perspective. Patients who lack the financial and institutional resources to be proactive about their health may also begin to feel a sense of disempowerment about being in control of their health in general. This sense of disempowerment, which is felt more commonly in low-income communities, may also contribute to the inequities we see in healthcare across the U.S. population.

Inequities in healthcare access and health outcomes in general are known as health disparities. Disparities are evident when there is a statistical overrepresentation of people in a category when compared to the population in general. For example, there are health disparities between ethnic minority groups in comparison to the U.S. norms (National Center for Health Statistics, 2011). Ethnic-minority, low–socioeconomic-status, immigrant, and older women suffer a disproportionate burden of breast and cervical cancer (Institute of Medicine, 1999). Although the number of new cervical cancer cases has declined overall, African American women have an incidence rate that remains 39% higher than that of non-Latina White women (Buki, Montoya, & Linares, 2012) Many federal entities have made the elimination of these disparities a major priority. For example, in 2000, Congress founded the National Center on Minority Health and Health Disparities with the specific mission of helping to reduce, and ultimately eliminate, health disparities. Through this initiative, each institute in the National Institutes of Health designed a plan for eliminating health disparities, each of which became part of a larger national strategic plan to reduce and ultimately eliminate health disparities (Institute of Medicine, 2006).

There are passionate debates about why health disparities exist. Some argue that some ethnic minority groups may be more susceptible to certain health problems (e.g., Native Americans and alcoholism). Others have argued that the stress of being an ethnic minority member results in physiological consequences that put communities of color at greater risk for health problems (Steffen, McNeilly, Anderson, & Sherwood, 2003). Still others postulate that it is not necessarily susceptibility as much as it is less effective healthcare behaviors due to a lack of access to the system or a lack of understanding how the system works. Imagine for example, a family of immigrants living in a rural part of the country. Not only may this family live far away from a doctor's office, but they may also lack the language skills (and be unable to converse with bilingual staff) to use the system effectively. It is possible that all the afore-mentioned factors play a role in explaining why health disparities exist.

Although disparities may be in part due to language barriers and to geographic distance from facilities, other sociocultural factors are also likely to be at work. For example, one's cultural norms around seeing doctors and engaging in routine exams may be a factor. Overall, African American women are twice as likely to die from cervical cancer as non-Latina White women (Buki et al., 2012). This may be explained in part by circumstance that African American women visit a gynecologist less often. With cancer such as cervical, breast, and colorectal types, the importance of regular exams among high-risk populations seems clear. Cancer is best diagnosed early. Early discovery and treat-ment leads to higher rates of treatment success. Therefore, it is important to do regular checkups once individuals pass the age of 50 (U.S. Preventive Services Task Force, 2002). Despite these recommen-dations, checkups for colorectal cancer follow the same pattern of low rates among the ethnic minor-ity elderly (National Center for Health Statistics, 2011). Shih, Zhao, and Elting (2006) studied various possible causes for these low rates. They find that the access issues of language, lack of health infor-mation on this topic, and culturally based perceptions of the screening procedures stand as barriers to these examinations.

In both of our opening stories, we find concerns about access and cost. The perception of the cost of regular medical checkups held back the individual in the first vignette from going until his ailment progressed to an untreatable stage. A lack of knowledge relating to health issues played an important role in both cases. They did not know the symptoms. The psychologist discovers that medical treatment can be expensive, that it is not available near her home where she needs it, and that her insurance cover-age is inadequate. She is in private practice, and therefore is a small business, which brings high insur-ance costs and lower benefits. Once her insurance runs out or is denied, she is left with no coverage. This is inevitably a bad set of scenarios.

**ADHERENCE AND COMPLIANCE.**    Beyond cost and access, there is the issue of the patient/consumer doing as instructed. This is called *adherence* or *compliance*. Haynes, McDonald, and Garg (2002) note that typical adherence runs about 50% for medication regimens. Lower rates of adherence are reported for prescriptions of changes in lifestyle—for example, changes in diet and exercise. So if adherence is so low, can anything be done to make patients more compliant? Following a review of research on adher-ence, McDonald, Garg, and Haynes (2002) report that short-term compliance (less than 2 weeks) can be increased with patient instruction, but long-term compliance takes a combination of instruction, social support, emphasis of the importance of the prescription, provision for positive feedback on compliance, and regular reminders of the regimen. This represents a cultural change in the patient's context or his or her social environment.

Using newer technologies such as the Internet, psychology might inform the manner in which compliance or adherence is measured and its effects on program success. An example of this is pre-sented by Manwaring, Bryson, and Goldschmidt (2008). Using adherence measures, the number of weeks in an Internet-based treatment program, the number of pages read over the Internet, the number of times engaged in online discussions, and the use of a computer-based booster program, Manwaring and colleagues (2008) found these measures to be a good gauge of patient compliance in an eating disorders program.

Other researchers in this area have studied whether particular subgroups of patients are more or less likely to be compliant with medical orders. For example, one group of researchers wanted to know who complies with instructions for physical exercise and who is not compliant. Butcher, Sallis, and

Mayer (2008) identified older adolescent girls and lower income youth as segments of the population who were less likely to follow up on exercise regimens. Using a 100-city sample, they found that these two groups did not adhere to physical activity guidelines as presented. Though Butcher and colleagues did not provide explanations for this finding, one could speculate that living in an inner city may present unique challenges to being physically active. In a neighborhood where there are safety concerns and a lack of recreational facilities, it may be much more challenging to find ways to increase one's physical exercise.

DiMatteo (2004) conducted a meta-analysis of studies examining medical adherence and the role of social support. The study aimed to examine what types of support might cause a patient to be more compliant. The results suggested functional social support (i.e., people giving help directly to the individual) to be more beneficial than structural social support (e.g., marital status, living alone or with others). Of the ways in which functional support was provided, practical social support (instrumental—providing information, lending a hand) was the best predictor of medical adherence, suggesting that a team approach to medical care is superior to an individual one. These patterns were helpful in devising interventions to increase following of medical instructions.

The former studies emphasized patient characteristics that were relevant to understanding compliance. However, it might not be surprising to know that some physician characteristics also influence patient compliance. In an earlier study of how physician characteristics related to patient adherence, DiMatteo and associates (1993) found that the physician's ratings of overall job satisfaction, the number of patients seen by the physician in a week, and his or her willingness to answer questions were all significantly predictive of patient compliance. Thus, one could conclude that a physician who liked what he or she was doing, was thoroughly engaged in the work, and communicated well with patients was more effective at providing the type of environment that maximized patient compliance. Such physicians also tend to have stronger relationships with their patients, which may make it more likely they want to be seen as "good patients."

From a number of the studies discussed, it seems obvious that supportive relationships and a broader network of support for healthy behaviors are both important. It was more than the correct technique or adequate technology; it was the ability of the medical system to reach out to the consumers/clients, connect with them, and then make a meaningful impact on the larger social context within which the consumers/clients reside. Given these findings, it is easier to see how a community psychologist might find important ways to contribute to improving the healthcare system.

## COMMUNITY PSYCHOLOGY AND THE HEALTHCARE SYSTEM

Revenson and Schiaffino (2000) argued that the cost versus benefit of our healthcare system indicated that things were not working. They proposed that the focus on preventive health services needed to be further developed and the emphasis on hospitals and emergency rooms as primary sites for receiving medical care needed to be reexamined. Because many of the physical illnesses that presently concern modern American medicine were related to lifestyle choices and habits, community psychology could help in changing these from unhealthy to healthy practices. They suggested that community intervention programs should incorporate sociocultural contexts, build off of community strengths, emphasize the adaptation of healthy behavior styles, seek change at the community level, and target communities, rather than individuals, for intervention. Among the intervention strategies they listed were mass media campaigns, community organizing, use of existing community institutions such as schools and churches, and social policy changes. We next examine how community psychology and community psychologists have contributed to these concepts.

## Prevention over Remediation

The Stanford Heart Disease Prevention Project served as an excellent example of a program aimed at public education of a targeted population on the topic of factors contributing to heart disease. The project reported on use of media (newspapers, radio, TV, printed matter) aimed at identified California coastal communities who were demographically at risk for heart disease in comparison to the population in general. The targeted communities showed significant improvement in heart disease–related factors in comparison to the one control community without the educational program (Maccoby & Altman, 1988). A second study on five cities produced similar findings in the two program-targeted urban sites compared to three reference-control cities (Farquhar et al., 1985; Flora, Jatilus, & Jackson, 1993). A follow-up study three years later showed these effects to have lasted (Winkleby, Taylor, Jatilus, & Fortmann, 1996). The intervention phase lasted for six years. Working with a multidisciplinary team, the Stanford Project showed the effectiveness of a primary preventive, universal population, targeted multimedia program that included radio and TV spots, flyers, and classes. The Stanford Project was similar to two other community-based disease prevention programs of that era: the Minnesota Heart Health Program (Luepker et al., 1994) and the Pawtucket Heart Health Program (Carleton, Lasater, Assaf, Feldman, & McKinlay, 1995). All of these programs attempted to change how individuals behaved within their community settings. They were multidisciplinary, and they involved the targeted communities in organizing and implementing programs.

Other population-focused prevention programs have been developed and run successfully. They used media along with multiple interventions within the community. These programs worked to ensure community involvement in project development. This involvement has helped establish and maintain new norms for behavior and new values to sustain healthy choices (DuRant, Wolfson, LaFrance, Balkrishnan, & Altman, 2006; Jason, 1998).

## Shifting Focus from Individuals to Groups, Neighborhoods, and Systems

Whereas large community interventions are clearly the focus of public health initiatives, the focus on groups, neighborhoods, and community systems has also been of interest to community psychology. Further discussion of the public health perspective occurs in the next chapter. However, suffice it to say that, as stated in previous chapters, the traditional health focus, be it physical or mental health, is on treatment of the individual. Broadening the focus of interventions from the individual to the community or neighborhood is a strength of the community psychology tradition. The public health model of studying the patterns of illness (i.e., epidemiology) and health and the factors that contribute to those patterns also contribute to a community research methodology. The previous section on prevention demonstrates the effectiveness of such interventions.

Stephens (2007) discussed the shift to health promotion efforts using community concepts. We earlier provided descriptions of the debates over how to define community—that is, whether it should be a matter of place or of identity (Campbell & Murray, 2004). Beyond these basic considerations, what community psychology has added to this model has been to define what variables contribute to the psychological awareness of neighborhood and community and how this has been used to advance efforts to influence entire groups. What were the natural boundaries to communities, who were the agents of change within those groups, how was the message effectively communicated, and how was the community awareness and motivation aroused (Altman & Wandersman, 1987; Imm, Kehres, Wandersman, & Chinman, 2006; Manzo & Perkins, 2006; Nicotera, 2007; Perkins, Florin, Rich, Wandersman, & Chavis, 1990; Shinn & Toohey, 2003)? An extensive body of literature has addressed these issues. The work of Wandersman and his colleagues has been previously cited in earlier chapters. Indicators of social cohesion versus social disorganization, defined by existence of local friendship networks, and participation in community organizations, as well as other neighborhood characteristics, have been shown to be associated with physical health indicators (Caughy, O'Campus, & Brodsky, 1999; Shinn & Toohey, 2003). **Goodness of fit** between individual and social environment—as defined by (1) similarities between the individual and the social environment, (2) the individual's needs and the environment's resources, and (3) the agreement of environmental features and individual preferences—has been linked to well-being (Shinn & Rapkin, 2000). Following a review of the community context variables studied in psychology, Shinn and Toohey (2003) caution against "context minimalization error," or a tendency to focus on the individual and to ignore the community/context that brings about behaviors and health outcomes. Community psychology has brought a focus on the larger picture. It has also helped conceptualize, develop, and evaluate systems addressing health issues. This has many implications for improving healthcare.

Snowden (2005) wrote of "population thinking," or consideration of given groups of people, how well they do in their environment, and the variables affecting that status. The focus was on the social mechanisms and how they work. What brought about and what maintained the population's health or illnesses? In Snowden's discussion, he cited the work done on poor communities as a good example of what these analyses yielded. Poverty placed communities at risk, but there have been poor communities where residents do well—that is, they were resilient, a concept discussed in Chapter 3. Studies of these resilient communities found them to have people who feel *responsible* for what happens and who *actively help* their communities maintain a positive orientation. Poverty was not what brings about the higher risks; it was that poverty made this positive orientation harder to maintain.

Bolland, Lian, and Formichella (2005) found measures of social disruption and social connectedness to predict levels of hopelessness in poor inner-city youth. It was not the poverty per se but the exposure to violence, worry, and trauma (**social disruption**) and the sense of community, warmth toward mother, and religiosity (**social connectedness**) that influenced the hopelessness, with disruption increasing and connectedness decreasing despair. Bolland (2003) had earlier found hopelessness to be related to risky behaviors. Therefore, any work on hopelessness was really work on risky behaviors. The community psychology orientation yielded social variables that have been demonstrated to have a link to a community's health. The lesson to be learned? Treat the social disruptions, intervene in hopelessness, and decrease risky behaviors.

## Building Systems

Community psychologists have long had interests in the creation of more functional systems and settings (Sarason, 1972/1999). Emshoff and associates (2007) described a program of collaboration building among community agencies that aimed to change systems of healthcare in Georgia. Lasker, Weiss, and Miller (2001) have defined *collaboration* as "a process that enables independent individuals and organizations to combine their human and material resources so they can accomplish objectives they are unable to bring about alone" (p. 183). Roussos and Fawcett's (2000) review of collaborations led them to the conclusion that the collaboration in itself brought about changes to the system. Specifically, collaboration led to an increase in efficiencies in the system (i.e., because duplication of services is reduced), and the overall functioning of the health system for an area was improved. Emshoff and colleagues (2007) found that changes in service delivery did occur in the first few years, that the number of meetings was directly related to greater changes, and that the longer term collaborative leadership helped bring about greater systems changes. The overall impression of the collaborative was that the successful ones could do more and could do it better. This would fit with the belief of Lasker and associates (2001) that when collaboration was best realized and created the opportunity for synergy among the elements, the result was more than the sum of its parts. The health community has come to realize that "most objectives . . . cannot be achieved by any single person, organization or sector working alone" (Lasker et al., 2001, p. 179).

This study of forming new systems to provide services and the effects on service provision have been within the purview of community psychology. These collaborative systems may represent the wave of the future for healthcare, with its attendant demands on cost and the need for a variety of expertise and equipment.

## Increasing Accessibility

**TIMELY INTERVENTIONS.**    There are several ways to consider accessibility problems, one of which has been discussed earlier in this chapter: the cost of services. Yet from a secondary prevention point of view, timely interventions, early in the process—for example, at first exposure to a risk factor—are one of the answers to the cost containment issue. As noted earlier, some of the costs of healthcare are related to lifestyle choices. These choices can and have been modified by psychological interventions at the community level.

Among the array of such programs is an early study on the reduction of a risky behavior: not using seatbelts for securing children in cars (Fawcett, Seekins, & Jason, 1987). Through collection of data on actual seatbelt usage and social opinion data on acceptability of requiring use, followed by strategic use of this information with legislatures, community psychologists were able to help in the passage of child seatbelt laws in the states of Kansas and Illinois. This program was successful before use of seatbelts came to national attention. These laws helped pave the way for the seatbelt laws found throughout the United States today. In today's world, most people would consider the use of seatbelts to be a normal behavior. However, this was not always the case. It is exciting to think that other health-promoting behaviors (e.g., healthy diets) might one day be viewed in such a "business as usual" fashion.

More recently, community psychology has provided research and programs in tobacco use, alcohol use, and safe sexual practices. These efforts are described and discussed in the next chapter. These are all health system interventions in that they are directly aimed at changing behavioral contributions to healthcare. Pregnancy prevention is a topic covered earlier in the text, within the chapter on social and health services. As noted there, infants of teen mothers have lower birth weight and higher mortality rates. Case in Point 10.1 takes a second look at pregnancy prevention and community perspectives on what can help.

As was discussed earlier in this chapter, two elements that affect healthcare are a willingness to take part in regular health visits and in increasing one's **health literacy** (knowledge of health-related issues). Having an annual checkup and being willing to visit a physician when experiencing symptoms of any health problem means that a person is willing to risk hearing bad news about his or her health (Rothman & Salovey, 1997). This mindset and the ability to respond to such news constructively are influenced by knowledge of procedures, cost, and the likelihood of treatment success. In addition, there are expectations and assumptions regarding the resources that one has to call on, if there is need for treatment. For example, it is often assumed that people trust physicians and will readily reach out to them when symptoms arise. Yet this is often not the case. Reluctance to go to the doctor delayed the diagnosis in this chapter's first story. Delaying the inevitable only places the potential patient at higher risk. Unfortunately, this behavior is typical of many ethnic minority community members, which may contribute to health disparities such as breast cancer deaths (Buki et al., 2012). Unfortunately, in the case presented in the story, waiting was fatal. So how can these disparities be addressed?

**DEALING WITH DIVERSE COMMUNITIES.**    Snowden (2006) studied a variety of clinic program variables believed to affect minority client use of mental health services in California. Looking at Medi-Cal (California's Medicaid program) patients, Snowden found that **outreach** (where clinic staff would go out into the community to meet people and, when needs were discovered, bring patients in to the clinic) helped increase Latino and Native American use of mental health services. For Asian Americans, having clinic staff who

## CASE IN POINT 10.1

# Teen Pregnancy Prevention

The U.S. teen pregnancy rate is the second highest among industrialized nations (Darrouch, Frost, & Singh, 2001; Kirby, 2007). In a study of five developed Western countries, Darrouch and associates (2001) found sexual activity in females before age 20 to be nearly equivalent (see Table 10.2), yet the pregnancy rates for the United States were notably higher (see Table 10.3). Among the reasons cited for this difference was that the U.S. women were less likely to take measures to prevent pregnancy.

Kirby's (2007) review of pregnancy prevention programs examined which ones had been successful. He considered only programs that were examined using experimental or quasi-experimental designs (see Chapter 2) and had an adequate sample size for meaningful statistical analyses. He found that comprehensive prevention programs that taught contraceptive procedures as well as encouraging

**TABLE 10.2   Percentage of Women Aged 20–24 Who Had First Intercourse before Age 20**

- Sweden: 86%
- France: 83%
- Canada: 75%
- Great Britain: 85%
- United States: 81%

**TABLE 10.3   Teenage Birth Rate per 1,000 Births**

- Sweden: 7
- France: 9
- Canada: 20
- Great Britain: 31
- United States: 49

abstinence could be effective. However, abstinence-only programs did not demonstrate positive effects (which lends support to the increased level of federal funding now available to more comprehensive sex education programs). Programs that focused on non-sexual protective factors, such as plans for the future, school performance, connections to family, and religion, were successful. Also, participation in service learning programs, such as volunteering in the community, proved to significantly decrease teen pregnancy rates. From program evaluations of a variety of teen pregnancy programs, a clear picture emerges. More comprehensive programs have demonstrated positive effects, and programs that are less comprehensive (e.g., abstinence only) do not have evidentiary support.

Beyond the evaluation of the specific programs, the importance of context to these programs was demonstrated in the implementation of a comprehensive, school- and community-based teen pregnancy prevention program in Kansas

(Paine-Andrews et al., 2002). This study found that the prevention program success varied as a function of the amount of community change that resulted from the program. Specifically, in areas that produced more system and program changes, the pregnancy rates dropped. In areas where fewer system and program changes occurred, the pregnancy rates did not drop.

Pursuing the goal of providing the appropriate contexts and capacities for implementation of effective teen pregnancy prevention programs, Rolleri, Wilson, Paluzzi, and Sedivy (2008) described their work at the national level with Healthy Teen Network and Education Training and Research Associates. Using a training model, they taught practitioners in the use of a logical process for defining interventions through the Behavior, Determinant, Intervention Logic model. This model called for a four-step process: goal definition, identifying behaviors to achieve the goal, identifying determinants to those behaviors, and identifying interventions to affect the determinants. Follow-up evaluations and future work with the practitioner systems have continued to build their understanding of the program and evaluation/research processes. The authors' work has helped in the implementation of prevention programs at the state level and built programs' capacities to do more science-based work.

were **bilingual** (speaking English and an Asian language) or **bicultural** (being familiar with American and Asian cultures) was associated with better care usage rates. In an unexpected finding of this study, having bilingual and bicultural receptionists led to decreases in Asian Americans receiving services, which may have to do with some element of stigma that Asian Americans may experience in initiating mental health services. For all groups, including Whites, increased numbers of mental health providers led to increased use rates. These findings are highly suggestive of ways for programs to increase health usage.

In an outreach and education program for New York state on breast cancer, Rapkin et al. (2006) used a partnership model between the state Department of Health and community-based organizations (CBOs). This program, called ACCESS, brought discussions of health information needs to specific community sites. From these discussions, interventions were developed for that particular site. Learning from the CBOs about the targeted communities, the program could devise information tailored for the population to be found in each given context. These site discussions resulted in more effective interventions and in building better relationships with the community organizations. At the end of the project, the CBOs requested more information and more opportunities to work with the program. The community program worked to bring about partnerships between the medical education center and the various sites (e.g., churches, youth groups, schools), which extended the reach of the program out into the neighborhoods. The program served as an entry point into these settings. The working relationships that developed seemed likely to be useful for future efforts at extending medical information beyond the traditional office or hospital settings. The program described was ecologically formulated to promote growth. This would be the ideal goal for any program, especially one that dealt with diversity in its many forms.

**RURAL HEALTH.**   Making treatment relevant to the community is important. This particularly applies in rural parts of the country. The ACCESS plan described in the last section was a good example of working to make the interventions fit the settings where they resided. These cancer education programs were in a variety of communities throughout New York, which includes both rural and urban settings. In other programs focused on the growth of rural health services, including the community in the process of determining needs and services has had good results. Such empowerment of the community is very much in the tradition of community psychology.

Two separate programs serving different parts of the country described similar approaches to community inclusion in definition of problems and in decision making. In North Dakota, organizations working in rural settings and in Native American communities held meetings to define the healthcare barriers and to ask how the rural health center could help (Moulton, Miller, & Offutt, 2007). From these conversations, strategic plans were devised and groups formed to address the problems identified. The engagement of the community in participating has resulted in more useful interventions for the targeted groups. A second study in a similar vein used a participation model (Hoshin) for engaging community members in defining goals, strategies, objectives, and action plans for health programs in rural Hawaii. What they found was a great deal of involvement and agreement within the participant groups. Among the common community needs identified were economic factors within the community (poverty, unemployment, insurance, ability to pay), drug use, lack of leadership, lack of health services or access to such services, lack of healthy activities for youth, and poor public education. These concerns are broadly defined and demonstrate an ecological perspective on the problems. All this emerges from community discussions. The concerns of rural health are more than a lack of medical doctors. They suggest that multilevel interventions for multideterminant problems are needed, along with a comprehension of these needs within the rural community contexts. Among the issues raised are those that might be characterized as social support and network resources. We examine some of the work on the importance of social support next; keep in mind that these considerations might be guided by models of stress, coping, and resilience described earlier.

## Social Support and Health

Studies of the health benefits of a good social support system have been a part of the community psychology literature for several decades (Wallston, Alagna, & DeVellis, 1983). In their early review of the existing work on social support and health benefits, Wallston and colleagues found few studies that clearly demonstrated the advantages of social support for overall health. However, there was research indicating such support was helpful in health recovery.

More than a decade later, however, a review of the literature by Uchino, Cacioppo, and Kiecolt-Glaser (1996) found studies suggesting that social support was beneficial to cardiovascular, endocrine, and immune system health. The precise physiological mechanisms that affected these relationships were unclear. However, theories explaining the relationship between social support and specific health outcomes were beginning to emerge. Social interactions have the potential to shape attitudes, beliefs, knowledge, and emotions about health problems, their prevention, and the importance of screening exams (Mobley, Kuo, Clayton, & Evans, 2009). Social networks consist of friends, family, colleagues, and other sources of contact (Katapodi, Falcione, Miaskowski, Dodd, & Waters, 2002) that may lay the foundation for information acquisition about health (e.g., through discussions within the family and peer education; Campos et al., 2008; McCloskey, 2009). Buki and associates (2012) argue that when patients do not have adequate support, their health literacy as well as follow-through with preventative behaviors may suffer.

An additional mechanism through which social support may affect health outcomes is an indirect one. Social support was seen to influence both behavioral and psychological processes, which then influenced physiological reactions related to positive health (Berkman, Glass, Brissette, & Seeman, 2000; Uchino, 2004). Findings are starting to more clearly demonstrate the physiological pathways from social support to the cardiovascular, endocrine, and immune systems (Uchino, 2004, 2006). Social support is a community variable. Interventions to improve social support may become a regular part of treatment prescription. Experimental studies are examining the impact of programs to improve the social connections of patients contending with medical conditions. If such treatments prove successful, new systems for treatment will need to be implemented for dealing with health promotion and health remediation.

## Summary

The healthcare system appears to be a natural place for the application of community psychology principles. Although there are a variety of healthcare systems in the world, the United States serves as our focal point. In this national example, we found a sophisticated and modern set of personnel and facilities, with vast amounts of money expended for care. Although U.S. technological and research capacities are among the world's best, with vast amounts of money in play, the outcomes still leave the United States ranking 26th in the world for longevity.

In analyzing areas of concern that contribute to this ranking, several issues arise. Among the more conspicuous are access and cost. Access can be defined in terms of timely medical information and the means to gain and use that information. Cost, of course, has to do with how much the individual and his or her family has to pay for this access. Clearly defined populations within the United States are at risk because of access and cost problems. These include those in rural settings, particular ethnic minority groups, and those without health insurance. A second identified area of concern regarding healthcare has to do with compliance issues. Of course, compliance may be influenced by cost and access, but there are socially driven ways to increase compliance.

In response to these concerns, community psychology argues for the advantages of prevention rather than reparative treatment; a focus on the efficiencies and benefits of a community, neighborhood, or group focus for intervention; knowledge and technologies for building systems of care; ways to increase accessibility; and knowledge of the healthy effects of social support. Although community psychology historically has had issues with the medical model, it has always been an advocate for the health model and the holistic approach. The challenge and the opportunity is to realize the potential for community psychology applied to health systems (Minden & Jason, 2002; Revenson & Schiaffino, 2000).

# 11

# Community Health and Preventive Medicine

*All human actions have one or more of these seven causes: chance, nature, compulsion, habit, reason, passion, and desire.*

—Aristotle, c. 384–322 BCE

Elizabeth is a freshman in college at a large state school. She considers herself similar to many of her peers—she drinks on the weekends and has occasionally blacked out. Elizabeth likes to have a good time, but she definitely thinks she doesn't have a problem. On homecoming weekend, she spends the day tailgating and pregame partying. In the evening, she attends several parties, where she takes multiple shots of vodka and plays various drinking games. At one of the parties, she runs into Jake from her chemistry class, who proceeds to flirt with her all evening. When Jake suggests that she come back to his place, Elizabeth eagerly joins him; he is cute, and she reminds herself that this is what college is all about. They end up having drunken sex, and in the morning Elizabeth realizes that in their inebriated state they did not use a condom. Her mind races: She is not taking birth control pills—what if she gets pregnant? Jake is a nice guy, but people say he gets around. What if he has a sexually transmitted disease (STD)? Where could she go for help?

Biological and natural sciences have made tremendous progress in recent decades, ranging from the first open heart surgery, to the cloned sheep named Dolly, to the morning-after pill and the so-called miracle drug Viagra (sildenafil). Yet, as discussed in Chapter 10, there exist great health disparities: Americans and people living in the industrialized world are dying from noncommunicable and often preventable diseases, whereas in the developing world people are dying of communicable diseases and easily treatable infections (Centers for Disease Control and Prevention [CDC], 2011a). Although the overall health status of Americans has improved greatly, there still exist great public health challenges. In 2009, there were more than 10,800 fatalities in crashes involving a driver with a BAC of .08 or higher, representing 32% of traffic fatalities for that year (National Highway Traffic Safety Administration, 2011). Infectious diseases (including some STDs) are at an all-time high, coupled with the emergence of drug-resistant bacteria and viruses (Morbidity and Mortality Weekly Report [MMWR], 2011). Globally, 33 million people are living with human immunodeficiency virus (HIV) (United Nations Programme on AIDS/HIV [UNAIDS], 2010). Collectively, these scenarios speak to the importance of community health and preventive medicine as integral components of a healthy lifestyle. With education and prevention campaigns, Elizabeth would have recognized her risky behavior and been able to access available resources.

To that end, this chapter examines six health issues from the perspectives of community psychology and preventive medicine; policy-based prevention targeting society in general or a single community are also discussed. These health issues were chosen for two main reasons. First, they have each received enormous attention in the media. Second, each is highly preventable if certain precautions are taken. Finally, a large number of people are affected or have the potential to be affected by these issues if no prevention efforts are made.

Statistics used to describe each of the health issues are drawn from various agencies in the U.S. Department of Health and Human Services (DHHS) and other federal (e.g., National Highway Traffic Safety Administration), state (e.g., Massachusetts Department of Public Health), national (e.g., American Public Health Association), and local (e.g., Asian and Pacific Islander Coalition on HIV/AIDS), as well as international (e.g., the United Nations Programme on HIV/AIDS [UNAIDS]), entities. Each agency or source has its own approach and method for estimating the extent of a health issue. For example, the Substance Abuse and Mental Health Services Administration (SAMHSA), an agency within the DHHS whose mission is providing substance-abuse treatment and services, conducts the National Household Survey on Drug Abuse targeting noninstitutionalized individuals age 12 and older nationwide. Another DHHS agency, the Centers for Disease Control and Prevention (CDC), whose mission is public health epidemiology and surveillance, conducts the **Youth Risk Behavior Surveillance System (YRBSS)**—a school-based survey—and also yields estimates of alcohol use. Given this variability and the lag time in reporting the latest findings, you are encouraged to check these various resources for their methodologies and updated information (see Table 11.1 for some examples).

**TABLE 11.1   Some Resources for Health-Related Statistics and Information**

| Agency | Source | Web Address |
|---|---|---|
| American Psychological Association | *APA Monitor* (June 2001, special issue on substance abuse) | www.apa.org |
| American Public Health Association | *The Nation's Health* | www.apha.org |
| Asian and Pacific Islander Coalition on HIV/AIDS | | www.apicha.org |
| Asian and Pacific Islander Wellness Center | | www.apiwellness.org |
| Centers for Disease Control and Prevention (including National Center for Health Statistics, Office on Smoking and Health) | *Morbidity and Mortality Weekly Report* Behavior Risk Factor Surveillance (adults only) Youth Risk Behavior Surveillance System | www.cdc.gov |
| Food and Drug Administration | | www.fda.gov |
| Legacy Foundation | | www.americanlegacy.org |
| National Institutes of Health (including National Cancer Institute, National Institute on Drug Abuse) | | www.nih.gov |
| Office of National Drug Control Policy | | www.whitehouse.gov/ondcp |
| Substance Abuse and Mental Health Services Administration | National Household Survey on Drug Abuse | www.samhsa.gov |
| United Nations Programme on HIV/AIDS | AIDS epidemic update Declaration of Commitment on HIV/AIDS | www.unaids.org |

# TOBACCO

## Extent of the Problem

According to the World Health Organization (2011), globally, tobacco use is the cause of more than 5 million deaths each year. According to the CDC (2011b):

- For every person who dies from a smoking-related disease, 20 more people suffer with at least one serious illness from smoking (e.g., heart disease, stroke, emphysema).
- Worldwide, current trends show that tobacco use will cause more than 8 million deaths annually by 2030.
- In the United States, tobacco use is responsible for about one in five deaths annually (i.e., about 443,000 deaths per year, and an estimated 49,000 of these smoking-related deaths are the result of secondhand smoke exposure).
- On average, smokers die 13 to 14 years earlier than nonsmokers.

Acetaldehyde (irritant)
Benzopyrene (cancer-causing agent)
Cadmium (used in car batteries)
Formaldehyde (embalming fluid)
Lead (nerve poison)
Nicotine (addictive drug)
*N*-Nitrosamines (cancer-causing agents)
Polonium-210 (radioactive element found in nuclear waste)
Uranium-235 (radioactive element used in nuclear weapons)

**FIGURE 11.1**   Some Ingredients in Smokeless Tobacco

Tobacco use is the leading preventable cause of death. Yet, each year, it causes more deaths than HIV, illegal drug use, alcohol use, motor vehicle injuries, suicides, and murders combined (CDC, 2011b). *Tobacco use* and *smoking* are often used interchangeably; note, however, that tobacco use also includes smokeless tobacco (see Figure 11.1), which is linked to various oral cancers.

The **National Household Survey on Drug Use and Health (NSDUH)** is the primary source of information on the prevalence, patterns, and consequences of drug and alcohol use and abuse in the general U.S. civilian noninstitutionalized population (including shelters, rooming houses, dormitories, and civilians living in military bases) aged 12 and older (see http://oas.samhsa.gov/nsduh/2k7nsduh/2k7results.cfm#Ch4). With regard to tobacco, results from the 2007 NSDUH survey indicated that 70.9 million Americans aged 12 or older were current tobacco product users, representing 28.6% of the population in that age range. In addition, young adults between the ages of 18 and 25 had the highest rate of current tobacco product use, comprising 41.8% of users. In terms of gender, the 2007 survey found that current use of a tobacco product was reported by a higher percentage of males (35.2%) among persons aged 12 or older than females (22.4%). In women aged 15 to 44, combined 2006 and 2007 data indicated that the rate of cigarette use in the past month was lower among pregnant women (16.4%) than among women who were not pregnant (28.5%). However, when isolating the women aged 15 to 17, the rate of cigarette smoking for pregnant women (24.3%) was significantly higher than for nonpregnant women (16%). The NSDUH also analyzes tobacco product use across several other determinants, including education, employment, and geographic area (SAMHSA, 2007).

The YRBSS is a nationwide survey funded by the CDC that monitors priority health-risk behaviors among youth and young adults, including 40 state surveys and 21 local surveys among students in grades 9 through 12 (MMWR, 2011). Findings indicated that, in 2010, 19.5% of students had smoked cigarettes on at least one day in the preceding 30 days ("current cigarette use"). White and Hispanic students were more likely (22.5% and 18%, respectively) than Black students (9.5%) to report current smoking. Overall, cigarette use in general was higher among male (19.8%) than female students (19.1%). In terms of age, older students were more likely to smoke than younger students. In 2010, only 5.2% of middle school students reported having smoked cigarettes. After decelerating considerably in recent years, the long-term decline in cigarette use, which began in the mid-1990s, came to a halt in the lower grades in 2010. Indeed, both 8th and 10th graders showed evidence of an increase in smoking in 2010, though the increases did not reach statistical significance (Johnston, O'Malley, Bachman, & Schulenberg, 2010). Perceived risk and societal disapproval had both leveled off some years ago, which may account for this trend.

Among women, cigarette smoking increases the grave risk for infertility, preterm delivery, stillbirth, sudden infant death syndrome (SIDS), and low birth weight (U.S. Department of Health and

Human Services, 2011). Birth weight is directly correlated with chances of child survival. Smoking also strongly contributes to ectopic pregnancy and spontaneous abortion (U.S. Department of Health and Human Services, 2011). Nevertheless, 13% to 17% of pregnant women continue to smoke throughout their pregnancies (U.S. Department of Health and Human Services, 2011).

Another way to appreciate the negative consequences of smoking is to calculate or estimate the money needed to provide medical and health-related services to people who are suffering or dying from smoking-related diseases or illnesses. These services include but are not limited to ambulatory care, prescription drugs, hospital care, home health services, and nursing home care. These services are used to calculate **state medical expenditures**—the financial cost to the state in providing medical and health-related services to people suffering from smoking-attributable diseases or illnesses (CDC, 2011b). During 2000–2004, cigarette smoking was estimated to be responsible for $193 billion in annual health-related economic losses in the United States ($96 billion in direct medical costs and approximately $97 billion in lost productivity) (MMWR, 2008).

Even nonsmokers are not safe from tobacco-related health issues. **Secondhand smoke,** formally called **environmental tobacco smoke (ETS),** is classified as a Group A (known human) carcinogen by the U.S. Environmental Protection Agency. In fact, more than 50 individual carcinogens have been identified in secondhand smoke (U.S. Department of Health and Human Services, 2006). Exposure to secondhand smoke alone causes approximately 49,400 deaths each year from heart or lung disease in nonsmokers (CDC, 2011b). Although there has been a decline in exposure of nonsmokers to secondhand smoke since 1986, secondhand smoke remains a major cause of premature death and disease among both children and adults (U.S. Department of Health and Human Services, 2006). Despite efforts to control tobacco in public areas, millions of American nonsmokers, children and adults alike, are still exposed to secondhand smoke, especially in their homes and workplaces (U.S. Department of Health and Human Services, 2006).

## Antitobacco Efforts

Since the establishment of the connection between tobacco use and lung cancer and several other health issues, antitobacco efforts have taken place at many levels, spanning from elementary school awareness programs to state-enforced smoking bans in restaurants. Based on the connection between smoking and lung cancer, the **National Cancer Institute (NCI),** as part of the U.S. National Institutes of Health, funds a number of smoking awareness and prevention programs. One program was the America Stop Smoking Intervention Study (ASSIST). The study, which took place from 1991 to 1999, was one of the largest government-funded demonstration projects to help states develop effective smoking reduction strategies. ASSIST provided funding for 17 states and found a noticeable decrease in per capita cigarette consumption among the states that experienced improvement in tobacco control policies. The study also sheds light on the latest evidence available with regard to state tobacco control programs: investing in state tobacco control programs that focus on strict policies and regulation is an important and effective strategy for reducing tobacco use (National Cancer Institute, 2004).

The American Legacy Foundation, "dedicated to building a world where young people reject tobacco and anyone can quit," is a foundation that has developed a number of programs to combat tobacco and cigarette smoking (American Legacy Foundation, 2008a). The foundation has been involved in antitobacco efforts from the national "Truth" youth smoking prevention campaign to research initiatives aimed at tobacco reduction and outreach programs that target smoking cessation among priority populations (American Legacy Foundation, 2008b). Among one of the foundation's most recent campaigns is the Smoke Free Movies Campaign. With the motivation of eliminating the deep smoking impressions left by Hollywood on youth, the campaign aims to make any new movie with smoking in it rated R, end brand appearances on the screen, and include antismoking ads before movies that contain tobacco of any sort (American Legacy Foundation, 2008a).

At the global level, the World Health Organization (2008c) has created a new landmark report that represents "the first in a series of WHO reports that will track the status of the tobacco epidemic and the impact of interventions implemented to stop it." The report outlines six policies as part of the WHO's MPOWER package that will serve to "counter the tobacco epidemic and reduce its deadly toll." The components of the MPOWER package consist of the following:

- Monitor tobacco use and prevention policies
- Protect people from tobacco smoke
- Offer help to quit tobacco use
- Warn about the dangers of tobacco
- Enforce bans on tobacco advertising, promotion, and sponsorship
- Raise taxes on tobacco

Despite a variety of antitobacco efforts, every year the tobacco industry spends millions of dollars in advertising and promoting tobacco (e.g., free coupons, or leather jackets with logos of the product). In 2006, cigarette companies spent $12.4 billion on advertising and promotional expenses in the United States alone, down from $13.1 billion in 2005, but more than double what was spent in 1997 (CDC, 2011b). In addition, the industry is quick to use image-based propaganda, which has been demonstrated to be effective with youth as well as the less educated. For instance, DiFranza and colleagues (1991) found that Joe Camel (a cartoon character smoking a Camel cigarette) was more readily recognized by children than Mickey Mouse. Although the U.S. government has implemented policies restricting the use of such characters in advertising in the United States, such images continue to be used in international markets. Based on the money spent on advertising alone, those who engage in antitobacco efforts (including the NCI and the WHO) are facing a Herculean task in creating effective antitobacco and antismoking public health efforts.

### Community-Based Approaches

Among the 15.7% of underage students (under 18) who reported being habitual smokers in 2009, 14% usually bought them on their own in a store or gas station, presumably without proof of age (MMWR, 2010a) suggesting that health-related legal policy (e.g., "No sale to minors") is just the first step in the fight for a smoke-free environment (Jason, Berk, Schnopp-Wyatt, & Talbot, 1999), and one that is obviously not adequate to stop the problem. Biglan and associates (1996) argued that

> many law enforcement officers feel that there are more important crimes to deal with and that judges will be annoyed if such cases are brought before them. In addition, if the value of reducing such sales has not been adequately publicized, there is a risk that enforcement will produce a backlash against tobacco control efforts. (p. 626)

These sentiments are still true today. So if laws are ineffective in curbing dangerous behaviors such as smoking, what other strategies would be more effective? Researchers in this field believe that members of a community must have a sense of ownership of health related problems, including how they view and implement health-related legal policy. To test this premise, Biglan and colleagues designed a five-component intervention program to reduce youth access to tobacco products in two small Oregon communities. The outcome of interest was the proportion of tobacco outlets in the community that were willing to sell tobacco products to youth.

Using a quasi-experimental design, Biglan and colleagues (1996) conducted their intervention in the two selected Oregon communities; two other similar communities did not receive the intervention.

Specifically, activities of *mobilization of community support* included a letter and signature campaign sought from members of various community sectors (e.g., school district, healthcare providers, and civic organizations) to produce a proclamation that tobacco would not be sold to youth. *Merchant education* involved visits and distribution of the proclamation to all tobacco outlets. A modified sting operation was employed to *change consequences to clerks* for selling or not selling tobacco to those under age 18. That is, those who complied with the law were rewarded each time with a gift certificate worth $2 for use in a local business. Those who violated the law were given a reminder of the law and the community proclamation of no sale of tobacco to youth. These activities were described in public media (e.g., newspapers) as part of the *publicity intervention strategy.* Finally, *owners of tobacco outlets were personally informed* about these activities (identities of clerks were masked). In brief, the five components represented a range of macro-level (e.g., mobilization of community) to micro-level (e.g., feedback to store owners) comprehensive community intervention strategies. Results indicated that tobacco outlets' willingness to sell tobacco products to youth was significantly lower in the intervention group than in the control group.

The research by Biglan and colleagues (1996) speaks to the importance of community-based involvement in augmenting health-related legal policy. Unfortunately, the significance of community norms and sentiment toward substance use may not be well understood by the population in general. Many people may not realize that their community as a whole can have an impact on issues such as tobacco access among youth. To explore the adult attitudes and beliefs surrounding the issue of restricting youth access to tobacco, Siegel and Alvaro (2003) conducted a study in two Arizona counties. According to their findings, an overwhelming majority of adults believed that it was easy for minors to get access to tobacco and that the parents of the youth purchasing tobacco were most responsible for the problem. Furthermore, most adults responded that "there is nothing that they or the community can do to stop minors who wish to purchase tobacco." Clearly, although there are proven cases in which the community at large can play a significant and important role in improving the status of a health-related issue, there is also a sense that individual community members do not understand their role as part of the fabric of the community. This sense of disempowerment is a social justice issue that affects many communities that are at highest risk for substance use problems.

## ALCOHOL

### Extent of the Problem

In addition to cigarettes, **alcohol** is a gateway drug to other drug use and abuse. In some ways, one could argue that alcohol, independent of its relationship to other drugs, is more of a health risk to young people than are all other drugs including tobacco. First, drugs like tobacco do the most damage when used over long periods of time, as opposed to alcohol, which can result in life-threatening circumstances in a single use (e.g., drunk driving accidents). Second, alcohol is perceived as a much more socially acceptable drug than is tobacco. For example, it is unlikely that there will be a day when consuming alcoholic beverages in a restaurant is banned the way that smoking has been banned in most restaurants. Third, although there is a legal age limit for both alcohol and tobacco, a disturbing number of underage youths have and will use alcohol at some point in their lives. For example, according to the 2009 YRBSS data (MMWR, 2010b), 72.5% of all students had had at least one drink of alcohol during their lifetimes. Furthermore, it appears that the age at which youths are having their first experiences with alcohol are quite young. For example, 21.1% of students had drunk alcohol for the first time before age 13 and 63.4% of 9th graders had already had their first experience with alcohol. Gender, age, and racial/ethnic differences served to further define the profile of students who drank alcohol by the time they reached 9th grade. For example, a higher percentage of females (66.4%) reported having drunk before by 9th grade than did males (60.8%). However, a higher percentage of males (23.7%) than females (18%) had had their first drink by age 13.

Nationwide, 41.8% of students were current alcohol users (or had least one drink of alcohol in the past 30 days). Current alcohol use also varied across gender, age, and racial/ethnic differences. For example, current alcohol use was more prevalent among White and Hispanic females (45.9% and 43.5%, respectively) than Black females (35.6%). Furthermore, 24.2% of all students had participated in episodic heavy drinking (at least five drinks of alcohol in a row within a couple of hours on more than one of the 30 days preceding the survey). Prevalence of episodic heavy drinking was higher among male (30%) 11th graders than among those who were female (26.5%). In addition, White students (27.8%) were more likely to have taken part in episodic heavy drinking than Black (13.7%) and Hispanic (24.1%) students.

In terms of trends that researchers have seen over the past several decades, alcohol use, including binge drinking, continued its longer term decline among teens, reaching historically low levels in 2010 (Johnston et al., 2010). Use has been in a long-term pattern of decline since about 1980, with the interruption of a few years in the early 1990s in which alcohol use increased along with the use of cigarettes and almost all illicit drugs. For example, among 12th graders in 1980, 41% admitted to having five or more drinks in a row on at least one occasion in the two weeks before the survey. This statistic fell to 28% by 1992, before its rebound in the 1990s, but has now fallen further, reaching 23% in 2010—a marked improvement (Johnston et al., 2010).

Alcohol use before or during sex is a major risk for unprotected sex (Cooper, 2002), which might result in unwanted pregnancy and acquisition of STDs (including HIV). According to the 2009 YRBSS data, nearly one-fifth (21.6%) of all students had used alcohol or drugs before their most recent sexual intercourse. (Overall, 34.2% of students were sexually active at the time of the survey.) Prevalence of drinking alcohol or using drugs before the last sexual intercourse was much higher among male (25.9%) than female (17.1%) students. In terms of racial/ethnic differences, White and Hispanic students (22.9% and 18.9%, respectively) were more likely to engage in this behavior than Black students (18%). Note, however, that a higher percentage of Black students (47.7%) reported being currently sexually active (had sexual intercourse with at least one person during the three months preceding the survey) than White and Hispanic students (32.0% and 34.6%, respectively).

Finally, **binge drinking** is a major issue associated with alcohol use and abuse that spans from college campuses to entire societies across the globe. The National Institute of Alcohol Abuse and Alcoholism defines binge drinking as "a pattern of drinking that brings a person's blood alcohol concentration (BAC) to 0.08% or above," a level that is usually reached by men after consuming five or more drinks and by women after consuming four or more drinks in a time span of approximately two hours. According to the CDC, binge drinking is associated with a multitude of health problems, from unintentional injuries and neurological damage to sexual dysfunction and liver disease (CDC, 2011e). In the United States, binge drinking makes up a large part of alcohol consumption. In fact, approximately 90% of alcohol consumed by youth under 21 years of age is in the form of binge drinks (Pacific Institute for Research and Evaluation, 2005). In addition, about 92% of adults who drink excessively report binge drinking within the past 30 days (Town, Naimi, Mokdad, & Brewer, 2006).

Might there be a cultural component to binge drinking? International research has examined use patterns in countries that are known to have higher levels of alcohol abuse and dependency. For example, for Russians, who have been found by several sources to drink less frequently but consume larger amounts of alcohol per occasion, binge drinking is a specific norm of alcohol consumption (Bobak et al., 2004; Jukkala, Makinen, Kislitsyna, Ferlander, & Vagero, 2008; Leinsalu, 2004; Simpura, Levin, & Mustonen, 1997). In their 2008 study, Jukkala and colleagues explained binge drinking as an important factor in Russia's mortality crisis and found binge drinking patterns to be related to an individual's "economic situations and social relations." Furthermore, gender was found to be an important factor in whether an individual would participate in binge drinking. Some of the key findings were as follows:

- Russian men with economic problems drink heavily, whereas women with economic problems drink less.
- Married Russian men binge drink as much as their nonmarried friends, whereas married women binge drink much less than their nonmarried friends.
- Russian women's drinking is concentrated in the context of friends, whereas men's occurs elsewhere.
- Drinking patterns indicate that Russian women and young people of both genders seem to be drinking more than they were previously.

Although the study sheds light on issues that justify worry with regard to the future of Russia's alcohol-related problems, it also makes important connections between individual health and the community (i.e., accepted norms around drinking) with regard to binge drinking. Because binge drinking is a possible contributor to the "extremely large gender gap in Russian mortality statistics," these connections can potentially serve as important points of emphasis in a community health approach to solving important public health issues (Jukkala et al., 2008). When addressing preventive health issues across the globe, it is necessary to assess the community in terms of its own unique cultural phenomena.

## Alcohol Safety Laws

In the United States, motor vehicle crashes are the leading cause of death for Americans between the ages of 2 and 34 years, and 41% of these fatal crashes involve alcohol (National Highway Traffic Safety Administration, 2008). Approximately one-third of driving while intoxicated (DWI) or driving under the influence (DUI) arrests each year involve individuals who were previously convicted of DWI or DUI (National Highway Traffic Safety Administration, 2008). Furthermore, impaired driving is the most frequently committed crime in the United States (National Highway Traffic Safety Administration, 2008).

Despite these grim statistics, alcohol-related deaths have been more controlled today than they were before the 1990s, due in part to a series of laws that have sought to limit and discourage alcohol-related driving incidents. In one study Voas, Tippetts, and Fell (2000) evaluated the effect of three major alcohol safety laws, including administrative license revocation laws, 0.10 illegal per se laws, and 0.08 illegal per se laws. The results of the study indicated that each of the three types of laws had a significant relationship to the downward trend in alcohol-related fatal crashes in the United States between 1982 and 1997. The study also pointed out that the significant decline in alcohol-related fatal crashes could not be attributed to one single law, but to the combined effect of several laws over time. However, as was the case with tobacco laws, the fact that such policies exist and are enforced cannot be the sole reason that drinking and driving is on the decline. Other factors, such as the media's attention to drinking-and-driving issues and increased use of sobriety checkpoints, were also identified as possibilities not tested in the model but that may also have contributed to the decline. The many contributors to increased alcohol safety on the road show the importance of implementing a comprehensive community approach when addressing preventive health issues such as limiting the number of deaths or injuries as a result of traffic accidents.

## A Community Psychology Approach

As argued earlier, health-related legal policy is most effective when people feel they are empowered to make informed choices and decisions, including why they should heed health advice by experts or government officials. A key component in this equation is that empowerment (and its effect on decision making) often begins at home (e.g., parents talk to their children about the good and bad of drinking, premarital sex) and at school (e.g., peers for prosocial behaviors). In other words, values and skills learned and supported by peer norms are thought to be instrumental in health-related decision-making processes. Thus, next is a brief review of a study using parent–child involvement as a strategy to address alcohol use among youth.

Spoth, Randall, Shin, and Redmond (2005) studied family- and school-based alcohol abuse prevention strategies' effects on ability to delay initiation and decrease regular use and weekly drunkenness in a large-scale randomized clinical study involving middle schoolers. The study compared the effectiveness of a family-focused program combined with a school-based intervention, a school-based intervention without the family program, and a no-treatment control group. The family-focused program was the Iowa Strengthening Families Program (Spoth, Redmond, & Shin, 2001; Spoth, Redmond, Shin, & Azevedo, 2004), and the school-based intervention was the Life Skills Training program (LST; Botvin,1996; Botvin, Baker, Dusenbury, Botvin, & Diaz, 1995).The family-focused intervention included seven sessions that involved parent education, youth skills building, and a joint family session where participants practiced their new skills with other families. The individual youth sessions focused on strengthening future goals, dealing with stress and strong emotions, increasing the desire to be responsible, and building skills to appropriately respond to peer pressure. Topics covered in parent sessions included discussing social influences on youth, understanding developmental characteristics of youth, providing nurturant support, dealing effectively with youth in everyday interactions, setting appropriate limits and following through with reasonable and respectful consequences, and communicating beliefs and expectations regarding substance use.

The primary goals of the 15-session LST are to promote skills development (e.g., social resistance, self-management, and general social skills) and to provide a knowledge base concerning the avoidance of substance use. Students are trained in the various LST skills through the use of interactive teaching techniques, including coaching, facilitating, role modeling, feedback, and reinforcement, plus homework exercises and out-of-class behavioral rehearsal. The results of their analyses revealed that the multicomponent intervention generally showed stronger results in intervention–control comparisons than did the control comparisons with LST only and the no-treatment control group, especially on measures of delaying initiation and weekly drunkenness. Unfortunately, there were not the same positive effects of regular use of alcohol.

Results from studies such as Spoth and associates (2005) suggest that although we have identified solid programs to prevent alcohol abuse in youth, we have not yet figured out how to minimize youths' temptation to use alcohol at all.

Vimpani (2005) states, however, that "much remains to be done to enable the promise of effective universal and targeted early intervention to be translated into policies, programs and practices." Thus, although many relationships between early alcohol intervention, the family, and the community have been established, existing programs that serve to take advantage of these important connections are still lacking.

## ILLICIT DRUGS → Opioid epidemic

### Extent of the Problem

Use of illicit drugs is a problem across the globe. According to the World Health Organization (2010), at least 15.3 million people in the world have drug use disorders. Drug use not only causes adverse personal and community health consequences, it is also the source of a huge economic and financial burden in terms of treatment for drug users in the short and long term. As a result, investing in drug treatment early on can limit future health and social costs. In fact, for every $1 invested in drug treatment, approximately $10 is saved in health and social costs (WHO, 2010).

In the United States, among other countries, youth drug use is a serious issue. According to the YRBSS survey (MMWR, 2010b), at least one instance of use ("ever used") of (1) **marijuana,** (2) **cocaine** (including powder, crack, and freebase), (3) illegal **injection drugs,** (4) illegal **steroids,** (5) **inhalants,** (6) **hallucinogenic drugs** (including LSD [lysergic acid diethylamide], acid, PCP [phencyclidine] [angel dust], mescaline, and mushrooms), (7) **heroin,** (8) **methamphetamine** (also known as "speed," "crystal," "crank," and "ice"), and (9) **ecstasy** (methylenedioxymethamphetamine, MDMA) was reported by 36.8%, 6.4%, 2.5%, 3.3%, 11.7%, 8.0%, 2.5%, 4.1%, and 6.7%, respectively, of all students. Less than 1 in 10 of all students (7.5%) had tried marijuana before 13 years of age. There were gender, grade, and racial/ethnic differences in this behavior. For example, male students (9.7%) were significantly more likely than female students (5%) to have tried marijuana before age 13. The study also began asking about prescription drug abuse, given its rise in popularity. Nationwide, 20% of students had taken prescription drugs (e.g., Oxy-Contin, Percocet, Vicodin, Adderall, Ritalin, or Xanax) without a doctor's prescription one or more times during their life. Overall, the prevalence of having ever taken prescription drugs without a doctor's prescription was higher among White (23.0%) than Black (11.8%) and Hispanic (17.2%) students. Compared to other illicit drugs that have been traditionally the concern of parents, it seems clear that more attention must be paid to prescription drug abuse given the easier access that exists to such drugs.

Marijuana was the most popular choice of drug—20.8% of all students had used marijuana one or more times during the 30 days preceding the survey. However, there is a great deal of variability in illegal drug use depending on such factors as gender, grade, and race/ethnicity. For example, male students were more likely than female students to have ever used marijuana (39.0% versus 34.3%) and illegal steroids (4.3% versus 2.2%), whereas females were more likely than males to have ever used inhalants (12.9% versus 10.6%). In addition, White and Hispanic students (6.3% and 9.4%, respectively) were more likely to report having ever used cocaine than Black students (2.9%).

In terms of trends of illicit drug use over the past few decades, according to Johnston and colleagues (2010), marijuana use, which had been rising among teens for the past two years, continued to rise in 2010 in all prevalence. This stands in stark contrast to the long, gradual decline that had been occurring over the preceding decade. Of particular relevance, **daily marijuana use** increased significantly in all three grades in 2010 and stands at 1.2%, 3.3%, and 6.1% in grades 8, 10, and 12. In other words, nearly 1 in 16 high school seniors today is a current daily, or near-daily, marijuana user. There was a significant increase in **heroin use using a needle** among 12th graders in 2010, with annual prevalence rising from 0.3% in 2009 to 0.7% in 2010. **Cocaine** and **powder cocaine** use continued gradual declines in all grades in 2010. **Sedative** use and use of **narcotics other than heroin**, which are reported only for 12th graders, similarly continued their slow, nonsignificant declines in 2010. The use of quite a number of drugs held fairly steady in 2010, including **LSD, hallucinogens other than LSD** taken as a class, **PCP, crack cocaine, heroin** without using a needle, **OxyContin, amphetamines (Ritalin** and **Adderall** specifically), **methamphetamine, crystal methamphetamine, tranquilizers, cough and cold medicines** taken to get high, several so-called "club drugs" (**Rohypnol, GHB,** and **ketamine),** and **anabolic steroids**. Johnston et al. (2010) also note that the drugs that are not down much from peak levels are the **narcotics other than heroin.**

The misuse of psychotherapeutic **prescription drugs** (amphetamines, sedatives, tranquilizers, and narcotics other than heroin) has become a more important part of the nation's drug problem in recent years. Use of most of these classes of drugs continued to increase beyond the point at which most illegal drugs ended their rise in the late 1990s; use of the latter group of illegal drugs has declined appreciably since then (Johnston et al., 2010). The proportion of 12th graders in 2010 reporting use of any of these prescription drugs without medical supervision in the prior year was 15.0%, up slightly from 14.4% in

2009 but a bit lower than in 2005, when it was 17.1%. Lifetime prevalence for the use of any of these drugs without medical supervision in 2010 was 21.6%.

Because most illicit drugs are not regulated for content, it is impossible for users to be sure exactly what they are consuming. Marijuana, for example, may be more dangerous for users today than it was 30 years ago. At the time of this writing, levels of THC, the psychoactive ingredient in marijuana, are at the highest recorded amount since scientific analysis of marijuana began at the end of the 1970s (Office of National Drug Control Policy, 2008). The outcome of the analysis of THC levels from the University of Mississippi's Potency Monitoring Project, released by the Office of National Drug Control Policy (ONDCP) and the National Institute on Drug Abuse (NIDA), is cause for authorities to be concerned. In the ONDCP press release on increased marijuana potency, John Walters, director of National Drug Control Policy and former President Bush's "drug czar," expressed his concern (echoed by Johnston et al., 2010) with the finding:

> Baby boomer parents who still think marijuana is a harmless substance need to look at the facts. Marijuana potency has grown steeply over the past decade, with serious implications in particular for young people, who may be not only at increased risk for various psychological conditions, cognitive deficits, and respiratory problems, but are also at significantly higher risk for developing dependency on other drugs, such as cocaine and heroin than are non-smokers.

Finally, there are many dire consequences due to illicit drug use, including but not limited to crime, domestic violence, illnesses, loss in productivity, and increases in STDs, including HIV/AIDS. For instance, of the 136 countries that reported injecting drug use, 93 reported HIV infection among the same population (WHO, 2010). This is just one statistic among many that demonstrates the fact that the effects of illicit drugs are far-reaching, penetrating societies far beyond the users themselves.

## Possible Solutions and Challenges

The **National Drug Control Strategy 2011 Annual Report** outlines several characteristics of the drug problem in the United States and the programs and interventions proposed or in place to combat the issues at hand. In May 2010, President Obama released the Administration's inaugural *National Drug Control Strategy,* a comprehensive approach to combat the public health and safety consequences posed by drug use (see http://www.whitehouse.gov/sites/default/files/ondcp/policy-and-research/2011strategyexecutive summary_0.pdf). A year later, the administration released an update building on that initial strategy. The *Strategy* establishes ambitious goals to reduce both drug use and drug-related consequences. This five-year plan aims to cut drug use among youth by 15%, drug-induced deaths and drug-related morbidity by 15%, and drugged driving by 10%. To achieve these goals, the *Strategy* focuses on seven core areas:

- Strengthening efforts to prevent drug use in our communities
- Seeking early intervention opportunities in health care
- Integrating treatment for substance use disorders into health care, and supporting recovery
- Breaking the cycle of drug use, crime, delinquency, and incarceration
- Disrupting domestic drug trafficking and production
- Strengthening international partnerships
- Improving information systems to better analyze, assess, and locally address drug use and its consequences

The report emphasizes the costs to the United State of drug abuse and addictions. Overall, the economic impact of illicit drug use on American society totaled more than $193 billion in 2007, the last year for which data are available. The report also echoes concern about the abuse of pharmaceutical drugs, mentioned earlier in this chapter and highlighted in the upcoming Case in Point 11.1.

CASE IN POINT 11.1

# Prescription Drug Misuse: Risk Factors for Problem Users

Prompted by data that documented that 10 million individuals, or 7% of the U.S. population, reported nonmedical use of prescription drugs (Substance Abuse and Mental Health Services Administration, 2000), Simoni-Wastila and Strickler (2004) set out to identify the risk factors associated with problem use of prescription drugs. Nonmedical prescription drug use encompasses a vast range of behaviors, from simple noncompliance to recreational use and serious abuse (Wesson, Smith, Ling, & Seymour, 1997).

Simoni-Wastila and Strickler first estimated the prevalence of problem use of prescription drugs using the National Household Survey on Drug Abuse. "Problem users" were identified based on meeting one of the following criteria for dependency/heavy use:

1. Inability to cut down
2. Getting less work done
3. Using substance in past month and being depressed, argumentative, anxious, or upset, feeling isolated, and/or having health problems and/or difficulty thinking clearly
4. Needing larger amounts
5. Experiencing withdrawal symptoms

In the study, identified problem users were analyzed based on race, age, gender, marital status, urbanicity, education, work status, health insurance, income, and general health status. The results showed that more than 8.2 million individuals, or 4% of the U.S. population, report some sort of past-year nonmedical use of prescription drugs annually. Furthermore, of these 8.2 million, 1.3 million individuals were categorized as "problem users of prescription drugs." Discovered risk factors for problem use included being female, being in poor or fair health, and drinking alcohol daily. Conversely, being young (under the age of 25 years) and employed full-time were found to protect against problem use. In addition, other factors, such as marital status, education, employment status, and income, were found to be uniquely associated with individual therapeutic classes of drugs. For example, being an unmarried woman above the age of 35 was found to increase an individual's likeliness of being a problem user of narcotic analgesics.

Simoni-Wastila and Strickler point out that their study, the first to estimate the prevalence of problem use of prescription drugs, illustrates a possible need for further risk factor identification and treatment for problem users of prescription drugs in the future. This case study shows that prescription drugs, although regulated and legal, can easily fall into the same category as illicit drugs in terms of their far-reaching effects and consequences for a population and may require the same community health measures necessary to address illicit drug problems in the United States and abroad.

---

Specifically, the largest number of past-year new users initiated drug use with psycho-pharmaceuticals, more than any other drug, including marijuana. In the past 10 years, drug-induced deaths—driven by prescription drugs—have more than doubled (National Drug Control Strategy, 2011). Whether or not the strategy will achieve its goals by 2015 remains to be seen, but reducing drug abuse and addiction appears to be a high priority of the current administration.

## SEXUALLY TRANSMITTED DISEASES

Susan Chandle debated whether to vaccinate her 12-year-old daughter, Alexandra, with the human papillomavirus (HPV) vaccine. It seemed odd to vaccinate against a sexually transmitted virus before her daughter became sexually active. She had barely spoken to Alexandra about sex and was uncomfortable even mentioning the premise of the vaccine. But Susan considered herself a vigilant mother and wanted to protect her daughter from the possibility of developing cervical cancer. She spoke to the doctor and weighed the pros and cons of the vaccine. The vaccine, known as Gardasil, was recently approved by the Food and Drug Administration (FDA) to provide complete immunity from the four most predominant strains of HPV. However, there are hundreds of strains of HPV; thus it is possible to have the vaccine and not be protected from all types of HPV or all forms of cervical cancer. Also, Susan was concerned this vaccine would embolden her daughter to believe she was protected against all STDs and thus engage in more sexual activity. In addition, the vaccine was costly; it required three doses at $120 per dose over a seven-month period and was not yet covered under the family's insurance plan. The vaccine was still relatively new, and the side effects and long-term health risk were unknown.

When she finally decided to vaccinate her daughter, she told her daughter that she was getting a vaccine to protect against cancer. Susan made no mention that HPV was sexually transmitted and decided to wait until Alexandra was taught about sex at school.

## Extent of the Problem

**Sexually transmitted diseases** (STDs) have long been considered a hidden epidemic of tremendous health and economic consequences. Many Americans are reluctant to address sexual health topics openly because of both the biological and social characteristics of these diseases. Although progress has been made in the treatment, diagnosis, and prevention of STDs, 19 million new infections occur each year in the United States (CDC, 2007b), with more than 340 million new cases of sexually transmitted bacterial and protozoal infections occurring throughout the world every year (WHO, 2010). Moreover, the United States has one of the highest rates of STDs in the industrialized world. In addition, adolescents (10- to 19-year-olds) and young adults (20- to 24-year-olds) are at the highest risk of contracting an STD. Table 11.2 is an overview of symptoms, prevalence, and modes of transmission of prevalent STDs.

The nature and impact of STDs are multifaceted. They pose a substantial economic burden; the direct medical costs associated with STDs are estimated as up to $14.7 billion annually. In 2000, there were 9 million new cases of STDs among 15- to 24-year-olds, and the direct economic burden of STDs was estimated to be $6.5 billion. Costs differ depending on specific the disease, with HPV having the highest direct medical cost ($2.9 billion) and syphilis the least ($3.6 million) (Chesson, Gift, & Pulver, 2004). Although many people experience few or no symptoms (and thus are never treated), diseases can still cause a great impact on personal health. For example, chlamydia, whether or not it is detected, may be the cause of a woman's infertility. Moreover, rates of STDs tend to be higher among drug users (both intravenous and nonintravenous [including alcohol] drug users). Epidemiological studies consistently demonstrate that concurrent STDs increase the transmission probability for HIV infection. In fact, it is the potent interaction between very early HIV infection and other sexually transmitted infections that could account for 40% or more of HIV transmissions (WHO, 2007).

## Possible Solutions and Challenges

Given the devastating toll that STDs take on both individuals and communities, what is known about their prevention? Because STDs are considered a global epidemic, organizations such as the World Health Organization have been very actively involved in increasing the ability of communities to decrease infection rates through prevention. There are several core elements to a public health approach to prevention and control of sexually transmitted infections, according to the WHO. Effective prevention and care can be achieved by use of a combination of responses. Services for prevention and for care of people with sexually transmitted infections should embrace a public health package that includes the following elements:

- Promotion of safer sexual behavior
- Promotion of early health-care–seeking behavior
- Introduction of prevention and care activities across all primary health-care programs, including sexual and reproductive health and HIV programs

**TABLE 11.2  Overview of Symptoms, Prevalence, and Modes of Transmission of STDs**

| Name | Symptoms | Transmission | Treatment | Prevalence |
|---|---|---|---|---|
| Chlamydia, *Chlamydia trachomatis* | Known as the "silent" disease, as many infected people show no symptoms<br><br>In women, symptoms may be abnormal vaginal discharge or burning sensation while urinating<br><br>In men, discharge from penis or burning sensation when urinating<br><br>If untreated, women can develop pelvic inflammatory disease | Transmitted during vaginal, anal, or oral sex<br><br>Transmitted by infected mother to her baby during vaginal childbirth | Can be easily treated and cured with antibiotics | More than 1 million infections in 2006 |
| Genital herpes<br><br>Herpes simplex virus, either type 1 (HSV-1) or type 2 (HSV-2) | Outbreak occurs within two weeks after initial infection<br><br>Primary episode includes blisters around the genitals or rectum that gradually give way to sores (ulcers)<br><br>Other outbreaks can appear weeks or months later, usually four to five outbreaks within a year, decreasing frequency over the years<br><br>Most people with HSV-2 infection never have sores or have unrecognizable signs | Virus released from the sores, but can also be released from skin that does not appear to have sores<br><br>HSV-1 causes "fever blisters" of the mouth and lips and can cause an infection of the genitals by oral–genital or genital–genital contact | No treatment to cure herpes, but antiviral medications shorten or prevent outbreaks<br><br>Daily suppressive therapy for symptomatic herpes to prevent transmission | 45 million people ages 12 and older have genital herpes<br><br>One out of five adolescents and adults have genital HSV<br><br>More common in women |
| Syphilis<br><br>Caused by bacterium *Treponema pallidum* | Many people do not have any symptoms for years but are at risk for later complications<br><br>Primary stage is the appearance of a single sore; if not treated, infection progresses to secondary stage<br><br>Secondary stage is characterized by skin rashes and mucous membrane lesion<br><br>Late and latent stages cause damage to the internal organs and difficulty coordinating muscle movements | Passed through direct contact with syphilis sore, sores occur commonly on external genitals and lips and mouth<br><br>Transmission during vaginal, anal, oral sex | Easy to cure in the early stages<br><br>Treated with injection of penicillin | Most syphilis cases occur in people aged 20–39 years<br><br>Between 2005 and 2006, syphilis cases increased by 11.8%<br><br>64% of cases in 2006 were among men who have sex with men |

**TABLE 11.2** *(Continued)*

| Name | Symptoms | Transmission | Treatment | Prevalence |
|---|---|---|---|---|
| Gonorrhea Caused by bacterium *Neisseria gonorrhoeae* | In men, symptoms include burning sensation while urinating or white, yellow, or green discharge from penis<br><br>Gonorrhea can cause epididymitis and lead to infertility if not treated<br><br>Women often experience mild or no symptoms and often symptoms mistaken for bladder or vaginal infections<br><br>If untreated, can cause pelvic inflammatory disease | Spread through contact with penis, vagina, mouth, or anus<br><br>Can be transmitted from mother to baby during delivery | Several antibiotics are used to treat gonorrhea, but the increasing number of drug-resistant strains is a cause of concern | In 2006, the rate of reported infections was 120.9 per 100,000 people<br><br>CDC estimates over 700,000 new cases each year |

*Source:* CDC (2006a). Reproduced by kind permission of UNAIDS, www.unaids.org.

- A comprehensive approach to case management that encompasses:
  - identification of the sexually transmitted infection;
  - appropriate antimicrobial treatment for the syndrome;
  - education and counseling on ways to avoid or reduce risk of infection with sexually transmitted pathogens, including HIV;
  - promotion of the correct and consistent use of condoms;
  - partner notification.

There has been sufficient evidence to show that condoms, when used correctly and consistently, are effective in protecting against the transmission of HIV and STDs to women and men. As was discussed in Chapter 7, it is important that sex education include instruction on the use of condoms as a cornerstone of a comprehensive approach. However, the WHO (2007) also recommends the following strategies as important in a successful prevention approach: promoting the correct use of male and female condoms, and their distribution; sexual abstinence; delaying sexual debut; and reducing the number of sexual partners. In settings where the infections are concentrated in high-risk populations, targeted interventions should be a priority, but not to the exclusion of education and other prevention and care services for the general population.

As is true with most prevention, targeting youths is typically more advantageous than waiting until adulthood. Accordingly, it is important to acknowledge that sexual behaviors have changed, especially among adolescents. The Kaiser Family Foundation reports a decline in the percentage of high school students engaging in sexual intercourse and an increase in contraceptive use among sexually active teens in the past decade. These both have contributed to a decreased pregnancy rate; however "about a third (34%) of young women become pregnant at least once before they reach the age of 20" (Kaiser Family Foundation, 2005a). These developments show that community-based public health programs have been effective in targeting youth. However, there still exist many barriers for adolescents to receive comprehensive reproductive care and services. These factors include state laws regarding parental consent, cost of care, few youth-friendly service delivery systems, and general ignorance of services available.

In the story that began this section, Susan decided to vaccinate her daughter despite her reluctance. By doing so, she is aiding in the fight to eliminate HPV. Currently HPV is the most common STD, and at least 50% of sexually active men and women will contract genital HPV at some point in their lives (CDC, 2004b). This scenario represents the discrepancies between culture, medical technology, and basic epidemiology. HPV poses a serious health risk that cannot be overlooked. The new technology offers a way of combating HPV, but it is by no means a cure. Multiple approaches in treatment and prevention are needed to address STDs. In addition, there needs to be a concerted effort by public health officials, schools, and parents in the realm of adolescent sexual health. Susan assumed that Alexandra's school would talk to her daughter, but conversations about sex must occur early and often.

## HIV AND AIDS

As discussed in the previous section, condom use is perhaps the most effective means of reducing the transmission of STDs, including HIV. However, given that the likelihood of all people using condoms, even with that knowledge, is very low, is there a way to inoculate against HIV? An AIDS vaccine is considered the safest, most inexpensive, effective, globally accessible, and practical means of controlling and ending the HIV/AIDS pandemic. However, HIV presents unique challenges for vaccine development because it does not have many of the viral features that vaccinologists have used to develop successful vaccines (Berkeley & Koff, 2007). In September 2007, the most promising vaccine failed in a large international human trial, and further development was halted. The HIV Vaccine Trail Network, a consortium including Merck, the National Institute of Allergy and Infectious Disease (NIAID), and academic members, used a new approach to develop immune response by generating T-cell response to limit viral load and disease progression (Sekaly, 2008). The STEP Trial, as it was known, consisted of immunizing close to 3,000 healthy HIV-negative participants. The vaccine was designed to produce visible cellular immunity, but it demonstrated no protection against infection. More alarmingly, the vaccine may have increased the risk of HIV transmission in some study participants (Altman, 2008).

The failure of the vaccine thus far demonstrates that the HIV/AIDS epidemic involves a complex infectious disease that a vaccine will not instantly cure. Not only does HIV pose an immunological challenge, it requires international cooperation by the medical community, governments, and other community leaders. Currently, the HIV/AIDS epidemic is one of the greatest challenges in public health.

### Overview

By the end of 2007, more than 33 million people were living with HIV worldwide. AIDS remains one of the top 10 causes of death globally and the primary cause of death in sub-Saharan Africa. Although 2007 marked a significant revision of global estimates of the AIDS epidemic due in part to better surveillance programs, AIDS remains a global crisis. Every day more than 6,800 people become infected with HIV, and slightly fewer than 6,000 people die from AIDS (UNAIDS, 2010). It is important to note that HIV is not the cause of AIDS. Rather, being HIV-positive weakens one's immune system, thus opening the door for opportunistic infections that lead to AIDS (see Figure 11.2).

---

Brain lesions (advanced stage of AIDS)
Frequent diarrhea
Loss of appetite
Low-grade fever that will not go away
Low T-cell count (below 400; T cells are involved in fighting infection)
Oral thrush (e.g., fungus inside the mouth)
Pneumonia
Skin lesions (e.g., Kaposi's sarcoma)
Swollen glands
Weight loss

---

**FIGURE 11.2**   Characteristics of People with HIV or AIDS

**TABLE 11.3**  Regional HIV Statistics and Features, End of 2007

| Region | Epidemic Started | Adults and Children Living with HIV/AIDS | Adult Prevalence (Age 15–49) | Adult and Child Deaths Due to AIDS |
|---|---|---|---|---|
| Sub-Saharan Africa | Late 1970s– early 1980s | 22.5 million | 5.0% | 1.6 million |
| North Africa and Middle East | Late 1980s | 380,000 | 0.3% | 25,000 |
| South and Southeast Asia | Late 1980s | 4.0 million | 0.3% | 270,000 |
| East Asia and Pacific | Late 1980s | 800,000 | 0.1% | 32,000 |
| Latin America | Late 1970s– early 1980s | 1.6 million | 0.5% | 58,000 |
| Caribbean | Late 1970s– early 1980s | 230,000 | 0.1% | 11,000 |
| Eastern Europe and Central Asia | Early 1990s | 1.6 million | 0.9% | 55,000 |
| Western and Central Europe | Late 1970s– early 1980s | 760,000 | 0.3% | 12,000 |
| North America | Late 1970s– early 1980s | 1.3 million | 0.6% | 21,000 |
| Oceania | Late 1970s– early 1980s | 75,000 | 0.4% | 12,000 |
| **Total** | | **33.2 million** | **0.8%** | **2.1 million** |

*Source:* UNAIDS (2007).

In the late 1970s and early 1980s, the medical community in the United States began to notice a strange disease, mostly infecting homosexual men and IV drug users. Very soon after, terms such as HIV, AIDS, and ARC (AIDS-related complex) became household words. Although HIV and AIDS were first recognized in homosexual men in this country, the disease has now been shown to infect all men, including heterosexual men, and women (see Table 11.3). Scientists and laypeople alike speculate about the origin of HIV and AIDS; theories range from the "green monkey theory" (a species of African monkey that is thought to be the genesis of the incurable disease) to biological warfare conducted by the U.S. Central Intelligence Agency. Still others (Eigen, 1993) have argued that HIV has been present in human beings for more than 120 years, just waiting for the right circumstances to attack the human immune system. Figure 11.3 presents some statements about AIDS to test your knowledge about this disease.

There have been encouraging developments in the battle against the AIDS epidemic, including improving prevention programs and increasing access to effective treatment. However, the number of people living with HIV continues to rise yearly. In many global regions, new HIV infections are concentrated among young people (15–24 years old). Sub-Saharan Africa bears most of the burden of disease—roughly two-thirds of all adults and children with HIV live there (UNAIDS, 2010).

## Extent of the Problem

In the United States, AIDS cases have been reported in all 50 states; however, 10 states/areas make up 71% of all reported cases. AIDS cases in the United States are concentrated in urban and southern areas,

Determine whether the following statements are true (T) or false (F):

1. Most infants born to mothers infected with HIV will test negative after 18 months.
2. The *window period* refers to the time between infection and the detection of antibodies in the blood.
3. Once you have tested positive for HIV, it is certain that you will develop AIDS.
4. *Confidential testing* means that you do not have to give your name when you get tested.
5. Latex condoms are an effective barrier to HIV.
6. You cannot get HIV if you are having sex with only one partner.
7. Oil-based lubricants should be used with latex condoms to prevent HIV.
8. In 2001, complications from AIDS was the leading cause of death for all Americans ages 25 to 44.

*Answers:* 1. F; 2. T; 3. T; 4. F; 5. T; 6. F; 7. F; 8. T

**FIGURE 11.3**    Test Your Knowledge of AIDS

with the District of Columbia having the highest case rate in the nation. In addition, AIDS has disproportionately affected racial and ethnic minorities, predominately Blacks and Latinos. More alarming is the demographic comparison of AIDS diagnoses and the U.S. population. For instance, whereas Blacks make up 12% of the population, they account for 49% of AIDS cases. In 2004, HIV was the fourth leading cause of death for Black men and the third for Black women aged 25–44 (Kaiser Family Fund, 2008b). The impact of HIV and AIDS among the various racial/ethnic minority communities can be gleaned and understood from at least three interrelated perspectives: (1) **knowledge, attitudes, beliefs, and behaviors (KABBs),** (2) **HIV testing,** and (3) **linkage to care.**

Although research on HIV/AIDS prevention and intervention indicates that KABBs alone are not sufficient for safer behavioral maintenance (staying HIV-negative or practicing safer behaviors among HIV-positive individuals) or changes for safer behaviors (Choi & Coates, 1994), misconception or less than optimal KABBs are likely to place people at risk. Researchers report that members of the African American community consistently underestimate their risk of contracting HIV. The CDC found that many sexually active Black women in North Carolina engaged in high-risk sexual behaviors. The reasons for involvement in these behaviors reported were:

> 1) financial dependence on male partners, 2) feeling invincible, 3) low self-esteem coupled with a need to feel loved by a male figure, and 4) alcohol and drug use. In addition, participant's proposed strategies for reducing HIV transmission among black women in North Carolina included 1) introducing HIV and STD educational activities in elementary and middle schools, 2) increasing condom availability and usage, and 3) integrating targeted HIV-education and prevention messages into church and community activities, as well as into media and popular culture. (MMWR, 2005b)

One barrier to combating the AIDS epidemic is HIV testing, which serves as a critical entry point to ensure linkage to care. In the three national surveys of household-based probability samples on which these figures are based, rates of testing were much higher for persons at increased risk (e.g., multiple sexual partners, IV drug use) for HIV. Twice as many people received HIV tests in private locations (medical offices, hospitals and emergency rooms, employee clinics, nursing homes, and at home via home testing kits) as in public locations (health departments, community clinics, HIV counseling and testing sites, family planning clinics, military and immigration sites, and STD clinics). Of those at increased risk for HIV, 70% had been tested for it. These patterns of findings suggest that there are at least two aspects to HIV testing: ability to access services and willingness to access services. Just because service is available does not mean that people (especially disenfranchised populations, including immigrants and refugees as well as those with limited English-speaking ability and some segments of racial/ethnic and cultural groups) will use it. In fact, available data indicate disparity in HIV testing among certain racial/ethnic and cultural groups. For example,

Asians and Pacific Islanders have one of the lowest testing rates. However, little is known about why people are unwilling to access HIV testing. Meanwhile, although the overall rates of HIV testing are high, more than half of the persons tested in public programs did not report that a health professional talked to them about HIV-related issues (KABBs) when they were tested, indicating that many either are not receiving counseling or are not recognizing their interaction with staff as counseling. The rate of counseling is even lower in private settings. These findings further underscore the complex relationship of KABBs, HIV testing, linkage to care, and most of all, their less than optimal effect in the fight against HIV. One theory, for example, acknowledges the relationship between an individual's sense of optimism and pessimism and HIV screening. A study of pregnant women in Ghana found that those who were most optimistic were not tested for HIV before pregnancy and had the least knowledge of HIV. This raises the question as to whether optimism translates into a denial or ignorance of potential risk. On the other hand, are pessimists better suited when it comes to HIV testing because they may be prepared for the worst (Moyer, Epko, Calhoun, Greene, Naik, Sippola et al., 2008)? These findings acknowledge that psychosomatic issues and emotional difficulties are involved in electing to test for HIV.

Prevention and testing alone cannot combat HIV. Treatment of HIV-positive individuals with **antiretrovirals (ARTs)** can extend their lives and increase quality of life. However, some argue that ARTs are expensive and the lack of health infrastructure in developing countries is a serious impediment to the delivery of treatment. However, Paul Farmer of Partners in Health created a successful HIV treatment program in rural Haiti, demonstrating that community-based approaches to HIV treatment in resource-poor settings are possible. Partners in Health provided directly observed therapy combined with **highly active antiretroviral therapy (HAART).** Each patient had an "accompagnateur" or health advocate (often a community health worker) who observed the ingestion of pills and provided emotional, moral, and social support. In addition, monthly meetings were offered to discuss illness and other concerns. The initial cohort responded extremely well to medicine, was less likely to be hospitalized, and reported higher morale. Farmer argues that the success of the HAART program in the poorest country in the Western hemisphere shows it can be implemented anywhere (Farmer et al., 2001).

## Complexities and Controversies

AIDS education raises many controversial questions. As part of education, should condoms be distributed in schools to prevent the spread of AIDS? If so, at what grade level? Such controversy has almost torn apart school systems across the nation. People with AIDS are growing impatient with the FDA in the regulation of experimental drugs and treatment criteria. To be treated, people must have more than 20 symptoms as defined by the CDC, the federal agency that oversees most HIV and AIDS surveillance. However, it took a lot of political lobbying before the CDC added to its list symptoms specific to women with AIDS (e.g., cervical cancer). Meanwhile, many people with AIDS have died from taking illegal treatments (usually smuggled into this country). The American Foundation for AIDS Research publishes a listing of all drugs for treating AIDS, including those that do not have FDA approval. The list is available free of charge.

On one hand, the pandemic has decreased in the United States and other industrialized countries due in large part to public health efforts and antiretroviral drugs. Yet in sub-Saharan Africa, AIDS continues to have devastating social, economic, political, and demographic consequences. Some argue that prevention and control in Africa has been based on earlier public models that were derived from policies from industrialized countries that did not take into account the nature of the epidemic (generalized rather than in specific risk groups) and African culture. In addition, a uniform global approach may not be suited to the extreme political and epidemiological diversity of the pandemic. Questions have arisen as to how to best tackle the epidemic in Africa. Should health officials require mandatory testing? How should limited funds be allocated within a country—on prevention or treatment? How do you combat stigma, discrimination, and the depression seen in HIV-positive individuals? What should be done when ARTs are available but there is not enough medical staff to administer them? Who should pay for treatment and testing? Should policies be made by local governments or international governing bodies such as the WHO or the World Bank?

Morality and politics aside, community psychologists and public health advocates have learned to use the public health model to slow down the spread of AIDS. After two decades of fighting the epidemic, it has been widely recognized that behavioral changes are paramount in preventing the transmission of HIV (National Commission on AIDS, 1993). Moreover, attitudinal variables are often viewed as determinants of compliance with HIV prevention recommendations (Fisher & Fisher, 1992). According to the Health Belief Model (Becker, 1974; Rosentock, 1986), readiness to perform health-related behaviors is seen as a function of perceived vulnerability, perceived severity of disease, perceived barriers to health-protective action, and feelings of self-efficacy concerning ability to protect oneself from disease. This meta-model has since been adapted or modified to meet the challenges and needs of the specific populations participating in HIV prevention programs.

## Possible Solutions: Community-Based Approaches

The preceding issues only scratch the surface of a very complex—and often volatile—problem. The virus is more than a biological epidemic; it has political and social valences, as well. It is beyond the scope of this chapter to review all solutions; however, a heuristic approach is to conceptualize solutions (with an emphasis on the principles of community psychology) along three interrelated dimensions: (1) prevention (KABBs), (2) HIV testing (see Case in Point 11.2), and (3) linkage to care (including psychosocial support; see Case in Point 11.3). The term *prevention* is used here in an inclusive sense to capture the overlap of primary, secondary, and tertiary modalities that occur in the AIDS literature and in the implementation of the clinical programs.

## CASE IN POINT 11.2

# Evaluation and Implementation of STD/HIV Community Intervention Program in Lima, Peru

Community programs focus on affecting the entire community to create widespread change in behavioral norms. The U.S. National Institute of Mental Health (NIMH) developed a collaborative model of community-level prevention focusing on mobilizing and training **community popular opinion leaders (CPOLs)** to promote healthy sexual behavior. NIMH is in the process of testing implications and effects of this intervention in Lima, Peru, in three different populations: men who identify as homosexual, women with multiple partners, and heterosexually identified men. This study looks at midterm evaluation of programs and

how to best implement STD prevention programs in low-income communities.

The program is based on Jeff Kelley and colleagues' Popular Opinion Leader model and adapts the four core elements (1) visible target population, (2) identification of CPOLs (criteria often include how popular, trusted, or respected they are among their peers), (3) training CPOLs over multiple sessions on theory-based prevention methods, and (4) goal setting with CPOLs.

The intervention in Peru is called *Qué te Cuentas* (What's up) and targets the young, urban, poor population where the HIV/STD epidemic is largely concen-

trated. Qué te Cuentas uses an innovative training approach and gives CPOLs information on sexuality, HIV and STDs, effective communication, and how to deliver nonthreatening, brief, and informal prevention messages. Researchers found the program to be overwhelmingly successful. CPOLs felt empowered by their position and ability to effect change in the community. Many CPOLs were surprised that conversations flowed easily at social spaces, including bars, soccer games, and homes. The intervention seems to be well accepted by the community, and a sense of ownership has developed among neighbors who

## (Continued)

perceive the intervention as a positive asset for the community.

Further evaluation of the program found that using CPOLs to disseminate STD prevention information created more culturally appropriate messages. Given the context of poverty and societal exclusion, CPOLs were given a chance to feel useful and a part of something. Initial findings also demonstrated that the intervention has directly changed CPOLs' knowledge, attitudes, and sexual risk behavior. In addition, the community has greater knowledge of how to prevent STDs and HIV (Maiorana et al., 2007). (See Community-Based Approaches for more information on this diffusion model.)

## The Bilingual Peer Advocate (BPA) Program

Nationwide, a majority of the Asian and Pacific Islanders (APIs) with AIDS/HIV are foreign-born individuals. In New York City, AIDS cases among APIs account for 95% of adult AIDS cases among APIs in the state and 13% of adult cases among APIs in the United States (Sy, Chng, Choi, & Wong, 1998).

Although they represent an expanding population (e.g., the highest growth rate from 1980 to 1990 in New York City) with increasing needs for HIV-related services, APIs are prevented from adequately accessing such services because of a number of barriers, including the following:

- Lack of culturally competent, linguistically accessible, and HIV-sensitive providers
- Lack of health insurance
- Distrust of institutions
- Stigma in API communities surrounding sex, substance use, homosexuality, illness, and death
- Lack of coordinated primary care and case-management services

Ideally, any API immigrant living with AIDS/HIV in New York City would be able to access any needed HIV-related service in the language that he or she speaks. In this ideal situation, the service would also be provided in a way that recognizes the cultural practices and attitudes of the client or patient. But given a tight funding environment, a lack of prioritization of API issues, and the numerous API languages and national and cultural groups, such an ideal is difficult to achieve. As part of a five-year national demonstration study (Chin & Wong, 2003), the Bilingual Peer Advocate (BPA) program, with its reliance on part-time peer workers, was designed to allow the Asian and Pacific Islander Coalition on HIV/AIDS (APICHA) to hire a large team of workers to meet the diverse language and cultural needs of APIs living with AIDS while also remaining within realistic cost parameters.

The program trains and maintains a corps of paid, part-time BPAs to act as language interpreters, cultural guides, and advocates for clients as they negotiate New York City's service system. In addition to helping service providers understand the clients' culture, BPAs are able to explain the culture of the health and social services to clients. BPAs are provided clinical supervision by three full-time case managers, one speaking Mandarin Chinese and two more speaking Japanese.

BPAs are paid because they commit more time to work and training than volunteers do. These individuals start with a three-day intensive training program and then receive a two- to three-hour follow-up training each month after. They are expected to be available on a regular basis; some are on call and carry beepers. BPAs work only part-time to retain a level of flexibility that full-time staff do not have and, more important, to allow APICHA to hire a broader range of individuals to represent more cultures and languages.

Currently, APICHA maintains a corps of 15 BPAs. Among them, they speak the following major languages: Bengali, Cantonese, English, Gujarati, Hindi, Japanese, Korean, Mandarin, Tagalog, Toisanese, and Urdu. Of APICHA's current 70-plus HIV-positive clients receiving comprehensive case management, 24 are being served by BPAs. Each month, BPAs spend about 8 to 12 hours working directly with clients, 3 to 5 hours conducting client outreach, 10 hours in travel, and 2 hours in training.

## OBESITY

Before concluding this chapter on behavioral health and the community psychology response, we consider a final health problem that has a uniquely American flavor: childhood obesity.

### Scope of the Problem

Within the past three decades, the percentage of children and adolescents who are overweight or obese has more than doubled (Ogden, Carroll, Curtin, Lamb, & Flegal, 2010). According to the most recent National Health and Nutrition Examination Survey (NHANES; Ogden et al., 2010), over a third of children ages 6 to 19 are obese (i.e., body mass index [BMI] for age at the 95th percentile or higher) or overweight (i.e., BMI for age at the 85th percentile or higher). Moreover, there are ethnic disparities in childhood obesity rates and rates of being overweight: African American and Latino/a children are at greater risk than their White counterparts (Ogden et al., 2010). Specifically, of children between the ages of 6 and 19, 43.0% of Mexican American children and 38.7% of African American children have BMIs at or above the 85th percentile, compared with 32.5% of White children. Across all racial and ethnic groups in this age range, the prevalence of children being overweight and childhood obesity appears roughly equivalent in boys and girls. However, some noteworthy gender disparities exist within specific racial groups. Forty-three percent of African American girls were overweight or obese, compared with 34.4% of African American boys. As is the case with other health problems, socioeconomic status (SES) is negatively associated with childhood obesity (Shrewsbury & Wardle, 2008). Thus, disparities in the prevalence of obesity are likely attributable to the confounding of SES and ethnic and racial group membership.

Although genetic factors are known to influence BMI (Mazzeo, Gow, & Bulik, 2012), the rapid increase in childhood obesity rates is considered primarily attributable to environmental factors. In fact, some leading scholars in the area have argued that obesity in Western society is caused by a "toxic environment" (Brownell, 2002) than includes too easily accessible calorie-dense foods, increases in sedentary behavior, and correspondent decreases in physical activity. Early intervention for obesity is important to prevent the development of obesity-related health problems, such as diabetes (Wang & Dietz, 2002). Further, quality of life among severely overweight children is significantly impaired, with some indication that it is worse than that of children with cancer (Schwimmer, Burwinkle, & Varni, 2003). Moreover, overweight children ages 10 to 17 are more than 20 times as likely to be obese in adulthood compared to their nonoverweight peers (Whitaker, Wright, Pepe, Seidel, & Deitz, 1997). Perhaps the strongest case to be made for early intervention, however, is that outcomes of adult obesity interventions are notoriously poor (Cooperberg & Faith, 2004; Mazzeo et al., 2012; Whitaker et al., 1997).

### Community Prevention Efforts

A few recent studies have begun to examine the effects of obesity prevention, although much more work is needed in this area (Carter & Bulik, 2008). Although one can imagine that teaching healthy eating habits and promoting recreational activity are key components of obesity prevention, as discussed in earlier chapters, knowing what is healthy and behaving in healthy ways are often compromised by contextual factors. For example, imagine a child growing up in a low-income neighborhood where healthy food is less available than is fast food. "Food deserts" may be one of the reasons that obesity is overrepresented in poor children, making it a health disparity. Add to the scenario that the family lives in a neighborhood that is unsafe, with random violence, and it becomes easier to understand why a family would struggle to "eat healthy" and exercise often. Because contextual constraints often keep individual children and families from attaining goals that promote health and well-being, scholars have designed prevention programs that target the community level. Two of the most common policy efforts to control obesity levels involve modifying school lunch programs and mandating BMI assessments in the schools.

The first community-based strategy for preventing obesity includes making significant changes in foods and snacks provided to children in schools, especially for children whose families lack the means or access necessary to provide nutritious food in the home. Although it is widely believed that changing meal choices at schools can help children eat better and potentially desire healthier foods in their home environment, few studies have decisively determined whether or not this actually occurs. For example, in a study involving middle school students, Schwartz and colleagues (Schwartz, Novak, & Fiore, 2009) investigated outcomes of an intervention targeting the removal of snacks of low nutritional value from schools. Six schools were involved in the study (three intervention, three control), and outcomes assessed by the researchers included changes in food consumption (both at school and at home) and dieting behavior. Results indicated that students in intervention program schools decreased their consumption of sugar-sweetened beverages and salty snacks of low nutritional value (e.g., chips) over the one-year study period. Meanwhile, students in the control group increased their consumption of these foods and beverages. Students in intervention program schools also increased their intake of water, nonartificially sweetened juice, less calorically/fat-dense salty snacks (e.g., pretzels), and healthy sweet snacks (e.g., fruit). Meanwhile, control group students' consumption of these foods and beverages was unchanged. However, there were no differences between groups in consumption of sweet snacks, such as ice cream. In addition, the program did not appear to have a significant effect on dietary intake in the home environment. Finally, there were no differences between groups in dieting behavior.

In a related study, Foster and associates (2008) investigated the effects of a school nutrition policy intervention (The School Nutrition Policy Initiative, SNPI) on fourth- to sixth-grade children from 10 schools with a high proportion of low-income students. As part of the SNPI, intervention program schools removed sodas, sugar-sweetened beverages, and snacks of low nutritional value from vending machines and cafeteria service. Water, low-fat milk, and nonartificially sweetened juice were the only beverages available in intervention program schools during the course of the project. In addition, school staff in the intervention program schools participated in nutrition education, and students were provided with 50 hours of nutrition education each school year. Students in intervention program schools were also offered incentives (e.g., raffle tickets for prizes) for the purchase of healthy foods.

Two years after the initiation of the SNPI, significantly fewer children in the intervention group had become overweight or obese (i.e., had a BMI at or above the 85th percentile for their age and sex), compared with the control group (Foster et al., 2008). Specifically, 15% of children in control schools became overweight during the study period (i.e., their BMIs moved from below the 85th to between the 85th and 95th percentiles), compared with 7.5% of children in the intervention schools. Moreover, the intervention was particularly effective for African American children, who were 41% less likely to be overweight at two-year follow-up than their African American peers in control schools. Data from the two studies reviewed here suggest that increasing nutritious foods available in school environments is a viable way to decrease obesity rates in children.

Another wide-scale intervention that has been used is school-based BMI screening. BMI screening is recommended by the Institute of Medicine as an important approach to the primary and secondary prevention of pediatric obesity (Institute of Medicine, 2004). BMI screening occurs regularly in many schools in the United States and other Westernized countries (Nihiser et al., 2007) and is even mandated in several U.S. states (Illinois, Maine, New York, Pennsylvania, Tennessee, and West Virginia) (Mazzeo et al., 2012). Proponents of school-based BMI screening note that it has several appealing features. It is a minimally invasive and relatively low-cost approach that can assess nearly all children and alert parents that their child might have a health concern (Mazzeo et al., 2012). In this sense, as has been argued (Morgan, 2008), BMI screening is analogous to routine vision and hearing screenings conducted in school settings. Given the vast numbers of uninsured families in the United States, many children might have no opportunity for routine BMI assessment outside of the school setting (Nihiser et al., 2007; Presswood, 2005). Results from BMI assessments are then communicated to parents (along with educational material about reducing obesity) on the assumption that if parents are unaware that their child's weight is a problem, they are obviously unlikely to facilitate behavioral changes that would address this issue.

So do such programs result in behavior changes? Few studies have assessed the impact of BMI screening programs. One that did was conducted by Chomitz, Collings, Kim, Kramer, and McGowan (2003). The authors compared a BMI screening program to a comparison group and found that parents in the BMI screening group whose children were overweight were more likely to seek medical treatment for their child compared to parents in the control group (25% vs. 7%). BMI screening group parents were also more likely to make changes in their children's diet and physical activity compared to parents in the comparison group. Mazzeo, Gow, Stern, and Gerke (2008), however, caution that the effectiveness of such programs is predicated on the ability of parents to communicate with their children about a potentially uncomfortable topic, given the stigma of being overweight in U.S. culture. Thus, in sum, these data suggest that prevention efforts should include **parents** and **incorporate information and skills training** regarding **communicating** with one's child about weight, appearance, and health.

Community-based approaches to obesity prevention appear to hold great promise. However, as is true with most programs, these approaches are not without their critics. For example, some disagree with the idea that foods should be presented as inherently "good" or "bad" (Mazzeo et al., 2012). A more acceptable way to categorize foods semantically may be as **foods to "promote"** versus **foods to "limit."** In addition, some eating disorder specialists have expressed significant concern that obesity prevention programs and policies will lead to extreme dieting among children (Cogan, Smith, & Maine, 2008). This is alarming because research has indicated that dieting is associated with the onset of eating disorder symptoms (Neumark-Sztainer et al., 2006). However, to date, research does not generally suggest that existing obesity interventions are associated with the onset of dieting in children or adolescents, at least at the aggregate level (Carter & Bulik, 2008). Nonetheless, some individuals, especially those with other underlying predispositions to develop an eating disorder (e.g., genetics), might be especially vulnerable to potential iatrogenic effects of obesity prevention. Thus, it is important that researchers not only evaluate the effects of their interventions at the aggregate level, but also track individual adverse events, including identifying individuals who develop eating pathology after exposure to obesity-related interventions (Carter & Bulik, 2008). Current data suggest such adverse outcomes will be relatively rare. However, as interventions and policies evolve and are more broadly disseminated, it will be important to rapidly identify such individuals, along with tracking characteristics that might have made them vulnerable to negative effects (Mazzeo et al., 2012).

## Summary

This chapter has reviewed six health issues: tobacco, alcohol, illicit drugs, STDs, HIV/AIDS, and obesity. These issues were examined from the perspectives of community psychology and preventive medicine; policy-based prevention (targeting a community) was also discussed (see Table 11.4). These issues were chosen for two main reasons: (1) They have each received enormous attention in the media, and (2) each is highly preventable. In addition, a large number of people are affected or have the potential to be affected if prevention does not occur.

**TABLE 11.4    Five Issues of Community Health and Preventive Medicine: A Snapshot**

| Issue | Extent of the Problem | Consequence | Possible Solution |
|---|---|---|---|
| Tobacco | • 23.0% of all adolescents smoked a cigarette at least once in past 30 days | • Smoking is a strong contributor to ectopic pregnancy and spontaneous abortion<br>• An estimated $72.7 billion in tobacco-related medical expenditures was recorded in 1993–2003 | • America Stop Smoking Intervention Study (ASSIST)<br>• Smoke Free Movies campaign |
| Alcohol | • 74.3% of all students have had at least one drink of alcohol during their lifetimes<br>• 25.6% of all students have used alcohol before age 13 | • 41% of fatal motor vehicle crashes involve alcohol<br>• Risk for contracting HIV is increased | • Parent–child skill building (Spoth, Redmond, Hockaday, & Yoo, 1996)<br>• Early intervention that involves the family and community |
| Illicit Drugs | • Marijuana—38.4% of students ever used<br>• Cocaine—7.6% of students ever used<br>• Injection drugs—2.1% of students ever used<br>• Steroids—4.0% of students ever used<br>• Inhalants—12.4% of students ever used<br>• Hallucinogenics—8.5% of students ever used<br>• Heroin—2.4% of students ever used<br>• Methamphetamine—6.2% of students ever used<br>• Ecstasy—6.3% of students ever used | • Users are consuming drugs without knowledge of unmonitored content and potential adverse health effects (rising THC levels in marijuana)<br>• HIV cases are directly linked to injection drug use worldwide<br>• Nonmedical use of prescription drugs is becoming just as high risk as "traditional" narcotics | • National Drug Control Strategy, 2008 (Office of National Drug Control Policy, 2008): early preventive programs, intervention and healing of current drug users, combating the market of illegal drugs |
| STDs | • In 2000, there were 9 million new cases of STDs among 15- to 24-year-olds | • Risk for contraction of HIV is increased<br>• New infections in mostly young people<br>• Direct economic burden of STDs is estimated to be $6.5 billion yearly | • Advisory Committee for HIV and STD Prevention (MMWR, 1998a)<br>• Community intervention (e.g., Peru) |

*(Continued)*

| TABLE 11.4 *(Continued)* | | | |
|---|---|---|---|
| Issue | Extent of the Problem | Consequence | Possible Solution |
| HIV/AIDS | • In 2004, HIV was the fourth leading cause of death for Black men and third for Black women aged 25–44.<br>• HIV deaths seen predominately in Africa | • Incurable disease with a long incubation period<br>• Resource allocation<br>• Stigma | • KABBs prevention and intervention<br>• HAART<br>• HIV testing |
| Obesity | • 33% of 6- to 19-year-olds | Higher rates of type 2 diabetes<br>Self-esteem issues | BMI Testing<br>Modified school lunch |

Internationally, tobacco is the cause of more than 5 million deaths each year (WHO, 2008c). In the United States alone, tobacco use (including smoking) is the number one preventable cause of death (U.S. DHHS, 2001b). Each year, tobacco use causes more deaths than HIV, illegal drug, alcohol use, motor vehicle injuries, suicides, and murders combined (U.S. DHHS, 2011; McGinnis & Foege, 1993). The American Legacy program has been effective in its antismoking efforts, as seen in its Truth youth smoking prevention and Smoke Free Movie campaigns. Biglan and colleagues illustrated the use of information and public policy to change behavior (cigarette sales to minors) for the good of the community. Biglan's research also demonstrated how various community services such as the police, elected officials, merchants, and psychologists can collaborate on programs for the community.

Like cigarette smoking, alcohol is a gateway drug to other drug use and abuse. More American students are consuming alcohol with 43.3% of students current alcohol users (or had least one drink of alcohol in the past 30 days) (MMWR, 2005a). Binge drinking is a major issue associated with alcohol use and abuse that spans from college campuses to entire societies across the globe. Research has shown that family greatly influences substance use and later misuse in young people. Other health policy–related research suggests that alcohol warning labels and

signs may be a useful way to inform women of child-bearing age about the danger of alcohol use during pregnancy.

Overall, illicit drug use has remained stable in this country. Globally, there are at least 15.3 million people in the world who have drug use disorders (WHO, 2008b). Yet certain drugs continue to be used by some segments of the population. For example, marijuana is the most popular drug used among youth and young adults. Consequences of illicit drug use include crimes, domestic violence, and other problems (e.g., increased HIV transmission). Proportionately, this country spends more money on law enforcement–related activities than on drug prevention, intervention, and treatment. Research has demonstrated the contribution of community psychology in preventing drug use; yet community psychologists need to take a more proactive role in advocating for more resources in prevention activities (i.e., other than law enforcement–related activities).

The United States has one of the highest rates of STDs in the industrialized world. Furthermore, epidemiological studies consistently demonstrate that concurrent STDs increase the transmission probability for HIV infection. Unfortunately, community psychologists have done little or no work in this area. It is recommended that the field of community psychology take a proactive role in heeding the recommendations of the Advisory Committee for HIV and

STD Prevention, including promoting sexuality as a healthy lifestyle.

In the absence of a cure or vaccine, prevention and information dissemination and behavioral intervention (e.g., the diffusion model) appear to be the only hope to slow the spread of HIV. Given that HIV/AIDS is also a political and social disease, coupled with the advent of new medical technologies, prevention takes on added dimensions and meanings beyond the traditional definition used in community health and community medicine.

Finally, obesity is considered an epidemic that is taking its toll on U.S. children. Racial disparities exist in prevalence rates of obesity just as they do for other health problems. The most commonly used community prevention strategies have included making systemic changes in foods and drinks available in public schools and including BMI assessments as mandatory components of health screenings conducted by schools. Although evidence suggests that these approaches may have a positive impact on children, they have yet to be implemented on a wide scale.

# Community/Organizational Psychology

*A business that makes nothing but business is a poor kind of business.*

—Henry Ford

As Sarah Anderson walked out the door of Harmony House, she glanced back at the building that had been her home away from home for the past eight months. She felt a sense of relief and a paradoxical sense of sadness as she exited for the last time. "What went wrong?" she wondered. "How could my job have become such a sore point in my life when only a few short months ago I accepted it so enthusiastically?"

Harmony House was run by a private nonprofit corporation that managed eight group homes for at-risk adolescents in Sarah's city. The adolescents were sent to the homes, including Harmony House, by judges, probation officers, schools, and parents. The group homes boasted of the ability to "turn kids around"—that is, get them off drugs, raise their school grades, and make them productive citizens again—in about six months.

A psychology major with a human services minor from a small liberal arts college, Sarah had been actively recruited by Harmony House after summer volunteer work there. Her grades were very good, and the combination of training in college and volunteer work plus her winning personality during interviews made her eagerly sought after by several community organizations. She had always wanted to be a case manager for one of them. Harmony House won her over because they offered the best salary, had an excellent training program, and had a good reputation. Harmony House seemed to be on the leading edge of innovations in treatment, which Sarah thought would give her the upper hand when she sought to move on to bigger and better agencies.

Idealistic and perhaps naïve, Sarah approached her first few days at Harmony House with immense enthusiasm. Her supervisor, Jan Hayes, mentored and coached her for the first few months. Sarah felt she was getting plenty of attention and good training under Jan. She was slowly developing a sense of confidence in handling each new difficult youth as he or she entered Harmony House.

Six months into her service, Sarah's career took a downturn that mirrored the changes occurring at corporate headquarters. Jan was moved from Harmony House to headquarters to become the chief trainer, and Sarah received a new supervisor who cared much less about mentoring her and more about keeping costs low. Sarah explained to her supervisor that she was fairly new to the job so would like to be mentored, but the new supervisor told her to stop complaining and start performing.

As the weeks passed, Sarah realized that not only was she without the tutelage and attention afforded her by Jan but that the budget cuts at the group home were taking their toll on the clients. The television broke, which left the youths with more free time than they needed. The furniture was in need of replacement, and the menu each day was much less appetizing. There were fewer field trips and fewer group therapy sessions, too. All these changes and others made the youths more discontented and harder to work with.

Sarah approached her supervisor and commented on these negative changes. His response was, "These are tough times; I have to make these cuts and changes. I suggest that if you think things are better elsewhere, you find another job." Sarah worked another two months before she resigned. She did not have any active job prospects, but she was so utterly dismayed with the changes at Harmony House that she felt she had to quit.

What would a community psychologist have to say about Sarah and her work situation? We review the organizational community's possible insights in this chapter.

## WHAT DO ORGANIZATIONAL AND COMMUNITY PSYCHOLOGY SHARE?

Community psychology examines the effects of social and environmental factors on behavior as it occurs in various levels in communities to produce beneficial change. To understand the effects of environmental factors or settings on individuals, one must understand something about the setting—in this case, organizations, whether they are private sector businesses, mental health clinics, prisons, or any other community organization. In fact, it is community psychology's position that it is futile to attempt to understand individuals apart from the settings or the contexts to which they belong (Keys & Frank, 1987; Trickett, 2009). This chapter looks at organizational psychology as it may relate to community psychology. Specifically, discussions cover ways that organizations can be conceptualized from a community perspective and how an organizational psychology might inform efforts to realize a community psychology.

## Organizational Psychology, Organizational Behavior

**Organizational psychology** approaches the examination of organizations from the perspective of the individual, whereas **organizational behavior** approaches the study of organizations from a systems perspective (Smither, 1998).

What do organizational psychology and organizational behavior have in common with community psychology? First, organizational specialists have developed theories and methodologies that go beyond the individual level of analysis (Riger, 1990; Shinn & Perkins, 2000). This is a goal of community psychology. For instance, from the study of organizations comes **organizational development (OD).** OD is a set of social science techniques designed to plan and implement long-term change in organizational settings for purposes of improving the effectiveness of organizational functioning and enhancing the individuals within the organizations (Baron & Greenberg, 1990; French & Bell, 1990). There is concern for both the organization and the individual within the organization (Beer & Walton, 1990). This focus is "in general the goals of I/O psychology . . . to better understand and optimize the effectiveness, health and well-being of both individuals and organizations" (Rogelberg, 2007, p. xxv).

An aspect of organizational psychology that parallels community psychology is the understanding that individuals and organizations have an active relationship—that is, an ever-changing, transactional relationship that occurs over an extended period of time (Keys & Frank, 1987; Maton, 2008). This is at the core of an ecological model of psychology (Kelly, 2006). For instance, at one point, an individual might be highly motivated to stay in an organization, whereas at another time, he or she may be motivated to leave, as did Sarah. Sometimes, just when a disgruntled individual wants to leave the organization, the organization needs that person and so seeks to retain him or her. The study of such dynamic relationships is pertinent to both community psychology and organizational psychology. In a review of 45 years' worth of articles in the *Journal of Applied Psychology* and the journal *Personnel Psychology*, Cascio and Aguinis (2008) identified job satisfaction, work teams, and organizational culture to be among the most popular topics in recent times (2003–2007).

## Ecology and Systems Orientation

Organizational scientists have a tradition of conducting research from an ecological perspective as well as a systems perspective (Foster-Fishman, Nowell, & Yang, 2007; Shinn & Perkins, 2000). They typically include multiple levels of a work setting (e.g., managers and employees) as well as coordinating mechanisms and processes in their research endeavors as they attempt to study and change the overall organization. It is this multilevel or holistic type of research that community psychologists hope to achieve, rather than endeavors focused merely on the individual.

Cascio (1995, 2010) challenged those in industrial/organization psychology to examine the shifts in work and technology, globalization, and the definitions of worth change the nature of organizations and leadership and management. He believed the worth of a worker shifted with changes in fundamental assumptions in business and the workplace. These paradigm shifts were important to new models for I/O psychology applications and research. For example, among the new ways of determining work performance might be "in situ" (in context) evaluations (Cascio & Aguinis, 2008).

## Distinctions

There is a point at which organizational and community psychology diverge from one another (Riger, 1990; Shinn & Perkins, 2000). In the field of organizational behavior, most efforts are aimed at improving **organizational efficiency and profits,** sometimes at the expense of the individuals in the organizations. Organizational efforts that benefit the individual are often incidental to the main task of improving the organization (Lavee & Ben-Ari, 2008; Riger, 1990). For instance, supervisory consideration of Sarah's concerns about budget cuts would focus on how it affected Harmony House and not on what would made Sarah happier. More specifically, suppose Sarah knew of a dangerous circumstance that might have resulted in Harmony House being sued, such as an elevator that was in disrepair. Her new supervisor might likely have listened to her, but not to please her. Rather, he would have been concerned about the financial well-being of the organization.

On the other hand, the primary aim in community psychology is to **enhance the functioning of individuals** in organizations (Shinn & Perkins, 2000). The intent is to **empower individuals within organizations** to create innovative solutions to the problems facing them, ensure that the innovations and changes are humanistic, and promote a sense of community within the organization (Peterson & Zimmerman, 2004). Community psychologists create a sense of community within an organization or a sense of belonging to the organization and hope to enhance human functioning. Organizational psychologists focus on the sense of community reducing turnover (Moynihan & Pandey, 2008).

Organizational psychology and community psychology may be linked in the use of **organizational theories** in community interventions and in the community research and perspectives that may inform organizational change (Keys, 2007). Though this relationship has some strong historical ties (e.g., Michigan State University's Ecological Psychology Program and University of Illinois at Chicago Circle's Organizational-Community Psychology Program's evolution into the Community and Prevention Research Program), Keys (2007) noted that these linkages were sometimes ignored or less evident in community psychologists' considerations.

## EVERYDAY ORGANIZATIONAL ISSUES

Why have this interest in organizations? People spend a great deal of their adult lives in organizations, particularly in their place of employment but also in volunteer, recreational, and educational groups. One's organizational affiliations often bring economic well-being, emotional security, happiness, a sense of self-esteem, and status, as well as the social rewards of belonging to a group and a sense of accomplishment (Schultz & Schultz, 1998). On the other hand, organizations can also frustrate and alienate people and cause much stress (Rubin & Brody, 2005). With that in mind, we turn to a sampling of the problems of today's organizations.

### Stress

Stress was discussed at length in Chapter 3 as a possible guiding model for community psychology studies or community psychologist interventions. For most, the workplace is one of the central **defining contexts** to one's identity. It can provide a source of both **pride and pain** (Blustein, 2008). Think about how, when we want to get to know someone, we ask what they do and who they work for. At least a third of our adult lives is usually spent working. The work setting changes and demands naturally affect our lives. Zohar (1999) found that work hassles are correlated with negative mood and later fatigue. And although stress from home can spill over into the workplace, the likelihood of **workplace stress** interfering with home life has been shown to be significantly greater (Mennino, Rubin, & Brayfield, 2005)

A person's experience within an organization can vary greatly because of many different variables. So we might expect that work stress and its causes are also quite varied (Rubin & Brody, 2005). Workers can be too busy *or* too bored. Interpersonal conflicts among coworkers may exist, or the individual may not feel competent or sufficiently trained to do the work. The job may be dangerous, such as working on a ward with violent individuals, or may be in a demanding and hazardous environment where noise, fumes, poor lighting, or the work itself can produce stress. There could be supervisory problems, too many or too few rules, or too much or too little structure.

Zohar (1997) proposed three types of work hassles: **role conflict** (when there are different and opposing work expectations, such as to be a friend but also to be able to criticize performance); **role ambiguity** (when it is unclear what one is expected to do, for example—not being told what the job expectations are); and **role overload** (there is just too much to do . . . empty the warehouse in 10 minutes, or do what used to be two full-time jobs).

The **workplace culture** has significant effects on negative work-to-home spillover of stress. The informal, often unspoken, expectations and values within the setting influence how much pressure people experience. For both males and females, time pressure on the job negatively influenced the work-to-home spillover. However, the perception of a "family friendly environment" and the ease with which one could take time out of the day for family-related events—that is, family-friendly cultural practices—seemed to ease the work-to-home intrusiveness (Mennino et al., 2005).

As a measure of stress-induced reactions, a link between everyday job **stress** and **alcohol and drug abuse** has been demonstrated (Frone, 2008). Early attempts to link overall alcohol and substance abuse to overall work stress were not consistently supportive to this position. But when the question was made explicit to a given context (a specific day with specific stressors), the work stress and substance abuse relationship appeared (How many drinks did you have at the end of that day?). Frone (2008) believed the stress-dampening efforts behind substance abuse were clearly demonstrated from these contextual data. Later findings suggested that a **permissive climate** at the workplace might encourage alcohol and drug use there (Frone, 2009) This climate was measured through three dimensions: substance availability, workplace descriptive norms, and workplace injunctive norms. In one estimate, 62% of a national sample reported that it was easy to bring alcohol into the workplace (Frone, 2012). However, this facilitative climate was in turn related to poor **safety**, to high levels of **strain**, and to poor **morale** in the workplace. These might be held within a definition of the workplace cultural context (O'Donnell, 2006) . The influence of the unspoken and assumed values and expectations, that is, culture, seemed critical to any consideration of workplace stress. If unchecked, this could lead to burnout.

## Stress Reduction

**Social support** from coworkers ameliorated the effects of stress and burnout in various community agencies (Bernier, 1998; Turnipseed, 1998). Snow, Swan, and Raghavan (2003) found in a sample of secretarial staff that both coping style and social support were predictive of reduced stress reactions. **Active coping** (dealing with the problem) led to the eventual lessening of stress symptoms (anxiety, depression, physical complaint), whereas **avoidance coping** (ignoring the problem, distracting oneself) did not. Having good social support increased active coping, which in turn led to fewer problems. A social support system helped the worker solve work problems. This would fit with the resilience models that were described and discussed in Chapter 3 resilience models.

Cautions are needed here, however. Social support often operates in complex ways in organizational settings (Schwarzer & Leppin, 1991). In some instances, social support can actually worsen the individual's situation (Grossi & Berg, 1991). Similarly, regard must be given to each person's cultural background and what kind of support is most appropriate for that person (Jay & D'Augelli, 1991).

Quillian-Wolever and Wolever (2003) wrote on work stress management programs. They note that these programs are based on the extensive research done on stress and coping (see Chapter 3). They propose a framework for program organization that addresses the multiple layers of the stress reaction: physical, cognitive, emotional, and behavioral. Among the interventions for physical and cognitive coping are exercise, with its positive effects on the entire organism (Freeman & Lawlis, 2001); massage therapy, which decreases muscle tension and enhanced immune functions (Zeitlin, Keller, Shiflett, Schleifer, & Bartlett, 2000); relaxation techniques leading to positive changes in several physiological indicators of stress (Cruess, Antoni, Kumar, & Schneiderman, 2000; Freeman, 2001); and meditation with its mental focusing and attendant positive immunological and neurological shifts (Davidson et al., 2003). Many techniques have been incorporated into stress management programs. The durability of these programs over time is less clear. Quillian-Wolever and Wolever (2003) conceptualize the stress management programs in terms of secondary prevention (dealing with early signs of dysfunction), yet describe universal prevention-educational programs for all workers.

The challenge to stress interventions, therefore, would be to devise environments that foster the protective and promoting factors for its members.

## Burnout

**Burnout** is a feeling of overall exhaustion that is the result of too much pressure and not enough sources of satisfaction (Maslach, Schaufeli, & Leiter, 2000; Moss, 1981). Burnout has three components:

1. The feeling of being drained or **exhausted**
2. **Depersonalizatio**n or insensitivity to others, including clients, and a kind of cynicism
3. A sense of **low personal accomplishment** or the feeling that one's efforts are futile (Jackson, Schwab, & Schuler, 1986; Leiter & Maslach, 2005)

Symptoms of burnout include loss of interest in one's job, apathy, depression, irritability, and finding fault with others. The quality of the individual's work also deteriorates, and the person often blindly and superficially follows rules and procedures (Schultz & Schultz, 1998)—topics discussed a little later in this chapter.

Burnout is most likely to affect organizational members who are initially eager, motivated, and perhaps idealistic (Van Fleet, 1991). Research has demonstrated that many individuals in community service organizations—including police officers, Social Security employees, social workers, teachers, and nurses—suffer from burnout (Adams, Boscarino, & Figley, 2006; Pines & Guendelman, 1995). You may have realized that many of these occupations are filled by women. Although an earlier study suggests that women suffer more from burnout than men (Pretty, McCarthy, & Catano, 1992), we have come to understand that there are no gender differences in burnout, but women's health may be more susceptible to work stressors (Toker, Shirom, Shapira, Berliner, & Melamed, 2005). Perhaps this was part of Sarah's problem; she was simply too burned out and was beginning to feel unhealthy, so she resigned. Poor fit between the person and the organization can also result in burnout (Maslach & Goldberg, 1998). For example, Xie and Johns (1995) examined the roles of **job scope** or job-related activities performed by the employee and burnout. They found that individuals who perceived a misfit between their abilities and the demands or scope of the job experienced higher burnout and stress.

Six organizational factors have been identified as contributing to burnout (Leiter & Maslach, 2004, 2005):

1. *Workload:* Overload of duties and responsibilities
2. *Control:* Lack of participation in decision making
3. *Reward:* Inadequate social, institutional, and/or monetary recognition
4. *Community:* Social support is wanting and lack of social integration
5. *Fairness:* Do not feel just or equitable environment, lack of reciprocity
6. *Values:* Incongruency of meaning and goals between individual and environment

Maslach and Leiter (2008) found that they could identify those who are at high risk for burnout by looking at the worker's perception of site **fairness** and earlier reports of **exhaustion** or **cynicism**. When the individual's expectations of fairness do not match those of the work site, the tendency to move toward exhaustion and cynicism increases. However, when work site fairness expectations are met, the individual seems to become more engaged (as opposed to burned out) with his or her work. These findings highlight both burnout and engagement tendencies as playing a role in burnout. Whereas Leiter and Maslach's (1998) earlier suggestion was to identify those who could stay energetic, involved, and feeling effective (i.e., engaged) versus those who would burn out, the later findings supported the role of the **perceived work environment** in determining these behaviors and attitudes. Fair settings retain personnel and maintain job effectiveness over time.

## Organizational Culture

Why is it that as individuals come and go from organizations, much as Sarah did, organizations do not seem to change much, even though their members do? The answer is organizational culture (Baron & Greenberg, 1990). Earlier in the history of its study, and as a narrower concept, organizational culture was referred to as *organizational climate.* Just as type A personality (e.g., hostile, competitive) is related to an individual's style, organizational culture is related to the personality of the organization. **Organizational culture** consists of the **beliefs, attitudes, values, and expectations** shared by most members of the organization (Schein, 1985, 1990). Once these beliefs and values are established, they tend to persist over time as the organization shapes and molds its members in its image. For example, can you recall how different all of the freshmen looked in appearance and dress your first week of classes? By senior year, many of these same students looked more similar because other students pressured them to conform to the organization's image. Students who most deviated from the campus norm often left rather than change.

Besides conformity, the prevailing organizational culture guides the organization's structure and processes. How decisions are made in the organization relates to its structure. For instance, whether decisions originate from the bottom, as when average organizational citizens participate in decisions, or from the top, when a centralized management makes the decisions, is part of the organization's structure (top and bottom) and processes (how the decision is made).

The organizational structure, including the decision-making system, also determines social class distinctions within organizations, such as status differences between executives and middle managers. The **distribution of power** is also likely to be affected by the organization's culture. If lower-level members make decisions, they will have more power than if they are not allowed to participate in decision making. Finally, organizational culture affects the ideology of the organization. If the organization views human nature as good, it will tend to allow subordinate participation (Tosi, Rizzo, & Carroll, 1986). If the culture emphasizes the development of human potential, then the members are more likely to be allowed to develop and create new ideas without much interference from the organization.

An **open culture,** one appreciative of human dignity and one that enhances human growth, is preferred by most organizational members and by most community psychologists. Open cultures foster a sense of community, better communication, and more empowerment, which can exist in an organization just as it may in neighborhoods (Detert & Edmondson, 2007; Klein & D'Aunno, 1986; Pretty & McCarthy, 1991). Such organizational cultures tend to foster employee commitment (Shadur, Kienzie, & Rodwell, 1999), among their other positive effects. However, when the culture is **repressive** in that it inhibits human growth or when there are huge gaps in what the organization professes to be and what it actually is (e.g., professing to have a positive culture that is negative in reality), high levels of member cynicism develop, performance deteriorates (Baron & Greenberg, 1990), and cohesiveness drops. Perhaps this is what happened to Sarah as she felt the disregard of her new supervisor flood over her.

Community psychologists are studying a phenomenon related to organizational culture: the sense of community within an organization. Chapter 1 discussed sense of community in some detail. *Sense of community* pertains to an individual's feeling that he or she is similar to others and that he or she and the other individuals in the setting belong there. There is a sense of "we-ness" and belonging coinciding with a sense of community.

Pretty and McCarthy (1991) explored the sense of community in men and women in corporations. They found that different features of the organization helped to predict the sense of community. What these characteristics were depended on gender and on position in the workplace. Male managers' sense of community was predicted by their perceptions of **peer cohesion** and **involvement**, whereas female managers' sense of community was predicted by their perceptions of **supervisor support, involvement**, and amount of **work pressure**.

Another aspect of organizational culture is the extent to which staff in the organization perceive a sense of empowerment; in fact, organizational culture provides an excellent framework for understanding and assessing the person–environment fit needed if empowerment is to succeed in organizations (Ambrose, Arnaud, & Schminke, 2008; Foster-Fishman & Keys, 1997). Empowerment in organizations was found to be related to employee effectiveness (Spreitzer, 1995). Pereira and Osburn (2008) reported in their review of quality circle research that work effectiveness was improved but employee attitudes toward work were not. What are the organizational characteristics that inspire empowerment? Using the case study method, Maton and Salem (1995) found at least four:

- A belief system that inspires growth, is strengths-based, and focuses beyond the individual
- An opportunity structure that is highly accessible
- A support system that is encompassing, is peer-based, and provides a sense of community
- Leadership that is inspiring, talented, shared, and committed to both the setting and the members

Such qualities very much parallel those of an open culture.

We are reminded of Leiter and Maslach's (2004, 2005) research on organizational factors related to burnout, mentioned earlier. The six dimensions of workload, control, reward, community, fairness, and values all fit within our discussions of organizational climate. Note that the fairness dimension proves pivotal in considerations of resiliency or burnout within the worksite (Maslach & Leiter, 2008). The importance of fairness and support as contextual factors has been demonstrated in a study of women and ethnic minority police officers in New York City (Morris, Shinn, & DuMont, 1999). Their commitment to the work was significantly influenced by these elements of organizational culture. The perception of fairness is important to everyone. It may be especially so for members of categories that have historically been discriminated against, such as a given gender or ethnic minority.

Elaborating on those aspects of organizational culture that encourage diversity, Bond (1999) describes a model of connectivity in which gender, race, and class might be appreciated within a work setting. **Connectivity** would result from (1) a culture of connection where people's reliance on each other to accomplish goals is known and appreciated, and (2) a recognition of multiple realities that notes many perspectives and invites participation in the creation of the narrative of what is real. She describes the creation of an organizational culture at odds with traditional American organizations' emphasis on individuality and autonomy and the norm of sameness.

As we can see, the consideration of what makes an organizational culture and what qualities of that culture encourage or sustain its members are very much a concern of community psychology. There has been increased focus on the ways in which organizational settings produce positive worker attitudes, or good citizens.

## Organizational Citizenship Behaviors

Organizational citizenship behaviors (OCBs) are the "contributions to the maintenance and enhancement of the social and psychological context that supports performance" (Organ, 1997, p. 91). Early work on these behaviors defined two different types of responses, the first an altruistic willingness to help others, and the second a conscientious willingness to meet the demands of the work setting. The second type of behavior is likened to being the "good soldier" (Organ, 1988).

Later conceptualizations of OCB have expanded these factors to include:

*Altruism*—helping of individuals

*Conscientiousness*—helping the organization to function

*Sportsmanship*—tolerating unexpected demands

*Courtesy*—helping others avoid problems

*Civic Virtue*—participating in the life of the organization (Organ, 1997; Lievens & Anseel, 2004)

Organ, Podsakoff, and Mackenzie (2006) have described *civic virtue* as an involvement with and responsibility for the life of the organization. *Sportsmanship*, or the willingness to do more without complaint for the good of the company, is also a more system-focused aspect of citizenship. Both of these are contrasted to the *altruism* factor, which is being helpful to individuals with whom one works. Coyne and Ong (2007) found that sportsmanship was a very good indicator of institutional commitment—that is, it was negatively related to intentions to leave a workplace. Similarly, Paillé and Grima (2012), in a study of white-collar French workers, found sportsmanship to be a strong predictor of commitment to the work organization.

Research has suggested that leader–member communications influence OCB (Truckenbrodt, 2000; Wayne & Green, 1993) and/or perceptions of system fairness (Organ, 1990; Schnake, 1991). Tepper (2000) wrote of "interactional justice," where "treating employees with respect, honesty, propriety, and sensitivity to their personal needs" (p. 179) contributed to an individual's commitment to the work setting.

Burroughs and Eby (1998) studied workplace sense of community and its relationship to OCB. Their sense of community scale had nine factors:

Sense of belonging (membership)

Coworker support (influence; expression of ideas)

Team orientation (integration; engaged and involved)

Emotional safety (shared emotional connection; mutual and trusting interaction)

Spiritual bond (anchored in common values and spirit)

Tolerance for differences (diversity is all right)

Neighborliness (help with advice and resources)

Collectivism (similarity with others)

Reflection (time for thinking out problems)

Of note, the four factors originally identified by McMillan and Chavis (1986) were present here in some form. McMillan and Chavis' four dimensions were: (1) membership, (2) influence, (3) integration and fulfillment of needs, and (4) shared emotional connection. However, Burroughs and Eby's (1999) work related context for sense of community produced dimensions reflecting this context. These nine factors combined into a single Psychological Sense of Community at Work measurement (PSCW). The PSCW was significantly related both to organizational citizenship behavior and to workers' job satisfaction.

The relationship between psychological sense of community and organizational outcomes was again shown in an Australian study (Purkiss & Rossi, 2007). Better sense of community was predictive of better workplace attachment, less absenteeism, and lower job turnover.

Recent refinements to the study of OCB and its impact on workers suggest differences in how we think about our team group (who we work with) and how we think about the larger organization or company.

Organizational support for the worker leads to commitment to the organization. Work team support leads to commitment to the team. Both organizational and team commitment result in OCB. However, job performance—that is, how well one does—is more related to team commitment. Loyalty to one's job is more a matter of commitment to one's organization. Change-oriented (being helpful to innovations within the setting) organizational citizenship behavior was found to be best predicted by employees' identification with their working group in combination with their openness to change when they felt a sense of control and power in their workplace. When the sense of control and power was not present, this prediction did not hold true (Seppälä, Lipponen, Bardi, & Pirttilä-Backman, 2012). In a related manner, perceived organizational support and psychological empowerment were positively related to organizational citizen behaviors. In turn, perceived psychological empowerment and organizational citizen behaviors positively related to overall job performance (Chiang & Hsieh, 2012).

These findings extend our understanding of behaviors in the workplace—in particular, the concept of being a "good citizen" or as Organ (1988) puts it, a "good soldier" in service to his or her work setting. The research highlights that the phenomenon is transactional in nature, with the setting needing to provide a reason for the "good citizenship" and the promise of better performance and loyalty.

## Work and Self-Concept

Work has consequences for our sense of well-being and how we feel about ourselves (Blustein, 2006, 2008; Fassinger, 2008; Fouad & Bynner, 2008; Lucas, Clark, Georgellis, & Diener, 2004).

> When people work or consider work, they are engaging in an overt and complex relationship with their social world. For many people, working is the 'playing field' of their lives, where their interactions with others and with existing social mores are most prominent with opportunities for satisfaction and . . . joy, as well as major challenges . . . and at times, pain. (Blustein, 2008, p. 232)

Given this importance of work to our self-definition, any holistic consideration of our functioning should include aspects of our working world.

## Dealing with a Diverse Workforce

Findings on the effects of group diversity on group functioning have been mixed over the past few decades of research. Tsui, Egan, and O'Reilly (1992) found that as workers became more different from their groups, absenteeism increased and the level of job commitment declined. This finding was strongest for Whites and for males. However, Huo (2003) has found that "super-ordinate" group membership could overcome "sub-ordinate" group memberships, so if identification with a company is powerful enough, individuals would come to ignore the other differences of race, gender, or other diversity designators. Mannix and Neale (2005) summarize the studies to date on diversity in the workplace as mixed in their results. They point out the importance of organizational context to the outcomes. They cite as an example Chatman and Spataro's (2005) finding that visibly different individuals were more cooperative within a business setting when collectivist values were emphasized over individualistic values. Following their review of the research on diversity in the workplace, Mannix and Neale (2005) provide three recommendations: (1) the types of tasks and goals given diverse teams should be carefully determined, because what is being asked of the team determines the dynamics within the team; (2) efforts to connect team members by establishing commonalities and similarities result in better group identity and effort; and (3) encouragement should be given to respect the minority voice, because the pressure to conform is a normal part of group processes. Ely and Thomas (2001) encourage a shift in rationale for diversity within business settings. They argue that a "learning and effectiveness" focus for diversification efforts would highlight the advantages to seeking different perspectives and the rewards that underlie the understanding of these perspectives. Diversity is important because we live in a diverse world. An awareness of the processes whereby diverse perspectives may be of value to group products and the manner in which these contributions may best serve the group can affect the integration of diverse populations and diverse perspectives into organizations. This knowledge derived from organizational psychology is certainly applicable to communities as a whole and community psychology in particular.

Organizations can promote diversity by encouraging a culture of connectedness and collaboration and of recognizing multiple realities (as opposed to insisting on a singular reality, determined by the historically empowered). To bring about change, the usefulness of "connected disruption," where the value of "both/and" challenges the value of the singular truth of the powerful and privileged, is suggested (Bond, 1999).

## Other Ecological Conditions

Size of organizations is important, too. Members of small organizations report more supportive environments, less discrimination, and more loyalty to the organization (MacDermid, Hertzog, Kensinger, & Zipp, 2001). On the other hand, large organizations often create negative conditions. For instance, Hellman, Greene, Morrison, and Abramowitz (1985) examined residential mental health treatment programs by measuring staff and client perceptions. Not surprisingly, the larger the program, the more the members experienced anxiety, held negative views of the psychosocial aspects of the organization, and perceived greater psychological distance from the organization.

However, size is just one consideration in cultural milieu. Examining the psychological sense of community (PSC) at work, Burroughs and Eby (1998) found that size of work group did not affect people's PSC. Rather, the individual's match between their personal goals and those of the organization significantly predicted PSC. In turn, the PSC related to job satisfaction, which related to loyalty, courtesy, and willingness to help within the organization.

The growing diversity in the workplace has produced other ecological considerations for organizations. Fassinger (2008) discussed the trends toward larger proportions of the workforce being women, people of color, sexual minorities, and people with physical disabilities. The impact of such shifts in the composition of organizations can be both beneficial and challenging. Case in Point 12.1 is an excellent illustration of the way organizational psychology and applied social psychology can make contributions to the concerns of the work setting ecology and its impact on a diverse workforce.

## CASE IN POINT 12.1

## Consulting on Diversity

In the 1990s, a New England company called on a team of community psychologists to help deal with diversity issues (Bond, 2007). A multiyear assessment and intervention followed. Previous work on systems-level change pointed out the positive effects of a culture that sought to "learn from diversity" (Kochan et al., 2002). Such deeper level attitudinal shifts brought more lasting changes within an organization's culture (Harrison, Price, & Bell,

1998; Harrison, Price, Gavin, & Florey, 2002; Thomas & Ely, 1996). The consultants sought to bring about more than superficial alterations in the company's numbers.

Using a social ecological perspective, the consultants were mindful of resources, the distribution of those resources, and the importance of understanding behaviors in context. Using a language of worker "needs and competencies" and company

"resources and demands," they looked at how actors and settings influenced each other. At the same time, given the nature of system interdependency, the consultants were aware that changes could be considered synergistic in nature. Small, specific changes could result in larger and wider alterations in attitudes and behaviors. The changes could be at the formal policy level or at the informal, cultural level (O'Donnell, 2006).

## CASE IN POINT 12.1

## *(Continued)*

To support diversity, they aimed to foster an organizational climate that emphasized:

- Understanding others in the context of their culture and their situation
- Shared goals and destiny (we all win or lose)
- An understanding and valuing of differences (along with appreciation of the larger social and historical forces that have brought about these differences)
- Taking responsibility for their effects on their environment (impact versus intent—what happens to others versus what an individual meant to do)

They also were respectful of individual experience—that is, the subjective world.

Facing changing local demographics and global markets, the company realized the need for change. With support from the top (president, human resources director), the consultants worked through a variety of departments, using existing leadership and work teams. The interventions were fitted to the situation, in collaboration with onsite workers. The phases to the intervention included needs assessment, setting the stage for collaboration, developing training appropriate for the site in collaboration with workers and leaders, providing training and dealing with group dynamics, assessing

change, and working for institutionalization of changes.

Outcomes of the various phases of this long-term intervention were measured both qualitatively and quantitatively. The results supported the effectiveness of the project in terms of attitudinal change and in terms of enhanced understanding of the nuances of what it means to support diversity in the given company context. Changes in the organizational culture were notable and included some measurable differences in both formal policies and informal practices along with some attendant changes in employment patterns (e.g., more diversity in the workplace, more diversity in leadership).

## TRADITIONAL TECHNIQUES FOR MANAGING PEOPLE

When Sarah left Harmony House, she was a discontented employee. She was not the only one hurt by her decision to leave, though. The organization also suffered. Harmony House would now have to recruit and select a replacement for Sarah as well as train and indoctrinate the new person. Clients might feel disoriented when they came looking for Sarah and could not find her. What do organizations traditionally do to attract and retain good members and manage poor members? Are these strategies helpful?

### Compensation Packages

Many of the traditional attempts by organizations to treat employees well or terminate them focus on the individual. An age-old method of motivating employees to work hard and work well is to manipulate compensation levels. In fact, setting compensation levels is often considered the primary function of many human resources management staffs (Milkovich & Boudreau, 1991). Interestingly, organizational members rarely mention pay as the job facet most related to job satisfaction. Nonetheless, one of the common ways organizations attempt to motivate their members is by adjusting compensation and benefits packages. One study showed that raising wage and salary levels was the most common response to reducing quitting in organizations (Bureau of National Affairs, 1981). However, in reality, pay adjustments only partially increase job satisfaction (Schultz & Schultz, 1998). Even when employees participate in their own performance reviews, which are often tied to compensation levels, satisfaction with pay remains unaffected (Morgeson, Campion, & Maertz, 2001).

Unfortunately, wage disparities between men and women have not been rectified. One study reports that women make 75% of what men make (American Association of University Women [AAUW],

2007). The wage difference appears to grow over time past college graduation, from 20% less 1 year postgraduation to 31% smaller 10 years postgraduation while controlling for occupation, hours working, and parenthood factors. Data from the U.S. Census (2009) placed women earning 77% of men's earnings and ethnic minorities at even greater disadvantage (African American women make 70 cents on the dollar; African American men make 74 cents; Hispanic or Latina women make about 60 cents; Hispanic men make almost 66 cents; AAUW, 2011). Note that earlier descriptions of burnout and of good citizenship both emphasize the need for fairness. One might wonder what Sarah was earning compared to her level of responsibilities, as well as her comparison points.

## Rules and Regulations

Organizations control member behavior by means of policies and regulations. Policy manuals and codes of ethics for employees have become quite common. Some policies are specific: "No gambling on company property." Others are less so: "Employees are expected to be loyal to the company." Add to this the multitude of public policies or federal and state legislation intended to regulate organizations and the individuals in them, and the total number of regulations is overwhelming. Federal Equal Employment Opportunity Guidelines and the Occupational Safety and Health Regulations alone would create a stack of policies higher than the average person is tall!

The extent to which employees follow organizational policies is unclear, but some classic studies of employee behavior indicate that not all organizational members appreciate regulations. In the classic study of the Western Electric Plant in Hawthorne, Illinois, the men of the bank wiring room purposely worked *below* the production standard set by their supervisors. Why? They believed that if they worked up to standard, their superiors would simply raise the standard (Roethlisberger & Dickson, 1939), thereby forcing the men to work harder. It is known today that in professional bureaucracies such as hospitals, universities, and other human services agencies, professionals prefer to operate according to their *own* codes rather than the formal policies of their organizations (Cheng, 1990; Mintzberg, 1979). Most organizational members have little say in the policies or regulations of their organization; that may be the primary reason they are discontented with the guidelines and violate the rules, as is often found in studies of organizational rules. In addition, rule violation can result in discipline, such as termination, demotion, or leave without pay. Atwater, Carey, and Waldman (2001) found that discipline is often perceived as unfair and that both recipients and observers consequently lose respect for the person administering the discipline as well as for the organization. Notably, the perception of fairness is seen as critical to work-setting stress (Maslach & Leiter, 2008). This appears to be a prime focus for anyone dealing with a work-setting community.

These traditional methods of regulating individuals in organizations have not typically been what community psychologists would recommend. Most were aimed at the individual within the organization. They neither addressed nor acknowledged the role that the context or the organization itself plays in producing and influencing individual behavior. However, there is a growing body of work focusing on the culture and the contexts of work. Findings have reinforced the advantages of fairness, empowerment, and the development of a sense of community.

We turn our attention to aspects of organizational change.

## OVERVIEW OF ORGANIZATIONAL CHANGE

### Reasons for Change

Organizations require change for a number of reasons, a few of which are mentioned briefly here. Pressures for change may be internal or external. **Internal pressures to change** come from within and include pressures from clients, staff, and supervisors. As in the case of Harmony House, internal budget pressures can force change. Organizations also sometimes change their focus or offer new or different services, which leads to further change.

Forces outside of the organization create **external pressures to change.** Government regulations, external competition, political and social trends, and other factors create the need for organizations to adapt. For example, the move to deinstitutionalize people who are mentally disabled has forced communities to provide alternative services, such as group homes. Both the availability of homes and the conditions in the institutions have been affected by this trend.

## Issues Related to Organizational Change

As already mentioned in Chapters 4 and 5, change is difficult. One reason organizational change is hard is because many organizational members resist change. They feel threatened by changes, perhaps because they do not feel competent to handle them or they do not want to put forth the effort to adapt to them. Similarly, some organizations are more difficult to change than others—for example, public sector organizations, which are often restricted by laws and civil service requirements (Shinn & Perkins, 2000).

There are other reasons change in organizations is complicated. Organizations are interdependent systems (Tosi et al., 1986). The people in the organization influence the organization, and the organization influences the people. One cannot be changed without changes occurring in the other. For example, suppose in his budget cuts, the Harmony House supervisor also decided to cut staff to save money. Fewer staff members means less attention to each youth; fewer staff members also means more work for the remaining staff. Hence, the services of the organization may start to decline; its reputation might also decline, and it would perhaps attract fewer clients and fewer qualified job applicants because of the budget cuts. Change also means a reallocation of resources and a change to the processes by which allocation is determined (Seidman & Tseng, 2011). This process is perceived to be fraught with risk (Stebbings & Braganza, 2009).

Difficulty in changing organizations also lies in the organizational tendency to look for change that fits within the existing organizational paradigm (Cheng, 1990). Changing organizations requires customizing the intervention and fitting the change to one the organization can understand, fitting the assumptions regarding operational paradigms (Constantine, 1991).

To ensure that change is indeed needed, change should commence with *action research*. The research can also address whether the organization is ready for change. Survey-guided feedback has been suggested as a viable method for monitoring organizational change (Shinn & Perkins, 2000). **Survey-guided feedback** involves the systematic collection of data from organizational members who also receive subsequent and repeated feedback about the changes.

Both need and readiness for change are generally prompted by dissatisfaction with the organization by its members (Baron & Greenberg, 1990). The age of the organization is also important, because there are different stages of development for community organizations (Bartunek & Betters-Reed, 1987). Some preliminary plan for change should also be in place, although a long-range plan may be better (Taber, Cooke, & Walsh, 1990). Such planning should involve staff and perhaps clients in all phases. Staff participation has a significant effect on both job satisfaction and self-esteem (Roberts, 1991; Sarata, 1984). Feeling empowered—that is, that one makes a difference and that one has some control over their work situation—is clearly related to positive feelings about what one does in the work setting as well as to one's effectiveness (Gregory, Albritton, & Osmonbekov, 2010; Spreitzer, Kizilos, & Nason, 1997).

Change in organizations can occur at the organizational level, the group level, or the individual level. Although some community psychologists might prefer to change the whole organization—the whole community, so to speak—often it is the subparts of the organization that are easiest to change. Next is an examination of selected organizational change methods.

## CHANGING ORGANIZATIONAL ELEMENTS

Change can occur at the top and all the way to the bottom of an organization. We consider possible changes in leadership style, which can influence how an organization functions, and then the processes by which organizational change can be facilitated. We finish with two examples of organizational change that have been attempted at the production level.

### Leadership

Eagly, Johannesen-Schmidt, and van Egan (2003) described and discussed the variety of ways in which leadership styles have been defined. Early studies spoke in terms of **task-focused** versus **interpersonally focused** leaders (Bales, 1950; Fiedler, 1971; Likert, 1961). The task-focused leader was interested in getting the work done the most efficient way possible. The interpersonally focused leader was concerned for the people in the process, worrying about how people feel and seeing the importance of the social climate and interpersonal relations as end products in and of themselves. An interesting development in understanding the effectiveness of these styles was studied and summarized by Fiedler (1971), who found the task focus style most effective in very favorable and unfavorable situations. On the other hand, the interpersonal focus style was best suited to nonextreme situations. He called this a **contingency model** for leadership style. (See Table 12.1.)

Other researchers distinguish between **democratic/participatory** styles and more **autocratic/directive** styles (Lewin & Lippett, 1938). The democratic leader asked for opinions and discussed the options with those to be affected. The autocratic leader made the decisions him- or herself and then acted. In a classic study on the effects of democracy versus autocracy leadership, Lewin, Lippett, and White (1939) found the autocratic style to yield more aggression and frustration in a children's group and the democratic style to result in more spontaneity. These initial findings have led to the study of leadership styles' effects on productivity and satisfaction. Gastil's (1994) meta-analysis of these studies on the two types of leadership yields mixed results. Although democratic styles brought more group satisfaction, the results were moderate at best. Neither democratic nor autocratic styles led to superior productivity.

Eagly and associates (2003) performed a meta-analysis of leadership studies using the newer categories of **transformational, transactional, or laissez-faire** styles (Bass, 1998). In the *transformational* style, the leader inspired through example, established trusting relationships, empowered those they

---

**TABLE 12.1    Examples of Three Leadership Styles**

Transformational—Interactions are positive and inspirational. You feel like a valued member of a team whose opinion is respected, valued, and sought out. You sense the leader's commitment to and interest in the work. This enthusiasm is contagious, and so you go seeking the leader when you have a good idea and take the initiative at times.

Transactional—The leader is seen and heard from when directives are being issued or feedback being provided. Often, seeing the leader could mean more work or feedback on what one has done. You work to complete tasks. There is a focus and a goal, and it is clear that your worth is determined by how well you follow orders.

Laissez faire—The leader is rarely seen or heard from in a meaningful way. S/he is absent from your work life. It feels as if you are working by yourself rather than in a workgroup or team that is interdependent on each other. Things can feel chaotic, unfocused, or not goal directed.

*Source:* Adapted from: Eagly, Johannesen-Schmidt, & van Engen (2003).

worked with, encouraged worker efforts, and worked for innovation. The *transactional* style was characterized by feedback on performance—positive when things were done well and negative when there were problems, intervening only when things were "exceptionally" bad. A third style of leadership, called *laissez-faire*, was one where the leader was absent and uninvolved. Eagly and colleagues found women to be more transformational and better at contingent rewarding, and men to be more transactional, using negative corrective feedback. Notably, both men and women preferred the leadership qualities in women. Women leaders were seen as inspiring better effort, being more effective, and resulting in better satisfaction with their leadership.

One might expect that there would be more women leaders, given these findings. But such is not the case. Later studies found that despite women's better leadership behaviors, the "definition" of a good leader remained "masculine" in nature (Koenig, Eagly, Mitchell, & Ristikari, 2011). Women faced the dilemma of being seen as nonfeminine when exhibiting good leadership skills (Eagly & Karau, 2002). Although the conceptual and research-based framework for understanding leadership and its effects on groups has been changed by the work of Eagly and her associates, the problem of gender-based expectations continues to plague organizations.

In an even more radical shift in understanding leadership, Wielkiewicz and Stelzner (2005) took exception to its person-centered focus. They argued that leadership was not a personal characteristic. Rather, leadership "emerged" from the interactions with a given context. Using James Kelly's (1968) ecological framework, Wielkiewicz and Stelzner argued that leadership was more process-driven and dynamic. Decisions were not made by the leader so much as they emerged from the interactions of those involved. Given this model, what was critical to leadership were the participatory structures and the genuineness of the interactions. Both structure and process were involved. The advantages of participation, diversity of opinion, and democracy were a part of the dynamic model.

Eagly and Chin (2010) have criticized the lack of research on diversity in leadership. What advantages are there to a leadership with a diverse background in times of increasingly diverse demographics? What new leadership models might emerge from expanded global and cultural backgrounds? And what happens when advantages have been demonstrated (such as women's superior transformational leadership style, mentioned earlier)? Community psychology would echo the need to answer these questions.

The work on gender and transformational leadership fit well with community psychology aspirations to diversity, empowerment, and relational processes. In Wielkiewicz and Stelzner's model, we see a proposal for a contextually driven, process-oriented model leadership. Finally, the dearth of work on diversity and leadership denies us information on new models, new skill repertoires, and more diverse understanding of leadership processes and what goes into the selection of leaders. Community psychology would, by its nature, find all of these issues and questions of interest.

## Reorganization

Several techniques may be employed for changing the whole organization or system; two are examined here. One change strategy is reorganization of the organization. **Reorganization** means that a structural change takes place; that is, the tasks, interpersonal relationships, reward system, or decision-making techniques are rearranged (Beer & Walton, 1990).

Organizations can also be reorganized by becoming linked to, affiliated with, or networked with other organizations. Networks, enabling systems, and umbrella organizations were discussed in an earlier chapter. Suffice it to say here that these "master" organizations help ensure the survival and success of their member organizations. However, competition, lack of coordinating mechanisms, and other factors can diminish the effectiveness of such federations. The power of collaboration is exemplified in Nowell's (2009) study of community organizations that networked to bring greater effectiveness to their work. She found that the member relationships were the best predictors of system changes and of willingness to organize and to change policies. If one was going to take the risk of committing to doing something, it was best if the partners knew each other. As described in the Crude Law of Social Relationships (Deutsch, 2000), the stronger the relationships, the more likely the cooperation. This is related to "social capital," or the value placed on the relationship to the person and/or to the system. (An example could be a group of friends whom you like and hold in high regard, who have done favors for you before. If that group calls on you to do them a favor, it is likely you will do it. In contrast, a group of people whom you barely know might ask for the same favor, and you might find it easy to decline.) However, in bringing about the actual coordination efforts, such as changing forms to get greater compatibility across agencies or developing explicit procedures for referrals, relationships themselves were insufficient. For achieving these specific types of activities, "strong leadership" and "decision-making capabilities" were necessary.

Foster-Fishman and colleagues (2007) provide a systems-based model for examining organizational and community systems and then using the findings to help direct change. Drawing on the earlier work based on Checkland's (1981) ideas of *soft systems,* Foster-Fishman and associates (2007) gather qualitative data to understand the subjective nature of the system targeted for change and the multiplicity of perspectives that make up the perception of the system. They also use a *system dynamics* theory (Forrester, 1969; Jackson, 2003) to look at feedback and interaction within the system, causes and consequences of action, and what brings about shifts in a system. By studying these patterns, the "levers for change" might be identified. When these levers are activated, the system as a whole changes. Foster-Fishman and coworkers believe that this richer and more complex paradigm provides a true picture of a system at work and helps devise meaningful shifts in what that system is. More linear and simplistic explanatory models lead to the proposal of one component interventions for system change, which by its nature leads to failure or at best serendipitous success. Foster-Fishman and colleagues (2007) argue that systems-level changes may not be always needed, but when they are, an understanding of the various parts of an organization and how the parts interact is critical to making changes. Systems theories are helpful to understanding and acting in organizations. We now look at two types of organizational change. Both emphasize the importance of interconnectedness and of empowerment of the workers within the organization.

## Quality of Work Life Programs

Another change that can be made throughout an organization is to introduce **quality of work life (QWL) programs**, or programs of participatory decision making that create long-term change in organizations. Recall that these programs include **participatory decision making**, designed to encourage democracy and staff motivation, satisfaction, and commitment. Such programs also foster career development and leadership by empowering or fostering decision making in others besides the leaders or managers already designated on the organizational chart (Hollander & Offerman, 1990). In QWL programs, the staff and possibly the clients design programs and action plans that they think will be effective and are well reasoned. The programs are then implemented and perhaps funded by higher levels in the organization. Such programs have been shown to be effective in improving organizational productivity as well as employee satisfaction in various settings (Baron & Greenberg, 1990). Some (Labianca, Gray, & Brass, 2000; Randolph, 2000) found that empowerment can be particularly elusive and a resisted concept in many organizations.

Managers have found that empowering those under them to participate in decision making in QWL programs can be a good idea (French & Bell, 1990). One example of a QWL program has been quality circles. In **quality circles**, small groups of volunteer employees (or volunteer clients of a community service) meet regularly to identify and solve problems related to organizational conditions. Quality circles can humanize organizational environments as well as increase participants' satisfaction with the organization (Baron & Greenberg, 1990). A meta-analysis of quality circle studies found that they have a moderate but significant effect on employee performance (Pereira & Osburn, 2007). If Sarah and other employees of Harmony House had participated in a quality circle, they might have realized that they were all discontented with the changes and developed innovative solutions to the organization's problems *before* staff turnover became high. Quality circles exemplify the "participation and democracy" work practices of empowerment theory, which have shown positive results (Klein, Ralls, Smith Major, & Douglas, 2000).

Hamilton, Basseches, and Richards (1985) suggested that the number of programs in communities that promote participatory decision making is steadily increasing, but several studies suggest that simply allowing participation in community organizations is hollow and therefore not beneficial. Prestby, Wandersman, Florin, Rich, and Chavis (1990) found that for individuals to continue to participate in block or neighborhood booster associations, benefits (such as getting to know one's neighbors better or learning a new skill such as public speaking) must exceed costs (such as feeling the association never gets anything done or having less time to spend with friends and family). Community organizations need to manage their incentive efforts so that participation by others results in satisfaction. Researchers have shown that quality circles improved employee satisfaction and performance (Klein et al., 2000). However, these results were short-lived without wider support. The larger ecological context played a critical role in the integration of these kinds of organizational changes.

Those living and working closest to the issues seemed best informed on how to address them. Quality circles and other participatory methods in organizations take advantage of this by empowering involved individuals to solve their own problems. Workplace effectiveness has been shown to improve (Klein et al., 2000; Pereira & Osburn, 2007). Yet efforts to change must be considered within the larger system (Kelly, 1980; Jackson, 2003).

## Team Building

One technique for improving groups in organizations is team building. **Team building** is an ongoing method in which group members are encouraged to work together in the spirit of cooperation that contributes to the group's sense of community. The purpose of team building is to *accomplish* goals and analyze tasks, member relations, and processes such as decision making in the group. In other words, the group is simultaneously the object of and a participant in the process. Teams are proving to be such a powerful force for empowerment that they form the basic building block for "intelligent organizations" (Pinchot & Pinchot, 1993). Three meta-analyses of team building across three decades have shown team building to be effective (Klein et al., 2009; Neuman, Edwards, & Raju, 1989; Svyantek, Goodman, Benz, & Gard, 1999). Klein and colleagues (2009) found team building to relate to better cognitive and emotional outcomes. As well, teamwork brought better processing—working through of problems— and better results.

Team building, or **team development,** as it is also known (Sundstrom, DeMeuse, & Futrell, 1990), has been used to improve staff services to clients at mental health agencies (Bendicsen & Carlton, 1990; Cohen, Shore, & Mazda, 1991), as well as to implement interventions in schools (Nellis, 2012) and improve the performance of both the corrections officers and staff at forensic (psychiatric) prisons (Miller, Maier, & Kaye, 1988). Some argue, however, that many employees resist teams primarily because of mistrust and low tolerance for change (Kirkman, Jones, & Shapiro, 2000).

The demand for team development consultation in business continues to grow along with research publications defining and explaining the processes (Offerman & Spiros, 2001; Stagl & Salas, 2008). Surveying members of the Academy of Management's Organizational Development and

## CASE IN POINT 12.2

# Managing Change

The assumption is that what managers do can influence worker well-being. Grant, Christianson, and Price (2007) considered how well-intentioned management decisions could bring negative as well as positive consequences. They found an abundant research literature on the positive effects of organizational interventions on employee well-being (Fisher, 2003; Judge, Thoresen, Bono, & Patton, 2001; Podsakoff, MacKenzie, Paine, & Bachrach, 2000).

On closer examination, they found that sometimes practices that brought increased satisfaction in one aspect of well-being brought decreases in well-being on another dimension. For example, when workers got increased responsibility, they reported greater psychological satisfaction with their work, but also reported increased stress and strain as the result of these changes

(Campion & McClelland, 1993). Also, if there were monetary incentives built into job performance, the resulting pay discrepancies could lead to social discord (Ferraro, Pfeffer, & Sutton, 2005; Munkes & Diehl, 2003). These have been seen as "trade-offs" in the efforts to bring about well-being.

Grant and associates (2007) proposed that an alternative way to think of these trade-off potentials was to consider them synergistically (that they could react together to bring about an even greater effect). This called for a broader conceptualization of who could be affected by changes and how the changes affected the larger system. So measurement of effects must examine more than the individual; it should include those around them. Also, measurements should be on several different aspects of well-being—physical,

psychological, and/or social. Grant and colleagues also recommended that managers think along longer timelines and be aware of the influence of historical influences on effects. Managers who have longer time horizons for their actions have happier workers (Bluedorn & Standifer, 2006). Finally, the recommendation was to seek deeper as well as broader data on workers (attitudes?) on a continuing basis. Companies that performed regular attitudinal surveys reported less job turnover, greater worker satisfaction, and better performance at the individual and company level (Huselid, 1995).

Clearly, driven by ecological considerations of complex effects and awareness of context and time dimensions, these recommendations use community perspectives as well as research bases to derive their directions.

Change Division, the authors find the two most often cited goals for training are goal setting and communication. The three areas with least adequate theory for practice are diversity issues, empowerment, and resource management. It is hard not to note that of these three areas, two come directly from the community psychology lexicon. In turn, note that the issues of team building (i.e., sharing of information, developing common goals, establishment of identity) are clearly skills that come from team building/organizational management studies.

All efforts at change need to be approached with caution. In Case in Point 12.2, we are reminded that systems are complex. Some outcomes are unintended and a long time in developing.

## Summary

Organizational and community psychology are related, with common origins in theory and applications (Shinn & Perkins, 2000). Whereas organizational psychology primarily focuses on the workplace, community psychology takes in a wider array of settings and interventions. They have much to learn from each other's research literature (Keys, 2007).

Organizational psychology addresses a wide variety of workplace topics: work stress, burnout, organizational culture, "good citizenship," diversity in the workforce. Notably, the conceptual models increasingly use ecological models, empowerment, and participation among their important factors.

Organizations and agencies that are better places to work provide better services and products to their clients. Historically, organizations have considered individual employees' characteristics rather than anything organizational to be the root of problems. Traditional techniques for managing problem individuals have been to alter compensation packages, or to institute rules and regulations. However, the development of new work models (or the return to older work models) provides alternatives to the dehumanizing, industrial-age conceptions of work and performance. How we think of leadership has been evolving away from a White, male model. Methods for changing the whole organization include reorganization—for example, creating smaller, friendlier work teams within a larger company or corporation. Another organizational strategy for change is to institute quality of work life programs. These are programs where staff members and perhaps clients participate in planning and designing the changes the organization needs.

The parallel course of organizational psychology and community psychology can be seen from this brief survey of work-setting topics.

# The Future of Community Psychology

*We are the dreams of our parents.*
—Deborah Iida, *Middle Son*

*Our human families have been extending and our empathy expanding for thousands of years.*
—Ehrlich and Ornstein, *Humanity on a Tightrope*

Mary's first choice for college was Cambridge University in England. Of course, she was eight years old at the time. When she finally applied to colleges several years later, she did not include Cambridge, but decided to try the American University of Paris. She was accepted. What surprised her parents was her willingness to even consider going away from home, much less away from Wisconsin and the Midwest. She had redefined her boundaries. The normal had expanded beyond her parents' horizons.

What she found in Paris was a student body and a faculty that was equally open to global and multicultural perspectives. They were happy to read novels from around the world as readily as those from the American, British, or French canon. She loved it. The university challenged her and her understanding of the world. She believed she was being prepared for the world in which she would live.

This story matches with other trends in colleges and universities. Study-abroad programs have existed for a long time, and they are now being used in record numbers. These programs encourage travel, exploration of global sites, and the development of an international perspective. At some U.S. colleges, more than half of the student body has studied abroad before graduation. One college we know of had students on all the world's continents at one time (including Antarctica). In similar ways, community psychology has grown beyond its original boundaries, and we are in areas never imagined by the original Swampscott, Massachusetts, "community psychologists." In what ways have we lived the dreams of the founders of the American movement? And in what ways have we gone beyond their horizons? Where are the challenges for today and tomorrow?

## THE ESTABLISHMENT OF INSTITUTIONAL MARKERS

The dream of community psychology seems to be born in "distant mists" by now. Yet it was really just a few academic generations ago that community psychology in the United States was formally born. From a set of ideas and concepts regarding the potential for psychology outside of the office and the laboratory, community psychology has developed a value system, an intervention focus, a skill set, and theories to direct our work in society and our research programs.

There are several markers of the establishment of this area of psychology. There is a *Handbook of Community Psychology* (Rappaport & Seidman, 2000). The *Annual Review of Psychology* publishes community psychology–oriented chapters with regularity (Table 13.1). The *Annual Review* is considered by many to be among the flagship publications in psychology (Robins, Gosling & Craik, 1999). It is ranked number one in citations by the Reuters Journal Citation Report (Annual Reviews, 2011).

**TABLE 13.1** *Annual Review of Psychology* Chapters on Community Psychology, Authors and Dates Since 1973 (First Chapter)

1. Cowen (1973)
2. Kessler and Albee (1975)
3. Kelly, Snowden, and Munoz (1977)
4. Sundberg, Snowden, and Reynolds (1978)
5. Bloom (1980)
6. Iscoe and Harris (1984)
7. Gesten and Jason (1987)
8. Heller (1990)
9. Levine, Toro, and Perkins (1993)
10. Reppucci, Woolard, and Fried (1999)
11. Shinn and Toohey (2003)
12. Trickett (2009)

---

**TABLE 13.2** Journals in Community and Preventive Psychology

---

*American Journal of Community Psychology*

*Journal of Community Psychology*

*Journal of Community and Applied Social Psychology*

*Global Journal of Community Psychology*

*Journal of Prevention and Intervention in the Community*

*Journal of Primary Prevention*

*Prevention Science*

---

There are also several research journals dedicated to community and preventive psychology (Table 13.2). Research universities are producing a steady stream of articles in community psychology journals. A review investigated which universities produced the most articles published in the *American Journal of Community Psychology* and the *Journal of Community Psychology* (Jason, Pokorny, Patka, Adams, & Morello, 2007). These universities were numbered among the top major research universities within the United States (Table 13.3).

A number of graduate programs can be found in community psychology or clinical-community psychology (as cited in Chapter 1). Because there are graduate programs, there are graduates in community psychology who in turn produce their own work. The future of community psychology seems established within the systems of psychology with regard to publications, institutions of higher education, and the products of these institutions—research and graduates.

---

**TABLE 13.3** Universities Publishing in the *American Journal of Community Psychology* and *Journal of Community Psychology*, 1973–2004

---

1. UCLA
2. Arizona State University
3. University of Illinois, Chicago
4. University of Michigan
5. Vanderbilt University
6. Michigan State University
7. University of Rochester
8. University of Illinois, Urbana–Champaign
9. Yale University
10. University of Maryland, College Park
11. University of California, Berkeley
12. DePaul University
13. Pennsylvania State University
14. New York University
15. University of South Carolina

---

*Source:* Jason et al. (2007).

Despite all these signs, Weinstein (2006) expressed concern over several institutional trends. She believed the number of identified community and clinical-community programs to be declining. Was this because there was no longer a need to make the distinction between clinical and community psychology perspectives, with clinical psychology embracing the concept of prevention and psychoeducation, or was it because there was decreasing interest in community psychology—in social justice, social change, and the systems-level interventions that would facilitate this change? Or was this an artifact of the historical and political cycle of the opening decade of the 21st century in the United States? Could shifts in political and social philosophy have affected interest in these programs? And could other changes bring renewed and greater interest in this area of psychology? Weinstein offered no answer, but cautioned community psychologists that they needed to attend to this possible decline. The struggles were not over.

## GROWING BEYOND NATIONAL BOUNDARIES

Beyond the U.S. borders, community psychology appears to continue to grow. Among the articles found in the *AJCP* and *JCP* for 2006 through 2011 was research derived from a variety of global settings (Table 13.4). These articles are representative of the growing international body of community psychology literature.

Lorion's (2007) editor's comments for the *Journal of Community Psychology* explicitly mentioned the expanded international composition of the journal's editorial board in a strategic decision to broaden perspectives beyond the United States. The *American Journal of Community Psychology* has psychologists from Japan, Brazil, and Chile on its Board of Editors. The "gatekeepers" for the journals have become international.

**TABLE 13.4** A Limited Selection of International Articles and Authors from the *American Journal of Community Psychology* and the *Journal of Community Psychology*

Stress and the role of religion in a South African township (Copeland-Linder, 2006)

Australian Aboriginal sense of community (Bishop, Colquhoun, & Johnson, 2006)

Israeli volunteer burnout (Kulik, 2006)

Jamaican attitudes toward mental illness (Jackson & Hetherington, 2006)

Filial piety and kinship care in Hong Kong (Cheung, Kwan, & Ng, 2006)

Italian crime (Amerio & Roccato, 2007)

Colombian violence (Brook, Brook, & Whiteman, 2007)

Canadian homeless youth (Kidd & Davidson, 2007)

Support systems for HIV/AIDS in South Africa (Campbell, Nair, & Maimane, 2007)

Help-seeking behavior of West African migrants (Knipscheer & Kleber, 2008)

Sense of community and prejudice in a heterogenous neighborhood of Milan, Italy (Castellini, Colombo, Maffeos, & Montali, 2011)

Afghan women's organization: education, community, and feminism (Brodsky et al., 2012)

Values as predictors of anticipated sociocultural adaptation among potential migrants from Russian to Finland (Yijälä, Lönnqvist, Jasinskaja, Lahti, & Verkasalo, 2012)

The analysis of the resilience of adults one year after the 2008 Wenchuan earthquake (Li, Xu, He, & Wu, 2012)

Adolescent religiosity and substance abuse in Mexico (Marsiglia, Ayers, & Hoffman, 2012).

There is a text on *Community Psychology and Social Change: Australian and New Zealand Perspectives* in its second edition (Thomas & Veno, 1996). A text on *Critical Community Psychology* (Kagan, Burton, Duckett, Lawthom, & Siddiquee, 2011) was written by a team out of Manchester, England. A text on *International Community Psychology* edited by Reich, Riemer, Prilleltensky, and Montero (2007) has chapters with contributors from Argentina-Uruguay, Canada, India, Australia, New Zealand, Japan, Hong Kong, Britain, Germany, Italy, Norway, Spain, Portugal, Israel, Poland, Greece, Turkey, Cameroon, Ghana, and South Africa. That means authors covered all the continents of the world except Antarctica.

The website for Division 27 of the American Psychological Association (Society for Community Research and Action) lists among its goals the promotion of an "international field of inquiry and action" (www.scra27.org). Besides the researchers and applied psychologists within the United States, community psychology has proponents from around the world. This is a long way from Swampscott, Massachusetts, where the American version of community psychology had its birth.

One future trend for community psychology is already well on its way. Community psychology has crossed borders and is well at work in Latin America, Europe, Africa, Asia, and the Pacific. One can see it in the study sites, the researchers and writers, and the graduate programs.

The original framers of the community psychology movement in the United States did not directly mention crossing international boundaries. Glidewell's (1966) discussion of "social change" anticipated the implications of a "shrinking globe" and what it would mean to our challenges:

> The population of the world moves about and one value system confronts another value system, as social systems grow in size, specialization and complexity, as the population shifts from rural to metropolitan areas, as mutual expectations become subject to much faster change, inter-personal and inter-group tensions rise. The tension may become a motivating force toward flexibility . . . or inducing emotional confusion and . . . rigidity. . . . Whether the tension provokes one or the other depends upon the capacity of the individual and the social organization to develop innovations. (p. 44)

Community psychology has acquired many of the systems-level markers of establishment in the United States. It also has growing recognition of its concepts, research, and applications in this "shrinking globe."

## A USEFUL PARADIGM

The various chapters in Part III of this text have demonstrated the usefulness of the community approach to various systems. Whether it is research and programs in the tertiary prevention of mental health problems, the promotion of well-being and the prevention of stress in business settings, the provision of alternative school programs, or community programs to prevent drug abuse and violence in youth, the application of community psychology principles can provide a useful and sturdy programmatic framework. In all cases, it is useful to consider the advantages of a preventive orientation to problems and of collaborative efforts in defining problems and solutions. Yet as the field matures and takes new directions, those who have applied its principles comment on their journey and the lessons learned along the way. These commentaries follow.

## COMMENTARIES

What would seasoned community psychologists bring to our attention as we move into the future? What hopes and cautions might they provide? The following section presents commentary on the research and applications of community psychology. They provide advice and direction for the present and the future.

**Julian Rappaport** (2005) cautioned against becoming too sure as to what was being studied or too set in how it was to be studied. He worried that the quest to be a "science" would lead to doctrinaire approaches of what was correct and acceptable versus incorrect and unacceptable. He would rather have us remember the rebellious origins of community psychology and the role of the community psychologist as a **"critical consciousness"** to the status quo. Community psychology should be where innovation and change can find a home. This means that the methodologies for discovery should be curious about the new and flexible. Having been influenced by Kuhn's schema of scientific revolutions, community psychology has always looked for the anomalies in the established and the traditional.

**Seymour Sarason** (2004) cautioned that the intervention process was not easily captured in the research literature. The methodological descriptions of studies could give an impression of a clean and linear process to community work. He did not believe this to be so. What he did believe was that the process of research and intervention was important. The **"before-the-beginning"** phase of development was rich with critical details. Before a "beginning," we establish the relationships with those in the community with whom we collaborate.

Who we are and who they are provides the meaningful context for whatever comes from the relationship. The contacts with community leaders and the community systems are the context that give birth to the eventual social action or research. Sarason raised the issue of people skills in the community process. He saw the ability to establish good relationships as essential to good community work. And he asked the question, can it be taught?

The beginning times were exciting, with new ways to conceptualize the problems of our society. **James Kelly** (2002) warned of the loss of this excitement, passion or **spirit** as the field matures. He too noted the difficulty of maintaining the balance between being a respected science and not being constrained by traditional designs or methodologies derived for the laboratory. He challenged us to be **adventuresome** in our research (Tolan, Keys, Chertak, & Jason, 1990, p. xvi). So we should be creative, and take a few chances in what we do. Although the field has succeeded in many ways, it must be careful to maintain its spirit of openness and willingness to disagree with the status quo. Kelly called for us to think beyond the ordinary and the confines of the psychological discipline. Among other ideas to help in doing this, he suggested increasing our use of interdisciplinary perspectives, increasing our use of culture- and systems-level focus (as opposed to the individual level), and adding community organizers (such as Saul Alinsky, 1971/1989) to our list of teachers.

**Rhona Weinstein** (2006) warned about the loss of community psychology's original initiatives. She challenged the field to raise its sights and work on **systems-level interventions**. Her top social priorities were to deal with "entrenched disparities and perceptions of the other." The disadvantaging differences were sustained because of our perceptions of others as different—*difference* meant the others were outsiders and therefore less worthy. The resulting discrepancies in treatment could be found in schooling advantages, health treatment opportunities, housing access, economic opportunities, and favoritism in the legal system. This broad band of disadvantage was a powerful systemic deterrent to achievement and advancement. At the heart of this system of advantage and disadvantage was the perception of "us" versus the "others" in our society, and how "they" deserved what they got. These structural advantages could not help but lead to advantages at the personal level. The advantages of an internal locus of control, a sense of self-efficacy, and an agentic attitude (willingness to act) have been clearly demonstrated. These personal styles have been found to be associated with favorable placement in our social structure. Contextual and environmental factors facilitate the development of advantageous or disadvantageous personality styles. For example, the problems of self-fulfilling prophecy and negative expectations within the school system have led to inequalities in schooling outcomes. Weinstein therefore argued for intervention **within the schools to address these negative expectations.**

**Stephen Fyson** (1999), following over 20 years of community work in the schools of Australia, discussed community psychology's efforts to resolve the tension between the One (individual) and the Many (collective). He believed that a **transformational sense of community** can bring together these two extreme positions. It is what Newborough (1995) called the *third position*. Between the "I" and the "they" is the "we." From what we understand of the importance of this perspective, the advantages that accumulate to the in-group, those who are perceived as a part of one's community, the "we," are substantial. The disadvantages of perception as a member of the out-group, those seen as not part of our community, the alien, the "they," are also substantial. Researchers have demonstrated the subtle and blatant ways in which these differences in membership continue to affect us (Gaertner & Dovidio, 2005).

**Lonnie Snowden** (2005) called for social and community analyses at the level of populations, in what he calls **population thinking**. From this perspective, population parameters were the level of analysis and focus and the "underlying processes and structures of social change" (p. 3) and maintenance. He cited as an example a study by Sampson, Raudenbush, and Earls (1997), who found collective efficacy to be the variable related to reduced crime in neighborhoods. So it is efficacy and not ethnic minority composition of those neighborhoods that was the critical variable to crime in a community. Snowden argued for the development of **prosocial norms** and practices as well as constructive traditions and institutions. In this manner, the disparities in our society could be more effectively addressed. The population level of thinking should lead to research uncovering the **social mechanisms** perpetuating these differences and to policy-level solutions for the attendant problems. For example, knowing that crime is based on collective efficacy and not on race should direct our interventions to empowerment.

**Rodney Watts** and **Irma Serrano-Garcia** (2003) presented a broad challenge in their call for a "**liberating community psychology**" engaged in **social and political power issues** that underlie the community's problems. They conceptualized the typical community concerns over violence, identity, stress, and education as the result of systems of oppression. Fostering an awareness of these systems, the intervention researchers helped groups change these systems. The importance of contexts and the need to create or re-create these contexts were the focus of interventions. The goal was to build systems to promote health as opposed to reacting to health problems once they arise. De Fatima Qunital de Freitas (2000) stated that among the guiding principles of community psychology in Brazil/Latin America was the realization that "it was clearly **political**." From an ecological point of view, the acknowledgment of this larger exosystem (Bronfenbrenner, 1979) seemed appropriate.

**Emory Cowen** (2000) believed in a shift from a risk and prevention model to **promotion** of growth, competency, and enhancement-of-life models. The community provided opportunities for successful development and the realization of potential. The focus of community psychology might be better placed on how various community contexts can **foster and develop trajectories for success**. With a better understanding of these trajectories and the factors that help bring them to fruition, our interventions may be positively focused on critical time frames and the adaptive capacities of communities and their members. Longitudinal studies of the effects of social competence are starting to discern the relationship between childhood competencies and the development of pathology over time (Burt, Obradovic, Long, & Masten, 2008).

For community psychologists to effectively work within the various cultural and ethnic communities, **Stanley Sue** (2006) focused on the need for cultural competencies. Three general processes were important to cultural competency. The first was "**scientific mindedness,**" or the formulation of hypotheses based on initial observations rather than preconceived conclusions based on group membership. Openness to reality was called for. The hypotheses could then be tested through observations. The second process was called "**dynamic sizing.**" An individual needed the skill to know when to generalize based on group membership and when to individualize. People did have commonalities in values and behaviors that came from social group regularities in practice. At the same time, each individual was unique. Knowing when and how to determine uniqueness and group commonalities was a skill. Finally, the process of acquiring "**culture-specific skills**" had to do with cultural knowledge. Any good clinician/counselor/therapist needed to understand the individual at these three levels, in order to fully comprehend their influences on behavior. Sue's work underscored the necessity for cultural competency in mental health settings. Several decades earlier, he had noted discrepancies in community mental health center use and in treatment outcomes (Sue, 1977). His 2006 article articulated the processes discovered to be necessary to correct these discrepancies.

**Cliff O'Donnell** and **Roland Tharp** (2012) wrote of the importance of culture in community psychology, proposing that "**cultural community psychology**" might better capture the nature of community work. They note that both culture and community emphasize the derivation of **shared meanings** resulting from the interactions of their members. The shared nature of meanings extends to "activity settings," in which repeated exposure to behaviors within that setting helped those within it to derive meaning. (Think of a family holiday gathering and how, over time, the holiday gains meaning for the people who regularly participate in those gatherings.) An understanding of culture is considered critical to the development of effective relationships within the community. Such an understanding will inform our conceptions of phenomena and processes as well as influence the ways in which we act and how we see outcomes.

**Bret Kloos** (2005) provided fair warning that community psychology must be sure not to become **too insular**. By having our own journals and our own conferences, we have been able to communicate more efficiently with each other, but at the same time we have become isolated from the broader field of psychology and from interdisciplinary settings. His challenge to community psychology was to continue to be relevant and continue to have an impact on the broad range of areas that affect the health of the community we hope to serve.

**Carolyn Swift** noted the role played by both "**real world**" and "academic" community psychologists throughout the history of the field. She saw difficulties with the two groups' appreciation of each other's contributions. Her challenge was for both groups to achieve a two-way admiration with attention to sharing leadership, responsibilities, and acknowledgments of contributions. "Such activities are likely to increase. . . . It will take each group reaching out to the other, not as outsiders but as partners . . ."(Wolff & Swift, 2008, p. 618).

**Tom Wolff** called for an active embrace of **politics** and **political activities** to foster system change. His own experience in building healthy communities verified the need for and effectiveness of such a focus. He too recommended better integration of the "real world" and the "academic world." Just as academics have been received into the community, the community should be invited into academia (Wolff & Swift, 2008).

**Prilleltensky** (2012) cautioned that psychology will "err on two counts: overestimating its importance for well-being, and not **paying sufficient attention to justice**" (p. 1). Making the argument that the literature in public health (Levy & Sidel, 2006), organizational development (Fujishiro & Heaney, 2009), interpersonal relations (Olson, DeFrain, & Skogrand, 2008), and personal well-being (Prilleltensky & Prilleltensky, 2006) supported the importance of justice to physical and psychological well-being, he states his belief that there was insufficient work in this area. Justice could be defined as **distributive** ("the equitable allocation of burdens and privileges," p. 6) and **procedural** ("fair, transparent . . . respectful treatment," p. 7). Both were important to our sense of justice. Community psychologists needed to pay attention to the conditions for justice and work to promote optimal and responsive conditions for justice processes to occur.

This sample of observations relating to the state of the field provides a fairly diverse sampling of community psychologists. Their common challenge to us is to be more ambitious in our thinking, to remember our humanity, with all its complexity, and to be bold in our ambitions. Community psychology can be applied to a variety of systems. We have reviewed a number of them. Yet the tendency has been to work on what Cowen (1985) would call *person-oriented programs*. After all, there are pressing needs at the personal level, and the outcomes are more immediate. However, the community psychologist perspective requires thinking in terms of both short-term outcomes, which demonstrate the usefulness of the paradigm, and longer term outcomes, which may be required to bring about systemic (r)evolution. Although there are many environmental demands for quick results, what we all desire is lasting change. These commentaries all argue for the importance of a long-term relationship with the community. They also call for respect, an understanding of similarities and differences within and between communities, openness to learning, and flexibility with regard to our own models and worldviews.

The theme of justice is also found in these comments. One would expect this, given community psychology's appreciation for diversity and for the problems that an unenlightened approach to differences can bring.

A community member once commented that the difference between the community psychologist and others who had come to do research before is that the community psychologist attends neighborhood events, celebrates the successes, and commiserates over the sorrows the community experiences. The psychologist becomes a part of the community in which she works. She is not "the professor" from the university, who flies in, hands out surveys, and leaves; she demonstrates her caring, concern, and connection with her community.

Having reviewed the status of current thinking and progress in the field, we turn our attention to areas for future work for community psychologists.

## ANSWERING THE PRESENT AND FUTURE NEEDS OF SOCIETY

As communities participate in defining the direction interventions should take (Jason, Keys, Suarez-Balcazar, Taylor, & Davis, 2004), the role of the community psychologist will continue to require us to use our understanding of how communities and systems work. The goal continues to be helping groups implement programs and interventions that they determine to be relevant. Though the obvious problems of crime, drug and alcohol abuse, serious mental illness, and the epidemic spread of HIV/AIDS are among the immediate issues facing all communities, we would add the challenges of developing an appreciation for differences; the search for compassion; sustainability and environmental concerns; disparities in opportunities in education, health, and economics; and the issues around an aging population and end-of-life care. These areas of warrant further study and possible intervention within the community psychology framework being used in the 21st century.

Christens, Hanlin, and Speer (2007) remind us that we must have a **social imagination**—we must be able to make the connection between the individual's experiences and the social systems that influence those experiences. From this ability to conceive of social systems linked to the personal, we can start to conceptualize community interventions. Social change (social, economic, political, environmental) is personal change. We have to be able to imagine things differently before we can make things different.

Boyd and Bright (2007) wrote of the potential in shifts of perspective from problem-focused to **opportunity-focused** research and intervention. Using a participatory research methodology called the appreciative inquiry technique, they engage poor rural communities in a process of defining problems and opportunities for their area. Appreciative inquiry asks neighborhood members to imagine what a community can do with the strength of its connections to each other and beyond. This is one way of gathering the resources available to a given group. Again, the emphasis is on being able to imagine what can be.

## Appreciation for Differences and the Search for Compassion

Differences can make contributions to our success. Different people bring different perspectives and different information to problem-solving situations. This diversity can come from background, experiences, or cultures. We usually associate this diversity with demographic variables, such as ethnicity, social class, geographic origin, or gender. This argument has been made with regard to educational or economic advantages (Bowen & Bok, 2000; Gurin, Nagda, & Lopez, 2004; Page, 2007). We are better informed, more open to differing opinions, and more comfortable with ideas beyond our typical range of thinking as the result of experiences with difference. In the end, this diversity can provide better decision making and more comfort with the pluralistic society found within the United States that is to be expected from expansion to global perspectives. The United States is indeed becoming more diverse (U.S. Census Bureau, 2011). Between 2000 and 2010, the total U.S. population grew by 9%. The fastest growing groups were Hispanic/Latino at 43% and Asian at 43%. Blacks grew approximately 12% and American Indian/Alaska Natives 18%. Those identifying as White grew 5.7%. Projections are that the combination of all "ethnic minority" groups will become a majority by 2050. Diversity will become the norm. Understanding it and how it may help is both future oriented and adaptive.

An appreciation of differences challenges the tendency to categorize and exclude based on superficial characteristics, such as physical appearance or demographic variables. This tendency to categorize can lead to advantages for those perceived to be in-group members. The definition of an in-group is based on establishment of shared characteristics (physical appearance, hometown, friends, and tasks). Community psychology may have some helpful perspectives on how these characteristics might be structured into social settings, so that an appreciation of the differences and a **compassionate** attitude is fostered—that is, an awareness of others' suffering and a willingness to help. This is certainly a positive human quality (Cassell, 2009). Although there is a wealth of psychological research on empathy and altruism (Batson, 2011; Batson, Ahmad, & Lishner, 2009), we have not yet seen empathy or compassion as dependent variables in the community literature; they would seem to be natural outcome variables for those interested in building community.

The area of resilience implies a compassionate community. Jason and Perdoux (2004) describe compassionate qualities in their text on "havens for community healing."

Cook (2012) reminds us that Sarason's definition of the public interest has to do with the individual, society and how the individual and society provide meaning and purpose to each other. Cook argues that

> through compassion we may begin to understand problems not as problems that affect just others, but as our problems. . . . Compassion will allow us to lose ourselves, our presumptions, and our preconceived notions and allow us to see the interconnections between each other. . . . Perhaps the study of compassion at all levels of analysis is the center of community psychology. (p. 223)

Ehrlich and Ornstein (2010) write on the importance of getting beyond our natural limitations for building community, and feeling empathy for others. The expanding human capacity to know others and to feel close and empathic is a part of our trajectory, but is hampered by our biological boundaries. Finding ways to accomplish this is a worthy ambition for community psychology.

What structural qualities facilitate the appreciation of differences? How can we help generate compassionate communities? At what stage can this occur? Jason and Moritsugu (2003) posed the question of how Buddhism and community psychology might have overlapping themes and challenges. In a book chapter on resilience, Greenberg, Riggs, and Blair (2007) discussed the development of resiliency and emotional intelligence. Could this be brought to bear on our community efforts? When and how can compassion be brought more explicitly into the work of community psychology? Or are we already studying it under another name?

## Sustainability and Environmental Concerns

Many people consider environmental concerns, global warming, and the waste of natural resources to be urgent international issues. The United Nations Framework Convention on Climate Change was entered into on March 21, 1994. Under this convention, governments from around the world joined in an effort to deal with the problems of greenhouse gases and carbon dioxide. The world's climate was recognized as a natural resource (see http://unfccc.int/essential_background/convention/items/ 2627.php; July 31, 2008). The reduction of greenhouse gases is the target for international strategies. What it requires is an overall consciousness regarding renewable resources to power the world.

Increases in energy costs have underscored the necessity of such concerns and brought the immediacy of this topic to prominence. Consumption practices are under discussion, and renewed efforts are being made to modify them. To the rest of the world, this realization may seem late in coming, but psychologically we know that this awareness and willingness to act are based on multiple factors.

These concerns and efforts have now evolved into the newer term of **sustainability.** Sustainability is different from purely environmental concerns in that sustainability is about maintaining a lifestyle; environmental concerns deal with not harming the planet (possibly a more abstract and indirect concept). We have seen a rapid multiplication of sites and services that claim to be "green" or working on "sustainability."

Community psychology can have some role in helping curb local community and national appetites for consumption of nonrenewable resources and instead learning to live in a finite world. Two articles provide examples of work in this area of sustainability and environment. The first is literally close to the Earth and at the personal level, a description of community garden projects (Okvat & Zautra, 2011). The community garden requires activity from its members. Tidball and Krasy (2007) believe that this style of gardening builds supportive and strong communities because of the creation of interdependency, the frequency of contacts, and the diversity of participants. Kuo (2001) found that being in "greenery" improved attention. Gardens could decrease isolation (Wakefield, Yeudall, Taron, Reynolds, & Skinner, 2007) and increase nutrition and activity levels (Stein, 2008). At the same time, gardens have a direct impact on the quality of the environment. Okvat and Zautra (2011) suggested that community psychologists help to develop, to sustain, and to research grassroots efforts on these gardens. Beyond this micro-level work, community psychology might aid in the creating a network of such gardens.

At a policy level, Quimby and Angelique (2011) examined people's perceived barriers to and facilitators for environmental advocacy. They surveyed individuals who had engaged in a pro-environment activity. They found that the primary reason respondents did not become more active was that they did not feel they could bring about change. Other factors were lack of time and money and lack of social support. The possible reasons for becoming active were a perception that others were doing the same—that is, there was a social norm for action.

Both Okvat and Zautra (2011) and Quimby and Angelique (2011) are informative for those who want to bring about action. They are examples of community psychology engaging in sustainability issues. There are of course many more questions. How do members of the community become more aware? How do we change our behaviors? How are these efforts sustained in a world where we find ourselves highly distractible? Once we have some of these answers, how do we successfully implement these programs within communities, across a nation, and around the world?

A lot of work can be done on placement of, attitudes toward, and practices to optimize the use of mass transit. Attitudes regarding alternative power sources, the construction of networks to support these alternatives, and the building of public will are also important. Lifestyle shifts away from the five-day work week could be studied. The definition of work sites (e.g., home, away from headquarters, distant from other workers) and work times (e.g., midnight to the early morning, staggered hours) could be researched, as well as work practices to adjust to these new definitions to accommodate personal preferences, spreading the load on the transportation infrastructure or global time frames.

Dean and Bush (2007) have described environmental organization processes, identifying five in particular that are relevant to these issues: problem analysis, impacting decision making, working on organizational relationships, involving the community, and transferring gained knowledge beyond the organization or project. They believe that the community psychology perspective can contribute to all of these processes.

## Disparities in Opportunity for Health, Education, and Economic Success

Prilleltensky and Fox (2007) discuss the relationship between wellness and justice. They argue that to feel one lives in a just society and has been treated justly contributes to one's sense of well-being. **Psychopolitical literacy** is the recognition of this relationship between societal conditions and psychological states. This is in the tradition of Freire's (1970) "pedagogy of the oppressed" mentioned in an earlier chapter.

Weinstein (2006) specifically called for studying the disparities in our society and mounting interventions to rectify them. These differences are attributed to social, cultural, or institutional barriers to equality of opportunity. Although the work on disparities is no small task, it is worthy of attention from a discipline that espouses justice and liberation among its principles. This goes beyond the appreciation of diversity. These disparities have historical roots, and shifts in these patterns require patient and persistent efforts at the local and policy levels. There are instances where addressing these disparities requires changes in patterns of power and reexamination of the basic assumptions regarding the social status quo. Beliefs in a just world and in the presence of equal opportunity may be among the basic assumptions of established life that need to be examined and changed. What structural obstacles exist to reduction of disparities? How are these obstacles vulnerable to influence? Community psychology may contribute to answering these questions. Is it a matter of empowerment? If so, Maton (2008) calls on community psychology to use what it has learned about empowering groups to foster these groups and their development. He presents the characteristics of successful empowered groups as having a central belief system, a clear and inspirational purpose, and an opportunity role structure. There need to be meaningful and engaging tasks for members; core activities that reinforce self-efficacy and skill development; a caring and supportive relational environment; leadership that is inspirational, motivating, has contact with most members, and is empowered to do things; and an organization that is open to learning and has bridges to the external environment (i.e., is not isolated). Wolff and Swift (2008) have already called for political involvement to deal with these kinds of issues. There are examples in the literature of community psychologists becoming involved in legislation (Jason & Rose, 1984) and policy change (Jason, 2012). There are surely many more instances where advocacy in the public area has been accomplished (work on domestic violence, alcohol and drug abuse, and health care disparities comes to mind). How might these processes empower more people and bring about the dissolution of social disparities?

## Aging and End of Life

Growing old and dying are two of the inevitabilities of life. The population in the United States is aging quickly (He, Sengupta, Velkoff, & DeBarros, 2005). U.S. Census estimates report that those over 65 years of age will double in numbers from 2000 to 2030. He and colleagues (2005) state that worldwide, there were approximately 420 million people over the age of 65 in 2000. Projections were made for

974 million people over 65 years old in 2030. Aging of the population is a global phenomenon. Japan, Hong Kong, and Sweden have the longest life expectancies at 82, 81.7, and 80.6 years. Some regions of the world will experience increases in their elderly population of approximately 200% to 300% between 2005 and 2050. The North American should see an increase of over 100%. These demographic pressures call for attention to the issues of aging.

What are the issues of aging? How does staying in a community help? How do we deal with the attendant concerns of death and dying? Karel, Gatz, and Smyer (2012) warn of problems of chronic physical illnesses, limitations on mobility, and dementia. LaVeist, Sellers, Brown, and Nickerson (1997) reported that extreme isolation for African American women (isolation defined by living alone and not seeing family or friends for over two years) was related to higher likelihood of death within five years. This was after controlling for physical conditions. In a later study of Hong Kong elderly by Cheng, Chan, and Phillips (2004) that combined qualitative interview and quantitative survey data, four factors were found to determine quality of life for this population:

Contributing to society (generativity)

Good relationships with family and friends

Good health

Comfortable material circumstances

In post survey interviews, the importance of interpersonal relationships and health was overwhelmingly endorsed. In a qualitative study of White American elderly, Farquhar (1995) found quality of life to be defined in terms of family, being active, social relationships, health, and material comfort. These community studies consistently emphasize the importance of social contact and social purpose, with noticeably greater significance than the more obvious health and material well-being factors.

Cheng and Heller (2009) point to issues of age discrimination and lack of support in old age, and the problems for elderly women that come with surviving to advanced age. They note that community psychology has neglected this population over the years. In a literature search in selected community journals, they could find only 40 articles on aging. They cite attitudinal issues within our profession and society as contributing to this lack of interest. Programmatic issues they believe community psychology could address include alternative long-term care; aging in place (staying in one's own home); empowerment of the elderly; and development of volunteer opportunities, family support, and community care.

These studies are helpful in guiding future programs related to aging. Although the field is silent on the topic of death and dying, one wonders what variables may play a role in the final phase of life—that is, having a good death. The topic of good aging and death and what that means seems quite appropriate for consideration in the context of community psychology.

## Summary

Community psychology has established itself over the past 40 years in many of the formal ways that one expects. There are journals devoted to the topic, a division in the American Psychological Association, and regular contributions made to the *Annual Review of Psychology* and other texts.

Commentaries on the state of the field have been offered by community psychologists of note.

Points are made on the accumulation of professional gains, but there remain cautions with regard to the need to preserve our original enthusiasm and to remain open to the revolutionary, continued focus on social and systems-level interventions, the need to promote well-being as well as prevent pathology, the applied nature of our field, the importance of social justice, and the reminder that the processes attendant to community change are long, complex, and based on human relationships.

Given the move to empower communities to help in defining issues and problems and how research and interventions are to be conducted, the direction of the field in terms of topics is harder to define. The obvious concerns over crime, mental illness, and drug and alcohol abuse are present but tend toward tertiary preventions.

Potential areas for growth and development include an appreciation for diversity and the development of compassion and of sustainability potential, rectifying social disparities in the many domains where they are found, and the issues of aging and death. Though not exhaustive, these topics have currency in today's society and bring possibilities for prevention and promotion to our conceptions of community.

## Final Reflections

Chapter 1 started with quotes from individuals who called us to action. When faced with social problems, they examined them, looked for solutions, and then moved forward, looking for feedback on the effectiveness of their actions. This is what a good community psychologist would do. The final chapter's opening quotes remind us of how far we have come and what our horizons might be.

The opening vignettes in Chapter 1 presented stories emphasizing the need for community for all people. We are also reminded that

> place characteristics provided cues about their personal histories as members of the community; communicated messages about the value and character of the community and its residents; defined social norms and behavior within the community; and provided markers that could remind residents of who they are and inspire a sense of possibility for who they could become. (Newell, Berkowitz, Deacon, & Foster-Fishman, 2006, p. 29)

The following excerpt from the novel *Volcano* by Garrett Hongo expresses the desire for home and community. Hongo speaks of land and a mountain, but in a metaphorical sense, he captures the feeling that community psychology endeavors to create.

> Years later, I was returning to Hawai'i to spend a week. . . . I stepped off the plane,

and when the full blast of the island's erotic and natal wind hit me, when I caught sight of Mauna Loa's[1] purple slopes disappearing into clouds, a sob of gratitude filled my chest. . . . What radiates as knowledge from that time is that there is a beauty in belonging to this earth and to its past. . . . Every singer of every mountain of magnificence in every land knows it. I wish you knowing. I wish you a land.

The land and the mountain are our communities. When we are grounded in them, we are connected to our heritage and our sources of strength. We may wander from that community, but we know when we are back and drawing on all that it can give us. Although it is a feeling, we also *know* it. The science of community psychology looks at how the community contributes to our resilience and how it has a hand in shaping us through its contexts. As we have reviewed in this text, science has made progress in discovering the variables of importance, and psychologists have used them in intervention. There have been both successes and challenges. As we suggest at the opening of this final chapter, the dreams of our founders have been put into action and in some ways have gone beyond their vision. Yet the work is far from complete. There are new dreams to be dreamed and realized. But that is for you, the student, to help determine.

---

[1]Mauna Loa is the largest volcano in the Hawaiian chain, situated on the biggest island in the archipelago.

# BIBLIOGRAPHY

Aber, J. L., Brooks-Gunn, J., & Maynard, R. A. (1995). Effects of welfare reform on teenage parents and their children. *Critical Issues for Children and Youths, 5,* 53–71.

Aber, M. S., Maton, K. I., & Seidman, E. (2011). *Empowering settings and voices for social change.* New York, NY: Oxford Press.

Abrahams, R. B., & Patterson, R. D. (1978–1979). Psychological distress among the community elderly: Prevalence, characteristics and implications for service. *International Journal of Aging and Human Development, 9,* 1–18.

Abrams, L. S. (2006). Listening to juvenile offenders: Can residential treatment prevent recidivism? *Child and Adolescent Social Work Journal, 23,* 61–85.

Ackerman, G., Anderson, B., Jensen, S., Ludwig, R., Montero, D., Plante, N., & Yanez, V. (2001). Crime rates and confidence in the police: America's changing attitudes toward crime and policy, 1972–1999. *Journal of Sociology & Social Welfare Special Issues, 28,* 43–54.

Adams, R. E. (1992). Is happiness a home in the suburbs? The influence of urban versus suburban neighborhoods on psychological health. *Journal of Community Psychology, 20,* 353–371.

Adams, R. E., Boscarino, J. A., & Figley, C. R. (2006). Compassion fatigue and psychological distress among social workers: A validation study. *American Journal of Orthopsychiatry, 76,* 103–108.

Adelman, H. S., & Taylor, L. (2003). Creating school and community partnerships for sub-stance abuse prevention programs. *Journal of Primary Prevention, 23*(3), 329–369.

Adelman, H. S., & Taylor, L. (2007). *Fostering school, family and community involvement: Effective strategies for creating safer schools and communities.* Portland, OR: Hamilton Fish Institute on School and Community Violence George Washington University and Northwest Regional Educational Laboratory.

Administration for Children and Families (2005). *Child maltreatment.* Retrieved from http://www.acf.hhs.gov

Administration for Children and Families (2006). Retrieved from http://www.acf.hhs.gov

Administration for Children and Families (2008). Retrieved from http://www.acf.hhs.gov

Administration for Children and Families (2010). *Child maltreatment.* Washington, DC: U.S. Department of Health and Human Services.

Afterschool Alliance, 2004. *America after 3 pm: A household survey on afterschool in America.* Retrieved from http://www.afterschoolaliance.org/researchFactSheets.cfm

Agency for Healthcare Research and Quality (2006). *National healthcare disparities report, 2006.* Rockville, MD. Retrieved from http://www.ahrq.gov/qual/nhdr06/nhdr06.htm

Alan Guttmacher Institute (2004). *Adolescent pregnancy.* Retrieved from http://www.nlm.nih.gov/medlineplus/ency/article/001516

Alan Guttmacher Institute (2006). *Facts on sex education in the United States.* Retrieved from http://www.guttmacher.org/pubs/fb_sexEd2006.html

Alanis, I., & Rodriguez, M. A. (2008). Sustaining a dual language immersion program: Features of success. *Journal of Latinos and Education, 7,* 305–319.

Albee, G. (1982). Preventing psychopathology and promoting human potential. *American Psychologist, 37*(9), 1043–1050.

Albee, G. W. (1998). The politics of primary prevention. *Journal of Primary Prevention, 19*(2), 117–127.

Albee, G. (2000). Commentary on prevention and counseling psychology. *The Counseling Psychologist, 28*(6), 845–853.

Albee, G. W., & Gullotta, T. (Eds.). (1997). *Primary prevention works.* Thousand Oaks, CA: Sage.

Albee, G. W., & Ryan, K. (1998). An overview of primary prevention. *Journal of Mental Health, 7*(5), 441–449.

Alderson, G., & Sentman, E. (1979). *How you can influence Congress: The complete handbook for the citizen lobbyist.* New York, NY: Dutton.

Alink, L. R., Cicchetti, D., Kim, J., & Rogosch, F. A. (2012). Longitudinal associations among child maltreatment, social functioning, and cortisol regulation. *Developmental Psychology, 48*(1), 224-236.

Alinsky, S. (1971). *Rules for radicals: A practical primer for realistic radicals.* New York, NY: Random House.

Alinsky, S. (1971/1989). *Rules for radicals.* New York, NY: Vintage

Allen, H., & Simonsen, C. E. (1992). *Corrections in America: An introduction.* New York, NY: Macmillan.

Allen, J. P., Seitz, V., & Apfel, N. H. (2007). The sexually mature teen as a whole person: New directions in prevention and intervention for teen pregnancy and parenthood. In A. J. Lawrence, S. J. Bishop-Josef, S. M. McLearn, K. Taaffe, & D. A. Phillips (Eds.), *Child development and social policy: Knowledge for action.* Washington, DC: American Psychological Association.

Allen, N. (2000). Welfare reform and women's poverty: Exploring the need for broader social change. *Community Psychologist, 33,* 11–13.

Allen, N. (2005). A multi-level analysis of community coordinating councils. *American Journal of Community Psychology, 35,* 49–63.

Allen-Meares, P., & Shore, D. A. (1986). A transactional framework for working with adolescents and their sexualities. Special issue: Adolescent sexualities: Overview and principles of intervention. *Journal of Social Work and Human Sexuality, 5,* 71–80.

Allport, G. W. (1954/1979). *The nature of prejudice.* Reading, MA: Addison-Wesley.

Altman, I. (1987). Community psychology twenty years later: Still another crisis in psychology? *American Journal of Community Psychology, 15,* 613–627.

Altman, L. (2008, March 26). Rethinking is urged on vaccine for AIDS. *The New York Times.* Retrieved from http://www.nytimes.com

Altman, I., & Wandersman, A. (1987). *Neighborhood and community environments.* New York, NY: Plenum Press.

Ambrose, M., Arnaud, A., & Schminke, M. (2008). Individual moral development and ethical climate: The influence of person–organization fit on job attitudes. *Journal of Business Ethics, 77*(3), 323–333.

American Association of University Women. (2007). *Behind the pay gap.* Washington, DC: American Association of University Women, Legal Advocacy Fund.

American Association of University Women. (2011, April). The simple truth about the gender pay gap. Retrieved from http://aauw.org/learn/research/upload/SimpleTruthAbout-PayGap1.pdf

American Legacy Foundation. (2008a). *Smoking in the movies.* Retrieved from http://www.americanlegacy.org/70.aspx

American Legacy Foundation. (2008b). *Who we are.* Retrieved from http://www.americanlegacy.org/whoweare.aspx

American Psychological Association (1985). *Standards for educational and psychological testing* (3rd ed.). Washington, DC: Author.

American Psychological Association. (2003). Guidelines on multicultural education, training, research, practice and organizational change for psychologists. *American Psychologist, 58*(3), 377–402.

American Psychological Association. (2005). *Report of the task force on urban psychology: Toward an urban psychology: Research, action, and policy.* Washington, DC: Author.

American Psychological Society. (1991). The importance of the citizen scientist in national science policy. *APS Observer, 4,* 10, 12, 23.

American Psychological Society. (1992, February). Schooling and literacy. *APS Observer Special Issue: The Human Capital Initiative,* 17–20.

American Youth Policy Forum. (2008). *Some things do make a difference for youth.* Retrieved from http://www.pyf.org.

Amerio, P., & Roccato, M. (2007). Psychological reactions to crime in Italy: 2002–2004. *Journal of Community Psychology, 35*(1), 91–102.

Anderson, J. E., Carey, J. W., & Taveras, S. (2000). HIV testing among the general US population and persons at increased risk: Information from national surveys, 1987–1996. *American Journal of Public Health, 90,* 1089–1095.

Anderson, L., Cooper, S., Hassol, L., Klein, D., Rosenblum, G., & Bennett, C. (1966). *Community psychology: A report of the Boston Conference on the Education of Psychologists for Community Mental Health.* Boston, MA: Boston University.

Angell, R. (1980, April 28). The sporting scene: A learning spring. *New Yorker,* 47–96.

Ajzen, I. (1985). From intensions to actions: A theory of planned behavior. In J. Kuhl & J. Beckman (Eds.), *Action-control: From cognition to behavior* (pp. 11–39). Heidelberg, Germany: Springer.

Ajzen, I. (1991). The theory of planned behavior. *Organizational Behavior and Human Decision Processes, 50,* 179–211.

Ajzen, I., & Fishbein, M. (Eds.). (1980). *Understanding attitudes and predicting social behavior.* Englewood Cliffs, NJ: Prentice Hall.

Annas, G. J., & Grodin, M. A. (1998). Human rights and maternal-fetal HIV transmission prevention trials in Africa. *American Journal of Public Health, 88,* 560–563.

Annual Reviews (2011). Annual Reviews rankings in Thomson Reuters Journal Citation Reports. Retrieved from http://www.annualreviews.org/page/about/isi-rankings

Anshel, M. H. (2000). A conceptual model and implications for coping with stressful events in police work. *Criminal Justice & Behavior, 27,* 375–400.

Applebaum, L. D., Lennon, M. C., & Lawrence, A. J. (2006). When effort is threatening: The influence of the belief in a just world on Americans' attitudes toward antipoverty policy. *Political Psychology, 27,* 387–402.

Appleyard, K., Egeland, B., & Sroufe, L. A. (2007). Direct social support for young high risk children: Relations with behavioral and emotional outcomes across time. *Journal of Abnormal Child Psychology, 35*(3), 443-457. doi:10.1007/s10802-008-9102-y

Arias, B. M. (2005). The impact of *Brown* on Latinos: A study of transformation of policy intentions. *Teachers College Record, 107,* 1974–1998.

Armour, M. P., & Umbreit, M. S. (2006). Victim forgiveness in restorative justice dialogue. *Victims & Offenders, 1,* 123–140.

Arnold, D. A., Ortiz, C., Curry, J. C., Stowe, R. M., Goldstein, N. E., Fisher, P. H., Zeljo , A., & Yershova, K. (1999). Promoting academic success and preventing disruptive behavior disorders through community partnership. *Journal of Community Psychology, 27,* 589–598.

Aronson, E. (2004). How the Columbine High School tragedy could have been prevented. *Journal of Individual Psychology, 60,* 355–560.

Aronson, E., Blaney, N., Stephan, C., Sikes, J., & Snapp, M. (1978). *The jigsaw classroom.* Beverly Hills, CA: Sage.

Aronson, E., Wilson, T. D., & Akert, R. M. (1999). *Social psychology.* New York, NY: Longman.

Aseltine, R., & DeMartino, R. (2004). An outcome evaluation of the SOS suicide prevention program. *American Journal of Public Health, 94,* 446-451.

Atwater, L., Carey, J., & Waldman, D. (2001). Gender and discipline in the workplace: Wait until your father gets home. *Journal of Management, 27*(5), 537–561.

Auerbach, J. D., Wypijewska, C., & Brodie, H. K. H. (Eds.). (1994). *AIDS and behavior: An integrated approach.* Washington, DC: National Academy Press.

Avert. (2008). Retrieved from http://www.avert.org/abstinence.htm

Ayers, T., Sandler, I., West, S., & Roosa, M. (1996). A dispositional and situational assessment of children's coping: Testing alternative models of coping. *Journal of Personality, 64,* 923–958.

Baba, Y., & Austin, D. M. (1989). Neighborhood environmental satisfaction, victimization, and social participation as determinants of perceived neighborhood safety. *Environment and Behavior, 21,* 763–780.

Bachrach, L. L. (1989). Deinstitutionalization: A semantic analysis. *Journal of Social Issues, 45,* 161–171.

Backer, T. E., Howard, E. A., & Moran, G. E. (2007). The role of effective discharge planning in preventing homelessness. *Journal of Primary Prevention, 28,* 229–243.

Bagby, W. (1981). *Contemporary American social problems.* Chicago, IL: Nelson-Hall.

Bahr, S. J., Armstrong, A. H., Gibbs, B. G., Harris, P. E., & Fisher, J. K. (2005). The reentry process: How parolees adjust to release from prison. *Fathering, 3,* 243–265.

Bair, J. P., & Greenspan, B. K. (1986). Teamwork training for interns, residents, and nurses. *Hospital and Community Psychiatry, 37,* 633–635.

Baker, D. B., & Benjamin, L. T. (2004). Creating a profession: The National Institute of Mental Health and the training of psychologists, 1946–1954. In W. E. Pickren & S. F. Schneider (Eds.), *Psychology and the National Institute of Mental Health: A historical analysis of science, practice, and policy* (pp. 181-207). Washington, DC: American Psychological Association.

Baker, J. (1998). Are we missing the forest for the trees? Considering the social context of school violence. *Journal of School Psychology, 36,* 29–44.

Baker, J. A. (2006). Contributions of teacher–child relationships to positive school adjustment during elementary school. *Journal of School Psychology, 44,* 211-229.

Baker, R. A. (1991). Modeling the school dropout phenomenon: School policies and prevention program strategies. *High School Journal, 74,* 203–210.

Bales, R. (1950). *Interaction process analysis: A method for the study of small groups.* Cambridge, MA: Addison-Wesley.

Balfanz, R., Herzog, L., & Mac Iver, D. J. (2007). Preventing student disengagement and keeping students on the graduation path in urban middle-grades schools: Early identification and effective interventions. *Educational Psychologist, 42(4),* 223–235.

Baltes, M. M., & Baltes, P. B. (Eds.). (1986). *The psychology of control and aging.* Hillsdale, NJ: Erlbaum.

Baltodano, H. M., Platt, D., & Roberts, C. W. (2005). Transition from secure care to the community: Significant issues for youth detention. *Journal of Correctional Education, 56,* 372–388.

Bandura, A. (1977). Self-efficacy: Toward a unifying theory of behavior change. *Psychological Review, 84,* 191–215.

Bandura, A. (1978). The self system in reciprocal determinism. *American Psychologist, 33*(4), 344-358.

Bandura, A. (1986). *Social foundations of thought and action: A social cognitive theory.* Englewood Cliffs, NJ: Prentice Hall.

Bandura, A. (1989). Human agency in social cognitive theory. *American Psychologist, 44*(9), 1175-1184.

Bandura, A. (1994). Social cognitive theory and exercise of control over HIV infection. In R. J. DiClemente and J. L. Peterson (Eds.), *Preventing AIDS: Theories and methods of behavioral interventions* (pp. 25–29). New York, NY: Plenum.

Bandura, A. (2000). Exercise of human agency through collective efficacy. *Current Directions in Psychological Science, 9*(3), 75–78.

Bandura, A. (2001). Social cognitive theory: An agentic perspective. *Annual Review of Psychology, 52,* 1–26.

Bandura, A. (2006). Toward a psychology of human agency. *Perspectives on Psychological Science, 1*(2), 164–180.

Banyard, V., & Miller, K. (1998). The powerful potential of qualitative research for community psychology. *American Journal of Community Psychology, 26*(4), 485–505.

Banziger, G., & Foos, D. (1983). The relationship of personal financial status to the utilization of community mental health centers in rural Appalachia. *American Journal of Community Psychology, 11,* 543–552.

Barak, G. (1991). *Gimme shelter: A social history of homelessness in contemporary America.* New York, NY: Praeger.

Barata, P. C., Gucciardi, E., Ahmad, F., & Stewart, D. E. (2006). Cross-cultural perspectives on research participation and informed consent. *Social Science and Medicine, 62*(2), 479–490.

Barker, R. G. (1965). Explorations in ecological psychology. *American Psychologist, 20,* 1–14.

Baron, R. A., & Greenberg, J. (1990). *Behavior in organizations* (3rd ed.). New York, NY: Allyn & Bacon.

Barrera, M. (2000). Social support research in community psychology. In J. Rappaport & E. Seidman (Eds.), *Handbook of community psychology* (pp. 215–245). New York, NY: Plenum.

Barrera, M., Castro, F. G., & Steiker, L. K. (2011). A critical analysis of approaches to the development of preventive interventions for subcultural groups. *American Journal of Community Psychology, 48*(3–4), 439–454.

Bartunek, J. M., & Betters-Reed, B. L. (1987). The stages of organizational creation. Special issue: Organizational perspectives in community psychology. *American Journal of Community Psychology, 15,* 287–303.

Bass, B. M. (1998). *Transformational leadership: Industrial, military, and educational impact.* Mahwah, NJ: Erlbaum.

Basso, R. V. J., Graham, J., Pelech, W., De Young, T., & Cardey, R. (2004). Children's street connections in a Canadian community. *International Journal of Offender Therapy and Comparative Criminology, 48,* 189–202.

Bassuk, E. L., & Rosenberg, L. (1988). Why does family homelessness occur? A case-control study. *American Journal of Public Health, 78,* 783–788.

Batson, C. (2011). *Altruism in humans.* New York, NY: Oxford University Press.

Batson, C. D., Ahmad, N., & Lishner, D. A. (2009). Empathy and altruism. In S. J. Lopez & C. R. Snyder (Eds.), *Oxford handbook of positive psychology* (pp. 417–426). New York, NY: Oxford University Press.

Batson, C. D., Batson, J., Todd, R. M., Brummett, B., Shaw, L., & Aldeguer, C. (1995). Empathy and the collective good: Caring for one of the others in a social dilemma. *Journal of Personality and Social Psychology, 68,* 619–631.

Bauman, Z. (2000). The deficiencies of community. *Responsive Community, 10,* 74–79.

Bayer, R. (1998). The debate over maternal-fetal HIV transmission prevention trials in Africa, Asia, and the Caribbean: Racist exploitation or exploitation of racism. *American Journal of Public Health, 88,* 567–570.

Bayley, B. K., & Andersen, J. D. (2006). Fear of crime among urban American youth. *Journal of Family and Consumer Sciences, 98,* 26–32.

Bazemore, G., Elis, L., & Green, D. L. (2007). The "independent variable" in restorative justice: Theory-based standards for evaluating the impact and integrity of vic-

tim sensitive process (Part II). *Victims & Offenders, 2,* 351–373.

Bazemore, G., & Stinchcomb, J. (2004). A civic engagement model of reentry: Involving community through service and restorative justice. *Federal Probation, 68,* 14–24.

Beacon Hill Institute for Public Policy Research. (1997, Winter). What charitable organizations have to say about volunteers. *NewsLink, 1.* Summary retrieved from http://www .bhi.sclas.suffolk.edu/NewsLink/vln2volun.html

Beaulieu, M., Dubé, M., Bergeron, C., & Cousineau, M. (2007). Are elderly men worried about crime? *Journal of Aging Studies, 21,* 336–346.

Becker, M. H. (1974). The health belief model and personal health behavior. *Health Education Monographs, 2,* 220–243.

Becker, M. H., & Maiman, L. A. (1980). Strategies for enhancing patient compliance. *Journal of Community Health, 6,* 113–115.

Beer, M., & Walton, E. (1990). Developing the competitive organization. *American Psychologist, 45,* 154–161.

Belcher, J. R. (1988). Are jails replacing the mental health care system for the homeless mentally ill? *Community Mental Health Journal, 24,* 185–195.

Bell, C. C. (2007). Review of Black males left behind. *International Journal of Men's Health, 6,* 167–168.

Bell, L. A. (1997). Theoretical foundations for social justice education. In M. Adams, L. A. Bell, & P. Griffin (Eds.), *Teaching for diversity and social justice: A sourcebook* (pp. 3–15). New York, NY: Routledge.

Belsky, J. (2006). Early child care and early child development: Major findings of the NICHD study of early child care. *European Journal of Developmental Psychology, 31,* 95–110.

Bendicsen, H., & Carlton, S. (1990). Clinical team building: A neglected ingredient in the therapeutic milieu. *Residential Treatment for Children and Youth, 8,* 5–21.

Benjamin, L. T., & Baker, D. B. (2004). The beginnings of psychological practice: Psychology's other occult doubles. *From Séance to Science: A History of the Profession of Psychology in America* (pp. 21–24). Belmont, CA: Wadsworth/Thomson Learning.

Benjamin, L., & Crouse, E. (2002). The American Psychological Association's response to *Brown versus the Board of Education*: The case of Kenneth B. Clark. *American Psychologist, 57,* 38–50.

Bennett, C. C., Anderson, L. S., Cooper, S., Hassol, L., Klein, D. C., & Rosenblum, G. (1966). *Community psychology: A report of the Boston Conference on the Education of Psychologists for Community Mental Health.* Boston, MA: Boston University and South Shore Mental Health Center.

Bennett, T. (1989). Factors related to participation in neighborhood watch schemes. *British Journal of Criminology, 29,* 207–218.

Benviente, G. (1989). *Mastering the politics of planning: Crafting credible plans and policies.* San Francisco, CA: Jossey-Bass.

Berkeley, S., & Koff, W. (2007). Scientific and policy challenges to development of an AIDS vaccine. *Lancet, 370*(9581), 94–101.

Berkman, L., Glass, T., Brissette, I., & Seeman, T. (2000). From social integration to health: Durkheim in the new millennium. *Social Science and Medicine, 51,* 843–857.

Bernal, G., & Sáez-Santiago E. (2006). Culturally centered psychosocial interventions. *Journal of Community Psychology, 34*(2), 121–132.

Bernal, G., Trimble, J., Burlew, A. K., & Leong, F. (Eds.) (2003). *Handbook of racial and ethnic minority psychology.* Thousand Oaks, CA: Sage.

Bernier, D. (1998). A study of coping: Successful recovery from severe burnout and other reactions to severe work-related stress. *Work & Stress, 12,* 50–65.

Bernstein, J., McNichol, E., & Nicholas, A. (2008). *Pulling apart: A state-by-state analysis of income trends.* Retrieved from http://www.epi.org/studies/pulling08/4–9–08sfp.pdf

Bhutta, Z. A. (2004). Beyond informed consent. *Bulletin of the World Health Organization, 82*(10), 771–778.

Biegel, D. (1984). Help seeking and receiving in urban ethnic neighborhoods: Strategies for improvement. In J. Rapport, C. Swift, & R. Hess (Eds.), *Studies in empowerment: Steps toward understanding and action.* New York, NY: Haworth.

Bierman, K. L., Coie, J. D., Dodge, K. A., Foster, E. M, Greenberg, M. T., Lochman, J. E., . . . Pinderhughes, E. E. (2007). Fast track randomized controlled trial to prevent externalizing psychiatric disorders: Findings from grades 3 to 9. *Journal of The American Academy of Child and Adolescent Psychiatry, 46*(10), 1250–1262.

Biglan, A., Ary, D., Koehn, V., Levings, D., Smith, S., Wright, Z., . . . Henderson, J. (1996). Mobilizing positive reinforcement in communities to reduce youth access to tobacco. *American Journal of Community Psychology, 24,* 625–638.

Biglan, A., & Taylor, T. K. (2000). Why have we been more successful in reducing tobacco use than violent crime? *American Journal of Community Psychology, 28,* 269–302.

Bilchik, S. (1998). *1998 report to Congress: Juvenile mentoring program.* Washington, DC: Office of Juvenile Justice and Delinquency Prevention.

Bilchik, S. (1999). *Promising strategies to reduce gun violence.* Washington, DC: Office of Juvenile Justice and Delinquency Prevention.

Bishop, B., Colquhoun, S., & Johnson, G. (2006). Psychological sense of community: An Australian aboriginal experience. *Journal of Community Psychology, 34,* 1–7.

Bishop, B., & Drew, N. (1998). The community psychologist as subtle change agent in the public policy arena. *Community Psychologist, 31,* 20–23.

Bishop, J. W., Scott, K. D., & Burroughs, S. M. (2000). Support, commitment, and employee outcomes in a team environment. *Journal of Management, 26*(6), 1113–1132. doi:10.1177/014920630002600603

Blakely, C. H., Mayer, J. P., Gottschalk, R. G., Schmidt, N., Davidson, W. S., Roitman, D. B., et al. (1987). The fidelity-adaptation debate: Implications of the implementation of public sector social programs. *American Journal of Community Psychology, 15,* 253–268.

Blakemore, J. L., Washington, R. O., & McNeely, R. L. (1995). The demography of aging. In P. K. H. Kim (Ed.), *Services to the aging and aged: Public policies and programs.* New York, NY: Garland.

Blaney, N. T., Stephan, C., Rosenfield, D., Aronson, E., & Sikes, J. (1977). Interdependence in the classroom: A field study. *Journal of Educational Psychology, 69,* 139–146.

Blom, G. E. (1986). A school disaster: Intervention and research aspects. *Journal of the American Academy of Child Psychiatry, 25,* 336–345.

Bloom, B. (1980). Social and community interventions. *Annual Review of Psychology, 31,* 111–142.

Bloom, B. L. (1984). *Community mental health: A general introduction.* Monterey, CA: Brooks/Cole.

Bloom, B. L., & Hodges, W. F. (1988). The Colorado Separation and Divorce Program: A preventive intervention program for newly separated persons. In R. Price, E. W. Cowen, R. P. Lorion, & J. Ramos-McKay (Eds.), *14 ounces of prevention.* Washington, DC: American Psychological Association.

Bloom, M. (1987). Toward a technology in primary prevention: Educational strategies and tactics. *Journal of Primary Prevention, 8,* 25–48.

Bluedorn, A., & Standifer, R. (2006). Time and the temporal imagination. *Academy of Management Learning and Education, 5,* 196–206.

Blustein, D. L. (2006). *The psychology of working: A new perspective for career development, counseling, and public policy.* Mahwah, NJ: Erlbaum.

Blustein, D. (2008). The role of work in psychological health and well being: A conceptual, historical and public policy perspective. *American Psychologist, 63,* 228–240.

Bobak, M., Room, R., Pikhart, H., Kubinova, R., Malyutina, S., Pajak, A., . . . Marmot, M. (2004). Contribution of drinking patterns in rates of alcohol related problems between three urban populations. *Journal of Epidemiology and Community Health, 58*(3), 238–242.

Bogat, A., & Jason, L. (1997). Interventions in the school and community. In R. T. Ammerman & M. Hersen (Eds.), *Handbook of prevention and treatment with children and adolescents: Intervention in the real world context* (pp. 134–154). New York, NY: Wiley.

Bogat, A., & Jason, L. (2000). Behaviorism and community psychology. In J. Rappaport & E. Seidman (Eds.), *Handbook of community psychology* (pp. 101–114). New York, NY: Kluwer/Plenum.

Boggiano, A. K., & Katz, P. (1991). Maladaptive patterns in students: The role of teachers' controlling strategies. *Journal of Social Issues, 47,* 35–52.

Bolland, J. M. (2003). Hopelessness and risk behavior among adolescents living in high poverty, inner city neighborhoods. *Journal of Adolescence, 26,* 145–158.

Bolland, J. M., Lian, B. E., & Formichella, C. M. (2005). The origins of hopelessness among inner-city African-American adolescents. *American Journal of Community Psychology, 36,* 293–306.

Bond, G. R., Miller, L. D., & Krumweid, R. D. (1988). Assertive case management in three CMHCs: A controlled study. *Hospital Community Psychiatry, 39,* 411–417.

Bond, G. R., Witheridge, T. F., Dincin, J., & Wasmer, D. (1991). Assertive community treatment: Correcting some misconceptions. *American Journal of Community Psychology, 19,* 41–51.

Bond, G. R., Witheridge, T. F., Dincin, J., Wasmer, D., Webb, J., & DeGraaf-Kaser, R. (1990). Assertive community treatment for frequent users of psychiatric hospitals in a large city: A controlled study. *American Journal of Community Psychology, 18,* 865–891.

Bond, M. (2004). Gender, race, and class in organizational contexts. *American Journal of Community Psychology, 27*(3), 327–355.

Bond, M. A. (1990). Defining the research relationship: Maximizing participation in an unequal world. In P. Jolan, C. Keep, F. Chertok, & L. Jason (Eds.), *Research community psychology: Issues of theory and methods* (pp. 183–184). Washington, DC: American Psychological Association.

Bond, M. A. (1998). Social policy, prevention, and interorganizational linkages. *Community Psychologist, 31,* 3–6.

Bond, M. A. (1999). Gender, race, and class in organizational contexts. *American Journal of Community Psychology, 27*(3), 327–355.

Bond, M. A. (2007). *Work place chemistry: Promoting diversity through organizational change.* Lebanon, NH: University Press of New England.

Bond, M. A., & Harrell, S. (2006). Diversity challenges in community research and action: The story of a special issue of AJCP. *American Journal of Community Psychology, 37,* 157–165.

Bond, M. A., Hill, J., Mulvey, A., & Terenzio, M. (2000). Weaving feminism and community psychology: An introduction to a special issue. *American Journal of Community Psychology, 28,* 585–597.

Bond, M. A., & Mulvey, A. (2000). A history of women and feminist perspectives in community psychology. *American Journal of Community Psychology, 28*(5), 599–630.

Bonhomme, J., Stephens, T., & Braithwaite, R. (2006). African-American males in the United States prison system: Impact on family and community. *Journal of Men's Health & Gender, 3,* 223–226.

Bootzin, R. R., Shadish, W. R., & McSweeney, A. J. (1989). Longitudinal outcomes of nursing home care for severely mentally ill patients. *Journal of Social Issues, 45,* 31–48.

Botvin, G. J. (1996). *Life skills training: Promoting heath and personal development.* Princeton, NJ: Princeton Health Press.

Botvin, G. J., Baker, E., Dusenbury, L., Botvin, E. M., & Diaz, T. (1995). Long-term follow-up results of a randomized drug abuse prevention trial in a White middle-class population. *Journal of the American Medical Association, 273,* 1106–1112.

Borum, R. (2000). Improving high risk encounters between people with mental illness and the police. *Journal of the American Academy of Psychiatry & Law, 28,* 332–337.

Bouey, P. D., Duran, B., Henrickson, M., Wong, F. Y., Haviland, L., Sember, R. E., & Lo, W. (1997). *A cultural competent model for HIV care: A conceptual framework for the collaborative evaluation of HIV services and care programs.* Unpublished manuscript [originally prepared for Ryan White CARE Act's Special Projects of National Significance, National Multi-Site Evaluation Program].

Bowen, W., & Bok, D. (2000), *The shape of the river: Long term consequences of considering race in university and college admissions.* Princeton, NJ: Princeton University Press.

Bowman, L. S., Stein, R. E. K., & Ireys, H. T. (1991). Reinventing fidelity: The transfer of social technology among settings. *American Journal of Community Psychology, 19,* 619–639.

Boyd, N., & Bright, D. (2007). Appreciative inquiry as a mode of action research for community psychology. *Journal of Community Psychology, 35*(8), 1019–1036.

Boyd-Zaharias, J. (1999, Summer). Project STAR. *American Educator,* 30–36.

Bracey, G. W. (2006). Locked up, locked out. *Phi Delta Kappan, 88,* 253–254.

Bradshaw, T. K. (1999). The community development society. *The Community Psychologist, 32,* 9–10.

Bradshaw, W., & Roseborough, D. (2005). Restorative justice dialogue: The impact of mediation and conferencing on juvenile recidivism. *Federal Probation, 69,* 15–21.

Branson, R. K. (1998). Teaching centered schooling has reached its upper limit: It doesn't get any better than this. *Current Directions in Psychological Science, 7,* 126–135.

Bravo, M., Rubio-Stipec, M., Canino, G. J., Woodbury, M. A., & Ribera, J. C. (1990). The psychological sequelae of disaster stress prospectively and retrospectively evaluated. *American Journal of Community Psychology, 18,* 661–680.

Breakey, W. R. (1996). *Integrated mental health services: Modern community psychiatry.* New York, NY: Oxford University Press.

Breiding, M. J., Black, M. C., & Ryan, G. W. (2008). Chronic disease and health risk behaviors associated with intimate partner violence—18 U.S. states/territories, 2005. *Annals of Epidemiology, 18,* 538–544.

Brewer, M. B. (1999). The psychology of prejudice: Ingroup love or outgroup hate? *Journal of Social Issues Special Issue: Prejudice and Intergroup Relations, 55,* 429–444.

Brissette, I., Scheier, M., & Carver, C. (2002). The role of optimism in social network development, coping and psychological adjustment during a life transition. *Journal of Personal and Social Psychology, 82,* 102–111.

Britt, C. L. (2000). Health consequences of criminal victimization. *International Review of Victimology, 8,* 63–73.

Britt T., Adler, A., & Bartone, P. (2001). Deriving benefits from stressful events: The role of engagement in meaningful work and hardiness. *Journal of Occupational Health Psychology, 6,* 53–63.

Brodsky, A. E. (2009). Multiple psychological senses of community in Afghan context: Exploring commitment and sacrifice in an underground resistance community. *American Journal of Community Psychology, 44*(3–4), 176–187.

Brodsky, A. E., Portnoy, G. A., Scheibler, J. E., Welsh, E. A., Talwar, G., & Carrillo, A. (2012). Beyond (the ABCs): Education, community, and feminism in Afghanistan. *Journal of Community Psychology, 40*(1), 159–181. doi:10.1002/jcop.20480

Brodsky, A., Senuta, K., Weiss, C., Marx, C., Loomis, C., Arteaga, S., & Castagnera-Fletcher, A. (2004). When one plus one equals three: The role of relationships and context in community research. *American Journal of Community Psychology, 33,* 229–241.

Brokaw, T. (1998). *The greatest generation.* New York, NY: Random House.

Broman, C. L., Hamilton, V. L., & Hoffman, W. S. (1990). Unemployment and its effects on families: Evidence from a plant closing study. *American Journal of Community Psychology, 18,* 643–659.

Bronfenbrenner, U. (1977). Toward an experimental ecology of human development. *American Psychologist, 32,* 513–531.

Bronfenbrenner, U. (1979). *The ecology of human development: Experiments by nature and design.* Cambridge, MA: Harvard University Press.

Bronfenbrenner, U. (1986, February). Alienation and the four worlds of childhood. *Phi Delta Kappan,* 430–436.

Bronfenbrenner, U. (1999). Environments in developmental perspective: Theoretical and operational models. In S. L. Friedman & T. D. Wachs (Eds.), *Measuring environment across the life span: Emerging methods and concepts.* Washington, DC: American Psychological Association.

Bronfenbrenner, U., & Morris, P. (2006). The bioecological model of human development. In R. Lerner, W. Damon & R. Lerner (Eds.), *Handbook of child psychology* (6th ed., pp. 793–828). New York, NY: John Wiley. doi:10.1002/9780470147658

Brook, J., Brook, D., & Whiteman, M. (2007). Growing up in a violent society: Longitudinal predictors of violence in Colombian adolescents. *American Journal of Community Psychology, 40*(1–2), 82–95.

Brooks, E. R., Zuniga, M., & Penn, N. E. (1995) The decline of public mental health in the United States. In C. V. Willie, P. P. Rieker, B. M. Kramer, & B. S. Brown (Eds.), *Mental health, racism, and sexism* (pp. 51–117). Pittsburgh, PA: University of Pittsburgh Press.

Brooks Gunn, J. (2004). Intervention and policy as change agents for young children. In P. L. Chase Lansdale, K. Kiernan, & R. J. Friedman (Eds.), *Human development across lives and generations. The potential for change.* (pp. 293–340). New York, NY: Cambridge University Press.

Brosnan, M. J., & Thorpe, S. J. (2006). An evaluation of two clinically-derived treatments for technophobia. *Computers in Human Behavior, 22,* 1080–1095.

Broussard, A. C., Mosley-Howard, S., & Roychoudhury, A. (2006). Using youth advocates for mentoring at-risk students in urban settings. *Children & Schools, 28,* 122–127.

Brown, B. B., Perkins, D. D., & Brown, G. (2003). Place attachment in a revitalizing neighborhood: Individual and block levels of analysis. *Journal of Environmental Psychology, 23,* 259–271.

Brown, B. B., Perkins, D. D., & Brown, G. (2004). Incivilities, place attachment, and crime: Block and individual effects. *Journal of Environmental Psychology, 24,* 359–371.

Brownell, K. D. (2002). The environment and obesity. In C. G. Fairburn & K. D. Brownell (Eds.), *Eating disorders and obesity* (2nd ed., pp. 433–438). New York, NY: Guilford.

Bruce, M. L., Takeuchi, D. T., & Leaf, P. J. (1991). Poverty and psychiatric status: Longitudinal evidence from the New Haven Epidemiologic Catchment Area Study. *Archives of General Psychiatry, 48,* 470–474.

Bruce, M., & Thornton, M. (2004). It's my world? Exploring Black and White perceptions of personal control. *Sociological Quarterly, 45,* 597–612.

Buckner, J. C. (1988). The development of an instrument to measure neighborhood cohesion. *American Journal of Community Psychology, 16,* 771–791.

Buhin, L., & Vera, E. M. (2009). Preventing racism and promoting social justice: Person-centered and environment-centered interventions. *Journal of Primary Prevention, 30,* 43–59.

Buki, L., Montoya, Y., & Linares, D. E. (2012). Ameliorating cancer disparities in medically underserved women: A community-based approach. In E. Vera (Ed.), *Oxford Handbook of Prevention in Counseling Psychology.* New York, NY: Oxford University Press.

Bullis, M., Yovanoff, P., & Havel, E. (2001). The importance of getting started right: Further examination of the facility-to-community transition of formerly incarcerated youth. *The Journal of Special Education, 38,* 80–94.

Burchard, J. D., Bruns, E. J., & Burchard, S. N. (2002). The wraparound approach. In B. J. Burns & K. Hoagwood (Eds.), *Community treatment for youth: Evidence-based interventions for severe emotional and behavioral disorders* (pp. 69–90). New York, NY: Oxford University Press.

Burchinal, M. R., Roberts, J. E., Riggins, Jr., R., Zeisel, S. A., Neebe, E., & Bryant, D.(2000), Relating quality of center-based child care to early cognitive and language development longitudinally. *Child Development, 71,* 339–357.

Bureau of Justice Statistics. (1993). *Highlights from 20 years of surveying crime victims.* Washington, DC: U.S. Department of Justice.

Bureau of Justice Statistics. (2006). *Criminal victimization.* Retrieved from http://www.ojp.usdoj.gov/bjs/abstract/cv06.htm

Bureau of Justice Statistics. (2007a). *Correctional authorities reported more than 6,000 allegations of sexual violence in prisons and jails during 2006.* Retrieved from http://www.ojp.usdoj.gov/bjs/pub/press/svrca06pr.htm

Bureau of Justice Statistics. (2007b). *Homicide trends in the U.S.: intimate homicide.* Retrieved from http://bjs.ojp.usdoj.gov/content/homicide/intimates.cfm

Bureau of Justice Statistics. (2008). *Probation and parole statistics.* Retrieved from http://www.ojp.usdoj.gov/bjs/pandp.htm

Bureau of Labor Statistics. (2007). *Employment characteristics of families summary.* Retrieved from http://www.bls.gov/news.release/famee.nr0.htm

Bureau of National Affairs. (1981). Job absence and turnover control. *Personnel Forum Survey no. 132.* Washington, DC: Author.

Burke, I. K., & Follingstad, D. R. (1999). Violence in lesbian and gay relationships: Theory, prevalence, and correlational factors. *Clinical Psychology Review, 19,* 487–512.

Burns, B. J., & Goldman, S. K. (Eds.). (1999). *Systems of Care: Promising practices in children's mental health, 1998 series: Vol. 4. Promising practices in wraparound for children with serious emotional disturbance and their families.* Washington, DC: Center for Effective Collaboration and Practice, American Institutes for Research.

Burns, B. J, Goldman, S. K., Faw, L., & Burchard, J. D. (1999). The wraparound evidence base. In B. J. Burns & S. K. Goldman (Eds.), *Systems of Care: Promising practices in children's mental health, 1998 series: Vol. 4. Promising practices in wraparound for children with serious emotional disturbance and their families* (pp. 77–100). Washington DC: Center for Effective Collaboration and Practice, American Institutes for Research.

Burns, T., Catty, J., Dash, M., Roberts, C., Lockwood, A., & Marshall, M. (2007). Use of intensive case management to reduce time in hospital in people with severe mental illness: Systematic review and meta-regression. *British Medical Journal, 335–336.* doi:10.1136/bmj.39251.599259.55

Burroughs, S. M., & Eby, L. T. (1998). Psychological sense of community at work: A measurement system and exploratory framework. *Journal of Community Psychology, 26,* 509–532.

Burt, K., Obradovic, J., Long, J., & Masten, A. (2008). The interplay of social competence and psychopathology over 20 years: Testing transactional and cascade models. *Child Development, 79*(2), 359–374.

Burt, M. R., Pearson, C., & Montgomery, A. E. (2007). Community-wide strategies for preventing homelessness: Recent evidence. *Journal of Primary Prevention, 23,* 213–228.

Burton, C. E. (2004). Segregation and Latino homicide victimization. *American Journal of Criminal Justice, 29,* 21–36.

Butcher, K., Sallis, J., & Mayer, J. (2008). Correlates of physical activity guideline compliance for adolescents in 100 U.S. cities. *Journal of Adolescent Health, 42,* 360–368.

Byrne, J. M. (2004). Introduction: Reentry—the emperor's new clothes. *Federal Probation, 69,* 1–2.

Byrne, J. M., & Taxman, F. S. (2004). Targeting for reentry: Inclusion/exclusion criteria across eight model programs. *Federal Probation, 68,* 53–61.

Cadena, B., Danziger, S., & Seefeldt, K. (2006). Measuring state welfare policy changes: Why don't they explain caseload and employment outcomes? *Social Science Quarterly, 87,* 798–807.

Caldwell, C. H., Kohn-Wood, L. P., Schmeelk-Cone, K. H., Chavous, T. M., & Zimmerman, M. A. (2004). Racial discrimination and racial identity as risk or protective factors for violent behaviors in African American young adults. *American Journal of Community Psychology, 33,* 91–105.

Campaign for Our Children. (2001). *About Campaign for Our Children.* Retrieved from http://www.cfoc.org.

Campbell, C., & Murray, M. (2004). Community health psychology: Promoting health analysis and action for social change. *Journal of Health Psychology, 9,* 187–195.

Campbell, C., Nair, Y., & Maimane, S. (2007). Building contexts that support effective community responses to HIV/AIDS: a South African case study. *American Journal of Community Psychology, 39,* 347–363.

Campbell, D. (1974). *Qualitative knowing in action research.* Paper presented at the annual meetings of the American Psychological Association, New Orleans, LA.

Campbell, D., & Stanley, J. (1963). *Experimental and quasi-experimental designs for research.* Chicago, IL: Rand McNally.

Campbell, R., Baker, C. K., & Mazurek, T. L. (1998). Remaining radical? Organizational predictors of rape crisis centers' social change initiatives. *American Journal of Community Psychology, 26,* 457–483.

Campbell, R., Gregory, K., Patterson, D., & Bybee, D. (2012). Integrating qualitative and quantitative approaches: An example of mixed methods research. In L. Jason & D. Glenwick (Eds.), *Methodological approaches to community-based research* (pp. 52–68). Washington, DC: American Psychological Association.

Campbell, R., & Wasco, S. (2000). Feminist approaches to social science: Epistemological and methodological tenets. *American Journal of Community Psychology, 28*(6), 773–791.

Campfield, K. M., & Hills, A. M. (2001). Effect of timing of critical incident stress debriefing on posttraumatic symptoms. *Journal of Posttraumatic Stress Special Issue, 14,* 327–340.

Campion, M., & McClelland, C.(1993). Interdisciplinary examination of the costs and benefits of enlarged jobs: A job design quasi-experiment. *Journal of Applied Psychology, 76,* 186–198.

Campos, B., Dunkel-Schetter, C., Abdou, C. M., Hobel, C. J., Glynn, L. M., & Sandman, C. A. (2008). Familialism, social support, and stress: Positive implications for pregnant Latinas. *Cultural Diversity and Ethnic Minority Psychology, 14*(2), 155–162.

Cantelon, S., & LeBoeuf, D. (1997, June). Keeping young people in school. Community programs that work. *Juvenile Justice Bulletin,* 1–9.

Caplan, G. (1964). *Principles of preventive psychiatry.* New York, NY: Basic Books.

Caplan, G. (1989). Recent developments in crisis intervention and the promotion of support service. *Journal of Primary Prevention, 10,* 3–25.

Caplan, N., Morrison, A., & Stambaugh, R. J. (1975). *The use of social science knowledge in policy decisions at the national level: A report to respondents.* Ann Arbor: Institute for Social Research, University of Michigan.

Caplan, R. D., Vinokur, A. D., Price, R. H., & van Ryn, M. (1989). Job seeking, reemployment, and mental health. *Journal of Applied Psychology, 74,* 759–769.

Caputo, R. K. (2003). Head Start, other preschool programs, and life success in a youth cohort. *Journal of Sociology & Social Welfare, 30,* 105–126.

Caputo, R. K. (2004). The impact of intergenerational Head Start participation on success measures among adolescent children. *Journal of Family and Economic Issues, 25,* 199–223.

Carbonell, J. (2003). *Baby boomers at the gate: Enhancing independence through innovation and technology.* U.S. Department of Health and Human Services. Retrieved from http://www.hhs.gov.asl.testify/t030520.html

Cargo, M., Grams, G. D., Ottoson, J. M., Ward, P., & Green, L. W. (2003). Empowerment as fostering positive youth development and citizenship. *American Journal of Health Behavior, 27,* 566–579.

Carleton, R., Lasater, T., Assaf, A., Feldman, H., & McKinlay, S. (1995). The Pawtucket Heart Health Program: Community changes in cardiovascular risk factors and projected disease risk. *American Journal of Public Health, 85,* 777–785.

Carlson, J., Watts, R. E., Maniacci, M. (2006). Consultation and psychoeducation. *Adlerian therapy: Theory and practice* (pp. 251–276). Washington DC: American Psychological Association.

Carmony, T., Lock, T., Crabtree, A., Keller, J., Yanasak, B., & Moritsugu, J. (2000). Teaching community psychology: A brief review of undergraduate courses. *Teaching of Psychology, 27,* 214–215.

Carnevale, P. J., & Pruitt, D. G. (1992). Negotiation and mediation. *Annual Review of Psychology, 43,* 531–582.

Carter, F. A., & Bulik, C. M. (2008). Childhood obesity prevention programs: How do they affect eating pathology and other psychological measures? *Psychosomatic Medicine, 70,* 363–371.

Carver, C. S., Scheier, M. F., & Weintraub, J. K. (1989). Assessing coping strategies: A theoretically based approach. *Journal of Personality and Social Psychology, 56*(2), 267–283.

Cascio, W. (1995). Whither industrial and organizational psychology in a changing world of work? *American Psychologist, 50,* 928–939.

Cascio, W. F. (2010). The changing world of work. In P. Linley, S. Harrington, & N. Garcea (Eds.), *Oxford handbook of positive psychology and work* (pp. 13–23). New York, NY: Oxford University Press.

Cascio, W. F., & Aguinis, H. (2008). Research in industrial and organizational psychology from 1963 to 2007: Changes, choices, and trends. *Journal of Applied Psychology, 93*(5), 1062–1081.

Cascio, W. F., & Aguinis, H. (2008). Staffing twenty-first-century organizations. *The Academy of Management Annals, 2*(1), 133–165. doi:10.1080/19416520802211461

Case, S., & Haines, L. (2007). Offending by young people: A further risk factor analysis. *Security Journal, 20,* 96–110.

Casper, L & Smith, K. (2002). Dispelling the myths: Self-care, class, and race. *Journal of Family Issues, 23,* 716–727.

Caspi, A., Taylor, A., Moffitt, T. E., & Plomin, R. (2000). Neighborhood deprivation affects children's mental health: Environmental risks identified in a genetic design. *Psychological Science, 11,* 338–342.

Cassinerio, C., & Lane-Garon, P. S. (2006). Changing school climate one mediator at a time: Year-one analysis of a school-based mediation program. *Conflict Resolution Quarterly, 23,* 447–460.

Cassell, E. J. (2009). Compassion. In S. J. Lopez & C. R. Snyder (Eds.), *Oxford handbook of positive psychology* (2nd ed., pp. 393–403). New York, NY: Oxford University Press.

Casswell, S. (2000). A decade of community action research. *Substance Use & Misuse Special Issue: Community Action and the Prevention of Alcohol-Related Problems at the Local Level, 35,* 55–74.

Castellini, F., Colombo, M., Maffeis, D., & Montali, L. (2011). Sense of community and interethnic relations: Comparing local communities varying in ethnic heterogeneity. *Journal of Community Psychology, 39*(6), 663-677.

Catalano, R. F., Bergland, M. L., Ryan, J. A., Lonczak, H. C., & Hawkins, J. D. (1999). *Positive youth development in the United States: Research findings on evaluations of positive youth development programs.* Washington, DC: Department of Health and Human Services, National Institute for Child Health and Human Development.

Catterall, J. S., & Stern, D. (1986). The effects of alternative school programs on high school completions and labor market outcomes. *Educational Evaluation and Policy Analysis, 8,* 77–86.

Cauce, A. (1990). A cautionary note about adventuresome research: Musings of a junior researcher. In P. Tolan, C. Keys, F. Chertok, & L. Jason (Eds.), *Researching community psychology: Issues of theory and methods* (p. 205). Washington, DC: American Psychological Association.

Caughy, M., O'Campus, P., & Brodsky, A. (1999). Neighborhoods, families and children: Implications for policy and practice. *Journal of Community Psychology, 27,* 615–633.

Cautin, R. (2011) A century of psychotherapy 1860–1960, In Norcross, J. VandenBos, G., Freedheim, D. (Eds.). *History of psychotherapy: Continuity and change* (2nd ed., pp. 3–38). Washington, D.C.: American Psychological Association.

Center on Philanthropy. (2001, April 18). *Report on the December 2000 Philanthropic Giving Index.* Retrieved from http://www.philanthropy.IUPUI.edu.

Centers for Disease Control and Prevention. (1996). *State behavioral risk factor surveillance system, 1993* [data tape]. Atlanta, GA: Author.

Centers for Disease Control and Prevention. (1999). *Teen pregnancy.* Retrieved from http://www.cdc.gov/nccdphp/teen.htm

Centers for Disease Control and Prevention. (2000). *CDC fact book 2000/2001.* Atlanta, GA: Author.

Centers for Disease Control and Prevention. (2004a). *HIV/AIDS surveillance report* (Vol. 16). Atlanta, GA: Author. Retrieved from http://www.cdc.gov/hiv/topics/surveillance/resources/reports/2004report/default.htm

Centers for Disease Control and Prevention. (2004b). *Report to Congress: Prevention of genital human papillomavirus infection.* Atlanta, GA: Author.

Centers for Disease Control and Prevention. (2006a). Epidemiology of HIV/AIDS United States, 1981–2004, *MMWR Weekly,* June 2, 2006/55(21), 589–592. Retrieved from cdc.gov/mmwr/preview/mmwrhtml/mm5521a2.htm

Centers for Disease Control and Prevention. (2006b). *HIV/AIDS Surveillance Report* (Vol. 18). Atlanta, GA: Department of Health and Human Services.

Centers for Disease Control and Prevention. (2007a). *Adolescent reproductive health: Teen pregnancy.* Retrieved from http://www.cdc.gov/reproductivehealth/adolescentreprohealth

Centers for Disease Control and Prevention. (2007b). *CDC fact sheet: The role of STD prevention and treatment in HIV prevention.* Atlanta, GA: Department of Health and Human Services.

Centers for Disease Control and Prevention. (2007c, Summer). Child maltreatment. *Facts at a Glance,* 1.

Centers for Disease Control and Prevention. (2008). Smoking-attributable mortality, years of potential life lost, and productivity losses—United States, 2000–2004. *Morbidity and Mortality Weekly Report, 57*(45), 1226–1228.

Centers for Disease Control and Prevention, National Center for Injury Prevention and Control, Centers for Disease Control and Prevention. (2010a). Cigarette use among high school students—United States, 1991–2009. *Morbidity and Mortality Weekly Report, 59*(26), 797–801. Retrieved from http://www.cdc.gov/mmwr/pdf/ss/ss5905.pdf

Centers for Disease Control and Prevention, National Center for Injury Prevention and Control. (2010b). The National Intimate Partner and Sexual Violence Survey. Retrieved from http://www.cdc.gov/violenceprevention/nisvs/index.html

Centers for Disease Control and Prevention. (2011a). *2010 sexually transmitted diseases surveillance.* Retrieved from http://www.cdc.gov/std/stats10

Centers for Disease Control and Prevention. (2011b). *Smoking and tobacco use*. Atlanta, GA: Author. Retrieved from http://www.cdc.gov/tobacco/data_statistics/fact_sheets/fast_facts/index.htm

Centers for Disease Control and Prevention, National Center for Injury Prevention and Control. (2011c). Assault all injury causes nonfatal injuries and rates per 100,000, all races, both sexes, ages 0 to 24. Web-based Injury Statistics Query and Reporting System (WISQARS) [online] (2008). Retrieved from: http://www.cdc.gov/injury/wisqars

Centers for Disease Control and Prevention. (2011d). *Teen pregnancy*. Retrieved from http://www.cdc.gov/teenpregnancy

Centers for Disease Control and Prevention. (2011e). *Fact sheets, binge drinking*. Retrieved from http://www.cdc.gov/alcohol/fact-sheets/binge-drinking.htm

Center for Prevention Research and Development. (2006). *Evidence-based practices for effective community coalitions*. Champaign: Center for Prevention Research and Development, Institute of Government and Public Affairs, University of Illinois. Retrieved from http://www.cprd.illinois.edu/files/CoalitionBestPractices.pdf

Chadee, D., Austen, L., & Ditton, J. (2007). The relationship between likelihood and fear of criminal victimization: Evaluating risk sensitivity as a mediating concept. *British Journal of Criminology, 47*, 133–153.

Chaffin, M. (2004). Is it time to rethink Healthy Start/Healthy Families? *Child Abuse & Neglect, 28*, 589–595.

Chan, C. K. (2004). Placing dignity at the center of welfare policy. *International Journal of Social Work, 47*, 227–239.

Chandler, M., & Proulx, T. (2006). Changing selves in changing worlds: Youth suicide on the fault-lines of colliding cultures. *Archives of Suicide Research, 10*(2), 125–140.

Chanley, V. A., Rudolph, T. J., & Rahn, W. M. (2000). The origins and consequences of public trust in government. *Public Opinion Quarterly, 54*, 239–256.

Chapman, J., & Ferrari, J. (1999). An introduction to community based service learning. In J. Ferrari & J. Chapman (Eds.), *Educating students to make a difference: Community based service learning* (pp. 1–3). New York, NY: Haworth Press.

Chapman, L. (2007). Closing thoughts. *American Journal of Health Promotion, 21*, 8.

Charkoudian, L. (2005). A quantitative analysis of the effectiveness of community mediation in decreasing repeat police calls for service. *Conflict Resolution Quarterly, 23*, 87–98.

Chatman, J., & Spataro, S. (2005). Using self-categorization theory to understand relational demographic based variations in people's responsiveness to organizational culture. *Academy of Management Journal, 48*, 321–331.

Chavis, D. M. (1993). A future for community psychology practice. *American Journal of Community Psychology, 21*, 171–183.

Chavis, D. M., Florin, P., & Felix, M. R. J. (1992). Nurturing grass roots initiatives for community development: The role of enabling systems. In T. Mizrahi & J. Morrison (Eds.), *Community organization and social administration: Advances, trends, and emerging principles*. Binghamton, NY: Haworth.

Chavis, D. M., Stucky, P. E., & Wandersman, A. (1983). Returning research to the community: A relationship between scientist and citizen. *American Psychologist, 38*, 424–434.

Chavis, D. M., & Wandersman, A. W. (1990). Sense of community in the urban environment: A catalyst for participation and community development. *American Journal of Community Psychology, 18*, 55–82.

Checkland, P. (1981). *Systems thinking: Systems practice*. Chichester, England: Wiley.

Checkoway, B. (2009). Community change for diverse democracy. *Community Development Journal, 44*(1), 5–21. doi:10.1093/cdj/bsm018

Cheng, S. (1990). Change processes in the professional bureaucracy. *Journal of Community Psychology, 18*, 183–193.

Cheng, S., Chan, A., & Phillips, D. (2004). Quality of life in old age: An investigation of well older persons in Hong Kong. *Journal of Community Psychology, 32*(3), 309–326.

Cheng, S., & Heller, K. (2009). Global aging: Challenges for community psychology. *American Journal of Community Psychology, 44*(1–2), 161–173. doi:10.1007/s10464-009-9244-x

Cherniss, C. (1999). Training in cultural competence: A survey of graduate programs in community research and action. *Community Psychologist, 32*, 22–23.

Chesson, H., Gift, T. L., & Pulver, A. L. S. (2004). The economic value of reductions in gonorrhea and syphilis incidence in the United States, 1990–2003. *Preventive Medicine, 43*, 411–415.

Cheung, C., Kwan, A., & Ng, S. (2006). Impacts of filial piety on preference for kinship versus public care. *Journal of Community Psychology, 34*, 617–634.

Cheung, F. M. C. (1986). Psychopathology among Chinese people. In M. H. Bond (Ed.), *The psychology of the Chinese people*. New York, NY: Oxford University Press.

Cheung, F. M. (1988). Surveys of community attitudes toward mental health facilities: Reflections or provocations? *American Journal of Community Psychology, 16*, 877–882.

Chiang, C., & Hsieh, T. (2012). The impacts of perceived organizational support and psychological empowerment on job performance: The mediating effects of organizational citizenship behavior. *International Journal of Hospitality Management, 31*(1), 180–190.

Child Welfare Information Gateway. (2006). *Child abuse and neglect fatalities: Statistics and interventions.* Retrieved from http://www.childwelfare.gov/pubs/factsheets/fatality.cfm

Children's Aid Society. (2008). *The Carrera Program.* Retrieved from http://www.childrensaidsociety.org/youth-development/carrera/components

Chilenski, S. M. (2011). From the macro to the micro: A geographic examination of the community context and early adolescent problem behaviors. *American Journal of Community Psychology, 48*(3–4), 352–364.

Chilenski, S. M., Greenberg, M. T., & Feinberg, M. E. (2007). Community readiness as a multidimensional construct. *Journal of Community Psychology, 35*(3), 347–365.

Chin, J. J., & Wong, F. Y. (2003). Improving access to care for cultural, linguistic and racial minorities: The Bilingual Peer Advocate Program of the Asian & Pacific Islander Coalition on HIV/AIDS. In J. Erwin, D. Smith, & B. S. Petersee (Eds.), *Ethnicity and HIV.* International Medical Press.

Chipperfield, J. (1993). Perceived barriers in coping with health problems: A twelve-year longitudinal study of survival among elderly individuals. *Journal of Aging and Health, 5,* 123–139.

Choi, B., Pang, T., Lin, V., Puska, P., Sherman, G., Goddard, M., . . . Clottey, C. (2005). Can scientists and policy makers work together? *Journal of Epidemiology & Community Health, 5,* 632–637.

Choi, J. J., Green, D. L., & Kapp, S. A. (2010). Victimization, victims' needs, and empowerment in victim offender mediation. *International Review of Victimology, 17*(3), 267–290.

Choi, K.-H., & Coates, T. J. (1994). Prevention of infection. *AIDS, 8,* 1371–1389.

Choi, N. G., & Wodarski, J. S. (1996). The relationship between social support and health status of elderly people: Does social support slow down physical and functional deterioration? *Social Work Research, 20,* 52–63.

Chomitz, V. R., Collings, J., Kim, J., Kramer, E., & McGowan, R. (2003). Promoting healthy weight among elementary school children via a health report card approach. *Archives of Pediatrics & Adolescent Medicine, 157,* 765–772.

Christens, B., Hanlin, C., & Speer, P. (2007). Getting the social organism thinking: Strategy for systems change. *American Journal of Community Psychology, 39*(3–4), 229–238.

Christensen, J. A., & Robinson, J. W. (1989). *Community development in perspective.* Ames: Iowa State University Press.

Christensen, L. (1988). Deception in psychological research. *Personality and Social Psychology Bulletin, 14,* 664–675.

Christenson, S. L., & Thurlow, M. L. (2004). School dropouts: Prevention considerations, interventions, and challenges. *Current Directions in Psychological Science, 13,* 36–39.

Christian, T. F. (1986). A resource for all seasons: A state-wide network of community dispute resolution centers. In J. Palenski & H. Launer (Eds.), *Mediation: Contexts and challenges.* Springfield, IL: Thomas.

Christie, C. A., Jolivette, K., & Nelson, M. (2007). School characteristics related to high school dropout rates. *Remedial and Special Education, 28,* 325–339.

Chronister, K. (2007). Contextualizing women domestic violence survivors' economic and emotional dependencies. *American Psychologist, 62,* 706–708.

Chronister, K., Brown, C., O'Brien, K., Wettersten, K. B., Burt, M., Falkenstein, C., & Shahane, A. (2009). Domestic violence survivors: Perceived vocational supports and barriers. *Journal of Career Assessment, 17,* 116–131.

Chronister, K. M., & McWhirter, E. H. (2006). An experimental examination of two career counseling programs for battered women. *Journal of Counseling Psychology, 53,* 151–164.

Cicchetti, D. (2004). An odyssey of discovery: Lessons learned through three decades of research on child maltreatment. *American Psychologist, 59*(8), 731–741.

Cicchetti, D. (2007). Intervention and policy implications of research on neurobiological functioning in maltreated children. In L. J. Aber, S. J. Bishop-Josef, S. M. Jones, K. Taffe, & D. A. Phillips (Eds.), *Child development and social policy: Knowledge for action.* Washington, DC: American Psychological Association.

Cicchetti, D., Rogosch, F. A., Gunnar, M. R., & Toth, S. L. (2010). The differential impacts of early physical and sexual abuse and internalizing problems on daytime cortisol rhythm in school-aged children. *Child Development, 81*(1), 252–269.

Cicchetti, D., Rogosch, F., & Toth, S. (2006). Fostering secure attachment in infants in maltreating families through preventive interventions. *Development and Psychopathology, 18,* 623–649.

Cicchetti, D., Toth, S. C., & Rogosch, F. A. (2000). The development of psychological wellness in maltreated children. In D. Cicchetti & J. Rappaport (Eds.), *The promotion of wellness in maltreated children and adolescents.* Washington, DC: Child Welfare League of America.

Cicchetti, D., & Toth, S. L. (1998). The development of depression in children and adolescents. *American Psychologist, 53*(2), 221–241.

Cicchetti, D., & Valentino, K. (2006). An ecological-transactional perspective on child maltreatment: Failure of the average expectable environment and its influence on child development. In D. Cicchetti & D. J. Cohen (Eds.), *Developmental psychopathology.* Hoboken, NJ: Wiley.

Cid, J. (2009). Is imprisonment criminogenic? A comparative study of recidivism rates between prison and suspended prison sanctions. *European Journal of Criminology, 6,* 459.

Clark, K. B. (1989). *Dark ghetto: Dilemmas of social power.* Hanover, NH: Wesleyan University Press.

Clark, K. B., & Clark, M. P. (1947). Racial identification and preference in Negro children. In T. M. Newcomb & E. L. Hartley (Eds.), *Readings in social psychology.* New York, NY: Holt.

Clark, R., Anderson, N., Clark, V., & Williams, D. (1999). Racism as a stressor for African Americans: A biopsychosocial model. *American Psychologist, 54,* 805–816.

Clarke, A. (2006). Coping with interpersonal stress and psychosocial health among children and adolescents: A meta-analysis. *Journal of Youth and Adolescence, 35,* 11–24.

Clary, E. G., & Snyder, M. (1999). The motivations to volunteer: Theoretical and practical considerations. *Current Directions in Psychological Science, 8,* 156–160.

Clipp, E., & Elder, G. (1996). The aging veteran of World War II: Psychiatric and life course insights. In P. Ruskin & J. Talbot (Eds.), *Aging and post traumatic stress disorder* (pp. 19–51). Washington, DC: American Psychiatric Press.

Cock, K., Mbori-Ngacha, D., & Marum, E. (2002). Shadow on the continent: Public health and HIV/AIDS in Africa in the 21st century. *Lancet, 360,* 67–72.

Coffee, J. N., & Pestridge, S. (2001, May). The career academy concept. *OJDP Fact Sheet,* 1–2.

Cogan, J. C., Smith, J. P., & Maine, M. D. (2008). The risks of a quick fix: A case against mandatory body mass index reporting laws. *Eating Disorders, 16,* 2–13.

Cohen, J. (2007). AIDS research: Promising AIDS vaccine's failure leaves field reeling. *Science, 318*(5847), 28–29.

Cohen, M. D., Shore, M. F., & Mazda, N. A. (1991). Development of a management training program for state mental health program directors. Special issue: Education in mental health administration. *Administration and Policy in Mental Health, 18,* 247–256.

Cohen, S., & Wills, T. (1985). Stress, social support and the buffering hypothesis. *Psychological Bulletin, 98,* 310–357.

Coleman, J. (1999). Social capital in the creation of human capital. In P. Dasgupta & I. Serageldin (Eds.), *Social capital: A multifaceted perspective* (pp. 13–39). Washington, DC: World Bank.

Coleman, R., & Widon, C. (2004). Childhood abuse and neglect and adult intimate relationships: A prospective study. *Child Abuse and Neglect, 28,* 1133–1151.

Coley, R. L., & Chase-Lansdale, P. L. (1998). Adolescent pregnancy and parenthood. *American Psychologist, 53,* 152–166.

Coley, R. L., Kuta, A., & Chase-Lansdale, P. L. (2000). An insider view: Knowledge and opinions of welfare from African American girls in poverty. *Journal of Social Issues Special Issue: The Impact of Welfare Reform, 56,* 707–726.

Coley, R. L., Lohman, B. J., Votruba-Drzal, E., Pittman, L. D., & Chase-Lansdale, P. L. (2007). Maternal functioning, time and money: The world of work and welfare. *Children and Youth Services Review, 29,* 721–741.

Coley, R, Morris, L., & Hernandez, D. (2004). Out of school care and problem behavior trajectories among low income adolescents: Individual, family, and neighborhood characteristics as added risks. *Child Development, 75,* 948–965.

Collier, A., Munger, M., & Moua, Y. (2012). Hmong mental health needs assessment: A community-based partnership in a small Mid-Western community. *American Journal of Community Psychology, 49*(1–2), 73–86.

Collins, C., & Yeskel, F. (2005). *Economic apartheid.* New York, NY: New Press.

Collins, M. E., & Mowbray, C. T. (2005). Higher education and psychiatric disabilities: National survey of campus disability services. *American Journal of Orthopsychiatry, 75*(2), 304–315.

Colman, R., & Widom, C. (2004). Childhood abuse and neglect and adult intimate relationships: A prospective study. *Child Abuse & Neglect, 28,* 1133–1151.

Compas, B. (2006). Psychobiological processes of stress and coping: Implications for resilience in children and adolescents—comments. *Annals of the New York Academy of Sciences, 1094,* 226–234.

Compas, B. E., Connor-Smith, J. K., Saltzman, H., Thomsen, A. H., & Wadsworth, M. (2001). Coping with stress during childhood and adolescence: Progress, problems, and potential. *Psychological Bulletin, 127,* 87–127.

Compas, B. E., Wagner, B. M., Slavin, L. A., & Vannatta, K. (1986). A prospective study of life events, social support, and psychological symptomatology during the transition from high school to college. *American Journal of Community Psychology, 14,* 241–257.

Connor, D. F., Doerfler, L. A., Volungis, A. M., Steingard, R. J., & Melloni, R. H. (2003). Aggressive behavior in abused children. In J. A. King, C. F. Ferris, & I. I. Lederhendler (Eds.), *Roots of mental illness in children* (pp. 79–90). New York, NY: New York Academy of Sciences.

Connors, M. M., & McGrath, J. W. (1997). The known, unknown, and unknowable in AIDS research in anthropology. *Anthropology Newsletter, 38,* 1–5.

Constantine, L. L. (1991). Fitting intervention to organizational paradigm. *Organization Development Journal, 9*(2), 41–50.

Conyne, R. K. (2004). *Preventive counseling: Helping people to become empowered in systems and settings* (2nd ed.). New York, NY: Brunner-Routledge.

Cook, S. L. (2012). In the public interest: Contemplating Seymour, sin, and a center. *Journal of Community Psychology, 40*(2), 223–226.

Cook, S. W. (1985). Experimenting on social issues: The case of school desegregation. *American Psychologist, 47,* 452–460.

Cook, T. D., & Shadish, W. R. (1986). Program evaluation: The worldly science. *Annual Review of Psychology, 37,* 193–232.

Cook, T. D., & Shadish, W. R. (1994). Social experiments: Some developments over the past fifteen years. In L. W. Porter & M. R. Rosenzweig (Eds.), *Annual review of psychology.* Palo Alto, CA: Annual Reviews.

Cooper, J. (2006). The digital divide: The special case of gender. *Journal of Computer Assisted Learning, 22,* 320–334.

Cooper, M. L. (2002). Alcohol use and risky sexual behavior among college students and youth: Evaluating the evidence. *Journal of Studies on Alcohol, 14,* 101–117.

Cooperberg, J., & Faith, M. S. (2004). Treatment of obesity II: Childhood and adolescent obesity. In J. K. Thompson (Ed.), *Handbook of eating disorders and obesity* (pp. 443–460). Hoboken, NJ: Wiley.

Copeland-Linder, N. (2006). Stress among black women in a south African township: The protective role of religion. *Journal of Community Psychology, 34*(5), 577–599.

Corcoran, J., & Pillai, V. K. (2007). Effectiveness of secondary pregnancy prevention programs: A meta-analysis. *Research on Social Work Practice, 17,* 5–18.

Cordner, G. W. (2000). A community policing approach to persons with mental illness. *Journal of the American Academy of Psychiatry & the Law, 28,* 326–331.

Corning, A., & Myers, D. (2002). Individual orientation toward engagement in social action. *Political Psychology, 23,* 703–729.

Coulton, C. J., & Korbin, J. E. (2007). Indicators of child well-being: Through a neighborhood lens. *Social Indicators Research, 84,* 349–361.

Coulton, C. J., Korbin, J. E., & Su, M. (1996). Measuring neighborhood context for young children in an urban area. *American Journal of Community Psychology, 24,* 5–32.

Coulton, C. J., Korbin, J., & Su, M. (1999). Neighborhoods and child maltreatment: A multi-level study. *Child Abuse & Neglect, 23,* 1019–1040.

Cowen, E. (1973). Social and community interventions. *Annual Review of Psychology, 24,* 423–472.

Cowen, E. L. (1980). The wooing of primary prevention. *American Journal of Community Psychology, 8,* 258–284.

Cowen, E. L. (1985). Person-centered approaches to primary prevention in mental health: Situation-focused and competence-enhancement. *American Journal of Community Psychology, 13*(1), 31–48.

Cowen, E. (1991). In pursuit of wellness. *American Psychologist. 46,* 404–408.

Cowen, E. (1994). The enhancement of psychological wellness: Challenges and opportunities. *American Journal of Community Psychology, 22*(2), 149–179.

Cowen, E. L. (1996). The ontogenesis of primary prevention: Lengthy strides and stubbed toes. *American Journal of Community Psychology, 24,* 235–249.

Cowen, E. L. (1997a). The coming of age of primary prevention research: Comments on Durlak and Wells's meta-analysis. *American Journal of Community Psychology, 25,* 153–167.

Cowen, E. L. (1997b). On the semantics and operations of primary prevention and wellness enhancement (or will the real primary prevention please stand up?). *American Journal of Community Psychology, 25,* 245–255.

Cowen, E. (2000). Community psychology and routes to psychological wellness. In J. Rappaport & E. Seidman (Eds.), *Handbook of community psychology* (pp. 79–99). New York, NY: Kluwer/Plenum.

Cowen, E. L., Hightower, A. D., Pedro-Carroll, J. L., Work, W. C., Wyman, P. A., & Haffey, W. G. (1996). *School-based prevention for children at risk.* Washington, DC: American Psychological Association.

Cox, R. S., & Perry, K. (2011). Like a fish out of water: Reconsidering disaster recovery and the role of place and social capital in community disaster resilience. *American Journal of Community Psychology, 48*(3–4), 395–411.

Coyne, I., & Ong, T. (2007). Organizational citizenship behavior and turnover intention: A cross-cultural study. *International Journal of Human Resource Management, 18*(6),1085–1097.

Crockett, L., Iturbide, M., Torres-Stone, R., McGinley, M., Raffaelli, M., & Carlo, G. (2007). Acculturative stress, social support and coping: Relations to psychological adjustment among Mexican American college students. *Cultural Diversity and Ethnic Minority Psychology, 13,* 347–355.

Crofford, L. J. (2007). Violence, stress, and somatic syndromes. *Trauma, Violence, & Abuse, 8,* 299–313.

Cromartie, S. P. (2007, July/August). Labor force status of families: A visual essay. *Monthly Labor Review, 130*(7), 35–41.

Crosby, R. A., & Holtgrave, D. R. (2005). The protective value of social capital against teen pregnancy: A state-level analysis. *Journal of Adolescent Health, 7,* 245–252.

Cross, W. (2006). Globalism, America's ghettos, and Black youth development. In C. Daiute, Z. Beykont, C. Higson-Smith, & L. Nucci (Eds.), *International perspectives on youth conflict and development* (pp. 269–288). New York, NY: Oxford University Press.

Crosson, M. T., & Christian, T. F. (1990). *The Community Dispute Resolution Centers Program annual report.* Albany, NY: Office of Court Administration.

Cruess, D., Antoni, M., Kumar, M., & Schneiderman, N. (2000). Reductions in salivary cortisol are associated with mood improvement during relaxation training among HIV-seropositive men. *Journal of Behavioral Medicine, 23*, 107–122.

Cuddy, A. J. C., Norton, M. I., & Fiske, S. T. (2005). This old stereotype: The pervasiveness and persistence of the elderly stereotype. *Journal of Social Issues, 61*, 267–285.

Currie, J. M. (2006). *The invisible safety net: Protecting the nation's poor children and families.* Princeton, NJ: Princeton University Press.

Cutrona, C. E., Russell, D. W., Hessling, R. M., Brown, P. A., & Murry, V. (2000). Direct and moderating effects of community context on the psychological well-being of African American women. *Journal of Personality & Social Psychology, 79*, 1088–1101.

Dandeneau, S., Baldwin, M., Baccus, J., Sakellaropoulo, M., & Pruessner, J. (2007). Cutting stress off at the pass: Reducing vigilance and responsiveness to social threat by manipulating attention. *Journal of Personality and Social Psychology, 93*, 651–666.

Daniel, P. T. K. (2004). Accountability and desegregation: *Brown* and its legacy. *Journal of Negro Education, 73*, 255–267.

Danish, S. J. (1983). Musings about personal competence: The contributions of sport, health, and fitness. *American Journal of Community Psychology, 11*, 221–240.

Danish, S. J., & Gullotta, T. P. (2000). *Developing competent youth and strong communities through after-school programming.* Washington, DC: Child Welfare League of America.

Danso, H. A., Sedlovskaya, A., & Suanda, S. H. (2007). Perceptions of immigrants: Modifying the attitudes of individuals higher in social dominance orientation. *Personality and Social Psychology Bulletin, 33*, 1113–1123.

Dapp, U., Anderson, J., von Rentein-Kruse, W., & Meier-Baumgartner, H. P. (2005). Active health promotion in old age: Methodology of a preventive intervention programme provided by an interdisciplinary health advisory team for independent old people. *Journal of Public Health, 13*, 122–127.

Darling, N., Bogat, A., Cavell, T., Murphy, S., & Sánchez, B. (2006). Gender, ethnicity, development, and risk: Mentoring and the consideration of individual differences. *Journal of Community Psychology, 34*(6), 765–779.

Darrock J. (2001). Teenage sexual and reproductive behaviour in developed countries: Can more progress be made? (Occasional Report No. 3). New York, NY: The Allan Guttmacher Institute.

Darrouch, J., Frost, J., & Singh, S. (2001). Differences in teenage pregnancy rates among five developed countries: The roles of sexual activity and contraceptive use. *Family Planning Perspectives, 33* (Nov–Dec), 244–250, 281.

Davey, C. L., Wootton, A. B., Cooper, R., & Press, M. (2005). Design against crime: Extending the reach of crime prevention through environmental design. *Security Journal, 18*, 39–51.

Davidson, L. M., & Demaray, M. K. (2007). Social support as a moderator between victimization and internalizing-externalizing distress from bullying. *School Psychology Review, 36*, 383–405.

Davidson, M. M., Schwartz, J., & Waldo, M. (2012). Preventing intimate partner violence. In E. Vera (Ed.), *Oxford handbook of prevention in counseling psychology.* New York, NY: Oxford University Press.

Davidson, R., Kabat Zinn, J., Schumacher, J., Rosenkranz, M., Muller, D., Santorelli, S., . . . Sheridan, J. (2003). Alterations in brain and immune function produced by mindfulness meditation. *Psychosomatic Medicine, 65*, 564–570.

Davidson, W. B., & Cotter, P. R. (1991). The relationship between sense of community and subjective well-being: A first look. *Journal of Community Psychology, 19*, 246–253.

Davis, D. M. (2004). Merry-go-round: A return to segregation and the implications for creating democratic schools. In De jure, de facto: Defining quality education 50 years beyond *Brown* [special issue]. *Urban Education, 39*, 394–407.

Davis, M. K., & Gidycz, C. A. (2000). Child sexual abuse prevention programs: A meta-analysis. *Journal of Clinical Child Psychology, 29*, 257–265.

Davis, P., & Cummings, E. (2006). Interparental discord, family process and developmental psychopathology. In D. Cicchetti & D. Cohen (Eds.), *Developmental psychopathology: Vol. 3. Risk, disorder and adaptation* (2nd ed., pp. 86–128). New York, NY: Wiley.

Davis, P., Sturge-Apple, M., Cicchetti, D., & Cummings, E. (2007). The role of child adrenocortical functioning in pathways between interparental conflict and child maladjustment. *Developmental Psychology, 43*, 918–930.

Davis, T. R., & Luthans, F. (1988). Service OD: Techniques for improving the delivery of quality service. *Organization Development Journal, 6*, 76–80.

Dean, A., & Lin, N. (1977). The stress-buffering role of social support. *Journal of Nervous and Mental Disease, 165*, 403–417.

Dean, J., & Bush, R. (2007). A community psychology view of environmental organization processes. *American Journal of Community Psychology, 40*, 146–166.

Deaux, K. (2006). A nation of immigrants: Living our legacy. *Journal of Social Issues, 62*, 633–651.

De Beus, K., & Rodriguez, N. (2007). Restorative justice practice: An examination of program completion and recidivism. *Journal of Criminal Justice, 35*(3), 337–347.

de Fatima Qunital de Freitas, M. (2000). Voices from the south: The construction of Brazilian community social psychology. *Journal of Community and Applied Social Psychology, 10,* 315–326.

DeFrances, C., & Smith, S. (1998). *Perceptions of neighborhood crime* (Bureau of Justice Statistics Special Report NCI 165811). Washington, DC: Department of Justice.

Delgado, G. (1986). *Organizing the movement: The roots and growth of ACORN.* Philadelphia, PA: Temple University Press.

Delongis, A., Coyne, J., Dakof, G., Folkman, S., & Lazarus, R. (1982). The relationship of daily hassles, uplifts and major life events to health status. *Health Psychology, 1,* 119–136.

Denham, S. A., & Almeida, M. C. (1987). Children's social problem-solving skills, behavioral adjustment, and interventions: A meta-analysis evaluating theory and practice. *Journal of Applied Developmental Psychology, 8,* 391–409.

D'Ercole, A., Skodol, A. E., Struening, E., Curtis, J., & Millman, J. (1991). Diagnosis of physical illness in psychiatric patients using Axis III and a standardized medical history. *Hospital and Community Psychiatry, 42,* 395–400.

Derogatis, L., & Coons, H. (1993). Self-report measures of stress. In L. Goldberger and S. Breznitz (Eds.), *Handbook of stress: Theoretical and clinical aspects* (2nd ed.). New York, NY: Free Press.

De Schipper, J. C., Van IJzendoorn, M. H., & Tavecchio, L. W. C. (2004). Stability in center day care: Relations with children's well-being and problem behavior in day care. *Social Development, 13,* 531–550.

Detert, J. R., & Edmondson, A. C. (2007). Why employees are afraid to speak. *Harvard Business Review, 85,* 23–30.

Deutsch, M. (2000). Cooperation and competition. In M. Deutsch, P. Coleman, & Marcus, C. E. (Eds.), *The handbook of conflict resolution.* San Francisco, CA: Jossey-Bass.

Dévieux, J. G., Malow, R., Lerner, B. G., Dyer, J. G., Baptista, L., Lucenko, B., & Kalichman, S. (2007). Triple jeopardy for HIV: Substance using severely mentally ill adults. *Journal of Prevention & Intervention in the Community, 33*(1–2), 5–18.

Devine, P. (1989). Prejudice and stereotypes: Their automatic and controlled components. *Journal of Personality and Social Psychology, 56,* 5–18.

Devine, P. (2005). Breaking the prejudice habit: Allport's inner conflict revisited. In J. Dovidio, P. Glick, & L. Budman (Eds.), *On the nature of prejudice: Fifty years after Allport* (pp. 327–342). Malden, MA: Blackwell.

DeVita, C. J. (1997). *Viewing nonprofits across the states: Changing civil society.* Retrieved from http://www.urban.org/periodcl/cnp_1.htm

De Wit, D. J., Lipman, E., Manzano-Munguia, M., Bisanza, J., Graham, K., Offord, D. R., . . . Shaver, K. (2006). Feasibility of a randomized controlled trial for evaluating Big Brothers Big Sisters community match program at the national level. *Children and Youth Services Review, 29,* 383–404.

Diamond, J. B. (2006). Still separate and unequal: Examining race, opportunity, and school achievement in "integrated" suburbs. *Journal of Negro Education, 75,* 495–505.

Diamond, P. M., & Schnee, S. B. (1990, August). *Tracking the costs of chronicity: Towards a redirection of resources.* Paper presented at the Annual Meeting of the American Psychological Association, Boston, MA.

Dickerson, S., & Kemeny, M. (2004). Acute stressors and cortisol responses: A theoretical integration and synthesis of laboratory research. *Psychological Bulletin, 130,* 355–391.

DiClemente, R. J., & Peterson, J. L. (Eds.). (1994). *Preventing AIDS: Theories and methods of behavioral interventions.* New York, NY: Plenum.

DiFranza, J. R., Richards, J. W., Paulman, P. M., Wolf-Gillespie, N., Fletcher, C., Jaffe, R. D., & Murray D (1991). RJR Nabisco's cartoon camel promotes Camel cigarettes to children. *Journal of the American Medical Association, 266,* 3149–3154.

DiMatteo, D., Sherbourne, C., Hays, R., Ordway, L., Kravitz, R., McGlynn, E., . . . Rogers, W. H. (1993). Physicians' characteristics influence patients' adherence to medical treatment: Results from the Medical Outcomes Study. *Health Psychology, 12,* 93–102.

DiMatteo, M. R. (2004). Social support and patient adherence to medical treatment: A meta-analysis. *Health Psychology, 23,* 207–218.

Division of Violence Prevention. (2010, September). *Injury prevention & control: Violence prevention.* Retrieved from http://www.cdc.gov/violenceprevention/intimatepartnerviolence/definitions.html

Dixon-Woods, M., Ashcroft, R. E., Jackson, C. J., Tobin, M. D., Kivits, J., Burton, P. R., & Samani, N. J. (2007). Beyond "misunderstanding": Written information and decisions about taking part in a genetic epidemiological study. *Social Science and Medicine, 65*(11), 2212–2222.

Dobmeyer, T. W., McKee, P. A., Miller, R. D., & Wescott, J. S. (1990). The effect of enrollment in a prepaid health plan on utilization of a community crisis intervention center by chronically mentally ill individuals. *Community Mental Health Journal, 26,* 129–137.

Dodge, K. A., Pettit, G. S., & Bates, J. E. (1997). How the experience of early physical abuse leads children to become chronically aggressive. In D. Cicchetti & S. L. Toth (Eds.), *Developmental perspectives on trauma: Theory, research, and intervention* (pp. 263–288). Rochester, NY: University of Rochester Press.

Doherty, G., Forer, B., Lero, D. S., Goelman, H., & LaGrange, A. (2006). Predictors of quality family child care. *Early Childhood Research Quarterly, 21,* 296–312.

Dohrenwend, B. S. (1978). Social stress and community psychology. *American Journal of Community Psychology, 6,* 1–14.

Domestic Abuse Intervention Programs. (2008). *History of the Duluth model.* Retrieved from http://www.theduluthmodel.org/history.php

Donn, J. E., Routh, D. K., & Lunt, I. (2000). From Leipzig to Luxembourg (via Boulder and Vail): A history of clinical psychology training in Europe and the United States. *Professional Psychology: Research and Practice, 31*(4), 423–428.

Dougherty, A. M. (2000). *Psychological consultation and collaboration.* Belmont, CA: Wadsworth.

Dovidio, J. F., & Gaertner, S. L. (1998). On the nature of contemporary prejudice: The causes, consequences, and challenges of divisive racism. In J. L. Eberhardt & S. T. Fiske (Eds.), *Confronting racism: The problem and the response.* Thousand Oaks, CA: Sage.

Dovidio, J. F., & Gaertner, S. L. (2004). Aversive racism. In Mark Zanna (Ed.), *Advances in experimental social psychology* (Vol. 36, pp. 1–52). San Diego, CA: Elsevier Academic Press.

Dovidio, J., Gaertner, S., & Kawakami, K. (2002). Implicit and explicit prejudice and interracial interaction. *Journal of Personality and Social Psychology, 82,* 62–68.

Dovidio, J., Gaertner, S. L., Nier, J. A., Kawakami, K., & Hodson, G. (2004). Contemporary racial bias: When good people do bad things. In A. G. Miller (Ed.), *The social psychology of good and evil.* New York, NY: Guilford.

Dovidio, J., Glick, P., & Budman, L. (Eds.). (2005). *On the nature of prejudice: Fifty years after Allport.* Malden, MA: Blackwell.

Dovidio, J. F., Johnson, J. D., Gaertner, S. L., Pearson, A. R., Saguy, T., & Ashburn-Nardo, L. (2010). Empathy and intergroup relations. In M. Mikulincer & P. R. Shaver (Eds.), *Prosocial motives, emotions, and behavior: The better angels of our nature* (pp. 393–408). Washington, DC: American Psychological Association.

Dowell, D. A., & Farmer, G. (1992). Community response to homelessness: Social change and constraint in local intervention. *Journal of Community Psychology, 20,* 72–83.

Dowler, K., & Zawilski, V. (2007). Public perceptions of police misconduct and discrimination: Examining the impact of media consumption. *Journal of Criminal Justice, 35,* 193–203.

Downing, J., & Harrison, T. C. (1990). Dropout prevention: A practical approach. *School Counselor, 38,* 67–74.

DuBois, D. L., Holloway, B. E., Valentine, J. C., & Cooper, H. (2002). Effectiveness of mentoring programs for youth: A meta-analytic review. *American Journal of Community Psychology, 30*(2), 157–197. doi:10.1023/A:1014628810714

Duffy, K. G. (1991). Introduction to community mediation programs: Past, present and future. In K. G. Duffy, J. W. Grosch, & P. V. Olczak (Eds.), *Community mediation: A handbook for practitioners and researchers.* New York, NY: Guilford.

Duffy, K. G., & Atwater, E. (2008). *Psychology for living.* Upper Saddle River, NJ: Prentice Hall.

Duffy, K. G., Grosch, J. W., & Olczak, P. V. (1991). *Community mediation: A handbook for practitioners and researchers.* New York, NY: Guilford.

Duffy, K. G., Olczak, P. V., & Grosch, J. W. (1993). *The influence of minority status on mediation outcome.* Paper presented to the International Association for Conflict Management, Henglehoef, Belgium.

Duffy, K. G., & Thompson, J. (1992). Community mediation centers: Humanistic alternatives to the court system, a pilot study. *Journal of Humanistic Psychology, 32,* 101–114.

Dumas, J. E., Rollock, D., Prinz, R. J., Hops, H., & Blechman, E. A. (1999). Cultural sensitivity: Problems and solutions in applied and preventive intervention. *Applied & Preventive Psychology, 8,* 175–196.

Dumont, M. P. (1982). [Review of *Private lives/public spaces,* by E. Baxter & K. Hopper, and *Shopping bag ladies,* by A. M. Rousseau.] *American Journal of Orthopsychiatry, 52,* 367–369.

Dupéré, V., & Perkins, D. D. (2007). Community types and mental health: A multilevel study of local environmental stress and coping. *American Journal of Community Psychology, 39,* 107–119.

DuRant, R. H., Wolfson, M., LaFrance, B., Balkrishnan, R., & Altman, D. (2006, March). An evaluation of a mass media campaign to encourage parents of adolescents to talk to their children about sex. *Journal of Adolescent Health, 38*(3), 298e1–289e9.

Durlak, J. A. (1983). Social problem-solving as a primary prevention strategy. In R. D. Felner, L. A. Jason, J. N. Moritsugu, & S. S. Farber (Eds.), *Prevention psychology: Theory, research, and practice.* New York, NY: Pergamon.

Durlak, J. A. (1995). *School-based prevention programs for children and adolescents.* Thousand Oaks, CA: Sage.

Durlak, J., & Weissberg, R. (2007). *The impact of after-school programs that promote personal and social skills.* Chicago, IL: Collaborative for Academic, Social, and Emotional Learning.

Durlak, J. A., Weissberg, R. P., Dymnicki, A. B., Taylor, R. D., & Schellinger, K. B. (2011). The impact of enhancing students' social and emotional learning: A meta-analysis of school-based universal interventions. *Child Development, 82,* 405–432.

Durlak, J. A., Weissberg, R. P., & Pachan, M. (2010). A meta-analysis of after-school programs that seek to promote personal and social skills in children and adolescents. *American Journal of Community Psychology, 45*(3–4), 294–309.

Durlak, J. A., & Wells, A. M. (1997). Primary prevention mental health programs for children and adolescents: A meta-analytic review. *American Journal of Community Psychology, 25,* 115–152.

Dworski-Riggs, D., & Langhout, R. (2010). Elucidating the power in empowerment and the participation in participatory action research: A story about research team and elementary school change. *American Journal of Community Psychology, 45*(3–4), 215–230.

Eagly, A., & Chin, J. (2010). Diversity and leadership in a changing world. *American Psychologist, 65*(3), 216–224.

Eagly, A., Johannesen-Schmidt, M., & van Engen, M. (2003). Transformational, transactional, and laissez-faire leadership styles: A meta-analysis comparing women and men. *Psychological Bulletin, 129*(4), 569–591.

Eagly, A. H., & Karau, S. J. (2002). Role congruity theory of prejudice toward female leaders. *Psychological Review, 109*(3), 573–598.

Earls, M., & Nelson, G. (1988). The relationship between long-term psychiatric clients' psychological well-being and their perceptions of housing and social support. *American Journal of Community Psychology, 16,* 279–293.

Eaves, C. (2001). The development and implementation of a crisis response team in a school setting. *International Journal of Emergency Mental Health Special Issue, 3,* 35–46.

Ebata, A. T., & Moos, R. H. (1991). Coping and adjustment in distressed and healthy adolescents. *Journal of Applied Developmental Psychology, 12*(1), 33–54.

Ebert-Flattau, P. (1980). *A legislative guide.* Washington, DC: Association for the Advancement of Psychology.

Eby, L. T., Allen, T. D., Evans, S. C., Ng, T., & Dubois, D. (2008). Does mentoring matter? A multidisciplinary meta-analysis comparing mentored and non-mentored individuals. *Journal of Vocational Behavior, 72*(2), 254–267. doi:10.1016/j.jvb.2007.04.005

Eckenrode, J., Ganzel, B., Henderson, C. R., Smith, E., Olds, D. L., Powers, J., . . . Sidora, K. (2000). Preventing child abuse and neglect with a program of nurse home visitation: The limiting effects of domestic violence. *Journal of the American Medical Association, 284,* 1385–1391.

Educational Conference on Psychiatry, Psychology and the Law. (1990). Dangerousness and discharge. *American Journal of Forensic Psychology, 8,* 19–58.

Edwards, D., Hunt, M. H., Meyers, J., Grogg, K. R., & Jarrett, O. (2005). Acceptability and student outcomes of a violence prevention curriculum. *Journal of Primary Prevention, 26,* 401–418.

Edwards, R. W., Jumper-Thurman, P., Plested, B. A., Oetting, E. R., & Swanson, L. (2001). Community readiness. Research to practice. *Journal of Community Psychology, 28,* 291–307.

Eggins, R. A., Reynolds, K. J., Oakes, P. J., & Mavor, K. I. (2007). Citizen participation in a deliberative poll: Factors predicting attitude change and political engagement. *Australian Journal of Psychology, 59*(2), 94–100.

Egeland, B. (2007). Understanding developmental processes of resilience and psychology: Implications for policy and practice. In A. S. Masten (Ed.), *Multilevel dynamics in developmental psychopathology: Pathways to the future* (pp. 83–117). New York, NY: Taylor & Francis/Erlbaum.

Ehrlich, P., & Ornstein, R. (2010). *Humanity on a tightrope: Thoughts on empathy, family, and big changes for a viable future.* Lanham, MD: Rowman & Littlefield.

Eigen, M. (1993). Viral quasispecies. *Scientific American, 269,* 42–49.

Eisenbraun, K. D. (2007). Violence in schools: Prevalence, prediction, and prevention. *Aggression and Violent Behavior, 12,* 459–469.

Eitle, D., D'Alessio, S. J., & Stolzenberg, L. (2006). Economic segregation, race, and homicide. *Social Science Quarterly, 87,* 638–657.

Elder, G. (1974). *Children of the Great Depression.* Chicago, IL: University of Chicago.

Elias, M. J., Gara, M., Ubriaco, M., Rothbaum, P. A., Clabby, J. F., & Schuyler, T. (1986). Impact of a preventative social problem solving intervention on children's coping with middle-school stressors. *American Journal of Community Psychology, 14,* 259–275.

Ellam, G., & Shamir, B. (2005). Organizational change and self concept. *Journal of Applied Behavioral Science, 41,* 399–421.

Elliott, K., & Urquiza, A. (2006). Ethnicity, culture, and child maltreatment. *Journal of Social Issues, 62,* 787–808.

Ellis, R. T. (1991). Perceptions, attitudes and beliefs of police recruits. *Canadian Police College Journal, 15,* 95–117.

Elvin, J. (2000, July 21). Is mental illness all in your head? *Insight on the News, 16,* 35.

Ely, R., & Thomas, D. (2001). Cultural diversity at work: The effects of diversity perspectives on work group processes and outcomes. *Administrative Science Quarterly, 46* (2), 229–273.

Embry, D. D., Flannery, D. J., Vazsonyi, A. T., Powell, K. E., & Atha, J. (1996). PeaceBuilders: A theoretically driven school based model for early violence prevention. *American Journal of Preventive Medicine, 12,* 91–100.

Emery, R. E., & Wyer, M. M. (1987). Divorce mediation. *American Psychologist, 42,* 472–480.

Emshoff, J., Darnell, A., Darnell, D., Erickson, S., Schneider, S., & Hudgins, R. (2007). Systems change as an outcome and a process in the work of community collaborative for health. *American Journal of Community Psychology, 39,* 255–267.

English, D. J., Upadhyaya, M. P., Litrownik, A. J., Marshall, J. M., Runyan, D. K., Graham, J. C., & Dubowitz, H. (2005). Maltreatment's wake: The relationship of maltreatment dimensions to child outcomes. *Child Abuse & Neglect, 29*(5), 597–619.

Entwisle, D. R., Alexander, K. L., & Olson, L. S. (2004). Temporary as compared to permanent high school dropout. *Social Forces, 82,* 1181–1205.

Entwisle, D. R., Alexander, K. L., & Olson, L. S. (2005). Urban teenagers: Work and dropout. *Youth & Society, 37,* 3–32.

Epel, E., Blackburn, E., Lin, J., Dhabhar, F., Adler, N., Morrow, J., & Cawthon, R. (2004, December 7). Accelerated telomere shortening in response to life stress. *Proceedings of the National Academy of Sciences, 101*(49), 17323–17324.

Eriksen, T. H. (2012). Xenophobic exclusion and the new right in Norway. *Journal of Community & Applied Social Psychology, 22*(3), 206–209. doi:10.1002/casp.2104

Erwin, P. G., Purvee, D., & Johannes, C. K. (2005). Involvement and outcomes in short-term interpersonal cognitive problem solving groups. *Counseling Psychology Quarterly, 18,* 41–46.

Espelage, D. L., & Low, S. (2012). Understanding and preventing adolescent bullying, sexual violence, and dating violence. In E. Vera (Ed.), *Oxford handbook of prevention in counseling psychology.* New York, NY: Oxford University Press.

Euser, E. M., van Ijzendoorn, M. H., Prinzie, P., & Bakermans-Kranenburg, M. J. (2011). Elevated child maltreatment rates in immigrant families and the role of socioeconomic differences. *Child Maltreatment, 16,* 63–73.

Evans, G. W. (2004). The environment of childhood poverty. *American Psychologist, 59,* 77–92.

Everly, G. S., Phillips, S. B., Kane, D., & Feldman, D. (2006). Introduction to and overview of group psychological first aid. *Brief Treatment and Crisis Intervention, 6,* 130–136.

Eysenck, H. J. (1952). The effects of psychotherapy: An evaluation. *Journal of Consulting Psychology, 16,* 319–324.

Eysenck, H. J. (1961). The effects of psychotherapy. In H. J. Eysenck (Ed.), *Handbook of abnormal psychology.* New York, NY: Basic Books.

Fagan, A. A., Van Horn, M. L., Hawkins, J. D., & Arthur, M. W. (2007). Using community and family risk and protective factors for community-based prevention planning. *Journal of Community Psychology, 35*(4), 535–555.

Fairweather, G. W. (1980). *The Fairweather lodge: A twenty-five year retrospective.* San Francisco, CA: Jossey-Bass.

Fairweather, G. W. (1986). The need for uniqueness. *American Journal of Community Psychology, 14,* 128–137.

Fairweather, G. W., & Davidson, W. S. (1986). *An introduction to community experimentation.* New York, NY: McGraw-Hill.

Fairweather, G., & Fergus, E. O. (1993). *Empowering the mentally ill: Theory and application.* Manchester, NH: Morgan Press.

Fairweather, G. W., Sanders, D. H., Maynard, H., & Cressler, D. L. (1969). *Community life for the mentally ill.* Chicago, IL: Aldine.

Fairweather, G. W., & Tornatzky, L. G. (1977). *Experimental methods for social policy research.* New York, NY: Pergamon.

Faith, M. S., Wong, F. Y., & Carpenter, K. M. (1995). Group sensitivity training: Update, meta-analysis, and recommendations. *Journal of Counseling Psychology, 42,* 390–399.

Farber, S. S., Felner, R. D., & Primavera, J. (1985). Parental separation/divorce and adolescents: An examination of factors mediating adaptation. *American Journal of Community Psychology, 13,* 171–186.

Farmer, P., Leandre, F., Mukherjee, J., Claude, M. S., Nevil, P., Smith-Fawzi, M., . . . Kim, J. (2001). Community-based approaches to HIV treatment in resource-poor settings. *Lancet, 345,* 404–409.

Farmer, T. W., Price, L. N., O'Neal, K. K., & Man-Chi, L. (2004). Exploring risk in early adolescent African-American youth. *American Journal of Community Psychology, 33,* 51–59.

Farquhar, M. (1995). Elderly people's definitions of quality of life. *Social Science and Medicine, 41,* 1439–1446.

Farquhar, J., Fortmann, S., Maccoby, N., Haskell, W., Williams, P., Flora, J., . . . Hulley, S. (1985). The Stanford Five-City Project: Design and methods. *American Journal of Epidemiology, 122,* 323–334.

Farreras, I. (2005). The historical context for National Institute of Mental Health support of American Psychological Association training and accreditation efforts. In W. E. Pickrens & S. F. Schneider, (Eds.), *Psychology and the National Institute of Mental Health: A historical analysis of science, practice, and policy* (pp. 153–179). Washington, DC: American Psychological Association.

Farrington, D. P., Gill, M., Waples, S. J., & Argomaniz, J. (2007). The effects of closed-circuit television on crime: Meta-analysis of an English national quasi multi-site evaluation. *Journal of Experimental Criminology, 3,* 21–38.

Farver, J. M., Xu, Y., Eppe, S., Fernandez, A., & Schwartz, D. (2005). Community violence, family conflict, and preschoolers' socioemotional functioning. *Developmental Psychology, 41,* 160–170.

Fassinger, R. (2008). Workplace diversity and public policy: Challenges, and opportunities for psychology. *American Psychologist, 63,* 252–268.

Fauth, R. C., Leventhal, T., & Brooks-Gunn, J. (2007). Welcome to the neighborhood? Long-term impacts of moving to low-poverty neighborhoods on poor children's and adolescents' outcomes. *Journal of Research on Adolescence, 17,* 249–282.

Fawcett, S. B. (1990). Some emerging standards for community research and action: Aid from a behavioral perspective. In P. Tolan, C. Kelp, F. Chertak, & L. Jason (Eds.), *Researching community psychology: Issues of theory and methods* (pp. 64–75). Washington, DC: American Psychology Association.

Fawcett, S. B., Paine-Andrew, A., Francisco, V. T., Schultz, J. A., Richter, K. P., Lewis, R. K., . . . Fisher, J. L. (1996). Empowering community health initiatives through evaluation. In D. M. Fetterman, S. Kaftarian, & A. Wandersman (Eds.), *Empowerment evaluation: Knowledge and tools for self-assessment and accountability* (pp. 161–187). Thousand Oaks, CA: Sage.

Fawcett, S. B., Seekins, T., & Jason, L. A. (1987). Policy research and child passenger safety legislation: a case study and experimental evaluation. *Journal of Social Issues, 43*(2), 133–148.

Federal Bureau of Investigation. (2010). *Crime in the U.S. 2010.* Retrieved from http://www.fbi.gov/about-us/cjis/ucr/crime-in-the-u.s/2010/crime-in-the-u.s.-2010

Federal Interagency Forum on Child and Family Statistics. (2008). *America's children: Key national indicators of well-being, 2008.* Retrieved from http://www.childstats.gov/americaschildren/tables.asp

Feldheusen, J. F. (1989, March). Synthesis of research on gifted youth. *Educational Leadership,* 6–11.

Felitti, V. J., Anda, R. F., Nordenberg, D., Williamson, D. F., Spitz, A. M., Edwards, V., . . . Marks, J. S. (1998). Relationship of childhood abuse and household dysfunction to many of the leading causes of death in adults: The Adverse Childhood Experiences (ACE) study. *American Journal of Preventive Medicine, 14*(4), 245–258.

Felner, R. D. (2000a). Educational reform as ecologically-based prevention and promotion. The project on high performance learning communities. In D. Cicchetti & J. Rappaport (Eds.), *The promotion of wellness in children and adolescents.* Washington, DC: Child Welfare League of America.

Felner, R. (2000b). Prevention in mental health and social intervention. In J. Rappaport & E. Seidman (Eds.), *Handbook of community psychology* (pp. 9–42). New York, NY: Kluwer/Plenum.

Felner, R. (2008). *School transitional environment project (STEP).* Retrieved from http://www.personal.psy.edu/dept/prevention/STEP.htm

Felner, R. D., Ginter, M., & Primavera, J. (1982). Primary prevention during school transitions: Social support and environmental structure. *American Journal of Community Psychology, 10,* 277–290.

Felner, R. D., Jason, L., Moritsugu, J., & Riger, S. (1983). *Preventive psychology: Theory, research and practice.* New York, NY: Pergamon Press.

Felner, R. D., Seitsinger, A. M., Brand, S., Burns, A., & Bolton, N. (2007). Creating small learning communities: Lessons from the project on high-performing learning communities about "what works" in creating productive, developmentally enhancing, learning contexts. In Promoting motivation at school: Interventions that work [Special issue]. *Educational Psychologist, 42,* 209–221.

Felton, B. (2005). Defining location in the mental health system: A case study of a consumer-run agency. *American Journal of Community Psychology, 36,* 373–386.

Ferguson, K. M., & Mindel, C. H. (2007). Modeling fear of crime in Dallas neighborhoods: A test of social capital theory. *Crime & Delinquency, 53,* 322–349.

Ferrari, J., Billows, W., Jason, L., & Grill, G. (1997). Matching the needs of the homeless with those of the disabled: Empowerment through caregiving. *Journal of Prevention and Intervention in the Community, 15,* 83–93.

Ferrari, J. R., & Jason, L. A. (1996). Integrating research and community service: Incorporating research skills into service learning experiences. *College Student Journal, 30,* 444–451.

Ferraro, F., Pfeffer, J., & Sutton, R. (2005). Economics language and assumptions: How theories become self-fulfilling. *Academy of Management Review,* 30, 8-24.

Fetterman, D. M., Kaftarian, S., & Wandersman, A. (Eds.). (1996). *Empowerment evaluation: Knowledge and tools for self-assessment and accountability.* Newbury Park, CA: Sage.

Fetterman, D. (2001). Empowerment evaluation and self-determination: A practical approach toward program improvement and capacity building. In N. Schneiderman, M. A. Speers, J. M. Silva, H. Tomes, & J. H. Gentry (Eds.), *Integrating behavioral and social sciences with public health* (pp. 321–350). Washington, DC: American Psychological Association.

Fetterman, D. (2005). A window into the heart and soul of empowerment evaluation: Looking through the lens of empowerment evaluation principles. In D. Fetterman & A. Wandersman (Eds.), *Empowerment evaluation principles in practice* (pp. 1–26). New York, NY: Guilford Press.

Fetterman, D. M., & Wandersman, A. (2005). *Empowerment evaluation principles in practice.* New York, NY: Guilford.

Fiedler, F. (1971). Validation and extension of the contingency model of leadership effectiveness: A review of empirical findings. *Psychological Bulletin, 76,* 128–148.

Fingeret, M.C., Warren, C. S., Cepeda-Benito, A., & Gleaves, D. (2006). Eating disorder prevention research: A meta-analysis. *Eating Disorders: The Journal of Prevention and Research, 14,* 191–213.

Finkelhor, S., & Jones, L. (2006). Why have child maltreatment and child victimization declined? *Journal of Social Issues, 62,* 685–716.

Firdion, J., & Marpsat, M. (2007). A research program on homelessness in France. *Journal of Social Issues, 63,* 567–587.

Fischer, C. S., Jackson, R. M., Stueve, C. A., Gerson, G., & McAllister-Jones, L. (1977). *Networks and places.* New York, NY: Free Press.

Fisher, A. T., Gridley, H., Thomas, D. R., & Bishop, B. (2008). Community psychology in Australia and Aotearoa/New Zealand. *Journal of Community Psychology, 36*(5), 649–660.

Fisher, (C. 2003). Why do lay people believe satisfaction and performance are correlated? Possible sources of a commonsense theory. *Journal of Organizational Behavior, 24,* 753–777.

Fisher, J. D., & Fisher, W. A. (1992). Changing AIDS-risk behavior. *Psychological Bulletin, 111,* 455–474.

Fishman, P. A., Thompson, E. E., Merikle, E., & Curry, S. J. (2006). Changes in health care costs before and after smoking cessation. *Nicotine & Tobacco Research, 8,* 393–401.

Fiske, S. T. (2004). Intent and ordinary bias: Unintended thought and social motivation create casual prejudice. *Social Justice Research, 17*(2), 117–127.

Fiske, S. T., Bersoff, D. N., Borgida, E., Deaux, K., & Heilman, M. E. (1991). Social science research on trial: Use of sex stereotyping research in *Price Waterhouse v. Hopkins. American Psychologist, 46,* 1049–1060.

Fiske, S., & Taylor, S. (2013). *Social cognition: From brains to culture.* New York, NY: Sage.

Flay, B. R., & Alfred, C. G. (2003). Long-term effects of the Positive Action program. *American Journal of Health Behavior, 27,* 6–21.

Flay, B. R., & Petraitis, J. (1991). Methodological issues in drug use prevention research: Theoretical foundation. In C. G. Leukefeld & W. J. Buoski (Eds.), *Drug abuse prevention intervention research methodology* (National Institute on Drug Abuse Research Monograph No. 107) (pp. 91–1761). Washington, DC: Superintendent of Documents, U.S. Government Printing Office.

Flick, U. (2007). Homelessness and health: Challenges for health psychology. *Journal of Health Psychology, 12,* 691–695.

Flora, J., Jatilus, D., & Jackson, C. (1993). The Stanford Five-City Heart Disease Prevention Project. In T. E. Backer & E. M. Rogers (Eds.), *Organizational aspects of health communication campaigns: What works?* (pp. 101–128). Thousand Oaks, CA: Sage.

Florin, P. (1989). *Nurturing the grassroots: Neighborhood volunteer organizations and American cities.* New York, NY: Citizen's Committee for New York City.

Florin, P., & Wandersman, A. (1990). An introduction to citizen participation, voluntary organizations, and community development: Insights for improvement through research. *American Journal of Community Psychology, 18,* 41–54.

Flouri, E., Mavroveli, S., & Tzavidis, N. (2010). Modeling risks: Effects of area deprivation, family socio-economic disadvantage and adverse life events on young children's psychopathology. *Social Psychiatry and Psychiatric Epidemiology, 45*(6), 611–619.

Flowers-Coulson, P. A., Kushner, M. A., & Bankowski, S. (2000). The information is out there, but is anyone getting it? Adolescent misconceptions about sexuality education and reproductive health and the use of the internet to get answers. *Journal of Sex Education & Therapy, 25,* 178–188.

Folkman, S., & Lazarus, R. S. (1980). An analysis of coping in a middle-aged community sample. *Journal of Health and Social Behavior, 21,* 219–239.

Folkman, S., & Moskowitz, J. (2000). Positive affect and the other side of coping. *American Psychologist, 55,* 647–654.

Ford, J. D., Ford, L. W., & D'Amelio, A. (2008). Resistance to change: The rest of the story. *Academy of Management Review, 33,* 362.

Ford, J. K. (2007). Building capability throughout a change effort: Leading the transformation of a police agency to community policing. *American Journal of Community Psychology, 39*(3–4), 321–334. doi:10.1007/s10464-007-9115-2

Forlenza, S. G. (1991). Mediation and psychotherapy: Parallel processes. In K. G. Duffy, T. W. Grosch, & P. V. Olczak (Eds.), *Community mediation: A handbook for practitioners and researchers.* New York, NY: Guilford.

Forrester, J. (1969). *Principles of system.* Cambridge, MA: Wright-Allen.

Foster, H. W., Greene, L. W., & Smith, M. S. (1990). A model for increasing access: Teenage pregnancy prevention. *Journal of Health Care for the Poor and Underserved, 1,* 136–146.

Foster, G. D., Sherman, S., Borradaile, K. E., Grundy, K. M., Vander Veur, S. S., Nachmani, J., . . . Shults, J. (2008). A policy-based school intervention to prevent overweight and obesity. *Pediatrics, 121,* e794–e802.

Foster-Fishman, P., & Behrens, T. (2007). Systems change reborn: Rethinking our theories, methods, and efforts in human services reform and community-based change. *American Journal of Community Psychology, 39*(3–4), 191–196.

Foster-Fishman, P. G., Berkowitz, S. L., Lounsbury, D. W., Jacobson, S., & Allen, N. A. (2001). Building collaborative capacity in community coalitions: A review and integrative framework. *American Journal of Community Psychology, 29*(2), 241–261.

Foster-Fishman, P. G., & Keys, C. B. (1997). The person/environment dynamics of employee empowerment: An organizational culture analysis. *American Journal of Community Psychology, 25,* 345–369.

Foster-Fishman, P. G., & Long, R. L. (2009). The challenges of place, capacity, and systems change. *The Foundation Review, 1*(1), 69–84.

Foster-Fishman, P., Nowell, B., & Yang, H. (2007). Putting the system back into system change: A framework for understanding and changing organizational and community systems. *American Journal of Community Psychology, 39,* 197–215.

Foster-Fishman, P. G., Nowell, B., Deacon, Z., Nievar, M. A., & McCann P. (2005). Using methods that matter: The impact of reflection, dialogue, and voice. *American Journal of Community Psychology, 36,* 275–291.

Foster-Fishman, P. G., Salem, D. A., Chibnall, S., Legler, R., & Yapchai, C. (1998). Empirical support for the critical assumptions of empowerment theory. *American Journal of Community Psychology, 26,* 507–536.

Fouad, N., & Bynner, J. (2008). Work transitions. *American Psychologist, 63,* 241–251.

Foundation Center. (2008). *Foundation giving grows across all program area*s (Foundation Center Reports). Retrieved from http://www.foundationcenter.org/media/news/pr_0802b.html

Fox, D., & Prilleltensky, I. (2007). Psychopolitical literacy for wellness and justice. *Journal of Community Psychology,* 793–805.

Fox, R. E., DeLeon, P. H., Newman, R., Sammons, M. T., Dunivin, D. L., & Baker, D. C. (2009). Prescriptive authority and psychology: A status report. *American Psychologist, 64*(4), 257–268.

Fozard, J. L., & Kearns, W. D. (2007). Technology, aging, and communication. In G. Lesnoff-Caravaglia (Ed.), *Gerontechnology: Growing old in a technological society.* Springfield, IL: Charles C. Thomas.

Fraga, M. F., Ballestar, E., Paz, M. F., Ropero, S., Setien, F., Ballestar, M. L., . . . Esteller, M. (2005). Epigenetic differences arise during the lifetime of monozygotic twins. *Proceedings of the National Academy of Science, 102*(30), 10604-10609. doi:10.1073/pnas.0500398102

Frank, J. D. (1983). Galloping technology, a new social disease. *Journal of Social Issues, 39,* 193–206.

Franklin, C., Grant, D., Corcoran, J., Miller, P. O., & Bultan, L. (1997). Effectiveness of prevention programs for adolescent pregnancy: A meta-analysis. *Journal of Marriage & the Family, 59,* 551–567.

Fraser, B. J., Williamson, J. C., & Tobin, K. G. (1987). Use of classroom and school climate scales in evaluating alternative high schools. *Teaching and Teacher Education, 219*–231.

Freedman, A. M. (1989). Mental health programs in the United States: Idiosyncratic roots. *International Journal of Mental Health, 18,* 81–98.

Freeman, L. (2001). Relaxation therapy. In L. Freeman & G. Lawlis (Eds.), *Mosby's complementary and alternative medicine: A research-based approach* (pp. 138–165). St. Louis, MO: Mosby.

Freeman, L., & Lawlis, G. (2001). Exercise as an alternative therapy. In L. Freeman & G. Lawlis (Eds.), *Mosby's complementary and alternative medicine: A research-based approach* (pp. 424–454). St. Louis, MO: Mosby.

Freeman, R. J., & Roesch, R. (1989). Mental disorder and the criminal justice system. *International Journal of Law and Psychiatry, 12,* 105–115.

Freiberg, J. H., & Lapoint, J. M. (2006). Research-based programs for preventing and solving discipline problems. In C. M. Evertson & C. S. Weinstein (Eds.), *Handbook of classroom management: Research, practice, and contemporary issues.* Mahwah, NJ: Erlbaum.

Freire, P. (1970). *Pedagogy of the oppressed.* New York, NY: Continuum.

Freire, P. (1994). *Pedagogy of hope.* New York, NY: Continuum.

Freisthler, B., Bruce, E., & Needell, B. (2007). Understanding geospatial relationship of neighborhood characteristics and rates of maltreatment for Black, Hispanic, and White children. *Social Work, 52,* 7–16.

French, W. L., & Bell, C. H. (1990). *Organizational development: Behavioral science interventions for organization improvement.* Englewood Cliffs, NJ: Prentice Hall.

Friedman, S. M., Neagius, A., Jose, B., Curtis, R., Goldstein, M., Sotheran, J., . . . DesJarlais, D. (1997). Network and sociohistorical approaches to the HIV epidemic among drug injectors. In L. Sherr, J. Catalano, & B. Hedge (Eds.), *The impacts of AIDS: Epidemiological and social aspects of HIV infection.* Chur, Switzerland: Harwood.

Frone, M. (2008). Are work stressors related to employee substance use? The importance of temporal context in assessments of alcohol and illicit drug use. *Journal of Applied Psychology, 93,* 199–206.

Frone, M. R. (2009). Does a permissive workplace substance use climate affect employees who do not use alcohol and drugs at work? A U.S. national study. *Psychology of Addictive Behaviors, 23,* 386–390.

Frone, M. R. (2012). Workplace substance use climate: Prevalence and distribution in the U.S. workforce. *Journal of Substance Use, 17,* 72–83.

Frost, D. M., & Ouellette, S. C. (2004). Meaningful voices: How psychologists, speaking as psychologists, can inform social policy. *Analyses of Social Issues and Public Policy,* 4, 219–226.

Frumkin, P. (2000). The face of the new philanthropy. *Responsive Community, 10,* 41–48.

Fujishiro, K., & Heaney, C. (2009). Justice at work, job stress, and employee health. *Health Education and Behavior, 36*(3), 487-504. doi:10.1177/1090198107306435

Fyson, S. (1999). Developing and applying concepts about community: Reflections from the field. *Journal of Community Psychology, 27*(3), 347–365.

Gabbidon, S. L., & Peterson, S. A. (2006). Living while Black: A state-level analysis of the influence of select social stressors on the quality of life among Black Americans. *Journal of Black Studies, 37,* 83–102.

Gaertner, S, & Dovidio, J. (1992). Toward the elimination of racism: The study of intergroup behavior. In R. M. Baird & S. E. Rosenbaum (Eds.), *Bigotry, prejudice and hatred: Definitions, causes and solutions* (pp. 203–207). Amherst, NY: Prometheus Books.

Gaertner, S., & Dovidio, J. (2005). Understanding and addressing contemporary racism: From aversive racism to the common in-group identity model. *Journal of Social Issues, 61,* 615–639.

Gaertner, S. L., Rust, M. C., Dovidio, J. F., & Bachman, B. A. (1996). The contact hypothesis: The role of a common ingroup identity on reducing intergroup bias. *Small Group Research, 25*(2), 224–249.

Gallagher, S., Phillips, A., Ferraro, A., Drayson, M., & Carroll, D. (2008). Social support is positively associated with the immunoglobulin M response to vaccination with pneumococcal polysaccharides. *Biological Psychology, 78*(2), 211–215.

Garbarino, J. (2001). *Making sense of school violence: Why do kids kill?* Washington, DC: American Psychiatric Press.

Garbarino, J., & Kostelny, K. (1992). Child maltreatment as a community problem. *Child Abuse and Neglect, 16,* 455–464.

Garbarino, J., & Kostelny, L. (1994). Neighborhood-based programs. In G. B. Melton & F. D. Barry (Eds.), *Protecting children from abuse and neglect: Foundations for a new strategy.* New York, NY: Guilford.

Garces, E., Thomas, D., & Currie, J. (2000, December). Longer term effects of Head Start. Retrieved from http://www.rand.org/labor/DRU/DRU2439.pdf

Garces, E., Thomas, D., & Currie, J. (2002). Longer-term effects of Head Start. *The American Economic Review, 92*(4), 999–1012.

García-Ramírez, M., Paloma, V., Suarez-Balcazar, Y., & Balcazar, F. (2009). Building international collaborative capacity: Contributions of community psychologists to a European network. *American Journal of Community Psychology, 44*(1–2), 116–122.

Garmezy, N. (1974). Children at risk. The search for the antecedents of schizophrenia: II. Ongoing research programs, issues and intervention. *Schizophrenia Bulletin, 9,* 55–125.

Garmezy, N., Masten, A. S., & Tellegen, A. (1984). The study of stress and competence in children: A building block for developmental psychopathology. *Child Development, 55,* 97–111.

Garmezy, N., & Streitman, S. (1974). Children at risk. The search for the antecedents of schizophrenia: I. Conceptual models and research methods. *Schizophrenia Bulletin, 8,* 14–90.

Gaylord-Harden, N., & Cunningham, J. (2009). The impact of racial discrimination and coping strategies on internalizing symptoms in African American youth. *Journal of Youth and Adolescence, 38,* 532–543.

Gaylord-Harden, N. K., Elmore, C. A., Campbell, C. L., & Wethington, A. (2011). An examination of the tripartite model of depressive and anxiety symptoms in African American youth: Stressors and coping strategies as common and specific correlates. *Journal of Clinical Child and Adolescent Psychology, 40,* 360–374. doi:10.1080/1537441 6.2011.563467

Gastil, J. (1994). A meta-analytic review of the productivity and satisfaction of democratic and autocratic leadership. *Small Group Research, 25,* 384–410.

Geen, R., Fender, L., Leos-Urbel, J., & Markowitz, T. (2001). *Welfare reform's effect on child welfare caseloads* (Assessing the New Federalism discussion paper No. 01-04). Washington, DC: Urban Institute.

Gendreau, P., Little, T., & Goggin, C. (1996). A meta-analysis of the predictors of adult offender recidivism: What works! *Criminology, 34*(4), 575–608. doi:10.1111/ j.1745-9125.1996

Genzuk, M. (2003). A synthesis of ethnographic research. Center for Multilingual, Multicultural Research Digital Papers Series (Eds.). Center for Multilingual, Multicultural Research, University of Southern California. Retrieved from http://www-bcf.usc.edu/~genzuk/Ethnographic_ Research.html

Gesten, E., & Jason, L. (1987). Social and community interventions. *Annual Review of Psychology, 38,* 427–460.

Gewirtz, A. H. (2007). Promoting children's mental health in family supportive housing: A community-university partnership for formerly homeless children and families. *Journal of Primary Prevention, 28,* 359–374.

Gignac, M. A. M., Kelloway, E. K., & Gottlieb, B. H. (1996). The impact of caregiving on employment: A mediational model of work-family conflict. *Canadian Journal of Aging, 15,* 525–542.

Gillespie, D. F., & Murty, S. A. (1994). Cracks in a postdisaster service delivery network. *American Journal of Community Psychology, 22,* 639–660.

Gillespie, J. F., Durlak, J., & Sherman, D. (1982). Relationship between kindergarten children's interpersonal problem solving skills and other indices of school adjustment: A cautionary note. *American Journal of Community Psychology, 10,* 149–153.

Gilley, A., Gilley, J. W., McConnell, C., & Veliquette, A. (2010). The competencies used by effective managers to build teams: An empirical study. *Advances in Developing Human Resources, 12*(1), 29–45. doi:10.1177/1523422310365720

Gilliam, M. L. (2007). The role of parents and partners in the pregnancy behaviors of young Latinas. *Hispanic Journal of Behavioral Sciences, 29,* 50–67.

Gilligan, C. (2011). *Joining the resistance.* Cambridge, MA: Harvard University Press.

Ginexi, E. M., Weihs, K., Simmens, S. J., & Hoyt, D. R. (2000). Natural disaster and depression: A prospective investigation of reactions to the 1993 Midwest floods. *American Journal of Community Psychology, 28,* 495–515.

Glaberson, W. (1990, February 19). Mean streets teach New Yorkers to just walk on by. *The New York Times,* pp. B1–B2.

Glaze, L., & Palia, S. (July, 2004). *Probation and parole in the United States, 2003.* Bureau of Justice Statistics. Retrieved from http://bjs.gov/index.cfm?ty=pbdetail&iid=1109

Gleason, P., & Dynarski, M. (2002). Do we know whom to serve? Issues in using risk factors to identify dropouts. *Journal of Education for Students Placed at Risk, 7*(1), 25–41.

Glenwick, D. S., & Jason, L. A. (Eds.). (1980). *Behavioral community psychology: Progress and prospects.* New York, NY: Praeger.

Glidewell, J. (1966). Perspectives in community health. In C. Bennett, L. Anderson, S. Cooper, L. Hassol, D. Klein, & G. Rosenblum (Eds.), *Community psychology: A report of the Boston Conference on the Education of Psychologists for Community Mental Health* (pp. 33–49). Boston, MA: Boston University and South Shore Mental Health Center.

Glidewell, J. (1987). Induced change and stability in psychological and social systems. *American Journal of Community Psychology, 15*(6), 741–772.

Glidewell, J. C. (1976). A theory of induced social change. *American Journal of Community Psychology, 4,* 227–239.

Golding, J. M., Potts, M. K., & Aneshensel, C. S. (1991). Stress exposure among Mexican Americans and non-Hispanic Whites. *Journal of Community Psychology, 19,* 37–59.

Goldring, E., Cohen-Vogel, L., Smrekar, C., & Taylor, C. (2006). Schooling closer to home: Desegregation policy and neighborhood contexts. *American Journal of Education, 112,* 335–362.

Gomby, D. S. (2000). Promise and limitations of home visitation. *Journal of the American Medical Association, 284,* 1430–1431.

Gomez, A., Dovidio, J., Huici, C., Gaertner, S. L., & Cuadrado, I. (2008). The other side of we: When outgroup members express common identity. *Personality and Social Psychology Bulletin, 34,* 1613–1626.

Gone, J. P. (2006). Research reservations: Response and responsibility in an American Indian community. *American Journal of Community Psychology, 37*(3–4), 333–340.

Gone, J. P. (2008). Mental health discourse as Western cultural proselytization. *Ethos, 36,* 310–315.

Gone, J. P. (2011). Is psychological science a-cultural? *Cultural Diversity and Ethnic Minority Psychology, 17*(3), 234–242.

Goodings, L., Locke, A., & Brown, S. D. (2007). Social networking technology: Place and identity in mediated communities. *Journal of Community & Applied Social Psychology, 17*(6), 463–476.

Goodman, A. M. (1990). A model for police officer burnout. *Journal of Business and Psychology, 5,* 85–99.

Goodrum, S. (2007). Victims' rights, victims' expectations, and law enforcement workers' constrains in cases of murder. *Law & Social Inquiry, 32,* 725–757.

Goodstein, L. D., & Sandler, I. (1978). Using psychology to promote human welfare: A conceptual analysis of the role of community psychology. *American Psychologist, 33,* 882–892.

Gore, A. (1990). Public policy and the homeless. *American Psychologist, 45,* 960–962.

Gottlieb, B. H. (1981). Social networks and social support in community mental health. In B. H. Gottlieb (Ed.), *Social networks and social support.* Beverly Hills, CA: Sage.

Gottlieb, B. (1997). Conceptual and measurement issues in the study of chronic stress. In B. Gottlieb (Ed.), *Coping with chronic stress* (pp. 3–37). New York, NY: Plenum.

Graber, J. A., Nichols, T., Lynne, S. D., Brooks-Gunn, J., & Botvin, G. J. (2006). A longitudinal examination of family, friend, and media influences on competent versus problem behaviors among urban minority youth. *Applied Developmental Science, 10,* 75–85.

Granovetter, M. (1973). The strength of weak ties. *American Journal of Sociology, 78,* 1360–1380.

Granovetter, M. (1983). The strength of weak ties: A network theory revisited. *Sociological Theory, 1,* 201–233.

Grant, A. M., Christiansen, M. K., & Price, R. H. (2007). Happiness, health, or relationships? Managerial practices and employee well-being tradeoffs. *Academy of Management Perspectives, 21*(3), 51–63.

Gray, P., & Chanoff, D. (1986). Democratic schooling: What happens to young people who have charge of their own education? *American Journal of Community Psychology, 94,* 182–213.

Gray, S., Sheeder, J., O'Brien, R., & Stevens-Simon, C. (2006). Having the best intentions is necessary but not sufficient: What would increase the efficacy of home visiting for preventing second teen pregnancies? *Prevention Science, 7,* 389–395.

Greatbatch, D., & Dingwall, R. (1989). Selective facilitation: Some preliminary observations on a strategy used by divorce mediators. *Law and Society Review, 23,* 613–641.

Greenberg, A. (1999). Defending the "American people." *Responsive Community, 9,* 52–58.

Greenberg, M., Riggs, N., & Blair, C. (2007). The role of preventive interventions in enhancing neurocognitive functioning and promoting competence in adolescence. In D. Romer & E. Walker (Eds.), *Adolescent psychopathology and the developing brain: Integrating brain and prevention science.* New York, NY: Oxford.

Greene, S. M., Anderson, E. R., Doyle, E. A., & Riedelbach, H. (2006). Divorce. In G. G. Bear & K. M. Minke (Eds.), *Children's needs III: Development, prevention, and intervention.* Washington, DC: National Association of School Psychologists.

Greenglass, E., Fiksenbaum, L., & Eaton, J. (2006). The relationship between coping, social support, functional disability and depression in the elderly. *Anxiety, Stress & Coping: An International Journal, 19,* 15–31.

Greenhouse, L. (July 1, 2007). In steps big and small, Supreme Court moved right. *The New York Times.* Retrieved from http://www.nytimes.com

Greenwood, D. J., Whyte, W. F., & Harkavy, I. (1993). Participatory action research as a process and as a goal. *Human Relations, 46,* 175–192.

Gregory, A., Henry, D. B., & Schoeny, M. E. (2007). School climate and implementation of a preventive intervention. *American Journal of Community Psychology, 40,* 250–260.

Gregory, B. T., Albritton, M. D., & Osmonbekov, T. (2010). The mediating role of psychological empowerment on the relationships between P–O fit, job satisfaction, and in-role performance. *Journal of Business and Psychology, 25*(4), 639–647. doi:10.1007/s10869-010-9156-7

Grob, G. N. (1991). *From asylum to community: Mental health policy in modern America.* Princeton, NJ: Princeton University Press.

Grogan-Kaylor, A. (2005). [Review of *One nation, underprivileged: Why American poverty affects us all.*] *Children and Youth Services Review, 27,* 687–689.

Grossi, E. L., & Berg, B. L. (1991). Stress and job dissatisfaction among correctional officers: An unexpected finding. *International Journal of Offender Therapy and Comparative Criminology, 35,* 73–81.

Gunn, P., Ratnesh, B., Nagda, A., & Lopez, G. E. (2004). The benefits of diversity in education for democratic citizenship. *Journal of Social Issues, 60,* 17–34.

Gurin, G., Veroff, J., & Field, S. (1960). *Americans view their mental health: A nationwide interview survey.* New York, NY: Basic Books.

Gurin, P., Nagda, B. A., & Lopez, G. (2004). The benefits of diversity in education for democratic citizenship. *Journal of Social Issues, 60*(1), 17–34.

Gutherie, R. V. (2003). *Even the rat was white: A historical view of psychology* (2nd ed.). Boston, MA: Allyn & Bacon.

Haber, M., Cohen, J., Lucas, T., & Baltes, B. (2007). The relationship between self-reported received and perceived social support: A meta-analytic review. *American Journal of Community Psychology, 39*(1–2), 133–144.

Hackerman, A. E. (1996). Intervening with the adolescent gang member: Understanding the spoken language. *Community Psychologist, 29,* 17–21.

Hadley-Ives, E., Stiffman, A. R., Elze, D., Johnson, S. D., & Dore, P. (2000). Measuring neighborhood and school environments: Perceptual and aggregate approaches. *Journal of Human Behavior in the Social Environment, 3,* 1–28.

Hagborg, W. J. (1988). A study of the intensity and frequency of crisis intervention for students enrolled in a school for the severely emotionally disturbed. *Adolescence, 23,* 825–836.

Hagestad, G. O., & Uhlenberg, P. (2005). The social separation of old and young: A root of ageism. *Journal of Social Issues, 61,* 343–358.

Halpern, D., & Nazroo, J. (2000). The ethnic density effect: Result from a national community survey of England and Wales. *International Journal of Social Psychiatry, 46,* 34–46.

Hamid, P. N., Yue, X. D., & Leung, C. M. (2003, Spring). Adolescent coping in different Chinese family environments. *Adolescence, 38,* 111–130.

Hamilton, S. F., Basseches, M., & Richards, F. A. (1985). Participatory-democratic work and adolescents' mental health. *American Journal of Community Psychology, 13,* 467–496.

Hamilton, S. F., Hamilton, M. A., Hirsch, B. J., Hughes, B. J., Hughes, J., King, J., & Maton, K. (2006). Community contexts for mentoring. *Journal of Community Psychology, 34,* 727–746.

Hammond, C., Linton, D., Smink, J., & Drew, S. (2007). *Dropout risk factors and exemplary programs.* Clemson, SC: National Dropout Prevention Center, Communities in Schools.

Hampton, C. V., Epstein, M. J., Johnson, D. B., & Reixach, K. A. (2004). Rochester, NY: Early childhood education intervention. *Community Psychologist, 37,* 42–47.

Handel, G. (1982). *Social welfare in Western society.* New York, NY: Random House.

Haney, C., Banks, C., & Zimbardo, P. (1973). Interpersonal dynamics in a simulated prison. *International Journal of Criminology and Penology, 1,* 69–97.

Hannon, L. E. (2005). Extremely poor neighborhoods and homicide. *Social Science Quarterly. Special Issues: Income, Poverty, and Opportunity, 86,* 1418–1434.

Harcourt, B. (2007, January 15). The mentally ill, behind bars. *The New York Times.* Retrieved from http://www.nytimes.com

Hardin, E., & Khan-Hudson, A. (2005). Elder abuse—"society's dilemma." *Journal of the National Medical Association, 97,* 91–94.

Harrington, C. (1985). *Shadow justice: The ideology and institutionalization of alternatives to court.* Westport, CT: Greenwood Press.

Harrison, D. A., Price, K. H., & Bell, M. P. (1998). Beyond relational demography: Time and the effects of surface- and deep-level diversity on group cohesion. *Academy of Management Journal, 41*(1), 96–107.

Harrison, D. A., Price, K. H., Gavin, J., & Florey, A. (2002). Time, teams, and task performance: Changing effects of surface and deep-level diversity on group functioning. *Academy of Management Journal, 45*(5), 10291045.

Haskins, R. (2005). Child development and child-care policy: Modest impacts. In D. B. Pillemer & S. H. White (Eds.), *Developmental psychology and social change: Research, history and policy.* New York, NY: Cambridge University Press.

Hatfield, A. B. (1997, September/October). Elderly individuals with mental illnesses: The overlooked and underserved generation. *NAMI Advocate,* pp. 13–18.

Hawkins, J. D., Van Horn, M. L., & Arthur, M. W. (2004). Community variation in risk and protective factors and substance use outcomes. *Prevention Science, 5*(4), 213–220.

Hawkins, R. P., Kreuter, M., Resnicow, K., Fishbein, M., & Dijkstra, A. (2008). Understanding tailoring in communicating about health. *Health Education Research, 23*(3), 454–466.

Hayes, S., & Cone, J. (1981). Reduction of residential consumption of electricity through simple monthly feedback. *Journal of Applied Behavior Analysis, 14*(1), 81–88.

Haynes, R. B., McDonald, H. P., & Garg, A. X. (2002). Helping patients follow prescribed treatment. *Journal of the American Medical Association, 288,* 2880–2883.

Hays, P. A. (2008). *Addressing cultural complexities in practice: Assessment, diagnosis, and therapy* (2nd ed.). Washington, DC: American Psychological Association.

He, W., Sengupta, M., Velkoff, V., & DeBarros, K. (December, 2005). *65+ in the United States: 2005.* Washington, D.C.: U.S. Department of Health and Human Services, National Institute on Aging and the U.S. Census Bureau. Retrieved from http://www.census.gov/PressRelease/www/releases/archives/aging_population/006544.html

Healy, K., & Smith, C. (1998). *Batterer programs: What criminal justice agencies need to know.* Washington DC: National Institute of Justice.

Hedeen, T. (2004). The evolution and evaluation of community mediation: Limited research suggests unlimited progress. *Conflict Resolution Quarterly, 22,* 101–133.

Hedegaard, M. (1996). The zone of proximal development as basis for instruction. In H. Daniels (Ed.), *An introduction to Vygotsky* (pp. 171–195). New York, NY: Routledge.

Heisterkamp, B. L. (2006). Conversational displays of mediator neutrality in a court-based program. *Journal of Pragmatics, 38,* 2051–2064.

Helgeson, V., & Cohen, S. (1996). Social support and adjustment to cancer: Reconciling descriptive, correlational and intervention research. *Journal of Health Psychology, 15,* 135–148.

Helping America's Youth. (2008). *The impact of caring adults in communities.* Retrieved from http://www.helpingamericasyouth.gov/facts.cfm

Heller, K. (1989a). Ethical dilemmas in community intervention. *American Journal of Community Psychology, 17,* 367–378.

Heller, K. (1989b). The return to community. *American Journal of Community Psychology, 17*(1), 1–15.

Heller, K. (1990). Social and community intervention. In L. W. Porter & M. R. Rosenzweig (Eds.), *Annual review of psychology.* Palo Alto, CA: Annual Reviews.

Heller, K., Jenkins, R., Steffen, A., & Swindle, R. W. (2000). Prospects for a viable community mental health system: Reconciling ideology, professional traditions, and political reality. In J. Rappaport & E. Seidman (Eds.), *Handbook of community psychology* (pp. 445–470). New York, NY: Plenum.

Heller, K., & Monahan, J. (1977). *Psychology and community change.* Oxford, England: Dorsey.

Heller, K., Price, R. H., Reinharz, S., Riger, S., & Wandersman, A. (1984). *Psychology and community change.* Homewood, IL: Dorsey.

Heller, K., Thompson, M. G., Trueba, P. E., Hogg, J. R., & Vlachos-Weber, I. (1991). Peer support telephone dyads for elderly women: Was this the wrong intervention? *American Journal of Community Psychology, 19,* 53–74.

Heller, K., Wyman, M. F., & Allen, S. M. (2000). Future directions for prevention science: From research to adoption. In C. R. Snyder & R. E. Ingram (Eds.), *Handbook of psychological change: Psychotherapy processes and practices for the 21st century.* New York, NY: Wiley.

Hellman, I. D., Greene, L. R., Morrison, T. L., & Abramowitz, S. I. (1985). Organizational size and perceptions in a residential treatment program. *American Journal of Community Psychology, 13,* 99–110.

Henderson, C. (2006). Review of Japan as a low-crime nation. *Journal of Forensic Psychiatry & Psychology, 17,* 356–358.

Henry, D., Guerra, N., Huesmann, R., Tolan, P., VanAcker, R., & Eron, L. (2000). Normative influences on aggression in urban elementary school classrooms. *American Journal of Community Psychology, 28,* 59–81.

Heppner, P. P., Heppner, M. J., Lee, D.-G., Wang, Y.-W., Park, H.-J., & Wang, L.-F. (2006). Development and validation of a collectivist coping styles inventory. *Journal of Counseling Psychology, 53,* 107–125.

Hersch, C. (1969). From mental health to social action: Clinical psychology in historical perspective. *American Psychologist, 24,* 906–916.

Hess, B. B., Markson, E. W., & Stein, P. J. (1991). *Sociology.* New York, NY: Macmillan.

Hetherington, E. M. (2003). Social support and the adjustment of children in divorced and remarried families. *Childhood, 10,* 237–254.

Hetherington, E. M., & Kelly, J. (2002). *For better or worse: Divorce reconsidered.* New York, NY: Norton.

Hill, J., Bond, M. A., Mulvey, A., & Terenzio, M. (2000). Methodological issues and challenges for a feminist community psychology: An introduction to a special issue. *American Journal of Community Psychology, 28,* 759–772.

Himle, D. P., Jayertne, S., & Thyness, P. (1991). Buffering effects of four social support types on burnout among social workers. *Social Work Research and Abstracts, 27,* 22–27.

Hingson, R., Heeren, T., & Winter, M. (1998). Effects of Maine's 0.05% legal blood alcohol level for drivers with DWI convictions. *Public Health Report, 113,* 440–446.

Hirsch, B. J., & David, T. G. (1983). Social networks and work/nonwork life: Action research with nurse managers. *American Journal of Community Psychology, 11,* 493–508.

Hitlan, R. T., Camillo, K., Zárate, M. A., & Aikman, S. N. (2007). Attitudes toward immigrant groups and the September 11 terrorist attacks. *Peace and Conflict: Journal of Peace Psychology, 13,* 135–152.

Hiltzik, M. (2011). *The New Deal: A modern history.* New York, NY: Free Press.

Hladikova, A., & Hradecky, I. (2007). Homelessness in the Czech Republic. *Journal of Social Issues, 63*(3), 607–622.

Hobfoil, S. E. (1998). Ecology, community, and AIDS prevention. *American Journal of Community Health, 26,* 133–144.

Hobfoil, S., & Vaux, A. (1993). Social support: Social resources and social context. In L. Goldberg & S. Breznitz (Eds.), *Handbook of stress: Theoretical and clinical aspects* (pp. 685–705). New York, NY: Free Press.

Hochschild, A. R. (2003). *The second shift.* New York, NY: Penguin.

Hofen, B., Karren, K., Frandsen, K., Smith, N. (1996). *Mind/body health: The effects of attitudes, emotions, and relationships.* Toronto, ON: Allyn & Bacon.

Hofferth, S. L. (1991). Programs for high risk adolescents: What works? Special issue: Service to teenage parents. *Evaluation and Program Planning, 14,* 3–16.

Holahan, C., Moos, R., & Bonin, L. (1997). Social support, coping, and psychological adjustment: A resources model. In G. Pierce, B. Lakey, I. Sarason, & B. Sarason (Eds.), *Sourcebook of social support and personality* (pp. 169–186). New York, NY: Plenum.

Holahan, J., & Cook, A. (2005). Changes in economic conditions and health insurance coverage, 2000–2004. *Health Affairs,* 498–508.

Hollander, E. P., & Offerman, L. (1990). Power and leadership in organizations. *American Psychologist, 45,* 179–189.

Hollingshead, A., & Redlich, C. (1958). *Social class and mental illness.* New York, NY: Wiley.

Holmes, T. H., & Rahe, R. H. (1967). The social readjustment rating scale. *Journal of Psychosomatic Research, 11,* 213–218.

Homan, M. (2010). *Promoting community change: Making it happen in the real world* (5th ed.). Independence, KY: Brooks Cole/Cengage.

Homan, M. S. (2011). *Promoting community change.* Belmont, CA: Brooks Cole.

Hong, L. (2000). Toward a transformed approach to prevention: Breaking the link between masculinity and violence. *Journal of American College Health, 48,* 269–279.

Houlette, M. A., Gaertner, S. L., Johnson, Kelly, M., Banker, B. S., Riek, B. M., & Dovidio, J. (2004). Developing a more inclusive social identity: An elementary school intervention. *Journal of Social Issues, 60,* 35–55.

House, J., Landis, K., & Umberson, D. (1988). Social relationships and health. *Science, 241,* 540–545.

Howard, J. (2003). Service-learning research: Foundational issues. In S. Billig & A. Waterman (Eds.), *Studying service-learning: Innovations in research methodology* (pp. 1–12). Mahwah, NJ: Erlbaum.

Howard, K. A., Flora, J., & Griffin, M. (1999). Violence-prevention programs in schools: State of the science and implications for future research. *Applied & Preventive Psychology, 8,* 197–215.

Hudiburg, R. (1990). *Comparing computer-related stress to computerphobia*. Retrieved from ERIC database. (ED 318986)

Hudiburg, R., & Necessary, J. (1996). Coping with computer stress. *Journal of Educational Computing Research, 15*(2), 113–124.

Hughey, J., Speer, P., & Peterson, N. A. (1999). Sense of community in community organizations: Structure and evidence of validity. *Journal of Community Psychology, 27,* 97–113.

Human Rights Watch (2003). *Ill equipped: U.S. prisons and offenders with mental illness*. Retrieved from http://www.hrw.org/sites/default/files/reports/usa1003.pdf

Hunter, A., & Riger, S. (1986). The meaning of community in community mental health. *Journal of Community Psychology, 14,* 55–71.

Huo, Y. (2003). Procedural justice and social regulation across group boundaries: Does subgroup identification undermine relationship-based governance? *Personality and Social Psychology Bulletin, 29,* 336–348.

Hurtado, S. (2005). The next generation of diversity and intergroup relations research. *Journal of Social Issues, 61,* 595–567.

Huselid, M. (1995). The impact of human resource management practices on turnover, productivity and corporate financial performance. *Academy of Management Journal, 38,* 635–672.

Hylander, I. (2004). Identifying change in consultee-centered consultation. In N. Lambert, J. Sandoval, & I. Hylander (Eds.). *Consultee-centered consultation* (pp. 373–389). Mahwah, NJ: Erlbaum.

Ialongo, N. S., Rogosch, F., Cicchetti, D., Toth, S., Buckley, J., Petras, H., & Neiderheiser, J. (2006). A developmental psychopathology approach to the prevention of mental health disorder. In D. Cicchetti & D. Cohen (Eds.), *Developmental psychopathology: Vol. 1. Theory and method* (2nd ed., pp. 968–1018). Hoboken, NJ: Wiley.

Ialongo, N. S., Werthamer, L., Kellam, S. G., Brown, C. H., Wang, S., & Lin, Y. (1999). Proximal impact of two first-grade preventive interventions on early risk behaviors for later substance abuse, depression, and antisocial behavior. *American Journal of Community Psychology, 27,* 599–642.

Imm, P., Kehres, R., Wandersman, A., & Chinman, M. (2006). Mobilizing communities for positive youth development: Lessons learned from neighborhood groups and community coalitions. In C. Gil & J. Rhodes (Eds.), *Mobilizing adults for positive youth development: Strategies for closing the gap between beliefs and behaviors* (pp. 137–157). New York, NY: Springer Science + Business Media.

*Improving HIV surveillance among American Indians and Alaska Natives in the United States, January, 2013.* (2013).

Retrieved from http://www.cdc.gov/hiv/strategy/nhas/pdf/strategy_nhas_native_americans.pdf

Independent Sector. (2006). *Facts and figures about charitable organizations*. Retrieved from http://www.indepedentsector.org

Institute of Medicine. (1999). *The unequal burden of cancer: An assessment of NIH research and programs for ethnic minorities and the medically underserved*. Washington, DC: National Academy Press.

Institute of Medicine. (2004). *Preventing childhood obesity: Health in the balance*. Washington, DC: National Institutes of Health.

Institute of Medicine. (2006). *Examining the health disparities research plan of the National Institutes of Health: Unfinished business*. Washington, DC: National Academies Press.

Institute of Medicine (2009). *Preventing mental, emotional, and behavioral disorders among young people*. Washington, DC: National Academies Press.

Iscoe, I. (1987). From Boston to Austin and points beyond: The tenacity of community psychology. *American Journal of Community Psychology, 15,* 587–590.

Iscoe, I. (1994). The early years of community psychology. *Community Psychologist, 28,* 22–23.

Iscoe, I., & Harris, L. (1984). Social and community interventions. *Annual Review of Psychology, 35,* 333–360.

Isenberg, D., Loomis, C., Humphreys, K., & Maton, K. (2004). Self-help research: Issues of power sharing. In L. A. Jason, C. B. Keys, Y. Suarez-Balcazar, R. R. Taylor, & M. L. Davis (Eds.), *Participatory community research: Theories and methods in action* (pp. 129–138). Washington, DC: American Psychological Association.

Ivancevich, J., Matteson, M., Freedman, S., & Phillips, J. (1990). Worksite stress management interventions. *American Psychologist, 45*(2), 252–261.

Jackson, C. T., Covell, N. H., Shear, K. M., & Zhu, C. (2006). The road back: Predictors of regaining preattack functioning among project liberty clients. *Psychiatric Services, 57,* 1283–1290.

Jackson, D., & Hetherington, L. (2006). Young Jamaicans' attitudes toward mental illness: Experimental and demographic factors associated with social distance and stigmatizing opinions. *Journal of Community Psychology, 34,* 563–576.

Jackson, M. (2003). *Systems thinking*. Chichester, England: Wiley.

Jackson, S. E., Schwab, R. L., & Schuler, R. S. (1986). Toward an understanding of the burnout phenomenon. *Journal of Applied Psychology, 71,* 630–640.

Jacobs, J. (1961). *The death and life of great American cities*. New York, NY: Random House.

Jacobs, J. (1961/2011). *The death and life of great American cities.* New York, NY: Vintage Books/Modern Library.

Jacobs, J. B. (1980). The prisoners' rights movement and its impacts, 1960–1980. In N. Morris & M. Tonry (Eds.), *Crime and justice: An annual review of research.* Chicago, IL: University of Chicago Press.

Jaenisch, R., & Bird, A. (2003). Epigenetic regulation of gene expression: How the genome integrates intrinsic and environmental signals. *Nature Genetics, 33,* 245–254. doi:10.1038/ng1089

Jahoda, M. (1958). *Current concepts of positive mental health.* New York, NY: Basic Books. Retrieved from http://www.archive.org/stream/currentconceptso00jaho#page/n5/mode/2up

James, D., & Glaze, L. (2006). *Mental health problems of prison and jail inmates* (Bureau of Justice Statistics Special Report). Washington, DC: U.S. Department of Justice, Office of Justice Programs.

Janz, N. K., & Becker, M. H. (1984). The health belief model: A decade later. *Health Education Quarterly, 11,* 1–47.

Jason, L. A. (1991). Participation in social change: A fundamental value of our discipline. *American Journal of Community Psychology, 19,* 1–16.

Jason, L. A. (1998). Tobacco, drug, and HIV preventive media. *American Journal of Community Psychology, 26,* 151–187.

Jason, L. (2012). Small wins matter in advocacy movements: Giving voice to patients. *American Journal of Community Psychology, 49*(3–4), 307–316.

Jason, L. A., Berk, M., Schnopp-Wyatt, D. L., & Talbot, B. (1999). Effects of enforcement of youth access laws on smoking prevalence. *American Journal of Community Health, 27,* 143–160.

Jason, L. A., Curran, T., Goodman, D., & Smith, M. (1989). A media-based stress management intervention. *Journal of Community Psychology, 17,* 155–165.

Jason, L. A., Davis, M., Suarez-Balcazar, Y., Keys, C., Taylor, R., Holtz Isenberg, D., & Durlak, J. (2003). Conclusion. In L. Jason, K. Keys, Y. Suarez-Balcazar, R. Taylor, & M. Davis (Eds.), *Participatory community research.* Washington, DC: American Psychological Association.

Jason, L., & Glenwick, D. (Eds.). (2002). *Innovative strategies for promoting health and mental health across the life span.* New York, NY: Springer.

Jason, L. A., & Glenwick,, D. S. (Eds.). (2012). *Methodological approaches to community-based research.* Washington, DC: American psychological Association

Jason, L. A., Gruder, C. L., Martins, S., Flay, B. R., Warnecke, R., & Thomas, N. (1987). Work site group meeting and the effectiveness of a televised smoking cessation intervention. *American Journal of Community Psychology, 15,* 57–72.

Jason, L., Hess, R., Felner, R., & Moritsugu, J. (1987a). Toward a multidisciplinary approach to prevention. *Prevention in Human Services, 5*(2), 1–10.

Jason, L. A., Hess, R., Felner, R. D., & Moritsugu, J. N. (Eds.). (1987b). *Prevention: Toward a multidisciplinary approach.* New York, NY: Haworth Press.

Jason, L. A., Kennedy, H. L., & Brackshaw, E. (1999). Television violence and children: Problems and solutions. In T. P. Gulotta & S. J. McElhaney (Eds.), *Violence in homes and communities: Prevention, intervention, and treatment.* Thousand Oaks, CA: Sage.

Jason, L. A., Keys, K., Suarez-Balcazar, Y., Taylor, R., & Davis, M. (Eds.). (2003). *Participatory community research.* Washington, DC: American Psychological Association.

Jason, L. A., La Pointe, P., & Bellingham, S. (1986). The media and self-help: A preventive community intervention. *Journal of Primary Prevention, 6,* 156–167.

Jason, L., & Moritsugu, J. (2003). The role of religion and spirituality in community building. In K. Dockett, G. Dudley-Grant, C. Bankart (Eds.), *Psychology and Buddhism: From individual to global community* (pp. 197–214). New York, NY: Kluwer Academic/Plenum.

Jason, L., & Perdoux, M. (2004). *Havens: Stories of true community healing.* Westport, CT: Praeger /Greenwood.

Jason, L., Pokorny, S., Parka, M., Adams, M., & Morello, T. (2007). Ranking institutional settings based on publications in community psychology journals. *Journal of Community Psychology, 35*(8), 967–979.

Jason, L. A., & Rose, T. (1984). Influencing the passage of child passenger restraint legislation. *American Journal of Community Psychology, 12*(4), 485–495. doi:10.1007/BF00896507

Jason, L. A., & Zolik, E. S. (1981). Modifying dog litter in urban communities. *American Journal of Public Health, 71*(7), 746–747.

Jay, G. M., & D'Augelli, A. R. (1991). Social support and adjustment to university life: A comparison of African-American and White freshman. *Journal of Community Psychology, 19,* 95–100.

Jemmott, J. B., & Jemmott, L. S. (1994). Intervention for adolescents in community settings. In R. J. DiClemente & J. L. Peterson (Eds.), *Preventing AIDS: Theories and methods of behavioral interventions* (pp. 141–174). New York, NY: Plenum.

Jenkins, R. A. (2010). Applied roles and the future of community psychology. *American Journal of Community Psychology, 45*(1–2), 68–72.

Johnson, D. (1991). Psychology in Washington: Why should government support science now that the Russians aren't competing? *Psychological Science, 2,* 133–134.

Johnson, S. (2007). *The ghost map: The story of London's most terrifying epidemic—and how it changed science, cities, and the modern world.* New York, NY: Riverhead Books/Penguin.

Johnston, D. F. (1980). *The handbook of social indicators: Success, characteristics, and analysis.* New York, NY: Garland STPM.

Johnston, L. D., O'Malley, P. M., & Bachman, J. G. (1993). *National survey results on drug use from monitoring the future study, 1975–1992.* Rockville, MD: National Institute on Drug Abuse.

Johnston, L. D., O'Malley, P. M., Bachman, J. G., & Schulenberg, J. E. (2010). *Monitoring the future national results on adolescent drug use: Overview of key findings, 2010.* Ann Arbor: The University of Michigan Institute for Social Research. Retrieved from http://monitoringthefuture.org/pubs/monographs/mtf-overview2010.pdf

Jones, D., Godwin, J., Dodge, K. A., Bierman, K. L., Coie, J. D., Greenberg, M. T., . . . Pinerhughes, E. E. (2010). Impact of the fast track prevention program on health services use by conduct-problem youth. *Pediatrics, 125*(1), e130–e136.

Jones, E. E., & Nisbett, R. E. (1971). *The actor and the observer: Divergent perceptors of the causes of behavior.* Morristown, NJ: General Learning Press.

Jones, J. (1997). *Prejudice and racism* (2nd ed.). New York, NY: McGraw-Hill.

Jones, J. (2003). TRIOS: A psychological theory of African legacy in American culture. *Journal of Social Issues, 59,* 217–242.

Joseph, M., & Ogletree, R. (1998). Community organizing and comprehensive community initiative. *Journal of Sociology and Social Welfare, 25,* 71–79.

Judge, T., Thoresen, C., Bono, J., & Patton, G. ((2001). The job satisfaction-job performance relationship: A qualitative and quantitative review. *Psychological Bulletin, 127,* 376–407.

Jukkala, T., Makinen, I. H., Kislitsyna, O., Ferlander, S., & Vagero, D. (2008). Economic strain, social relations, gender, and binge drinking in Moscow. *Social Science & Medicine, 66,* 663–674.

Kagan, C., Burton, M., Duckett, P., Lawthom, R., & Siddiquee, A. (2011). *Critical community psychology.* Oxford, England: Wiley-Blackwell.

Kaiser Family Foundation. (2005a). *U.S. teen sexual activity.* Menlo Park, CA: Author.

Kaiser Family Foundation. (2010). *Generation M2: Media in the lives of 8- to 18-year-olds.* Menlo Park, CA: Author.

Kalafat, J., & Elias, M. (1995). Suicide prevention in an educational context: Broad and narrow foci. *Suicide and Life Threatening Behavior, 25,* 123–133.

Kamradt, B. (2000). Wraparound Milwaukee: Aiding youth with mental health needs. *Juvenile Justice, 7,* 14–23.

Kanner, A. D., Coyne, J. C., Schaefer, C., & Lazarus, R. S. (1981). Comparison of two models of stress management: Daily hassles and uplifts versus major life events. *Journal of Behavioral Medicine, 4,* 1–39.

Kaplan, C. P., Turner, S. G., & Badger, L. W. (2007). Hispanic adolescent girls' attitudes toward school. *Child & Adolescent Social Work Journal, 24,* 173–193.

Kaplan, G. (1994). Reflections on present and future research on bio-behavioral risk factors. In S. Blumenthal, K. Matthews, & S. Weiss (Eds.), *New research frontiers in behavioral medicine: Proceedings of the national conference.* Washington, DC: NIH Publications.

Karavidas, M., Lim, N. K., & Katsikas, S. L. (2005). The effects of computers on older adult users. *Computers in Human Behavior, 21,* 697–711.

Karcher, M. J. (2005). The effects of developmental mentoring and high school mentors' attendance on their younger mentees' self-esteem, social skills, and connectedness. *Psychology in the Schools, 42,* 65–77.

Karel, M. J., Gatz, M., & Smyer, M. A. (2012). Aging and mental health in the decade ahead: What psychologists need to know. *American Psychologist, 67*(3), 184–198.

Karim, Q. A., Karim, S. S. A., Coovadia, H. M., & Susser, M. (1998). Informed consent for HIV testing in a South African Hospital: Is it truly informed and truly voluntary? *American Journal of Public Health, 88,* 637–640.

Katapodi, M. C., Facione, N. C., Miaskowski, C., Dodd, M. J., & Waters, C. (2002). The influence of social support on breast cancer screening in a multicultural community sample. *Oncology Nursing Society, 29*(5), 845–852.

Katz, D. (1983). Factors affecting social change: A social psychological interpretation. *Journal of Social Issues, 39,* 25–44.

Kaufman, J. S., Crusto, C. A., Quan, M., Ross, E., Friedman, S. R., O'Reilly, K., & Call, S. (2006). Utilizing program evaluation as a strategy to promote community change: Evaluation of a comprehensive community-based family violence initiative. *American Journal of Community Psychology, 38*(3–4), 191–200.

Kaufman, J. S., Ross, E., Quan, M. A., O'Reilly, K., & Crusto, C. A. (2004). Building the evaluation capacity of community-based organizations: The Bridgeport Safe Start Initiative. *Community Psychologist, 37*(4), 45–47.

Kaufman, K., Gregory, W. L., & Stephan, W. (1990). Maladjustment in statistical minorities within ethnically unbalanced classrooms. *American Journal of Community Psychology, 18,* 757–765.

Kawakami, K., Phills, C. E., Steele, J. R., & Dovidio, J. F. (2007). Distance makes the heart grow fonder: Improving implicit racial attitudes and interracial interactions through approach behaviors. *Journal of Personality and Social Psychology, 92,* 957–971.

Kazden, A. E. (1980). *Research design in community psychology.* New York, NY: Harper & Row.

Kazden, A. (2010). *Reconsidering clinical psychology.* The James McKeen Cattell Fellow Award Address at the American Psychological Society Convention, Boston, MA.

Kazdin, A. E., & Blasé, S. L. (2011a). Rebooting psychotherapy research and practice to reduce the burden of mental illness. *Perspectives on Psychological Science, 6*(1), 21–37.

Kazdin, A. E., & Blasé, S. L. (2011b). Interventions and models of their delivery to reduce the burden of mental illness: Reply to commentaries. *Perspectives on Psychological Science, 6*(5), 507–510.

Keen, B., & Jacobs, D. (2009). Racial threat, partisan politics, and racial disparities in prison admissions: A panel analysis. *Criminology, 47*(1), 209-238.

Keinan, G. (1997). Social support, stress, and personality: Do all women benefit from their husband's presence during childbirth? In G. Pierce, B. Lakey, I. Sarason, & B. Sarason (Eds.), *Sourcebook of social support and personality* (pp. 409–427). New York, NY: Plenum.

Kellam, S. G., Koretz, D., & Moscicki, E. K. (Eds.). (1999a). Prevention science, part I [Special issue]. *American Journal of Community Psychology, 27,* 461–595.

Kellam, S. G., Koretz, D., & Moscicki, E. K. (Eds.). (1999b). Prevention science, part II [Special issue]. *American Journal of Community Psychology, 27,* 697–731.

Keller, T. E. (2007). Youth mentoring: Theoretical and methodological issues. In T. D. Allen & L. T. Eby (Eds.), *The Blackwell handbook of mentoring: A multiple perspectives approach.* Malden, MA: Blackwell.

Kelly, C., & Breinlinger, S. (1996). *The social psychology of collective action: Identity, injustice, and gender.* Washington, DC: Taylor & Francis.

Kelly, G. W. R., & Ekland-Olson, S. (1991). The response of the criminal justice system to prison overcrowding: Recidivism patterns among four successive parolee courts. *Law and Society Review, 25,* 601–620.

Kelly, H. H. (1973). The process of causal attribution. *American Psychologist, 28,* 107–128.

Kelly, J. (1966). Ecological constraints on mental health services. *American Psychologist, 21,* 535–539.

Kelly, J. (1968). Toward an ecological conception of preventive interventions. In J. Carter (Ed.), *Research contributions from psychology to community mental health* (pp. 75–99). New York, NY: Behavioral Publications.

Kelly, J. (May, 6, 1980). *On the conservation of community leadership: An ecological view.* Invited Address at the Western Psychological Association meetings, Honolulu, Hawaii.

Kelly, J. G. (1986a). An ecological paradigm: Defining mental health consultation as a preventative service. *Prevention in the Human Services, 4,* 1–36.

Kelly, J. G. (1986b). Context and process: An ecological view of the interdependence of practice and research. *American Journal of Community Psychology, 14,* 581–589.

Kelly, J. G. (1990). Changing contexts and the field of community psychology. *American Journal of Community Psychology, 18,* 769–792.

Kelly, J. G. (1999). Contexts and community leadership: Inquiry as an ecological expedition. *American Psychologist, 54*(11), 953–961.

Kelly, J. (2002). The Seymour Sarason Award address: The spirit of community psychology. *American Journal of Community Psychology, 30,* 43–63.

Kelly, J. G. (2005). The National Institute of Mental Health and the founding of the field of community psychology. In W. R. Pickren & S. F. Schneider (Eds.), *Psychology and the National Institute of Mental Health: A historical analysis of science, practice, and policy* (pp. 233–259). Washington, DC: American Psychological Association.

Kelly, J. G. (2006). *Becoming ecological: An expedition into community psychology.* New York, NY: Oxford University Press.

Kelly, J. G. (2010). Ecological thinking: Four qualities. *Análise Psicológica, 28*(3), 389–393.

Kelly, J., Azelton, L., Lardon, C., Mock, L., Tandon, S., & Thomas, M. (2004). On community leadership: Stories about collaboration in action research. *American Journal of Community Psychology, 33*(3–4), 205–216.

Kelly, J., Dassoff, N., Levin, I., & Schreckengost, J. (1988). A guide to conducting prevention research in the community: First steps. *Prevention in Human Services, 6*(1), 174.

Kelly, J., Snowden, L., & Munoz, R. (1977). Social and community interventions. *Annual Review of Psychology, 28,* 323–361.

Kelly, K. D., Caputo, T., & Jamieson, W. (2005). Reconsidering sustainability: Some implications for community-based crime prevention. *Critical Social Policy, 25,* 306–324.

Kelsey, J. L., Thompson, W. D., & Evans, A. S. (1986). *Methods in observational epidemiology.* New York, NY: Oxford University Press.

Kennedy, C. (1989). Community integration and well-being: Toward the goals of community care. *Journal of Social Issues, 45,* 65–78.

Kennedy, M. (2006). On your guard. *American School & University, 78,* 40–48.

Kenyon, D., & Carter, J. S. (2011). Ethnic identity, sense of community, and psychological well-being among Northern Plains American Indian youth. *Journal of Community Psychology, 39*(1), 1–9.

Keppel, B. (2002). Kenneth B. Clark in the patterns of American culture. *American Psychologist, 57*(1), 29–37.

Kerlinger, F. N. (1973). *Foundations of behavioral research.* New York, NY: Holt, Rinehart & Winston.

Kessler, M., & Albee, G. (1975). Primary prevention. *Annual Review of Psychology, 26,* 557–591.

Kessler, R. C., Chiu, W., Demler, O., & Walters, E. (2005). Prevalence, severity, and comorbidity of 12-month DSM-IV disorders in the national comorbidity survey replication. *Archives of General Psychiatry, 62,* 617–627.

Kessler, R. C., McGonagle, K. A., Zhao, S., Nelson, C. B., Hughes, M., Eshleman, S., . . . Kendler, K. (1994). Lifetime and 12-month prevalence of DSM-III-R psychiatric disorders in the United States: Results from the national comorbidity survey. *Archives of General Psychiatry, 51,* 8–19.

Kettner, P. M., Daley, J. M., & Nichols, A. W. (1985). *Initiating change in organizations of communities: A macro practice model.* Monterey, CA: Brooks Cole.

Key, J. D., O'Rourke, K., Judy, N., & McKinnon, S. A. (2005–2006). Efficacy of a secondary adolescent pregnancy prevention: An ecological study before, during and after implementation of the second chance club. *International Quarterly of Community Health Education, 24,* 231–240.

Keyes, C. L. M. (2007). Promoting and protecting mental health as flourishing: A complementary strategy for improving national mental health. *American Psychologist, 62*(2), 95–108.

Keys, C. (2007). Foreward to the special issue: Exploring the intersection of organization studies and community psychology. *Journal of Community Psychology, 35,* 277–280.

Keys, C. B., & Frank, S. (1987). Organizational perspectives in community psychology [Special issue]. *American Journal of Community Psychology, 15.*

Khoury-Kassabri, M., Benbenishty, R., Astor, R. A., & Zeira, A. (2004). The contributions of community, family, and school variables to student victimization. *American Journal of Community Psychology, 34,* 187–204.

Kidd, S., & Davidson, L. (2007). "You have to adapt because you have no other choice": The stories of strength and resilience of 208 homeless youth in New York City and Toronto. *Journal of Community Psychology, 35*(2), 219–238.

Kidd, S., & Kral, M. (2005). Practicing participatory action research. *Journal of Counseling Psychology, 52*(2), 187–195.

Kiernan, M., Toro, P. A., Rappaport, J., & Seidman, E. (1989). Economic predictors of mental health service utilization: A time-series analysis. *American Journal of Community Psychology, 17,* 801–820.

Kiesler, C. A. (1980). Mental health policy as a field of inquiry for psychology. *American Psychologist, 35,* 1066–1080.

Kiesler, C. A. (1992). Mental health policy: Doomed to fail. *American Psychologist, 47,* 1077–1082.

Kim, J., & Cicchetti, D. (2010). Longitudinal pathways linking child maltreatment, emotion regulation, peer relations, and psychopathology. *Journal of Child Psychology and Psychiatry, 51*(6), 706–716.

Kim, M. M., & Ford, J. D. (2006). Trauma and post-traumatic stress among homeless men: A review of current research. *Journal of Aggression, Maltreatment, & Trauma, 13,* 1–22.

Kimbro, R. T., Bzostek, S., Goldman, N., & Rodríguez, G. (2008). Race, ethnicity, and education gradient in health. *Health Affairs, 27,* 361–372.

King, R. H. (2004). The *Brown* decade. *Patterns of Prejudice, 38,* 333–353.

Kirby, D. (2007). *Emerging answers 2007: New research findings on programs to reduce teen pregnancy* (Report of The National Campaign to Prevent Teen and Unplanned Pregnancy). Retrieved from http://www.thenationalcampaign .org/resources/reports.aspx

Kirkman, B. L., Jones, R. G., & Shapiro, D. L. (2000). Why do employees resist teams? Examining the "resistance barrier" to work team effectiveness. *International Journal of Conflict Management, 11,* 74–92.

Kirmeyer, S. L., & Dougherty, T. W. (1988). Workload, tension, and coping: Moderating effects of supervisor support. *Personnel Psychology, 41,* 125–139.

Kitchen, C. D. (1991). Crisis intervention using reality therapy for adult sexual abuse victims. *Journal of Reality Therapy, 10,* 34–39.

Kite, M. E., Stockdale, G. D., Whitley, B. E., & Johnson, B. T. (2005). Attitudes toward younger and older adults: An updated meta-analytic review. *Journal of Social Issues, 61,* 241–266.

Klaw, E. L., & Humphreys, K. (2000). Beyond abstinence: Life stories of Moderation Management mutual help group members. *Contemporary Drug Problems, 27,* 779–803.

Kleck, G. (1991). *Point blank: Guns and violence in America.* New York, NY: De Gruyter.

Klein, C., DiazGranados, D., Salas, E., Le, H., Burke, C., Lyons, R., et al. (2009). Does team building work?. *Small Group Research, 40*(2), 181–222. doi:10.117/ 1046408328821

Klein, D. (1987). The context and times at Swampscott: My story. *American Journal of Community Psychology, 12,* 515–517.

Klein, J. (2005). America is from Mars, Europe from Venus: How the United States can learn from Europe's social work response to school shootings. *School Social Work Journal, 30,* 1–24.

Klein, K. J., & D'Aunno, T. A. (1986). Psychological sense of community in the workplace. *Journal of Community Psychology, 14,* 365–377.

Klein, K. J., Ralls, R. S., Smith Major, V., & Douglas, C. (2000). Power and participation in the workplace: Implications for empowerment theory, research, and practice. In J. Rappaport & E. Seidman (Eds.), *Handbook of community psychology.* New York, NY: Plenum.

Kleinman, J. C., & Madanas, J. H. (1985). The effects of maternal smoking, physical stature, and educational attainment on the incidence of low birthweight. *American Journal of Epidemiology, 121,* 843–855.

Kling, R. (2000). Learning about information technologies and social change: The contribution of social informatics. *Information Society, 16,* 217–232.

Kloos, B. (2005). Community science: Creating an alternative place to stand? *American Journal of Community Psychology, 35,* 259–267.

Kloos, B., Hill, J., Thomas, E., Wandersman, A., Elias, M. J., & Dalton, J. H. (2011). *Community psychology: Linking individuals and communities* (3rd ed.). Belmont, CA: Wadsworth.

Knipscheer, J. W., & Kleber, R. J. (2008). Help seeking behavior of West Africans in the Netherlands. *Journal of Community Psychology, 36*(7), 915–928.

Knitzer, J. (2007). Putting knowledge into policy: Toward an infant-toddler policy agenda. In Infant mental health in early Head Start [Special issue]. *Infant Mental Health Journal, 28,* 237–245.

Koch, T., & Kralik, D. (2006). *Participatory action research in health care.* Oxford, England: Blackwell.

Koch, W. (January 1, 2006). Poll: Washington scandals eating away public trust. *USA Today.* Retrieved from http://www.usatoday.com

Kochan, T., Bezrukova, K., Ely, R., Jackson, S., Joshi, A., Jehn, K., . . . Thomas, D. (2002, October). The effects of diversity on business performance: report of the diversity research network. Retrieved from http://www.shrm.org/about/foundation/research/Documents/kochan_fulltext.pdf

Koegel, P., Burnam, M. A., & Farr, R. K. (1990). Substance adaptation among homeless adults in the inner city of Los Angeles. *Journal of Social Issues, 46,* 83–107.

Koenig, A. M., Eagly, A. H., Mitchell, A. A., & Ristikari, T. (2011). Are leader stereotypes masculine? A meta-analysis of three research paradigms. *Psychological Bulletin, 137*(4), 616–642.

Kofkin Rudkin, J. (2003). *Community psychology: Guiding principles and orienting concepts.* Upper Saddle River, NJ: Prentice Hall.

Kohlberg, L. (1984). *Essays on moral development: Vol. 2. The nature and validity of moral stages.* San Francisco, CA: Harper & Row.

Koizumi, R. (2000). Anchor points in transitions to a new school environment. *Journal of Primary Prevention, 20,* 175–187.

Kooyman, I., & Walsh, E. (2011). Societal outcomes in schizophrenia. In D. Weinberger & P. Harrison (Eds.), *Schizophrenia* (3rd ed., pp. 644–665). Oxford, England: Wiley-Blackwell.

Korbin, J. E., & Coulton, C. J. (1996). The role of neighbors and the government in neighborhood-based child protection. *Journal of Social Issues, 52,* 163–176.

Kosic, A., & Phalet, K. (2006). Ethnic categorization of immigrants: The role of prejudice, perceived acculturation strategies, and group size. *International Journal of Intercultural Relations, 30,* 769–782.

Kotch, J., Blakely, C., Brown, S., & Wong, F. (1992). *A pound of prevention: The case for universal maternity care in the US.* Washington, DC: American Public Health Association.

Kral, M. J., Idlout, L., Minore, J. B., Dyck, R. J., & Kirmayer, L. J. (2011). Unikkaartuit: Meanings of well-being, unhappiness, health, and community change among Inuit in Nunavut, Canada. *American Journal of Community Psychology, 48*(3–4), 426–438.

Kral, M. J., García, J. I., Aber, M. S., Masood, N., Dutta, U., & Todd, N. R. (2011). Culture and community psychology: Toward a renewed and reimagined vision. *American Journal of Community Psychology, 47*(1–2), 46–57.

Kranz, D. H. (1998). Predictors of homelessness among families in New York City: From shelter request to housing stability. *American Journal of Public Health, 88,* 1651–1657.

Kreisler, A., Snider, A. B., & Kiernan, N. E. (1997). Using distance education to educate and empower community coalitions: A case study. *International Quarterly of Community Health Education, 17,* 161–178.

Krueger, P. M., Bond Huie, S. A., Rogers, R. G., & Hummer, R. A. (2004). Neighbourhoods and homicide mortality: An analysis of race/ethnic differences. *Journal of Epidemiology & Community Health, 58,* 223–230.

Kruger, D. J., Reischl, T. M., & Gee, G. C. (2007). Neighborhood social conditions mediate the association between physical deterioration and mental health. *American Journal of Community Psychology, 40,* 261–271.

Kuhn, T. (1962/1996). *The structure of scientific revolutions.* Chicago, IL: University of Chicago Press.

Kuehner, C., Huffziger, S., & Liebsch, K. (2009). Rumination, distraction, and mindful self-focus: Effects on mood, dysfunctional attitudes, and cortisol stress response. *Psychological Medicine, 39,* 219–228.

Kulik, L. (2006). Burnout among volunteers in the social services: The impact of gender and employment status. *Journal of Community Psychology, 34,* 541–561.

Kumper, K. L., & Alvarad, R. (2003). Family strengthening approaches for the prevention of youth problem behaviors. *American Psychologist, 58,* 457–465.

Kumpfer, K. L., Alvarado, R., Smith, P., & Bellamy, N. (2002). Cultural sensitivity and adaptation in family based interventions. *Prevention Science, 3,* 241–246.

Kuo, F. (2001). Coping with poverty: Impacts of environment and attention in the inner city. *Environmental Behavior, 33,* 5–34.

Kuo, F. E., Sullivan, W. C., Coley, R. L., & Brunson, L. (1998). Fertile ground for community: Inner-city neighborhood common spaces. *American Journal of Community Psychology, 26,* 823–852.

Labianca, G., Gray, B., & Brass, D. J. (2000). A grounded model of organizational schema change during empowerment. *Organization Science, 11,* 235–257.

Ladson-Billings, G. (2006). From the achievement gap to the education debt: Understanding achievement in US schools. *Educational Researcher, 35,* 3–12.

Laguna, K., & Babcock, R. L. (1997). Computer anxiety in young and older adults: Implications for human-computer interactions in older populations. *Computers in Human Behavior, 13,* 317–326.

Lahm, K. F. (2008). Inmate-on-inmate assault. *Criminal Justice and Behavior, 35,* 120–137.

Lakes, K. D., Vaughn, E., Jones, M., Burke, W., Baker, D., & Swansen, J. M. (2012). Diverse perceptions of the informed consent process: Implications for the recruitment and participation of diverse communities in the National Children's Study. *American Journal of Community Psychology, 49,* 215–232.

Lal, S. (2002). Giving children security: Mamie Phipps Clark and the racialization of child psychology. *American Psychologist, 57*(1), 20–28.

Lamb, M. E., & Ahnert, L. (2006). Nonparental child care: Context, concepts, correlations, and consequences. In K. A. Renninger, I. E. Sigel, W. Damon, & R. M. Lerner (Eds.), *Handbook of child psychology: Vol. 4. Child psychology in practice.* Hoboken, NJ: Wiley.

Lambert, E. Y. (Ed.). (1990). *The collection and interpretation of data from hidden populations* (NIDA Monograph No. 98). Rockville, MD: NIDA.

Lambert, M. J., & Barley, D. E. (2001). Research summary on the therapeutic relationship and psychotherapy outcome. *Psychotherapy: Theory, Research, Practice, Training, 38,* 357–361.

Lambert, S. F., Ialongo, N. S., Boyd, R. C., & Cooley, M. R. (2005). Risk factors for community violence exposure in adolescence. *American Journal of Community Psychology, 36,* 29–48.

Landers, S. (1989). Homeless children lose childhood. *APA Monitor, 20*(12), 1, 33.

Langan, P. A., & Levin, D. J. (2002). *Recidivism of prisoners released in 1994* (Bureau of Justice Statistics Special Report NCJ 193427). Washington, DC: U.S. Department of Justice. Retrieved from http://bjs.ojp.usdoj.gov/content/pub/pdf/rpr94.pdf

Langer, L. J., & Rodin, J. (1976). The effects of choice and enhanced personal responsibility for the aged: A field experiment in an institutional setting. *Journal of Personality and Social Psychology, 34,* 191–198.

Langhout, R. D. (2004). Facilitators and inhibitors of positive school feelings: An exploratory study. *American Journal of Community Psychology, 34,* 111–127.

La Piere, R. T. (1934). Attitudes and actions. *Social Forces, 13,* 230–237.

Laracuenta, M., & Denmark, F. L. (2005). What can we do about school violence? In F. L. Denmark, H. H. Krause, R. W. Wesner, E. Midlarsky, E. Gielen, & P. Uwe (Eds.), *Violence in schools: Cross-national and cross-cultural perspectives.* New York, NY: Springer.

Lasker, R., Weiss, E., & Miller, R. (2001). Partnership synergy: A practical framework for studying and strengthening the collaborative advantage. *Milbank Quarterly, 79*(2), 179–205.

Latimer, J., Dowden, C., & Muise, D. (2005). The effectiveness of restorative justice practices: A meta-analysis. *Prison Journal, 85,* 127–144.

Latkin, C. A., Mandell, W., Vlahov, D., Oziemkowska, M., & Celentano, D. (1996). The long-term outcome of a personal network-oriented HIV prevention intervention for injection drug users: The SAFE study. *American Journal of Community Psychology, 24,* 341–364.

Lavee, Y., & Ben-Ari, A. (2008). The association between daily hassles and uplifts with family and life satisfaction: Does cultural orientation make a difference? *American Journal of Community Psychology, 1–2,* 89–98.

LaVeist, T., Sellers, R., Brown, K., & Nickerson, K. (1997). Extreme social isolation, use of community-based senior support services, and mortality among African American elderly women. *American Journal of Community Psychology, 25*(5), 721–732.

Lavoie, K. L., & Barone, S. (2006). Prescription privileges for psychologists: A comprehensive review and critical analysis of current issues and controversies. *CNS Drugs, 20*(1), 51–66.

Lavoie, F., & Brunson, L. (2010). La pratique de la psychologie communautaire. *Canadian Psychology/Psychologie Canadienne, 51*(2), 96–105.

Lawson, A., & Rhode, D. L. (1993). *The politics of pregnancy: Adolescent sexuality and public policy*. New Haven, CT: Yale University Press.

Lazarus, R. (1999). *Stress and emotion: A new synthesis*. New York, NY: Springer.

Lazarus, R. S., & Folkman, S. (1984). *Stress, appraisal, and coping*. New York, NY: Springer.

Lee, D. L., & Ahn, S. (2011). Racial discrimination and Asian mental health: A meta-analysis. *The Counseling Psychologist, 39*, 463–489.

Lee, T., & Breen, L. (2007). Young people's perceptions and experiences of leaving school early: An exploration. *Journal of Community & Applied Social Psychology, 17*, 329–346.

Legault, L., Green-Demers, I., & Pelletier, L. (2006). Why do high school students lack motivation in the classroom? Toward an understanding of academic motivation and the role of social support. *Journal of Educational Psychology, 98*, 567–582.

Lehr, C. A., Johnson, D. R., Bremer, C. D., Cosio, S., & Thompson, M. (2004). *Essential tools. Increasing rates of school completion: Moving from policy and research to practice*. Minneapolis, MN: National Center on Secondary Education and Transition, College of Education and Human Development, University of Minnesota.

Lehr, U., Seiler, E., & Thomae, H. (2000). Aging in cross-cultural perspective. In L. Comunian & U. P. Gielen (Eds.), *International perspectives on human development*. Lengerich, Germany: Pabst Science.

Leigh, B. C., & Stall, R. (1993). Substance abuse and risky behavior for exposure to HIV: Issues in methodology, interpretation, and prevention. *American Psychologist, 48*, 1035–1045.

Leinsalu, M. (2004). *Troubled transitions: Social variation and long-term trends in health and mortality in Estonia*. Stockholm: Almqvist & Wiksell.

Leiter, M., & Maslach, C. (1998). Burnout. In H. Friedman (Ed.), *Encyclopedia of mental health*. San Diego, CA: Academic Press.

Leiter, M. P., & Maslach, C. (2004). Areas of work life: A structured approach to organizational predictors of job burnout. In P. Perrewe & D. Ganster (Eds.), *Research in occupational stress and well being* (Vol. 3, pp. 91–134). Oxford, England: Elsevier.

Leiter, M. P., & Maslach, C. (2005). A mediation model of job burnout. In A. Antoniou & C. Cooper (Eds.), *Research companion to organizational health psychology* (pp. 544–564). Cheltenham, England: Edward Elger.

Lempert, R., & Sanders, J. (1986). *An invitation to law and social science*. New York, NY: Longman.

Leonard, P. A., Dolbeare, C. N., & Lazere, E. B. (1989). *A place to call home: The crisis in housing for the poor*. Washington, DC: Center on Budget and Policy Priorities and Low Income Housing Information Service.

Lerner, R. M. (1995). *America's youth in crisis: Challenges and options for programs and policies*. Thousand Oaks, CA: Sage.

Leserman, J., & Drossman, D. A. (2007). Relationship of abuse history to functional gastrointestinal disorders and symptoms. *Trauma, Violence, & Abuse, 8*, 331–343.

Lesesne, C. A., Lewis, K. M., White, C. P., & Green, D. C. (2008). Promoting science-based approaches to teen pregnancy prevention: Proactively engaging the three systems of interactive systems framework. *American Journal of Community Psychology, 41*, 379–393.

Lettieri, D. J., Sayers, M., & Pearson, H. W. (Eds.). (1984). *Theories on drug abuse: Selected contemporary perspectives* (National Institute on Drug Abuse Research Monograph No. 30). Washington, DC: Superintendent of Documents, U.S. Government Printing Office.

Leventhal, T., & Brooks-Gunn, J. (2004). A randomized study of neighborhood effects on low income children's educational outcomes. *Developmental Psychology, 40*, 488–507.

Levey, B., & Sidel, V. (Eds.). (2006). *Social injustice and public health*. New York, NY: Oxford University Press.

Levi, Y., & Litwin, H. (1986). *Communities and cooperatives in participatory development*. Brookfield, VT: Gower Press.

Levine, I. S., & Huebner, R. D. (1991). Homeless persons with alcohol, drug, and mental disorders. *American Psychologist, 46*, 1113–1114.

Levine, M. (1988). An analysis of mutual assistance. *American Journal of Community Psychology, 16*, 167–188.

Levine, M. (1998). Prevention and community. *American Journal of Community Psychology, 26*, 189–206.

Levine, M. (1999, Spring). Prevention and progress. *Community Psychologist, 32*, 11–14.

Levine, M. & Perkins, D. (1987). Principles of community psychology: Perspectives and applications. New York: NY: Oxford University Press.

Levine, M., & Perkins, D. V. (1997). *Principles of community psychology: Perspectives and applications*. 2nd Ed. New York, NY: Oxford University Press.

Levine, M., Perkins, D., & Perkins, D. (2004). *Principles of community psychology. Perspectives and applications*, Third Edition. New York, NY: Oxford University Press.

Levine, M., Toro, P. A., & Perkins, D. V. (1993). Social and community interventions. In L. W. Porter & M. R. Rosenzweig (Eds.), *Annual review of psychology*. Palo Alto, CA: Annual Reviews.

Levine, M. D. (1986). Working it out: A community re-creation approach to crime prevention. *Journal of Community Psychology, 14*, 378–390.

Leviton, L. C. (1989). Theoretical foundations of AIDS prevention programs. In R. O. Valdiserri (Ed.), *Preventing AIDS: The design of effective programs* (pp. 42–90). New Brunswick, NJ: Rutgers University Press.

Levy, D., Splansky, G. L., Strand, N. K., Atwood, L. D., Benjamin, E. J., Blease, S., . . . Murabito, J. M. (2010). Consent for genetic research in the Framingham heart study. *American Journal of Medical Genetics, 152*(A), 1250–1256.

Levy, B., & Sidel, V. (2006). *Social injustice and public health.* New York, NY: Oxford University Press.

Levy, L. H. (2000). Self-help groups. In J. Rappaport & E. Seidman (Eds.), *Handbook of community psychology.* New York, NY: Plenum.

Lewin, K. (1936). *Principles of topological psychology.* New York, NY: McGraw-Hill.

Lewin, K. (1946). Action research and minority problems. *Journal of Social Issues, 2*(4), 34–46.

Lewin, K. (1948). *Resolving social conflict.* New York, NY: Harper.

Lewin, K. (1951). *Field theory in social science.* New York, NY: Harper & Row.

Lewin, K., & Lippett, R. (1938) An experimental approach to the study of autocracy and democracy. A preliminary note. *Sociometry, 1,* 292–300.

Lewin, K., Lippett, R., & White, R. (1939) Patterns of aggressive behavior in experimentally created "social climates." *Journal of Social Psychology 10,* 271–299.

Li, M., Xu, J., He, Y., and Wu, Z. (2012). The analysis of the resilience of adults one year after the 2008 Wenchuan earthquake, *Journal of Community Psychology, 40,* 860–870.

Lievens, F., & Anseel, F. (2004). Confirmatory factor analysis and invariance of an organizational citizenship behaviour measure across samples in a Dutch-speaking context. *Journal of Occupational and Organizational Psychology, 77*(3), 299–306.

Light, D., & Keller, S. (1985). *Sociology.* New York, NY: Knopf.

Likert, R. (1961). *New patterns of management.* New York, NY: McGraw-Hill.

Lin, N., Simonre, R., Ensel, W., & Kuo, W. (1979). Social support, stressful life events, and illness: A model and an empirical test. *Journal of Health and Social Behavior, 20,* 108–119.

Lindemann, E. (1944). Symptomatology and management of acute grief. *American Journal of Psychiatry, 151* (2): 155–160.

Linney, J. A. (1990). Community psychology into the 1990's: Capitalizing opportunity and promoting innovation. *American Journal of Community Psychology, 18,* 1–17.

Linney, J. (2005). Might we practice what we've preached? Thoughts on the special issue papers. *American Journal of Community Psychology, 35,* 253–258.

Lippett, R., Watson, J., & Westley, B. (1958). *The dynamics of planned change.* New York, NY: Harcourt, Brace, & World.

Liptak, A. (February, 29, 2008). U.S. imprisons one in 100 adults, report finds. *The New York Times.* Retrieved from http://www.nytimes.com

Liptak, A. (2008, April 23). U.S. prison population dwarfs that of other nations. *The New York Times.* Retrieved from http://www.nytimes.com

Liu, E., & Hanauer, N. (2011). *The gardens of democracy.* Seattle: Sasquatch Books.

Lohr, S. (October 31, 2006). Computing 2016, what won't be possible? *The New York Times.* Retrieved from http://www.nytimes.com

Long, D., & Perkins, D. (2003). Confirmatory factor analysis of the Sense of Community Index and development of a brief SCI. *Journal of Community Psychology, 31,* 279–296.

Loo, C., Fong, K. T., & Iwamasa, G. (1988). Ethnicity and cultural diversity: An analysis of work published in community psychology journals, 1965–1985. *Journal of Community Psychology, 16,* 332–349.

Lopez, G. E. (2004). Interethnic contact, curriculum, and attitudes in the first year of college. *Journal of Social Issues, 60,* 75–94.

Lorion, R. P. (1983). Evaluating preventive interventions: Guidelines for the serious social change agent. In R. Felner, L. Jason, J. Moritsugu, & S. Farber (Eds.), *Preventive psychology: Theory, research and practice* (pp. 251–268). New York, NY: Pergamon.

Lorion, R. P. (1990) Developmental analyses of community phenomena. In P. Tolan, C. Keys, F. Chertok, & L. Jason (Eds.), *Researching community psychology* (pp. 32–41). Washington, DC: American Psychological Association.

Lorion, R. P. (1991). Targeting preventive interventions: Enhancing risk estimates through theory. *American Journal of Community Psychology, 19,* 859–865.

Lorion, R. (2007). From the editor. *Journal of Community Psychology, 35*(1), 1–2.

Lorion, R. P. (2011). Understanding Sarason's concepts of school cultures and change: Joining a community in school improvement efforts. *American Journal of Community Psychology, 48*(3–4), 147–156.

Lösel, F. (2007). Counterblast: The prison overcrowding crisis and some constructive perspectives for crime policy. *Howard Journal of Criminal Justice, 46,* 512–519.

Loukaitou-Sideris, A., & Eck, J. E. (2007). Crime prevention and active living. *American Journal of Health Promotion. Special Issue: Active Living Research, 21,* 380–389.

Loukes, A., Suzuki, R., & Horton, K. D. (2006). Examining social connectedness as a mediator of school climate effects. *Journal of Research on Adolescence, 16*, 491–502.

Lounsbury, J. W., Leader, D. S., Meares, E. P., & Cook, M. P. (1980). An analytic review of research in community psychology. *American Journal of Community Psychology, 8*, 415–441.

Love, J. M., Tarullo, L. B., Raikes, H., & Chazan-Cohen, R. (2006). Head Start: What do we know about its effectiveness? What do we need to know? In K. McCartney & D. Malden (Eds.), *Blackwell handbook of early childhood development*. Malden, MA: Blackwell.

Lovell, A. M. (1990). Managed cases, drop-ins, drop-outs, and other by-products of mental health care. *American Journal of Community Psychology, 18*, 917–921.

Lowenthal, M. F., & Haven, C. (1968). Interaction and adaptation: Intimacy as a cultural variable. *American Sociological Review, 33*, 20–30.

Lucas, R. E., Clark, A. E., Georgellis, Y., & Diener, E. (2004). Unemployment alters the set point for life satisfaction. *Psychological Science, 15*(1), 8–13.

Lucksted, A., McFarlane, W., Downing, D., Dixon, L., & Adams, C. (2012). Recent developments in family psychoeducation as an evidence based practice. *Journal of Marital and Family Therapy, 38*(1), 101–121.

Ludwig, J., & Phillips, D. (2007). The benefits and costs of Head Start. *Social Policy Report, 21*, 1–20.

Luepker, R., Murray, D., Jacobs, D., Mittelmark, M., Bracht, N., Carlaw, R., . . . Elmer, P. (1994). Community education for cardiovascular disease prevention: Risk factor changes in the Minnesota Heart Health Program. *American Journal of Public Health, 84*, 1383–1393.

Luke, D. A. (2005). Getting the big picture in community science: Methods that capture context. *American Journal of Community Psychology, 35*(3–4), 185–200.

Lukens, E., & McFarlane, W. (2004). Psychoeducation as evidence-based practice: Considerations for practice, research, and policy. *Brief Treatment and Crisis Intervention, 4*, 205–225.

Lukens, E. P., & McFarlane, W. R. (2006). Psychoeducation as evidence-based practice: Considerations for practice, research, and policy. In A. R. Roberts, K. R. Yeager (Eds.), *Foundations of evidence-based social work practice* (pp. 291–313). New York, NY: Oxford University Press.

Lussier, G., Deater-Deckland, K., Dunn, J., & Davies, L. (2002). Support across two generations: Children's closeness by grandparents following parental divorce and remarriage. *Journal of Family Psychology, 16*, 363–376.

Lustig, J. L., Wolchik, S. A., & Braver, S. L. (1992). Social support in chumships and adjustment in children of divorce. *American Journal of Community Psychology, 20*, 391–393.

Lynch, M. (2006). Children exposed to community violence. In M. M. Feerick & G. B. Silverman (Eds.), *Children exposed to violence*. Baltimore, MD: Brookes.

Maccoby, N., & Altman, D. (1988). Disease prevention in communities: The Stanford Heart Disease Prevention Program. In R. Price, E. Cowen, R. Lorion, & J. Ramos-McKay (Eds.), *Fourteen ounces of prevention: A casebook for practitioners* (pp. 165–174). Washington, DC: American Psychological Association.

MacDermid, S. M., Hertzog, J. L., Kensinger, K. B., & Zipp, J. F. (2001). The role of organizational size and industry in job quality and work-family relationships. *Journal of Family & Economic Issues Special Issue, 22*, 119–126.

MacKenzie, D. L., Wilson, D. B., Armstrong, G. S., & Gover, A. R. (2001). The impact of boot camps and traditional institutions on juvenile residents: Perceptions, adjustment, and change. *Journal of Research in Crime & Delinquency Special Issue, 38*, 279–313.

Macy, B. A., & Izumi, H. (1993). Organizational change, design, and work innovation: A meta-analysis of 131 North American field studies—1961–1991. In R. W. Woodman & W. A. Pasmore (Eds.), *Research in organizational change and development* (Vol. 7). Greenwich, CT: JAI.

Madera, E. J. (1986). A comprehensive approach to promoting mutual AIDS self-help groups: The New Jersey Self-Help Clearinghouse model. *Journal of Voluntary Action Research, 15*, 57–63.

Magee Quinn, M., Kavale, K. A., Mathur, S. R., Rutherford, R. B., & Forness, S. R. (1999). A meta-analysis of social skill interventions for students with emotional or behavioral disorders. *Journal of Emotional & Behavioral Disorders, 7*, 54–64.

Magnuson, K. A., & Waidfugel, J. (2005). Early childhood care and education: Effects on ethnic and racial gaps in school readiness. *Future of Children, 15*, 169–196.

Magura, S., Goldsmith, D. S., Casriel, C., & Lipton, D. S. (1988). Patient-staff governance in methadone maintenance treatment: A study in participative decision making. *Narcotic and Drug Research, 23*, 253–278.

Mahalingam, R. (2006). *Cultural psychology of immigrants*. Mahwah, NJ: Erlbaum.

Maiorana, A., Kegeles, S., Fernandez, P., Salazar, X., Caceres, C., Sandoval, C., . . . Coates, T. (2007). Implementation and evaluation of an HIV/STD intervention in Peru. *Evaluation and Program Planning, 30*, 82–93.

Maloy, K. A., Darnell, J., Nolan, L., Kenney, K., & Cyprien, S. (2000). *Effect of the 1996 welfare and immigration reform laws on immigrants' ability and willingness to access Medicaid and health care services: Findings from four metropolitan sites* (Vol. 1). Washington, DC: Center for Health Services Research and Policy, George Washington University School of Public Health and Health Services.

Mann, J., Tarantola, D., & Netter, T. (1992). *AIDS in the world*. Cambridge, MA: Harvard University Press.

Manning, M., Homel, R., & Smith, C. (2010). A meta-analysis of the effects of early developmental prevention programs in at-risk populations on non-health outcomes in adolescence. *Children and Youth Services Review, 32*(4), 506–519.

Mannix, E., & Neale, M. (2005). What differences make a difference? *Psychological Science in the Public Interest, 6,* 31–55.

Manwaring, J., Bryson, S., & Goldschmidt, A. (2008). Do adherence variables predict outcome in an online program for the prevention of eating disorders? *Journal of Consulting and Clinical Psychology, 76,* 341–346.

Manzo, L., & Perkins, D. (2006). Finding common ground: The importance of place attachment to community participation and planning. *Journal of Planning Literature, 20,* 335–350.

Marchel, C., & Owens, S. (2007). Qualitative research in psychology: Could William James get a job? *History of Psychology, 10*(4), 301–324.

Marcus-Newhall, A., & Heindl, T. R. (1998). Coping with interracial stress in ethnically diverse classrooms: How important are Allport's contact conditions? In Understanding and resolving national and international group conflict [Special issue]. *Journal of Social Issues*, 54, 813–830.

Marsiglia, F., Ayers, S. L., & Hoffman, S. (2012). Religiosity and adolescent substance use in Central Mexico: Exploring the influence of internal and external religiosity on cigarette and alcohol use. *American Journal of Community Psychology, 49*(1–2), 87–97. doi:10.1007/s10464-011-9439-9

Marin, G. (1993). Defining culturally appropriate community interventions: Hispanics as a case study. *Journal of Community Psychology, 21,* 149–161.

Marlatt, G. A., & Gordon, J. R. (1985). *Relapse prevention: Maintenance strategies in the treatment of addictive behaviors*. New York, NY: Guilford.

Marlowe, L. (1971). *Social psychology: An interdisciplinary approach to human behavior*. Oxford, England: Holbrook, 1971.

Martin, J., & Hall, G. N. (1992). Thinking Black, thinking internal, thinking feminist. *Journal of Counseling Psychology, 39,* 509–514.

Martin, P., Lounsbury, D., & Davidson II, W. (2004). AJCP as a vehicle for improving community life: An historic-analystic review of the journal's contents. *American Journal of Community Psychology, 34,* 163–173.

Martin-Baró, I. (1994). *Writings for a liberation psychology*. Cambridge, MA: Harvard University Press.

Maruyama, G. (2003). Disparities in educational opportunities and outcomes: What do we know and what can we do? *Journal of Social Issues, 59,* 653–676.

Marx, J. D., & Hopper, F. (2005). Faith-based versus fact-based social policy: The case of teenage pregnancy prevention. *Social Work, 50,* 280–282.

Mashburn, A. J. (2008). Quality of social and physical environments in preschools and children's development of academic, language, and literacy skills. *Applied Developmental Science, 12,* 113–127.

Maslach, C., & Goldberg, J. (1998). Prevention of burnout: New perspectives. *Applied and Preventive Psychology, 7,* 63–74.

Maslach, C., & Jackson, D. (1981). *Maslach burnout inventory manual*. Palo Alto, CA: Consulting Psychologist Press.

Maslach, C., & Leiter, M. P. (2008). Early predictors of job burnout and engagement. *Journal of Applied Psychology, 93,* 498–512.

Maslach, C., Schaufeli, W. B., & Leiter, M. P. (2000). Job burnout. *Annual Review of Psychology, 52,* 397–422.

Massachusetts Department of Public Health. (1991). *Handbook on smoking laws and regulations for Massachusetts Communities*. Boston, MA: Author.

Masten, A. (2001). Ordinary magic: Resilience processes in development. *American Psychologist, 56,* 227–238.

Masten, A. S. (2009). Ordinary magic: Lessons from research on resilience in human development. *Education Canada, 49*(3), 28–32.

Masten, A., & Coatsworth, J. (1998). The development of competence in favorable and unfavorable environments. *American Psychologist, 53*(2), 205–220.

Masten, A., & Obradovic, J. (2006). Competence and resilience in development. *Annals of the New York Academy of Sciences, 1094,* 13–27.

Maton, K. I. (1988). Social support, organizational characteristics, psychological well being, and group appraisal in three self-help group populations. *American Journal of Community Psychology, 16,* 53–78.

Maton, K. (2000). Making a difference: The social ecology of social transformation. *American Journal of Community Psychology, 28,* 25–57.

Maton, K. (2008). Empowering community settings: Agents of individual development, community betterment, and positive social change. *American Journal of Community Psychology, 41*(1–2), 4–21.

Maton, K., Seidman, E., & Aber, M. (2011). Empowering settings and voices for social change: An Introduction. In M. Aber, K. Maton, & E. Seidman (Eds.), *Empowering settings and voices for social change* (pp. 1–11). New York, NY: Oxford University Press.

Maton, K. I., & Brodsky, A. E. (2010). Empowering community settings: Theory, research, and action. In M. Aber, K. Maton, E. Seidman (Eds.), *Empowering settings and voices for social change* (pp. 38–64). New York, NY: Oxford University Press.

Maton, K. I., Levanthal, G. S., Madera, E. J., & Julien, M. (1989). Factors affecting the birth and death of mutual help groups: The role of national affiliation, professional involvement, and member focal point. *American Journal of Community Psychology, 17,* 643–671.

Maton, K. I., Meissen, G. J., & O'Conner, P. (1993). The varying faces of graduate education in community psychology: Comparisons by program type and program level. *Community Psychologist, 26,* 19–21.

Maton, K. I., Perkins, D. D., Altman, D. G., Guitierrez, L., Kelly, J. G., Rappaport, J., & Saegert, S. (2006). Community-based interdisciplinary research: Introduction to the special issue. *American Journal of Community Psychology, 38,* 1–8.

Maton, K. I., Perkins, D. D., & Saegert, S. (2006). Community psychology at the crossroads: Prospects for interdisciplinary research. *American Journal of Community Psychology, 38,* 9–21.

Maton, K. I., & Salem, D. A. (1995). Organizational characteristics of empowering community settings: A multiple case approach. *American Journal of Community Psychology, 23,* 631–656.

Maton, K. I., Seidman, E., & Aber, M. (2010). Empowering settings and voices for social change: An introduction. In M. S. Aber, K. I. Maton & E. Seidman (Eds.), *Empowering settings and voices for social change* (pp. 1–11). New York, NY: Oxford University Press. doi:10.1093/acprof:oso/9780195380576.003.0001

Matthews, D. B. (1991). The effects of school environment on intrinsic motivation of middle-school children. *Journal of Humanistic Education and Development, 30,* 30–38.

Mawby, R. (1986). Fear of crime and concern over the crime problem among the elderly. *Journal of Community Psychology, 14,* 300–306.

Mayer, J. P., & Davidson, W. S. (2000). Dissemination of innovation as social change. In J. Rappaport & E. Seidman (Eds.), *Handbook of community psychology.* New York, NY: Plenum.

Mays, V., Cochran, S., & Barnes, N. (2007). Race, race-based discrimination, and health outcomes among African Americans. *Annual Review of Psychology, 58,* 201–225.

Mazzeo, S. E., Gow, R. W., & Bulik, C. (2012). Integrative approaches to the prevention of eating disorders and obesity in youth: Progress, pitfalls and possibilities. In E. Vera (Ed.), *Oxford handbook of prevention in counseling psychology.* New York, NY: Oxford University Press.

Mazzeo, S. E., Gow, R. W., Stern, M., & Gerke, C. K. (2008). Developing an intervention for parents of overweight children. *International Journal of Child and Adolescent Health, 1,* 355–364.

McAlister, A. (2000). Action-oriented mass communication. In J. Rappaport & E. Seidman (Eds.), *Handbook of community psychology.* New York, NY: Plenum.

McBride, T. D., Calsyn, R. J., Morse, G. A., Klinkenberg, W. D., & Allen, G. A. (1998). Duration of homeless spells among severely mentally ill individuals: A survival analysis. *Journal of Community Psychology, 26,* 473–490.

McCaughey, B. G. (1987). U.S. Navy Special Psychiatric Rapid and Intervention Team (SPRINT). *Military Medicine, 152,* 133–135.

McCave, E. L. (2007). Comprehensive sexuality education vs. abstinence-only sexuality education: The need for evidence-based research and practice. *School Social Work Journal, 32,* 14–28.

McCloskey, J. (2009). Promotores as partners in a community-based diabetes intervention program targeting Hispanics. *Family & Community Health, 32*(1), 48–57.

McConnell, A., Rydell, R., & Strain, L. (2008). Forming implicit and explicit attitudes toward individuals: Social group association cues. *Journal of Personality and Social Psychology, 94*(5), 792–807.

McDonald, H. P., Garg, A. X., Haynes, R. B. (2002). Interventions to enhance patient adherence to medication prescriptions: scientific review. *Journal of the American Medical Association, 288,* 2868–2879.

McGee, R. (2004). *The last imaginary place: A human history of the Arctic world.* Toronto, Canada: Key Porter—Canadian Museum of Civilization.

McGillis, D. (1997). *Community mediation programs: Developments and challenges.* Washington, DC: U.S. Department of Justice.

McGinnis, J., & Foege, W. H. (1993). Actual causes of death in the United States. *Journal of American Medical Association, 270,* 2207–2212.

McGrath, J. E. (1983). Looking ahead by looking backwards: Some recurrent themes about social change. *Journal of Social Issues, 39,* 225–239.

McGrath, R. E., & Sammons, M. (2011). Prescribing and primary care psychology: Complementary paths for professional psychology. *Professional Psychology: Research and Practice, 42*(2), 113–120.

McIntosh, N. J. (1991). Identification of properties of social support. *Journal of Organizational Behavior, 12,* 201–217.

McIntyre, J. J. (2007). *Impact of media violence on children.* Testimony before the U.S. Senate Committee on Commerce, Science, and Transportation. Washington, DC: Public Policy Office of the American Psychological Association.

McMahon, S. D., & Jason, L. A. (2000). Social support in a worksite smoking intervention: A test of theoretical modes. *Behavior Modification, 24,* 184–201.

McMillan, D. W., & Chavis, D. M. (1986). Sense of community: A definition and theory. *Journal of Community Psychology, 14*(1), 6–23.

McNeal, R. B. (1997). High school dropouts: A closer examination of school effects. *Social Science Quarterly, 78*, 209–222.

Meade, J. (1991). Turning on the bright lights. *Teacher Magazine*, 36–42.

Medway, F. J., & Updyke, J. F. (1985). Meta-analysis of consultation outcome studies. *American Journal of Community Psychology, 13*, 489–505.

Meehan, T. (1986). Alternatives to lawsuits. *Alternatives to Legal Reform, 6*, 9–12.

Meehl, P. E. (1954). *Clinical versus statistical prediction*. Minneapolis: University of Minnesota Press.

Meehl, P. E. (1960). The cognitive activity of the clinician. *American Psychologist, 15*, 19–27.

Melamed, S., Kushnir, T., & Meir, E. I. (1991). Attenuating the impact of job demands: Addictive and interactive effects of perceived control and social support. *Journal of Vocational Behavior, 39*, 40–53.

Mellow, J., & Dickinson, J. M. (2006). The role of prerelease handbooks for prisoner reentry. *Federal Probation, 70*, 70–76.

Melton, G. B. (2000). Community change, community stasis, and the law. In J. Rappaport & E. Seidman (Eds.), *Handbook of community psychology*. New York, NY: Plenum.

Méndez-Negrete, J., Saldaña, L. P., & Vega, A. (2006). Can a culturally informed after-school curriculum make a difference in teen pregnancy prevention? Preliminary evidence in the case of San Antonio's escuelitas. *Families in Society, 87*, 95–104.

Menec, V., Button, C., Blandford, A., & Morris-Oswald, T. (2007). *Age-Friendly Cities Project: A report prepared for the City of Portage la Prairie*. Centre on Aging: University of Manitoba. Retrieved from http://www.city-plap.com/corporate/pdf/Portage%20Report%20May%202007%20-%20Final.pdf

Mennino, S. F., Rubin, B. A., & Brayfield, A. (2005). Home-to-join and job-to-home spillover: The impact of company policies and workplace culture. *The Sociological Quarterly, 46*, 107–135.

Miao, T. A., Umemoto, K., Gonda, D., & Hishinuma, E. S. (2011). Essential elements for community engagement in evidence-based youth violence prevention. *American Journal of Community Psychology, 48*(1–2), 120–132.

Miers, R., & Fisher, A. T. (2002). Being church and community: Psychological sense of community in a local parish. In A. T. Fisher, C. C. Sonn, B. J. Bishop, A. T. Fisher, C. C. Sonn, & B. J. Bishop (Eds.), *Psychological sense of community: Research, applications, and implications* (pp. 141–160). New York, NY: Kluwer Academic/Plenum.

Milburn, N. G., Gary, L. E., Booth, J. A., & Brown, D. R. (1991). Conducting research in a minority community: Methodological considerations. *Journal of Community Psychology, 19*, 3–12.

Milkovich, G. T., & Boudreau, J. W. (1991). *Human resource management*. Homewood, IL: Irwin.

Miller, L. S., Zhang, X., Rice, D., & Max, W. (1998). State estimates of total medical expenditures attributable to cigarette smoking, 1993. *Public Health Report, 113*, 447–458.

Miller, N., Brewer, M. B., & Edwards, K. (1985). Cooperative interaction in desegregated settings: A laboratory analogue. *Journal of Social Issues, 41*, 63–79.

Miller, R. D., Maier, G. J., & Kaye, M. S. (1988). Orienting the staff of a new maximum security forensic facility. *Hospital and Community Psychiatry, 39*, 780–781.

Milne, A. (1985). Mediation or therapy—which is it? In S. C. Grebe (Ed.), *Divorce and family mediation*. Rockville, MD: Aspen.

Minden, J., & Jason, L. (2002). Preventing chronic health problems. In L. Jason & D. Glenwick (Eds.), *Innovative strategies for promoting health and mental health across the life span* (pp. 227–243). New York, NY: Springer.

Mintzberg, H. (1979). *The structuring of organizations*. Englewood Cliffs, NJ: Prentice Hall.

Mischel, W. (1968). *Personality and assessment*. Mahwah, NJ: Erlbaum.

Mischel, W. (2004). Toward an integrative science of the person, *Annual Review of Psychology, 55*, 1–22.

Mishara, B. L. (1997). Effects of different telephone intervention styles with suicidal callers at two suicide prevention centers: An empirical investigation. *American Journal of Community Psychology, 25*, 861–885.

Mitchell, R. E. (1982). Social networks and psychiatric clients: The personal and environmental context. *American Journal of Community Psychology, 10*, 387–402.

Mobley, L R., Kuo, T., Clayton, L. J., & Evans, W. D. (2009). Mammography facilities are accessible, so why is utilization so low? *Cancer Causes & Control, 20*(6), 1017–1028.

Moffitt, T. (1993). Adolescence-limited and life-course-persistent antisocial behavior: A developmental taxonomy. *Psychological Review, 100*(4), 674–701.

Molina, L. E., & Wittig, M. A. (2006). Relative importance of contact conditions in explaining prejudice reduction in a classroom context: Separate and equal? *Journal of Social Issues, 62*, 489–509.

Molnar, J. (1988). *Home is where the heart is: The crisis of homeless children and families in New York City*. New York, NY: Bank Street College of Education.

Molnar, J. M., Rath, W. R., & Klein, T. P. (1990). Constantly compromised: The impact of homelessness on children. *Journal of Social Issues, 46,* 109–124.

Moos, R. (1973). Conceptualizations of human environments. *American Psychologist, 28*(8), 652–665.

Moos, R. H. (1994). *Work environment scale manual: Development, applications, research* (3rd ed.). Palo Alto, CA: Consulting Psychologists Press.

Moos, R. (2003). Social contexts: Transcending their power and their fragility. *American Journal of Community Psychology, 31*(1–2), 1–13.

Moradi, B., & Yoder, J. D. (2012). The psychology of women. In E. Altamaier & J. I. Hansen (Eds.), *Oxford handbook of counseling psychology* (pp. 346–374). New York, NY: Oxford University Press.

Morbidity and Mortality Weekly Report. (1997). *State-specific prevalence of cigarette smoking among adults, and children's and adolescents' exposure to environmental tobacco smoke—United States, 1996, 46,* 1038–1043. Atlanta, GA: Author.

Morbidity and Mortality Weekly Repor.t (1998a, September 11). *Preventing emerging infectious diseases: A strategy for the 21st century, 47* (no. RR-15). Atlanta, GA: Author.

Morbidity and Mortality Weekly Report. (1998b, October 9). *Incidence of initiation of cigarette smoking—United States, 47* (No. 39, pp. 837–840). Atlanta, GA: Author.

Morbidity and Mortality Weekly Report. (1998c, August 14). *Youth Risk Behavior Surveillance—United States, 1997, 47* (No. SS-3). Atlanta, GA: Author.

Morbidity and Mortality Weekly Report. (2005a). *Annual smoking-attributable mortality, year of potential life lost, and productivity losses—United States, 1997–2001* (pp. 54, 625–628). Atlanta, GA: Author.

Morbidity and Mortality Weekly Report. (2005b). *HIV Transmission among Black women—North Carolina, 2004.* Retrieved from http://www.cdc.gov/mmwr/preview/mmwrhtml/mm5404a2.htm

Morbidity and Mortality Weekly Report. (2006, June 9). *Youth risk behavior surveillance—United States, 2005, 47* (No. SS-5, pp. 1–108). Atlanta, GA: Author.

Morbidity and Mortality Weekly Report. (2008). *Smoking attributable mortality, years of life lost, and productivity losses, United States, 2000–2004.* Retrieved from http://www.cdc.gov/tobacco/data_statistics/mmwrs/byyear/2008/mm5745a3/intro.htm

Morbidity and Mortality Weekly Report. (2010a). *Tobacco use among middle and high school students, United States, 2000–2009.* Retrieved from http://www.cdc.gov/mmwr/preview/mmwrhtml/mm5933a2.htm?s_cid=mm5933a2_e%0D0a

Morbidity and Mortality Weekly Report. (2010b). *Youth risk behavior surveillance, United States, 2009.* Retrieved from http://www.cdc.gov/mmwr/pdf/ss/ss5905.pdf

Morbidity and Mortality Weekly Report. (2011a). *Summary of notable diseases, United States, 2010.* Retrieved from http://www.cdc.gov/mmwr/mmwr_nd

Morbidity and Mortality Weekly Report. (2011b). *Youth risk behavior surveillance, United States, 2011.* Retrieved from http://www.cdc.gov/mmwr/preview/mmwrhtml/ss6104a1.htm?s_cid=ss6104a1_w

Morgan, L. (2008). BMI . . . a weighty issue. *School Nurse News, 25,* 24–26.

Morgan, M., & Vera, E., (2012). Prevention and psychoeducation in counseling psychology. In E. Altamaier & J. Hansen (Eds.), *Oxford handbook of counseling psychology* (pp. 529–544). New York, NY: Oxford University Press.

Morgeson, F. P., Campion, M. A., & Maertz, C. P. (2001). Understanding pay satisfaction: The limits of a compensation system implementation. *Journal of Business & Psychology Special Issue, 16,* 133–149.

Morgenstern, J., Blanchard, K. A., Kahler, C., Barbosa, K. M., McCrady, B. S., & McVeigh, K. H. (2008). Testing mechanisms of action for intensive case management. *Addiction, 103*(3), 469–477.

Moritsugu, J., & Sue, S. (1983). Minority status as a stressor. In R. Felner, L. Jason, J. Moritsugu, & S. Farber (Eds.), *Preventive psychology.* New York, NY: Pergamon.

Morris, A., Shinn, M., & DuMont, K. (1999). Contextual factors affecting the organizational commitment of diverse police officers: A levels of analysis perspective. *American Journal of Community Psychology, 27,* 75–105.

Morton, C., Peterson, N. A., Speer, P., Reid, R., & Hughey, J. (2012). Applying geographic information systems to community research. In L. Jason, C. Keys, Y. Suarez-Balcazar, R. Taylor, & M. Davis (Eds.), *Participatory community research: Theories and methods in action* (pp. 205–220). Washington, DC: American Psychological Association.

Moses, D. J., Kresky-Wolff, M., Bassuk, E. L., & Brounstein, P. (2007). Guest editorial: The promise of homelessness prevention. *Journal of Primary Prevention, 28,* 191–197.

Moss, L. (1981). *Management stress.* Reading, MA: Addison-Wesley.

Moulton, P., Miller, M., & Offutt, S. (2007). Identifying rural health care needs using community conversations. *Journal of Rural Health, 23*(1), 92–96.

Mowbray, C. T. (1979). A study of patients treated as incompetent to stand trial. *Social Psychiatry, 14,* 31–39.

Mowbray, C. T. (1990). Community treatment for the seriously mentally ill: Is this community psychology? *American Journal of Community Psychology, 18,* 893–902.

Mowbray, C. T. (1999). The benefits and challenges of supported education: A personal perspective. *Psychiatric Rehabilitation Journal, 22*(3), 248–254.

Mowbray, C. T., Herman, S. E., & Hazel, K. (1992). Subgroups and differential treatment needs of young adults with long-term severe mental illness. *Psychosocial Rehabilitation Journal, 16*, 45–62.

Mowbray, C. T., & Moxley, D. P. (2000). Deinstitutionalization. In A. E. Kazdin (Ed.), *Encyclopedia of psychology* (Vol. 2, pp. 459–462). New York, NY: Oxford University Press.

Moyer, C. A., Ekpo, G., Calhoun, C., Greene, J., Naik, S., Sippola, E., . . . Anderson, F. (2008). Quality of life, optimism/pessimism, and knowledge and attitudes toward HIV screening among pregnant women in Ghana. *Women's Health Issues*, x, 1–9.

Moynihan, D. R., & Pandey, S. K. (2008). The ties that bind: Social networks, person-organization value fit, and turnover intention. *Journal of Public Administration Research and Theory, 18*, 205–227.

Mrazek, P., & Haggerty, R. (1994). Reducing risks for mental disorders: Frontiers for preventive intervention research. *National Academy of Sciences, Institute of Medicine, Division of Biobehavioral Sciences & Mental Disorders, Committee on Prevention of Mental Disorders* (p. 605). Washington, DC: National Academies Press.

Muenchow, S., & Marsland, K. W. (2007). Beyond baby steps: Promoting the growth and development of U.S. child-care policy. In J. L. Aber, S. J. Bishop-Josef, S. M. Jones, K. T. McLearn, & D. Phillips (Eds.), *Child development and social policy: Knowledge for action*. Washington, DC: American Psychological Association.

Muha, D. G., & Cole, C. (1990). Dropout prevention and group counseling: A review of the literature. *High School Journal, 74*, 76–80.

Muir, E. (Winter 2000–2001). Smaller schools. *American Educator,* 40–46.

Muller, R. T., & Diamond, T. (1999). Father and mother physical abuse and child aggressive behaviour in two generations. *Canadian Journal of Behavioural Science/Revue Canadienne Des Sciences Du Comportement, 31*(4), 221–228. doi:10.1037/h0087091

Munger, R. L. (1998). *The ecology of troubled children: Changing children's behavior by changing the places, activities, and people in their lives.* Cambridge, MA: Brookline Books.

Munkes, J.,& Diehl, M. (2003). Matching or competition? Performance comparison processes in an idea generation task. *Group Processes and Intergroup Relations, 6*, 305–320.

Muñoz, M., Panadero, S., Santos, E. P., & Quiroga, M. A. (2005). Role of stressful life events in homelessness: An intragroup analysis. *American Journal of Community Psychology, 35*, 35–46.

Murphy, S. E., & Halpern, D. (2006). Vison for the future of work and family interaction. In D. F. Halpern & S. E. Murphy (Eds.). *From work-family balance to work-family interaction.* Mahwah, NJ: Erlbaum.

Murray, B. (2000, January). The degree that almost wasn't: The PsyD comes of age. *Monitor on Psychology.* Retrieved from http://www.apa.org/monitor/jan00/ed1.aspx

Myers, W. C., Catalano, G., Sanchez, D. L., & Ross, M. M. (2006). HIV/AIDS among prisoners. In F. Fernandez & P. Ruiz (Eds.), *Psychiatric aspects of HIV/AIDS.* Philadelphia, PA: Lippincott Williams & Wilkins.

Nadel, H., Spellmann, M., Alvarez-Canino, T., Lausell-Bryant, L., & Landsberg, G. (1996). The cycle of violence and victimization: A study of the school-based intervention of multidisciplinary youth violence-prevention program. *American Journal of Preventive Medicine, 12,* 109–119.

Naisbett, J., & Aburdene, P. (1990). *Megatrends 2000.* New York, NY: William Morrow.

Nation, M., Crusto, C., Wandersman, A., Kumpfer, K. L., Seybolt, D., Morrissey-Kane, E., & Davino, K. (2003). What works in prevention: Principles of effective prevention programs. *American Psychologist, 58,* 449–456.

National Campaign to Prevent Teen and Unwanted Pregnancy. (2012). *Teen pregnancy prevention.* Retrieved from http://www.teenpregnancy.org/data/genlfact.asp

National Cancer Institute. (2004, June 16). *American Stop Smoking Intervention Study (ASSIST) evaluation: Questions and answers.* Retrieved from http://www.cancer.gov/newscenter/qa/2004/assistqanda

National Center for Education Statistics. (2007). *Numbers and rates of public high school dropouts: School year 2004–2005.* Washington, DC: Author.

National Center for Education Statistics. (2008). *What are the dropout rates of high school students?* Retrieved from http://www.Nces.ed.gov/fastfacts/display.asp?id=16

National Center for Education Statistics. (2011). *Fast facts: English language learners.* Washington DC: Institute of Education Sciences. Retrieved from http://nces.ed.gov/fastfacts/display.asp?id=96

National Center for Health Statistics. (2003). *Vital statistics of the United States, 2003, Volume 1, Natality.* Retrieved from http://www.cdc.gov/nchs/products/vsus.htm

National Center for Health Statistics. (2007a). *Teen birth rate rises for first time in 15 years.* Retrieved from http://www.cdc.gov/nchs/pressroom/07newsreleases/teenbirth.htm

National Center for Health Statistics. (2007b). *Health, United States, 2007.* Washington, DC: U.S. Government Printing Office. Retrieved from http://www.cdc.gov/nchs/hus.htm

National Center for Health Statistics, Centers for Medicare and Medicaid Services. (2011). *National health expenditure data.* Retrieved from https://www.cms.gov/NationalHealthExpendData/25_NHE_Fact_Sheet.asp#TopOfPage

National Center on Shaken Baby Syndrome. (2011). *Frequently asked questions about Shaken Baby Syndrome.* Retrieved from http://www.dontshake.org/sbs.php?topNavID=3&subNavID=28&navID=95

National Coalition Against Domestic Violence. (2010). *Family violence prevention and services act: Funding need: $175 million.* Retrieved from http://www.ncadv.org/files/statecomparisonFVPSA.pdf

National Coalition for the Homeless. (1999). *NCH factsheets 1–3.* Retrieved from http://www.nationalhomeless.org

National Coalition for the Homeless. (2006). *A dream denied: The criminalization of homelessness in U.S. cities.* Washington, DC: Author.

National Coalition for the Homeless (2007a). *How many people experience homelessness? NCH Fact Sheet #2.* Washington, DC: Author.

National Coalition for the Homeless (2007b). Who is homeless? *NCH Fact Sheet #3.* Washington, DC: Author.

National Coalition for the Homeless (2009, July). *Mental illness and homelessness.* Retrieved from http://www.nationalhomeless.org/factsheets/Mental_Illness.pdf

National Coalition for the Homeless. (2011). *How many people experience homelessness?* Washington, DC: Author. Retrieved from http://nationalhomeless.org/factsheets/How_Many.html

National Center on Elder Abuse. (2005). *Elder abuse prevalence and incidence.* Washington, DC: Author. Retrieved from http://www.ncea.aoa.gov/ncearoot/Main_Site/pdf/publication/FinalStatistics050331.pdf

National Center on Secondary Education and Transition. (2008). *Increasing rates of school completion: Moving from policy and research to practice: A manual for policymakers, administrators, and educators.* Retrieved from http://www.ncset.org/publications/essentialtools/dropout/part3.3.09.asp

National Coalition of STD Directors. (2008). *National guidelines for Internet-based STD/HIV prevention.* Washington, DC: US. Government Printing Office.

National Commission on AIDS. (1993). *Behavioral and Social Sciences and the HIV/AIDS Epidemic.* Washington, D.C. (1990).

National Crime Prevention Council. (1989). The success of community crime prevention. *Canadian Journal of Criminology, 31,* 487–506.

National Drug Control Strategy. (2008). *2008 annual report.* Washington, DC: White House.

National Drug Control Strategy. (2011). *Executive summary.* Washington DC: National Drug Control Strategy. Retrieved from http://www.whitehouse.gov/sites/default/files/ondcp/policy-and-research/2011strategyexecutivesummary_0.pdf

National Highway Traffic Safety Administration. (1995, February). *Repeat DWI offenders in the United States* (NHTSA Technology Series No. 85). Washington, DC: Author.

National Highway Traffic Safety Administration. (1996). *Traffic safety facts 1995: Alcohol.* Washington, DC: Author.

National Highway Traffic Safety Administration. (1997). *Setting limits, saving lives: The case for. 08% BAC laws* (Pub. No. DOT HS 808 524). Washington, DC: Author.

National Highway Traffic Safety Administration. (2008, January). Repeat intoxicated driver laws. *Traffic Safety Facts Laws.*

National Highway Traffic Safety Administration. (2011). *Traffic safety facts.* Washington, DC: U.S. Department of Transportation. Retrieved from http://www.nrd.nhtsa.dot.gov/Pubs/811385.pdf

National Institute of Alcohol Abuse and Alcoholism. (2004). NIAAA council approves definition of binge drinking. *NIAAA Newsletter, 3,* 3.

National Institute of Child and Human Development, Early Child Care Research Network. (2001). Nonmaternal care and family factors in early development: An overview of the NICHD Study of Early Child Care. *Journal of Applied Developmental Psychology, 22,* 457–492.

National Institute of Child and Human Development. (2006). *Study of early child care and youth development.* Washington, DC: U.S. Government Printing Office.

National School Safety and Security Services (2008). *School violence facts & figures.* Retrieved from http://www.schoolsecurity.org/trends/school-violence.html

National Science Foundation. (2003). *Science and technology: Public attitudes and public understanding.* Retrieved from http://www.nsf.gov/sbe/srs/seind02/c7/c7h.htm

National Survey on Drug Use and Health. (2008). *Results from the 2007 NHSDUH: National findings.* Washington, DC: SAMHSA. Retrieved from http://oas.samhsa.gov/nsduh/2k7nsduh/2k7results.cfm#Ch4

Nation's Health. (1998, October). *DWI deaths reach historic low: Proportion falls below 40 percent of first time on record.* Washington, DC: Author.

Nation's Health. (2001, August). *Arizona smoking rates decline.* Washington, DC: Author.

Nellis, L. M. (2012). Maximizing the effectiveness of building teams in response to intervention implementation. *Psychology in the Schools, 49*(3), 245–256. doi:10.1002/pits.21594

Nelson, D., & Simmons, B. (2003). Health psychology and work stress: A more positive approach. In J. Quick & L.

Tetrick (Eds.), *Handbook of occupational health psychology* (pp. 97–119).Washington, DC: American Psychological Association.

Nelson, G., Aubrey, T., & Lafrance, A. (2007). A review of the literature on the effectiveness of housing and support, assertive community treatment, and intensive case management interventions for persons with mental illness who have been homeless. *American Journal of Orthopsychiatry, 77*(3), 350–361.

Nelson, G., Ochocka, J., Griffin, K., & Lord, J. (1998). "Nothing about me, without me." Participatory action research with self-help/mutual aid organizations for psychiatric consumer survivors. *American Journal of Community Psychology, 26,* 881–912.

Nelson, G., & Prilleltensky, I. (2010). (Eds.). *Community psychology: In pursuit of liberation and well-being.* New York, NY: Palgrave Macmillan.

Nelson, G., Prilleltensky, I., & MacGillivary, H. (2001). Building value-based partnerships: Toward solidarity with oppressed groups. *American Journal of Community Psychology, 29*(5), 649–677.

Nemoto, T., Wong, F. Y., Ching, A., Chng, C. L., Bouey, P., Henrickson, M., & Sember, R. E. (1998). HIV seroprevalence, risk behaviors, and cognitive factors among Asian and Pacific Islander American men who have sex with men: A summary and critique of empirical studies and methodological studies. *AIDS Education and Prevention, 10* (Supplement A), 31–47.

Neuman, G. A., Edwards, J. E., & Raju, N. S. (1989). Organizational development interventions: A meta-analysis of their effects on satisfaction and other attitudes. *Personnel Psychology, 42,* 461–489.

Neumark-Sztainer, D., Wall, M. M., Haines, J. I., Story, M. T., Sherwood, N. E., & van den Berg, P. A. (2007). Shared risk and protective factors for overweight and disordered eating in adolescents. *American Journal of Preventive Medicine, 33,* 359–369.

Newborough, J. (1992). Toward community: A third position. *American Journal of Community Psychology, 23*(1), 9–37.

Newbrough, J. R., & Chavis, D. M. (Eds.). (1986). Psychological sense of community, I: Forward. *American Journal of Community Psychology, 14,* 3–5.

Newell, B. L., Berkowitz, S. L., Deacon, Z., & Foster-Fishman, P. (2006). Revealing the cues within community places: Stories of identity, history, and possibility. *American Journal of Community Psychology, 37*(1–2), 29–46.

Newman-Carlson, D., & Horne, A. (2004). Bully busters: A psychoeducational intervention for reducing bullying behavior in middle school students. *Journal of Counseling and Development, 82,* 259–267.

Nicotera, N. (2007). Measuring neighborhood: A conundrum for human service researchers and practitioners. *American Journal of Community Psychology, 40,* 26–51.

Nihiser, A. J., Lee, S. M., Wechsler, H., McKenna, M., Doom, E., Rienold, C., . . . Grummer-Strawn, L. (2007). Body mass index measurement in schools. *Journal of School Health, 77,* 651–671.

Nikelly, A. G. (1990). *Political activism: A new dimension for community psychology.* Paper presented to the Annual Convention of the American Psychological Association, Boston, MA.

Norcross, J., Freedheim, D., & VandenBos, G. (2011). Into the future: Retrospect and prospect in psychotherapy. In Norcross, J. VandenBos, G., & Freedheim, D. (Eds.). *History of psychotherapy: Continuity and change* (2nd ed., pp. 743–760). Washington, DC: American Psychological Association.

Nores, M., Belfield, C. R., Barnett, S. W., & Schweinhart, L. (2005). Updating the economic impacts of the High/Scope Perry Preschool Program. *Educational Evaluation and Policy Analysis, 27,* 245–261.

Novotney, L. C., Mertinko, E., Lange, J., & Baker, T. K. (2000, September). Juvenile mentoring program: A progress review. *Juvenile Justice Bulletin,* 1–8.

Nowell, B. (2009). Profiling capacity for coordination and systems change: The relative contribution of stakeholder relationships in interorganizational collaboratives. *American Journal of Community Psychology, 44*(3–4), 196–212.

Nowell, B., & Foster-Fishman, P. (2011). Examining multisector community collaboratives as vehicles for building organizational capacity. *American Journal of Community Psychology, 48*(3–4), 193–207.

O'Connell, J. J. (2007). The need for homelessness prevention: A doctor's view of life and death on the streets. *Journal of Primary Prevention, 28,* 199–203.

O'Donnell, C. (2006). Beyond diversity: Toward a cultural community psychology. *American Journal of Community Psychology, 37*(1–2), 1–7.

O'Donnell, C., & Ferrari, J. (2000). Employment in community psychology: The diversity of opportunity. *Journal of Prevention and Intervention in the Community, 19*(2):1–4.

O'Donnell, C. R., & Tharp, R. G. (2012). Integrating cultural community psychology: Activity settings and the shared meanings of intersubjectivity. *American Journal of Community Psychology, 49*(1–2), 22–30.

O'Donnell, C. R., & Williams, I. (2013). The buddy system: A 35-year follow-up of criminal offenses. *Clinical Psychological Science, 1,* 54–66.

Offerman, L., & Spiros, R. (2001). The science and practice of team development: Improving the link. *Academy of Management Journal, 44,* 376–392.

Office of Head Start. (2007). *Statistical fact sheet fiscal year 2007.* Washington, DC: Administration for Children and Families.

Office of Head Start. (2012). *Statistical fact sheet fiscal year 2009*. Washington, DC: Administration for Children and Families.

Office of Justice Programs. (2006). *Methamphetamine use increasing among state and federal prisoners*. Washington, DC: Department of Justice.

Office of Justice Programs. (2007). *Urban and suburban crime rates stable from 2005 to 2006* (Press release). Washington, DC: Department of Justice.

Office of Juvenile Justice and Delinquency Programs. (2008a). *Model programs*. Retrieved from http://www.dsgonline.com/mpg2.5/TitleV_MPG_Table_Ind_Rec.asp?ed=390.

Office of Juvenile Justice and Delinquency Prevention. (2008b). *Safe Start: Promising approaches for communities*. Retrieved from http://www.safestartcenter.org.

Office of National Drug Control Policy. (1998). *The national drug control strategy, 1998. A ten-year plan*. Washington, DC: Author.

Office of National Drug Control Policy. (2008, June 12). New report finds highest-ever levels of THC. *Office of National Drug Control Policy Press Release*. Retrieved from http://www.whitehousedrugpolicy.gov/news/press08/061208.html

Office of Smoking and Health. (2001). *Women and smoking: A report of the Surgeon General*. Atlanta, GA: U.S. Department of Health and Human Services, Public Health Service, CDC.

Ogden, C. L., Carroll, M. D., Curtin, L. R., Lamb, M. M., & Flegal, K. M. (2010). Prevalence of high body mass index in U.S. children and adolescents, 2007-2008. *Journal of the American Medical Association, 303*, 242–249.

Okamato, Y. (2007). A comparative study of homelessness in the United Kingdom and Japan. *Journal of Social Issues, 63*, 525–542.

Okazaki, S., & Saw, A. (2011). Culture in Asian American community psychology: Beyond the East-West binary. *American Journal of Community Psychology, 47*, 144–156.

Okvat, H. A., & Zautra, A. J. (2011). Community gardening: A parsimonious path to individual, community, and environmental resilience. *American Journal of Community Psychology, 47*(3–4), 374–387.

Olatunji, A. N. (2005). Dropping out of high school among Mexican-origin youths: Is early work experience a factor? *Harvard Educational Review, 75*, 286–306.

Olds, D. (1997). The prenatal early infancy project: Preventing child abuse and neglect in the context of promoting maternal and child health. In D. A. Wolfe, R. J. McMahon, & R. D. Peters (Eds.), *Child abuse: New directions in prevention and treatment across the lifespan*. Thousand Oaks, CA: Sage.

Olds, D. L. (2005). The nurse-family partnership: Foundations in attachment theory and epidemiology. In L. J. Berlin, Y. Ziv, L. Amaya-Jackson, & M. T. Greenberg (Eds.), *Enhancing early attachments: Theory, research, intervention and policy. Duke series in child development and public policy*. New York, NY: Guilford.

Olds, D. L. (2006). The nurse-family partnership: An evidence-based prevention intervention. In Early preventive intervention and home visiting [Special issue]. *Infant Mental Health Journal, 27*, 5–25.

Olds, D. L. (2007). Preventing crime with prenatal and infancy support of parents: The nurse-family partnership. *Victims & Offenders: Special Issue on Early Intervention, 2*, 205–225.

Olds, D. L. (2010). The nurse-family partnership. In B. M. Lester & J. D. Sparrow (Eds.), *Nurturing children and families: Building on the legacy of T. Berry Brazleton* (pp. 192–203). Hoboken, NJ: Wiley.

Olds, D. L., Eckenrode, J., & Kitzman, H. (2005). Clarifying the impact of the nurse-family partnership on child maltreatment: Response to Chaffin (2004). *Child Abuse & Neglect, 29*, 229–233.

Olds, D., Henderson, C., Chamberlin, R., & Tetelbaum, R. (1986). Preventing child abuse and neglect: A randomized trial of nurse home visitation. *Pediatrics, 78*, 65–78.

Olds, D., Hill, P., & Rumsey, E. (1998, November). Prenatal and early childhood nurse home visitation. *Juvenile Delinquency Bulletin*, 1–7.

Olds, D. L., Kitzman, H., Hanks, C., Cole, R., Anson, E., Sidora-Arcoleo, K., . . . Bondy, J. (2007). Effects of nurse home visiting on maternal and child functioning: Age 9 follow up of a randomized trial. *Pediatrics, 120*, e832–e845.

Olfson, M. (1990). Assertive community treatment. An evaluation of experimental evidence. *Hospital Community Psychiatry, 41*, 631–641.

Olson, D., DeFrain, J., & Skogrand, L. (2008). *Marriages and families: Intimacy, diversity, and strengths* (6th ed.). New York, NY: McGraw-Hill.

Olson, M. R. (1991). Supportive growth experiences of beginning teachers. *Alberta Journal of Educational Research, 37*, 19–30.

Olson, M., & Cohen, A. A. (1986). An alternative approach to the training of residential treatment. *Residential Group Care and Treatment, 3*, 65–88.

O'Neill, L., & McGloin, J. M. (2007). Considering the efficacy of situation crime prevention in schools. *Journal of Criminal Justice, 35*, 511–523.

O'Neill, P. (1989). Responsible to whom? Responsible to what? Some ethical issues in community intervention. *American Journal of Community Psychology, 17*(3), 323–341.

O'Neill, P., Duffy, C., Enman, M., Blackman, E., & Goodwin, J. (1988). Cognition and citizen participation in social action. *Journal of Applied Sociology, 18*, 1067–1083.

Opulente, M., & Mattaini, M. A. (1997). Toward welfare that works. *Research on Social Work Practice, 7,* 115–135.

Organ, D. (1988). *Organizational citizenship behavior: The good soldier syndrome.* Lexington, MA: Lexington.

Organ, D. (1990). The motivational basis of organizational citizenship behavior. In B. M. Staw & L. Cummings (Eds), *Research in organizational behavior* (Vol. 12, pp. 43–72). Greenwich, CT: JAI.

Organ, D. W. (1997). Organizational citizenship behavior: It's construct clean-up time. *Human Performance, 10*(2), 85–97. doi:10.1207/s15327043hup1002_2

Organ, D., Podsakoff, P., & MacKenzie, S. (2006). *Organizational citizenship behavior: Its nature, antecedents, and consequences.* Thousand Oaks, CA: Sage.

Orthner, D. K., & Randolph, K. A. (1999). Welfare reform and high school dropout patterns for children. *Children and Youth Services Review, 21,* 881–900.

Ortmann, R. (2000). The effectiveness of social therapy in prison—A randomized experiment. In Advising criminal justice policy through experimental evaluations: international views [Special issue]. *Crime & Delinquency, 46,* 214–232.

Oskamp, S. (1984). *Applied social psychology.* Englewood Cliffs, NJ: Prentice Hall.

Ostermeyer, M. (1991). Conducting the mediation. In K. G. Duffy, J. W. Grosch, & P. V. Olizak (Eds.), *Community mediation: A handbook for practitioners and researchers.* New York, NY: Guilford.

Oxley, D. (2000). The school reform movement. In J. Rappaport & E. Seidman (Eds.), *Handbook of community psychology.* New York, NY: Plenum.

Pacific Institute for Research and Evaluation in Support of the Office of Juvenile Justice and Delinquency Prevention Enforcing the Underage Drinking Laws Program (2005). *Drinking in America: Myths, realities, and prevention policy* [Brochure]. Washington, DC: Author.

Padilla, A., Ruiz, R., & Alvarez, R. (1975). Community mental health services for the Spanish-speaking/surnamed. *American Psychologist, 9,* 892–905.

Page, S. (2007). *The difference: How the power of diversity creates better groups, firms, schools, and societies.* Princeton, NJ: Princeton University Press.

Paillé, P., & Grima, F. (2011). Citizenship and withdrawal in the workplace: Relationship between organizational citizenship behavior, intention to leave current job and intention to leave the organization. *Journal of Social Psychology, 151*(4), 478–493.

Paine-Andrews, A., Fisher, J., Patton, J., Fawcett, S., Williams, E., Lewis, R., & Harris, K. (2002). Analyzing the contribution of community change to population health outcomes in an adolescent pregnancy prevention initiative. *Health Education & Behavior, 29,* 183–193.

Palmer, T., & Wedge, R. (1989). California's juvenile probation camps: Findings and implications. *Crime and Delinquency, 35,* 234–253.

Paluk, E. L. (2006). Diversity training and intergroup contact: A call to action research. *Journal of Social Issues, 62,* 577–595.

Pargament, K. I. (1986). Refining fit: Conceptual and methodological challenges. *American Journal of Community Psychology, 14,* 677–684.

Parks, G. (October 2000). The High/Scope Perry Preschool Project. *Juvenile Justice Bulletin, 1–8.*

Patchin, J. W., Huebner, B. M., McCluskey, J. D., Varano, S. P., & Bynum, T. S. (2006). Exposure to community violence and childhood delinquency. *Crime & Delinquency, 52,* 307–332.

Patrikakou, E., & Weissberg, R. P. (2000). Parents' perceptions of teacher outreach and parent involvement in children's education. *Journal of Prevention & Intervention in the Community, 20,* 103–119.

Pattavina, A., Byrne, J. M., & Garcia, L. (2006). An examination of citizen involvement in crime prevention in high-risk versus low-to-moderate risk neighborhoods. *Crime & Delinquency, 52,* 203–231.

Patterson, D. (1990). Gaining access to community resources: Breaking the cycle of adolescent pregnancy. *Journal of Health Care for the Poor and Underserved, 1,* 147–149.

Patton, M. (1997). *Utilization-focused evaluation: The new century text* (3rd ed.). Thousand Oaks, CA: Sage.

Pedersen, P. (2008). Ethics, competence, and professional issues in cross-cultural counselling. In P. Pedersen, J. Draguns, W. Lonner, & J. Trimble (Eds.), *Counselling across cultures* (6th ed., pp. 5–20). Los Angeles, CA: Sage.

Pedersen, P., Draguns, J., Lonner, W., & Trimble, J. (Eds.). (2008). *Counselling across cultures* (6th ed.). Los Angeles, CA: Sage.

Pederson, P. (1997). *Culture centered counseling interventions.* New York, NY: Sage.

Pederson, P. B., Carter, R. T., & Ponterotto, J. G. (1996). The cultural context of psychology: Questions for accurate research and appropriate practice. *Cultural Diversity and Mental Health, 2*(3), 205–216.

Pedro-Carroll, J. (1997). The children of divorce intervention program: Fostering resilient outcomes for school-aged children. In G. W. Albee & T. P. Gullotta (Eds.), *Primary prevention works.* Thousand Oaks, CA: Sage.

Pedro-Carroll, J. L. (2005a). Fostering resilience in the aftermath of divorce: The role of evidence-based programs for children. In Prevention: Research, policy, and evidence-based practice [Special issue]. *Family Court Review, 43,* 52–64.

Pedro-Carroll, J. L. (2005b). Research, policy, and evidence-based practice. In Prevention: Research, policy, and evidence-based practice [Special issue]. *Family Court Review, 43,* 18–21.

Peel, N., Bartlett, H., & McClure, R. (2004). Healthy aging: How is it defined and measured? *Australasian Journal on Ageing, 23,* 115–119.

Pentz, M. A. (2000). Institutionalizing community-based prevention through policy change. *Journal of Community Psychology, 28,* 257–270.

Pereira, G., & Osburn, H. (2007). Effects of participation on performance and employee attitudes: A quality circles meta-analysis. *Journal of Business and Psychology, 22,* 145–153.

Perkins, C. A. (1997). *Special report: Age patterns of victims of serious violent crimes.* Washington, DC: Bureau of Justice Statistics.

Perkins, D. D. (1988). The use of social science in public interest litigation: A role for community psychologists. *American Journal of Community Psychology, 16,* 465–485.

Perkins, D. D., Bess, K. D., Cooper, D. G., Jones, D. L., Armstead, T., & Speer, P. W. (2007). Community organizational learning: Case studies illustrating a three-dimensional model of levels and orders of change. *Journal of Community Psychology, 35*(3), 303–328.

Perkins, D. D., Brown, B. B., & Taylor, R. B. (1996). The ecology of empowerment: Predicting participation in community organizations. *Journal of Social Issues, 52,* 85–110.

Perkins, D. D., Florin, P., Rich, R. C., Wandersman, A., & Chavis, D. M. (1990). Participation and the social and physical environment of residential blocks: Crime and community context. *American Journal of Community Psychology, 18,* 83–115.

Perkins, D. D., & Taylor, R. B. (1996). Ecological assessments of community disorder: Their relationship to fear of crime and theoretical implications. *American Journal of Community Psychology, 24,* 63–107.

Perkins, D. D., & Zimmerman, M. A. (1995). Empowerment theory, research, and application. *American Journal of Community Psychology, 23,* 569–579.

Perry, B. L. (2011). The labeling paradox: Stigma, the sick role, and social networks in mental illness. *Journal of Health and Social Behavior, 52*(4), 460–477.

Peterson, J. L. (1998). Introduction to the special issue: HIV/AIDS prevention through community psychology. *American Journal of Community Psychology, 26,* 1–5.

Peterson, N. A., & Reid, R. J. (2002). Paths to psychological empowerment in an urban community: Sense of community and citizen participation in substance abuse prevention activities. *Journal of Community Psychology, 31*(1), 25–38.

Peterson, N. A., Speer, P., & Hughey, J. (2006). Measuring sense of community: A methodological interpretation of a factor structure debate. *Journal of Community Psychology, 34,* 453–469.

Peterson, N. A., Speer, P., & McMillan, D. (2008). Validation of a Brief Sense of Community Scale: Confirmation of a principle theory of "sense of community." *Journal of Community Psychology, 36,* 61–73.

Peterson, N. A., & Zimmerman, M. A. (2004). Beyond the individual: Toward a nomological network of organizational empowerment. *American Journal of Community Psychology, 1–2,* 129–141.

Pettigrew, T. F. (1998). Intergroup contact theory. *Annual Review of Psychology, 49,* 65–85.

Pettigrew, T. F. (2004). Justice deferred a half century after *Brown v. Board of Education. American Psychologist, 59,* 521–529.

Pettigrew, T., & Meertens, R. W. (1995). Subtle and blatant prejudice in Western Europe. *European Journal of Social Psychology, 25,* 57–75.

Pfeifer, M. (2005). *The state of Hmong-American studies.* Paper presented at the Hmong National Conference, Fresno, CA. Retrieved from http://www.hmongstudies.com/HNDPresentation2005.pdf

Phares, J. E. (1991). *Introduction to personality.* New York, NY: HarperCollins.

Phares, J. E., & Chaplin, W. F. (1997). *Introduction to personality.* New York, NY: Longman.

Philliber, S., Kaye, J., & Herrling, S. (2001) *The national evaluation of the Children's Aid Society Carrera-Model Program to prevent teen pregnancy.* Accord, NY: Philliber Research Associates.

Phillip, K., & Hendry, L. B. (2000). Making sense of mentoring or mentoring making sense? Reflections on the mentoring process by adult mentors with young people. *Journal of Community & Applied Social Psychology, 10,* 211–223.

Phillips, D. A. (2000). Social policy and community psychology. In J. Rappaport & E. Seidman (Eds.), *Handbook of community psychology.* New York, NY: Plenum.

Phillips, D. A., Howes, C., & Whitebook, M. (1992). The social policy context of child care: Effects on quality. *Journal of Community Psychology, 20,* 25–50.

Pieterse, A. L., Todd, N. R., Neville, H., A., & Carter, R. T. (2012). Perceived racism and mental health among Black American adults: A meta-analytic review. *Journal of Counseling Psychology, 59,* 1–9.

Pinchot, G., & Pinchot, E. (1993). *The end of bureaucracy and the rise of the intelligent organization.* San Francisco, CA: Berrett-Koehler.

Pickren, W. (2005). Science, practice, and policy: An introduction to the history of psychology and the national institute of mental health. In W. Pickren & S. Schneider (Eds.), *Psychology and the national institute of mental health: A historical analysis of science, practice, and policy* (pp. 3–15). Washington, DC: American Psychological Association.

Pickren, W., & Schneider, S. (Eds.), *Psychology and the national institute of mental health: A historical analysis of science, practice, and policy*. Washington, DC: American Psychological Association.

Pickren, W., & Tomes, H. (2002). The legacy of Kenneth B. Clark to the APA: The Board of Social and Ethical Responsibility for Psychology. *American Psychologist, 57*(1), 51–59.

Pines, A., & Guendelman, S. (1995). Exploring the relevance of burnout to Mexican blue-collar women. *Journal of Vocational Behavior, 47,* 1–20.

Piven, F. F., & Cloward, R. A. (1996). Welfare reform and the new class war. In M. B. Lykes, A. Banuazizi, R. Liem, & M. Morris (Eds.), *Myths about the powerless: Contesting social inequalities.* Philadelphia, PA: Temple University Press.

Plante, T. (2005). *Contemporary clinical psychology* (2nd ed.). Hoboken, NJ: Wiley.

Plante, T. (2011). *Contemporary clinical psychology* (3rd ed.). New York, NY: Wiley.

Podsakoff, P. M., MacKenzie, S. B., Paine, J., & Bachrach, D. G. (2000). Organizational citizenship behaviors: A critical review of the theoretical and empirical literature and suggestions for future research. *Journal of Management, 2000 Yearly Review, 26,* 513–563.

Pogrebin, M. R., & Poole, E. D. (1987). Deinstitutionalization and increased arrest rates among the mentally disordered. *Journal of Psychiatry and Law, 15,* 117–127.

Pogrebin, M. R., & Regoli, R. M. (1985). Mentally disordered persons in jail [Editorial]. *Journal of Community Psychology, 13,* 409–412.

Pong, S. L., & Ju, D. B. (2000). The effects of change in family structure and income on dropping out of middle and high school. *Journal of Family Issues, 21,* 147–169.

Popper, K. R. (1957/1990). Philosophy of science: A personal report. In C. A. Mace (Ed.), *British philosophy in the mid-century.* London, England: Allen & Unwin.

Popper, K. R. (1968). *The logic of scientific discovery.* New York, NY: Harper Torchbooks.

Popovich, P. M., Gullekson, N., Morris, S., & Morse, B. (2008). Comparing attitudes towards computer usage by undergraduates from 1986 to 2005. *Computers in Human Behavior, 24,* 986–992.

Porter, B. E. (2001). Empowerment-based interventions are not useful. *Community Psychologist, 34,* 22–23.

Poteat, V. P., Mereish, E. H., DiGiovanni, C. D., & Koenig, B. (2011). The effects of general and homophobic victimization on adolescents' psychosocial and educational concerns: The importance of intersecting identities and parent support. *Journal of Counseling Psychology, 58,* 597–609.

Portzky, G., & van Heeringen, K. (2006). Suicide prevention in adolescents: A controlled study of the effectiveness of a school-based psychoeducational program. *Journal of Child Psychology and Psychiatry, 47,* 910–918.

Presser, L., & Hamilton, C. A. (2006). The micropolitics of victim-offender mediation. *Sociological Inquiry, 76,* 316–342.

Presswood, R. F. (2005). School health report card. *School Nurse News, 22,* 27–32.

Prestby, J., & Wandersman, A. (1985). An empirical exploration of a framework of organizational viability: Maintaining block organization. *Journal of Applied Behavioral Sciences, 21,* 287–305.

Prestby, J., Wandersman, A., Florin, P., Rich, R., & Chavis, D. (1990). Benefits, costs, incentive management and participation in volunteer organizations: A means to understanding and promoting empowerment. *American Journal of Community Psychology, 18,* 117–150.

Pretty, G. M., & McCarthy, M. (1991). Exploring the psychological sense of community among women and men of the corporation. *Journal of Community Psychology, 19,* 351–361.

Pretty, G. M., McCarthy, M. E., & Catano, V. M. (1992). Psychological environments and burnout: Gender considerations within the corporation. *Journal of Organizational Behavior, 13,* 701–711.

Prevatt, F., & Kelly, F. D. (2003). Dropping out of school: A review of intervention programs. *Journal of School Psychology, 41*(5), 377–395.

Prezza, M., Amici, M., Tiziana, R., & Tedeschi, G. (2001). Sense of community referred to the whole town: Its relations with neighboring, loneliness, life satisfaction, and area of residence. *Journal of Community Psychology, 29,* 29–52.

Prezza, M., & Pacilli, M. G. (2007). Current fear of crime, sense of community and loneliness in Italian adolescents: The role of autonomous mobility and play during childhood. *Journal of Community Psychology, 35*(2), 151–170. doi:10.1002/jcop.20140

Price, R. (1983). The education of a prevention psychologist. In R. Felner, L. Jason, J. Moritsugu, & S. Farber (Eds.), *Preventive psychology: Theory, research and practice* (pp. 290–296). New York, NY: Pergamon.

Price, R. H. (1985). Work and community. *American Journal of Community Psychology, 13,* 1–12.

Price, R. H. (1990). Whither participation and empowerment? *American Journal of Community Psychology, 18,* 163–167.

Price, R. H., Cowen, E. L., Lorion, R. P., & Ramos-McKay, J. (1988). *14 ounces of prevention.* Washington, DC: American Psychological Association.

Prilleltensky, I. (1997). Values, assumptions, and practices: Assessing the moral implications of psychological discourse and action. *American Psychologist, 52,* 517–535.

Prilleltensky, I. (2008). The role of power in wellness, oppression and liberation: The promise of psychopolitical validity. *Journal of Community Psychology, 36*(2), 116–136.

Prilleltensky, I. (2009). Community psychology: Advancing social justice. In D. Fox, I. Prilleltensky, & S. Austin (Eds.), *Critical psychology: An introduction* (2nd ed., pp. 126–143). London, England: Sage.

Prilleltensky, I. (2012). Wellness as fairness. *American Journal of Community Psychology, 49,* 1–21.

Prilleltensky, I., & Fox, D. (2007). Psychopolitical literacy for wellness and justice. *Journal of Community Psychology, 35*(6), 793–805.

Prilleltensky, I., & Prilleltensky, O. (Eds.). (2006). *Promoting well-being: Linking personal, organizational, and community change.* Hoboken, NJ: Wiley.

Primavera, J. (1999). The unintended consequences of volunteerism: Positive outcomes for those who serve. *Journal of Prevention & Intervention in the Community, 18,* 125–140.

Primavera, J., & Brodsky, A. (2004). Introduction to the special issue on the process of community research and action. *American Journal of Community Psychology, 33,* 177–180.

Prince-Embury, S., & Rooney, J. F. (1995). Psychological adaptation among residents following restart of Three Mile Island. *Journal of Traumatic Stress, 8,* 47–59.

Proescholdbell, R. J., Roosa, M. W., & Nemeroff, C. J. (2006). Component measures of psychological sense of community among gay men. *Journal of Community Psychology, 34*(1), 9–24.

Public Health Service. (1980). *Toward a national plan for the chronic mentally ill.* Washington, DC: U.S. Department of Health and Human Services.

Purich, D. (1992). *The Inuit and their land: The story of Nunavut.* Toronto, ON: Lorimer.

Purkiss, R. B., & Rossi, R. J. (2007). Sense of community: A vital link between leadership and wellbeing in the workplace. In A. Glendon, B. M. Thompson, & B. Myors, (Eds.), *Advances in organisational psychology* (pp. 281–300). Bowen Hills, Australia: Australian Academic Press.

Quigley, R. (2005). Building strengths in the neighborhood. *Reclaiming Children and Youth, 14,* 104–106.

Quillian-Wolever, R., & Wolever, M. (2003). Stress management at work. In J. Quick & L. Tetrick (Eds.), *Handbook of occupational health psychology* (pp. 355–375). Washington, DC: American Psychological Association.

Quimby, C. C., & Angelique, H. (2011). Identifying barriers and catalysts to fostering pro-environmental behavior: Opportunities and challenges for community psychology. *American Journal of Community Psychology, 47*(3–4), 388–396.

Quintana, S., Vogel, M., & Ybarra, V. (1991). Meta-analysis of Latino students' adjustment in higher education. *Hispanic Journal of Behavioral Sciences, 13*(2), 155–168.

Rader, N. E., May, D. C., & Goodrum, S. (2007). An empirical assessment of the "threat of victimization": Considering fear of crime, perceived risk, avoidance, and defensive behaviors. *Sociological Spectrum, 27,* 475–505.

Rafferty, Y. (1990). Testimony on behalf of Advocates for Children of New York and the American Psychological Association to the oversight hearings on homelessness. House of Representatives, Washington, DC.

Rafferty, Y., & Shinn, M. (1991). The impact of homelessness on children. *American Psychologist, 46,* 1170–1179.

Rafferty, Y., Shinn, M., & Weitzman, B. (2004). Academic achievement among formerly homeless adolescents and their continuously housed peers. *Journal of School Psychology, 42,* 179–199.

Rahe, R., Meyers, M., Smith, M., Kjaer, G., & Holmes, T. (1964). Social stress and illness onset. *Journal of Psychosomatic Research, 8,* 35–44.

Raikes, J. A., Raikes, H. H., & Wilcox, B. (2005). Regulation, subsidy receipt and provider characteristics: What predicts quality in child care homes? *Early Childhood Research Quarterly, 20,* 164–184.

Ramey, C. T., Ramey, S. L., & Lanzi, R. (2006). Children's health and education. In K. A. Renninger & I. E. Siegel (Eds.), *Handbook of child psychology: Vol. 4. Child psychology in practice* (6th ed., pp. 864–892). Hoboken, NJ: Wiley.

Ramey, S. L., & Ramey, C. T. (2003). Understanding efficacy of early educational programs: Critical design, practice, and policy issues. In A. J. Reynolds, M. C. Wang, & H. J. Wallberg (Eds.), *Early childhood programs for a new century.* Washington, DC: Child Welfare League of America.

Ramirez, M. (1999). *Psychotherapy and counseling with minorities.* Boston, MA: Allyn & Bacon.

Randolph, W. A. (2000). Re-thinking empowerment: Why is it so hard to achieve? *Organizational Dynamics, 29,* 94–107.

Rank, M. R. (2005). *One nation, underprivileged: Why American poverty affects us all.* New York, NY: Oxford University Press.

Rapkin, B. D., Massie, M. J., Janskym, E. J., Lounsbury, D. W., Murphy, P. D., & Powell, S. (2006). Developing a partnership model for cancer screening with community-based organizations: The ACCESS Breast Cancer Education and Outreach Project. *American Journal of Community Psychology, 38*(3–4), 153–164.

Rappaport, J. (1977). *Community psychology: Values, research, and action.* New York, NY: Holt, Rinehart & Winston.

Rappaport, J. (1981). In praise of paradox: A social policy of empowerment over prevention. *American Journal of Community Psychology, 9,* 1–25.

Rappaport, J. (1987). Terms of empowerment/exemplars of prevention: Toward a theory for community psychology. *American Journal of Community Psychology, 15,* 121–148.

Rappapon, J. (1984). Studies in empowerment: Introduction to the issues. *Prevention in Human Services, 3*(2–3),1–7.

Rappaport, J. (1990). Research methods and the empowerment social agenda. In P. Tolan, C. Keys, F. Chertok, & L. Jason (Eds.), *Researching community psychology: Issues of theory and methods.* Washington, DC: American Psychological Association.

Rappaport, J. (2000). Community narratives: Tales of terror and joy. *American Journal of Community Psychology, 28*(1), 1–24.

Rappaport, J. (2005). Community psychology is (thank god) more than science. *American Journal of Community Psychology, 35,* (3–4), 231–238.

Rappaport, J., & Seidman, E. (Eds.). (2000). *Handbook of community psychology.* New York, NY: Kluwer/Plenum.

Rappaport, J., Seidman, E., Toro, P., McFadden, L. S., Reischl, T. M., Roberts, L. J., . . . Zimmerman, M. A. (1985). Collaborative research of a mutual help organization. *Social Policy, 15,* 12–24.

Rappaport, J., Swift, C., & Hess, P. (Eds.). (1984). *Studies in empowerment: Steps toward understanding and action.* New York, NY: Haworth.

Rasmussen, A., Aber, M., & Arvinkumar, B. (2004). Adolescent coping and neighborhood violence: Perceptions, exposure, and urban youths' efforts to deal with danger. *American Journal of Community Psychology, 33,* 61–75.

Ratcliffe, J. H., Taniguchi, T., Groff, E., & Wood, J. (2011). The Philadelphia Foot Patrol Experiment: A randomized controlled trial of police patrol effectiveness in violent crime hotspots, *Criminology, 49*(3), 795–831.

Ratiu, I. S. (1986). A workshop on managing in a multicultural environment. In International management and development [Special issue]. *Management Education and Development, 17,* 252–256.

Raviv, A., Erel, O., Fox, N. A., Leavitt, L. A., Raviv, A., Dar, I., . . . Greenbaum, C. (2001). Individual measurement of exposure to everyday violence among elementary schoolchildren across various settings. *Journal of Community Psychology, 29,* 117–140.

Redeinstitutionalization. (1986, August 25). *The New York Times,* p. A18.

Reese, L. E., & Vera, E. M. (2007). Culturally responsive prevention: Scientific and practical considerations of community-based programs. *The Counseling Psychologist,* 763–778.

Reich, J. W., & Zautra, A. J. (1991). Experimental and measurement approaches to internal control in at-risk older adults. *Journal of Social Issues, 47,* 143–158.

Reich, S. M., & Reich, J. A. (2006). Cultural competence in interdisciplinary collaborations: A method for respecting diversity in research partnerships. *American Journal of Community Psychology, 38*(1–2), 51–62.

Reich, S., Riemer, M., Prilleltensky, I., & Montero, M. (Eds.) (2007). *International community psychology: History and theories.* New York, NY: Springer.

Reid, R. J., Peterson, N. A., Hughey, J., & Garcia-Reid, P. (2006). School climate and adolescent drug use: Mediation effects of violence victimization in the urban high school context. *Journal of Primary Prevention, 27,* 281–292.

Rein, M., & Schon, D. A. (1977). Problem setting in policy research. In C. H. Weiss (Ed.), *Using social research in public policy making.* Lexington, MA: Lexington Books.

Reiss, D., & Price, R. H. (1996). National research agenda for prevention research: The National Institute of Mental Health Report. *American Psychologist, 51,* 1109–1115.

Reppucci, N. D. (1987). Prevention and ecology: Teen-age pregnancy, child sexual abuse, and organized youth sports. *American Journal of Community Psychology, 15,* 1–22.

Reppucci, N., Woolard, J., & Fried, C. (1999). Social, community, and preventive interventions. *Annual Review of Psychology, 50,* 387–418.

Resnicow, K., & Braithwaite, R. (2001). Cultural sensitivity in public health. In R. Braithwaite & S. Taylor (Eds.), *Health issues in the Black community* (2nd ed., pp. 516–542). San Francisco, CA: Jossey-Bass.

Resnicow, K., Solar, R., Braithwaite, R., Ahluwalia, J., & Butler, J. (2000). Cultural sensitivity in substance abuse prevention. *Journal of Community Psychology, 28,* 271–290.

Revenson, T., D'Augelli, A., French, S., Hughes, D., Livert, D., Seidman, E., . . . Yoshikawa, H. (2002). *Ecological research to promote social change: Methodological advances from community psychology.* New York, NY: Kluwer Academic/Plenum.

Revenson, T., & Schiaffino, K. (2000). Community-based health interventions. In J. Rappaport & E. Seidman (Eds.), *Handbook of community psychology* (pp. 471–493). New York, NY: Kluwer Academic/Plenum.

Reyes, O., Gillock, K. L., Kobus, K., & Sanchez, B. (2000). A longitudinal examination of the transition into senior high school for adolescents from urban, low-income status, and predominantly minority backgrounds. *American Journal of Community Psychology, 28,* 519–544.

Reyes, O., & Jason, L. (1991). An evaluation of a high school dropout prevention program. *Journal of Community Psychology, 19*(3), 221–230.

Rhodes, J. E. (2008). Improving youth mentoring interventions through research-based practice. *American Journal of Community Psychology, 41,* 35–42.

Rhodes, J. E., Spencer, R., Keller, T. E., Liang, B., & Noam, G. (2006). A model for the influence of mentoring relationships on youth development. *Journal of Community Psychology, 34,* 691–707.

Richmond, C., Ross, N., & Egeland, G. (2007). Social support and thriving health: A new approach to understanding the health of indigenous Canadians. *American Journal of Public Health, 97,* 1827–1833.

Riger, S. (1989). The politics of community intervention. *American Journal of Community Psychology, 17,* 379–383.

Riger, S. (1990). Ways of knowing and organizational approaches to community psychology. In P. Tolan, C. Keys, F. Chertak, & L. Jason (Eds.), *Researching community psychology.* Washington, DC: American Psychological Association.

Riger, S. (1993). What's wrong with empowerment. *American Journal of Community Psychology, 21,* 279–292.

Riley, D. A., Roach, M. A., Adams, D., & Edie, D. (2005). Section III—policy affecting and evaluation of quality: From research to policy: In search of an affordable statewide system for rating child care quality. In Early childhood program quality [Special issue]. *Early Education and Development, 16,* 493–504.

Rixon, R., & Erwin, P. G. (1999). Measure of effectiveness in a short-term interpersonal cognitive problem-solving programme. *Counseling Psychology Quarterly, 12,* 87–93.

Roak, K. S. (1991). Facilitating friendship formation in late life: Puzzles and challenges. *American Journal of Community Psychology, 19,* 103–110.

Roberts, A. R., & Everly, G. S. (2006). A meta-analysis of 36 crisis intervention studies. *Brief Treatment and Crisis Intervention, 6,* 10–21.

Roberts, D. G. (1991). I don't get no respect. *Organization Development Journal, 9,* 55–60.

Robins L., Helzer J., Weissman M., Orvaschel, H., Gruenberg, E., Burke, J., & Regier, D. (1984). Lifetime prevalence of specific psychiatric disorders in three sites. *Archives of General Psychiatry, 41*(10), 949–958.

Robins, R., Gosling, S., & Craik, K. (1999). An empirical analysis of trends in psychology. *American Psychologist, 54,* 117–128.

Robinson, M. B. (2000). From research to policy: Preventing residential burglary through a systems approach. *American Journal of Criminal Justice, 24,* 169–179.

Robinson, W. L. (1990). Data feedback and communication to the host setting. In P. Tolan, C. Keys, F. Chertak, & L. Jason (Eds.), *Researching community psychology: Issues of theory and methods.* Washington, DC: American Psychological Association.

Roccato, M., Russo, S., & Vieno, A. (2011). Perceived community disorder moderates the relation between victimization and fear of crime. *Journal of Community Psychology, 39*(7), 884–888. doi:10.1002/jcop.20470

Rodin, J., & Langer, E. J. (1977). Long-term effects of a control-relevant intervention with the institutionalized aged. *Journal of Personality and Social Psychology, 35,* 897–902.

Rodin, J., Timko, C., & Harris, S. (1986). The construct of control: Biological and psychological correlates. In C. Eisdorfer, M. P. Lawson, & G. I. Maddoy (Eds.), *Annual review of gerontology and geriatrics.* New York, NY: Springer.

Rodriguez, N. (2005). Restorative justice, communities, and delinquency: Whom do we reintegrate? *Criminology & Public Policy, 4,* 103–130.

Rodriguez, N. (2007). Restorative justice at work: Examining the impact of restorative justice resolutions on juvenile recidivism. *Crime and Delinquency, 53,* 355–379.

Roesch, R. (1988). Community psychology and the law. *American Journal of Community Psychology, 14,* 451–463.

Roethlisberger, F. J., & Dickson, W. J. (1939). *Management and the worker: An account of a research program conducted by the Western Electric Company, Chicago.* Cambridge, MA: Harvard University Press.

Rogelberg, S. G. (2007). Introduction. In S. Rogelber (Ed.), *Encyclopedia of industrial and organizational psychology* (Vol. 1, pp. xxxv–xxxvii). Thousand Oaks, CA: Sage.

Rogers, E. M. (1982). *Diffusion of innovations.* New York, NY: Free Press.

Roh, S., & Oliver, W. M. (2005). Effects of community policing upon fear of crime: Understanding the causal linkage. *Policing, 28,* 640–683.

Rohrer, L. M., Cicchetti, D., Rogosch, F. A., Toth, S. L., & Maughan, A. (2011). Effects of maternal negativity and of early and recent recurrent depressive disorder on children's false belief understanding. *Developmental Psychology, 47*(1), 170–181.

Rokeach, M. (1960). *The open and closed mind.* New York, NY: Basic Books.

Roll, J. M., & Habemeier, W. (1991, April). *Gender differences in coping with potential victimization.* Paper presented at the Annual Meeting of the Eastern Psychological Association, New York.

Rolleri, L., Wilson, M., Paluzzi, P., & Sedivy, V. (2008). Building capacity of state adolescent pregnancy prevention coalitions to implement science-based approaches. *American Journal of Community Psychology, 41*(3–4), 225–234.

Romano, J., & Hage, S. (2000). Prevention and counseling psychology: Revitalizing commitments for the 21st century. *The Counseling Psychologist, 28*, 733–763.

Romeo, R., & McEwan, B. (2006). Stress and the adolescent brain. *Annals of the New York Academy of Sciences, 1094*, 202–214.

Roosa, M. W., Weaver, S. R., White, R. M. B., Tein, J., Knight, G. P., Gonzales, N., & Saenz, D. (2009). Family and neighborhood fit or misfit and the adaptation of Mexican Americans. *American Journal of Community Psychology, 44*(1–2), 15–27.

Roscigno, V. J., Tomaskovic-Devey, D., & Crowley, M. (2006). Education and the inequalities of place. *Social Forces, 84*, 2121–2145.

Rose-Gold, M. S. (1992). Intervention strategies for counseling at-risk adolescents in rural school districts. *School Counselor, 39*, 122–126.

Rosenberg, Y. (2006). Talking 'bout our generation. *Fortune, 153*, 106.

Rosenfeld, S. (1991). Homelessness and rehospitalization: The importance of housing for the chronic mentally ill. *Journal of Community Psychology, 19*, 60–69.

Rosenhack, R., Kasprow, W., Frisman, L., & Liu-Mares, W. (2003). Cost-effectiveness of supported housing for homeless persons with mental illness. *Archives of General Psychiatry, 60*, 940–951.

Rosenhan, D. L. (1973). On being sane in insane places. *Science, 179*, 250–258.

Rosenthal, D., & Rotheram-Borus, M. J. (2005) Young people and homelessness. *Journal of Adolescence, 28*, 167–169.

Rosenthal, R., & Jacobson, L. V. (1968). *Pygmalion in the classroom: Teacher expectation and pupils' intellectual development*. New York, NY: Holt.

Rosentock, I. M. (1986). Why people use health services. *Milburn Memorial Fund Quarterly, 44*, 94–127.

Ross, C. E., & Jang, S. J. (2000). Neighborhood disorder, fear, and mistrust: The buffering role of social ties with neighbors. *American Journal of Community Psychology, 28*, 401–420.

Ross, J., Bradley, E., & Busch, S. (2006). Use of health care services by lower-income and higher-income uninsured adults. *Journal of the American Medical Association, 295*, 2027–2036.

Ross, L. (2006). Where do we belong? Urban adolescents' struggle for place and voice. *American Journal of Community Psychology, 37*, 293–301.

Ross, R. R., Altmaier, E. M., & Russell, D. W. (1989). Job stress, social support, and burnout among counseling center staff. *Journal of Counseling Psychology, 36*, 464–470.

Rossell, C. H. (1988). How effective are voluntary plans with magnet schools? *Educational Evaluation and Policy Analysis, 10*, 325–342.

Rossi, P. H. (1989). *Down and out in America: The origins of homelessness*. Chicago, IL: University of Chicago Press.

Rossi, P. H. (1990). The old homeless and the new homelessness in historical perspective. *American Psychologist, 45*, 954–959.

Rothman, A., & Salovey, P. (1997). Shaping perceptions to motivate healthy behavior: The role of message framing. *Psychological Bulletin, 121*, 3–19.

Rothman, J. (1974). Three models of community organization practice. In F. Cox, J. Erlich, J. Rothman, & J. Tropman (Eds.), *Strategies of community organization: A book of readings* (2nd ed.). Itasca, IL: Peacock.

Rotter, J. (1966). Generalized expectancies for internal versus external control of reinforcements. *Psychological Monographs, 80*, Whole No. 609.

Rouget, B., & Aubry, J. (2007). Efficacy of psychoeducational approaches on bipolar disorders: A review of the literature. *Journal of Affective Disorders, 98*(1–2), 11–27.

Rountree, P. W. (1998). A reexamination of the crime-fear linkage. *Journal of Research in Crime and Delinquency, 35*, 341–372.

Roussos, S. T., & Fawcett, S. (2000). A review of collaborative relationships as a strategy for improving community health. *Annual Review of Public Health, 21*, 369–402.

Rubin, B. A., & Brody, C. J. (2005). Contradictions of commitment in the new economy: Insecurity, time, and technology. *Social Science Research, 34*, 843–851.

Ruggiero, K., & Taylor, D. (1997). Why minority group members perceive or do not perceive the discrimination that confronts them: The role of self-esteem and perceived control. *Journal of Personality and Social Psychology, 72*(2), 373–389.

Runyan, D., Wattam, C., Ikeda, R., Hassan, F., & Ramiro, L. (2002). Child abuse and neglect by parents and caregivers. In E. Krug, L. I. Dahlberg, J. A. Mercy, A. B. Zwi, & R. Lozano (Eds.), *World report on violence and health*. Geneva: World Health Organization.

Runyan, D. K., Shankar, V., Hassan, F., Hunter, W. M., Jain, D., Paula, C. S., . . . Isabel, A. (2010). International variations in harsh child discipline. *Pediatrics, 126*(3), pp. e701–e711.

Rutter, M. (1981). The city and the child. *American Journal of Orthopsychiatry, 51*, 610–625.

Rutter, M. (1985). Resilience in the face of adversity: Protective factors and resistance to psychiatric disorder. *British Journal of Psychiatry, 147*, 598–611.

Rutter, M. (1987). Psychosocial resilience and protective mechanisms. *American Journal of Orthopsychiatry, 57*, 316–331.

Rutter, M. (2006). Implications of resiliency concepts for scientific understanding. *Annals of the New York Academy of Sciences, 1094,* 1–12.

Ryan, J. P., & Yang, H. (2005). Family contact and recidivism: A longitudinal study of adjudicated delinquents in residential care. *Social Work Research, 29,* 31–39.

Ryan, W. (1971). *Blaming the victim.* New York, NY: Pantheon.

Ryerson Espino, S. L., & Trickett, E. J. (2008). The spirit of ecological inquiry and intervention research reports: A heuristic elaboration. *American Journal of Community Psychology, 42*(1–2), 60–78.

Saegert, S., & Winkel, G. (2004). Crime, social capital, and community participation. *American Journal of Community Psychology, 34,* 219–233.

Salazar, J. M. (1988, August). *Psychology and social change in Latin America.* Paper presented at the Annual Convention of the American Psychological Association, Atlanta, GA.

Salem, D. A. (1990). Community-based services and resources: The significance of choice and diversity. *American Journal of Community Psychology, 18,* 909–915.

Salmi, S., Voeten, M. J. M., & Keskinen, E. (2000). Relation between police image and police visibility. *Journal of Community and Applied Social Psychology, 10,* 433–447.

Salmi, S., Voeten, M., & Keskinen, E. (2005). What citizens think about the police: Assessing actual and wished-for frequency of police activities in one's neighbourhood. In Community policing [Special issue]. *Journal of Community & Applied Social Psychology, 15,* 1888–2002.

Sameroff, A. J., & Chandler, M. J. (1975). Reproductive risk and the continuum of caretaker causality. In F. D. Horowitz (Ed.), *Review of child development research* (Vol. 4). Chicago, IL: University of Chicago Press.

Sammons, Morgan T. (2011). Pharmacotherapy. In J. Norcross, G. VandenBos, & D. Freedheim (Eds.). *History of psychotherapy: Continuity and change* (2nd ed. pp. 516–532) Washington, DC: American Psychological Association.

Sammons, M. T., & Brown, A. (1997). The department of defense psychopharmacology demonstration project: An evolving program for postdoctoral education in psychology. *Professional Psychology: Research and Practice, 28,* 107–112.

Sammons, M. T., Gorny, S. W., Zinner, E. S., & Allen, R. P. (2000). Prescriptive authority for psychologists: A consensus of support. *Professional Psychology: Research And Practice, 31*(6), 604–609. doi:10.1037/0735-7028.31.6.604

Sampson, R., & Groves, W. (1989). Community structure and crime: Testing social-disorganization theory. *American Journal of Sociology, 94*(4), 774.

Sampson, R., & Raudenbush, S. (1999). Systematic social observation of public spaces: A new look at disorder in urban neighborhoods. *American Journal of Sociology, 105*(3), 603–651.

Sampson, R. J., Raudenbush, S. W., & Earls, F. (1997). Neighborhoods and violent crime: A multilevel study of collective efficacy. *Science, 277,* 918–924.

Sandler, I. (1980). Social support resources, stress, and maladjustment of poor children. *American Journal of Community Psychology, 8,* 41–52.

Sandler, I., Braver, S., & Gensheimer, L. (2000) Stress. In J. Rappaport & E. Seidman (Eds.), *Handbook of community psychology.* New York, NY: Kluwer/Plenum.

Sandler, I. N., & Keller, P. A. (1984). Trends observed in community psychology training descriptions. *American Journal of Community Psychology, 12,* 157–164.

Sansone, R. A., Fine, M. A., & Chew, R. (1988). A longitudinal analysis of the experiences of nursing staff on an inpatient eating disorder unit. *International Journal of Eating Disorders, 7,* 125–131.

Sarason, S. B. (1972/1999). *The creation of settings and the future societies.* San Francisco, CA: Jossey-Bass.

Sarason, S. B. (1974). *The psychological sense of community: Prospects for a community psychology.* San Francisco, CA: Jossey-Bass.

Sarason, S. B. (1976a). Community psychology and the anarchist insight. *American Journal of Community Psychology, 4,* 246–259.

Sarason, S. B. (1976b). Community psychology, networks, and Mr. Everyman. *American Journal of Community Psychology, 18,* 317–328.

Sarason, S. B. (1978). The nature of problem solving in social action. *American Psychologist, 33,* 370–380.

Sarason, S. B. (1983). *Schooling in America: Scapegoat and salvation.* New York, NY: Free Press.

Sarason, S. (1984). Community psychology and public policy: Missed opportunity. *American Journal of Community Psychology, 12*(2), 199–207.

Sarason, S. B. (1997). The public schools: America's Achilles heel. *American Journal of Community Psychology, 25,* 771–786.

Sarason, S. (2004). What we need to know about intervention and interventionists. *American Journal of Community Psychology, 33*(3–4), 275–277.

Sarason, S. B., Carroll, C. F., Maton, K., Cohen, S., & Lorentz, E. (1977). *Human services and resource networks.* San Francisco, CA: Jossey-Bass.

Sarata, B. P. V. (1984). Changes in staff satisfactions after increases in pay, autonomy, and participation. *American Journal of Community Psychology, 12,* 431–445.

Scales, P. (1990). Developing capable young people: An alternative strategy for prevention programs. *American Journal of Community Psychology, 10,* 420–438.

Scarr, S. (1998). American child care today. *American Psychologist, 53*(2), 95–108.

Scarr, S., & Eisenberg, M. (1993). Child care research: Issues, perspectives, and results. *Annual Review of Psychology, 44,* 613–644.

Schafer, J. A., Huebner, B. M., & Bynum, T. G. (2006). Fear of crime and criminal victimization: Gender-based contrasts. *Journal of Criminal Justice, 34,* 285–301.

Scheckner, S., Rollin, S. A., Kaiser-Ulrey, C., & Wagner, R. (2004). School violence in children and adolescents: A meta-analysis of the effectiveness of current interventions. In E. R. Gerler (Ed.), *Handbook of school violence.* New York, NY: Haworth.

Schein, E. H. (1985). How culture forms, develops and changes. In R. H. Kilmann, M. J. Saxton, & R. Serpa (Eds.), *Gaining control of the corporate culture.* San Francisco, CA: Jossey-Bass.

Schein, E. H. (1990). Organizational culture. *American Psychologist, 45,* 109–119.

Schiaffino, K. M. (1991). Fine-tuning theory to the needs of the world: Responding to Heller et al. *American Journal of Community Psychology, 19,* 99–102.

Schinke, S. P. (1998). Preventing teenage pregnancy: Translating research knowledge. *Journal of Human Behavior in the Social Environment, 1,* 53–66.

Schnake, M. (1991). Organizational citizenship: A review, proposed model, and research agenda. *Human Relations, 44*(7), 735–759. doi:10.1177/001872679104400706

Schneider, S. (2005). Reflections on psychology and the national institute of mental health. In W. Pickren & S. Schneider (Eds.), *Psychology and the national institute of mental health: A historical analysis of science, practice, and policy* (pp. 17–28). Washington, DC: American Psychological Association.

Schubert, M., & Borkman, T. (1991). An organizational typology for self-help groups. *American Journal of Community Psychology, 19,* 769–787.

Schuck, A. M., & Widom, C. S. (2005). Understanding the role of neighborhood context in the long-term criminal consequences of child maltreatment. *American Journal of Community Psychology, 36,* 207–222.

Schueller, S. M. (2009). Promoting wellness: Integrating community and positive psychology. *Journal of Community Psychology, 37*(7), 922–937.

Schuller, N. (2006). Older people, crime and justice. *Community Safety Journal, 5,* 37–43.

Schultz, D., & Schultz, S. (1990). *Psychology and industry today.* New York, NY: Macmillan.

Schultz, D., & Schultz, S. E. (1998). *Psychology and work today.* Upper Saddle River, NJ: Prentice Hall.

Schulz, R., & Heckhausen, J. (1996). A life span model of successful aging. *American Psychologist, 51,* 702–714.

Schur, L. A., & Kruse, D. L. (2000). What determines voter turnout? Lessons from citizens with disabilities. *Social Science Quarterly, 81,* 571–587.

Schwartz, J. P., Waldo, M., & Daniels, D. (2005). Gender role conflict and self-esteem: Predictors of partner abuse in court referred men. *Psychology of Men and Masculinity, 6,* 109–113.

Schwartz, M. B., Novak, S. A., & Fiore, S. S. (2009). The impact of removing snacks of low nutritional value from middle schools. *Health Education and Behavior, 36,* 999–1011.

Schwartz, S., & Boodell, D. (2009). *Dreams from the monster factory: A tale of prison, redemption, and one woman's fight to restore justice to all.* New York, NY: Scribner.

Schwarzer, R., & Leppin, A. (1991). Social support and health: A theoretical and empirical overview. *Journal of Social and Personal Relations, 8,* 99–127.

Schweinhart, L. J. (2006). The High/Scope approach: Evidence that participatory learning in early childhood contributes to human development. In N. F. Watt, C. Ayoub, R. H. Bradley, J. E. Puma, & W. A. LeBoeuf (Eds.), *The crisis in youth mental health: Critical issues and effective programs: Vol. 4. Early intervention programs and policies. Child psychology and mental health.* Westport, CT: Praeger.

Schweinhart, L. J. (2007). Crime prevention by the High/Scope Perry Preschool Program. In Early intervention [Special issue]. *Victims & Offenders, 2,* 141–160.

Schweinhart, L. J., & Weikart, D. (1998). High/Scope Perry Preschool Program effects at age twenty-seven. In J. Crane (Ed.), *Social programs that work.* New York, NY: Sage.

Schweitzer, J. H., Kim, J. W., & Mackin, J. R. (1999). The impact of the built environment on crime and fear of crime in urban neighborhoods. *Journal of Urban Technology, 6,* 59–74.

Schwimmer, J. B., Burwinkle, T. M., & Varni, J. W. (2003). Health-related quality of life of severely obese children and adolescents. *Journal of the American Medical Association, 289,* 1813–1819.

Scileppi, J. A., Teed, E. L., & Torres, R. D. (2000). *Community psychology: A common sense approach to mental health.* Upper Saddle River, NJ: Prentice Hall.

Scott, E. K., London, A. S., & Edin, K. (2000). Looking to the future: Welfare-reliant women talk about their job aspirations in the context of welfare reform. In The impact of welfare reform [Special issue]. *Journal of Social Issues, 56,* 727–746.

Scully, J., Tosi, H., & Banning, K. (2000). Life event check-lists: Revisiting the social readjustment rating scale after 30 years. *Educational and Psychological Measurement, 60*(6), 864–876.

Searight, H. R., & Goldberg, M. A. (1991). The Community Competence Scale as a measure of functional daily living skills. *Journal of Mental Health Administration, 18*(2), 128–134.

Searight, H. R., Oliver, J. M., & Grisso, J. T. (1986). The community competence scale in the placement of the deinstitutionalized mentally ill. *American Journal of Community Psychology, 14*, 291–301.

Sears, R., Rudisill, J., & Mason-Sears, C. (2006). *Consultation skills for mental health professionals*. Hoboken, NJ: Wiley.

Secrist, Z. S. (2006). *Perceptions and knowledge of Hmong high school students regarding mental health* (Unpublished doctoral dissertation). University of Wisconsin–Stout, Menomonie, WI.

Seekins, T., & Fawcett, S. B. (1987). Effects of a poverty-clients agenda on resource allocations by community decision-makers. *American Journal of Community Psychology, 15*, 305–322.

Seidman, E. (1983). Unexamined premises of social problem solving. In E. Seidman (Ed.), *Handbook of social intervention*. Beverly Hills, CA: Sage.

Seidman, E. (1988). Back to the future, community psychology: Unfolding a theory of social intervention. *American Journal of Community Psychology, 16*, 3–24.

Seidman, E. (1990). Pursuing the meaning and utility of social regularities for community psychology. In P. Tolan, C. Keys, F. Chertak, & L. Jason (Eds.), *Researching community psychology: Issues of theory and methods*. Washington, DC: American Psychological Association.

Seidman, E., & Rappaport, J. (1974). You have got to have a dream, but it's not enough. *American Psychologist, 29*(7), 569–570.

Seidman, E., & Rappaport, J. (1986). *Redefining social problems*. New York, NY: Springer.

Seidman, E., & Tseng, V. (2011). Changing social settings: A framework for action. In M. S. Aber, K. I. Maton, & E. Seidman (Eds.), *Empowering settings and voices for social change* (pp. 12–37). New York, NY: Oxford University Press.

Seitz, V., Apfel, N., & Efron, C. (1977). *Long-term effects of early intervention: A longitudinal investigation*. Paper presented at the Annual Meeting of the American Association for the Advancement of Science, Denver, CO.

Seitz, V., Apfel, N., & Rosenbaum, L. (1991). Effects of an intervention program for pregnant adolescents: Educational outcomes at two years post partum. *American Journal of Community Psychology, 19*(6), 11–30.

Sekaly, R. (2008). The failed HIV Merck vaccine study: A step back or a launching point for future vaccine development? *Journal of Experimental Medicine, 205*(1), 7–12.

Seligman, M. E. P. (1975). *Helplessness: On depression, development, and death*. San Francisco, CA: Freeman.

Seligman, M. (2001). Positive psychology, positive prevention, and positive therapy. In C. R. Snyder & S. Lopez (Eds.), *Handbook of positive psychology* (pp. 3–12). New York, NY: Oxford University Press.

Seligman, M. E. P., & Csikszentmihalyi, M. (2000). Positive psychology: An introduction. *American Psychologist, 55*, 5–14.

Selye, H. (1936). A syndrome produced by diverse nocuous stimuli. *Journal of Neuropsychiatry and Clinical Neurosciences, 138*, 32.

Selye, H. (1956). *The stress of life*. New York, NY: McGraw-Hill.

Selye, H. (1974). *Stress without distress*. Philadelphia, PA: Lippincott.

Selznick, P. (2000). Reflections on responsibility: More than just following the rules. *Responsive Community, 10*, 57–61.

Sennett, R. (2003). *Respect: The formation of character in an age of inequality*. London, England: Allen Lane.

Seppälä, T., Lipponen, J., Bardi, A., & Pirttilä-Backman, A. (2012). Change-oriented organizational citizenship behaviour: An interactive product of openness to change values, work unit identification, and sense of power. *Journal of Occupational and Organizational Psychology, 85*(1), 136–155. doi:10.111/j.2044-8325.2010.02010.x

Serrano-Garcia, I. (1990). Implementing research: Putting our values to work. In P. Tolan, C. Keys, F. Chertak, & L. Jason (Eds.), *Researching community psychology: Issues of theory and methods*. Washington, DC: American Psychological Association.

Serrano-Garcia, I. (1994). The ethics of the powerful and the power of ethics. *American Journal of Community Psychology, 22*, 1–20.

Serrano-García, I. (2011). Contradictions and consistencies: Rappaport's contributions to community psychology (1968–2007). In M. S. Aber, K. I. Maton, & E. Seidman (Eds.), *Empowering settings and voices for social change* (pp. 207–231). New York, NY: Oxford University Press.

Serrano-Garcia, I., Lopez, M. M., & Rivera-Medena, E. (1987). Toward a social-community psychology. *Journal of Community Psychology, 15*, 431–446.

Seyfried, S. F. (1998). Academic achievement of African American preadolescents: The influence of teacher perceptions. *American Journal of Community Psychology, 26*, 381–402.

Shadish, W. R. (1990). Defining excellence criteria in community research. In P. Tolan, C. Keys, F. Chertak, & L. Jason

(Eds.), *Researching community psychology: Issues of theory and methods.* Washington, DC: American Psychological Association.

Shadish, W., Cook, T., & Campbell, D. (2002). *Experimental and quasi-experimental designs for generalized causal inference.* Boston, MA: Houghton Mifflin.

Shadish, W. R., Cook, T. D., & Leviton, L. C. (1991). *Foundations of program evaluation: Theories of practice.* Newbury Park, CA: Sage.

Shadish, W. R., Lurigio, S. J., & Lewis, D. A. (1989). After deinstitutionalization: The present and future of mental health long-term care policy. *Journal of Social Issues, 45,* 1–15.

Shadish, W. R., Thomas, S., & Bootzin, R. R. (1982). Criteria for success in deinstitutionalization: Perceptions of nursing homes by different interest groups. *American Journal of Community Psychology, 10,* 553–566.

Shadur, M. A., Kienzle, R., & Rodwell, J. J. (1999). The relationship between organizational climate and employee perceptions of involvement: The importance of support. *Group & Organization Management, 24,* 479–503.

Shaheen, G., & Rio, J. (2007). Recognizing work as a priority in preventing or ending homelessness. *Journal of Primary Prevention, 28,* 341–358.

Shakow, D. (2002). Clinical psychology seen some 50 years later. In W. E. Pickren & D. A. Dewsbury (Eds.), *Evolving perspectives on the history of psychology* (pp. 433–451). Washington, DC: American Psychological Association.

Shapira, N., Barak, A., & Gal, I. (2007). Promoting older adults' well-being through Internet training and use. *Aging & Mental Health, 11,* 477–484.

Sharstein, S. (2000). Whatever happened to community mental health? *Psychiatric Services, 51,* 612–620.

Sheldon, S. B., & Epstein, J. L. (2004). Getting students to school: Using family and community involvement to reduce chronic absenteeism. *School Community Journal, 14,* 39–56.

Shepherd, M. D., Schoenberg, M., Slavich, S., Wituk, S., Warren, M., & Meissen, G. (1999). Continuum of professional involvement in self-help groups. *Journal of Community Psychology, 27,* 39–53.

Shih, Y., Zhao, L, & Elting, L. (2006). Does Medicare coverage of colonoscopy reduce racial/ethnic disparities in cancer screening among the elderly? *Health Affairs, 25,* 1153–1162.

Shin, R. Q., Kendall, M. A. (2012). Dropout prevention: A (re) conceptualization through the lens of social justice. In E. Vera (Ed.), *Oxford handbook of prevention in counseling psychology.* New York, NY: Oxford University Press.

Shinn, M. (1992). Homelessness: What is a psychologist to do? *American Journal of Community Psychology, 20,* 1–24.

Shinn, M. (1997). Family homelessness: State or trait. *American Journal of Community Psychology, 25,* 755–769.

Shinn, M. (2007). International homelessness: Policy, sociocultural, and individual perspectives. *Journal of Social Issues, 63,* 657–677.

Shinn, M., & Gillespie, C. (1993). *Structural vs. individual explanation for homelessness: Implications for intervention.* Paper presented at the Ninth Annual Northeast Community Psychology Conference, New York.

Shinn, M., Gottlieb, J., Wett, J. L., Bahl, A., Cohen, A., & Ellis, D. B. (2007). Predictors of homelessness among older adults in New York City: Disability, economic, human and social capital and stressful events. *Journal of Health Psychology, 12,* 696–708.

Shinn, M., Lehmann, S., & Wong, N. W. (1984). Social interaction and social support. *American Journal of Community Psychology, 40,* 55–76.

Shinn, M., Morch, H., Robinson, P. E., & Neuer, R. A. (1993). Individual, group, and agency strategies for coping with job stressors in residential child care programmes. *Journal of Community and Applied Social Psychology, 3,* 313–324.

Shinn, M., & Perkins, D. N. T. (2000). Contributions from organizational psychology. In J. Rappaport & E. Seidman (Eds.), *Handbook of community psychology.* New York, NY: Plenum.

Shinn, M., & Rapkin, B. (2000). Cross-level analysis without cross-ups. In J. Rappaport & E. Seidman (Eds.), *Handbook of community psychology* (pp. 669–695). New York, NY: Kluwer Academic/ Plenum.

Shinn, M., & Toohey, S. (2003). Community contexts of human welfare. *Annual Review of Psychology, 54,* 427–259.

Shinn, M., & Tsemberis, S. (1998). Is housing the cure for homelessness? In X. Arriaga & S. Oskamp (Eds.), *Addressing community problems: Psychological research and interventions.* Thousand Oaks, CA: Sage.

Shinn, M., & Weitzman, B. C. (1990). Research on homelessness: An introduction. *Journal of Social Issues, 46,* 1–11.

Shinn, M., Weitzman, B. C., Strojanovic, D., Knickman, J. R., Jimenez, L., Duchon, L., . . . Kranz, D. H. (1998). Predictors of homelessness among families in New York City: From shelter request to housing stability. *American Journal of Public Health, 88,* 1651–1657.

Shivy, V. A., Wu, J. J., Moon, A. E., Mann, S. C., & Eacho, C. (2007). Ex-offenders reentering the workforce. *Journal of Counseling Psychology, 54,* 466–473.

Shpungin, E., & Lyubansky, M. (2006). Navigating social class roles in community research. *American Journal of Community Psychology, 37,* 227–235.

Shrewsbury, V., & Wardle, J. (2008). Socioeconomic status and adiposity in childhood: a systematic review of cross-sectional studies 1990–2005. *Obesity, 16,* 275–294.

Shumaker, S. A., & Brownell, A. (1984). Toward a theory of social support: Closing conceptual gaps. *Journal of Social Issues, 40,* 11–36.

Shumaker, S. A., & Brownell, A. (1985). Introduction: Social support interventions. *Journal of Social Issues, 41,* 1–4.

Shure, M. B. (1997). Interpersonal cognitive problem-solving: Primary prevention of high-risk behaviors in the preschool and primary years. In G. W. Albee & T. P. Gullotta (Eds.), *Primary prevention works.* Thousand Oaks, CA: Sage.

Shure, M. B. (1999, April). Preventing violence the problem-solving way. *Juvenile Justice Bulletin,* 1–10.

Shure, M. B., & Spivack, G. (1988). Interpersonal cognitive problem solving. In R. H. Price, E. L. Cowan, R. P. Lorion, & J. Ramos-McKay (Eds.), *14 ounces of prevention: A casebook for practitioners.* Washington, DC: American Psychological Association.

SIECUS National Guidelines Task Force (2004). *Guidelines for comprehensive sexuality education* (3rd ed.). Washington, DC: Sexuality Information and Education Council of the United States.

Siegel, J. T., & Alvaro, E. M. (2003). Youth tobacco access: Adult attitudes, awareness, and perceived self-efficacy in two Arizona counties. *Journal of Community Health, 28,* 439–449.

Siegel, J., & Kuykendall, D. A. (1990). Loss, widowhood, and psychological distress among the elderly. *Journal of Consulting and Clinical Psychology, 58,* 519–524.

Silka, L. (2007). Immigrants in the community: New opportunities, new struggles. *Analysis of Social Issues and Public Policy, 7,* 75–91.

Simmons, B. (2000). *Eustress at work: Accentuating the positive* (Unpublished doctoral dissertation). Oklahoma State University, Tulsa.

Simmons, B., & Nelson, D. (2001). Eustress at work: The relationship between hope and health in hospital nurses. *Health Care Management Review, 26,* 7–18.

Simoni-Wastila, L., & Strickler, G. (2004). Risk factors associated with problem use of prescription drugs. *American Journal of Public Health, 94,* 266–268.

Simpura, J., Levin, B. M., & Mustonen, H. (1997). Russian drinking in the 1990s: Patterns and trends in international comparison. In J. Simpura & B. M. Levin (Eds.), *Demystifying Russian drinking. Comparative studies from the 1990s* (pp. 79–107). Helsinki: STAKES.

Sims, B., Yost, B., & Abbott, C. (2005). Use and nonuse of victim services programs: Implications from a statewide survey of crime victims. *Criminology & Public Policy, 4,* 361–383.

Singer, M. (1994a). AIDS and the health crisis of the US urban poor: The perspective of critical medical anthropology. *Social Science and Medicine, 39,* 931–948.

Singer, M. (1994b). Implementing a community-based AIDS prevention program for ethnic minorities: The Comunidad y Responsibilidad Project. In J. P. Van Vugt (Ed.), *AIDS prevention and services: Community based research* (pp. 59–92). Westport, CT: Gergin and Garvey.

Singer, M., & Borrero, M. (1984). Indigenous treatment for alcoholism: The evidence for Puerto Rican spiritism. *Medical Anthropology, 8,* 246–273.

Singer, M., Flores, C., Davison, L., Burke, G., Castillo, Z., Scaon, K., & Rivera, M. (1990). SIDA: The economic, social, and cultural context of AIDS among Latinos. *Medical Anthropology Quarterly, 4,* 73–117.

Singer, M., & Weeks, M. R. (1996). Preventing AIDS in communities of color: Anthropology and social prevention. *Human Organization, 55,* 488–492.

Singh, S., & Darrock, J. (2000). Adolescent pregnancy and childbearing: Levels and trends in developed countries. *Family Planning Perspectives, 32,* 14–23.

Singleton, J. (2000). Women caring for elderly family members: Shaping non-traditional work and family initiatives. *Journal of Comparative Family Studies, 31,* 367–375.

Siska, D. (1998, March/April). Boom time. *Foundation News and Commentary.* Retrieved from http://www.cof.org/fnc/28growth.htm#Growth

Skinner, B. F. (1974). *About behaviorism.* New York, NY: Vintage.

Skinner, E., Edge, K., Altman, J., & Sherwood, H. (2003). Searching for the structure of coping: A review and critique of category systems for classifying ways of coping. *Psychological Bulletin, 129*(2), 216–269.

Skogan, W., Hartnett, S., Bump, N., & Dubois, J. (2008). *Evaluation of CeaseFire-Chicago.* Washington, DC: National Institute of Justice/JCJRS. Retrieved from http://www.ncjrs.gov/App/publications/abstract.aspx?ID=249182

Slavin, R. E. (1985). Cooperative learning: Applying contact theory in desegregated schools. *Journal of Social Issues, 41,* 45–62.

Slavin, R. (1996). Research on cooperative learning and achievement: What we know, what we need to know. *Contemporary Educational Psychology, 21,* 43–69.

Smart Growth. (2008). *Private foundations.* Retrieved from http://www.epa.gov/smartgrowth/topics/private_foundations.htm

Smith, H. P. (2006). Violent crime and victim compensation: Implications for social justice. *Violence and Victims, 21,* 307–322.

Smith, L. (2009). Enhancing training and practice in the context of poverty. *Training and Education in Professional Psychology, 3,* 84–93.

Smith, S. J., Easterlow, D., Munro, M., & Turner, K. M. (2003). Housing as health capital: How health trajectories and housing paths are linked. *Journal of Social Issues, 59,* 501–546.

Smither, R. D. (1998). *The psychology of work and human performance.* New York, NY: Longman.

Smyth, J., & McInerney, P. (2007). Living on the edge: A case of school reform working for disadvantaged adolescents. *Teachers College Record, 109,* 1123–1170.

Snow, D., Swan, S., & Raghavan, C. (2003).The relationship of work stressors, coping and social support to psychological symptoms among female secretarial employees. *Work & Stress, 17,* 241–263.

Snowden, L. R. (1987). The peculiar successes of community psychology: Service delivery to ethnic minorities and the poor. *American Journal of Community Psychology, 15,* 575–586.

Snowden, L. R. (1992). Community psychology and the "severely mentally ill." *Community Psychologist, 25,* 3.

Snowden, L. (2005). Racial, cultural and ethnic disparities in health and mental health: Toward theory and research at community levels. *American Journal of Community Psychology, 35,* 1–8.

Snowden, L. (2006). Strategies to improve minority access to public mental health services in California: Description and preliminary evaluation. *Journal of Community Psychology, 34,* 225–235.

Snowden, L. R., Martinez, M., & Morris, A. (2000). Community psychology and ethnic minority populations. In J. Rappaport & E. Seidman (Eds.), *Handbook of community psychology.* New York, NY: Plenum.

Social Security Online. (2005). *Cost of living adjustments for 2005.* Retrieved from http://www.ssa.gov/cola/colafacts2005.htm

Society for Community Research and Action. (1994). *Final report of the task force on homeless women, children, and families.* Washington, DC: American Psychological Association.

Society for Community Research and Action. (2007). *Practice Task Force report.* Washington, DC: American Psychological Association.

Solarz, A., & Bogat, G. A. (1990). When social support fails: The homeless. *Journal of Community Psychology, 18,* 79–96.

Solomon, D., Watson, M., Battisch, V., Schaps, E., & Delucchi, K. (1996). Creating classrooms that students experience as communities. *American Journal of Community Psychology, 24,* 719–748.

Sosin, M., Piliavin, I., & Westerfelt, H. (1990). Toward a longitudinal analysis of homelessness. *Journal of Social Issues, 46,* 157–174.

South, S. J., Haynie, D. L., & Bose, S. (2007). Student mobility and school dropout. *Social Science Research, 36,* 68–94.

Southwick, S. M., Morgan, C. A., Vythilingam, M., & Charney, D. (2006). Mentors enhance resilience in at-risk children and adolescents. *Psychoanalytic Inquiry, 26,* 577–584.

Spears, R., & Haslam, S. (1997). Stereotyping and the burden of cognitive load. In R. Spears, P. J. Oakes, N. Ellemers, & S. Haslam (Eds.), *The social psychology of stereotyping and group life* (pp. 171–207). Malden, MA: Blackwell.

Speer, P., Dey, A., Griggs, P., Gibson, C., Lubin, B., & Hughey, J. (1992). In search of community: An analysis of community psychology research from 1984–1988. *American Journal of Community Psychology, 20,* 195–209.

Speer, P., & Hughey, J. (1995). Community organizing: An ecological route to empowerment and power. *American Journal of Community Psychology, 23,* 729–748.

Speigel, H. (1987). Coproduction in the context of neighborhood development. *Journal of Voluntary Research, 16,* 54–61.

Spillman, B. C., & Pezzin, L. E. (2000). Potential and active family caregivers: Changing networks and the "sandwich generation." *Millbank Quarterly, 78,* 347–374.

Spitzer, R. J. (1999, Summer). The gun dispute. *American Educator,* 10–17.

Spivack, G., & Marcus, J. (1987). Marks and classroom adjustment as early indicators of mental health at age twenty. *American Journal of Community Psychology, 15,* 35–56.

Spoth, R. (1997). Challenges in defining and developing the field of rural mental disorder preventive intervention research. *American Journal of Community Psychology, 25,* 425–448.

Spoth, R., Randall, G., Shin, C., & Redmond, C. (2005). Randomized study of combined universal family and school preventive interventions: Patterns of long-term effects on initiation, regular use, and weekly drunkenness. *Psychology of Addictive Behaviors, 19,* 372–381.

Spoth, R., Redmond, C., Hockaday, C., & Yoo, S. (1996). Protective factors and young adolescent tendency to abstain from alcohol use: A model using two waves of intervention study data. *American Journal of Community Psychology, 24,* 749–770.

Spoth, R., Redmond, C., & Shin, C. (2001). Randomized trial of brief family interventions for general populations: Adolescent substance use outcomes four years following baseline. *Journal of Consulting and Clinical Psychology, 69,* 627–642.

Spoth, R., Redmond, C., Shin, C., & Azevedo, K. (2004). Brief family intervention effects on adolescent substance initiation: School-level curvilinear growth curve analyses six years following baseline. *Journal of Consulting and Clinical Psychology, 72,* 535–542.

Sprague, J., & Hayes, J. (2000). Self-determination and empowerment: A feminist standpoint analysis of talk about disability. *American Journal of Community Psychology, 28,* 671–695.

Spreitzer, G. M. (1995). An empirical test of a comprehensive model of intrapersonal empowerment in the workplace. *American Journal of Community Psychology, 23,* 601–629.

Spreitzer, G. M., Kizilos, M. A., & Nason, S. W. (1997). A dimensional analysis of the relationship between psychological empowerment and effectiveness, satisfaction, and strain. *Journal of Management, 23*(5), 679–704.

Stack, L. C., Lannon, P. B., & Miley, A. D. (1983). Accuracy of clinicians' expectancies for psychiatric rehospitalization. *American Journal of Community Psychology, 11,* 99–113.

Stadler, C., Feifel, J., Rohrmann, S., Vermeiren, R., & Poustka, F. (2010). Peer-victimization and mental health problems in adolescents: Are parental and school support protective? *Child Psychiatry and Human Development, 41,* 371–386. doi:10.1007/s10578-010-0174-5

Stagl, K. C., & Salas, E. (2008). Best practices in building more effective teams. In R. J. Burke, C. L. Cooper, R. J. Burke & C. L. Cooper (Eds.), *Building more effective organizations: HR management and performance in practice* (pp. 160–182). New York, NY: Cambridge University Press.

Stanko, E. A. (2003). *The meanings of violence.* London, England: Routledge.

Stanton, A., Kirk, S., Cameron, C., & Danoff-Burg, S. (2000). Coping through emotional approach: Scale construction and validation. *Journal of Personality and Social Psychology, 78,* 1150–1169.

Stanton, A., & Low, C. (2012). Expressing emotions in stressful contexts: Benefits, moderators, and mechanisms. *Current Directions in Psychological Science, 21,* 124–128.

Stearns, E., Moller, S., Blau, J., & Potochnick, S. (2007). Staying back and dropping out: The relationship between grade retention and school dropout. *Sociology of Education, 80,* 210–240.

Stebbings, H., & Braganza, A. (2009). Exploring continuous organizational transformation: Morphing through network interdependence. *Journal of Change Management, 9*(1), 27–48.

Steffen, A. M. (1996). Community psychology's response to the promises and problems of aging. *The Community Psychologist, 29,* 19–21.

Steffen, P. R., McNeilly, M., Anderson, N., & Sherwood, A. (2003). Effects of perceived racism and anger inhibition on ambulatory blood pressure in African Americans. *Psychosomatic Medicine, 65*(5), 746–750.

Stein, C., & Mankowski, E. (2004). Asking, witnessing, interpreting, knowing: Conducting qualitative research in community psychology. *American Journal of Community Psychology, 33*(1–2), 21–35.

Stein, L., & Test, M. A. (1985). The training in community living model: A decade of experience. In *New directions for mental health services* (Vol. 26). San Francisco, CA: Jossey-Bass.

Stein, L. I., & Test, M. A. (1980). An alternative to mental hospital treatment. I: Conceptual model, treatment program, and clinical evaluation. *Archives of General Psychiatry, 37,* 392–397.

Stein, M. (2008). Community gardens for health promotion and disease prevention. *International Journal of Human Caring, 12,* 47–52.

Stephens, C. (2007). Community as practice: Social representations of community and their implications for health promotion. *Journal of Community and Applied Social Psychology, 17,* 103–114.

Sternberg, L. (2004). Risk-taking in adolescence. *Annals of the New York Academy of Science, 1021,* 108.

Stipek, D., & Hakuta, K. (2007). Strategies to ensure that no child starts from behind. In L. J. Aber, S. J. Bishop-Josef, S. M. Jones, K. Taffe, & D. A. Phillips (Eds.), *Child development and social policy: Knowledge for action.* Washington, DC: American Psychological Association.

Stoiber, K. C., & McIntyre, J. (2006). Adolescent pregnancy and parenting. In G. G. Bear & K. M. Minke (Eds.), *Children's needs III: Development, prevention, and intervention.* Washington, DC: National Association of School Psychologists.

Stokols, D. (2006). Toward a science of transdisciplinary action research. *American Journal of Community Psychology, 38*(1–2), 63–77.

Storch, M., Gaab, J., Küttel, Y., Stüssi, A.-C., & Fend, H. (2007). Psychoneuroendocrine effects of resource-activating stress management training. *Health Psychology, 26*(4), 456–463.

Strange, J., Sherman, L., Angel, C. M., & Woods, D. J. (2006). Victim evaluations of face-to-face restorative justice conferences: A quasi-experimental analysis. *Journal of Social Issues, 62,* 281–306.

Strom, K., & MacDonald, J. (2007). The influence of social and economic disadvantage on racial patterns in youth homicide over time. *Homicide Studies, 11,* 50–69.

Strother, C. R. (1987). Reflections on the Stanford Conference and subsequent events. *American Journal of Community Psychology, 15,* 519–522.

Struening, E. L., & Padgett, D. K. (1990). Physical health status, substance use and abuse, and mental disorders among homeless adults. *Journal of Social Issues, 46,* 65–81.

Strumer, S., Snyder, M., & Omoto, A. (2005). Prosocial emotions and helping: The moderating role of group membership. *Journal of Personality and Social Psychology, 88,* 532–546.

Suarez-Balcazar, Y., Davis, M., Ferrari, J., Nyden, P., Olsen, B., & Alverez, A. (2004). University-community partnerships: A framework and an exemplar. In L. Jason, C. Keys, Y. Suarez-Balcazar, R. Taylor, & M. Davis (Eds.), *Participatory community research: Theories and methods in action* (pp. 105–120). Washington, DC: American Psychological Association.

Suarez-Balcazar, Y., Durlak, J. A., & Smith, C. (1994). Multicultural training practices in community psychology programs. *American Journal of Community Psychology, 22,* 785–798.

Substance Abuse and Mental Health Services Administration. (2000). *Summary of findings from the 1999 National Household Survey on Drug Abuse* (Publication No. 00-3466). Rockville, MD: U.S. Department of Health and Human Services, Substance Abuse and Mental Health Services Administration.

Substance Abuse and Mental Health Services Administration. (2007). *Results from the 2006 National Survey on Drug Use and Health: National findings.* Rockville, MD: SAMHSA Office of Applied Studies.

Sue, D., Bucceri, J., Lin, A., Nadal, & Torino, G. (2007). Racial microaggressions and the Asian American experience. *Cultural Diversity and Ethnic Minority Psychology, 13,* 72–81.

Sue, D., Sue, D. W., Sue, D., & Sue, S. (2013). *Understanding abnormal behavior* (10th ed.). New York, NY: Wadsworth.

Sue, D. W. (2010). *Microaggressions in everyday life: Race, gender, and sexual orientation.* Hoboken, NJ: Wiley.

Sue, D. W., Bingham, R. P., Porché-Burke, L., & Vasquez, M. (1999). The diversification of psychology: A multicultural revolution. *American Psychologist, 54,* 1061–1069.

Sue, D. W., & Sue, D. (2008). *Counseling the culturally diverse: Theory and practice* (5th ed.). Hoboken, NJ: Wiley.

Sue, S. (1977). Community mental health services: Some optimism, some pessimism. *American Psychologist, 32,* 616–624.

Sue, S. (1999). Science, ethnicity, and bias: Where have we gone wrong? *American Psychologist, 54*(12), 1070–1077.

Sue, S. (2003). In defense of cultural competency in psychotherapy and treatment. *American Psychologist, 58,* 964–970.

Sue, S. (2006). Cultural competency: From philosophy to research and practice. *Journal of Community Psychology, 34,* 273–245.

Sue, S., & Sue, L. (2003). Ethnic research is good science. In G. Bernal, J. E. Trimble, A. K. Burlew, & F. T. L. Leong (Eds.), *Handbook of racial and ethnic minority psychology* (pp. 198–207). Thousand Oaks, CA: Sage.

Sundberg, N. D. (1985). The use of future studies in training for prevention and promotion in mental health. *Journal of Primary Prevention, 6,* 98–114.

Sundberg, N., Snowden, L., & Reynolds, W. (1978). Toward assessment of personal competence and incompetence in life situations. *Annual Review of Psychology, 29,* 179–221.

Sundstrom, E., DeMeuse, K. P., & Futrell, D. (1990). Work teams. *American Psychologist, 45,* 120–133.

*Surgeon General's call to action to promote sexual health and responsible sexual behavior.* (2001). Retrieved from http://www.surgeongeneral.gov/library/sexualhealth/call.htm

Susser, E., Moore, R., & Link, B. (1993). Risk factors for homelessness. In H. K. Armenian, L. Gordis, J. L. Kelsey, M. Levine, & S. B. Thacker (Eds.), *Epidemiologic reviews* (Vol. 15). Baltimore, MD: Johns Hopkins University School of Hygiene and Public Health.

Susser, E., Valencia, E., & Conover, S. (1993). Prevalence of HIV infection among psychiatric patients in a New York City men's shelter. *American Journal of Public Health, 83,* 55–57.

Sutton, R. M., & Farrall, S. (2005). Gender, socially desirable responding and the fear of crime: Are women really more anxious about crime? *British Journal of Criminology, 45,* 212–224.

Svec, H. (1987). Youth advocacy and high school dropout. *High School Journal, 70,* 185–192.

Svyantek, D. J., Goodman, S. A., Benz, L. L., & Gard, J. (1999). The relationship between organizational characteristics and team building success. *Journal of Business & Psychology, 14,* 265–283.

Swift, C., & Levin, G. (1987). Empowerment: An emerging mental health technology. *Journal of Primary Prevention, 8,* 71–94.

Sy, F. S., Chng, C. L., Choi, S. T., & Wong, F. Y. (1998). Epidemiology of HIV and AIDS among Asians and Pacific Islander Americans. *AIDS Education and Prevention, 10* (Supplement A), 4–18.

Szasz, T. S. (1961). *The myth of mental illness.* New York, NY: Dell.

Taber, T. D., Cooke, R. A., & Walsh, J. T. (1990). A joint business-community approach to improve problem solving by workers displaced in a plant shutdown. *Journal of Community Psychology, 18,* 19–33.

Talbott, J. A. (1975). Current clichés and platitudes in vogue in psychiatric vocabularies. *Hospital and Community Psychiatry, 26,* 530.

Tartaglia, S. (2006). A preliminary study for a new model of sense of community. *Journal of Community Psychology, 34,* 25–36.

Taulé-Lunblad, J., Galbavy, R., & Dowrick, P. (2000). Putting the cool into after school: Responsive after-school community learning centers. *Community Psychologist, 33,* 33–34.

Tausig, M. (1987). Detecting "cracks" in mental health service systems: Application of network analytic techniques. *American Journal of Community Psychology, 15,* 337–351.

Taxman, F. S. (2004). The offender and reentry: Supporting active participation in reintegration. *Federal Probation, 68,* 31–35.

Taylor, C., & Taylor, V. (2007). Hip hop is now: An evolving youth culture. *Reclaiming Children and Youth, 15,* 210–213.

Taylor, R. B., & Shumaker, S. A. (1990). Local crime as a natural disaster: Implications for understanding the relationship between disorder and fear of crime. *American Journal of Community Psychology, 18,* 619–641.

Taylor, S. E. (1986–1987). The impact of an alternative high school program on students labeled "deviant." *Educational Research Quarterly, 11,* 8–12.

Taylor, S. E., Helgeson, V. S., Reed, G. M., & Skokan, L. A. (1991). Self-generated feelings of control and adjustment to physical illness. *Journal of Social Issues, 47,* 91–110.

Tebbs, J. (2012). Philosophical foundations of mixed methods: Implications for research practice. In L. Jason & D. Glenwick (Eds.), *Methodological approaches to community-based research* (pp. 13–32). Washington, DC: American Psychological Association.

Tepper, B. J. (2000). Consequences of abusive supervision. *Academy of Management Journal, 43*(2), 178–190.

The National Campaign to Prevent Teen and Unplanned Pregnancy. (2012). *Federal funding streams for teen pregnancy prevention.* Washington DC: Author. Retrieved from http://www.thenationalcampaign.org/policymakers/PDF/Overview_FedFundingStreams_2011.pdf

Thoits, P. (1984). Explaining distributions of psychological vulnerability: Lack of social support in the face of life stress. *Social Forces, 63*(2), 453–481.

Thoits, P. (1985). Social support and psychological well being: Theoretical possibilities. In I. Sarason & B. Sarason (Eds.), *Social support: Theory, research and application* (pp. 51–72). Netherlands: Martinus Nijhoff.

Thoits, P. (1986). Social support as coping assistance. *Journal of Consulting and Clinical Psychology, 54,* 416–423.

Thomas, D., & Ely, R. (1996, September 1). Making difference matter: A new paradigm for managing diversity. *Harvard Business Review,* 79–90.

Thomas, D., & Veno, A. (Eds.) *Community psychology and social change: Australian and New Zealand perspectives* (2nd ed.). Palmerston North, New Zealand: Dunmore Press.

Thomas G. P. (2010). *Contemporary clinical psychology* (3rd ed.). New York, NY: Wiley.

Thomas, E., Rickel, A. U., Butler, C., & Montgomery, E. (1990). Adolescent pregnancy and parenting. *Journal of Primary Prevention, 10,* 195–206.

Thomas, J. (2008). *Crime rates in the United States remain at 30-year lows.* Retrieved from http://www.america.gov/st/washfile-english/%202005/September/200509281446271.

Thomas, W., & Collier, V. (2003). The multiple benefits of dual language. *Educational Leadership, 61,* 61–64.

Thompson, M. P., & Norris, F. H. (1992). Crime, social status and alienation. *American Journal of Community Psychology, 20,* 97–119.

Thompson, S. C., & Spacespan, S. (1991). Perceptions of control in vulnerable populations. *Journal of Social Issues, 47,* 1–21.

Thorpe, S. J., & Brosnan, M. J. (2007). Does computer anxiety reach levels which conform to DSM IV criteria for specific phobia? *Computers in Human Behavior, 23,* 1258–1272.

Tice, C. H. (1991). Developing informal networks of caring through intergenerational connections in school settings. *Marriage and Family Review, 16,* 377–389.

Tidball, K., & Krasy, M. (2007). From risk to resilience: What role for community greening and civic ecology in cities? In A. Wals (Ed.) *Social learning toward a sustainable world: Principles, perspectives and praxis* (pp. 149–164). Wageningen, The Netherlands: Wageningen Academic.

Tierney, J. P. Grossman, J. B., & Resch, N. (1995). *Making a difference: An impact study of Big Brother/Big Sister.* Philadelphia, PA: Public/Private Ventures.

Timothy, T. (2004). *Clinical psychology.* Florence, KY: Wadsworth.

Tobler, W. (1970). A computer movie simulating urban growth in the Detroit region. *Economic Geography, 46*(2), 234–240.

Tobler, N. S., Ronna, M., Ochshorn, P., Marshall, D. G., Streke, A., & Stackpole, K. M. (2000). School-based adolescent drug prevention programs: 1998 meta-analysis. *Journal of Primary Prevention, 20,* 275–336.

Toker, S., Shirom, A., Shapira, I., Berliner, S., & Melamed, S. (2005). The association between burnout, depression, anxiety, and inflammation biomarkers: C-reactive protein and fibrinogen in men and women. *Journal of Occupational Health Psychology, 10,* 344–362.

Tolan, P., Keys, C., Chertak, F., & Jason, L. (1990). *Researching community psychology.* Washington, DC: American Psychological Association.

Tompsett, C. J., Toro, P. A., Guzicki, M., Manrique, M., & Zatakia, J. (2006). Homelessness in the United States: Assessing changes in prevalence and public opinion, 1993–2001. *American Journal of Community Psychology, 37,* 47–61.

Toro, P. A. (1990). Evaluating professionally operated and self-help programs for the seriously mentally ill. *American Journal of Community Psychology, 18,* 903–907.

Toro, P. (2005). Community psychology: Where do we go from here? *American Journal of Community Psychology, 35*(1–2), 9–16.

Toro, P. A. (2007). Toward an international understanding of homelessness. *Journal of Social Issues, 63,* 461–481.

Torrey, E. F. (1997, June). The release of the mentally ill from institutions: A well-intentioned disaster. *Chronicle of Higher Education,* B4–B5.

Tosi, H. L., Rizzo, J. R., & Carroll, S. J. (1986). *Managing organizational behavior.* Marshfield, MA: Pitman.

Toth, S. L., Pickreign Stronach E., Rogosch, F. A., Caplan, R., & Cicchetti, D. (2011). Illogical thinking and thought disorder in maltreated children. *Journal of the American Academy of Child and Adolescent Psychiatry, 50(7),* 659–668.

Town, M., Naimi, T. S., Mokdad, A. H., & Brewer, R. D. (2006). Health care access among U.S. adults who drink alcohol excessively: missed opportunities for prevention. *Preventing Chronic Disease, 3,* A53.

Townley, G., & Kloos, B. (2011). Examining the psychological sense of community for individuals with serious mental illness residing in supported housing environments. *Community Mental Health Journal, 47*(4), 436–446.

Townley, G., Kloos, B., Green, E. P., & Franco, M. M. (2011). Reconcilable differences? Human diversity, cultural relativity, and sense of community. *American Journal of Community Psychology, 47*(1–2), 69–85.

Traynor, M. P., Begay, M. E., & Glantz, S. A. (1993). New tobacco industry strategy to prevent local tobacco control. *Journal of the American Medical Association, 270,* 479–486.

Trickett, E. (1996). A future for community psychology: The contexts of diversity and the diversity of contexts. *American Journal of Community Psychology, 24,* 209–234.

Trickett, E. (2009). Community psychology: Individuals and interventions in community context. *Annual Review of Psychology, 60,* 395–419.

Trickett, E. J., Beehler, S., Deutsch, C., Green, L., Hawe, P., McLeroy, K., . . . Trimble, J. E. (2011). Advancing the science of community-level interventions. *American Journal of Public Health, 101,* 1410–1419.

Trickett, E. J., McConahay, J. B., Phillips, D., & Ginter, M. A. (1985). Natural experiments and the educational context: The environment and effects of an alternative inner-city public school on adolescents. *American Journal of Community Psychology, 13,* 617–643.

Trickett, E., Watts, R., & Birman, D. (Eds.). (1994). *Human diversity: Perspectives on people in context.* San Francisco, CA: Jossey-Bass.

Trimble, J. E. (2001). A quest for discovering ethnocultural themes. In J. G. Ponterotto, J. M. Casas, L. A. Suzuki, & C. M. Alexander (Eds.), *Handbook of multicultural counseling* (2nd ed., pp. 3–13). Thousand Oaks, CA: Sage.

Trimble, J., & Fisher, C. (Eds.) (2006). *The handbook of ethical research with ethnocultural populations and communities.* New York, NY: Sage.

Trimble, J. E., Scharrón-del Río, M. R., & Bernal, G. (2010). The itinerant researcher: Ethical and methodological issues in conducting cross-cultural mental health research. In D. C. Jack & A. Ali (Eds.), *Silencing the self across cultures: Depression and gender in the social world* (pp. 73–95). New York, NY: Oxford University Press.

Trimble, J., Trickett, E., Fisher, C., & Goodyear, L. (2012). A conversation on multicultural competence in evaluation. *American Journal of Evaluation, 33*(1), 112–123.

Trotter, R. T. (1995). Drug use, AIDS, and ethnography: Advanced ethnographic research methods exploring the HIV epidemic. In R. H. Needle, S. G. Gesner, & R. T. Trotter (Eds.), *Social networks, drug abuse, and HIV transmission* (pp. 38–53). Rockville, MD: National Institute on Drug Abuse.

Truckenbrodt, Y. (2000). The relationship between leader-member exchange and commitment and organizational citizenship behavior. *Acquisition Review Quarterly, 7*(3), 233–242. Retrieved from http://webharvest.gov/peth04/20041019050221/http://www.dau.mil/pubs/arq/2000arq/truck.pdf

Tseng, V., & Seidman, E. (2007). A systems framework for understanding social settings. *American Journal of Community Psychology, 39*(3–4), 217–228.

Tseng, V., & Seidman, E. (2011). Changing social settings: A framework for action. In M. Aber, K. Maton, & E. Seidman (Eds.), *Empowering settings and voices for social change* (pp. 1237). New York, NY: Oxford University Press.

Tsui, A., Egan, T., & O'Reilly, C. (1992) Being different: Relational demography and organizational attachment. *Administrative Science Quarterly, 37,* 549–579.

Turman, K. M. (2001, January/February). Crime victims. *National Criminal Justice Reference Service catalog,* p. 14.

Turner, J. B., Kessler, R. C., & House, J. S. (1991). Factors facilitating adjustment to unemployment: Implications for intervention. *American Journal of Community Psychology, 19,* 521–524.

Turnipseed, D. L. (1998). Anxiety and burnout in the health care work environment. *Psychological Reports, 82,* 627–642.

Uchino, B. (2004). *Social support and physical health: Understanding the health consequences of relationships.* New Haven, CT: Yale University Press.

Uchino, B. (2006). Social support and health: A review of physiological processes potentially underlying links to disease outcomes. *Journal of Behavioral Medicine, 29,* 377–387.

Uchino, B., Cacioppo, J., & Kiecolt-Glaser, J. (1996). The relationship between social support and physiological processes: A review with emphasis on underlying mechanisms and implications for health. *Psychological Bulletin, 119*(3), 488–531.

UNAIDS. (2007). *AIDS epidemic update.* Geneva, Switzerland: WHO Library Cataloguing, World Health Organization.

Unger, D. G., & Wandersman, A. (1985). The importance of neighbors: The social, cognitive and affective components of neighboring. *American Journal of Community Psychology, 13,* 139–170.

Unger, D. G., & Wandersman, L. P. (1985b). Social support and adolescent mothers: Action research contributions to theory and application. *American Journal of Community Psychology, 41,* 29–45.

United Nations Programme on AIDS/HIV. (2010). *Global report.* Geneva, Switzerland: UNAIDS. Retrieved from http://www.unaids.org/globalreport/documents/20101123_GlobalReport_full_en.pdf

U.S. Census Bureau (2004). *U.S. Interim projections by age, sex, race, and Hispanic origin.* Retrieved from http://www.census.gov/ipc//www/interimproj

U.S. Census Bureau. (2007). *Household income rises, poverty rate declines, number of uninsured up.* Retrieved from http://www.census.gov/Press-Release/www/releases/archives/income_wealth/010583.html

U.S. Census Bureau. (2008). *The 2008 statistical abstracts.* Washington, DC: Author.

U.S. Census Bureau. (2009). *Income, poverty, and health insurance coverage in the United States: 2008.* Retrieved from http://www.census.gov/prod/2009pubs/p60-236.pdf

U.S. Census Bureau. (2011, March). *Overview of race and Hispanic origin: 2010.* Retrieved from http://www.census.gov/prod/cen2010/briefs/c2010br-02.pdf

U.S. Department of Education. (1998). *Guide to safe schools.* Washington, DC: Author.

U.S. Department of Health and Human Resources. (2003). *STD in adolescents and young adults: Special focus profiles.* Washington, DC: U.S. Government Printing Office.

U.S. Department of Health and Human Resources. (2006). *STD surveillance national profile.* Washington, DC: U.S. Government Printing Office.

U.S. Department of Health and Human Services. (1998). *Profile of homelessness.* Retrieved from http://www.aspe.os.dhhs.gov/progsys/homeless/profile.htm

U.S. Department of Health and Human Services. (2000). *Healthy people 2000: National health promotion and disease prevention objectives.* DHHS publication no. (PHS) 91–50212. Washington, DC: Superintendent of Documents, U.S. Government Printing Office.

U.S. Department of Health and Human Services. (2001a). *Head Start factsheet 2001.* Retrieved from http://www.acf.dhhs.gov/programs/hsb/about/fact2001.htm

U.S. Department of Health and Human Services. (2001b). *Women and smoking: A report of the Surgeon General.* Atlanta, GA: U.S. Department of Health and Human Services, Centers for Disease Control and Prevention, National Center for Chronic Disease Prevention and Health Promotion, Office on Smoking and Health.

U.S. Department of Health and Human Services. (2004). *The health consequences of smoking: A report of the Surgeon General.* Atlanta, GA: U.S. Department of Health and Human Services, Centers for Disease Control and Prevention, National Center for Chronic Disease Prevention and Health Promotion, Office on Smoking and Health.

U.S. Department of Health and Human Services. (2006). *The health consequences of smoking: A report of the Surgeon General.* Atlanta, GA: US Department of Health and Human Services, Centers for Disease Control and Prevention, Office on Smoking and Health.

U.S. Department of Health and Human Services. (2010). Health, United States, 2009. Retrieved December 1, 2011 from http://www.cdc.gov/nchs/data/hus/hus09.pdf

U.S. Department of Health and Human Services. (2011). *Smoking and your health.* Retrieved November 10, 2011 from http://betobaccofree.hhs.gov/health-effects/smoking-health/

U.S. Department of Health and Human Services, Centers for Disease Control and Prevention. (2008, April 2). *Alcohol and public health—binge drinking.* Retrieved from http://www.cdc.gov/alcohol.quickstats/binge_drinking.htm

U.S. Department of Justice. (1997). *What you can do if you are a victim of crime.* Washington, DC: Author.

U.S. Department of Labor, Bureau of Labor Statistics. (2006). *Futurework: Trends and challenges for work in the 21st century.* Retrieved from http://www.dol.gov/oasam/programs/history/herman/reports/futurework/report/chapter4/main.htm

U.S. Preventive Services Task Force. (November, 2002). Screening for colorectal cancer: U.S. Preventive Services Task Force recommendation statement. *Annals of Internal Medicine, 149*(9). Retrieved from http://www.annals.org/cgi/content/full/0000605-200811040-00243v1.

U.S. Surgeon General. (1999). *Mental health: A report of the U.S. Surgeon General.* Retrieved from http://www.surgeon-general.gov/library/mentalhealth/home.html

Vacca, J. S. (2004). Educated prisoners are less likely to return to prison. *Journal of Correctional Education, 55,* 297–315.

Vacha-Haase, T., & Duffy, M. (2012). Counseling psychologists working with older adults. In E. Altamaier & J. I. Hansen (Eds.), *Oxford handbook of counseling psychology* (pp. 480–502). New York, NY: Oxford University Press.

Valdiserri, R. O., West, G., Moore, M., Darrow, W. W., & Hinman, A. R. (1992). Structuring HIV prevention services delivery systems on the basis of social science theory. *Journal of Community Health, 17,* 259–269.

Valenti, M., & Campbell, R. (2009). Working with youth on LGBT issues: Why gay-straight alliance advisors become involved. *Journal of Community Psychology, 37*(2), 228–248.

Valentiner, D., Holohan, C., & Moos, R. (1994). Social support, appraisals of event controllability, and coping: An integrative model. *Journal of Personality and Social Psychology, 66,* 1094–1102.

Vandell, D., & Posner, J. (1999), Conceptualization and measurement of children's afterschool environments. In S. L. Friedman & T. D. Wachs (Eds.), *Measuring environments across the life span* (pp. 167–196). Washington, DC: American Psychological Association.

Vandell, D., Reisner, E., Pierce, K., Brown, B., Lee, D., Bolt, D., & Pechman, E. (2006). The study of promising afterschool programs: Examination of longer term outcomes after two years of program experience. Retrieved from http://www.wcer.wisc.edu/childcare/statements/html

Van Fleet, D. D. (1991). *Behavior in organizations.* Boston, MA: Houghton Mifflin.

Van Heeringen, C. (2001). *Understanding suicidal behavior. The process approach to research and treatment.* Chichester, England: Wiley.

Van Houtte, M. (2005). Climate or culture? A plea for conceptual clarity in school effectiveness research. *School Effectiveness and School Improvement, 16,* 71–89.

Varmus, H., & Satcher, D. (1997). Ethical complexities of conducting research in developing countries. *New England Journal of Medicine, 337,* 1003–1005.

Vartonian, T. P., & Gleason, P. M. (1999). Do neighborhood conditions affect high school dropout and college graduation rates? *Journal of Socio-Economics, 28,* 21–41.

Vaux, A. (1991). Let's hang up and try again: Lessons learned from a social support intervention. *American Journal of Community Psychology, 19,* 85–90.

Velleman, R. B., Templeton, L. J., & Copello, A. G. (2005). The role of the family in preventing and intervening with substance use and misuse: A comprehensive review of family interventions, with a focus on young people. *Drug and Alcohol Review, 24,* 93–109.

Vera, E., Bena, K., Dick, L., Blackmon, S., Gomez, K., Jorgenson, K., . . . Steele, J. (2012). Stress, coping, and subjective well-being in urban adolescents: The moderating roles of humor and venting. *Youth and Society,* in press.

Vera, E., Caldwell, J., Clarke, M., Gonzales, R., Morgan, M., & West, M. (2007). The Choices Program: Multisystemic interventions for enhancing the personal and academic effectiveness of urban adolescents of color. *The Counseling Psychologist, 35,* 779–796.

Vera, E. M., & Polanin, M. (2012). Prevention and counseling psychology: A simple yet difficult commitment. In E. Vera (Ed.), *Handbook of prevention in counseling psychology.* New York, NY: Oxford University Press.

Vera, E. M., & Speight, S. (2003). Multicultural competence, social justice, and counseling psychology: Expanding our roles. *The Counseling Psychologist, 31,* 253–272.

Vera, E., Vacek, K., Coyle, L., Stinson, J., Mull, M., Doud, K., . . . Langrehr, K. J. (2011). An examination of culturally-relevant stressors, coping, ethnic identity, and subjective well being in urban, ethnic minority adolescents. *Professional School Counseling, 15,* 55–66.

Vidal, A. P. C., Howitt, A. M., & Foster, K. P. (1986). *Stimulating community report? An assessment of the local initiative support corporation.* Cambridge, MA: John F. Kennedy School of Government.

Vidmar, N. (1992). Procedural justice and alternative dispute resolution. *Psychological Science, 3,* 224–228.

Vieno, A., Perkins, D. D., Smith, T. M., & Santinello, M. (2005). Democratic school climate and a sense of community in school: A multilevel analysis. *American Journal of Community Psychology, 36,* 327–341.

Vimpani, G. (2005). Getting the mix right: Family, community and social policy interventions to improve outcomes for young people at risk of substance misuse. *Drug and Alcohol Review, 24,* 111–125.

Vincent, T. A. (1990). A view from the hill: The human element in policy making on Capitol Hill. *American Psychologist, 45,* 61–64.

Vitaliano, P., DeWolfe, D., Maiuro, R., Russo, J., & Katon, W. (1990). Appraised changeability of a stressor as a modifier of the relationship between coping and depression: A test of the hypothesis of fit. *Journal of Personality and Social Psychology, 59,* 582–592.

Vivolo, A. M., Matjasko, J. L., & Massetti, G. M. (2011). Mobilizing communities and building capacity for youth violence prevention: The National Academic Centers of Excellence for Youth Violence Prevention. *American Journal of Community Psychology, 48*(1–2), 141–145.

Voas, R. B., Tippetts, A. S., & Fell, J. (2000). The relationship of alcohol safety laws to drinking drivers in fatal crashes. *Accident Analysis and Prevention, 32,* 483–492.

Vogelman, L. (1990). Psychology, mental health care and the future: Is appropriate transformation in post-apartheid South Africa possible? *Social Science and Medicine, 31,* 501–505.

Wagner, B., Compas, B., & Howell, D. (1988). Daily and major life events: A test of an integrative model of psychosocial stress. *American Journal of Community Psychology, 16*(2), 189–205.

Wahl, O. F. (2012). Stigma as a barrier to recovery from mental illness. *Trends in Cognitive Sciences, 16,* 9–10.

Wakefield, S., Yeudall, F., Taron, C., Reynolds, J., & Skinner, A. (2007). Growing urban health: Community gardening in South East Toronto. *Health Promotion International, 22,* 92–101.

Walfish, S., Polifka, J. A., & Stenmark, D. E. (1986). The job search in community psychology: A survey of recent graduates. *American Journal of Community Psychology, 14,* 237–240.

Walker, C. R., & Walker, S. G. (1990). The citizen and the police: A partnership in crime prevention. *Canadian Journal of Criminology, 32,* 125–135.

Walker, I., & Crogan, M. (1998). Academic performance, prejudice, and the jigsaw classroom: New pieces to the puzzle. *Journal of Community & Applied Social Psychology, 8,* 381–393.

Walker, L. E. (1999). Psychology and domestic violence around the world. *American Psychologist, 54*(1), 21–29.

Walker, L., & Greening, R. (2010). Huikahi Restorative Circles: A public health approach for reentry planning. *Federal Probation, 74*(1), 43–47.

Walker, L., Sakai, T., & Brady, K. (2006). Restorative circles—a reentry planning process for Hawaii inmates. *Federal Probation, 70,* 33–38.

Wallerstein, N., & Bernstein, S. (1988). Empowerment education: Freire's idea adapted to health education. *Health Education Quarterly, 15,* 379–394.

Wallston, B., Alagna, S., & DeVellis, B. (1983). Social support and physical health. *Health Psychology, 2,* 367–391.

Walsh, M. E., & Jackson, J. H. (2005). Psychological services for children and families who are homeless. In R. G. Steele & M. C. Roberts (Eds.), *Handbook of mental health services for children, adolescents, and families.* New York, NY: Kluwer.

Walsh, R. T. (1987). A social historical note on the formal emergence of community psychology. *American Journal of Community Psychology, 15,* 523–529.

Wandersman, A., & Florin, P. (2000). Citizen participation and community organizations. In J. Rappaport & E. Seidman (Eds.), *Handbook of community psychology.* New York, NY: Plenum.

Wandersman, A., Florin, P., Friedman, R., & Meier, R. (1987). Who participates, who does not and why? An analysis of voluntary neighborhood organizations in the United States and Israel. *Sociological Forum, 2,* 534–555.

Wandersman, A., Hallman, W., & Berman, S. (1989). How residents cope with living near a hazardous waste landfill: An example of substantive theorizing. *American Journal of Community Psychology, 17,* 575–584.

Wandersman, A., Kloos, B., Linney, J., & Shinn, M. (2005). Science and community psychology: Enhancing the vitality of community research and action. *American Journal of Community Psychology, 35,* 105–106.

Wandersman, A., Morrissey, E., Davino, K., Seybolt, D., Crusto, C., Nation, M., . . . Imm, P. (1998). Comprehensive quality programming and accountability: Eight essential strategies for implementing successful prevention programs. *Journal of Primary Prevention, 19,* 3–30.

Wandersman, A., & Nation, M. (1998). Urban neighborhoods and mental health: Psychological contributions to understanding toxicity, resilience, and interventions. *American Psychologist, 53,* 647–656.

Wang, G., & Dietz, W. H. (2002). Economic burden of obesity in youths aged 6 to 17 years: 1979-1999. *Pediatrics, 109,* e81.

Ward, T., & Stewart, C. (2003). Criminogenic needs and human needs: A theoretical model. *Psychology, Crime and Law, 9*(2), 125–143.

Wardlaw, D. M. (2000). Persistent themes in the history of community psychology: A preliminary analysis of *The Community Psychologist* or do we have an identity after all? *Community Psychologist, 33,* 15–18.

Warner, R. (1989). Deinstitutionalization: How did we get where we are? *Journal of Social Issues, 45,* 17–30.

Warren, M. R. (2005). Communities and schools: A new view of urban education reform. *Harvard Educational Review, 75*(2), 133–173.

Warren-Sohlberg, L., Jason, L. A., Orosan-Weine, A. M., Lantz, G. D., & Reyes, O. (1998). Implementing and evaluating preventive programs for high-risk transfer students. *Journal of Educational & Psychological Consultation, 9,* 309–324.

Wasik, B. H., Ramey, C. T., Bryant, D. M., & Sparling, J. J. (1990). A longitudinal study of two early intervention strategies: Project CARE. *Child Development, 61,* 1682–1696.

Watters, J., & Biernacki, P. (1989). Targeted sampling options for the study of hidden populations. *Social Problems, 36,* 416–430.

Watts, R. J. (1992). Elements of a psychology of human diversity. *Journal of Community Psychology, 20,* 116–131.

Watts, R., & Serrano-Garcia, I. (2003). The quest for a liberating community psychology: An overview. *American Journal of Community Psychology, 31,* 73–78.

Watts-English, T., Fortson, B. L., Gibler, N., Hooper, S. R., & De Bellis, M. D. (2006). The psychobiology of maltreatment in childhood. *Journal of Social Issues, 62,* 717–736.

Watzlawick, P., Weakland, J., & Fisch, R.(1974). *Change: Principles of problem formation and problem resolution.* New York, NY: Norton.

Way, M., Reddy, R., & Rhodes, J. (2007). Students' perceptions of school climate during the middle school years: Associations with trajectories of psychological and behavioral adjustment. *American Journal of Community Psychology, 40,* 194–213.

Wayne, S. J., & Green, S. A. (1993). The effects of leader-member exchange on employee citizenship and impression management behavior. *Human Relations, 46*(12),1431–1440. doi:10.1177/001872679304601204

Weaver, J. (1986). Therapeutic implications of divorce mediation. *Mediation Quarterly, 12,* 75–90.

Webb, D. H. (1989). PBB: An environment contaminant in Michigan. *Journal of Community Psychology, 17,* 30–46.

Webster-Stratton, C., & Reid, M. J. (2007). Incredible Years Parents and Teachers Training Series: A Head Start partnership to promote social competence and prevent conduct problems. In P. Tolan, J. Szapocznik, & S. Sambrano (Eds.), *Preventing youth substance abuse: Science-based programs for children and adolescents.* Washington, DC: American Psychological Association.

Wechsler, H., Dowdall, G. W., Maenner, G., Gledhill-Hoyt, L., & Lee, H. (1998). Changes in binge drinking and related problems among American college students between 1993 and 1997: Results of the Harvard School of Public Health College Alcohol Study. *American College Health, 47,* 51–55.

Weed, D. S. (1990, August). *Providing consultation to primary prevention programs: Applying the technology of community psychology.* Paper presented at the Annual Convention of the American Psychological Association, Boston, MA.

Weeks, M. R. (1990). *Community outreach prevention effort: Designs in culturally appropriate AIDS intervention.* Hartford, CT: Institute for Community Research.

Weeks, M. R., Schensul, J. J., Williams, S. S., Singer M., & Grier, M. (1995). AIDS prevention for African-American and Latina women: Building culturally and gender-appropriate intervention. *AIDS Education and Prevention, 7,* 251–263.

Weeks, M. R., Singer, M., Grier, M., Hunte-Marrow, J., & Haughton, C. (1991). *Project COPE: Preventing AIDS among injection drug users and their sex partners.* Hartford, CT: Institute for Community Research.

Weikart, D. P., & Schweinhart, L. J. (1997). High/Scope Perry Preschool Program. In G. W. Albee & T. P. Gullotta (Eds.), *Primary prevention works.* Thousand Oaks, CA: Sage.

Weinberg, R. B. (1990). Serving large numbers of adolescent victim-survivors: Group interventions following trauma at school. *Professional Psychology Research and Practice, 21,* 271–278.

Weinstein, R. S. (1990). The universe of alternatives in schooling: The contributions of Seymour B. Sarason to education. *American Journal of Community Psychology, 18,* 359–369.

Weinstein, R. S. (2002). *Reaching higher: The power of expectations in schooling.* Cambridge, MA: Harvard University Press.

Weinstein, R. (2006). Reaching higher in community psychology: Social problems, social settings, and social change. *American Journal of Community Psychology, 37*(1–2), 9–20.

Weinstein, R. S., Soule, C. R., Collins, F., Cone, J., Mehlhorn, M., & Simontacchi, K. (1991). Expectations and high school change: Teacher-researcher collaboration to prevent school failure. *American Journal of Community Psychology, 19,* 333–362.

Weissberg, R., Kumpfer, K., & Seligman, M. (2003). Prevention that works for children and youth: An introduction. *American Psychologist, 58*(6–7), 425–432.

Weitzer, R., & Tuch, S. A. (2005). Racially biased policing: Determinants of citizen perceptions. *Social Forces, 83,* 1009–1030.

Weitzman, B. C., Knickman, J. R., & Shinn, M. (1990). Pathways to homelessness among New York City families. *Journal of Social Issues, 46*(4), 125–140.

Well, S. S., Holme, J. J., Atanda, A. K., & Revilla, A. T. (2005). Tackling racial segregation one policy at a time: Why school desegregation only went so far. *Teachers College Record, 107,* 2141–2177.

Wells, W. (2007). Type of contact and evaluations of police officers: The effects of procedural justice across three types of police-citizen contact. *Journal of Criminal Justice, 35,* 612–621.

Wemmers, J., & Cyr, K. (2005). Can mediation be therapeutic for crime victims? An evaluation of victims' experiences in mediation with young offenders. *Canadian Journal of Criminology and Criminal Justice, 47,* 527–554.

Werner, E., & Smith, R. (2001). *Journeys from childhood to midlife: Risk, resilience, and recovery.* Ithaca, NY: Cornell University Press.

Wesson, D. R., Smith, D. E., Ling, W., & Seymour, R. B. (1997). Sedative-hypnotics and tricyclics. In J. H. Lowinson, *Substance abuse a comprehensive textbook* (3rd ed.). Baltimore, MD: Williams & Wilkins.

Western Regional Advocacy Project (2006). *Without housing: Decades of federal housing cutbacks, massive homelessness and policy failures.* San Francisco, CA: Author.

Wheaton, B. (1997). The nature of chronic stress. In B. Gottlieb (Ed.), *Coping with chronic stress* (pp. 43–103). New York, NY: Plenum.

Whitaker, R. C., Wright, J. A., Pepe, M. S., Seidel, K. D., & Deitz, W. H. (1997). Predicting obesity in young adulthood from childhood and parental obesity. *New England Journal of Medicine, 337,* 869–873.

White, R. W. (1959). Motivation reconsidered: The concept of competence. *Psychological Review, 66,* 297–333.

Whitfield C. L., Dube S. R., Felitti V. J., & Anda R. F. (2005). Adverse childhood experiences and hallucinations. *Child Abuse and Neglect, 29*(7), 797–810.

*WHO Report on the Global Tobacco Epidemic, 2008: The MPOWER package* (2008). Geneva: World Health Organization.

Widom, C., DuMont, K., & Czaja, S. (2007). A prospective investigation of major depressive disorder and comorbidity in abused and neglected children grown up. *Archives of General Psychiatry, 64,* 49–56.

Widom, C., Marmorstein, N., & White, H. (2006). Childhood victimization and illicit drug use in middle adulthood. *Psychology of Addictive Behaviors, 20,* 394–403.

Wielkiewicz, R., & Stelzner, S. (2005). An ecological perspective on leadership theory, research and practice. *Review of General Psychology, 9,* 326–341.

Wilcox, B. (1981). Social support, life stress, and psychological adjustment: A test of the buffering hypothesis. *American Journal of Community Psychology, 9*(4), 371–386.

Wilcox, B. L., Robbennolt, J. K., O'Keeffe, J. E., & Pynchon, M. E. (1996). Teen nonmarital childbearing and welfare: The gap between research and political discourse. *Journal of Social Issues, 52,* 71–90.

Wilczenski, F. L., & Coomey, S. M. (2007). *A practical guide to service learning: Strategies for positive development in schools.* New York, NY: Springer Science.

Wilke, L. A., & Speer, P. W. (2011). The mediating influence of organizational characteristics in the relationship between organizational type and relational power: An extension of psychological empowerment research. *Journal of Community Psychology, 39*(8), 972–986.

Wilkinson, D. (2007). The multidimensional nature of social cohesion: Psychological sense of community, attraction, and neighboring. *American Journal of Community Psychology, 40,* 214–229.

Wilkinson-Lee, A. M., Russell, S. T., & Lee, F. C. H. (2006). Practitioners' perspectives on cultural sensitivity in Latina/o teen pregnancy prevention. *Family Relations, 55,* 376–389.

Williams, D. (2004). Improving race relations in higher education: The jigsaw classroom as a missing piece to the puzzle. *Urban Education, 39,* 316–344.

Williams, K. R., & Guerra, N. G. (2007). Prevalence and predictors of Internet bullying. *Journal of Adolescent Health, 41,* S41–S21.

Williamson, T., Ashby, D., & Webber, R. (2006). Classifying neighbourhoods for reassurance policing. *Policing & Society, 16*(2), 189–218.

Willis, T. A. (1991). Comments on Heller, Thompson, Trueba, Hogg and Vlachos-Weber: Peer support telephone dyads for elderly women. *American Journal of Community Psychology, 19,* 75–83.

Willowbrook plan worked. (1982, September 4). *The New York Times,* p. 20.

Wilson, G., & Lester, D. (1998). Suicide prevention by e-mail. *Crisis Intervention and Time-Limited Treatment, 4,* 81–87.

Wilson, G. T., O'Leary, K. D., & Nathan, P. (1992). *Abnormal psychology.* Englewood Cliffs, NJ: Prentice Hall.

Wilson, J. B., Ellwood, D. T., & Brooks-Gunn, J. (1996). Welfare-to-work through the eyes of children. In P. L. Chase-Lansdale & J. Brooks-Gunn (Eds.), *Escape from poverty: What makes a difference for children?* New York, NY: Cambridge University Press.

Winkleby, M., Taylor, C., Jatulis, D., & Fortmann, S. (1996). The long-term effects of a cardiovascular disease prevention trial: The Stanford Five City Project. *American Journal of Public Health, 86,* 1773–1779.

Wisconsin (WI) Department of Health and Family Services. (2001). *Findings from focus groups: Select populations in Dane County* (Briefing Paper No. 3). Madison: Wisconsin State Planning Grant.

Withy, K., Andaya, J., Mikami, J., & Yamada, S. (2007). Assessing health disparities in rural Hawaii using the Hoshin facilitation method. *Journal of Rural Health, 23*(1), 84–88.

Wittig, M. A., & Schmitz, J. (1996). Electronic grassroots organizing. *Journal of Social Issues, 52,* 53–69.

Wolfe, D. A., Wekerle, C., Gough, B., Reitzel-Jaffe, D., Grasley, C., Pittman, A., . . . Stumpf, J. (1996). *The youth relationships manual: A group approach with adolescents for the prevention of woman abuse and the promotion of healthy relationships.* Thousand Oaks, CA: Sage.

Wolfe, D. A., Wekerle, C., Scott, K., Straatman, A-L., & Grasley, C. (2004). Predicting abuse in adolescent dating relationships over one year: The role of child maltreatment and trauma. *Journal of Abnormal Psychology, 113,* 406–415.

Wolfe, D. A., Wekerle, C., Scott, K., Straatman, A.-L., Grasley, C., & Reitzel-Jaffe, D. (2003). Dating violence prevention with at-risk youth: A controlled outcome evaluation. *Journal of Consulting and Clinical Psychology, 71,* 279–291.

Wolff, T. (1987). Community psychology and empowerment: An activist's insights. *American Journal of Community Psychology, 15,* 151–166.

Wolff, T. (2010). *The power of collaborative solutions: Six principles and effective tools for building healthy communities.* San Francisco, CA: Jossey-Bass.

Wolff, T., & Swift, C. (2008). Reflections on "real-world" community psychology. *Journal of Community Psychology, 36*(5), 609–625.

Wollert, R., & The Self-Help Research Team. (1987). The Self-Help Clearinghouse concept: An evaluation of one program and its implications for policy and practice. *American Journal of Community Psychology, 15,* 491–508.

Wombacher, J., Tagg, S. K., Bürgi, T., & MacBryde, J. (2010). Measuring sense of community in the military: Cross-cultural evidence for the validity of the Brief Sense of Community Scale and its underlying theory. *Journal of Community Psychology, 38*(6), 671–687.

Wong, F. Y., Blakely, C. H., & Worsham, S. L. (1991). Techniques and pitfalls of applied behavioral science research: The case of community mediation. In K. G. Duffy, J. W. Grosch, & P. V. Olczak (Eds.), *Community mediation: A handbook for practitioners and researchers* (pp. 35–41). New York, NY: Guilford.

Wong, F. Y., & Bouey, P. D. (2001). *Substance use/HIV health among urban Native Indians.* Unpublished manuscript, George Washington University School of Public Health and Health Services, Washington, DC.

Wong, N. T., Zimmerman, M. A., & Parker, E. A. (2010). A typology of youth participation and empowerment for child and adolescent health promotion, *American Journal of Community Psychology, 46*(1–2), 100–114.

Woodin, E. M., & O'Leary, D. (2009). Theoretical approaches to the etiology of partner violence. In D. J. Whitaker & J. R. Lutzker (Eds.) *Preventing partner violence: Research and evidence-based intervention strategies* (pp. 41–65). Washington, DC: American Psychological Association.

Woodward, T. G. (2008). Using protective factors to change the future of corrections. *Corrections Today, 70,* 76–77.

Woolpert, S. (1991). Victim-offender reconciliation programs. In K. G. Duffy, J. W. Grosch, & P. V. Olczak (Eds.), *Community mediation: A handbook for practitioners and researchers.* New York, NY: Guilford.

Worchel, S., Cooper, J., & Goethals, G. R. (1991). *Understanding social psychology.* Pacific Grove, CA: Brooks/Cole.

Worchel, S., & Lundgren, S. (1991). The nature of conflict and conflict resolution. In K. G. Duffy, J. W. Grosch, & P. V. Olczak (Eds.), *Community mediation: A handbook for practitioners and researchers.* New York, NY: Guilford.

Work, W. C., Cowen, E., Parker, G. R., & Wyman, P. A. (1990). Stress resilient children in an urban setting. *Journal of Primary Prevention, 11,* 3–17.

Work, W. C., & Olsen, K. H. (1990). Evaluation of a revised fourth grade social problem solving curriculum: Empathy as a moderator of adjustive gain. *Journal of Primary Prevention, 11,* 143–157.

World Drug Report. (2010). Retrieved from http://www.unodc.org/unodc/en/data-and-analysis/WDR-2010.html

World Health Organization. (2004). *Managing child abuse: A handbook for medical officers.* New Delhi, India: Author.

World Health Organization. (2007). *Behavioural interventions for HIV positive prevention in developing countries: a systematic review and meta-analysis.* Retrieved from http://www.who.int/bulletin/volumes/88/8/09-068213/en

World Health Organization. (2008a). *Global health indicators. World health statistics 2008* (pp. 36–46). Retrieved from http://www.who.int/whosis/whostat/2008/en/index.html

World Health Organization. (2008b). *WHO facts and figures.* Retrieved on June 13, 2008, from http://www.who.int/substance_abuse/facts/en

World Health Organization. (2008c). *Tobacco free initiative.* Retrieved from http://www.who.int/tobacco/mpower/en

World Health Organization. (2010). *World health report.* Retrieved from http://www.who.int/whr/en

World Health Organization. (2011). *Global health indicators.* Geneva, Switzerland: Author. Retrieved from http://www.who.int/gho/publications/world_health_statistics/EN_WHS2011_Part2.pdf

World Health Organization. (2012). *Global strategy for the prevention and control of sexually transmitted infections: 2006–2015.* Retrieved from http://whqlibdoc.who.int/publications/2007/9789241563475_eng.pdf

Wright, S. C., Aron, A., McLaughlin-Volpe, T., & Ropp, S. A. (1997). The extended contact effect: Knowledge of cross-group friendships and prejudice. *Journal of Personality and Social Psychology, 73,* 73–90.

Wright, S., & Cowen, E. L. (1985). The effects of peer teaching on student perceptions of class environment, adjustment, and academic performance. *American Journal of Community Psychology, 13,* 417–432.

Wrosch, C., Dunne, E., Scheier, M. F., & Schulz, R. (2006). Self-regulation of common age-related challenges: Benefits for older adults' psychological and physical health. *Journal of Behavioral Medicine, 29,* 299–306.

Xie, J. L., & Johns, G. (1995). Job scope and stress: Can job scope be too high? *Academy of Management Journal, 38,* 1288–1309.

Yates, M., & Youniss, J. (1998). Community service and political identity development in adolescence. In Political development: Youth growing up in a global community [Special issue]. *Journal of Social Issues, 54,* 495–512.

Yang, P., & Barrett, N. (2006). Understanding public attitudes towards Social Security. *International Journal of Social Welfare, 15,* 95–109.

Yasuda, T. (2009). Psychological sense of community in university classrooms: Do achievement goal orientations matter? *College Student Journal, 43*(2), 547–561.

Yick, A. (2006). Role of culture and context: Ethical issues in research with Asian Americans and immigrants in intimate violence. *Journal of Family Violence, 22*(5), 277–285.

Yijälä, A., Lönnqvist, J., Jasinskaja-Lahti, I., & Verkasalo, M. (2012). Values as predictors of anticipated socio-cultural adaptation among potential migrants from Russia to Finland. *Journal of Community and Applied Social Psychology, 22*(2), 95–110. doi:10.1002/casp.1104

Yodanis, C. (2004). Gender inequality, violence against women, and fear: A cross-national test of the feminist theory of violence against women. *Journal of Interpersonal Violence, 19,* 655–675.

Yoon, O., & Joo, H. (2005). A contextual analysis of crime rates: The Korean case. *Crime, Law and Social Change, 43,* 31–55.

Young, I. M. (1990). *Justice and the politics of difference.* Princeton, NJ: Princeton University Press.

Youngstrom, E., Weist, M., & Albus, K. E. (2003). Exploring violence exposure, stress, protective factors and behavioral problems among inner-city youth. *American Journal of Community Psychology, 32,* 115–129.

Yunus, M. (1999, November). The Grameen Bank. *Scientific American,* 114–119.

Yunus, M. (2007). *Grameen bank at a glance.* Retrieved from http://www.grameen-info.org/bank/GBGlance.htm

Zarit, S. H., Pearlin, L., & Schaie, K. W. (2003). Personal control in social and life course contexts. In S. H. Zarit, L. Pearlin, & K. W. Schaie (Eds.), *Social impact on aging.* New York, NY: Springer.

Zeitlin, D., Keller, S., Shiflett, S., Schleifer, S., & Bartlett, J. (2000). Immunological effects of massage therapy during acute academic stress. *Psychosomatic Medicine, 62,* 83–84.

Zeldin, S. (2004). Youth as agents of adult and community development: Mapping the process and outcomes of youth engaged in organizational governance. *Applied Development Science, 8*(2), 75–90.

Zhong, L. Y., & Broadhurst, R. G. (2007). Building little safe and civilized communities: Community crime prevention with Chinese characteristics? *International Journal of Offender Therapy and Comparative Criminology, 51,* 52–67.

Zigler, E. (1990). Shaping child care policies and programs in America. *American Journal of Community Psychology, 18,* 183–216.

Zigler, E. (1994). Reshaping early childhood intervention to be a more effective weapon against poverty. *American Journal of Community Psychology, 22,* 37–48.

Zigler, E. F., & Gilman, E. D. (1998). Day care and early childhood settings: Fostering mental health in young children. *Child and Adolescent Psychiatric Clinics of North America, 7,* 483–498.

Zigler, E. F., & Goodman, J. (1982). The battle for day care in America: A view from the trenches. In E. F. Zigler & E. W.

Gordon (Eds.), *Day care: Scientific and social policy issues.* Boston, MA: Auburn House.

Zigler, E., & Lang, M. (1991). *Childcare choices.* New York, NY: Free Press.

Zigler, E. F., & Muenchow, S. (1992). *Head Start: The inside story of America's most successful educational experiment.* New York, NY: Basic Books.

Zimmerman, M. (1995). Psychological empowerment: Issues and illustrations. *American Journal of Community Psychology, 23*(5), 581–599.

Zimmerman, M. (2000). Empowerment theory: Psychological, organizational and community levels of analysis. In J. Rappaport, & E. Seidman (Eds.), *Handbook of community psychology* (pp. 43–63). New York, NY: Kluwer Academic/Plenum.

Zimmerman, M. A., Ramírez-Valles, J., & Maton, K. L. (1999). Resilience among urban African American male adolescents: A study of the protective effects of sociopolitical control on their mental health. *American Journal of Community Psychology, 27,* 733–751.

Zimmerman, M. A., & Rappaport, J. (1988). Citizen participation, perceived control, and empowerment. *American Journal of Community Psychology, 16,* 725–750.

Zimmerman, M. A., & Zahniser, J. H. (1991). Refinements of sphere-specific measures of perceived control: Development of a sociopolitical control scale. *Journal of Community Psychology, 19*(2), 189–204.

Zippay, A. (1990–1991). The limits of intimates: Social networks and economic status among industrial workers. In Applications of social support and social network interventions in direct practice [Special issue]. *Journal of Applied Social Sciences, 15,* 75–95.

Zirkel, S., & Cantor, N. (2004). 50 years after *Brown v. Board of Education:* The promise and challenge of multicultural education. *Journal of Social Issues, 60,* 1–14.

Zlotnick, C., Robertson, M. J., & Lahiff, M. (1999). Getting off the streets: Economic resources and residential exits from homelessness. *Journal of Community Psychology, 27,* 209–224.

Zohar, D. (1997). Predicting burnout with a hassle based measure of role demands. *Journal of Occupational Behavior,* 101–115.

Zohar, D. (1999). When things go wrong: The effect of daily work hassles on effort, exertion and negative mood. *Journal of Occupational and Organizational Psychology, 72,* 265–283.

Zugazaga, C. (2004). Stressful life event experiences of homeless adults: A comparison of single men, single women, and women with children. *Journal of Community Psychology, 32,* 643–654.

# NAME INDEX

# SUBJECT INDEX